Implementing Interactive Learning Strategies in Higher Education

Elena Aurel Railean
Information Society Development Institute, Moldova

A volume in the Advances in Higher Education and Professional Development (AHEPD) Book Series

Published in the United States of America by
IGI Global
Information Science Reference (an imprint of IGI Global)
701 E. Chocolate Avenue
Hershey PA, USA 17033
Tel: 717-533-8845
Fax: 717-533-8661
E-mail: cust@igi-global.com
Web site: http://www.igi-global.com

Copyright © 2024 by IGI Global. All rights reserved. No part of this publication may be reproduced, stored or distributed in any form or by any means, electronic or mechanical, including photocopying, without written permission from the publisher.
Product or company names used in this set are for identification purposes only. Inclusion of the names of the products or companies does not indicate a claim of ownership by IGI Global of the trademark or registered trademark.

Library of Congress Cataloging-in-Publication Data

CIP Data in progress

British Cataloguing in Publication Data
A Cataloguing in Publication record for this book is available from the British Library.

All work contributed to this book is new, previously-unpublished material.
The views expressed in this book are those of the authors, but not necessarily of the publisher.

For electronic access to this publication, please contact: eresources@igi-global.com.

Advances in Higher Education and Professional Development (AHEPD) Book Series

Jared Keengwe
University of North Dakota, USA

ISSN:2327-6983
EISSN:2327-6991

MISSION

As world economies continue to shift and change in response to global financial situations, job markets have begun to demand a more highly-skilled workforce. In many industries a college degree is the minimum requirement and further educational development is expected to advance. With these current trends in mind, the **Advances in Higher Education & Professional Development (AHEPD) Book Series** provides an outlet for researchers and academics to publish their research in these areas and to distribute these works to practitioners and other researchers.

AHEPD encompasses all research dealing with higher education pedagogy, development, and curriculum design, as well as all areas of professional development, regardless of focus.

Coverage

- Adult Education
- Assessment in Higher Education
- Career Training
- Coaching and Mentoring
- Continuing Professional Development
- Governance in Higher Education
- Higher Education Policy
- Pedagogy of Teaching Higher Education
- Vocational Education

IGI Global is currently accepting manuscripts for publication within this series. To submit a proposal for a volume in this series, please contact our Acquisition Editors at Acquisitions@igi-global.com or visit: http://www.igi-global.com/publish/.

The (ISSN) is published by IGI Global, 701 E. Chocolate Avenue, Hershey, PA 17033-1240, USA, www.igi-global.com. This series is composed of titles available for purchase individually; each title is edited to be contextually exclusive from any other title within the series. For pricing and ordering information please visit http://www.igi-global.com/book-series/advances-higher-education-professional-development/73681. Postmaster: Send all address changes to above address. Copyright © IGI Global. All rights, including translation in other languages reserved by the publisher. No part of this series may be reproduced or used in any form or by any means – graphics, electronic, or mechanical, including photocopying, recording, taping, or information and retrieval systems – without written permission from the publisher, except for non commercial, educational use, including classroom teaching purposes. The views expressed in this series are those of the authors, but not necessarily of IGI Global.

Titles in this Series
For a list of additional titles in this series, please visit: www.igi-global.com/book-series

Best Practices to Prepare Writers for Their Professional Paths
Carissa A. Barker-Stucky (Carnegie Writers, Inc., USA) and Kemi Elufiede (Carnegie Writers, Inc., USA)
Information Science Reference • copyright 2024 • 300pp • H/C (ISBN: 9781668490242) • US $165.00 (our price)

Enhancing Higher Education and Research With OpenAI Models
Şirvan Şen Demir (Süleyman Demirel University, Turkey) and Mahmut Demir (Isparta University of Applied Sciences, Turkey)
Information Science Reference • copyright 2024 • 308pp • H/C (ISBN: 9798369316665) • US $165.00 (our price)

A Cross-Cultural Examination of Women in Higher Education and the Workplace
Reem A. Abu-Lughod (Royal University for Women, Bahrain & School of Social Sciences and Education, California State University, Bakersfield, USA)
Information Science Reference • copyright 2024 • 315pp • H/C (ISBN: 9798369301029) • US $165.00 (our price)

Global Perspectives on Decolonizing Postgraduate Education
Mishack Thiza Gumbo (University of South Africa, South Africa) Michael Gaotlhobogwe (University of Botswana, Botswana) Constantino Pedzisai (Chinhoyi University of Technology, Zimbabwe) Zingiswa Mybert Monica Jojo (Rhodes University, South Africa) and Christopher B. Knaus (University of Washington, Tacoma, USA & University of South Africa, South Africa)
Information Science Reference • copyright 2024 • 339pp • H/C (ISBN: 9798369312896) • US $230.00 (our price)

701 East Chocolate Avenue, Hershey, PA 17033, USA
Tel: 717-533-8845 x100 • Fax: 717-533-8661
E-Mail: cust@igi-global.com • www.igi-global.com

Table of Contents

Preface xvii

Chapter 1
Interactive Learning Strategies in Higher Education: From Enhanced Lecture to Team-Based Learning 1
    Elena Aurel Railean, Information Society Development Institute, Moldova

Chapter 2
Active Learning Strategies in Higher Education 32
    Manjari Sharma, Christ University, India
    Sharad Gupta, Christ University, India

Chapter 3
Social Emotional Learning Strategies in Higher Education 68
    S. C. Vetrivel, Kongu Engineering College, India
    V. P. Arun, JKKN College of Engineering and Technology, India
    T. P. Saravanan, Kongu Engineering College, India
    R. Maheswari, Kongu Engineering College, India

Chapter 4
Cognitive and Metacognitive Strategies of Learning in Higher Education 95
    Anne Liz Job, PES University, India
    Srishti Muralidharan, PES University, India

Chapter 5
Empowering Minds: Cognitive Learning Strategies for Higher Education Success 123
    R. Sridevi, Christ University, India
    P. Ashokkumar, PSG College of Arts and Science, India
    V. Sathish, PSG College of Arts and Science, India

Chapter 6
Adaptive Intelligence Revolutionizing Learning and Sustainability in Higher Education: Enhancing Learning and Sustainability With AI............................. 151
    Bianca Ifeoma Chigbu, University of Fort Hare, South Africa
    Ikechukwu Umejesi, University of Fort Hare, South Africa
    Sicelo Leonard Makapela, Walter Sisulu University, South Africa

Chapter 7
From Compliance to Transformation: Jain University's Journey With the NEP 177
    Patcha Bhujanga Rao, Jain University (Deemed), India

Chapter 8
Innovative Teaching Strategies in Higher Education and Their Impact on Overall Educational Effectiveness: A Theoretical Model and Instrument Development 214
    Srinivasan Moharkonda Balakrishnan, Christ University, India
    S. R. Deepika, Christ University, India
    Priyadarshini Moharkonda Srinivasan, Christ University, India

Chapter 9
Interactive Learning in Library Instruction: Fostering Student Engagement Through Engaging Activities 241
    N. Meeramani, Srinivas University, Mangalore, India
    Divakara Bhat, Srinivas University, Mangalore, India

Chapter 10
Multimedia Cloud Data Warehouse Design for Knowledge Sharing in the University Environment: A Proposed Digital Solution 273
    Godwin Nse Ebong, University of Salford, UK
    Ugochukwu Okwudili Matthew, Hussaini Adamu Federal Polytechnic, Nigeria
    Babatunde Olofin, Enugu State University, Nigeria
    Nneoma Andrew-Vitalis, University of Hertfordshire, UK
    Lateef Olawale Fatai, University of Salford, UK
    Ajibola Olaosebikan Waliu, Southampton Solent University, UK
    David Oyewumi Oyekunle, University of Salford, UK
    Matthew Abiola Oladipupo, University of Salford, UK

Chapter 11
The Impact of Digital Textbooks on Student Engagement in Higher
Education: Highlighting the Significance of Interactive Learning Strategies
Facilitated by Digital Media 301
    Jayalakshmi Jayaraman, Christ University, India
    Jyothi Aane, Christ University, India

Chapter 12
Nursing Students' Experiences of Peer Group Teaching: A Cooperative
Learning Approach 329
    Daniel Opotamutale Ashipala, University of Namibia, Namibia

Chapter 13
Interactive Learning Strategies in Teaching Corporate Finance 349
    V. Rajesh Kumar, Alliance University, India
    Ravi Darshini, St. Joseph's Institute of Management, India

Chapter 14
Teacher Educators and Technology Integration With Preservice Teachers 381
    Brooke Urbina, The Chicago School, USA
    Aubrey Statti, The Chicago School, USA
    Kelly M. Torres, The Chicago School, USA

Chapter 15
Exploring Factors Contributing to a Failure Rate in Bachelor of Nursing
Science Programme in Namibia 410
    Daniel Opotamutale Ashipala, University of Namibia, Namibia
    David N. Sakeus, University of Namibia, Namibia

Chapter 16
Teaching Human Resource Management in Law Schools: A Scrutiny of
Pedagogies for Critical and Reflective Teaching Practice 429
    Prageetha G. Raju, Rainbow Management Research Consultants, India

Compilation of References 455

About the Contributors 501

Index 509

Detailed Table of Contents

Preface xvii

Chapter 1
Interactive Learning Strategies in Higher Education: From Enhanced Lecture
to Team-Based Learning 1
    Elena Aurel Railean, Information Society Development Institute,
        Moldova

In higher education, interactive learning strategies are a means of encouraging students to participate actively in their education, frequently with the aid of technology. Technology should assist digital pedagogy rather than the other way around. This chapter applies metasystems learning design theory to summarize the diversity of interactive learning strategies in higher education. Based on the hypothesis that interactive learning strategies result in guaranteed learning outcomes, it is clear that passive teaching techniques impact the methodology of traditional lectures and teams. Therefore, within the context of global education, this chapter critically explores 21st-century interactive learning strategies as a response to the following research question: What are the most effective interactive learning strategies in higher education? This chapter describes global trends in the implementation of interactive learning strategies in higher education, which situated current instructional-learning-assessment practices within a framework of critical deconstruction.

Chapter 2
Active Learning Strategies in Higher Education 32
    Manjari Sharma, Christ University, India
    Sharad Gupta, Christ University, India

This chapter investigates active learning strategies in higher education, showcasing five innovative learning strategies conducted with students. These strategies include starting and managing a small business to understand entrepreneurship, recording transactions according to accounting principles, and engaging in role-play as members of international organizations like the IMF and World Bank to negotiate projects. Additionally, students create short films on specific topics to explore creative storytelling and communication. These experiential learning activities aim to provide comprehensive insights into practical and theoretical knowledge applications.

Chapter 3
Social Emotional Learning Strategies in Higher Education 68
    S. C. Vetrivel, Kongu Engineering College, India
    V. P. Arun, JKKN College of Engineering and Technology, India
    T. P. Saravanan, Kongu Engineering College, India
    R. Maheswari, Kongu Engineering College, India

Social emotional learning (SEL) has gained increasing recognition as a vital component of education, particularly in the context of higher education institutions. This chapter provides a detailed overview of the key concepts, strategies, and implications of integrating SEL into higher education settings. Social emotional learning encompasses a range of skills and competencies that enable individuals to understand and manage their emotions, develop positive interpersonal relationships, and make responsible decisions. In the higher education landscape, the focus on SEL strategies has emerged as a response to the evolving needs of students and the recognition that academic success is closely intertwined with emotional well-being. This chapter explores the foundational principles of SEL and its relevance in higher education, emphasizing the positive impact on students' personal and academic development.

Chapter 4
Cognitive and Metacognitive Strategies of Learning in Higher Education 95
    Anne Liz Job, PES University, India
    Srishti Muralidharan, PES University, India

This chapter provides a broad understanding of the areas of cognition and metacognition and their significance in higher education settings. The chapter encompasses not only the theory and the knowledge related to these thinking processes, but also provides tools in the fields of thinking for educators to implement. The chapter delves into a detailed description of cognitive strategies including elaboration, repetition, distributed practice, and the dual coding hypothesis, and metacognitive strategies, such as goal setting, metacognitive regulation and reflection. Additionally, the chapter explores frameworks such as VAK, Bloom's taxonomy and mental models, by which cognitive and metacognitive strategies can be integrated to enhance learning outcomes. The chapter also provides research evidence, proving the effectiveness of cognitive and metacognitive strategies in the context of higher education.

Chapter 5
Empowering Minds: Cognitive Learning Strategies for Higher Education
Success 123
    R. Sridevi, Christ University, India
    P. Ashokkumar, PSG College of Arts and Science, India
    V. Sathish, PSG College of Arts and Science, India

It takes more than just passive information consumption to meet the expectations of higher education. This chapter delves into the efficacy of cognitive learning processes, providing students with useful tools to improve their understanding, memory, and critical thinking abilities. The authors enable learners to actively engage with information, develop deeper comprehension, and attain academic greatness by exploring evidence-based tactics such as interleaving, spaced retrieval, and elaboration. The authors also discuss common issues that students in higher education encounter, like information overload and procrastination, and offer solutions to help students get past these obstacles and maximize their educational opportunities. Lastly, the authors stress the value of metacognition and exhort students to evaluate their own learning experiences and modify their approach as necessary. The purpose of this chapter is to help as an invaluable means for both educators and students, fostering a culture of empowered learning in higher education

Chapter 6
Adaptive Intelligence Revolutionizing Learning and Sustainability in Higher
Education: Enhancing Learning and Sustainability With AI............................. 151
    Bianca Ifeoma Chigbu, University of Fort Hare, South Africa
    Ikechukwu Umejesi, University of Fort Hare, South Africa
    Sicelo Leonard Makapela, Walter Sisulu University, South Africa

This chapter examines the incorporation of adaptive intelligence in higher education, focusing on its influence on conventional learning approaches and long-lasting educational strategies. Adaptive intelligence merges artificial intelligence with human cognition to provide personalized learning by utilizing real-time customisation and data analysis. Adaptive intelligence enhances sustainability by integrating sustainability principles into the learning process in a dynamic manner. The chapter discusses obstacles such resource constraints, instructor opposition, and ethical issues. The significance of ethical AI usage, educator engagement, and continuous research is emphasized to maximize adaptive intelligence's potential in creating a sustainable and inclusive educational system. The text ends by addressing future research and practical consequences with the goal of establishing a robust educational system that accommodates individual learning requirements, incorporates sustainability principles, and equips students to navigate contemporary challenges.

Chapter 7
From Compliance to Transformation: Jain University's Journey With the NEP 177
  Patcha Bhujanga Rao, Jain University (Deemed), India

This abstract explores the transformative journey of Jain deemed-to-be university (JDTBU) in alignment with the National Education Policy (NEP) of India. JDTBU initially transitioned from compliance to transformation, adhering to NEP guidelines through curriculum revisions and fostering interdisciplinary learning and skill development. Recognizing the NEP's transformative potential, JDTBU embraced a holistic and innovative learning environment by implementing collaborative and experiential learning approaches to cultivate critical thinking and creativity in students. This transformation further involved faculty development initiatives focused on student engagement and technology integration, alongside research and industry partnerships to enhance the practical relevance of learning outcomes. JDTBU's commitment to continuous improvement ensures ongoing alignment with NEP objectives, aiming to create a learning ecosystem that promotes innovation, social responsibility, and lifelong learning.

Chapter 8
Innovative Teaching Strategies in Higher Education and Their Impact on Overall Educational Effectiveness: A Theoretical Model and Instrument Development 214
  Srinivasan Moharkonda Balakrishnan, Christ University, India
  S. R. Deepika, Christ University, India
  Priyadarshini Moharkonda Srinivasan, Christ University, India

This book chapter delves into pioneering teaching methods in higher education and their impact on educational efficacy. It delves into the shift from traditional teaching to collaborative and experiential learning, emphasizing how these methods foster engagement and active involvement. The chapter scrutinizes leading pedagogical innovations and their effects, crafting a research model and assessment tool to gauge their efficacy. This tool blends quantitative and qualitative metrics for a comprehensive evaluation, offering insights for educators, administrators, and policymakers. By amalgamating theory, empirical data, and practical insights, the chapter advances understanding and provides a guide for educators and researchers to explore, implement, and assess these strategies, ultimately enriching educational outcomes and student success in diverse higher education landscapes.

Chapter 9
Interactive Learning in Library Instruction: Fostering Student Engagement Through Engaging Activities 241
    N. Meeramani, Srinivas University, Mangalore, India
    Divakara Bhat, Srinivas University, Mangalore, India

Library instruction is important for students' information literacy and academic success. This chapter explores interactive learning strategies to improve engagement and learning outcomes during library instruction sessions. It discusses the benefits of interactive learning in fostering participation, critical thinking, and information literacy development in students. The chapter highlights the importance of interactive learning experiences in library instruction, including hands-on activities, group discussions, and experiential learning. It emphasizes the role of librarians in creating engaging experiences, using technology to enhance student interaction, and overcoming potential barriers such as limited resources and time constraints. The chapter stresses the need for innovative teaching methods to promote student engagement and information literacy development.

Chapter 10
Multimedia Cloud Data Warehouse Design for Knowledge Sharing in the
University Environment: A Proposed Digital Solution 273
    Godwin Nse Ebong, University of Salford, UK
    Ugochukwu Okwudili Matthew, Hussaini Adamu Federal Polytechnic,
        Nigeria
    Babatunde Olofin, Enugu State University, Nigeria
    Nneoma Andrew-Vitalis, University of Hertfordshire, UK
    Lateef Olawale Fatai, University of Salford, UK
    Ajibola Olaosebikan Waliu, Southampton Solent University, UK
    David Oyewumi Oyekunle, University of Salford, UK
    Matthew Abiola Oladipupo, University of Salford, UK

The desire for homogeneity in the execution of national policy on information communication technologies (ICTs) for tertiary education in Nigeria has been updated through progressive inclusion in the national policy with regard to ICTs use in education. In evaluating the progress made towards the sustainable development goals, the policy highlighted the necessity of ICTs in achieving the national technology objectives. In this paper, the authors argued that developments in ICT policy with regard to the implementation of National Research and Education Networks (NRENs) should adopt a bottom-up approach in order to establish contributions in the Nigeria Education Research Network (NgREN) in the direction of improving educational quality and research output geared toward sustainable national development. The research's findings showed that integrating ICTs into educational mainstream management is essential for academic success, effectiveness, globalization, and job satisfaction that incorporates electronic changes for opportunities in the digital age.

Chapter 11
The Impact of Digital Textbooks on Student Engagement in Higher
Education: Highlighting the Significance of Interactive Learning Strategies
Facilitated by Digital Media 301
 Jayalakshmi Jayaraman, Christ University, India
 Jyothi Aane, Christ University, India

The introduction of digital textbooks in higher education has revolutionized student engagement and educational outcomes through interactive learning strategies. This study examines the effectiveness of digital textbooks in enhancing student engagement compared to traditional print textbooks. Using a mixed-methods design, the research involves undergraduate and postgraduate students from various disciplines. Preliminary findings suggest that digital textbooks with features like multimedia, annotations, quizzes, and collaborative tools significantly boost student engagement and cater to diverse learning styles. The study also reveals a positive correlation between digital textbooks and academic performance, emphasizing the potential for deeper understanding and long-term knowledge retention. The research advocates for higher education institutions to incorporate digital textbooks to modernize resources, improve learning outcomes, and increase student satisfaction by leveraging digital technology to meet evolving educational needs.

Chapter 12
Nursing Students' Experiences of Peer Group Teaching: A Cooperative
Learning Approach 329
 Daniel Opotamutale Ashipala, University of Namibia, Namibia

Peer teaching is a rapidly developing educational method that enhances student learning through a variety of collaborative and cooperative educational strategies. In Namibia, little research exists on how nursing students experiences the use of peer teaching in nursing and midwifery education. The purpose of this chapter is to explore and describe nursing students' experiences on the use of peer group teaching as a learning method in nursing and midwifery education. The results revealed nursing students positive and negative experiences with suggestions for improvement. Findings from this chapter may help identify strengths and weaknesses in the use of peer group teaching for learning purposes in nursing and midwifery education.

Chapter 13
Interactive Learning Strategies in Teaching Corporate Finance 349
    V. Rajesh Kumar, Alliance University, India
    Ravi Darshini, St. Joseph's Institute of Management, India

Students pursuing management education, in either undergraduate or graduate program, are exposed to all the functional areas of management viz., Marketing management, human resource management, production and operations management, and financial management (or corporate finance). The interesting feature of teaching/learning financial management is that 'what is discussed in the classroom' and 'what happens in a company boardroom' are the same. A student can better understand the depth, width and nuances of the course titled 'Corporate Finance' when the discussion on the course provides 'experiential learning.' This chapter provides an idea and framework for teachers regarding the approach to teaching this course, how to make it interactive and how to make the course offer practical exposure to the actual financial decision-making in companies.

Chapter 14
Teacher Educators and Technology Integration With Preservice Teachers 381
    Brooke Urbina, The Chicago School, USA
    Aubrey Statti, The Chicago School, USA
    Kelly M. Torres, The Chicago School, USA

The mission of this chapter is to provide teachers with the knowledge and benefits of utilizing the TPACK framework and the SAMR model to guide the use of technology, so they can empower students for the digital age, through primarily focusing on the importance of the role of teacher educators in the training of preservice teachers. To overcome deficiencies in skills, knowledge, and abilities related to the instruction of technology integration, the focus for preparation should be turned to the teacher educators themselves. Combining the constructivist theory with the TPaCK framework, the study aimed to make a connection to the relevance of this theoretical framework in conjunction with technology integration to adequately prepare preservice teachers for the classroom. Overall, the study found that gaps exist among consistency of skills in teacher educators when it comes to technology integration, and a need to close this gap was clearly identified, defining it is the responsibility of the university teacher educator faculty to ensure that happens.

Chapter 15
Exploring Factors Contributing to a Failure Rate in Bachelor of Nursing
Science Programme in Namibia 410
    Daniel Opotamutale Ashipala, University of Namibia, Namibia
    David N. Sakeus, University of Namibia, Namibia

Academic failure among tertiary students remains a worldwide phenomenon, yet the extent of these failures and their precipitating factors are not well understood. In Namibia, factors that contribute to the failure rate in the Bachelor of Nursing Science degree are not extensively researched. The objectives of this chapter are thus to assess and describe the factors that contribute to the failure rate in the Bachelor of Nursing Science degree at a Namibian university. This chapter's findings revealed that the poor academic performance of students in the Bachelor of Nursing degree is influenced by personal factors, such as a lack of interest and absenteeism, as well as academic factors, such as inadequate curriculum content, ineffective teaching methods, the rarity of some procedures, and inappropriate attitudes amongst some registered nurses.

Chapter 16
Teaching Human Resource Management in Law Schools: A Scrutiny of
Pedagogies for Critical and Reflective Teaching Practice 429
    Prageetha G. Raju, Rainbow Management Research Consultants, India

Many courses of higher education emerged for being ideological but later graduated into something more critical and reflective; HRM is one such course. A number of studies tried to address teaching HRM in a responsible, reflective, and critical manner. At this point, it is to be noted that HRM teaching is getting essential to students given the trend for integrated programmes in India and abroad. But how HRM should be taught to students pursuing integrated programmes still remains unanswered. There is dearth of literature regarding the context, the content, the perspectives, and the pedagogies of HRM for non-business students. So, how should HRM be taught? The author established the context to teach HRM in non-business schools, personally developed teaching materials, and gradually emerged into incorporating tested models to foster criticality and reflection. Two interventions, viz., project pedagogy and critical studies in HRM, are used to teach HRM to law students.

Compilation of References 455

About the Contributors 501

Index 509

Preface

Nowadays, learning happens everywhere, at all times, and in real and virtual environments. Higher education faces the challenge of teaching students to use interactive strategies for achievement of the successful lifelong learning competencies. Both educators and learners seek to attain these competencies because digital tools and environments provide the necessary resources to allow us to perceive the world of education as inclusive and accessible to all. Both educators and learners seek to attain these competencies because digital tools and environments provide the necessary resources to allow us to perceive the world of education as inclusive and accessible to all. However, digital tools and environments create also a disconnect between the classical theory of learning and instruction practice, and, as a result, traditional teaching and assessment methods need to be updated. We might call this an example of convergence between teaching and assessment, the coming together of two or more disparate disciplines or educational technologies for better learning outcomes, or, perhaps more properly, a synergism between cognitive and non-cognitive systems, where two disparate factors are combining for a valuable effect that is better than the sum of teaching and assessment. To address this dilemma, *Implementing Interactive Learning Strategies in Higher Education* offers a comprehensive framework and insights for conceptual research in university pedagogy to help managers and instructors address students' learning needs.

Implementing interactive learning strategies in higher education is expected to become one of the best solutions. In theory, interactive learning strategies are based on the active learning approach and its practical applications (Tong, 2001). Unlike the teaching paradigm, which depends on the one-way transfer of knowledge through passive learning—such as listening to a teacher-centered lecture—active learning has been proposed based on the learning paradigm., 'Active learning includes all kinds of learning beyond the mere one-way transmission of knowledge in lecture-style classes (= passive learning). It requires engagement in activities (writing, discussion, and presentation) and externalizing cognitive processes in the activities' (Mizokami, 2018, p. 79). However, this definition is based on the assumption that learning is, first of all, a cognitive activity. Second, active learning strategies foster the development of social, metacognitive, affective, psychomotor, and interpersonal skills and competencies, reflecting the ongoing changes in society. Third, because learning is about curiosity, motivation, and insight, adaptive learning cannot lead to active learning. From this perspective, the adaptive learning strategy refers to the capacity of the learner to self-regulate the variables of the learning process (i.e. skills, energy, health) toward lifelong valuable learning outcomes.

Interactive learning is more about the interaction between teacher(s), student(s), content and context. Examples of some of the techniques, especially for school classroom strategies, have been explored and well-documented in scientific literature (Barker, 1994; Buehl, 2023). Such learning strategies use, for instance, active reading with deep understanding or argumentation through reading, writing, speaking, and listening in a digital learning environment. However, to foster learning in higher education is important to motivate students to learn through collaboration and cooperation. This task is important because of the risks of failure in the social decisions related to climate change, the emergence of new technologies, and cognitivization.

How can interactive learning strategies be implemented in higher education? This book attempts to answer this question by bringing together contributions from prominent researchers and practitioners actively involved in all aspects of teaching, learning, and assessment. Three factors – "academic third mission" (Spânu, P., Ulmeanu, M. E., & Doicin, 2024) through community engagement and social impact of specialists with higher education, as well as rapidly increasing use of microlearning/microcredentials and nano learning in higher education and the need in understanding how to develop professional competence – have caused a resurgence of interest amongst university professors in interactive learning strategies design, development and control. In addition, greater curiosity than ever before is being shown in more interactive learning strategies, as evidenced by the number of books, journal articles, and conference papers devoted to topics such as active learning, adaptive learning, interactive learning, affordable learning, scaffolding, metacognitive learning strategies, teacher training.

The book focuses on reflective analysis active and interactive learning strategies, cognitive and metacognitive approaches, and social-emotional learning techniques. Active learning strategies encourage students to think, debate, research, and create. Interaction, or a scenario in which two or more students or objects equipped with artificial intelligence converse with or respond to one another, is the basis of interactive learning strategies. There are, at least, three models of interactions a) student-lecturer interaction, b) student-student interaction, and c) student–content. Providing feedback on assignments, learning journals, or other reflective activities; taking part in discussion boards or chats; sending out regular announcements summarizing the previous week or outlining the upcoming week; mentoring individual

Preface

students; and working with small groups of students assigned to assist in teaching portions of the course (peer teaching) are examples of student-lectures interaction. Activities that involve student-student interaction encompass group projects, case studies, peer instruction, role-playing, synchronous and asynchronous discussions or debates, collaborative brainstorming, peer review of selected work, and more. However, student-content interaction is a case of scientific debate because encompasses both interactions with "ideas" through immediate feedback, as well as the more tangible interactions students have with the course materials through reading/video discussions or reflections, simulations, web quests, quizzes and tutorials with text, still images, audio, and/or video, all of these accomplished with delayed feedback.

THE CHALLENGES

Changing the design of traditional teaching environments, advances in digital technologies based on artificial intelligence, and the importance of metacognition and successful learning strategies in higher education pose several global challenges for the sustainability of higher education. The main problem is that higher education has become an open system and, as such, education is produced in a diversity of learning environments, both physical and virtual. The vitality of education is determined by the interdependence between motivation, the performance of lifelong learning, and the need for competitive specialists. For these reasons, it is proposed that the multifaceted nature of higher education and its learning strategies be studied from the perspective of Metasystems Learning Design Theory.

The kernel of Metasystem Learning Design Theory is a student's action, defined as the capacity to capacity of a student to learn and re-learn in a diversity of learning environments. The added value of the theory is in the comprehensive understanding of the dynamicity of the rapid diversification of learning environments in the open education system and their impact on (meta)cognitive mechanisms of learning and models of knowledge management. Unfortunately, this task is not easy. Research suggests that three psychological conditions are important: a) metacognition and successful learning strategies, b) ecosystem of learning and communication, and c) digital assessment. Based on survey funding Railean, Trofimov & Aktas (2021) suggest that students are motivated to learn in a diversity of learning environments where the management of the self-regulated learning capacity is more important than teaching. Motivation is a personalized construct of motive, energy, and intellect. For these reasons, it is important to relate the concept of motivation to a stimulus in the environment, whether real or virtual, that captures the learner's attention and increases interest in exploring phenomena, processes, or learning objects. In other words, learners do not have a universally accepted or socially determined intrinsic motivation. Motivation is a complex (meta)cognitive-affective construct, "coordinated" by the learner toward solving specific problems or tasks. Understanding the factors that determine or inhibit intrinsic motivation remains a problem.

THE ORGANISATION OF THE BOOK

Chapter 1 "Interactive Learning Strategies: From Enhanced Lectured to Team-based Learning" summarizes the variety of interactive learning strategies from the perspective of metasystems learning design theory. Emphasis is placed on the guaranteed learning outcomes that come from using interactive learning strategies. These outcomes can be updated situationally based on an individual's lifetime capacity for learning and relearning. The chapter critically examines 21st-century interactive learning strategies within the framework of global education and reports some results of practical applications. To place current instructional, learning, and assessment practices within a framework of critical deconstruction, it describes global trends in the implementation of interactive learning strategies in higher education.

Chapter 2 "Active Learning Strategies in Higher Education" investigates active learning strategies in higher education, showcasing five innovative learning strategies conducted with students. These strategies include starting and managing a small business to understand entrepreneurship, recording transactions according to accounting principles, and engaging in role-play as members of international organizations like the IMF and World Bank to negotiate projects. Additionally, students create short films on specific topics to explore creative storytelling and communication. These experiential learning activities aim to provide comprehensive insights into practical and theoretical knowledge application.

Chapter 3 "Social Emotional Learning Strategies in Higher Education" provides a detailed overview of the key concepts, strategies, and implications of integrating SEL into higher education settings. Social Emotional Learning encompasses a range of skills and competencies that enable individuals to understand and manage their emotions, develop positive interpersonal relationships, and make responsible decisions. In the higher education landscape, the focus on SEL strategies has emerged as a response to the evolving needs of students and the recognition that academic success is closely intertwined with emotional well-being. This chapter explores the foundational principles of SEL and its relevance in higher education, emphasizing the positive impact on students' personal and academic development.

Chapter 4 "Cognitive and Metacognitive Strategies of Learning in Higher Education" begins with a report that UNESCO (2023) describes higher education as a rich cultural and scientific asset that enables personal development and promotes economic, technological, and social changes through knowledge sharing, creativity,

Preface

and research. Higher education institutions should give students the affordable tools they need to adapt to rapidly changing environments and job markets. All these tools include cognitive and metacognitive strategies. The authors found that effectively designed cognitive strategies of learning empower students to excel in professional settings and real-world scenarios.

Chapter 5 "Empowering Minds: Cognitive Learning Strategies for Higher Education Success" delves into the efficacy of cognitive learning processes, providing students with useful tools to improve their understanding, memory, and critical thinking abilities. We enable learners to actively engage with information, develop deeper comprehension, and attain academic greatness by exploring evidence-based tactics such as interleaving, spaced retrieval, and elaboration. We also discuss common issues that students in higher education encounter, like information overload and procrastination, and offer solutions to help students get past these obstacles and maximize their educational opportunities. Lastly, we stress the value of metacognition and exhort students to evaluate their own learning experiences and modify their approach as necessary. The purpose of this chapter is to help as an invaluable means for both educators and students, fostering a culture of empowered learning in higher education.

Chapter 6 "Adaptive Intelligence Revolutionizing Learning and Sustainability in Higher Education: Enhancing Learning and Sustainability with AI" explores the use of adaptive intelligence in higher education, emphasizing how it affects traditional teaching methods and long-term learning strategies. It is concluded that personalized learning strategies combine artificial intelligence and human cognition through data analysis and real-time customization. To fully utilize adaptive intelligence's potential in building a sustainable and inclusive educational system for higher education emphasizes the importance of ethical AI use, educator engagement, and research to create a strong educational system that can adapt to the unique needs of each student and integrate sustainability principles.

Chapter 7 "From Compliance to Transformation: Jain Deemed-to-be University's Journey with the NEP" explores the transformative journey of Jain Deemed-to-be University (JDTBU) in alignment with the National Education Policy (NEP) of India. JDTBU initially transitioned from compliance to transformation, adhering to NEP guidelines through curriculum revisions and fostering interdisciplinary learning and skill development. Recognizing the NEP's transformative potential, JDTBU embraced a holistic and innovative learning environment by implementing collaborative and experiential learning approaches to cultivate critical thinking and creativity in students. This transformation further involved faculty development initiatives focused on student engagement and technology integration, alongside research and industry partnerships to enhance the practical relevance of learning outcomes. JDTBU's commitment to continuous improvement ensures ongoing alignment with NEP objectives, aiming to create a learning ecosystem that promotes innovation, social responsibility, and lifelong learning.

Chapter 8 "Innovative Teaching Strategies in Higher Education and Their Impact on Overall Educational Effectiveness: A Theoretical Model and Instrument Development" delves into pioneering teaching methods in higher education and their impact on educational efficacy. It delves into the shift from traditional teaching to collaborative and experiential learning, emphasizing how these methods foster engagement and active involvement. The chapter scrutinizes leading pedagogical innovations and their effects, crafting a research model and assessment tool to gauge their efficacy. This tool blends quantitative and qualitative metrics for a comprehensive evaluation, offering insights for educators, administrators, and policymakers. By amalgamating theory, empirical data, and practical insights, the chapter advances understanding and provides a guide for educators and researchers to explore, implement, and assess these strategies, ultimately enriching educational outcomes and student success in diverse higher education landscapes.

Chapter 9 "Interactive Learning in Library Instruction: Fostering Student Engagement Through Engaging Activities" explores interactive learning strategies to improve engagement and learning outcomes during library instruction sessions. It discusses the benefits of interactive learning in fostering participation, critical thinking, and information literacy development in students. The chapter highlights the importance of interactive learning experiences in library instruction, including hands-on activities, group discussions, and experiential learning. It emphasizes the role of librarians in creating engaging experiences, using technology to enhance student interaction, and overcoming potential barriers such as limited resources and time constraints. The chapter stresses the need for innovative teaching methods to promote student engagement and information literacy development.

Chapter 10 "Multimedia Cloud Data Warehouse Design for Knowledge Sharing in the University Environment: A Proposed Digital Solution" argues that developments in ICT policy with regard to the implementation of National Research and Education Networks (NRENs) should adopt a bottom-up approach in order to establish contributions in the Nigeria Education Research Network (NgREN) in the direction of improving educational quality and research output geared toward sustainable national development. The research's findings showed that integrating ICTs into educational mainstream management is essential for academic success, effectiveness, globalization, and job satisfaction that incorporates electronic changes for opportunities in the digital age.

Chapter 11 "The Impact of Digital Textbooks on Student Engagement in Higher Education: Highlighting the Significance of Interactive Learning Strategies Facilitated by Digital Media" examines the effectiveness of digital textbooks in enhancing student engagement compared to traditional print textbooks. Using a mixed-methods

Preface

design, the research involves undergraduate and postgraduate students from various disciplines. Preliminary findings suggest that digital textbooks with features like multimedia, annotations, quizzes, and collaborative tools significantly boost student engagement and cater to diverse learning styles. The study also reveals a positive correlation between digital textbooks and academic performance, emphasizing the potential for deeper understanding and long-term knowledge retention. The research advocates for higher education institutions to incorporate digital textbooks to modernize resources, improve learning outcomes, and increase student satisfaction by leveraging digital technology to meet evolving educational needs.

Chapter 12 "Nursing Students' Experiences of Peer Group Teaching: A Cooperative Learning Approach" explores and describes nursing students' experiences on the use of peer group teaching as a learning method in nursing and midwifery education. The results reveal nursing students positive and negative experiences with suggestions for improvement. Findings from this chapter may help identify strengths and weaknesses in the use of peer group teaching for learning purposes in nursing and midwifery education.

Chapter 13 "Interactive Learning Strategies in Teaching Corporate Finance" presents a typical lesson plan for teaching "Corporate Finance" using interactive learning strategies. It is concluded that corporate finance is a management course, the learning of which can be made most interactive through role plays, analysis of financial statements and other contents of the annual report, case studies, simulations, spreadsheet modeling, and experience sharing (Guest Lectures) by Industry professionals, industry visits, games, recorded lectures, and mini research projects.

Chapter 14 "Teacher Educators and Technology Integration With Preservice Teachers" provides teachers with the knowledge and benefits of utilizing the TPACK framework and the SAMR model to guide the use of technology, so they can empower students for the digital age, through primarily focusing on the importance of the role of teacher educators in the training of preservice teachers. To overcome deficiencies in skills, knowledge, and abilities related to the instruction of technology integration, the focus for preparation should be turned to the teacher educators themselves. Combining the constructivist theory with the TPaCK framework, the study aimed to make a connection to the relevance of this theoretical framework in conjunction with technology integration to adequately prepare preservice teachers for the classroom. Overall, the study found that gaps exist among consistency of skills in teacher educators when it comes to technology integration, and a need to close this gap was clearly identified, defining it is the responsibility of the university teacher educator faculty to ensure that happens.

Chapter 15 'Exploring Factors Contributing to a Failure Rate in Bachelor of Nursing Science Programme in Namibia' assesses and describes the factors that contribute to the failure rate in the Bachelor of Nursing Science degree at a Namibian university. This chapter's findings revealed that the poor academic performance of students in the Bachelor of Nursing degree is influenced by personal factors, such as a lack of interest and absenteeism, as well as academic factors, such as inadequate curriculum content, ineffective teaching methods, the rarity of some procedures, and inappropriate attitudes amongst some registered nurses.

Chapter 16 "Teaching Human Resource Management in Law Schools: A Scrutiny of Pedagogies for Critical and Reflective Teaching Practice" describes many courses of higher education that emerged for being ideological but later graduated into something more critical and reflective; HRM is one such course. A number of studies tried to address teaching HRM in a responsible, reflective, and critical manner. At this point, it is to be noted that HRM teaching is getting essential to students given the trend for integrated programmes in India and abroad. But, how HRM should be taught to students pursuing integrated programmes, still remains unanswered. There is dearth of literature regarding the context, the content, the perspectives and pedagogies of HRM for non-business students. So, how should HRM be taught? The author established the context to teach HRM in non-business school, developed own teaching materials, and gradually emerged into incorporating tested model to foster criticality and reflection. Two interventions, viz., project pedagogy and critical studies in HRM are used to teach HRM to law students.

The book is a vital resource for professionals and researchers seeking to navigate the frontier of higher education. Whether you're an educator, administrator, or executive concerned with global education and citizenship, this book offers practical solutions to the complex challenges faced by modern universities.

Elena Aurel Railean

Information Society Development Institute, Moldova

REFERENCES

Barker, P. (1994). Designing interactive learning. In *Design and production of multimedia and simulation-based learning material* (pp. 1–30). Springer Netherlands. 10.1007/978-94-011-0942-0_1

Buehl, D. (2023). *Classroom strategies for interactive learning.* Routledge. 10.4324/9781032680842

Mizokami, S. (2018). Deep active learning from the perspective of active learning theory. *Deep active learning: Toward greater depth in university education*, 79-91.

Railean, E., Trofimov, V., & Aktas, D. (2021). Learning Resource Management from Investigating Intrinsic Motivation in Various Learning Environments. In: *Proceedings of the Fourteenth International Conference on Management Science and Engineering Management. Advances in Intelligent Systems and Computing.* Springer, Cham. 10.1007/978-3-030-49889-4_12

Spânu, P., Ulmeanu, M. E., & Doicin, C. V. (2024). Academic Third Mission through Community Engagement: An Empirical Study in European Universities. *Education Sciences*, 14(2), 141. 10.3390/educsci14020141

Tong, S. (2001). *Active learning: theory and applications.* Stanford University.

Chapter 1
Interactive Learning Strategies in Higher Education:
From Enhanced Lecture to Team-Based Learning

Elena Aurel Railean
https://orcid.org/0000-0002-7893-9742
Information Society Development Institute, Moldova

ABSTRACT

In higher education, interactive learning strategies are a means of encouraging students to participate actively in their education, frequently with the aid of technology. Technology should assist digital pedagogy rather than the other way around. This chapter applies metasystems learning design theory to summarize the diversity of interactive learning strategies in higher education. Based on the hypothesis that interactive learning strategies result in guaranteed learning outcomes, it is clear that passive teaching techniques impact the methodology of traditional lectures and teams. Therefore, within the context of global education, this chapter critically explores 21st-century interactive learning strategies as a response to the following research question: What are the most effective interactive learning strategies in higher education? This chapter describes global trends in the implementation of interactive learning strategies in higher education, which situated current instructional-learning-assessment practices within a framework of critical deconstruction.

DOI: 10.4018/979-8-3693-3559-8.ch001

Copyright © 2024, IGI Global. Copying or distributing in print or electronic forms without written permission of IGI Global is prohibited.

INTRODUCTION

Researchers who approach interactive learning strategies as a contested practice in higher education assert that the term 'learning outcomes' emerge out of an arduous process of negotiation between theoreticians and practicians and this process produces a contentious curriculum fraught with misaligned perspectives to global anthropocentric challenges and social transformations. The dispute over the rapid diversification of interactive learning strategies exists because defined learning outcomes within the course curriculum are instilled with characteristics of actual students that either perpetuate the status quo of learning in a diversity of environments or challenge dominant paradigms narrative in pedagogy to be transformed from cognitive to metacognitive.

Interactive learning strategies aim to make learning a priority. In higher education, one of the most powerful strategies to make learners more engaged in professional learning is to make it interactive. However, there are three psychopedagogical conditions: a) metacognition and successful learning strategies, b) digital assessment, and c) ecosystem of learning and communication. Thus, metacognition is the main assumption for successful learning strategies.

Ecological education (EE) is concerned with the 'symbiotic relationship between human beings and nature' (Judson, 2010). EE also focuses on the relationship between humankind and the Earth. However, the term 'ecological' stemming from the term 'ecology' (the study of the Earth's household) refers to how human beings are connected with the environment. In digital pedagogy, the ecological belief is nurtured by models emphasizing relationships between people in the context (i.e., place-based education) of the learning process (i.e., learning is holistic, cooperative, and collaborative) and of the administrative processes (i.e., collective or/and cooperative decision-making, collaboration and cooperation).

The ecological focus in interactive learning strategies brings together holistic and contextual pedagogies. 'The holistic approach involves the development of such knowledge, skills, and values which should enable learners to become active, democratic and responsible citizens capable of making informed decisions' (Badjanova and Ilisko, 2015). However, EE is more than holistic; it is also contextual because it 'connects' learners with specific places and memorable events in their lives. Relating learning *to context* and *in context* is a way to engage learners in transcending traditional borders of 'discipline' to multiple learning environments for a more holistic understanding of the world. Even though EE has until recently been conducted mostly in environmental education, EE practices have noticeably seeped into the context of the **ecosystem**. Nevertheless, we lack a global perspective on how ecosystem models have been applied and the results for the improvement of learning and communication design. In response, this study offers a systematic review of the scientific literature on ELC to gain a better understanding of the features of published studies, their bibliographic and bibliometric data, and, in particular, the results they report regarding the practice and effects of ecosystem models on learning and communication.

THEORETICAL UNDERPINNINGS OF ECOSYSTEM-BASED LEARNING DESIGN

Active learning is an approach where learners participate in the learning process by building knowledge and understanding. To process and subsequently comprehend new material, learners must draw connections between new information and ideas and their prior knowledge. This active process of making sense of the world can happen during a variety of educational endeavors. It can be compared to a passive method of instruction where the speaker talks mainly "at" the class and presumes they will understand without further clarification. Active learning requires active (interactive) learning strategies. In theory, interactive learning strategies are based on constructivism theory which states that learners construct or build their understanding primarily through social interaction with others. The kernel of such strategies is the integrity of student-centered, inquiry-based, problem-based, discovery, and/or experiential learning.

Interactive learning strategies must be considered a state of a metasystem in an ecosystem. The metasystem is a system of systems. According to Metasystem Transition Theory, 'metasystem occurs when living systems achieve higher system organization from the controlled coordination (i.e., control system X) of previously disparate subsystems (i.e., A1+A2+A3=B). Metasystems separate two different levels of organization' (Last, 2015, p. 2). However, as was noted by Heylighen (2000), living organizations generate complexity that manifests as hierarchical and developmentally constrained cybernetic controls. The proper feature of such systems is their autonomy, but autonomy is "autonomy in living systems is a feature of self-production (autopoiesis), and that a living system is properly characterized only as a network of processes of production of components that is continuously, and recursively, generated and realized as a concrete entity (unity) in the physical space, by the interactions of the same components that it produces as such a network. This organization I call the autopoietic organization, and any system that exhibits it is an autopoietic system in the space in which its components exist; in this sense, living systems are autopoietic systems in the physical space." (Maturana, 1975).

An ecosystem, the concept developed by Tansley (1935), refers to a biological assemblage interacting with its associated physical environment and located in a specific place. In the opinion of Schowalter (2022), the ecosystem is the integration of the biotic community with its abiotic environment. Subsequently, the idea of an ecosystem was linked to social structures and/or management schemes and procedures. Moreover, the term '*ecosystem*' is connected to the idea of integrating the biological community with its physical environment. However, as was noted by Schowalter (2022), ecosystems differ in their structure and functions. The structure can be described by the amount, diversity, and distribution of biotic and abiotic factors, but the functions are described by how communities transfer energy and nutrients among biotic and abiotic pools and control other environmental conditions. Human-dominated ecosystems can be described using the same metrics as those used to describe natural communities.

'Biocoenosis' and 'biotope' are the kernel terms of the ecosystem terminology. A biocoenosis (i.e., biocoenosis, biocenose, biocoenose, biotic community, biological community, ecological community, life assemblage) is a community of associated organisms. Biotope (from gr. *bios* = life and *topos* = place, home, environment) refers to '*the habitat together with its recurring associated community of species, operating together at a particular scale*' (Connor et al., 1997). However, the English term '*habitat*' is used to define the place of a community occupied by a species, or a population, while 'biotope' refers to the environment with material, energetic, and informational resources. The structure of the ecosystem includes inorganic and organic elements and substances; a climate regime (temperature, pressure, humidity); producers (most of which are green plants); e) macro consumers and j) micro consumers as well as inhibitors or stimulants.

In pedagogy and knowledge management, the term "ecosystem" first appeared in 1960, following the widespread use of personal computers and information systems in classrooms. The ecosystems approach was first applied theoretically to comprehend the structure and relationships between different systems to identify and control emergent characteristics and forecast disturbance effects. However, with the emergence of digital technologies in education, the concept of the ecosystem was applied to some e-learning technologies. For instance, according to Chang and Guetl (2007), the learning ecosystem consists of stakeholders incorporating the whole chain of the learning process and the learning utilities, or the learning environments, within specific boundaries. A learning community is an organization of learners and stakeholders (i.e., lecturers, tutors, content providers, experts, and technology support and management staff). In other words, the learning ecosystem is an ecological system, which has 'all the components needed to implement an e-learning solution' (Lohmosavi et al., 2013).

Regarding the e-learning ecosystem, Van de Heyde and Siebrits (2019) highlight the idea of a dynamic, ever-evolving, and living system of human and non-human resources, in which the most important feature is the constant and fluid dialogue between its components. At the same time, academic developers and lecturers aligned tools, resources, and pedagogies with the needs of students engaged in the e-learning environment, in supporting individual learning imperatives. These top-down and bottom-up continuous processes represent the kernel of the modern e-learning ecosystem. However, for the affordability of top-down and bottom-up processes is important to plan, design, develop, and implement interactive learning strategies.

The other reason is the global shift from operational objectives to *learning outcomes*. The Bologna process, which embraces learning outcomes, is still in its early stages of change in higher education. According to CEDEFOP (2008), learning outcomes are statements of what a learner knows, understands, and can do after completion of learning. How to design and implement a learning outcomes approach in higher education? On the one hand, there are some issues. First, terms of learning outcomes and competencies are interchanged. Second, learning outcomes are often called competencies. Third, as the result of the emergence of *socle commun* in France, competencies are defined as a combination of essential knowledge, skills, abilities, and attitudes. Therefore, every competency ought to be obtained from several disciplines, and every discipline ought to aid in the acquisition of multiple competencies. On the other hand, higher university pedagogy is focused on two main types of goals, that are a) goals to strive towards lifelong learning competencies and b) metacognitive goals to be attained by students within their studies. The metacognitive goals of students refer to lifelong learning competencies of students, which include, but are not limited to *metacognitive knowledge* and/or *metacognitive competencies.*

Prioritizing learning outcomes is often seen as a sign of and a precursor to a new metaparadigm in teaching, learning, and assessment. But there is a contradiction between traditional (cognitive and behavioral) and non-traditional (constructivist) approaches. Advocates of traditional models view learning as accumulative, factual, and replicable with a focus on the individual activity of each student. Vice versa, advocates of non-traditional models prioritize active (constructive) learning environments with a balance of conceptual and practical activities. In sum, according to the active learning (constructivist) theories, learning is a social process in which students and teachers constantly engage with their diverse contexts and give knowledge its meaning.

Ecosystem-Based Models of Learning And Interactivity

The global roadmap focuses on understanding the differences between learner-centered learning environments and the learning ecosystem. In general terms, 'the concept of learning environment, in the new pedagogical paradigm, adds a sociological dimension to those features as learning environments are understood as different learning situations which are characterized by activities taking place between teachers and pupils in a framework that comprises several structural factors consisting of resources and roles' (Midoro, 2006, p. 42). The concept of the learning environment was analyzed based on the findings of Lane et al. (2021). Differences between the concepts of *learning environment* and *learning ecosystem* are presented in Table 4.

Table 1. The main differences between learning environment and the learning ecosystem

Criteria	Learning environment	Learning Ecosystem
learning environment	a place that may or may not support life, competence, or experience growth	an inherently dynamic living environment in which the place and its inhabitants are interdependent
learning activity	learner-centered, interactive	ecosystem-centred, dynamic
content developer	teacher, an expert in the field	content is created collaboratively
learner activity	transformation of facts, quality of understanding, identification of solutions	learners actively employ and experience the technologies, conventions, and practices of/in the 'real' and digital worlds
assessment	multiple-choice items, criterion-referenced tests, all-inclusive portfolios	learners can maintain control of their work (digital artifacts) both during and following the completion of their study

There are various models of ecosystem-based learning design. One of these refers to a 'domain-specific work-integrated learning ecosystem' (Fergusson et al., 2021), described as a valued approach to higher education pedagogies at the intersection of two concepts: *learning ecosystems* and *work-integrated learning*. The concept of *learning ecosystems*', also known as learning communities and networks of practice, refers to learning hubs – the place where learning and communication take place over time via connectors and collaborative actions.

Lane et al. (2021) reviewed the pedagogical opportunities offered by a fully open learning ecosystem. In their opinion, 'learning ecosystem' is the common term of the international consortium of open education resource universities to meet the needs of students and stakeholders by promoting the open-source Next Generation Digital Learning Ecosystem (NGDLE), offering 'OER-based micro-courses with pathways to gain stackable micro-credentials, convertible to academic credit toward recognized university qualifications' (Lane et al., 2021). This learning ecosystem can reach learners wherever they are. However, not all of the studies reported such favorable outcomes. Msweli, Twinomurinzi, and Ismail (2022) found differences between learning design before and after the global COVID-19 pandemic and observed that instructional designers focus on more flexible *microcredentials* – credentialing short, interactive, and available online and sector- or practice-focused educational systems that follow competency-based professional learning pathways and can be completed in the individual's own time.

The design of STEM/STEAM/STEMx as a learning ecosystem is an opportunity to understand that in real environments, learning refers to multiple processes that occur in a nonlinear manner. An interesting result was described by Allen et al., 2020: 'As we continue to develop innovative STEM learning models that emphasize hands-on, mind-on 'project-based' learning to foster curiosity, questioning, creativity, and innovation, meaningful assessments of and for learning are vital' (p. 85). However, in the planning of a lesson, it is important to consider the idea of *ecosystem degradation*. Each ecosystem is a part of nature, and the 'connections' between biocoenosis and biotope are continuous but based on ecological principles, norms, and rules. Currently, developments in technology and the irresponsible use of digital devices have increased issues of learning and communication and ecosystem degradation.

Aminatun et al. (2022) developed Android modules based on local wisdom ecosystem materials. After the dissemination of the module among high school students, they observed that the problem-solving design module was better perceived than the project-based learning design. Therefore, the use of the Android module as a digital platform is a perspective in learning design that aims to understand the specific features of the local ecosystem. The ecosystem of learning for the active engagement of students through all life, the main idea of Becker's research, refers to a complex and dynamic organization that fosters links between student-led engagement, institutional engagement, and society to create virtuous circles. This model of the learning ecosystem has committed to exploring and exploiting the synergies between formal education and civic engagement to impact campuses and communities, including the global community.

These approaches make ELC an innovative practice that responds to what ecologists tell us concerning the relationships between biocoenosis and biotope, as it implies the special place of each learner in an ecosystem and the correlation between students and self-regulated lifelong learners in a diversity of learning environments. In my research, earlier findings have revealed that ELC offers professionals in education the chance to redesign learning spaces, curricula, and course materials and rethink pedagogy. The emerging third mission university model labeled the 'ecosystem model' – as defined by Knudsen (et al., 2021) – and leading to a collaboration between public and private actors of education is not only about generating profit for a university but also about interacting with business partners, policymakers and clusters to create value for society.

THE MAIN FOCUS OF THE CHAPTER

Learning Strategies

The ideas and actions a learner use to increase task performance and gain knowledge are referred to as learning strategies. When someone describes how they approach learning and how they can use data, information, and knowledge throughout their life, it's called that person has a 'learning strategy'. In university education, how can one create a workable learning strategy? It is widely recognized that training in suitable information-processing strategies can improve a person's ability to obtain and use data, information, and knowledge most suitably. However, learning strategies have many classifications. For instance, according to Dansereau (2019), there are primary and support strategies. Thus, support strategies are used to keep the student's mental state appropriate for learning, while primary strategies—such as comprehension and memory strategies - are used to work directly with the text material (e.g., concentration strategies). Therefore, learning strategies are specific actions taken by learners or groups of learners under the guidance of teachers to make learning more efficient and sustainable.

Learning strategies are not independent; rather, they are closely associated with the learner's innate learning styles, motivation to learn and other aspects of personality (Figure 1).

Interactive Learning Strategies in Higher Education

Figure 1. Learning strategies and personality

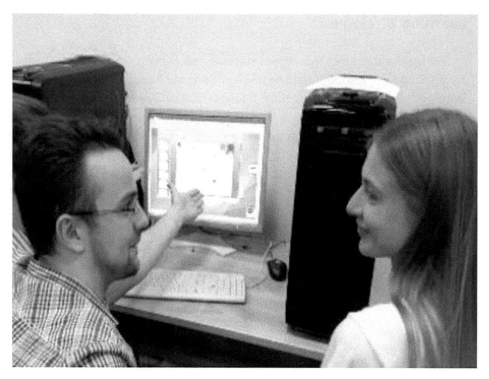

From this perspective, learning strategies are cognitive, metacognitive, and socio affective. Cognitive learning strategies are related to the cognitive styles of students (a psychological construct relating to how individuals process information) and may include repetition, summarizing, guessing meaning from context, etc. Metacognitive learning strategies are related to metacognition, thinking, and decision-making capacity. These strategies regulate the learning process from the perspective of learners' motivation to learn and involve thinking about planning, monitoring, evaluation, and regulation of the learning process. Socio-affective learning strategies deal with emotions, motivation, demonstration of success in diversity of learning environments.

Ironically, metacognitive and socio-affective learning strategies hinge on cognitive educational outcomes – even in learning for a profession - thus it creates a scenario in which one student or a small team of students is more 'active' than others (Figure 2).

Figure 2. The initiative in learning strategies

The metacognitive outcome of learning strategy, however, generates a branding response for the 'new normal' in higher education in which liquid skills (i.e. hard skills, soft skills, green skills) rank at the top in comparison to the learning outcome of cognitive strategies like specialized knowledge, skills, attitude or so on Finally, socio-affective learning strategies, including cognitive and/or spiritual intelligence, have influenced the emergence of global trends in the implementation of interactive learning strategies in higher education. Knowledge acquisition is directly impacted by cognitive learning strategies, while learning is facilitated by socio-affective and metacognitive learning strategies. Thus, when instructional / learning designers implement interactive learning strategies in higher education, it significantly impacts the quality of learning outcomes of students and, therefore, their lifelong capacity to learn for success.

Interactive Learning Strategies

Interactive learning is a pedagogical approach that incorporates active learning and social networking into course design and delivery. It has emerged as a result of the widespread use of digital technology and digital communication among students. Simply put, interactive learning is learning that requires student participation through class and small group discussions as well as through exploration of interactive learning materials, both physical and digital. Examples of interactive learning strategies include asking questions, soliciting opinions, getting students to make short presentations, analyzing case studies, and making and using audio, video, and other sources to prompt dialogue and debate. Regarding collaboration between students, interactive learning strategies may be classified as individual, group, and collaborative activities.

Brainstorming

The most used strategy is *brainstorming* applied to foster group creativity by which ideas and thoughts are shared among members spontaneously. It aims to reach solutions to practical problems. "Brainstorming is a method of generating ideas, clarifications, and solutions; therefore, there is a strong connection between brainstorming productivity and domain learning" (Gogus, 2012). A review of brainstorming techniques in higher education was conducted by Al-Samarraie and Hurmuzan (2018), who identified traditional/verbal, nominal, and electronic techniques of brainstorming. In traditional/verbal brainstorming students actively participate in active dialogue and interaction by verbally sharing their ideas one at a time. In his opinion, the most realistic solution in a university setting is *electronic brainstorming*. With the help of brainstorming apps like MindMeister, Padlet, Popplet, Trello, Miro, Lucidchart, Brainstormer, BookWidgets mind map widget Wrap up!, Mentimeter, and many others, the university professor can actively engage their students in active learning for better and more affordable learning outcomes.

Well-designed learning strategies for brainstorming sessions have the following limits:

1. set a time limit between 15 and 60 minutes
2. target a problem by a defined question, plan, or goal and *stay* on topic
3. no judgment or criticism so that no one should be negative about any idea
4. encourage all ideas so that everyone feels *free* to blurt out ideas
5. aim for quantity because the sifting-and-sorting process comes later
6. build on ideas focusing on associations of "and" and "but"
7. stay visual with diagrams and posts
8. allow one conversation at a time showing respect to everyone's ideas.

To capture ideas in brainstorming sessions is important to play "scribe" and mark every idea on the board or write down all ideas as they come, and share these with the group (Figure 3).

Figure 3. The role of personality in brainstorming

Here can be used brainstorming and its sibling approaches – *brain-dumping* (for individuals), *brainwriting*, and *brain walking* (for group-and-individual mixes), *self-assessment strategies and control* etc. that promote active engagement with the course versus traditional pedagogical tactics of learning in university settings. However, risks arose as a result of psychopedagogical aspects of learning, including students' personality and his /her motivation to be engaged in own learning or/and for benefits of team. First, in a brainstorming session is important to take care of *harnessing synergy* because leveraging the collective thinking towards a variety of potential solutions with introverts and extroverts may focus the discussion to the extreme in which extroverts are in the majority. Second, in brainstorming is vital to stick to the problem relevant to the part of the discussion problem for which the brainstorming session was designed.

Exit Slips or Exit Tickets

In appropriate contexts, a pedagogical game strategy is a mix of formative and diagnostic assessment, which can be used for the purpose of deciding when to sit for formal evaluation.

Figure 4. Game strategy in university pedagogy

By using the exit ticket, instructors with an active student can establish a feedback loop whereby they gather data, take action on it, and then gather more data to foster trust and improve student engagement, learning, and sense of belonging. This strategy is best used at the end of the lecture. For questions can be used a picture or a template like *BookWidgets* or Mentimeter

However, exit tickets can be used in many other ways. First, exit tickets are affordable to assess the knowledge of the students and their level of understanding of the material. For this is important to allow students to rate their comprehension of the lesson from 0-to-3 or to identify the right response from the list. Second, students may write a response to the question they have related to the lesson's concept. Questions are: How hard did you work today? What do you think we accomplished in the small group activity? Third, lecturers collect feedback on instructional strategies and create an open communication line with the professor. Questions: How well did the video improve your learning? Did you enjoy working as a group? Why or why not? Do you think all participants were able to contribute to the seminar discussion? What can I do to help you in this course? Fourth, but not the last the lecturer asks the students to write for one minute on a specific question, like "What was the most important thing you learned from previous course?"

There are a few recommendations for designing an effective exit ticket learning strategy. First, frequent exit ticket assignments can help students form good habits and metacognitive strategies related to how to learn about own learning, but they can also get tedious if they are given too often. Second, students can be as honest as possible when answering an anonymous exit ticket, but it is more challenging to respond to specific queries or issues brought up in the ticket. Third, an exit ticket can serve as a substitute for an attendance sheet.

Buzz Session

Buzz session is an interactive learning strategy in which students come together in session groups that focus on a single topic. This may include elements of peer assessment strategy – a learning strategy which refers to 'the process of having the learners critically reflect upon, and perhaps suggest grades for, the learning of their peers' (Robets, 2016). In a buzz session every student offer idea and thought to each group. Encouragement of dialogue and cooperation between the students in each group is crucial (Figure 5).

Figure 5. Psychopedagogical aspects of buzz session with the game elements

Everyone ought to gain knowledge from one another's opinions and experiences. The teacher could provide the class with some discussion starters to spark the conversation. According to Vinacke (1957) in a buzz session, a question is posed to a group. The members are then asked to turn to a neighbour (or to form convenient groups) and to engage in discussion for several minutes. There is no preparation, no formality, and no systematic efforts to organize the groups, nor to follow up the discussion other than in simple and general ways. Nowadays, the question can be generated by artificial intelligence, but active learning should remain a priority.

Buzz session strategy is essential for building genuine pragmatic situations that assist higher institutions to effectively train future teachers or school psychologists as professionals with the capacity to learn through life thereby meeting global societal demands. However, more time must be spent by university lecturers in preparation for the buzz session to complete tasks, respond to inquiries, and establish the lecture's context and pedagogical design of interactive learning environment. Interactive scenarios, case studies, real images, multimedia could be included in a buzz session. When students collaborate and brainstorm with one another under the direction of their facilitator, it is beneficial for the sustainability of lifelong learning capacity.

Misconception Check

This interactive learning strategy aims to discover students' misconceptions by analyzing their capacity to identify the correct answer when given a false fact in learning with or without a digital learning environment. The learning strategy encourages students to think deeply and wager all the possibilities related to the studied material (Figure 6).

Figure 6. The misconception check strategy with info on digital screen

Most researchers and practitioners are in agreement that for interactive learning strategies to work well, it is important for the instructor to provide clear and concise guidelines, and to maintain the ultimate responsibility for the final grades. As was noted by Fisher and Frey (2014), checking for understanding is part of a formative assessment system in which faculty members know exactly what students are getting out of the lecture. For this outcome, it is recommended to use interoperability of feed-up, feedback, and feed-forward. The role of interactive feedback is to establish a purpose, scope, clear objectives, or learner target(s) so that students understand the goal of the instruction and teaching strategies are easily aligned with the lectures'

motivation to learn. Immediate feedback is important for responding to activity. Ideally, feedback occurs when students' complete tasks so they continue to master more deeply the studied content. If learning is the goal of student, instructor does not limit feedback to summative review but provides formative feedback that students could use to improve their performance and to learn through understanding.

Feedforward is a (meta)process used by learner in a group to improve his/her performance of learning how to learn or how to prove what was learn, but here the problem of allocating a uniform mark to all members of a group needs to be taken into account. For teacher, the role of feedforward is to get data for planning instruction and interventions. Moreover, in the misconception check strategy is important to make the difference between errors and mistakes. Typically, errors occur because of the lack of knowledge, but mistakes are due to fatigue, carelessness, or intention. Faculty members who are familiar with a student's prior work may be able to identify errors or mistakes. When we see a mistake, it seems out of character, especially if we have witnessed the student complete the same task correctly in the past. The teacher, in this case, possesses the power that dictates the outcome of the student-curriculum relationship.

Circle the Questions

In this learning strategy, instructor uses a) a worksheet with a list of questions related to the studied topic and asks students to circle (or check) the ones they don't know the answers to or b) digital assessment test with a list of correct / incorrect answers which will be analysed by immediate feedback. Then, in the first situation the teacher created corners concerning different questions that were circled. Students work on the extra exercises and explanations in the corners, individually and receive feedback, either individual or social.

In a digital learning environment, the student may be engaged in a human-computer communication. However, this multimodal form of communication is a form of integrity between various *input* (i.e. keyboard typing, mouse clicking, screen touching) and *output* (i.e. human abilities like perception, cognition, language) channels. The most frequently encountered problem is that in passive digital learning environment, even it is used interactive feedback as a secure of learning, the learner is a less active user of digital learning environment in which knowledge is provided. This problem can best be countered by ensuring that all students do not solve the same task or adding questions, which require reflection and real problem solving (Figure 7).

Figure 7. Interactive learning strategy with elements of human-computer communication

But this raised a problem. Studies have indicated that education and training are intensely social endeavors. Creating learning communities that are secure and trustworthy is crucial to the learning process. Because students will all have circled different questions, instructors have to give each student or each group of students a different and personalized order to visit the corners and answer questions. One of the key components of this interactive learning strategy is responding to all questions. University teachers can strengthen relationships, foster trust, and assist individuals in expressing their needs, wants, and feelings. Equity, concentration, connection, and inclusion amongst all participants are made possible by the "circle" format. Moreover, "circle the question" may be improved by the "ask the winner" strategy. In this situation, instructor asks students to silently solve a problem on the board. After disclosing the solution, it tells those who answered correctly to raise their hands (and keep them raised). To better understand the question and how to answer it the next time, all other students are required to speak with who raised their hand.

Think, Pair, and Share

Think, pair, and share is an interactive learning strategy developed by Frank Lyman in which a university lecturer sets a problem or a question around the studied topic and pairs up students to collaborate on understanding the main concept. Many ways of teaching with this strategy have been suggested in scientific literature, such as 'setting' a provocative question, studding case studies important for students and so on. But the most reliable and fair strategies would seem to include a high level of peer assessment within the group themselves. Each pair of students has enough time to reach the proper conclusion and to share it in the voice (Figure 8).

Figure 8. Interactive learning strategies in training of in-service teachers

The process is straightforward: the teacher asks a question and then instructs the class to consider their responses in silence. The lecturers could ask them to write down students' unique responses as an alternative or may give them anywhere from 10 seconds to five minutes to work alone, depending on the difficulty of the question and how long they believe the activity should last. After that, students may compare or debate their answers in pairs with a partner. Lastly, a few students are randomly selected to provide a summary of the conversation.

A similar learning strategy is *"pair-share-repeat"*. In this strategy, the instructor asks students to find a new partner and share the wisdom of the old partnership with this new partner to brainstorm the main ideas of the studied material. The teacher may assist students in two roles: one of the teacher and the other – of the student. The teacher's function is to sketch the main points, while the student's role is to cross off points on his list and come up with points that the teacher missed. An alternative learning strategy is called "wisdom from another". Using this strategy, the faculty member pairs up students and asks them to discuss their findings following a creative or brain-storming session. Then, he or she requests volunteers who thought their partner's work was noteworthy or engaging. It was observed that students frequently share their work less publicly than those of their peers.

Interactive Debating

One well-known learning strategy is debating, which stimulates students' minds and helps them grasp the material in greater depth. Since the term's inception, debating has been used to describe the process of weighing various points of view and making conclusions. According to Mont (2014), debating can be a group activity in which participants attempt to persuade others to agree with their points of view, or it can be a personal experience in which each participant uses communication to help formulate his or her viewpoint. In the debate process, students are expected to conduct background research, evaluate the reliability of sources, rank their points of view, think of original and useful ways to present their positions, hear opposing viewpoints, analyze them, and come up with a counterargument. All of this work is done in groups. Students grow a deeper comprehension of the material and take greater ownership of their understanding as a result.

Interactive debating is a strategy of active learning, which devolves deeper into peer interaction and requires higher level of knowledge and understanding how to solve a real situation (Figure 9).

Interactive Learning Strategies in Higher Education

Figure 9. Interactive debating in training of future teachers

There are various forms of planning interactive debating strategy. For instance, in a debate with optimists/pessimists students should take opposite emotional sides of a case study, statement, or topic following a teacher that encourages them to be empathetic and truly "live" the case study. Then, in a forced debate students must defend the opposite side of their personal opinion. It pushes them to question their convictions and occasionally teaches them to see the world through a different lens. One half of the class, for example, takes one position, and the other half takes the other position. Students face one another as they form a line. To allow all students to discuss the matter, each student may only speak once (Figure 10).

Figure 10. The strategy of a forced interactive debate

In another version of the interactive debating strategy, the teacher posts a statement like '*Anything can be found on Google and learning is not important*' and students, divided into four groups, argue their own from the perspective of SWOT analysis methodology (where S- Strengths, W- Weaknesses, O- opportunities, and T- Threats).

An interactive debating strategy can be done through an oral and written task. For instance, in a '*peer review writing task*' students exchange drafts of assessment with a partner. After reading the essay, the partner responds in three paragraphs: the first highlights the essay's advantages, the second addresses its shortcomings, and the third describes the revisions the partner would make if it were an essay. This strategy may be accomplished by digital technologies allowing students to use one of the self-assessment strategies or networking in a digital environment. Among self-assessment strategies are selfie/emoticon roulette, Instagram story, and lesson Tweet (with hashtag).

Interactive Group Learning Strategies

Board Rotation

In this strategy, students are divided into different groups. Each group is assigned to a board. One topic/question is assigned per board. Each group moves on to the next board after writing their response. Here, they jot down their response beneath the preceding group's initial response. The teacher allows students to circle the room until every group has covered every board.

Pick the Winner

Group the students and assign them to work on the same subject or issue. Allow them to write down or digitally record a response or plan. Ask the groups to switch places with a group that is close by so they can assess each other's responses. Give each group a few minutes to come together, then ask them to choose the best response between the two options to be given to the class as a whole.

Movie Application

Students work in groups to analyze examples of films that utilize a topic or event that was covered in class, attempting to point out both the good and bad things that the filmmakers did. Consider films that present historical, geographical, or celebrity biographies.

Interactive Gamification

Gamification of education, which should not be confused with game-based learning (which is more limited in scope), is the use of game elements to influence or motivate behavior in non-gaming contexts. Students will be encouraged to learn more independently and effectively if gamification is used in higher education. The main justification for this is that it fosters relationships between members of an academic community by promoting competition and teamwork. A gamification is a great tool for accomplishing this goal. Whether an instructor is teaching in-person or virtually, it is crucial to be aware of the social aspects of teaching and learning. Additionally, a gamified learning process can help your students become fully engaged with the material and develop a positive attitude toward self-regulated learning. Examples of interactive learning games are crossword puzzles, pair-matching games, bingo games, jigsaw puzzles, and memory games.

FUTURE RESEARCH DIRECTIONS

The ecosystem of learning and communication is the core concept of green pedagogy – the science of education in the Anthropocene period, which is characterized by specifics of living in the time in which human thinking, action, and activities influence not only the climate and natural environment but also the natural mechanism of learning and communication. An increasing number of people virtually connect to, communicate, and learn in various geographical areas and learning spaces. This global ecosystem is more than a simple network of digital devices; it is a metasystem of people, devices, networking, and various linkages, both spatial and temporal because it ensures the exchange of matter, energy, and information.

On the one hand, the 'integration' of people's intelligence into the 'intelligence' of digital devices and artifacts leads to novel models of human-machine communications. On the other hand, the internet, sensors, and embedded systems multiply power through an intelligent combination of mental, physical, and mechanical factors, leading to the emergence of digital citizenship, defined as the successful engagement of individuals with digital technologies and a participative culture. In all these processes, the student should be 'situated' in the real world of learning and communication. Therefore, to understand ELC and its impact on learning outcomes, it is important to first study the meaning of humans in the world.

Shifting the educational paradigm from the design of learner-centered learning environments to the acceptance of ELC allows us to reflect on *global risks* – a large-scale phenomenon that impacts society, economics, politics, and educational science. In this regard, pedagogy should take into account the fact that learning consists of multiple conscious-unconscious, often hidden processes; that natural learning capacity cannot be developed without communication in a social environment; and that human minds are governed not only by 'mechanical' norms and laws but also by quantum laws, even if their nature cannot be understood with research methods.

Each ecosystem consists of dynamically changing environments formed because of ecological processes that are 'non-linear, multi equilibrium and full of surprises', as was noted by Berkes et al. (2009). 'We use the term "ecological processes" to events (as milestones) that link humans with the environment and, therefore, allow them to adapt actions and behavior to changing environments' (Railean, 2019). However, to manage this effect, it is important to balance hard skills (i.e., knowledge) and liquid skills (i.e., learning and communication literacy).

The global ecosystem includes various models of open, distance, and remote education. As was noted by Uden (2019), the digital environment is a self-sustaining ecosystem with all the tools and surroundings necessary to achieve the desired educational outcomes, but where organisms interact with one another and with their physical environment, if they are aware of their unique role, must be in balance between all aspects of the ecosystem. Braescu (2019), who observed communication gaps, agreed with this idea and found that dysfunctionalities are induced by human nature and may be considered a result of discrepancies between the flow of data, information, and knowledge and old patterns of teaching and learning. Therefore, in an ecosystem, it is important to be aware of the balance between holistic and personalized learning and spaces for communication. Interactive learning strategies should ensure this dynamic equilibrium.

CONCLUSION

The education ecosystem consists of two interrelated aspects: learning and communication. The first aspect relies on the fact that an ecosystem is a community of organisms together with their physical environments, and the second relies on the ecosystem being a system of ecological relationships. Stability within the system is upheld because *'the relationship between the different organisms is such that each member mutually supports the continued existence of the other members and of the system itself'* (van der Heyde and Siebrits, 2019). Thus, the ecosystem has two important aspects – its components and the relationship. For this, it is important to develop liquid skills. There are many ways to develop liquid skills. According to Marisi (2019), learners should be guided to develop scaffolding thinking, reflect on learning, and use the most appropriate cognitive and metacognitive strategies for context. In the opinion of Mikhalsky (2019), 'ecosystem integrates a new image of the future (if it does not fit the context of its metasystem), and it tunes up the ecosystem aligning to some new qualities of the new order, or a new state'. Therefore, the ecosystem requires a connection to learning and communication for professional growth.

This chapter discusses the place of interactive learning strategies in an ecosystem of learning and communication in higher education. The ecosystem approach indicates that interactive learning strategies will immensely outperform the learning environment approach due to their affordability in serving self-assessment needs of students. In addition, we envision that developing student 'thinking and learning skills', 'ecosystem of learning and communication', 'interactive learning strategies' are candidates for the conceptualization of new normal in university education.

REFERENCES

Al-Samarraie, H., & Hurmuzan, S. (2018). A review of brainstorming techniques in higher education. *Thinking Skills and Creativity*, 27, 78–91. 10.1016/j.tsc.2017.12.002

Allen, P. J., Brown, Z., & Noam, G. G. (2020). STEM Learning Ecosystems: Building from Theory toward a Common Evidence Base. *International Journal for Research on Extended Education*, 8(1), 80–96.

Aminatun, T., Subali, B., Dwiyani, A., Prihartina, I., & Meliana, D. (2022). Developing Android-Based Mobile through Local Ecosystem Materials to Improve Thinking Skills of High School Students. *Anatolian Journal of Education*, 7(1), 73–82. 10.29333/aje.2022.716a

Anbalagan, G. (2019). Learning Ecosystem for Open and Distance Learning. In Railean, E. (Ed.), *Handbook of Research on Ecosystem-Based Theoretical Models of Learning and Communication* (pp. 124–138). IGI Global. 10.4018/978-1-5225-7853-6.ch007

Becker, J. (2019). Bard College: An Ecosystem of Engagement. *Journal of Community Engagement and Higher Education at Indiana State University*, 11(1), 38–52.

Bhat, J. R., & Alqahtani, S. A. (2021). 6G ecosystem: Status and future perspective. *IEEE Access : Practical Innovations, Open Solutions*, 9, 43134–43167. 10.1109/ACCESS.2021.3054833

Cardak, O., & Dikmenli, M. (2016). Student Science Teachers' Ideas about the Degradation of Ecosystems. *International Education Studies*, 9(3), 95–103. 10.5539/ies.v9n3p95

CEDEFOP. (2008). *Conceptual, political, and practical developments in Europe*. European Centre for the Development of Vocational Training. https://www.cedefop.europa.eu/files/4079_en.pdf

Chang, V., & Guetl, C. e-Learning ecosystem (ELES) – A holistic approach for the development of more effective learning environment for small-and-medium-sized enterprises (SMEs). In: *Proceedings of the Inaugural IEEE International Conference on Digital Ecosystems and Technologies*. IEEE. 10.1109/DEST.2007.372010

Dansereau, D. F. (2014). Learning strategy research. In *Thinking and learning skills* (pp. 209–239). Routledge.

Donnelly, R., & Maguire, T. (2020). Building Digital Capacity for Higher Education Teachers: Recognising Professional Development through a National Peer Triad Digital Badge Ecosystem. European Journal of Open. *Distance and E-Learning*, 23(2), 1–19.

Fergusson, L., van der Laan, L., Imran, S., & Ormsby, G. (2021). The Development of Work-Integrated Learning Ecosystems: An Australian Example of Cooperative Education. *International Journal of Work-Integrated Learning*, 22(1), 25–40.

Fisher, D., & Frey, N. (2014). *Checking for understanding: Formative assessment techniques for your classroom*. ASCD.

Gogus, A. (2012). Brainstorming and learning. *Encyclopedia of the Sciences of Learning*. Springer. 10.1007/978-1-4419-1428-6_491

Gonzalez-Zamar, M., & Abad-Segura, E. (2021). Visual Arts in the University Educational Ecosystem: Analysis of Schools of Knowledge. *Education Sciences*, 11(4), 184. 10.3390/educsci11040184

Gütl, C., & Chang, V. (2008). Ecosystem-based theoretical models for learning in environments of the 21st century. [iJET]. *International Journal of Emerging Technologies in Learning*, 3(1), 3. 10.3991/ijet.v3i1.742

Heylighen, F. (2000). Evolutionary transitions: How do levels of complexity emerge? *Complexity*, 6, 53–57. 10.1002/1099-0526(200009/10)6:1<53::AID-CPLX1008>3.0.CO;2-O

Johnson, D. W., Johnson, R. T., & Smith, K. A. (1991). *Cooperative learning: increasing college faculty instructional productivity*. ASHE/ERIC Higher Education.

Judson, G. (2010). *A new approach to ecological education: Engaging students' imaginations in their world*. Peter Lang Publishing.

Kato, S., Galán-Muros, V., & Weko, T. (2020). *The emergence of alternative credentials*. (OECD Education Working Papers, No. 216). OECD Publishing. https://doi.org/10.1787/19939019

Khozali, N., & Karpudewan, M. (2020). An Interdisciplinary Facebook Incorporated STEM Education Strategy in Teaching and Learning of Dynamic Ecosystems. *Eurasia Journal of Mathematics, Science and Technology Education*, 16(11), em1902. 10.29333/ejmste/8704

Knudsen, M. P., Frederiksen, M. H., & Goduscheit, R. C. (2021). New forms of engagement in third mission activities: A multi-level university-centric approach. *Innovation (North Sydney, N.S.W.)*, 23(2), 209–240. 10.1080/14479338.2019.1670666

Lane, D. C., & Goode, Cl. (2021). Open for All: The OERu's Next Generation Digital Learning Ecosystem. *International Review of Research in Open and Distance Learning*, 22(4), 146–163. 10.19173/irrodl.v23i1.5763

Last, C. (2015). Human metasystem transition (HMST) theory. *Journal of Ethics and Emerging Technologies*, 25(1), 1–16. 10.55613/jeet.v25i1.36

Li, M., Hung, M., Hsian, W., Heung, W., Chiu, M., & Wang, S. (2019). Teaching Ecosystem Design: Teachers' Satisfaction with the Integrated Course Service System. *Education Sciences*, 9(3), 232. 10.3390/educsci9030232

Lohmosavi, V., Nejad, A. F., & Hosseini, E. M. (2013). E-learning ecosystem based on serviceoriented cloud computing architecture. In: *Proceedings of the 5th Conference on Information and Knowledge Technology*. IEEE. 10.1109/IKT.2013.6620032

Marisi, R. (2019). Developing the Students' Thinking and Learning Skills in the Instrumental Lesson. In Railean, E. (Ed.), *Handbook of Research on Ecosystem-Based Theoretical Models of Learning and Communication* (pp. 40–65). IGI Global. 10.4018/978-1-5225-7853-6.ch003

Matthew, J. (2021). The PRISMA 2020 statement: An updated guideline for reporting systematic reviews. *BMJ (Clinical Research Ed.)*, 2021, 372. https://www.bmj.com/content/372/bmj.n71

Maturana, H. R. (1975). The organization of the living: A theory of the living organization. *International Journal of Man-Machine Studies*, 7(3), 313–332. 10.1016/S0020-7373(75)80015-0

Meepung, T., Pratsri, S., & Nilsook, P. (2021). Interactive Tool in Digital Learning Ecosystem for Adaptive Online Learning Performance. *Higher Education Studies*, 11(3), 70–77. 10.5539/hes.v11n3p70

Midoro, V. (2016). *A common European Framework for Teachers' Professional Profile in ICT for Education*. Edizioni MENABO Didactica.

Mikhalsky, A. V. (2019). The Ecology of Social Practice in Language, Communication, and Constructing the Future. In Railean, E. (Ed.), *Handbook of Research on Ecosystem-Based Theoretical Models of Learning and Communication* (pp. 66–85). IGI Global. 10.4018/978-1-5225-7853-6.ch004

Mont, M. (2014). The Use of Debates in Higher Education Classrooms. *Adult Education Research Conference*. New Prairie Press. https://newprairiepress.org/aerc/2014/roundtables/23

Msweli, N. T., Twinomurinzi, H., & Ismail, M. (2022). The International Case for Micro-Credentials for Life-Wide and Life-Long Learning: A Systematic Literature Review. *Interdisciplinary Journal of Information, Knowledge, and Management*, 17, 151–190. 10.28945/4954

Niemi, H. (2021). Education Reforms for Equity and Quality: An Analysis from an Educational Ecosystem Perspective with Reference to Finnish Educational Transformations. *Center for Educational Policy Studies Journal*, 11(2), 13–35. 10.26529/cepsj.1100

Pita, M., Costa, J., & Moreira, A. (2021). The Effect of University Missions on Entrepreneurial Initiative across Multiple Entrepreneurial Ecosystems: Evidence from Europe. *Education Sciences*, 11(762), 1–20. 10.3390/educsci11120762

Pitts, W., & Lehner-Quam, A. (2019). Engaging the Framework for Information Literacy for Higher Education as a Lens for Assessment in ePortfolio Social Pedagogy Ecosystem for Science Teacher Education. *International Journal of ePortfolio, 1*, 29-44. https://academicworks.cuny.edu/cgi/viewcontent.cgi?article=1391&context=le_pubs

Railean, E. (2019). *Handbook of Research on Ecosystem-Based Theoretical Models of Learning and Communication*. IGI Global. 10.4018/978-1-5225-7853-6

Ricaurte, P. (2016). Pedagogies for the open knowledge society. *International Journal of Educational Technology in Higher Education*, 13(1), 1–10. 10.1186/s41239-016-0033-y

Sahlberg, P., & Oldroyd, D. (2010). Pedagogy for economic competitiveness and sustainable development. *European Journal of Education*, 45(2), 280–299. 10.1111/j.1465-3435.2010.01429.x

Schowalter, T. D. (2022). Ecosystem structure and function. *Insect Ecology: An Ecosystem Approach*. Science Direct. https://www.sciencedirect.com/science/article/pii/B9780323856737000046

Uden, L. (2019). E-Learning Ecosystems Through the Co-Creation of Value From Service Ecosystems. In Railean, E. (Ed.), *Handbook of Research on Ecosystem-Based Theoretical Models of Learning and Communication* (pp. 106–123). IGI Global., 10.4018/978-1-5225-7853-6.ch006

van de Heyde, V., & Siebrits, A. (2019). The ecosystem of e-learning model for higher education. *South African Journal of Science*, 115(5/6), 78–83. 10.17159/sajs.2019/5808

Vinacke, W. E. (1957). Some variables in buzz sessions. *The Journal of Social Psychology*, 45(1), 25–33. 10.1080/00224545.1957.9714283

Weinstein, C. E., & Mayer, R. E. (1986). The teaching of learning strategies. In Wittrock, M. C. (Ed.), *Handbook of research in teaching* (Vol. 3, pp. 315–327). Macmillan.

KEY TERMS AND DEFINITIONS

Interactive Learning: A pedagogical approach that incorporates social networking and urban computing into course design and delivery with a more hands-on, real-world process of relaying information in classrooms; a technique of teaching-learning-assessment that seeks to get students actively engaged in the learning process, often through the use of technology.

Interactive Learning Materials: Interactive resources and/or tools that can contain any combination of text, images, audio, or video and are designed to teach a specific learning outcome.

Interactive Learning Strategies: Teaching, learning, and assessment strategies, which are focused on thinking, debates, and decision making.

Meaningful Learning Environment: The learning space in which technology is integrated into teaching, learning, and assessment and is focused on collaboration, connection, and interaction.

Chapter 2
Active Learning Strategies in Higher Education

Manjari Sharma
Christ University, India

Sharad Gupta
https://orcid.org/0000-0002-4994-3523
Christ University, India

ABSTRACT

This chapter investigates active learning strategies in higher education, showcasing five innovative learning strategies conducted with students. These strategies include starting and managing a small business to understand entrepreneurship, recording transactions according to accounting principles, and engaging in role-play as members of international organizations like the IMF and World Bank to negotiate projects. Additionally, students create short films on specific topics to explore creative storytelling and communication. These experiential learning activities aim to provide comprehensive insights into practical and theoretical knowledge applications.

INTRODUCTION

Active learning represents a transformative shift in the educational landscape of higher education, moving away from traditional passive learning methods towards more engaging, participatory instructional techniques. Traditional learning methods, often characterized by passive lecture formats, have been criticized for their inability to fully engage students or promote deep understanding. These methods frequently result in student passivity and disengagement, limiting opportunities for critical thinking and active involvement in the learning process.

DOI: 10.4018/979-8-3693-3559-8.ch002

Copyright © 2024, IGI Global. Copying or distributing in print or electronic forms without written permission of IGI Global is prohibited.

In contrast, active learning approaches are grounded in the understanding that students learn best when they are actively involved in the learning process, not merely as receivers of information but as dynamic participants in their educational journey. This approach not only addresses the shortcomings of traditional methods but also aligns with contemporary educational needs that prioritize critical thinking, collaboration, and practical application of knowledge.

This chapter aims to explore the multifaceted impact of active learning strategies on higher education, highlighting its benefits, challenges, and the diverse methodologies employed across different disciplines. Active learning involves methods that engage students directly in the learning process, prompting them to read, write, discuss, or engage in problem-solving activities. These strategies range from complex group projects to simple class discussions, and their significance in higher education cannot be overstated. They enhance student learning outcomes, foster deeper engagement with course content, and encourage the development of critical thinking and problem-solving skills (Freeman et al., 2014; Prince, 2004).

The importance of active learning in higher education is well-documented, with numerous studies indicating that actively engaging students in the learning process leads to improved academic performance and higher levels of student satisfaction (Michael, 2006; Kuh et al., 2005). These strategies are particularly vital in today's globalized world, where the ability to think critically and work collaboratively in diverse teams is highly valued. Active learning not only supports the acquisition of knowledge but also helps students develop essential life skills that are crucial for their professional and personal success beyond the classroom (Baepler et al., 2016).

Table 1. A comparison between active learning and interactive learning

Aspect	Active Learning	Interactive Learning
Definition	Instructional methods that actively engage students in the learning process.	Strategies that focus on the interaction between students and instructors and among students.
Focus	Student engagement with content.	Interaction and communication among participants.
Key Characteristics	• Student-centered • Promotes critical thinking • Hands-on activities • Deep learning	• Interaction-focused • Encourages collaboration • Real-time feedback • Dynamic learning environment
Examples	• Problem-based learning • Think-pair-share • Peer instruction • Case studies	• Group discussions • Simulations • Interactive lectures • Role-playing

continued on following page

Table 1. Continued

Aspect	Active Learning	Interactive Learning
Goals	• Enhance critical thinking • Improve retention • Foster deeper understanding	• Develop communication skills • Promote collaboration • Facilitate immediate feedback
Techniques	• Discussions • Group projects • Hands-on activities • Problem-solving	• Peer teaching • Group work • Technology-facilitated collaboration • Real-time interactions
Benefits	• Better retention of material • Higher test scores • Improved critical thinking	• Enhanced collaborative skills • Better communication skills • Increased student satisfaction
Research Support	• Freeman et al. (2014): Active learning improves student performance in STEM	• Michael (2006): Interaction increases student engagement and learning
Implementation Challenges	• Requires active participation • Can be time-consuming to plan	• Requires effective facilitation • Can be challenging in large classes
Why Choose to Report	• Proven effectiveness in enhancing student outcomes • Increases student engagement • Fosters critical thinking and problem-solving skills	• Active learning is adaptable across various disciplines and educational settings

Active Learning Strategies are instructional approaches that actively engage students in the learning process. Unlike traditional lecture-based teaching, where students passively receive information, active learning requires students to participate in meaningful learning activities and think about what they are doing. These strategies encourage students to discuss, practice, and apply the material they are learning, fostering deeper understanding and retention.

Key Characteristics of Active Learning Strategies:
a. **Student-Centered**: Focuses on students' active participation.
b. **Engagement:** Involves students in activities such as discussions, problem-solving, case studies, and collaborative projects.
c. **Critical Thinking**: Promotes analysis, synthesis, and evaluation of content.
d. **Feedback**: Provides opportunities for immediate feedback from peers and instructors.

Examples of Active Learning Strategies:
a. **Think-Pair-Share:** Students think about a question individually, discuss their thoughts with a partner, and then share their ideas with the larger group.
b. **Problem-Based Learning**: Students work on complex, real-world problems and seek solutions collaboratively.
c. **Peer Teaching**: Students take turns teaching each other under the supervision of the instructor.

d. **Case Studies**: Students analyze and discuss real-life scenarios to apply theoretical knowledge.

Why Active Learning Strategies?

Research has shown that active learning strategies significantly improve student performance, understanding, and retention. For example, Freeman et al. (2014) found that active learning increases student performance in science, engineering, and mathematics compared to traditional lecturing. These strategies not only help students grasp the material better but also develop essential skills such as critical thinking and problem-solving, which are crucial for their academic and professional success (Prince, 2004; Bonwell & Eison, 1991).

Bridge Between Strategy and Method

In educational practice, the terms "strategy" and "method" are often used interchangeably, but they have distinct meanings:

Strategy: A strategy is a broad, overarching plan or approach designed to achieve a specific educational goal. It outlines the general direction and principles guiding the teaching process. For example, the strategy of active learning emphasizes student engagement and participation to enhance learning outcomes.

Method: A method is a specific technique or procedure used to implement a strategy. It involves concrete steps and actions taken by the instructor to facilitate learning. Methods are the practical tools that bring strategies to life in the classroom.

Relationship Between Strategy and Method:

a. **Strategy as the Plan**: The strategy provides the "why" and "what" – it sets the vision and goals for the learning experience. For instance, the active learning strategy aims to engage students and develop their critical thinking skills.

b. **Method as the Execution**: The method provides the "how" – it specifies the actions and techniques to achieve the strategic goals. For example, think-pair-share, problem-based learning, and peer teaching are methods that execute the active learning strategy.

The goals of this chapter are to:

(a) Provide an overview of various active learning strategies and their pedagogical foundations.

(b) Discuss the benefits and challenges associated with implementing active learning in higher education.

(c) Highlight case studies and empirical research that showcase the effectiveness of active learning methodologies.

(d) Offer insights into future trends and directions in active learning research and practice.

THEORETICAL FRAMEWORK

This section discusses these theories in detail, integrating them with practical applications to illustrate how they manifest in real educational settings.

(a) **Constructivism:** Constructivism posits that learning is an active, constructive process where learners build new knowledge upon the foundation of their previous knowledge. According to this theory, learning is more effective when students are actively involved in constructing their own understanding rather than passively receiving information. Vygotsky's concept of the Zone of Proximal Development highlights the importance of scaffolded learning, where the educator helps the student extend their current skills and knowledge base through active engagement (Vygotsky, 1978). In practice, this approach is crucial in active learning environments where students are encouraged to explore, question, and challenge the material presented to them (Fosnot, 2005). For instance, in a classroom setting, a constructivist approach might involve students working on group projects where they must apply theoretical knowledge to solve real-world problems, thereby constructing new understandings through collaboration and discussion.

(b) **Experiential Learning:** Experiential learning, advanced by Kolb (1984), emphasizes the role of experience in the learning process. Kolb's Experiential Learning Theory argues that effective learning occurs through a cycle of experiencing, reflecting, thinking, and acting, which engages learners in a continuous process of adaptation and learning (Kolb, 1984). In the context of higher education, this means structuring activities that allow students to engage directly with material, reflect on their experiences, derive insights, and apply these insights in real-world or simulated scenarios. For example, in medical education, experiential learning can be implemented through clinical simulations where students practice medical procedures in a controlled environment, reflect on their performance, and receive feedback to improve their skills.

(c) **Social Learning Theory:** Social Learning Theory, articulated by Bandura (1977), stresses the importance of observing, modeling, and imitating the behaviors, attitudes, and emotional reactions of others. In active learning, this translates into collaborative projects and peer-learning sessions where students learn from each other's insights and feedback, enhancing the learning experience through social interaction (Bandura, 1977). A practical application of this theory can be seen in peer review activities where students critique each other's work, offering constructive feedback and learning through the process of giving and receiving critiques. This not only reinforces their understanding but also develops their ability to evaluate and improve their work critically.

(d) **Empirical Support and Integration:** Empirical support for these theories is robust. Freeman et al. (2014) demonstrates that active learning strategies in STEM education significantly improve students' academic performance and retention rates compared to traditional lecturing methods. Similarly, Prince's (2004) meta-analysis confirms that active learning techniques such as problem-based learning and inquiry-based learning substantially enhance engineering education by aligning with diverse learning styles and increasing engagement and retention (Prince, 2004).

Further research by Michael (2006) highlights that active learning fosters critical thinking and problem-solving skills as it requires students to analyze, synthesize, and evaluate information actively. This is echoed in studies by Kuh et al. (2005), who found that engagement through active learning is strongly correlated with higher levels of student achievement, satisfaction, and overall college success. Additionally, Baepler et al. (2016) discuss the logistical and pedagogical benefits of active learning classrooms, which are designed to facilitate a dynamic learning environment through physical and curricular modifications that promote interaction and engagement.

(e) **Practical Applications:** The practical applications of these theoretical frameworks in active learning environments are vast and varied. For example, constructivist approaches can be seen in project-based learning where students undertake extensive projects that require them to apply classroom knowledge to real-world scenarios. Experiential learning is often implemented through internships and practicums where students gain hands-on experience in their field of study. Social learning is frequently facilitated through group work and peer assessments, encouraging students to learn from and with each other.

Figure 1. Conceptual framework: Model for active learning in higher education

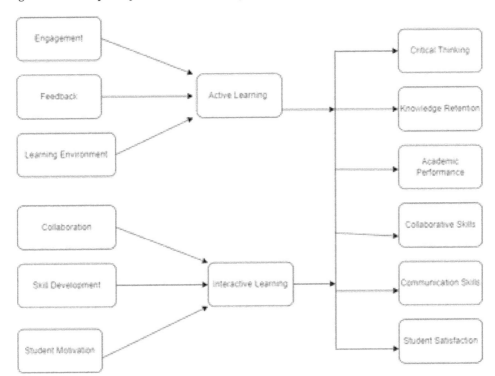

BENEFITS OF ACTIVE LEARNING

This section delves into the various advantages of active learning, each supported by empirical evidence and theoretical insights, demonstrating why it is a preferred strategy in modern educational practices.

(a) **Improved Student Engagement and Motivation:** Active learning strategies significantly increase student engagement by involving them directly in the learning process. Techniques such as problem-solving, group discussions, and hands-on activities encourage students to participate actively, enhancing their motivation and interest in the subject matter. This engagement is crucial for deep learning and helps prevent the passivity often seen in lecture-based formats. Prince (2004) notes that active involvement in learning activities maintains student interest and fosters a sense of ownership over their education, leading to sustained motivation and higher levels of engagement. For example, in a physics course, interactive engagement methods have shown to improve student performance significantly compared to traditional lectures (Hake, 1998).

(b) **Enhanced Understanding and Retention:** By engaging students in active learning, educators facilitate a deeper understanding of course material. Deslauriers et al. (2019) found that students taught through active learning strategies performed better on subsequent tests, indicating that these methods enhance retention and comprehension. This is particularly relevant in complex subjects where understanding foundational concepts is critical for advanced learning. For instance, Crouch and Mazur (2001) demonstrated that peer instruction in physics courses led to significantly improved conceptual understanding and retention compared to traditional teaching methods.

(c) **Development of Critical Thinking and Problem-Solving Skills:** Active learning fosters critical thinking and problem-solving skills by requiring students to analyze, synthesize, and evaluate information as part of the learning process. Michaelsen et al. (2004) highlight that group work and collaborative projects, common in active learning settings, challenge students to think critically as they confront real-world problems and scenarios. These activities demand that students apply theoretical knowledge to practical situations, enhancing their analytical and problem-solving abilities. For example, engineering education often employs problem-based learning (PBL) to develop students' capacity to tackle complex engineering challenges creatively and effectively.

(d) **Improved Communication Skills:** Active learning often involves discussions and presentations, which help students develop stronger communication skills. These skills are essential not only in academic settings but also in professional environments. Astin (1993) emphasizes that the ability to articulate thoughts clearly and collaborate effectively with others is greatly enhanced through active learning methodologies. Engaging in group discussions, peer reviews, and collaborative projects provides students with ample opportunities to practice and refine their communication skills, preparing them for the demands of the professional world.

(e) **Greater Student Satisfaction and Positive Attitudes:** Students report higher satisfaction and more positive attitudes toward courses that employ active learning strategies. According to a study by Baepler et al. (2014), students appreciate the interactive and engaging nature of active learning classes, which often leads to a more enjoyable learning experience compared to traditional lectures. This positive attitude towards learning can enhance overall academic success and foster a lifelong love of learning.

(f) **Better Performance in Assessments:** Numerous studies have shown that students who participate in active learning environments perform better on exams and other assessments than those who do not. Hake (1998) demonstrated that interactive engagement methods resulted in significantly improved test scores in physics courses, a trend observed across various disciplines. This improvement in performance is attributed to the deeper understanding and retention facilitated by active learning strategies, as well as the development of critical thinking and problem-solving skills.

(g) **Increased Inclusivity:** Active learning can be particularly beneficial in diverse classrooms where students come with different backgrounds and learning styles. Freeman et al. (2014) argue that active learning strategies are more adaptable to various learning needs, helping to close achievement gaps between different groups of students. By providing multiple ways for students to engage with the material, active learning creates a more inclusive learning environment that supports the success of all students.

(h) **Preparation for Professional Careers:** The collaborative and hands-on nature of active learning prepares students for the teamwork and problem-solving they will encounter in their professional lives. Felder and Brent (2003) discuss how the skills developed through active learning, such as collaboration and critical thinking, are highly valued in the workplace. These skills are essential for professional success and are increasingly emphasized in today's job market, where employers seek individuals who can work effectively in teams and tackle complex problems.

(i) **Flexibility in Teaching:** Active learning offers flexibility in teaching methods, allowing educators to adapt their instructional techniques to better meet the needs of their students. This adaptability is crucial in responding to the dynamic demands of the educational landscape. For instance, Light (2001) highlights the importance of flexible teaching strategies in creating effective learning environments that can accommodate diverse student populations and learning preferences.

(j) **Fostering Lifelong Learning Skills**: Finally, active learning encourages the development of lifelong learning skills. Bransford et al. (2000) note that active learning helps students learn how to learn, equipping them with the skills to manage their own learning throughout their lives. This ability to self-direct their learning is essential for continual personal and professional development, enabling students to adapt to new challenges and opportunities beyond the classroom.

ACTIVE LEARNING STRATEGIES

This section explores several prominent active learning strategies, providing detailed examples and empirical support to illustrate their effectiveness across different disciplines.

(a) **Collaborative Learning**: Collaborative learning involves students working together in groups to solve problems, complete projects, or understand new concepts. This approach not only enhances critical thinking skills but also promotes greater retention of information and higher student satisfaction. Johnson and Johnson (1999) argue that collaborative learning environments where students work towards shared goals foster the development of interpersonal skills and improve group dynamics. An example of successful implementation can be seen in medical education, where students work in teams to diagnose patient cases, fostering an environment of peer learning and practical engagement (Smith and MacGregor, 1992).

(b) **Problem-Based Learning (PBL):** Problem-Based Learning centers around student-driven problem solving. Barrows (1986) describes PBL as an educational approach that organically integrates theory and practice by engaging students in solving real-world problems, thus preparing them for professional practice. Engineering education has benefited greatly from PBL, where students are often tasked with developing solutions to complex engineering problems, enhancing their technical skills and practical knowledge (Duch et al., 2001). For instance, a PBL approach in a civil engineering course might involve students designing a sustainable urban drainage system, requiring them to apply theoretical concepts to practical challenges.

(c) **Flipped Classrooms**: The flipped classroom is a pedagogical model where the typical lecture and homework elements of a course are reversed. Pre-class video lectures allow for in-class time to be dedicated to exercises, projects, or discussions, thus enhancing student engagement and learning outcomes. A notable case study in computer science education involved using the flipped classroom to teach algorithms, resulting in improved student performance and more interactive class sessions (Lage et al., 2000). This model allows students to engage with the material at their own pace before class and then apply what they have learned during interactive, hands-on activities.

(d) **Technology-Enhanced Learning**: Incorporating technology into learning environments can greatly enhance the reach and efficacy of educational practices. Means et al. (2013) report that online and blended learning environments, which use technology extensively, can produce learning outcomes superior to those of solely face-to-face instruction. An example is the use of virtual reality in architectural education, where students can interact with 3D models of buildings, enhancing their understanding of spatial relationships and design principles (Dalgarno & Lee, 2010). Additionally, online platforms can facilitate collaborative learning and interactive discussions, even in large classes.

(e) **Case-Based Learning**: Case-based learning involves students analyzing real or simulated scenarios to apply theoretical knowledge to practical situations. This method is widely used in law, business, and medical schools to develop critical thinking and decision-making skills. For example, Harvard Business School's case method immerses students in real-world business challenges, requiring them to analyze complex situations and propose strategic solutions. This approach not only reinforces theoretical knowledge but also enhances students' ability to think on their feet and communicate their ideas effectively.

(f) **Inquiry-Based Learning**: Inquiry-based learning encourages students to investigate questions, problems, or scenarios, promoting deeper engagement with the material. This method fosters curiosity and independent learning by allowing students to explore topics of interest and develop their research skills. In a biology course, for instance, students might investigate the impact of environmental changes on local ecosystems, requiring them to formulate hypotheses, conduct experiments, and analyze data. This approach helps students develop scientific literacy and critical thinking skills.

(g) **Role-Playing and Simulations**: Role-playing and simulations involve students taking on roles and acting out scenarios to explore complex issues and develop practical skills. These methods are particularly effective in disciplines such as law, international relations, and healthcare, where understanding different perspectives and practicing decision-making are crucial. In a nursing program, students might simulate emergency medical situations, allowing them to practice their clinical skills and decision-making under pressure. These activities not only enhance practical skills but also build confidence and teamwork.

(h) **Service Learning**: Service learning integrates community service with academic learning, allowing students to apply their knowledge in real-world contexts while addressing community needs. This approach fosters civic responsibility and enhances learning by connecting classroom content with practical experience. For example, a social work program might involve students working with local non-profits to address issues such as homelessness or substance abuse, providing them with hands-on experience while contributing to the community. Service-learning projects enhance students' understanding of social issues and develop their problem-solving and leadership skills.

(i) **Peer Teaching**: Peer teaching involves students teaching their peers, either through formal presentations or informal study groups. This strategy reinforces the teacher-students' understanding of the material and provides a collaborative learning environment for their peers. Research shows that students often ben-

efit from peer explanations that use relatable language and perspectives. In a chemistry course, students might take turns presenting complex concepts to the class, fostering a deeper understanding and encouraging collaborative learning.
(j) **Socratic Seminars**: Socratic seminars involve guided, open-ended discussions where students explore complex ideas and develop critical thinking skills. This method encourages deep engagement with the material and helps students articulate and defend their viewpoints. In a philosophy course, a Socratic seminar might involve discussing ethical dilemmas, requiring students to analyze different perspectives and develop coherent arguments. These discussions promote active listening, respectful debate, and critical analysis.

STUDENT ENGAGEMENT AND COLLABORATION

Student engagement and collaboration are fundamental to the success of active learning strategies. These elements not only enhance the learning experience but also develop essential skills that are invaluable in both academic and professional contexts. This section explores how active learning methods foster deeper student interaction and collaboration, leading to improved educational outcomes.

(a) **Enhanced Student Engagement**: Active learning strategies significantly increase student engagement by requiring active participation in learning activities. Research shows that methods such as problem-solving, group discussions, and hands-on projects not only maintain student interest but also deepen their understanding of the subject matter. Prince (2004) highlights that when students are actively involved in their learning process, they exhibit higher motivation and engagement. This active involvement fosters a sense of ownership and investment in learning, which naturally leads to higher engagement levels.

For example, in a large introductory biology course, incorporating active learning techniques such as think-pair-share and interactive simulations has been shown to increase student attendance and participation significantly. These methods require students to engage with the material actively, discuss concepts with their peers, and apply their knowledge in practical scenarios, thereby enhancing their engagement and understanding.

(b) **Fostering Collaboration**: Collaboration is a cornerstone of active learning strategies. Through activities such as group projects and peer teaching, students learn to work effectively with others, which enhances their collaborative skills. Johnson and Johnson (1999) emphasize that cooperative learning environments where students work together to achieve shared goals promote the development of interpersonal skills and significantly improve group dynamics.

In practice, collaborative learning can take various forms. For instance, in a business management course, students might work in teams to develop a comprehensive business plan. This project would require them to integrate knowledge from various disciplines, delegate tasks, communicate effectively, and solve problems collaboratively. Such activities not only reinforce academic content but also develop essential skills like teamwork, communication, and leadership.

(c) **Development of Communication and Teamwork Skills:** Active learning environments naturally cultivate communication and teamwork skills. Engaging in discussions and collaborative projects requires students to articulate their thoughts clearly, listen to others, and negotiate solutions. Astin (1993) notes that such interactions are invaluable for developing effective communication skills. Furthermore, the requirement to work as part of a team on complex tasks mirrors many workplace environments, preparing students for future professional collaboration.

For example, in a law school setting, students might participate in moot court competitions, where they must present legal arguments, respond to counterarguments, and collaborate with their team to develop a cohesive case strategy. These activities hone their public speaking, critical thinking, and teamwork skills, providing them with a robust foundation for their legal careers.

(d) **Soft Skills Enhancement**: The role of active learning in developing soft skills extends beyond communication and collaboration to include critical thinking, adaptability, and leadership. By engaging students in challenging tasks, active learning encourages them to think critically and creatively, adapt to new situations, and occasionally take on leadership roles within their groups. Michaelsen et al. (2004) assert that these experiences are crucial for building confidence and competence in managing diverse professional scenarios.

For instance, in a public health course, students might be tasked with designing and implementing a community health intervention. This project would require them to conduct research, analyze data, develop a strategic plan, and work collaboratively with community stakeholders. Through this process, students not only apply their academic knowledge but also develop vital soft skills such as project management, leadership, and adaptability.

(e) **Implications for Higher Education**: The implications of enhanced engagement and collaboration through active learning are profound. They not only improve academic outcomes but also prepare students for the complexities of modern work environments, where soft skills are increasingly valued alongside technical abilities. By embedding active learning strategies into curricula, educational institutions can better prepare students to be effective, adaptive, and collaborative professionals.

CHALLENGES AND SOLUTIONS

This section explores common challenges and offers practical solutions to facilitate the successful integration of active learning methodologies.

Common Challenges

(a) **Resistance from Faculty and Students**: One of the primary challenges in implementing active learning strategies is resistance from both faculty and students. Faculty members may be reluctant to adopt active learning due to unfamiliarity with these methods or skepticism about their efficacy. Traditional lecture-based teaching is deeply ingrained in higher education, and shifting to a more interactive approach can be daunting. Additionally, students accustomed to passive learning may resist active learning due to the increased accountability and effort it demands.

(b) **Logistical Issues**: Active learning often requires flexible classroom spaces that can accommodate group work and other dynamic activities. Traditional lecture halls, with fixed seating and limited space for movement, are not conducive to these kinds of activities. This logistical challenge can limit the implementation of active learning strategies, particularly in institutions with aging infrastructure.

(c) **Resource Constraints**: Implementing active learning can require additional resources such as technology for interactive learning and training for faculty. These requirements may be challenging for institutions with limited budgets. Furthermore, active learning approaches often necessitate smaller class sizes to be effective, which can increase the demand for more faculty and classroom spaces.

Proposed Solutions and Best Practices

(a) **Faculty Development and Support**: Providing faculty with training and resources to implement active learning is crucial. Workshops, seminars, and peer mentoring can help faculty understand the benefits of active learning and how to effectively incorporate these strategies into their teaching. Ebert-May et al. (2011) emphasize the importance of ongoing professional development to ensure faculty are equipped with the skills and confidence needed to facilitate active learning environments. Additionally, creating a community of practice where faculty can share experiences and strategies can foster a supportive culture that encourages innovation in teaching.

(b) **Redesigning Learning Spaces**: To overcome logistical challenges, institutions can invest in redesigning classrooms to support active learning. This can include flexible seating arrangements, access to technology, and spaces that promote collaboration among students. Whiteside et al. (2010) highlight the importance of designing learning environments that are conducive to active learning. For example, classrooms can be equipped with movable furniture, whiteboards, and digital displays to facilitate group work and interactive activities.

(c) **Incremental Implementation**: Rather than implementing active learning strategies wholesale, gradual implementation can help ease resistance. Starting with small, manageable changes can demonstrate the benefits of active learning and build support among faculty and students. Froyd et al. (2013) suggest piloting active learning techniques in select courses or modules before scaling up to entire programs. This approach allows for adjustments based on feedback and ensures a smoother transition.

(d) **Leveraging Technology**: Using technology to facilitate active learning can help manage resource constraints by providing scalable solutions that enhance student engagement. Online tools and learning management systems can support collaborative learning and interactive activities even in large classes. Graham et al. (2013) note that blended learning environments, which combine online and face-to-face instruction, can effectively integrate active learning strategies while optimizing resource use. For example, virtual collaboration tools can enable group work and discussions beyond the physical classroom, expanding the reach and flexibility of active learning.

(e) **Cultivating a Supportive Culture**: Building a culture that values innovative teaching and continuous improvement can help mitigate resistance and encourage the adoption of active learning. Recognizing and rewarding faculty who use active learning strategies can also promote wider acceptance and adoption. Hativa (1995) underscores the importance of institutional support in fostering a culture of teaching excellence. This can include providing grants for pedagogical innovation, showcasing successful active learning initiatives, and integrating active learning into faculty evaluation and promotion criteria.

(f) **Resource Allocation and Strategic Planning**: Addressing resource constraints requires strategic planning and resource allocation. Institutions can prioritize investments in technology and infrastructure that support active learning. Additionally, seeking external funding through grants and partnerships can supplement institutional budgets. For example, collaborative grants from educational foundations or government agencies can provide the necessary funding for classroom redesigns and faculty development programs.

ASSESSMENT AND EVALUATION

This section explores different assessment strategies and how they can be aligned with active learning objectives to accurately measure student learning.

Formative and Summative Assessments

Assessments in active learning environments can generally be categorized into formative and summative assessments. Formative assessments are ongoing evaluations conducted throughout the learning process, providing immediate feedback to students and instructors. These assessments, such as quizzes, peer reviews, and reflective journals, allow for real-time adjustments to teaching methods and help ensure that learning objectives are being met (Nicol & Macfarlane-Dick, 2006). For example, in a flipped classroom, frequent low-stakes quizzes can help gauge student understanding of pre-class materials, allowing instructors to tailor subsequent in-class activities accordingly.

Summative assessments, on the other hand, evaluate student learning at the end of an instructional period, providing a comprehensive measure of how well students have achieved the course objectives. Examples include final exams, projects, and presentations. In active learning settings, summative assessments can be designed to reflect the collaborative and interactive nature of the learning environment, incorporating group projects or capstone presentations that require students to synthesize and apply their knowledge (Angelo & Cross, 1993).

Formative Assessments are ongoing assessments that provide continuous feedback to both instructors and students about learning progress. These assessments help identify learning gaps and guide instructional adjustments. Examples include quizzes, in-class activities, and homework assignments.

Summative Assessments evaluate student learning at the end of an instructional period, such as a unit, course, or semester. These assessments aim to measure the extent to which students have achieved the learning objectives. Examples include final exams, end-of-term projects, and standardized tests.

Digital Assessment and the Importance of Immediate Feedback

Digital Assessment tools are transforming both formative and summative assessments by providing new ways to measure and enhance student learning. Digital tools include online quizzes, interactive assignments, and real-time polling that provide immediate feedback to students.

Formative Digital Assessments:

a. **Online Quizzes and Polls:** Tools like Kahoot, Quizlet, and Google Forms can be used to quickly assess student understanding and adjust instruction accordingly.
b. **Interactive Assignments**: Platforms such as Edmodo and Canvas allow for the submission and instant grading of assignments, providing timely feedback.

Summative Digital Assessments:

a. E-portfolios: Students compile their work over a period of time, reflecting their learning progress and achievements.
b. Online Exams: Digital platforms like Moodle and Blackboard facilitate comprehensive assessment of student learning over a term.

Importance of Immediate Feedback:

Immediate feedback helps students recognize their learning gaps and correct misconceptions promptly. This real-time adjustment is crucial for reinforcing learning and enhancing retention. Research shows that timely feedback significantly impacts student learning outcomes (Hattie & Timperley, 2007).

Alignment with Learning Objectives

To ensure assessments accurately measure student learning, they must align with the objectives of the active learning environment. This alignment can be achieved by:

(a) **Clearly Defining Learning Objectives**: Before designing assessments, instructors must establish clear learning objectives that reflect the goals of the active learning environment. These objectives should encompass both content knowledge and soft skills such as critical thinking, communication, and collaboration, which are central to active learning strategies (Biggs & Tang, 2011). For example, in a problem-based learning course, objectives might include the ability to apply theoretical knowledge to real-world problems and work effectively in teams.

(b) **Designing Assessments That Reflect Active Learning:** Assessments should mirror the interactive nature of the learning process, emphasizing practical application and real-world problem-solving. For instance, group projects or case studies can evaluate both content knowledge and students' ability to work collaboratively, reflecting the core objectives of active learning (Fink, 2013). A business course might assess students through a group project that requires them to develop a marketing plan for a new product, integrating various business concepts and teamwork.

(c) **Incorporating Self and Peer Assessment**: In active learning environments, self and peer assessment can provide valuable insights into student learning. These assessments encourage students to reflect on their progress and give constructive feedback to peers, reinforcing collaborative skills and fostering a culture of continuous improvement (Topping, 1998). For example, in a seminar-style course, students might be asked to provide peer feedback on presentations, helping to develop critical evaluation skills.

(d) **Ensuring Consistency Between Teaching Methods and Assessments**: The assessment methods should be consistent with the active learning strategies used in the classroom. For example, if the course heavily relies on group work and discussions, assessments should evaluate both individual and group performance, ensuring that they capture the full scope of student learning (Ramsden, 2003). In a STEM course, this might involve a combination of individual exams and group lab reports.

Benefits of Active Learning Assessments

By aligning assessments with active learning objectives, instructors can create a comprehensive evaluation system that:

(a) **Accurately Measures Learning Outcomes**: Consistent assessments provide a holistic view of student learning, capturing both content knowledge and practical skills developed through active learning activities. For instance, a capstone project in an engineering course can demonstrate students' ability to apply theoretical knowledge to design and build a functional prototype.

(b) **Provides Continuous Feedback**: Formative assessments allow for immediate feedback, helping students and instructors identify areas for improvement and make necessary adjustments to enhance learning outcomes (Black & Wiliam, 1998). This iterative process ensures that students are continuously developing their skills and knowledge.

(c) **Encourages Lifelong Learning Skills**: Self and peer assessments help develop critical reflection and feedback skills, which are essential for lifelong learning and professional development (Nicol & Macfarlane-Dick, 2006). These assessments foster a mindset of continuous improvement and self-directed learning, preparing students for the demands of their future careers.

Innovative Assessment Techniques

Incorporating innovative assessment techniques can further enhance the effectiveness of active learning environments:

(a) **Portfolio Assessments**: Portfolios provide a comprehensive record of student learning over time, showcasing a range of skills and accomplishments. This method allows students to reflect on their progress and demonstrates their ability to integrate and apply knowledge across different contexts. For example, an education student might compile a portfolio that includes lesson plans, reflections, and feedback from teaching practicums.

(b) **Simulations and Role-Playing**: These techniques provide realistic scenarios where students can apply their knowledge and skills in a controlled environment. In a medical course, simulations might involve diagnosing and treating virtual patients, providing a practical assessment of clinical skills.

(c) **Peer-Led Workshops**: In peer-led workshops, students take on the role of instructors, teaching specific topics to their classmates. This method assesses both their understanding of the material and their ability to communicate it effectively.

CASE STUDIES

This section provides detailed case studies from different institutions, highlighting the implementation, outcomes, and lessons learned from incorporating active learning.

A. Case Study 1: University of Washington – SCALE-UP Initiative

i. Background: The University of Washington (UW), a large public research university, implemented the SCALE-UP (Student-Centered Active Learning Environment for Undergraduate Programs) initiative to transform its large introductory physics courses. These courses, which typically enroll over 200 students, faced significant challenges such as low student engagement and high dropout rates. The traditional lecture-based format was insufficient in addressing the diverse learning needs and preferences of the students, many of whom struggled to grasp complex scientific concepts through passive listening alone.

ii. **Institutional Details**: The SCALE-UP initiative was implemented within the Department of Physics at the University of Washington. This department serves a diverse student population, including undergraduates majoring in physics, engineering, and other science-related fields. The demographics of the students involved in these courses included a mix of first-year and second-year students, with varying degrees of prior knowledge and academic preparation. The initiative aimed to create a more inclusive and engaging learning environment that could cater to this diversity and improve overall student outcomes.

iii. **Specific Context and Challenges**: Implementing SCALE-UP required a significant overhaul of existing classroom spaces and teaching practices. Traditional lecture halls with fixed seating were not conducive to the collaborative and interactive nature of active learning. Additionally, there was initial resistance from faculty members who were accustomed to lecture-based instruction and skeptical about the efficacy of new pedagogical approaches.

The physics courses targeted by the SCALE-UP initiative involved complex subjects that required a deep understanding of theoretical principles and their practical applications. The size of the classes posed logistical challenges in facilitating group work and ensuring that all students actively participated in learning activities. Moreover, there was a need to provide adequate training and support to faculty to help them transition to active learning methodologies effectively.

iv. **Opportunities**: Despite these challenges, the initiative presented unique opportunities to leverage modern educational technologies and redesign learning spaces to better support student-centered learning. The University of Washington saw the potential to not only improve student performance and retention rates but also to foster a culture of innovation in teaching and learning across the institution. By addressing the specific needs of their diverse student body, the university aimed to create a scalable model of active learning that could be applied to other disciplines and courses in the future.

v. **Implementation**: The transition to the SCALE-UP model involved several key steps:

Active Learning Strategies in Higher Education

    a. **Classroom Redesign**: Classrooms were reconfigured to facilitate team-based learning, with round tables seating nine students each, equipped with laptops and whiteboards. This layout enabled group discussions and collaborative problem-solving.

    b. **Faculty Training**: Instructors received extensive training in active learning techniques, focusing on how to guide discussions, foster student engagement, and manage classroom dynamics. Workshops and peer mentoring programs were established to support faculty during the transition.

    c. **Curriculum Restructuring**: The curriculum was redesigned to emphasize hands-on activities, peer teaching, and collaborative problem-solving. Traditional lectures were replaced with interactive sessions where students worked on problems and projects in groups.

vi. **Outcomes:** The SCALE-UP initiative led to significant improvements in student engagement, satisfaction, and academic performance. Quantitative data showed that students in SCALE-UP classrooms had higher test scores and retention rates compared to those in traditional lecture-based courses. Specifically, there was a 30% improvement in student performance on standardized tests and a 40% increase in retention rates.

Student feedback indicated higher levels of engagement and satisfaction with the interactive learning environment. Students reported that the hands-on activities and collaborative problem-solving helped them understand and retain complex concepts better than traditional lectures.

vii. **Theoretical Integration**: This case study illustrates the application of constructivist principles, where students actively construct knowledge through collaborative problem-solving. It also highlights the role of social learning theory, as peer teaching facilitated learning through observation and interaction. The SCALE-UP model aligns with experiential learning theory, emphasizing the importance of hands-on activities and real-world problem-solving.

viii. **Lessons Learned**: The success of the SCALE-UP initiative underscores the importance of faculty development and the need for institutional support in redesigning learning spaces. High-quality instructional materials, comprehensive faculty training, and a supportive learning environment are crucial for the successful implementation of active learning strategies. Future efforts will focus on expanding these methods to other courses and disciplines, continually refining the approach based on feedback from students and educators.

B. Case Study 2: Stanford University – Flipped Classroom in Computer Science

    i. **Background**: Stanford University, a leading institution known for its innovation in education and technology, implemented a flipped classroom model in its introductory computer science courses. These courses, often enrolling between 100 to 150 students, were traditionally taught using lecture-based methods. However, the department recognized the need for a more interactive approach to improve student engagement and understanding of complex computational concepts. The flipped classroom model was seen as a solution to address these needs by making the best use of both in-class and out-of-class time.

ii. **Institutional Details**: The flipped classroom initiative was introduced in the Department of Computer Science at Stanford University, targeting introductory courses such as CS 106A: Programming Methodology. This course is a foundational class for computer science majors and attracts students from various disciplines who seek to acquire programming skills. The student demographic was diverse, including first-year undergraduates, non-computer science majors, and international students with varying levels of prior experience in programming.

iii. **Specific Context and Challenges**: Implementing the flipped classroom model involved significant changes to both the course structure and the roles of instructors and students. Traditionally, the course relied heavily on in-class lectures for delivering content, with students completing homework assignments independently. The new model required students to watch pre-recorded video lectures before attending class, thereby freeing up in-class time for interactive exercises, problem-solving sessions, and group discussions.

One of the primary challenges was ensuring that students were adequately prepared for in-class activities by engaging with the video content beforehand. This required a shift in student habits and self-discipline. Additionally, the faculty needed training to effectively facilitate interactive sessions and manage classroom dynamics that foster collaboration and active learning.

Another logistical challenge was the production of high-quality video lectures that could effectively replace live lectures. This involved investing in video production resources and creating engaging, comprehensible content that students could easily follow on their own.

iv. **Opportunities:** The flipped classroom model presented several opportunities to enhance student learning outcomes. By moving lectures online, students could learn at their own pace, pausing and replaying content as needed to fully grasp the material. This approach was particularly beneficial for students with varying levels of prior knowledge, as it allowed them to review difficult concepts multiple times.

In-class time was transformed into a collaborative learning environment where students could apply the concepts they learned online to practical problems. This not only reinforced their understanding but also developed their problem-solving and teamwork skills. The new model encouraged active participation and peer learning, as students worked together on coding exercises and received immediate feedback from instructors and classmates.

v. **Implementation:** The transition to a flipped classroom involved several key steps:
   a. **Preparation of Video Lectures**: High-quality video lectures covering all course content were created. These videos were designed to be engaging and accessible, using animations and practical examples to illustrate complex concepts.
   b. **Faculty Training**: Instructors participated in workshops and training sessions to learn how to facilitate active learning in the classroom. They were trained to guide discussions, oversee group work, and provide real-time assistance to students.
   c. **Classroom Redesign**: Classrooms were reconfigured to support group activities, with movable furniture and access to collaborative tools. This setup encouraged interaction and made it easier for instructors to engage with students.

vi. **Outcomes:** The flipped classroom approach led to significant improvements in student performance, engagement, and satisfaction. Students reported a deeper understanding of the material, as they could actively apply theoretical concepts during in-class activities. Attendance and participation rates increased, and the interactive nature of the classes fostered a more supportive learning environment.

Quantitative data showed that students in the flipped classroom performed better on assessments compared to those in traditional lecture-based courses. For instance, the average exam scores increased by 15%, and the pass rate improved by 10%. Qualitative feedback from students highlighted their appreciation for the flexibility and interactivity of the flipped model.

vii. **Theoretical Integration**: This case study exemplifies the application of experiential learning theory, where students learn through doing and reflection. By engaging in hands-on activities and collaborative problem-solving, students construct their understanding of programming concepts. The flipped classroom also aligns with constructivist principles, as it allows students to build on their prior knowledge at their own pace and in their own style.

viii. **Lessons Learned**: The success of the flipped classroom at Stanford underscores the importance of preparation and support in implementing active learning strategies. High-quality instructional materials and faculty training are crucial for effective execution. Moreover, fostering a classroom environment that encourages interaction and collaboration can significantly enhance learning outcomes. Future efforts will focus on expanding the flipped model to other courses and continually refining the approach based on student feedback and performance data.

C. Case Study 3: Harvard University – Problem-Based Learning in Medical Education
   i. **Background:** Harvard Medical School (HMS), renowned for its leadership in medical education, adopted a problem-based learning (PBL) approach to enhance its medical curriculum. This approach was introduced to address the limitations of traditional lecture-based instruction, which often failed to engage students deeply or develop their critical thinking and clinical reasoning skills. By focusing on real-world clinical problems, PBL aims to better prepare students for the complexities of medical practice.
   ii. **Institutional Details**: The PBL initiative was implemented in the pre-clinical years at Harvard Medical School, targeting courses in human biology, pathology, and clinical skills. These courses are integral to the first and second years of medical education and involve a diverse group of students, including both domestic and international enrollees with varying educational backgrounds and levels of clinical experience. The objective was to foster a more interactive and student-centered learning environment.
   iii. **Specific Context and Challenges**: The PBL approach at HMS required a fundamental shift from traditional didactic teaching to small-group, student-centered learning. In this model, students work in small groups to analyze clinical cases, identify learning objectives, research relevant information, and discuss their findings collaboratively. This approach posed several challenges:

a. **Faculty Training**: The transition to PBL necessitated comprehensive training for faculty members to effectively facilitate small-group discussions and guide students without directly providing answers. This required a change in mindset from being the primary source of knowledge to a facilitator of learning.

b. **Curriculum Redesign**: The curriculum had to be restructured to integrate clinical cases that were relevant, challenging, and aligned with learning objectives. This involved a significant effort in designing and validating cases that could effectively stimulate critical thinking and clinical reasoning.

c. **Assessment Methods**: Traditional assessment methods, such as multiple-choice exams, were not sufficient to evaluate the skills developed through PBL. There was a need to develop new assessment tools that could measure problem-solving abilities, teamwork, and application of knowledge in clinical contexts.

   iv. **Opportunities:** Despite these challenges, the PBL approach presented several opportunities to enhance medical education at HMS:

a. **Enhanced Clinical Reasoning**: By working through real-world clinical cases, students could develop and refine their clinical reasoning and decision-making skills. This hands-on approach helped bridge the gap between theoretical knowledge and practical application.
b. **Development of Soft Skills**: PBL sessions promoted the development of essential soft skills such as teamwork, communication, and leadership. Students learned to collaborate effectively, articulate their thoughts, and lead discussions, which are critical skills in medical practice.
c. **Lifelong Learning**: PBL encouraged students to take responsibility for their own learning, fostering a culture of lifelong learning and continuous professional development. Students developed the skills to seek out information, critically evaluate sources, and apply knowledge to new situations.

   v. **Implementation:** The implementation of PBL at Harvard Medical School involved several key steps:

a. **Faculty Development**: Extensive workshops and training programs were conducted to prepare faculty for their new roles as facilitators. These sessions focused on techniques for guiding discussions, fostering critical thinking, and assessing student performance.
b. **Case Development:** A dedicated team of educators and clinicians developed a series of clinical cases that covered a wide range of medical conditions and scenarios. Each case was designed to be challenging and relevant, requiring students to integrate knowledge from multiple disciplines.
c. **Assessment Reform**: New assessment tools were introduced to evaluate the outcomes of PBL. These included oral examinations, reflective essays, and peer assessments that focused on problem-solving abilities, teamwork, and the application of knowledge.

   vi. **Outcomes:** The adoption of PBL at Harvard Medical School led to significant improvements in student engagement, satisfaction, and performance. Students reported that PBL sessions were more engaging and enjoyable compared to traditional lectures. They appreciated the opportunity to apply their knowledge to real-world problems and develop their clinical reasoning skills.

Quantitative data showed that students in PBL courses performed better on clinical skills assessments and demonstrated higher levels of critical thinking and problem-solving abilities. Additionally, there was an increase in student satisfaction and a greater sense of preparedness for clinical rotations.

   vii. **Theoretical Integration:** This case study illustrates the application of experiential learning and constructivist principles in medical education. By engaging in hands-on problem-solving and collaborative learning, students construct their understanding of medical concepts and develop essential clinical skills.

The PBL approach aligns with social learning theory as well, as students learn from each other's insights and experiences through group discussions.

viii. **Lessons Learned:** The success of PBL at Harvard Medical School highlights the importance of faculty development, curriculum redesign, and assessment reform in implementing active learning strategies. The initiative demonstrated that PBL can effectively enhance clinical reasoning, teamwork, and lifelong learning skills. Future efforts will focus on expanding PBL to other courses and continually refining the approach based on student feedback and educational research.

FUTURE DIRECTIONS

This section explores these trends, including the integration of artificial intelligence (AI) and virtual reality (VR), and discusses how active learning strategies can be scaled and integrated into traditional educational models.

Integration of Artificial Intelligence

AI is revolutionizing education, particularly in active learning environments. It offers a variety of tools and applications that can enhance learning experiences and outcomes:

(a) **Adaptive Learning Platforms**: AI-powered adaptive learning platforms can personalize educational content based on individual student needs, allowing for more tailored and effective instruction (DuBoulay, 2016). These platforms analyze student performance and adjust content delivery accordingly, ensuring that learners are consistently challenged at an appropriate level. For instance, an AI system in a mathematics course can provide additional problems for students struggling with a concept while offering advanced topics to those who have mastered the basics.

(b) **Automated Feedback**: AI can provide immediate, personalized feedback to students, enhancing their learning process. Automated grading tools, for instance, offer instant evaluation and guidance on assignments, helping students understand and correct mistakes in real-time (Gartner, 2020). This immediate feedback loop is particularly beneficial in large classes where individual feedback from instructors may be limited.

(c) **Intelligent Tutoring Systems**: AI-based tutoring systems simulate one-on-one instruction, offering guided practice and support that mimic traditional tutoring sessions. These systems have been shown to improve learning outcomes by providing targeted assistance and practice opportunities (Graesser et al., 2017). For example, an AI tutor in a language course can provide personalized practice exercises and conversational practice tailored to each student's proficiency level.

Virtual Reality in Active Learning

VR is another emerging technology with significant potential to transform active learning strategies:

(a) **Immersive Learning Experiences**: VR offers immersive, interactive environments that allow students to engage with content in new and innovative ways. This is particularly beneficial in fields such as science and medicine, where VR simulations can create realistic scenarios for students to explore and practice skills (Dalgarno & Lee, 2010). For instance, medical students can use VR to simulate surgical procedures, gaining hands-on experience in a controlled, risk-free environment.

(b) **Remote Learning Opportunities**: VR can expand access to active learning environments by allowing students to participate in interactive, collaborative experiences from remote locations. This makes education more inclusive and accessible, particularly for students in geographically isolated or underserved areas (Pantelidis, 2010). Virtual classrooms can simulate a traditional classroom experience, enabling real-time interaction and collaboration among students and instructors.

(c) **Real-World Application**: VR environments can simulate real-world challenges and scenarios, enabling students to apply their knowledge and skills in practical contexts. For example, VR-based business simulations allow students to manage virtual companies, developing their decision-making and problem-solving skills in a risk-free environment (Johnson, 2021). These simulations provide a practical, hands-on learning experience that enhances theoretical understanding.

Scaling Active Learning Strategies

To effectively scale active learning strategies and integrate them into traditional educational models, several considerations must be addressed:

(a) **Curriculum Design**: Active learning strategies should be incorporated into the curriculum in a way that aligns with traditional educational objectives. This requires careful planning to ensure that interactive activities complement course content and learning goals (Biggs & Tang, 2011). For instance, integrating active learning modules within existing courses can provide a balanced approach that combines traditional and innovative teaching methods.

(b) **Faculty Training and Support**: Providing faculty with the necessary training and support to implement active learning strategies is crucial. This includes workshops, peer mentoring, and access to resources that help instructors adopt new teaching methods effectively (Ebert-May et al., 2011). Institutions can create professional development programs focused on active learning, ensuring that faculty are well-equipped to facilitate interactive and engaging classrooms.

(c) **Classroom Infrastructure**: Scaling active learning strategies requires adaptable classroom environments that support interactive activities. This includes flexible seating arrangements, access to technology, and spaces that facilitate collaboration and group work (Whiteside et al., 2010). Investing in modern classroom designs that support active learning can significantly enhance the learning experience.

(d) **Technology Integration**: Leveraging technology is essential for scaling active learning strategies. Online platforms, collaborative tools, and other digital resources can facilitate interactive learning experiences even in large classes, making active learning accessible to a wider range of students (Graham et al., 2013). For example, using learning management systems to support flipped classrooms can provide students with the flexibility to engage with content at their own pace while participating in interactive activities during class time.

Emerging Trends and Research

As we look to the future, several emerging trends and areas of research hold promise for further advancing active learning strategies:

(a) **Gamification**: Incorporating game elements into learning can increase student motivation and engagement. Research is exploring how gamification can be effectively integrated into active learning environments to enhance educational outcomes (Deterding et al., 2011). For example, using competitive elements, such as leaderboards and badges, can motivate students to actively participate and achieve learning goals.

(b) **Learning Analytics**: The use of learning analytics involves analyzing data on student performance and engagement to inform instructional design and decision-making. This approach can provide insights into the effectiveness of active learning strategies and help educators tailor their methods to better meet student needs (Siemens & Long, 2011). By tracking student interactions and outcomes, educators can identify areas for improvement and implement data-driven strategies.

(c) **Personalized Learning Pathways**: Advances in technology enable the creation of personalized learning pathways that cater to individual student needs and preferences. This approach can ensure that each student receives the support and challenges necessary for their personal development (Pane et al., 2015). Personalized learning pathways can adapt to student progress, providing customized resources and activities that align with their learning goals.

Future Research Directions

Active learning has been widely recognized for its role in enhancing student engagement, critical thinking, and knowledge retention. However, its integration within interactive learning strategies presents a rich avenue for future research.

Understanding the interplay between active and interactive learning can provide deeper insights into optimizing educational practices.

Role of Active Learning in Interactive Strategies

Active learning can serve as the foundation for interactive learning strategies by ensuring that students are not only engaged but also actively participating in their learning process. By integrating active learning within interactive strategies, educators can create a more dynamic and effective learning environment (Bonwell & Eison, 1991).

Impact on Student Outcomes

Future research should explore how the combination of active and interactive learning strategies impacts various student outcomes, such as:

a. **Academic Performance**: Investigating whether the integration of these strategies leads to higher grades and better understanding of course material (Freeman et al., 2014).
b. **Engagement and Motivation**: Assessing how these combined strategies influence student motivation and engagement levels (Prince, 2004).
c. **Skill Development**: Examining the development of critical thinking, problem-solving, and collaborative skills through the use of active and interactive learning (Bonwell & Eison, 1991).

Implementation and Scalability

Another area for future research is the practical implementation and scalability of these combined strategies. This includes:

a. **Technological Integration**: Exploring the use of emerging technologies, such as artificial intelligence and virtual reality, to support and enhance active and interactive learning.
b. **Large-Scale Implementation**: Studying the effectiveness of these strategies in large classroom settings and diverse educational contexts (Railean, 2020).

Inclusivity and Accessibility

Research should also focus on how active and interactive learning strategies can be made more inclusive and accessible. This includes:

a. **Addressing Diverse Learning Needs**: Investigating how these strategies can be adapted to meet the needs of students with different learning styles and abilities (Prince, 2004).
b. **Reducing Barriers to Participation**: Identifying and mitigating potential barriers to student participation in active and interactive learning activities.

Longitudinal Studies

Long-term studies are needed to assess the sustained impact of active and interactive learning strategies on student success. These studies can provide valuable data on:

a. **Career Readiness:** Evaluating how these strategies prepare students for their future careers and lifelong learning (Freeman et al., 2014).

b. **Lifelong Learning**: Investigating the role of active and interactive learning in fostering a culture of continuous learning and adaptation.

CONCLUSION

Active learning strategies have demonstrated their transformative potential in higher education, offering a dynamic, interactive approach that enhances student engagement, understanding, and performance. This chapter has explored the theoretical foundations, practical applications, and future directions of active learning, providing a comprehensive overview of its benefits and challenges. As educators and policymakers seek to implement these strategies, the following actionable takeaways and future research directions can guide their efforts.

Active learning strategies have been shown to significantly enhance student engagement, critical thinking, and knowledge retention, making them essential components of effective educational practices. These strategies shift the focus from passive reception of information to active participation, fostering a deeper understanding of the subject matter.

Formative and Summative Assessments, when integrated with digital tools, provide continuous feedback that is crucial for student learning. The use of digital assessments not only facilitates timely feedback but also supports a more comprehensive evaluation of student performance, aligning with the advancements discussed by Railean (2020). Immediate feedback, in particular, helps students quickly identify and address learning gaps, thereby reinforcing their understanding and retention of the material (Hattie & Timperley, 2007).

The relationship between strategy and method is crucial in educational practices. Strategies provide the overarching goals and vision for student learning, while methods are the specific techniques used to achieve these goals. Understanding this relationship helps educators design more effective learning experiences that actively engage students and promote critical thinking.

The future research directions outlined in this chapter highlight the need for further exploration into the integration of active learning within interactive strategies. By examining the impact on student outcomes, implementation and scalability, inclusivity and accessibility, and conducting longitudinal studies, researchers can provide deeper insights into optimizing educational practices.

Active Learning in Interactive Strategies:

Role: Active learning serves as the foundation for interactive learning strategies by ensuring active student participation.

Impact: Combined strategies enhance academic performance, engagement, motivation, and skill development.

Implementation: Effective use of technology and adaptation to diverse educational contexts are crucial for scalability.

Inclusivity: Strategies should be designed to address diverse learning needs and reduce barriers to participation.

Long-Term Impact: Sustained use of these strategies can significantly improve career readiness and foster a culture of lifelong learning.

By continuing to research and refine these strategies, educators can create more dynamic, inclusive, and effective learning environments that better prepare students for the challenges of the future.

Actionable Takeaways

(a) **Integrate Theory with Practice**: Ensure that theoretical discussions are consistently linked with practical applications. For instance, after introducing a theoretical framework, immediately provide real-world examples or case studies that illustrate how the theory can be applied in educational settings.

(b) **Enhance Faculty Development**: Invest in ongoing professional development for faculty. Offer workshops, seminars, and peer mentoring programs that equip educators with the skills and confidence to implement active learning strategies effectively. Creating a supportive community of practice can encourage the adoption and refinement of these methods.

(c) **Redesign Learning Spaces**: Adapt classroom environments to support active learning. Flexible seating arrangements, access to technology, and spaces that facilitate group work and interaction are essential. Institutions should prioritize investments in modernizing classrooms to create conducive environments for active learning.

(d) **Leverage Technology**: Utilize technology to enhance and scale active learning. AI-powered adaptive learning platforms, automated feedback systems, and virtual reality simulations can provide personalized, immersive learning experiences. Online collaborative tools can support active learning even in large classes, making these strategies more accessible.

(e) **Gradual Implementation**: Start small by integrating active learning strategies incrementally. Pilot programs or individual courses can demonstrate the benefits of these methods, building support among faculty and students. Use feedback from these pilots to refine and expand active learning initiatives.

(f) **Align Assessments with Learning Objectives**: Design assessments that reflect the interactive nature of active learning. Incorporate both formative and summative assessments that measure content knowledge and practical skills. Use self and peer assessments to develop critical reflection and feedback skills.

(g) **Foster a Culture of Innovation**: Cultivate an institutional culture that values innovative teaching and continuous improvement. Recognize and reward faculty who successfully implement active learning strategies. Encourage experimentation and the sharing of best practices.

(h) **Focus on Inclusivity**: Ensure that active learning strategies are adaptable to diverse learning needs and backgrounds. Tailor activities to support inclusivity and close achievement gaps, providing equitable opportunities for all students to succeed.

Future Research Directions

(a) **Technology Integration**: Investigate the long-term impacts of integrating emerging technologies such as AI and VR in active learning environments. Research should focus on how these technologies can enhance engagement, retention, and learning outcomes across various disciplines.

(b) **Scalability of Active Learning**: Examine strategies for scaling active learning in large classes and diverse educational settings. Studies should explore the effectiveness of blended learning models and the use of online platforms to support active learning in larger cohorts.

(c) **Impact on Soft Skills Development**: Conduct longitudinal studies to assess how active learning strategies contribute to the development of soft skills such as critical thinking, communication, and collaboration. Understanding the long-term benefits of these skills in professional contexts can provide valuable insights.

(d) **Personalized Learning Pathways**: Explore the effectiveness of personalized learning pathways that adapt to individual student needs. Research should examine how adaptive learning technologies can provide customized educational experiences and support diverse learning styles.

(e) **Equity and Inclusivity**: Investigate how active learning strategies can be designed and implemented to promote equity and inclusivity in higher education. Studies should focus on identifying best practices for supporting underrepresented and marginalized student populations.

(f) **Professional Development Models**: Evaluate different models of professional development for faculty implementing active learning. Research should identify the most effective approaches to training and supporting educators in adopting these strategies.

By addressing these actionable takeaways and future research directions, educators and policymakers can effectively implement and refine active learning strategies, ensuring that they enhance student learning and prepare students for the complexities of the modern world. Through continuous innovation and a commitment to excellence, active learning will continue to evolve as a cornerstone of 21st-century education.

REFERENCES

Alé-Ruiz, R., Martínez-Abad, F., & del Moral-Marcos, M. T. (2023). Academic engagement and management of personalised active learning in higher education digital ecosystems. *Education and Information Technologies*. Advance online publication. 10.1007/s10639-023-12358-4

Angelo, T. A., & Cross, K. P. (1993). *Classroom Assessment Techniques: A Handbook for College Teachers*. Jossey-Bass.

Astin, A. W. (1993). *What Matters in College? Four Critical Years Revisited*. Jossey-Bass.

Baepler, P., Walker, J. D., & Driessen, M. (2014). It's not about seat time: Blending, flipping, and efficiency in active learning classrooms. *Computers & Education*, 65, 227–236. 10.1016/j.compedu.2014.06.006

Bandura, A. (1977). *Social Learning Theory*. Prentice Hall.

Barrows, H. S. (1986). A taxonomy of problem-based learning methods. *Medical Education*, 20(6), 481–486. 10.1111/j.1365-2923.1986.tb01386.x3796328

Biggs, J., & Tang, C. (2011). *Teaching for Quality Learning at University*. Open University Press.

Black, P., & Wiliam, D. (1998). Assessment and classroom learning. *Assessment in Education: Principles, Policy & Practice*, 5(1), 7–74. 10.1080/0969595980050102

Black, P., & Wiliam, D. (1998). Inside the Black Box: Raising Standards Through Classroom Assessment. *Phi Delta Kappan*, 80(2), 139–148.

Bonwell, C. C., & Eison, J. A. (1991). ASHE-ERIC Higher Education Report: Vol. 1. *Active Learning: Creating Excitement in the Classroom*. School of Education and Human Development, George Washington University.

Bransford, J., Brown, A., & Cocking, R. (2000). *How People Learn: Brain, Mind, Experience, and School*. National Academy Press.

Crouch, C. H., & Mazur, E. (2001). Peer Instruction: Ten years of experience and results. *American Journal of Physics*, 69(9), 970–977. 10.1119/1.1374249

Dalgarno, B., & Lee, M. J. W. (2010). What are the learning affordances of 3-D virtual environments? *British Journal of Educational Technology*, 41(1), 10–32. 10.1111/j.1467-8535.2009.01038.x

Deslauriers, L., McCarty, L. S., Miller, K., Callaghan, K., & Kestin, G. (2019). Measuring actual learning versus feeling of learning in response to being actively engaged in the classroom. *Proceedings of the National Academy of Sciences of the United States of America*, 116(39), 19251–19257. 10.1073/pnas.182193611631484770

Detyna, M., Granelli, F., & Betts, T. (2023). Exploring the effect of a collaborative problem-based learning simulation within a technology-enhanced learning environment on tutor perceptions and student learning outcomes. *Journal of Education and Training Studies*, 12(1), 53. Advance online publication. 10.11114/jets.v12i1.6499

DuBoulay, B. (2016). Artificial intelligence as an effective tutor. *IEEE Intelligent Systems*, 31(6), 38–43.

Duch, B. J., Groh, S. E., & Allen, D. E. (Eds.). (2001). *The Power of Problem-Based Learning*. Stylus Publishing, LLC.

Ebert-May, D., Derting, T. L., Hodder, J., Momsen, J. L., Long, T. M., & Jardeleza, S. E. (2011). What we say is not what we do: Effective evaluation of faculty professional development programs. *Bioscience*, 61(7), 550–558. 10.1525/bio.2011.61.7.9

Felder, R. M., & Brent, R. (2003). Learning by Doing. *Chemical Engineering Education*, 37(4), 282–290.

Fink, L. D. (2013). *Creating Significant Learning Experiences: An Integrated Approach to Designing College Courses*. Jossey-Bass.

Fosnot, C. T. (Ed.). (2005). *Constructivism: Theory, perspectives, and practice*. Teachers College Press.

Freeman, S., Eddy, S. L., McDonough, M., Smith, M. K., Okoroafor, N., Jordt, H., & Wenderoth, M. P. (2014). Active learning increases student performance in science, engineering, and mathematics. *Proceedings of the National Academy of Sciences of the United States of America*, 111(23), 8410–8415. 10.1073/pnas.131903011124821756

Froyd, J. (2013). Five major shifts in 100 years of engineering education. *Proceedings of the IEEE*, 101(6).

Gartner. (2020). *Magic Quadrant for Artificial Intelligence*. Gartner.

Graesser, A. C. (2017). Intelligent tutoring systems. In *International Handbook of the Learning Sciences*. Routledge.

Graham, C. R. (2013). Designing asynchronous online discussion environments: Recent progress and possible future directions. *Computer Education*.

Graham, C. R., Woodfield, W., & Harrison, J. B. (2013). A framework for institutional adoption and implementation of blended learning in higher education. *The Internet and Higher Education*, 18, 4–14. 10.1016/j.iheduc.2012.09.003

Hake, R. R. (1998). Interactive-engagement versus traditional methods: A six-thousand-student survey of mechanics test data for introductory physics courses. *American Journal of Physics*, 66(1), 64–74. 10.1119/1.18809

Harlen, W. (2013). *Assessment & Inquiry-Based Science Education: Issues in Policy and Practice*. Global Network of Science Academies.

Hativa, N. (1995). The department-wide approach to improving faculty instruction in higher education: A qualitative evaluation. *Research in Higher Education*, 36(4), 377–413. 10.1007/BF02207904

Hattie, J., & Timperley, H. (2007). The power of feedback. *Review of Educational Research*, 77(1), 81–112. 10.3102/003465430298487

Henderson, C. (2012). Faculty development for physics instructors: A case study of a workshop using active learning. *Physical Review Special Topics. Physics Education Research*.

Johnson, C. (2021). Virtual Reality in Business Education: Opportunities and Challenges. *Business Horizons*.

Johnson, D. W., & Johnson, R. T. (1999). *Learning together and alone: Cooperative, competitive, and individualistic learning* (5th ed.). Allyn & Bacon.

Johnson, D. W., Johnson, R. T., & Smith, K. A. (1998). Cooperative learning returns to college: What evidence is there that it works? Change. *Change*, 30(4), 26–35. 10.1080/00091389809602629

Kolb, D. A. (1984). *Experiential Learning: Experience as the source of learning and development*. Prentice-Hall.

Kuh, G. D., Kinzie, J., Schuh, J. H., & Whitt, E. J. (2005). *Student Success in College: Creating Conditions That Matter*. Jossey-Bass.

Lage, M. J., Platt, G. J., & Treglia, M. (2000). Inverting the classroom: A gateway to creating an inclusive learning environment. *The Journal of Economic Education*, 31(1), 30–43. 10.1080/00220480009596759

Light, G. (2001). *Making the Most of College: Students Speak Their Minds*. Harvard University Press. 10.4159/9780674417502

Means, B., Toyama, Y., Murphy, R., Bakia, M., & Jones, K. (2013). *Evaluation of Evidence-Based Practices in Online Learning: A Meta-Analysis and Review of Online Learning Studies*. U.S. Department of Education.

Michael, J. (2006). Where's the evidence that active learning works? *Advances in Physiology Education*, 30(4), 159–167. 10.1152/advan.00053.200617108243

Michaelsen, L. K., Knight, A. B., & Fink, L. D. (2004). *Team-Based Learning: A Transformative Use of Small Groups in College Teaching. Sterling.* Stylus Publishing.

Nicol, D. J., & Macfarlane-Dick, D. (2006). Formative assessment and self-regulated learning: A model and seven principles of good feedback practice. *Studies in Higher Education*, 31(2), 199–218. 10.1080/03075070600572090

Pantelidis, V. S. (2010). *Reasons to use virtual reality in education and training courses and a model to determine when to use virtual reality.* Themes in Science and Technology Education.

Paul, R., & Elder, L. (2008). *The Miniature Guide to Critical Thinking: Concepts and Tools*. Foundation for Critical Thinking Press.

Prince, M. (2004). Does active learning work? A review of the research. *Journal of Engineering Education*, 93(3), 223–231. 10.1002/j.2168-9830.2004.tb00809.x

Railean, E. A. (2020). Pedagogy of New Assessment, Measurement, and Testing Strategies in Higher Education: Learning Theory and Outcomes. In Railean, E. (Ed.), *Assessment, Testing, and Measurement Strategies in Global Higher Education* (pp. 1–19). IGI Global. 10.4018/978-1-7998-2314-8.ch001

Ramsden, P. (2003). *Learning to Teach in Higher Education*. Routledge. 10.4324/9780203507711

Smith, B. L., & MacGregor, J. T. (1992). What is collaborative learning? In A. S. Goodsell, M. R. Maher, V. Tinto, B. L. Smith, & J. MacGregor (Eds.), *Collaborative Learning: A Sourcebook for Higher Education* (Vol. 2, pp. 10-30). National Center on Postsecondary Teaching, Learning, and Assessment, Syracuse University.

Topping, K. (1998). Peer Assessment Between Students in Colleges and Universities. *Review of Educational Research*, 68(3), 249–276. 10.3102/00346543068003249

Vygotsky, L. S. (1978). *Mind in Society: The development of higher psychological processes*. Harvard University Press.

Walsh, G. (2015). Implementing innovations in global health care: Financial sustainability in the social sector. *Health Affairs*.

Whiteside, A. (2010). Making the case for space: Three years of empirical research on learning environments. *EDUCAUSE Quarterly*.

Yao, J. (2023). *Exploring experiential learning: Enhancing secondary school chemistry education through practical engagement and innovation*. Education, Health, and Social Sciences., 10.54097/ehss.v22i.12508

Zitha, I., Mokganya, G., & Sinthumule, O. (2023). Innovative strategies for fostering student engagement and collaborative learning among extended curriculum programme students. *Education Sciences*.

Chapter 3
Social Emotional Learning Strategies in Higher Education

S. C. Vetrivel
https://orcid.org/0000-0003-3050-8211
Kongu Engineering College, India

V. P. Arun
JKKN College of Engineering and Technology, India

T. P. Saravanan
Kongu Engineering College, India

R. Maheswari
Kongu Engineering College, India

ABSTRACT

Social emotional learning (SEL) has gained increasing recognition as a vital component of education, particularly in the context of higher education institutions. This chapter provides a detailed overview of the key concepts, strategies, and implications of integrating SEL into higher education settings. Social emotional learning encompasses a range of skills and competencies that enable individuals to understand and manage their emotions, develop positive interpersonal relationships, and make responsible decisions. In the higher education landscape, the focus on SEL strategies has emerged as a response to the evolving needs of students and the recognition that academic success is closely intertwined with emotional well-being. This chapter explores the foundational principles of SEL and its relevance in higher education, emphasizing the positive impact on students' personal and academic development.

DOI: 10.4018/979-8-3693-3559-8.ch003

INTRODUCTION

Conceptual Framework

The conceptual framework for Social Emotional Learning (SEL) strategies in higher education is grounded in the understanding that academic success is not solely determined by cognitive abilities but also by the development of social and emotional skills. SEL encompasses a range of competencies, including self-awareness, self-regulation, social awareness, relationship skills, and responsible decision-making. In the higher education context, this framework aims to foster a holistic approach to student development, acknowledging the significance of emotional intelligence alongside academic achievement (Anderson et al., 2019). Firstly, the conceptual framework emphasizes the integration of SEL into the academic curriculum. This involves designing courses and educational activities that explicitly address and cultivate social and emotional skills. For instance, professors can incorporate collaborative projects, reflective exercises, and discussions that promote self-awareness and interpersonal skills. By weaving SEL principles into the fabric of academic content, students can experience a seamless integration of emotional intelligence and subject matter expertise. Secondly, the framework acknowledges the role of educators as key facilitators of SEL. Faculty members are encouraged to model and embody social and emotional competencies, creating an environment that promotes positive relationships, empathy, and effective communication. Professional development opportunities for instructors can include training on incorporating SEL into their teaching methods, as well as strategies for supporting students' emotional well-being. Another crucial aspect of the conceptual framework involves creating a campus culture that values SEL. This includes developing policies and practices that prioritize students' mental and emotional health, providing resources such as counseling services, and fostering a sense of community (Railean, 2017). Institutional commitment to SEL is essential for creating an atmosphere where students feel supported, respected, and able to thrive both academically and emotionally. Furthermore, the conceptual framework recognizes the importance of assessment and evaluation in gauging the effectiveness of SEL strategies in higher education (Barlow et al., 2018). This involves developing tools and metrics to measure students' social and emotional growth, providing valuable feedback for continuous improvement. Assessment can encompass both qualitative and quantitative methods, including self-report surveys, peer evaluations, and academic performance indicators. Lastly, the conceptual framework for SEL strategies in higher education emphasizes the need for collaboration among various stakeholders, including faculty, administrators, students, and external partners. Interdisciplinary collaboration can enhance the impact of SEL initiatives by drawing on diverse perspectives and expertise. Moreover, engagement with employers and industry leaders can help align SEL competencies with the skills demanded in the workforce, ensuring that higher education remains relevant to students' future success.

Importance of SEL in Academic Settings

Social and Emotional Learning (SEL) plays a crucial role in academic settings as it contributes significantly to the overall well-being and success of students. SEL encompasses a set of skills and competencies that enable individuals to understand and manage their emotions, build positive relationships, and make responsible decisions. In academic settings, where students are not only acquiring knowledge but also developing as individuals, SEL fosters an environment conducive to both academic and personal growth. One of the key aspects of SEL is the promotion of a positive and inclusive school climate. When students feel a sense of belonging and safety in their academic environment, they are more likely to engage actively in their learning. Positive relationships between students and teachers, as well as among peers, create a supportive atmosphere that enhances overall well-being and contributes to a positive attitude towards learning. SEL also plays a vital role in improving students' interpersonal skills, which are essential for collaboration and teamwork (Bellocchi, 2019). Academic success often requires effective communication, conflict resolution, and cooperation. Through SEL, students develop skills such as empathy, active listening, and effective communication, which not only improve their relationships with others but also enhance their ability to work collaboratively on academic tasks and projects. Furthermore, SEL contributes to the development of essential life skills. Students who are proficient in SEL are better equipped to cope with stress, manage their time effectively, and set realistic goals (Railean, 2019b). These skills are not only beneficial in the academic realm but also prepare students for the challenges they may face in their future personal and professional lives. SEL provides a foundation for resilience, adaptability, and a positive attitude towards overcoming obstacles. Academic settings often emphasize cognitive development, but SEL recognizes the importance of emotional intelligence. Students who are emotionally intelligent can regulate their emotions, which positively impacts their ability to focus, concentrate, and manage stress. This, in turn, enhances their academic performance and overall learning experience (Belfield et al., 2015). Moreover, SEL contributes to the prevention of negative behaviors such as bullying, substance abuse, and violence. By fostering a positive school culture that emphasizes empathy, respect, and responsible decision-making, SEL programs create an environment where such behaviors are less likely to occur. This not only ensures a safer learning environment but also allows students to focus on their academics without the distractions and negative influences associated with these behaviors.

Overview of SEL Competencies

Social and Emotional Learning (SEL) competencies are a set of skills and abilities that encompass a wide range of emotional intelligence, interpersonal skills, and self-awareness. These competencies are crucial for individuals to navigate and succeed in various aspects of life, including relationships, work, and personal well-being. There are five core SEL competencies identified by leading experts and educational organizations, including the Collaborative for Academic, Social, and Emotional Learning (CASEL): self-awareness, self-management, social awareness, relationship skills, and responsible decision-making. Self-awareness is the foundation of SEL, involving an individual's ability to recognize and understand their own emotions, thoughts, and values. It also includes having a clear understanding of one's strengths and weaknesses. This competency is essential for individuals to develop a strong sense of identity, establish positive relationships, and make informed decisions. Self-management refers to the ability to regulate and control one's emotions, behaviors, and impulses. It involves setting and achieving goals, demonstrating resilience in the face of challenges, and maintaining a positive outlook (Bond & Castagnera, 2006). Effective self-management is crucial for individuals to cope with stress, adapt to changes, and maintain a healthy balance in their lives. Social awareness focuses on the ability to understand and empathize with others' perspectives and experiences. It includes recognizing and appreciating diversity, as well as demonstrating empathy and compassion. Socially aware individuals are more likely to form positive relationships, collaborate effectively, and contribute to a supportive and inclusive community. Relationship skills encompass the ability to establish and maintain healthy and positive relationships with others. This includes effective communication, active listening, cooperation, and conflict resolution. Developing strong relationship skills is essential for building a supportive social network and thriving in both personal and professional settings. Responsible decision-making involves the ability to make thoughtful and ethical choices by considering the well-being of oneself and others. It requires weighing potential consequences, evaluating different perspectives, and demonstrating integrity. Individuals with strong responsible decision-making skills are better equipped to navigate complex situations and contribute positively to their communities.

THEORETICAL FOUNDATIONS OF SEL IN HIGHER EDUCATION

Psychological Theories Supporting SEL

Social and Emotional Learning (SEL) is grounded in various psychological theories that highlight the importance of developing emotional intelligence, social awareness, and interpersonal skills. These theories provide a foundation for understanding the psychological mechanisms behind SEL and offer insights into its effectiveness. Here are some key psychological theories supporting SEL:

- **Emotional Intelligence (EI) Theory:** Developed by Daniel Goleman, EI theory posits that emotional intelligence is a crucial component of personal and social success. It consists of four components: self-awareness, self-management, social awareness, and relationship management (Boothe et al., 2018). SEL programs often draw upon these components to enhance emotional intelligence, helping individuals recognize, understand, and regulate their own emotions, as well as empathize with others.
- **Attachment Theory:** Proposed by John Bowlby and Mary Ainsworth, attachment theory emphasizes the significance of early emotional bonds between caregivers and children (Railean & Railean, 2020). SEL programs recognize the impact of secure attachments on emotional and social development. They aim to foster positive relationships and a sense of security, addressing the emotional needs that arise from early attachment experiences.
- **Social Cognitive Theory:** Albert Bandura's Social Cognitive Theory highlights the role of observational learning, modeling, and imitation in the development of behavior. SEL programs leverage this theory by incorporating role modeling and observational learning to promote positive social behaviors and communication skills.
- **Erikson's Psychosocial Development:** Erik Erikson's theory outlines eight stages of psychosocial development, with each stage presenting a unique social and emotional challenge. SEL aligns with Erikson's emphasis on the importance of mastering these challenges for overall well-being and successful development.
- **Mindfulness and Self-Regulation Theories:** SEL often integrates principles from mindfulness and self-regulation theories, emphasizing the cultivation of attention, emotional awareness, and impulse control. Practices such as meditation and mindful breathing are commonly used in SEL programs to enhance self-regulation skills.

- **Positive Psychology:** Positive psychology, pioneered by Martin Seligman, focuses on cultivating strengths and virtues to promote well-being. SEL aligns with the positive psychology framework by emphasizing the development of positive character traits, resilience, and a positive mindset in individuals.
- **Cognitive-Behavioral Theory:** SEL interventions frequently draw from cognitive-behavioral theories, emphasizing the interplay between thoughts, feelings, and behaviors. These programs aim to help individuals recognize and reframe negative thought patterns, fostering more positive social interactions and emotional well-being.
- **Self-Determination Theory (SDT):** SDT, developed by Edward Deci and Richard Ryan, posits that individuals are motivated by the innate psychological needs for autonomy, competence, and relatedness. SEL programs support autonomy by providing students with choices, enhance competence by developing social and emotional skills, and promote relatedness by fostering positive relationships.

Cognitive and Emotional Development in Young Adults

Cognitive development in young adults is a multifaceted process that involves the growth and refinement of thinking, reasoning, problem-solving, and decision-making skills. One prominent theory that sheds light on cognitive development is Jean Piaget's stages of cognitive development. According to Piaget, young adults typically fall into the formal operational stage, which spans from adolescence into adulthood. During this stage, individuals develop abstract thinking abilities, allowing them to conceptualize hypothetical scenarios and engage in complex problem-solving. In young adulthood, cognitive abilities continue to evolve as individuals confront a variety of challenges in education, work, and personal relationships. This period is characterized by an increased capacity for critical thinking, metacognition, and the ability to reflect on one's own thoughts and actions. Young adults often demonstrate more advanced reasoning skills, enabling them to consider multiple perspectives and approach problems with a greater level of sophistication (Brooks & Brooks, 1999). Cognitive development in this stage is closely tied to experiences, education, and exposure to diverse ideas, contributing to the formation of a well-rounded and adaptable cognitive framework. Emotional development in young adults is a parallel and interconnected process that involves the regulation and expression of emotions. Erik Erikson's psychosocial stages of development highlight the importance of establishing a sense of identity during young adulthood. This period is characterized by the psychosocial crisis of intimacy versus isolation, where individuals seek to form deep and meaningful connections with others while also maintaining a sense of independence and self-identity. Emotionally, young adults may experience heightened levels of self-awareness, empathy, and the ability to navigate complex social relationships. Emotional regulation becomes more refined during this stage, allowing individuals to manage stress, cope with challenges, and regulate their emotions in a socially appropriate manner. The formation of intimate relationships, whether romantic or platonic, plays a crucial role in emotional development, providing opportunities for emotional expression, support, and personal growth. Furthermore, young adults may grapple with the development of a stable and realistic self-concept, integrating various aspects of their identity, values, and aspirations. This process often involves self-reflection, exploration of personal values, and alignment of one's goals with their evolving sense of self. Emotional intelligence, the ability to recognize and understand one's own emotions and those of others, tends to increase during young adulthood, facilitating more effective communication and interpersonal skills.

Connection to Positive Psychology

Social and Emotional Learning (SEL) and Positive Psychology share a significant connection, both emphasizing the importance of fostering well-being and personal development. SEL refers to the process of acquiring and applying the knowledge, attitudes, and skills necessary to understand and manage emotions, set and achieve positive goals, feel and show empathy for others, establish and maintain positive relationships, and make responsible decisions. Positive Psychology, on the other hand, focuses on the scientific study of what makes life worth living and emphasizes the promotion of positive emotions, strengths, and overall well-being. One key connection between SEL and Positive Psychology lies in their shared goal of enhancing individual and collective happiness (Caine & Caine, 1994). SEL programs provide individuals with the tools to develop emotional intelligence, a crucial aspect of positive psychology. By understanding and managing emotions effectively, individuals can cultivate positive emotions and resilience, contributing to overall life satisfaction. Positive Psychology complements SEL by providing a theoretical framework and evidence-based practices that promote happiness and well-being, reinforcing the objectives of SEL programs. Furthermore, both SEL and Positive Psychology underscore the importance of building positive relationships and fostering a sense of belonging. SEL programs often include components focused on interpersonal skills, communication, and empathy, which align with Positive Psychology's emphasis on the significance of social connections in promoting happiness. Positive relationships contribute significantly to an individual's well-being, and both SEL and Positive Psychology recognize the reciprocal relationship between positive emotions and fulfilling social connections. Additionally, SEL and Positive Psychology share an interest in the concept of strengths and virtues. Positive Psychology identifies individual strengths and virtues as key factors in flourishing, while SEL programs often incorporate the identification and development of personal strengths. By fostering a strengths-based approach, both disciplines empower individuals to leverage their unique qualities for personal growth and contribute positively to their communities. SEL and Positive Psychology also intersect in their focus on goal-setting and personal development. SEL programs guide individuals in setting and achieving positive goals, aligning with Positive Psychology's emphasis on the pursuit of meaningful objectives to enhance overall life satisfaction. The connection lies in the shared belief that personal growth and goal attainment contribute significantly to an individual's sense of purpose and well-being.

SEL COMPETENCIES FOR HIGHER EDUCATION

Self-Awareness and Self-Management

Social and Emotional Learning (SEL) competencies play a crucial role in the development of students in higher education, preparing them for success in both academic and personal aspects of their lives. Two fundamental components of SEL are self-awareness and self-management. Self-awareness is the foundational aspect of emotional intelligence. In the context of higher education, it involves students' ability to recognize and understand their emotions, strengths, weaknesses, values, and goals. This competency enables students to gain insight into how their emotions influence their thoughts and behaviors, fostering a deeper understanding of themselves. Self-aware individuals are better equipped to navigate the challenges of higher education, form meaningful relationships, and make informed decisions. In a higher education setting, self-awareness is nurtured through reflective practices, such as journaling, self-assessments, and mindfulness activities. Professors and educators can encourage students to engage in self-reflection, prompting them to explore their motivations, beliefs, and reactions to different situations. This process not only enhances emotional intelligence but also fosters a greater sense of identity and purpose, crucial for personal and academic growth. Moving on to self-management, this competency builds upon self-awareness by empowering students to regulate their emotions and behaviors effectively (Chen, 2017). In higher education, where academic pressures, deadlines, and social interactions can be demanding, self-management skills are essential for maintaining focus, resilience, and a positive mindset. Self-management in the higher education context involves setting and achieving academic and personal goals, time management, stress management, and the ability to adapt to change. Students with strong self-management skills can navigate the complex demands of their academic journey, prioritize tasks effectively, and bounce back from setbacks with resilience. Educators can support the development of self-management by teaching stress reduction techniques, providing tools for effective time management, and encouraging a growth mindset that embraces challenges as opportunities for learning.

Social Awareness and Relationship Skills

Social Awareness and Relationship Skills are integral components of Social and Emotional Learning (SEL) competencies in higher education. These competencies aim to equip students with the skills and knowledge necessary for successful interpersonal interactions, collaboration, and navigating diverse social contexts. Social Awareness involves the ability to understand and empathize with the feelings, needs, and perspectives of others. In higher education, this encompasses recognizing and appreciating the diversity within the campus community. Students are encouraged to develop cultural competence, embracing different backgrounds, ethnicities, and perspectives (Conley, 2015). Social Awareness also involves understanding social norms, ethics, and the impact of one's actions on others. It fosters a sense of responsibility and accountability for contributing positively to the social fabric of the academic environment. Building Social Awareness in higher education involves activities such as group discussions, case studies, and experiential learning opportunities. These activities help students explore and appreciate different cultural perspectives, challenging biases, and promoting open-mindedness. Campus initiatives that promote inclusivity, equity, and diversity contribute significantly to enhancing social awareness among students. Relationship Skills, another vital SEL competency, focus on building and maintaining positive relationships. In the context of higher education, this involves effective communication, conflict resolution, and collaboration. Students are encouraged to develop strong interpersonal skills, including active listening, clear communication, and the ability to work collaboratively with diverse groups of people. In higher education settings, Relationship Skills are often developed through group projects, team-based activities, and extracurricular involvement. These experiences provide students with opportunities to practice effective communication, resolve conflicts, and collaborate with peers who may have different perspectives and strengths. Building these skills prepares students for the complex interpersonal dynamics they may encounter in both academic and professional settings. To further enhance Relationship Skills, higher education institutions may offer workshops, seminars, and training programs focused on communication, teamwork, and conflict resolution (Courey et al., 2012). These initiatives not only contribute to the personal development of students but also prepare them for success in their future careers, where effective collaboration and relationship-building are often critical.

Responsible Decision-Making

Responsible Decision-Making is a critical component of Social and Emotional Learning (SEL) competencies for higher education, encompassing a set of skills that enable individuals to make thoughtful and ethical choices in various academic, personal, and social contexts. This competency is rooted in the understanding that decisions have consequences, not only for oneself but also for others and the community at large. Higher education institutions play a crucial role in fostering these skills, preparing students to navigate complex situations and contribute positively to society. Within the framework of SEL, Responsible Decision-Making involves a multi-step process. First, students need to develop self-awareness, understanding their own values, emotions, and goals. This self-awareness forms the foundation for considering how their decisions align with personal principles and aspirations. Next, students must demonstrate social awareness by understanding the perspectives and feelings of others, recognizing the potential impact of their decisions on different stakeholders. In higher education settings, responsible decision-making often requires critical thinking skills. Students should be equipped to analyze information, evaluate potential outcomes, and consider ethical implications. This includes assessing the short-term and long-term consequences of decisions and recognizing the interconnectedness of choices within the broader community. Institutions can facilitate this by incorporating ethical reasoning and decision-making frameworks into their curricula, encouraging students to think beyond immediate gratification and weigh the broader societal implications of their choices. Collaboration and communication skills are also integral to responsible decision-making. Higher education institutions can provide opportunities for students to engage in group projects, discussions, and debates, allowing them to practice effective communication and negotiation (Durlak et al., 2011). Through these experiences, students learn to navigate diverse perspectives, compromise when necessary, and make decisions that consider the collective well-being. Furthermore, institutions should create a supportive and inclusive environment that encourages students to seek guidance from peers, faculty, and counseling services when faced with challenging decisions. By fostering a culture that values open communication and mentorship, higher education institutions contribute to the development of responsible decision-making skills.

INTEGRATING SEL INTO THE CURRICULUM

Incorporating SEL Into Academic Programs

Integrating Social-Emotional Learning (SEL) into academic programs is a critical approach to fostering holistic student development. SEL focuses on developing key skills such as self-awareness, self-regulation, social awareness, relationship skills, and responsible decision-making. By seamlessly incorporating SEL into the curriculum, educators can create an environment that nurtures not only cognitive growth but also emotional intelligence.

To begin with, embedding SEL into academic programs requires a comprehensive understanding of the core competencies associated with SEL. This knowledge allows educators to identify natural connections between these competencies and academic subjects, ensuring a seamless integration. For instance, a history lesson could incorporate discussions about empathy and perspective-taking, while a math class might emphasize teamwork and collaboration through group projects (Gardner, 2006; Greenberg et al., 2016). This approach helps students see the relevance of SEL skills in various aspects of their academic journey. Furthermore, explicit instruction is essential to ensure students grasp the concepts and practices associated with SEL. Dedicated lessons or activities can be incorporated into the curriculum, focusing on building emotional intelligence and interpersonal skills. These lessons may include mindfulness exercises, role-playing scenarios, and reflective writing to encourage self-awareness and effective communication. Teachers can also model SEL behaviors, providing real-life examples of how these skills are applicable both inside and outside the classroom. Moreover, creating a positive and supportive classroom culture is pivotal to the success of integrating SEL into academic programs. Teachers should establish a safe space where students feel comfortable expressing their thoughts and emotions. Encouraging open communication and active listening fosters a sense of belonging and helps build strong teacher-student relationships, which are crucial for the overall success of SEL initiatives. Assessment and feedback mechanisms should be integrated to evaluate students' progress in developing SEL skills. This can be done through self-assessments, peer evaluations, and teacher feedback on social and emotional growth. Recognizing and celebrating students' achievements in these areas reinforces the importance of SEL and encourages continued development.

Designing SEL-Focused Courses

Designing Social-Emotional Learning (SEL)-focused courses within the framework of integrating SEL into the curriculum requires a thoughtful and comprehensive approach. First and foremost, educators must identify the specific SEL competencies they aim to address, such as self-awareness, self-regulation, social awareness, relationship skills, and responsible decision-making. Once these competencies are determined, the course content can be developed to align with these goals. The curriculum design should be interdisciplinary, weaving SEL principles into subjects like language arts, mathematics, science, and social studies. This integration ensures that students not only acquire academic knowledge but also develop the emotional intelligence necessary for personal and social success. For example, a language arts lesson could focus on empathetic storytelling, while a science class might explore the emotional impact of environmental issues (Hasson, 2015). Instructional methods should be varied to cater to diverse learning styles, incorporating interactive activities, group discussions, role-playing, and real-world applications. The courses should provide opportunities for students to reflect on their emotions and behaviors, fostering self-awareness. Additionally, teaching strategies should emphasize the importance of positive relationships and effective communication, promoting social awareness and relationship skills.

Assessment in SEL-focused courses should go beyond traditional tests and exams. Instead, educators can implement formative assessments, reflective journals, and project-based evaluations that gauge students' emotional and social growth. This approach allows for a more holistic understanding of a student's development, going beyond academic achievements to measure their interpersonal skills and emotional well-being.

Professional development for teachers is crucial to the success of SEL-focused courses. Educators need training on incorporating SEL principles into their teaching methods and managing the unique challenges that may arise when addressing emotional and social development. Collaborative planning sessions can facilitate the sharing of best practices and ensure a consistent approach across the curriculum. Furthermore, creating a positive and inclusive classroom environment is integral to SEL integration. Teachers should establish clear expectations for behavior, foster a sense of belonging, and implement strategies for conflict resolution. The physical layout of the classroom can also be designed to encourage collaboration and open communication.

Interdisciplinary Approaches to SEL

Interdisciplinary approaches to Social and Emotional Learning (SEL) involve integrating SEL concepts and practices seamlessly into various academic subjects, fostering a holistic development of students. By intertwining SEL with the curriculum, educators can create an environment where students not only gain academic knowledge but also develop crucial social and emotional skills that are essential for success in both school and life. One key aspect of this approach is the identification of natural intersections between SEL and different subjects. For instance, literature classes can explore characters' emotional intelligence and empathy, history classes can delve into the impact of social and emotional factors on historical events, and math classes can incorporate problem-solving scenarios that require collaboration and communication. This multidisciplinary approach not only reinforces SEL concepts but also demonstrates the real-world applicability of these skills. Furthermore, interdisciplinary SEL approaches encourage collaborative teaching among educators from various disciplines. Teachers can work together to design lessons that seamlessly integrate both academic content and SEL components. This collaborative effort fosters a school culture that prioritizes social and emotional development, creating a more cohesive and supportive learning environment (Keefer et al., 2018). Incorporating SEL into the curriculum also involves providing educators with the necessary training and resources. Teachers need to be equipped with the knowledge and skills to integrate SEL seamlessly into their lessons. Professional development programs can offer guidance on how to infuse SEL into different subjects, ensuring that teachers feel confident in delivering effective SEL instruction. Moreover, interdisciplinary SEL approaches emphasize the importance of assessment and evaluation. While traditional academic assessments measure cognitive understanding, SEL assessments evaluate students' emotional intelligence, interpersonal skills, and self-awareness. This comprehensive evaluation system provides a more accurate picture of a student's overall development, recognizing the significance of both academic and socio-emotional growth.

PROMOTING SEL THROUGH CAMPUS CULTURE

Creating a Positive and Inclusive Campus Climate

Creating a positive and inclusive campus climate is crucial for promoting Social and Emotional Learning (SEL) through campus culture. This initiative involves fostering an environment that prioritizes emotional well-being, empathy, and respect among students, faculty, and staff. To achieve this, schools can implement various strategies. First and foremost, establishing clear expectations for behavior and communication helps set a foundation for a positive campus climate. This includes promoting open dialogue and active listening, creating spaces where diverse perspectives are valued, and addressing any incidents of discrimination or exclusion promptly.

In addition, integrating SEL into the curriculum can be instrumental in fostering emotional intelligence, self-awareness, and interpersonal skills. Incorporating SEL lessons into various subjects and extracurricular activities enables students to practice these skills in real-life situations, contributing to a more supportive and harmonious campus environment. Schools may also consider implementing SEL programs that involve community-building activities, group discussions, and workshops to enhance students' emotional regulation, interpersonal communication, and conflict resolution skills. Moreover, creating a sense of belonging for all students is paramount (Kolb, 1984). This involves acknowledging and celebrating diversity, promoting cultural competence, and providing resources and support for underrepresented groups. School leaders can actively involve students in decision-making processes, ensuring their voices are heard and valued in shaping the campus culture. Collaborating with community organizations, hosting inclusive events, and celebrating cultural awareness months are also effective ways to enhance the sense of community and belonging. Finally, fostering positive relationships between students, faculty, and staff is essential. Implementing mentorship programs, promoting positive teacher-student interactions, and providing professional development opportunities for educators to enhance their SEL skills contribute to a more supportive and inclusive campus climate. By prioritizing SEL through campus culture, schools can create an environment that not only supports academic success but also nurtures the social and emotional well-being of all its members.

Faculty and Staff Development for SEL

Faculty and staff development plays an important role in promoting Social-Emotional Learning (SEL) through campus culture. Recognizing that educators serve as the foundation for fostering a positive and supportive learning environment, investing in their professional growth becomes paramount. The development initiatives should focus on equipping faculty and staff with the necessary knowledge, skills, and resources to integrate SEL practices seamlessly into their teaching methods and interpersonal interactions. Workshops, training sessions, and ongoing professional development opportunities can empower educators to understand the principles of SEL, cultivate self-awareness, and effectively implement SEL strategies within the classroom and broader campus community (Lubit & Lubit, 2019; Nussbaum, 2001). Furthermore, administrators should encourage a collaborative approach that enables educators to share best practices, exchange ideas, and collectively contribute to a school-wide culture that prioritizes social and emotional well-being. By nurturing the personal and professional development of faculty and staff, educational institutions can create a ripple effect, fostering a positive campus culture that prioritizes the holistic development of students and prepares them for success in both academic and social spheres.

Student Engagement and Leadership

Promoting social-emotional learning (SEL) through campus culture is essential for nurturing well-rounded individuals, and student engagement and leadership play pivotal roles in this transformative process. When students actively participate in their educational experience, they not only develop a deeper understanding of academic content but also cultivate crucial interpersonal and emotional skills (Palmer, 2015). Campus culture that emphasizes SEL creates an environment where students feel valued, supported, and connected to their peers and educators. Student engagement is fostered through interactive learning experiences, collaborative projects, and extracurricular activities that encourage teamwork, communication, and empathy. Leadership opportunities further amplify SEL by empowering students to take on responsible roles, make decisions, and contribute to the positive development of their school community. Through student-led initiatives, clubs, and programs, young leaders emerge, equipped with the social and emotional competencies necessary for success in both academic and real-world contexts. In essence, a robust focus on student engagement and leadership within the framework of promoting SEL through campus culture not only enhances the educational experience but also prepares students for a lifetime of personal and professional success.

ASSESSMENT AND MEASUREMENT OF SEL IN HIGHER EDUCATION

Tools and Instruments for Evaluating SEL Competencies

In the realm of higher education, the assessment and measurement of Social and Emotional Learning (SEL) competencies are pivotal for fostering holistic student development. To effectively gauge SEL competencies, a diverse array of tools and instruments is utilized, encompassing both quantitative and qualitative approaches. Surveys and self-report questionnaires, such as the Social Emotional Learning Assessment Scale (SELAS), are commonly employed to measure students' self-perceived abilities in areas like self-awareness, self-management, social awareness, relationship skills, and responsible decision-making (Railean, 2017). Additionally, observational tools like the Classroom Assessment Scoring System (CLASS) allow educators and researchers to assess social and emotional interactions within educational settings. Performance assessments, such as role-playing scenarios or case studies, provide a more practical evaluation of how students apply SEL competencies in real-world situations. Furthermore, emerging technologies like virtual reality simulations enable immersive and interactive assessments, offering a dynamic and engaging method for evaluating SEL skills. These tools collectively contribute to a comprehensive understanding of students' social and emotional development, guiding educators in tailoring interventions and curricula to enhance SEL competencies within higher education settings.

Longitudinal Studies on SEL Impact

Longitudinal studies examining the impact of Social and Emotional Learning (SEL) within the context of higher education assessment and measurement have become increasingly essential in understanding the sustained effects of SEL interventions on students' personal and academic development. These studies involve tracking the same group of individuals over an extended period, allowing researchers to observe changes and patterns in their social and emotional competencies. SEL interventions in higher education aim to enhance students' self-awareness, interpersonal skills, and emotional regulation, contributing to their overall well-being and academic success. Through rigorous assessment and measurement methods, such as surveys, self-reports, and behavioral observations, researchers can gather valuable data to evaluate the long-term effectiveness of SEL programs (Railean, 2019b). Longitudinal studies offer insights into the persistence of SEL outcomes, shedding light on whether improvements in social and emotional skills endure beyond the immediate intervention period. This comprehensive understanding is crucial for institutions seeking evidence-based practices to inform future SEL implementation strategies in higher education settings.

TECHNOLOGY AND INNOVATION IN SEL

With the integration of digital tools, educational platforms, and artificial intelligence, SEL initiatives have become more accessible, engaging, and personalized. Technology facilitates real-time feedback, tracking progress, and tailoring interventions to individual needs. Virtual reality and augmented reality applications provide immersive experiences that simulate various social situations, enabling learners to practice and develop emotional intelligence in a safe environment. Additionally, innovative apps and online platforms offer interactive modules, games, and multimedia content designed to enhance self-awareness, relationship-building skills, and responsible decision-making. Furthermore, data analytics and machine learning algorithms are employed to assess students' emotional states, identifying patterns and trends that educators can use to provide targeted support (Railean & Railean, 2020). The intersection of technology and SEL is creating a dynamic and responsive framework for nurturing essential life skills in the digital age. As technology continues to advance, it holds the potential to revolutionize SEL, making it more inclusive, adaptive, and effective in preparing individuals for the complexities of the 21st century.

GLOBAL PERSPECTIVES ON SEL IN HIGHER EDUCATION

Global perspectives on Social and Emotional Learning (SEL) in higher education underscore the increasing recognition of its vital role in fostering holistic student development and success. SEL in higher education transcends traditional academic measures, acknowledging the importance of emotional intelligence, interpersonal skills, and resilience in preparing students for a rapidly changing global landscape. Across the globe, educational institutions are incorporating SEL into their curricula, emphasizing the cultivation of self-awareness, social awareness, responsible decision-making, relationship skills, and self-management. The global perspective on SEL recognizes that these competencies not only contribute to academic achievement but also equip students with the essential life skills necessary for personal and professional success. Additionally, international collaboration and cultural sensitivity are integral components of SEL in higher education, promoting a diverse and inclusive learning environment that prepares students to navigate the complexities of our interconnected world. As countries continue to share best practices and adapt to the evolving needs of their societies, SEL in higher education emerges as a critical component in shaping well-rounded, empathetic, and globally-minded individuals.

INSTITUTIONAL POLICIES AND SEL

Institutional policies play a crucial role in shaping the educational landscape, and their integration with Social and Emotional Learning (SEL) is essential for fostering holistic student development. These policies establish the framework within which schools operate, influencing not only academic practices but also the overall well-being of students. SEL is a paradigm that recognizes the importance of emotional intelligence, self-awareness, and interpersonal skills in shaping successful and resilient individuals (Railean, 2019a; Rakovan, 2018). When institutional policies align with SEL principles, a conducive environment is created where educators are empowered to prioritize students' social and emotional growth alongside academic achievements. This integration ensures that schools not only focus on imparting knowledge but also emphasize the cultivation of essential life skills, such as empathy, self-regulation, and effective communication. By fostering a supportive atmosphere through institutional policies, schools can contribute significantly to the emotional and social development of students, preparing them for a well-rounded and successful future.

CHALLENGES AND EMERGING TRENDS IN SEL IMPLEMENTATION

Implementing Social and Emotional Learning (SEL) in educational settings is crucial for nurturing well-rounded individuals equipped with essential life skills. However, this endeavor comes with its set of challenges and evolving trends that educators and policymakers must address to ensure its effectiveness and sustainability. One significant challenge in SEL implementation is the need for comprehensive teacher training and support. Educators must possess a deep understanding of SEL concepts, pedagogy, and effective instructional strategies to integrate them seamlessly into their teaching practices. Additionally, ongoing professional development opportunities are essential to equip teachers with the skills and knowledge necessary to adapt to diverse student needs and classroom dynamics. Another obstacle is the integration of SEL into existing curriculum standards and assessment frameworks. While SEL competencies are increasingly recognized as essential for academic success and overall well-being, there is often a disconnect between academic priorities and the integration of SEL into the curriculum (Vetrivel et al., 2024). Aligning SEL goals with academic standards and incorporating them into assessments without overburdening teachers and students requires careful planning and collaboration among stakeholders. Furthermore, addressing equity and inclusivity is paramount in SEL implementation. Socioeconomic disparities, cultural differences, and varying levels of access to resources can impact students' ability to engage with SEL initiatives effectively. Schools must prioritize strategies that ensure all students, regardless of background or circumstance, have equitable access to high-quality SEL instruction and support services. This may involve culturally responsive teaching practices, targeted interventions for marginalized groups, and community partnerships to address external factors affecting students' social and emotional well-being. In addition to challenges, there are emerging trends shaping the future of SEL implementation. One trend is the increasing use of technology as a tool for delivering SEL instruction and support (Weissberg et al., 2015). Digital platforms, apps, and online resources offer new opportunities for personalized learning, data-driven insights, and remote access to SEL programming. However, careful consideration must be given to issues of digital equity, data privacy, and the need for human connection and interaction in fostering social and emotional development. Another trend is the emphasis on holistic approaches to SEL that extend beyond the classroom walls. Recognizing the influence of family, community, and out-of-school experiences on students' social and emotional development, schools are increasingly adopting multi-systemic approaches that involve parents, caregivers, mental health professionals, and community organizations. Collaborative efforts that bridge the gap between school, home, and community environments can reinforce SEL skills and create a more supportive ecosystem for students to thrive.Top of Form

STUDENT SUPPORT SERVICES AND SEL

Student Support Services (SSS) is important in fostering a positive and inclusive learning environment by addressing the diverse needs of students. In tandem with Social-Emotional Learning (SEL), these services aim to promote the holistic development of students, encompassing not only academic success but also emotional well-being. SEL provides students with the necessary skills to navigate social situations, manage emotions, and build healthy relationships (Reicher, 2010). The integration of SSS and SEL enhances the overall educational experience by equipping students with tools to cope with stress, develop resilience, and foster a sense of belonging within the school community. Through personalized counseling, mentorship programs, and targeted interventions, Student Support Services ensure that each student receives the necessary support to thrive academically and emotionally (Schneider et al., 2013). By recognizing the interconnectedness of academic and social-emotional development, schools can create an environment that empowers students to reach their full potential and prepares them for success in both their academic and personal lives.

EMERGING BEST PRACTICES IN SEL IMPLEMENTATION

Best practices in SEL implementation encompass a range of strategies and approaches that promote the holistic development of students' social and emotional skills within educational settings. By implementing these best practices, schools can create a comprehensive and effective SEL program that supports the social, emotional, and academic development of all students. Some key best practices include:

- **Explicit Instruction**: Providing direct instruction in SEL competencies such as self-awareness, self-management, social awareness, relationship skills, and responsible decision-making. This involves teaching specific skills and strategies through structured lessons and activities.

- **Integration Across Curriculum**: Integrating SEL into various subject areas and classroom activities to reinforce learning and demonstrate the relevance of SEL skills across contexts. This helps students see the connections between social and emotional competencies and academic success.
- **Positive School Climate**: Creating a supportive and inclusive school environment where students feel safe, respected, and valued. This includes promoting positive relationships among students and between students and teachers, as well as implementing clear behavior expectations and consequences.
- **Teacher Training and Support**: Providing ongoing professional development and support for educators to effectively integrate SEL into their teaching practices (Wong, 2016). This includes training in SEL concepts, pedagogy, and classroom management techniques, as well as opportunities for collaboration and peer learning.
- **Family and Community Engagement**: Involving families, caregivers, and community members in SEL initiatives to reinforce learning and promote consistency between home and school environments. This can include workshops, events, and resources for parents, as well as partnerships with community organizations.
- **Data-Informed Decision Making**: Collecting and analyzing data on students' social and emotional competencies to inform instruction, intervention, and program evaluation. This may involve using formal assessments, surveys, and observational data to track progress and identify areas for improvement.
- **Culturally Responsive Practices**: Recognizing and respecting the cultural backgrounds, values, and experiences of students and integrating culturally relevant content and perspectives into SEL instruction. This helps ensure that SEL initiatives are inclusive and accessible to all students.
- **Trauma-Informed Approaches**: Adopting trauma-informed practices that recognize the impact of adverse experiences on students' social and emotional well-being and create safe and supportive learning environments. This includes providing resources and support for students who have experienced trauma and implementing strategies to promote resilience and healing.

FUTURE RESEARCH DIRECTIONS

Social and Emotional Learning (SEL) has gained significant attention in recent years as educators, researchers, and policymakers recognize its importance in fostering holistic development in students (Schutte & Loi, 2014). As we look towards the future, several emerging trends and directions are shaping the landscape of SEL, enhancing its impact on educational outcomes and well-being. One prominent trend is the integration of technology into SEL programs. With the rise of digital learning platforms and tools, educators are exploring innovative ways to incorporate SEL into virtual and hybrid learning environments. This includes the development of interactive applications, virtual reality experiences, and online resources that support students' emotional intelligence, self-awareness, and interpersonal skills. The use of technology not only extends the reach of SEL programs but also provides opportunities for personalized and adaptive learning experiences. Another future direction in SEL involves a greater emphasis on cultural responsiveness and equity (Srinivasan, 2019). Recognizing the diverse backgrounds and experiences of students, educators are increasingly incorporating culturally relevant content and practices into SEL curricula. This includes acknowledging and addressing systemic inequities, promoting inclusivity, and ensuring that SEL programs resonate with students from various cultural, racial, and socio-economic backgrounds (Railean, 2019a). The goal is to create more equitable and accessible SEL interventions that meet the unique needs of all students. Mindfulness and well-being are becoming central components of SEL programs. Educators are recognizing the importance of teaching students skills to manage stress, build resilience, and prioritize their mental health. Mindfulness practices, such as meditation and breathing exercises, are being integrated into daily routines to help students develop self-regulation and coping mechanisms. The emphasis on well-being extends beyond the individual to include a focus on creating positive and supportive school climates that foster a sense of belonging and connection. Collaboration between schools, families, and communities is a growing trend in SEL. Recognizing that social and emotional development occurs in various settings, educators are seeking ways to strengthen partnerships with parents, caregivers, and community organizations (Tantillo Philibert, 2018). This collaborative approach ensures that SEL is reinforced across different environments, creating a more comprehensive and consistent support system for students. Schools are increasingly involving parents in SEL activities, providing resources for families, and engaging community stakeholders to enhance the overall impact of SEL initiatives. Assessment and measurement tools for SEL are evolving to provide more nuanced insights into students' social and emotional competencies (The M.C. Escher Foundation, 2020). Traditional standardized testing is being complemented by innovative assessment methods that capture qualitative data on students' interpersonal skills, self-awareness, and decision-making abilities. This shift towards more holistic evaluation aligns with the multifaceted nature of SEL and allows educators to tailor interventions based on individual student needs.

CONCLUSION

The integration of Social Emotional Learning (SEL) strategies in higher education represents a crucial and transformative approach to fostering holistic student development. As we navigate the complex landscape of academia, it becomes evident that academic success is not solely determined by cognitive abilities but is intrinsically linked to emotional intelligence, interpersonal skills, and self-awareness. SEL strategies empower students to navigate challenges, build meaningful relationships, and cultivate resilience in the face of adversity. Higher education institutions that prioritize SEL are not only preparing students for academic excellence but are also contributing to the creation of well-rounded, emotionally intelligent individuals equipped to thrive in both their personal and professional lives. The positive impact of SEL extends beyond the classroom, shaping a society that values empathy, collaboration, and emotional well-being. As educators and institutions continue to recognize the importance of SEL, we are poised to witness a paradigm shift in higher education that places the development of the whole person at its core.

REFERENCES

Anderson, V., Rabello, R., Wass, R., Golding, C., Rangi, A., Eteuati, E., & Waller, A. (2019). Good teaching as care in higher education. *Higher Education*, 79.

Barlow, A. T., Watson, L. A., Tessema, A. A., Lischka, A. E., & Strayer, J. F. (2018). Inspection-Worthy Mistakes: Which? And Why? *National Council of Teachers of Mathematics*, 24, 384–391.

Belfield, C., Bowden, A. B., Klapp, A., Levin, H., Shand, R., & Zander, S. (2015). The Economic Value of Social and Emotional Learning. *Journal of Benefit-Cost Analysis*, 6(3), 508–544. 10.1017/bca.2015.55

Bellocchi, A. (2019). Early career science teacher experiences of social bonds and emotion management. *Journal of Research in Science Teaching*, 56(3), 322–347. 10.1002/tea.21520

Bond, R., & Castagnera, E. (2006). Peer Supports and Inclusive Education: An Underutilized Resource. *Theory into Practice*, 45(3), 224–229. 10.1207/s15430421tip4503_4

Boothe, K. A., Lohmann, M. J., Donnell, K. A., & Hall, D. D. (2018). Applying the Principles of Universal Design for Learning (UDL) in the College Classroom. *The Journal of Special Education Apprenticeship*, 7(3), 1–13. 10.58729/2167-3454.1076

Brooks, J. G., & Brooks, M. G. (1999). *In Search of Understanding: The Case for Constructivist Classrooms*. Association for Supervision and Curriculum Development.

Caine, R. N., & Caine, G. (1994). *Making Connections: Teaching and the Human Brain*. Addison-Wesley Publishing Company.

Chen, J. C. (2017). Nontraditional Adult Learners: The Neglected Diversity in Postsecondary Education. *SAGE Open*, 7(1), 1–12. 10.1177/2158244017697161

Conley, C. S. (2015). SEL in higher education. In *Handbook of Social and Emotional Learning: Research and Practice* (pp. 197–212). The Guilford Press.

Courey, S. J., Tappe, P., Siker, J., & LePage, P. (2012). Improved Lesson Planning with Universal Design for Learning (UDL). *Teacher Education and Special Education*, 36(1), 7–27. 10.1177/0888406412446178

Durlak, J. A., Weissberg, R. P., Dymnicki, A. B., Taylor, R. D., & Schellinger, K. B. (2011). The impact of enhancing students' social and emotional learning: A meta-analysis of school-based universal interventions. *Child Development*, 82(1), 405–432. 10.1111/j.1467-8624.2010.01564.x21291449

Gardner, H. (2006). *Multiple Intelligences: New Horizons in Theory and Practice.* Basic Books.

Greenberg, M. T., Brown, J. L., & Abenavoli, R. M. (2016). *Teacher Stress and Health: Effects on Teachers, Students, and Schools.* Edna Bennett Pierce Prevention Research Center, Pennsylvania State University.

Hasson, G. (2015). *Understanding Emotional Intelligence.* Pearson Education.

Keefer, K., Parker, J. D. A., Saklofske, D. H., & Saklofskenald, H. (2018). *Emotional Intelligence in Education: Integrating Research with Practice.* Springer. 10.1007/978-3-319-90633-1

Kolb, D. A. (1984). *Experiential Learning: Experience as The Source of Learning And Development.* Prentice Hall.

Lubit, R., & Lubit, R. (2019). Why Educators Should Care About Social and Emotional Learning? *New Directions for Teaching and Learning*, 2019(160), 19–32. 10.1002/tl.20362

Nussbaum, M. C. (2001). *Upheavals of Thought: The Intelligence of Emotions.* Cambridge University Press. 10.1017/CBO9780511840715

Palmer, D. C. (2015). Visualization and analysis of crystal structures using CrystalMaker software. *Zeitschrift für Kristallographie. Crystalline Materials*, 230(9-10), 559–572. 10.1515/zkri-2015-1869

Railean, E. (2017). Metacognition in Higher Education: Successful Learning Strategies and Tactics for Sustainability. In *Metacognition and Successful Learning Strategies in Higher Education* (pp. 1-21). IGI Global. https://doi.org/10.4018/978-1-5225-2218-8.ch00

Railean, E. (2019a). *Anticipating Competence Development With Open Textbooks: The Case of Liquid Skills in Metasystems Learning Design of Open Textbooks: Emerging Research and Opportunities.* IGI Global., 10.4018/978-1-5225-5305-2.ch005

Railean, E. A. (2019b). Education Ecosystems in the Anthropocene Period: Learning and Communication. In *Handbook of Research on Ecosystem-Based Theoretical Models of Learning and Communication* (pp. 1-19). IGI Global. 10.4018/978-1-5225-7853-6.ch001

Railean, E. A. (2020). Pedagogy of New Assessment, Measurement, and Testing Strategies in Higher Education: Learning Theory and Outcomes. In Railean, E. (Ed.), *Assessment, Testing, and Measurement Strategies in Global Higher Education* (pp. 1–19). IGI Global. 10.4018/978-1-7998-2314-8.ch001

Rakovan, J. (2018). Computer Programs for Drawing Crystal Shapes and Atomic Structures. *Rocks and Minerals*, 93(1), 60–64. 10.1080/00357529.2018.1383832

Reicher, H. (2010). Building inclusive education on social and emotional learning: Challenges and perspectives—A review. *International Journal of Inclusive Education*, 14(3), 213–246. 10.1080/13603110802504218

Robertson, D. L. (2020). Adult Students in U.S. Higher Education: An Evidence-Based Commentary and Recommended Best Practices. *Innovative Higher Education*, 45(2), 121–134. 10.1007/s10755-019-09492-8

Schneider, T. R., Lyons, J. B., & Khazon, S. (2013). Emotional intelligence and resilience. *Personality and Individual Differences*, 55(8), 909–914. 10.1016/j.paid.2013.07.460

Schutte, N. S., & Loi, N. M. (2014). Connections between emotional intelligence and workplace flourishing. *Personality and Individual Differences*, 66, 134–139. 10.1016/j.paid.2014.03.031

Srinivasan, M. (2019). *SEL Every Day: Integrating Social and Emotional Learning with Instruction in Secondary Classrooms*. W.W. Norton & Company.

Tantillo Philibert, C. (2018). *Everyday SEL in High School: Integrating Social-Emotional Learning and Mindfulness into Your Classroom*. Routledge.

The M.C. Escher Foundation. (2020). *M.C. Escher—Image Categories—Symmetry*. MC Escher Foundation. https://www.mcescher.com/gallery/symmetry/ (accessed on 27 July 2020).

U.S. Census Bureau. (2013). *School Enrollment in the United States: 2011*. Suitland-Silver Hill.

U.S. Department of Education. (2018). *40th Annual Report to Congress on the Implementation of the Individuals with Disabilities Education Act, Parts B and C*. ED PUBS, Education Publications Center, Washington, DC, USA.

Vetrivel, S. C., & Mohanasundaram, T. (2024a). Flourishing on Campus: Promoting Mental Health and Coping Skills in Higher Education Institutions. In Aloka, P. (Ed.), *Mental Health Crisis in Higher Education* (pp. 294–311). IGI Global. 10.4018/979-8-3693-2833-0.ch017

Vetrivel, S. C., & Mohanasundaram, T. (2024b). Beyond the Blackboard: Embracing Hybrid Learning Spaces. In Omona, K., & O'dama, M. (Eds.), *Global Perspectives on Micro-Learning and Micro-Credentials in Higher Education* (pp. 10–28). IGI Global. 10.4018/979-8-3693-0343-6.ch002

Vetrivel, S. C., Sowmiya, K. C., Arun, V. P., Saravanan, T. P., & Maheswari, R. (2024). Guiding Principles for Youth-Centric Development: Ethical AI. In *Zeinab Zaremohzzabieh, Rusli Abdullah, Seyedali Ahrari, Exploring Youth Studies in the Age of AI (ch-17)*. IGI Global. 10.4018/979-8-3693-3350-1

Weissberg, R. P., Durlak, J. A., Domitrovich, C. E., & Gullotta, T. P. (2015). Social and emotional learning: past, present, and future. In *Handbook of Social and Emotional Learning: Research and Practice* (pp. 3–19). The Guilford Press.

Wong, C. (2016). *Emotional Intelligence at Work: 18-Year Journey of A Researcher*. Taylor & Francis Group.

KEY TERMS AND DEFINITIONS

Academic Performance: A measure of a student's success in their educational endeavors, typically evaluated through grades, test scores, and other assessments of knowledge and skills.

Artificial Intelligence (AI): The simulation of human intelligence in machines that are programmed to think like humans and mimic their actions. In the context of SEL, AI can be used to create personalized learning experiences and provide adaptive feedback.

Assessment Tools: Instruments and methods used to evaluate the effectiveness of SEL programs. These tools can include surveys, interviews, observational checklists, and other measures to assess changes in social and emotional competencies.

Career Readiness: The level of preparation a student has to enter and succeed in the workforce. This includes not only academic knowledge but also skills such as communication, teamwork, problem-solving, and emotional intelligence.

Collaborative Research: Research conducted by teams of people from different fields or institutions working together to address a common research question or goal. In the context of SEL, this can include educators, psychologists, sociologists, and policymakers.

Cultural Adaptation: The process of adjusting SEL strategies to fit the cultural norms, values, and practices of different groups. This ensures that SEL programs are relevant and effective across diverse populations.

Higher Education: The stage of learning that occurs at universities, colleges, and other institutions offering degrees beyond the secondary education level. This includes undergraduate, graduate, and postgraduate studies.

Interdisciplinary Research: A research approach that integrates methods and perspectives from different academic disciplines to provide a more comprehensive understanding of a complex issue, such as SEL.

Mental Health: A state of well-being in which an individual realizes their own potential, can cope with the normal stresses of life, can work productively, and is able to contribute to their community. SEL programs aim to support and enhance students' mental health.

Policy Implementation: The process of putting policies into action within institutions. This involves translating research findings into practical guidelines, strategies, and procedures that can be adopted by educational institutions.

Resilience: The ability to recover quickly from difficulties and adapt well in the face of adversity, trauma, or stress. SEL strategies often aim to build resilience in students.

Social Emotional Learning (SEL): A process through which individuals acquire and apply the knowledge, attitudes, and skills necessary to understand and manage emotions, set and achieve positive goals, feel and show empathy for others, establish and maintain positive relationships, and make responsible decisions.

Socio-Economic Context: The social and economic circumstances that influence individuals' lives and opportunities. In SEL research, understanding socio-economic context helps tailor interventions to meet the needs of students from various backgrounds.

Chapter 4
Cognitive and Metacognitive Strategies of Learning in Higher Education

Anne Liz Job
https://orcid.org/0009-0004-9867-1933
PES University, India

Srishti Muralidharan
PES University, India

ABSTRACT

This chapter provides a broad understanding of the areas of cognition and metacognition and their significance in higher education settings. The chapter encompasses not only the theory and the knowledge related to these thinking processes, but also provides tools in the fields of thinking for educators to implement. The chapter delves into a detailed description of cognitive strategies including elaboration, repetition, distributed practice, and the dual coding hypothesis, and metacognitive strategies, such as goal setting, metacognitive regulation and reflection. Additionally, the chapter explores frameworks such as VAK, Bloom's taxonomy and mental models, by which cognitive and metacognitive strategies can be integrated to enhance learning outcomes. The chapter also provides research evidence, proving the effectiveness of cognitive and metacognitive strategies in the context of higher education.

DOI: 10.4018/979-8-3693-3559-8.ch004

THE PROCESSES OF COGNITION AND METACOGNITION

The term cognition stems from the Latin word 'cognoscere' meaning 'to know'. It encompasses a wide range of mental processes, such as perception, memory, logical reasoning, attention and problem solving. Cognition constitutes the basis of human intelligence and behavior, and is essential in enabling individuals to adapt to the ever-changing VUCA (Volatile-Uncertain-Complex-Ambiguous) world around them. The frontal lobe of the human brain is primarily responsible for higher level mental activities such as logical analysis and problem-solving. An individual's awareness of their own cognitive processes is termed cognitive awareness, or metacognition.

The term metacognition originates from the Greek word 'meta' meaning 'beyond' and the Latin word 'cognoscere' meaning 'to know'. It was coined by James H. Flavell in the 1970s, who defined it as one's knowledge concerning one's own cognitive processes or anything related to them or "thinking about thinking" (Wikipedia contributors, 2024b). It involves knowing when one knows, knowing when one doesn't, and knowing what to do when one doesn't know. Metacognitive awareness is a measure of how aware an individual is of their own cognitive processes, including thoughts, emotions, memory, and attention.

While cognition and metacognition are deeply intertwined, there exists a definite distinction between the two processes. Metacognition begins when awareness of one's cognitive processes is the focus. This implies that, while cognition encompasses various mental processes including thinking, memory, attention, and perception, metacognition comprises an awareness of these mental processes.

For instance, when a student is attempting to solve a complex mathematical equation, cognition is employed when deliberating possible methods to arrive at the solution. However, when the student is engaging in self-regulation to determine the reason for their inability to solve the equation, which might be insufficient practice, they are engaging in the act of metacognition. As a result of engaging in such reflection, the student would become self-aware, possibly leading to them undertaking practice, so as to perfect their mathematical skills.

Therefore, engaging in the process of metacognition could encourage individuals to invest in their personal development by enhancing their cognitive abilities. In the context of knowledge acquisition in higher education students, this investment in personal growth could manifest itself in productive endeavors, including an engagement in deep subject understanding, and overall efficiency in learning.

COGNITIVE AND METACOGNITIVE STRATEGIES OF LEARNING

The strategies and practices that can be employed to improve and enhance one's cognitive abilities, such as memory, and problem-solving skills, and ultimately facilitate knowledge acquisition and academic performance, are referred to as cognitive learning strategies. These strategies include elaboration, repetition, and distributed practice, and these could be highly effective when employed by higher education students in their learning. Professors and students in the field of higher education have greatly benefited from employing these strategies, and this has always been a highly concentrated topic of research.

Another vastly explored subject is the utilization of metacognitive strategies in education. "Metacognitive strategies are techniques to help students develop an awareness of their thinking processes as they learn. These techniques help students focus with greater intention, reflect on their existing knowledge versus information they still need to learn, recognize errors in their thinking, and develop practices for effective learning" (*Metacognitive Strategies (How People Learn) | Center for Teaching Innovation*, n.d.). Metacognitive strategies are employed in educational environments to optimize learning outcomes. It includes the processes of goal setting, planning, monitoring and evaluation, and metacognitive reflection, all of which require deep contemplation.

IMPORTANCE AND SCOPE

The application of cognitive and metacognitive strategies in one's learning endeavors could prove to be highly advantageous, leading to both an improvement in academic performance and a boost in one's level of comprehension and understanding. Employing cognitive strategies in learning can result in an improvement in one's cognitive capabilities, and memory performance. Effectively utilizing the processes of elaboration, repetition and mnemonics can facilitate deep understanding and encoding of information in long term memory. Engaging in self-regulation through the implementation of metacognitive strategies could lead to an improvement in problem-solving and decision-making capabilities.

Metacognitive strategies place a focus on monitoring, evaluating, and appropriately modifying one's methods of studying and acquiring information. Due to the emphasis on self-regulatory behaviors, metacognitive strategies inculcate a sense of responsibility in students, which manifests itself in the expression of an internal locus of control. This internal locus of control encourages students to exercise control over their own results and academic outcomes, contrary to an external locus of control, which leads to individuals attributing academic outcomes to external events, outside of their control, such as the instructor's capabilities and the difficulty of assessments.

According to Vrugt, A., and Oort, F. J. (2008), "One key assumption of all theories of metacognition is that knowledge and regulation of cognition are mutually correlated (e.g. Jacobs & Paris, 1987; Flavell, 1979). However, this positive relationship does not occur when metacognitive knowledge is incorrect, since incorrect metacognitive knowledge about their learning processes prevents students from amending this knowledge (Veenman et al., 2006)". This highlights the need to impart correct, and effective metacognitive knowledge to students so as to enable them to achieve and perform to the fullest of their potential. Awareness and utilization of metacognitive strategies could not only enhance students' academic performance, but also prepare the population for future hurdles, various challenges, and effective decision-making.

In higher education settings, an in-depth understanding of the subject matter is crucial for efficient performance in prospective career paths. In the listed examples that follow, the cognitive and metacognitive aspects of various streams are highlighted:

- For example, in the field of education, it is crucial to have a deep level understanding of the subject while in psychology the emphasis would be on reflection and self-regulation.
- Similarly in main stream career fields, the same rules apply. In Business management, decision-making and knowledge about customer satisfaction play a crucial role while in Engineering and Technology development of new products using nascent technologies and sciences for advancing humanity is of utmost importance.
- In non-main stream career fields too, there is a similar pattern. In Sports, physical and mental health of players and team coherence greatly influence performance while for those in the Creative Arts, perception and self-expression through reflection is the central theme.

LIMITATIONS

Despite the numerous advantages associated with the application of metacognitive and cognitive strategies to learning in university settings, several factors operate as limitations, hindering their effective implementation. These factors are as elaborated below:

- Cognitive and metacognitive strategies place an emphasis on the mental activities of the brain, effectively de-emphasizing the influence of emotions on

- these processes. The current emotional disposition of an individual could greatly affect their motivation, preventing them from effectively employing these strategies. For instance, if an individual is experiencing high levels of stress, they would tend not to prioritize the implementation of cognitive and metacognitive strategies as it could lead to cognitive overload, and might instead engage in behaviors that lead to an improvement in emotional well-being.
- Measuring changes in cognition is a challenging procedure as it is highly subjective. It is greatly dependent on an individual's emotional state and capabilities, and can be influenced by a multitude of factors, such as age, health conditions, genetics, experience and environment. Cognition and metacognition are complex processes that involve a wide range of mental activities, including attention, memory, perception, decision-making and problem-solving, making then difficult to measure using a single scale.
- Assessments that measure cognitive capabilities often tend to neglect the influence of learning through experience. For instance, tests conducted prior to the implementation of cognitive and metacognitive strategies could influence the results of tests conducted after their implementation. Therefore, a comparison between the two sets of results might not be an accurate representation of change in performance.
- Higher education learning involves the transfer of an immense amount of information from the teaching instructor to the students. While the application of cognitive and metacognitive strategies would greatly benefit the students in acquiring this knowledge, the time, effort, and amount of practice required for their implementation is immense. Thus, this leads to a focus on the teaching of subject-related material, over the instruction of cognitive and metacognitive strategies.
- Cognitive and metacognitive strategies of learning are highly advantageous, as highlighted in the previous section. However, most strategies are either unknown to most, or their application is viewed as much too complex to be undertaken.
- While instructors and students might be aware of cognitive and metacognitive strategies, and their methods of implementation, the practical application of these methods might be complicated. Translating theories to practice is a complex, time-taking procedure, leading to a general preference for their avoidance. This can be referred to as the theory-practice gap.

COGNITIVE LEARNING STRATEGIES

Importance

A comprehensive understanding of the course content among higher education students would empower them to excel in professional settings and real-world scenarios. The significance of cognitive strategies in fostering this depth of comprehension is immense as they facilitate impactful learning. Students can leverage the techniques described in this chapter to fully realize the benefit.

The Cognitive Strategies of Learning

The most notable and beneficial cognitive strategies that can be employed by teaching professionals and university students, along with practices to implement these strategies are as listed below.

Elaboration

The process of elaboration involves expanding one's knowledge by constantly engaging with, and adding detail to information, in order to strongly encode it in memory. The ultimate goal of the technique of elaboration is to enhance understanding and improve retention. Retaining the information acquired through learning, in long-term memory could greatly benefit students, and could prove to be crucial in both examination and professional settings.

"Memories form when repeated neural stimulation strengthens synapses-the connections between nerve cells. Proteins are needed to stabilize the long-lasting synaptic connections required for long-term memories". (Einstein Researchers Discover How Long-Lasting Memories Form in the Brain | Albert Einstein College of Medicine, n.d.). The research study found that repeated presentation of a stimulus triggers the cyclic production of proteins, leading to their accumulation at the synapses, thus "cementing" the memories into place. (Einstein Researchers Discover How Long-Lasting Memories Form in the Brain | Albert Einstein College of Medicine, n.d.).

The process of elaboration facilitates the formation of strong neural connections. Elaboration can be performed in multiple ways, and could be adapted to the classroom setting as discussed below:

Mnemonic Strategies. Any strategy that aids with the retention and retrieval of memory is classified as a 'Mnemonic Strategy'. Acronyms and acrostics are common forms of mnemonics. This process involves associating complex terms with simpler words, well known to one, for ease of retrieval. For instance, a commonly used acrostic to remember the planets in the solar system is 'My Very Educated Mother Just Served Us Noodles". In the given example, the first alphabet of each word represents the initial letter of each of the eight planets. (My – Mercury; Very – Venus; Educated – Earth; Mother – Mars; Just – Jupiter; Served – Saturn; Us – Uranus; Noodles – Neptune). A familiar Acronym is VIBGYOR, which is used to remember the colors in a rainbow, in the sequence of their appearance.

Therefore, employing mnemonic strategies facilitates ease of memory encoding as the contractions used can be modified to suit personal preferences.

Forming Associations. This technique involves establishing relationships between new information, and information that was previously acquired, and encoded strongly in the long-term memory.

According to the network model of memory, proposed by Allan Collins and Ross Quillian in the late 1960s, information is stored as an interconnected web of ideas, and nodes of information are connected to each other through strong and weak links. These links explain how thoughts move from one concept to another deeply connected concept, without much conscious effort. For instance, when thinking of the sky, one automatically relates it to the color blue. This flow of thought occurs due to the links that connect "nodes" (Kamiya & Airth, 2023) of memories.

The network model can be employed to improve memory encoding through the concept of 'Redintegration'. Redintegration is defined as "the restoration of the whole of something from a part of it" (Wikipedia contributors, 2023). In memory processes, this can be described as the reconstruction of a chain of related memories, starting with one memory. For instance, if an individual's memory for the mathematical concept of calculus is activated, it might lead to memories of the classroom where they were trained in the subject, of the professor who instructed them, and related episodic memories of instances in that classroom, or interactions with the professor.

When a student is being instructed in a given concept, relating the concept to pre-existing knowledge, could greatly enhance memory retention. This method could prove to be advantageous because it can be adjusted based on the personal experiences and preferences of the learner. Students could form an elaborative network of interconnected memories by relating newly learned concepts to personal examples and instances.

Chunking. When attempting to memorize a large amount of data, the process of chunking, which includes classifying elements into related groups, could aid in the process of memory retention. Primarily, chunking improves short-term memory. However, due to its meaningful nature of organization, it can also indirectly benefit long-term memory. An example of this could be memorizing a grocery list containing the following elements – Milk, orange juice, tomatoes, potatoes, wheat, sugar, and salt. In order to remember this list, one might categorize it into three groups – Liquids, vegetables, and solids. By doing so, one forms categories or groups into which each item fits, facilitating ease of recall.

Repetition

The process of repetition involves repeated exposure to information over time, in order to strengthen the neural pathways, and enhance the retrieval and retention of that information. "When stimuli are learned by repetition, they are remembered better and retained for a longer time" (Zhan, Guo, Chen & Yang, 2018). Though employing repetition to improve memory performance has proven to be effective, deployment of certain strategic methods could further improve these results. These methods include 'spaced learning' and 'distributed practice' developed based on Hermann Ebbinghaus' forgetting curve theory.

Spaced Learning and Distributed Practice

Hermann Ebbinghaus (1850-1909), a German philosopher, was a pioneer in the experimental study of memory. He was the first to describe the forgetting curve, a theory he conceptualized after performing experiments on his own memory.

Ebbinghaus' experiments constituted using lists of meaningless three-lettered combinations (such as "XOB" or "MEK"), which he called 'nonsense syllables'. He would memorize a list of nonsense syllables until he could recite it without error. After a brief interval of time, he would attempt to recite the list, and would make note of the number of times he had to repeat the list before he was as proficient in it as he was after the first learning session. He would continue to carry out this process at definite intervals of time. Through this experiment, he developed the forgetting curve, that represents the rate at which information is forgotten, when no effort is made to relearn or retain it. The curve, as depicted in Figure 1 is plotted on a graph, with the x-axis representing the time, in hours, days, weeks or months, and the y-axis representing the percentage of information retained in memory.

Figure 1. Ebbinghaus' forgetting curve

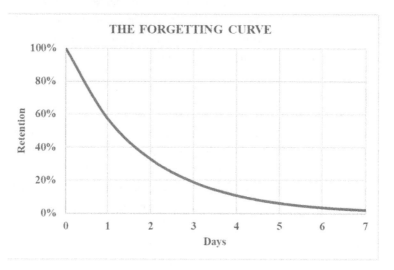

As displayed in Figure 1, the forgetting curve has a slope that is observed to be steepest during the period immediately following learning. As time goes on, the slope gradually becomes less steep. This indicates that the rate of forgetting is highest immediately after learning, and most of the acquired information is forgotten during this time. Gradually, the rate of forgetting slows down, and a small percentage of acquired information is retained for a long period of time after learning takes place.

Figure 2. Ebbinghaus' forgetting curve with distributed practice

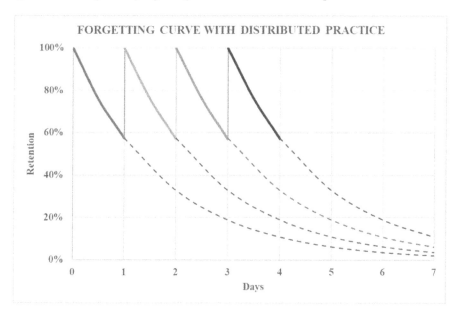

Based on Ebbinghaus' findings, researchers developed the 'spaced learning' technique that enhances the retention of information in memory. Spaced repetition is defined as the act of reviewing new information at key moments on the Forgetting Curve, so as to reduce the rate at which one forgets. (MindTools | Home, n.d.). It involves spacing out study sessions strategically, so as to counter the phenomenon of forgetting, by revisiting learned information. Every instance of recalling information reduces the steepness of the forgetting curve, and this is especially effective when the learning sessions are placed at key points on the curve. Figure 2 displays the key moments on the forgetting where revision could prove to be most efficient.

The first study session is ideally placed a few hours after initial encoding, while the next is placed a few days following the first session. The time gap is eventually increased to weeks, then months. The amount of time between each review session is gradually increased as time goes by. Engaging in this process ultimately leads to the encoding of information in long-term memory.

Bjork (1994), through a thorough review of literature on the effects of memory and meta-memory training on human beings, stated that "The long-term advantages of distributing practice sessions over time have been demonstrated repeatedly for more than a century, tracing back over the entire history of controlled research on human memory." More recent research conducted by Kang (2016) demonstrated that "spaced practice can improve students' memory for essential facts and concepts, which in turn facilitates more complex learning and problem solving". These statements illustrate the benefits associated with utilizing distributed practice and spaced learning during the learning process.

Therefore, the technique of spaced repetition can be implemented in students' daily learning habits by encouraging them to engage in distributed practice sessions. For instance, if a particularly complex concept was taught to them during class, they could revise it at the end of the day. The next revision could be scheduled about a day later, and the next, 3 days after the one preceding it. Following this, the student could revise the information with a week's gap, gradually increasing this period to a month. By employing this technique, students would be able to regularly keep up with their course material, while simultaneously reducing the stress they might have undergone during the exam season, because the information they need to learn has already been encoded in their long-term memory.

While the steep slope of the forgetting curve indicates that memory weakens very quickly immediately after learning, there are multiple aspects that influence memory which must be taken into consideration. According to MindTools | Home (n.d.), learning and retention of information are influenced by how the information is presented to an individual, how meaningful the information is to the individual, and the feelings and emotions experienced by them during encoding. When information is meaningful to an individual, it is retained better in their memory. Ebbinghaus chose to perform his experiment using meaningless combinations of letters, in order to account for and prevent this influence (MindTools | Home, n.d.).

Since retention is greatly impacted by the manner in which material is presented, professors and teaching instructors could facilitate efficient learning by ensuring that information is presented in interesting ways, capturing the students' attention. Another prominent advantage of employing distributed practice is as illustrated by Kang (2016), "Incorporating spaced practice into education can be a cost-effective approach—learning becomes more durable in the same amount of time (relative to massed practice), and this can lead to future savings because less time needs to be spent on relearning content that has been forgotten, leaving more time for other productive learning activities". Overall, the spaced repetition technique is both efficient in the learning process and time-effective.

Dual Coding Hypothesis

Allan Paivio (1925-2016), a professor of psychology at the University of Ontario, introduced the Dual Coding hypothesis in 1971. According to this theory, information presented to an individual undergoes simultaneous processing through two channels – the visual channel and the verbal channel (Wikipedia contributors, 2024). When a stimulus is presented, the verbal and visual components of the stimulus are processed simultaneously, but through separate channels. However, since the two components of the stimuli are presented at the same time, an association between the two aspects is formed in the learner's mind.

Due to the encoding of two kinds of stimuli, both visual and verbal, two pathways for the retrieval of the information are created. Consequently, when a learner recalls either the verbal or the visual stimulus, their memory for the other type of stimulus is activated. The presence of two pathways simplifies the process of retrieval, reducing cognitive load. Therefore, the use of Dual Coding prevents cognitive overload, and facilitates easier retrieval.

In the realm of higher education, quick and effortless retrieval are essential. A reduction in cognitive load enables students to focus more on the process of understanding, which would greatly enhance their performance in the professional sphere, while simultaneously reducing the emphasis on memory and rote learning.

The process of Dual Coding can be employed in classroom settings in the following ways:

- Technology can be leveraged by the use of Microsoft's PowerPoint presentations and videos. Presentations employ visuals such as images and animations, along with text or audio. The implementation of teaching through presentations in the classroom setting would enable students to encode information both visually and verbally, thus improving retention.
- Students can be taught effective note-taking techniques, where they are instructed to utilize both text and visuals, such as images, sketches and diagrams that would enhance their understanding, and enable effective retention of content.
- Throughout the process of studying, students should be encouraged to engage with both the text and the visuals accompanying the text in the textbooks. Doing so would enable them to encode the acquired information through two associated pathways, consequently improving memory, retention, and understanding.

On the whole, the theory of Dual Coding developed by Allan Paivio could prove to be highly beneficial to students pursuing higher education, when employed appropriately. Learners should be encouraged to engage entirely with their course material so as to advance understanding.

Research Evidence

According to Winn et al. (2019), "Cognitive learning strategies are strategies that improve a learner's ability to process information more deeply, transfer and apply information to new situations, and result in enhanced and better-retained learning". In an experiment to examine the effects of training in cognitive strategies on clinical teachers, Winn et al. (2019) designed a training session that taught 5 cognitive learning strategies – Interleaving, spaced retrieval, elaboration, reflection and generation. 161 teachers participated in the session, at the end of which 52 participants filled a commitment-to-change form that evaluated the level of implementation each individual expected themselves to carry out. 6 weeks after the termination of the program, 24 of these teachers completed a follow-up survey, through which it was revealed that 82% of responders had implemented a change in their teaching methodologies based on the knowledge acquired through the workshop. The imparting of cognitive strategies of learning led to a positive behavioral modification in instructors, which in turn, was predicted to highly benefit the students under their instruction.

Through a thorough analysis of literature on the topic of distance education, Boström, L., Collen, C., Damber, U., Gidlund, U. (2021) studied the most effective study strategies employed by students, especially after the onset of COVID-19. The papers included in the analysis mainly constituted empirical research, along with a small number of qualitative research studies. The most effective strategies utilized by students in distance education learning was found to include cognitive strategies, self-efficacy, and retention strategies, all of which can be classified as cognitive and metacognitive strategies. It was also found by Boström et al. (2021) that technology facilitated the use of the right type of strategies and devices to improve learning outcomes and academic success. The teaching strategies utilized by instructors for effective distance learning was found to include flexibility, planning, and impactful interaction with students to facilitate effective knowledge acquisition and encourage critical thinking among learners.

METACOGNITIVE LEARNING STRATEGIES

Importance

Metacognitive strategies can be employed in a wide variety of settings to promote critical thinking, and self-reflection. Metacognitive strategies of learning, when employed in higher education settings, facilitate self-regulation and reflection, which in-turn promote learning. Learning is the end goal of education, thus highlighting the need to impart knowledge of metacognitive strategies to students and professors. This knowledge is especially crucial in higher education settings as it would directly influence career performance.

The Metacognitive Strategies of Learning

The most prominent and useful metacognitive strategies that can be employed by university students, along with practices to implement these strategies are as listed below.

Goal Setting

Goal setting is the process of identifying desired outcomes and creating a plan to achieve those outcomes. One of the most popular model for Goal setting is SMART and it stands for -S – Specific, M – Measurable, A – Attainable, R- Relevant and T – Time bound.Metacognition is about becoming cognizant of one's own thinking process. Deploying a model like SMART helps optimize the cognitive process. This model provides a roadmap for the learner to identify and chart out the right course of action to achieve their goals.

When goals are specific, the student is aware of what is outside the scope of the goal, and what is within its scope. This helps bring in the required clarity which is a quintessential aspect of goal setting. The next important feature of goals, is measurability. Drucker (1966), through his book *The Effective Executive* popularized the idea that "what gets measured, gets improved". The underlying idea is to understand the data relating to one's goals, and to plan accordingly.

The third aspect of goal setting is attainability. A goal is motivating only if it has the right amount of challenge, it must not be too easy nor be too hard to achieve. The fourth feature is Relevant which means the goal needs to be aligned with the values and long term objectives.

The fifth aspect, time bound, is what keeps students motivated to achieve their goals. A sense of achievement comes when the goal is met within the specified timeline. The expected time to complete a task must neither be too short and ambitious, nor be left undefined.

Metacognitive Regulation

Metacognitive regulation is the ability to control and adjust one's thoughts and behaviors. Planning, Monitoring and Evaluation are the three stages of metacognitive regulation. As explained in the topic above, goal setting is a strategy which requires planning and serves as a pre requisite to regulation. A well planned goal is a good starting point for achieving success, however, the rest of the stages of implementation and post-implementation are equally vital for a student to succeed in their mission.

During the process of implementation, there can be a list of questions that the individual can ask to ensure that they stay close to the plan formulated to achieve the goal. These questions can be listed by educators and students and can be modified to suit the different needs of the students. However, at an advanced stage, these questions serve the very purpose of increasing one's awareness while undertaking the tasks.

A good monitoring system can be built into a plan. A SMART goal will be time bound and will also include checks in place to continuously monitor and review the plan. Thus, the implementation process will continue to stay relevant and aligned to the outcomes that the student sets out to achieve.

The plethora of digital tools now available can be leveraged to suit the outcomes of the students and will serve as aids to both students and teachers. Most of these tools are available at little to no cost.

Metacognitive Reflection

Metacognitive Reflection, in sequence, is the step that follows goal setting and metacognitive regulation. However, it could be prudent to employ it during the implementation stage too. Metacognitive reflection is a powerful strategy, the power of pausing to think and considering the right course of action. It involves identifying whether the strategy currently being employed by a learner requires changes, how to implement these changes, whether the time allocation for each step in the plan is reasonable, and whether it is in line with the initial plan. These are questions that a learner will have while they have set out on learning a new subject. These metacognitive strategies ensure that the learner and the teacher are on the right track and can make changes on the go, rather than waiting until the end. Applying these metacognitive strategies would not only ensure a greater success of the outcomes, but also minimal errors during the implementation process. Based on the success of these outcomes, the teachers can create a repository of questions for the students to ask themselves, thus maximizing both efficiency and effectiveness of their learning.

Research Evidence

According to Abdellah (2015), Metacognition has been one of the most vastly explored concepts among researches in the field of psychology. As a contribution to the pre-existing literature, a study was conducted by Abdellah (2015) to determine the relationship between metacognitive awareness, academic achievement and teaching performance. 75 pre-service female teachers in Ajman University were randomly selected to participate in the study. They were given the Metacognitive Awareness Inventory developed by John H. Schraw and Robert W. Dennison, which was used to measure metacognitive awareness, and the Teaching Performance Checklist, which was used to assess their teaching performance. Metacognitive awareness and academic achievement were found to be directly related. A positive relationship between metacognitive awareness and teaching performance was also established through the study.

This demonstrated a favorable influence of metacognitive awareness on both teaching and learning performance, demonstrating that students and instructors alike, benefit from the implementation of these strategies. To efficiently teach students how to successfully implement these strategies in their own learning, it is crucial for instructors and tutors to be aware of and utilize these strategies themselves. This approach would aid professors guide students in effectively using their knowledge of these strategies, while also benefitting from the knowledge themselves, and enhancing their teaching methodologies.

Aloqleh and Teh (2019) conducted a study in order to investigate the effect of metacognition on the academic achievement of the students of Jordanian University. In the research, 440 first year students of Jordanian University belonging to the faculty of Education were given 2 questionnaires, Part A of which collected information about students' level of metacognitive awareness, while Part B about the students' GPAs. Through statistical analyses, the relationship between metacognition and academic achievement was calculated. It was established that a high level of metacognition was related to higher grades achieved by students.

Jain, D., Tiwari, G. K., Awasthi, I. D. (2017) conducted a research study to investigate the impact of metacognition and gender on academic achievement and outcome. 522 UG and PG students in India aged between 17 and 28 years were the participants. The Metacognitive Awareness Inventory developed by John H. Schraw and Robert W. Dennison, and the Academic Adjustment Scale developed by Manuel Martinez-Pons were used to measure the metacognitive awareness and academic adjustment of the participants. Academic outcome was measured by the percentage of marks or GPA obtained by the students. It was found that metacognition and academic achievement are directly related. Metacognitive awareness accounted for significant variance in academic lifestyle, achievements, adjustment, and outcome.

This direct connection between academic achievement and the employment of metacognitive strategies in learning by university students is noteworthy.

INTEGRATING COGNITIVE AND METACOGNITIVE STRATEGIES

Importance

While the very application of cognitive and metacognitive strategies by learners calls for a more conscious and concerted effort, the integration of these strategies is natural and fluid. "When it comes to learning strategies, using cognitive and metacognitive strategies improves learning outcomes" (Zeitlhofer, Hormann, Mann, Hallinger & Zumbach, 2023). Self-regulated learning and online learning calls for a better integration of Cognitive and metacognitive learning strategies.

The Strategies

A combination of cognitive and metacognitive strategies are employed to enhance learning. A description of how these frameworks can be used to enhance learning in higher education settings, is as described below:

VAK (Visual-Auditory-Kinesthetic)

Among the several learning models that exist in higher education, one of the most popular one is the VAK model. It is based on the notion that there are different ways in which students process information, and each student has a preferred way of learning. This preferred learning style also known as dominant mode is consistent for all learning. The subject could vary between sciences and arts and the preferred style for a given individual will remain be one of the three. This model, which later on also included 'Reading/Writing' commonly known as VARK, was developed by educational psychologists Walter Burke Barbe and Neil Fleming in the 1920s.

The main ideas of VARK based on Fleming and Baume (2006) are as follows (Guide to Types of Learning Styles, 2024):

- "Students' preferred learning modes have a significant influence on their behavior and learning.
- Students' preferred learning modes should be matched with appropriate learning strategies.
- Information that is accessed through students' use of their modality preferences shows and increase in their levels of comprehension, motivations, and metacognition".

Table 1 displays the characteristics of visual, auditory and kinesthetic learners.

Table 1. Differences between visual – auditory – kinesthetic learners

VISUAL learners	AUDITORY learners	KINESTHETIC learners
• Like to see images and pictures	• Like to listen to lectures and sounds	• Like to do and create things
• Imagine concepts and draw things	• Repeat word aloud and prefer listening to sounds, mnemonic devices	• Engage in hands-on activities
• Graphs, flowcharts are important in a presentation	• Podcasts, audio tapes with good voice clarity	• Puzzles, models and moving around
• Written instructions	• Verbal instructions	• Discussing with others

Understanding and applying the VAK model, accepts the diversity of each learner and allows the teacher to customize the learning style best suited to each learner. This means that the lessons will allow room for students to engage in different learning activities and also eventually gain an understanding into the style that suits them the most.

Without an awareness of this diverse style, it is most likely for a teacher to slip into their dominant style or also to engage in the style that is most accessible in any situation. Also, if a student is exposed only to one particular style, their rate of absorption of a topic and their depth of understanding and hence their learning can get limited.

"Some researchers who were interested in confirming Fleming's finding conducted some studies about VAK learning model. Rambe and Zainuddin (2014) showed that VAK learning model significantly affected students' achievement in writing especially writing recount text. Another study conducted by Lista, Atmowardoyo, and Salija (2015) also proved that the VAK was effective to improve students' writing ability" (Ramadian, Cahyono, & Suryati, 2019).

VAK celebrates the human diversity and allows the teacher to expose the students to the different styles, and also through metacognitive steps, help the student identify their styles. This in turn could increase their participation and their motivation to ensure successful learning outcomes for every student. Understanding one's style is also important while choosing Self-regulated Learning activities which is gaining popularity in higher education and beyond. Through a deeper understanding of one's preferred mode, a metacognition strategy is to choose and design learning to one's most preferred mode. However, students learn not only through their most preferred style but through a combination of the other learning styles as well. By exposure, reflection and recognizing one's preference, the learner is more empowered to design the best learning solutions for themselves.

Bloom's Taxonomy

While several models of education existed before the Bloom's model, it was the 1950s post war period that saw a team of researchers from fields of education and psychology come together to work on a classification of education objectives. This team under the leadership of Benjamin Bloom created a framework which included several aspects involved in the learning process. Until then, the focus of education was more on rote learning and following instructions clearly.

The team noted the need to classify the education objectives to make it feasible for teachers to create goals, activities, and assessments to ensure maximum learning effectiveness in classrooms. Bloom's taxonomy has been one of the most popular models of education for decades and it has been modified from its original forms to accommodate not just higher education learning but also the Learning and Development departments of organizations, successfully transferring learning; technical and behavioral to employees in their organizations.

In this section, the Bloom's taxonomy will be discussed in detail, and the changes the model has undergone to accommodate several aspects will also be noted. Table 2 displays the changes the model has undergone from 1956 to 2001. The versatility of the model lies in how alongside the cognitive domains, the affective (learner's interests, attitudes and feelings, their motivation to learn) and the psychomotor domains (motor skills) together can be accommodated to create metacognitive strategies, empowering educators and learners alike. This is also known as 'KSA' Knowledge-Skills-Attitudes and is at the base of the competency framework for many organizations.

Table 2. Evolution of Bloom's taxonomy

Year 1956	Year 2001
Knowledge	Remember
Comprehension	Understand
Application	Apply
Analysis	Analyze
Synthesis	Evaluate
Evaluation	Create

The revised framework uses verbs or gerunds as compared to nouns in the original framework. It also gave an opportunity for the teachers to see the relationship between the objectives of the content being taught which is in the cognitive realm. Once these objectives are set, the teachers can further examine and decide how that content needs to be taught to maximize these outcomes. Further on, the model also makes possible for teachers to design the timing and quality of assessments. The how and when come under the metacognitive realm. This interplay between the cognitive and metacognitive is another area of flexibility that this model allows.

This directly rolled into learning objectives for every level, well-crafted lesson plans for the courses and appropriate assessments at the beginning and the end of the course, resulting in a robust plan for students to know where they stand at the beginning of a course, and to be aware of what they will achieve by the end.

The opportunity for educators to identify objectives, lesson plans and assessments and for learners to reflect and know their roadmap demonstrates how cognitive and metacognitive come together through this model of learning.

A description Bloom's framework in detail and how these levels of learning can be applied in a learning environment will currently be discussed. It is imperative to start at the bottom and work one's way up of the pyramid. The lower level skills require less cognitive processes, but, however are the foundation for the higher level skills. The higher order skills call for deeper learning and a greater degree of cognitive processing. In the journey of moving from the lower order to higher order processing, application of metacognition is vital for a successful outcome.

While Bloom's framework focuses on cognitive processes, it's the application of the metacognitive that helps address the issue of 'the hows and the whens' while deploying the framework. For instance, while moving up the ladder from Remembering to Understanding, one need to bear in mind, how quickly new concepts need to introduced, when and how to reinforce them and how to test them.

The first stage is Remember and this is about recalling the facts and basic concepts. It is the ability of the learner to define, duplicate, list, memorize, repeat and state these facts and concepts. This does not warrant comprehension.

That is where the next stage comes in, Understand. At this stage, it is not just recalling the concepts but about explaining them. The learner's ability to classify, describe, explain, identify, locate, recognize, report, select and translate is what this stage demands. So the skills of paraphrasing and comparing are displayed here.

Once this is conquered, the learner then moves to the next stage of learning: Apply. This is about using the newly acquired information in situations, and includes executing, implementing, solving, demonstrating, interpreting, operating, scheduling and sketching. With knowledge of one's strengths, preferences and, goal setting, all metacognitive processes can be applied both during and in between these stages.

Moving up the pyramid, the learner reaches the Analyze stage. Drawing connections between the different ideas, which means differentiating, organizing, relating, comparing, contrasting, distinguishing, examining, experimenting, questioning and testing. This stage is about Critical thinking, the learner distinguishes facts from opinions and breaks down information into different useful components.

The higher stages on the pyramid distinguishably call for higher order thinking and at these stages the metacognitive processing unfolds and integrates with the cognitive processing.

The next in the hierarchy is the Evaluate stage where the learner can take a stand or decision and justify it. This is about appraising, arguing, defending, judging, selecting, supporting, valuing, critiquing and weighing the ideas and concepts based on the knowledge and application they have acquired so far.

The final hallmark of learning as per the revised Bloom's framework is Create. Producing new or original work depending on the subject or course. It is about assembling, designing, constructing, conjecturing, developing, formulating, authoring and investigating.

A concept cannot be understood without first remembering it, cannot be applied without understanding it. It can only be analyzed, based on the results of applying it, and can be defended and critiqued by evaluating it and finally moving on to create something entirely new based on the information gathered by the conclusions in the evaluation.

While designing the course based on this framework, the objectives, the lesson plans and the assessment, the learner and the educator can see the progress and take necessary steps to ensure the motivational needs are also met. This is closely connected to Carol Dweck's Growth Mindset concept as here the learner is sufficiently and appropriately challenged and through the feedback of the assessments, channelized to move up on the pyramid.

Bloom's taxonomy enables the learner to understand their KSA (Knowledge, Skill and Attitude) at the end of each course. Blending the cognitive and metacognitive is at the heart of this framework. The student will have clear and concise goals to achieve during the course. "These explicit goals and expectations in class can also help guide students in the right direction – which is a great application of metacognition within Bloom's taxonomy" (Persaud, 2023).

Bloom's taxonomy can also be applied in online classes. Learning now is not always limited to classrooms, it also occurs through online classes. The versatility of the Bloom's model makes it possible to design the course based on the requirement in each of the stages. Questions, activities, exercises and assessments, could be customized to suit online learning as effectively as they suit classroom settings. "Each of Blooms' taxonomy levels is designed with active learning in mind. This way, students feel a responsibility for their learning" (Persaud, 2023). This demonstrates the importance of the integration of cognitive and metacognitive strategies in enabling effective learning.

As with any model, there is always a new approach and a new light in which the Bloom's taxonomy can be applied. Some experts argue that the pyramid approach could be discouraging for a student who would like to create something faster than waiting until reaching the top of the pyramid. This calls for a circular representation of the Blooms' framework rather than the current pyramid one.

Mental Models

"Mental Models are simplified representations, concepts, and frameworks that allow us to quickly understand ourselves and our world" (ModelThinkers, n.d.).

"Mental models are like a map, they retain the key information while ignoring the irrelevant details. Models concentrate the world into understandable and useable chunks" (Farnam Street, 2023).

Mental models are akin to a toolkit. Just like the variety of tools in a carpenter's toolbox enables them to function better, more number of mental models and the ability to switch between them, helps an individual solve complex problems.

Metacognitive knowledge and experience is not about having stable or fixed knowledge, it is about the fluidity of the knowledge and experience which then serve as an improvised way to view the world and its workings. This is the most important skill for a successful life, learning to learn, constantly breaking and forming new mental models. Late Charlie Munger (1924-2023), who was the vice president of Berkshire Hathaway, prescribes to a latticework of mental models. Most individuals stick to a range of familiar mental models rather than a variety of them. Possessing a greater number of mental models provides a new approach to thinking and decision making. This enables one to view problems through a variety of lenses rather than the limited few that one is used to (ModelThinkers, n.d.-b).

This constant awareness of one's cognition and the ability to strategically use the different mental models is the metacognitive nature of thinking which multiplies and far supersedes the quality of cognition associated with sticking to a familiar range of models.

There are four types of mental models as defined by ModelThinkers (n.d.) – The Invisible Models, Routine Models, Contextual Models and Powerful Models.

The Invisible Models. This encompasses all the mental thought processes that take place unconsciously, that is, when one is not consciously engaging in thought, including unconscious biases and the mental shortcuts that one has created in one's mind over the years. This can range from fleeing upon seeing a snake on the street, to disliking the person who has an exact opposite view point as one's. Biases and heuristics rule decision-making when the conscious brain is not paying attention. While one may not be aware of it, Invisible Models are what one uses most of the time. An example of an invisible model is, 'If it is a flight attendant, it must be a woman and a pilot must be a man'.

The Routine/Basic Models. These are the models that an individual has consciously built, and over a period of time, become second nature to them. These are the frameworks required in an individual's routine life to save time and to simplify life. Remembering basic recipes while cooking, organizing one's workplace, weekly wardrobe choice, are instances of decisions that can be made with relative ease. These decisions enable one to save up energy for critical decisions, and helps avoid decision fatigue.

The Contextual Models. In these models, second order thinking starts to show. These are models that one has built through unique and specific experiences. For instance, knowing how to get things done while staying within University norms is a situation-specific model built by students. These might be developed through specialist study or cycles of personal experience and reflection within one's context, and they enable one to act in one's specific environment or domain. As an educator, planning assessments based on the amount of time one's students have received to experiment the new topic, is another instance of this model.

Powerful Models. These are the tried and tested mental models which can hold their ground in varied contexts. They are highly applicable in different situations, and across domains. For instance, compounding is as much applicable in a relationship as it is in investments. There are multiple models under these powerful mental models, and they are widely applied in various fields. For example, the *Circle of Competence*, is a model that Charlie Munger stated his biggest strategy rested on, and *First Principle Thinking,* Elon Musk's most widely used mental model for his innovations.

Mental models are highly adaptable, and their application can be extended to a variety of contexts. They can be adapted to higher education settings, where they could prove to be useful in problem-solving, planning, goal setting, and modifying learning strategies. As a result of employing effective mental models, one could enhance learning outcomes, and make the best of university education. Beyond the university setting, these models could be used in any aspect of life, including career and professional contexts, where they would enable an individual to utilize their time effectively, preventing cognitive overload, and producing success.

Research Evidence

Zeitlhofer et al. (2023) conducted a study to examine the effect of employing cognitive and metacognitive prompts on the memory performance of students in digital learning environments. The sample chosen for this study consisted of 100 learners, who were divided into three conditions, which were, learning with cognitive prompts, learning with metacognitive prompts and learning without prompts. The prompts administered were questions that promoted reflection and facilitated deeper understanding. A comparison between pre and post-tests revealed an improvement in performance in all three groups. While both groups that received prompts showed a greater improvement in performance than the control condition, the group that received cognitive prompts obtained the highest scores, demonstrating the greatest increase in knowledge. The findings of the research suggest that introducing cognitive and metacognitive prompts and strategies in lectures might greatly benefit learning outcomes, and improve performance.

Almarzouki, H. S., Khan, A., Al-Mansour, M., Al-Jifree, H. M., (2023) conducted a research to investigate the effects of cognitive and metacognitive prompts on learning performance of medical students. It involved 36 participants who were assigned to either the Interventional or the control group condition based on their Grade Point Average (GPA) scores, in order maintain uniformity between the two conditions. The Interventional group attended a lecture where cognitive strategies were employed, while the Traditional group attended a traditional lecture where these strategies were not utilized. In order to compare performance prior to and after the completion of the lecture, a pre-test and post-test was conducted for both the groups. Pre-test results showed that the mean score achieved by both groups was very similar, while post-test results displayed a significantly higher score achieved by the Interventional group than the Traditional group. The inference drawn based on the outcomes of the study was that training while employing cognitive strategies was far more beneficial, and led to enhanced academic outcomes, as compared to training in the traditional method.

"Based on the cognitive theory and memory model, different strategies have been suggested to maintain learners' attention and improve their memory. For example, changing the tone or position during lectures, using cues or challenging questions, beginning a lecture with a review or summary slide to help learners create a link between their current understanding and the incoming new knowledge. These strategies would ensure information retention in the working memory and its availability for further processing" (Almarzouki et al., 2023).

CONCLUSION

The chapter highlights some of the most important aspects of how cognition and metacognition can not only impact the academic community, but also its far reaching impact on people's careers and how they can incorporate the very skill of learning for life-long success.

The four W's (When, where, what and why) and the one H (How) are the tools that encapsulate the processes of cognition and metacognition. Answering the questions why, what and where, is in the cognitive domain, while the questions how and when enable one to move to the metacognitive realm.

This chapter provides a broader understanding of the areas of cognition and metacognition and their significance in higher education settings. These processes are inevitably intertwined with the learning and mastery of any subject. The chapter encompasses not only the theory and the knowledge related to these thinking processes, but also provides hands on tools in the fields of thinking for one to implement.

Each student has a preferred learning style. The strategies provided in this chapter enable them to explore and adopt the one best suited to them for their distinct style of learning. Learners can experiment with combinations of the various learning strategies, employing cognitive and metacognitive strategies together, in order to enhance learning outcomes. In case some of these strategies do not work efficiently for a given individual, through the processes of monitoring and evaluation, they can recognize these strategies, and substitute them with ones that yield better results.

Cognitive and metacognitive strategies require planning, making their implementation a time-consuming process. Instructors could divide course topics to ensure that each type of learner acquires some amount of knowledge through their preferred method of learning. However, tailoring the course to suit the preference of each of their students could become a tedious process for instructors. This emphasizes the importance of imparting the knowledge of these strategies to the students themselves so as to enable them to enhance and improve their own knowledge acquisition. Universities and other higher educational institutions are recommended to take into account the time it requires to plan an effective learning program, catering to the diverse needs of the students.

REFERENCES

Abdellah, R. (2015). Metacognitive Awareness and its Relation to Academic Achievement and Teaching Performance of Pre-service Female Teachers in Ajman University in UAE. *Procedia: Social and Behavioral Sciences*, 174, 560–567. 10.1016/j.sbspro.2015.01.707

Albert Einstein College of Medicine. (n.d.). *Einstein Researchers Discover How Long-Lasting Memories Form in the brain*. Albert Einstein College of Medicine. https://www.einsteinmed.edu/news/10988/einstein-researchers-discover-how-long-lasting-memories-form-in-the-brain/#:~:text=They%20form%20when%20repeated%20neural,required%20for%20long%2Dterm%20memories

Almarzouki, H. S., Khan, A., Al-Mansour, M., Al-Jifree, H. M., Abuznadah, W., & Althubaiti, A. (2023). Effectiveness of Cognitive Strategies on Short-Term Information Retention: An Experimental Study. *Health Professions Education*. Research Gate. https://www.researchgate.net/publication/369912992_Effectiveness_of_Cognitive_Strategies_on_Short-Term_Information_Retention_An_Experimental_Study

Aloqleh, A. M. A., & Teh, K. S. M. (2019). The Effectiveness of Metacognition on Academic Achievement among the Jordanian Universities Students. *International Journal of Academic Research in Business & Social Sciences*, 9(9). 10.6007/IJARBSS/v9-i9/6315

Bjork, R. A. (1994). *Memory and metamemory considerations in the training of human beings*. MIT Press. 10.7551/mitpress/4561.003.0011

Boström, L., Collén, C., Damber, U., & Gidlund, U. (2021). A Rapid Transition from Campus to Emergent Distant Education; Effects on Students' Study Strategies in Higher Education. *Education Sciences*, 11(11), 721. 10.3390/educsci11110721

Cornell University. (n.d.). *Metacognitive Strategies (How People Learn)*. Center for Teaching Innovation. https://teaching.cornell.edu/teaching-resources/teaching-cornell-guide/teaching-strategies/metacognitive-strategies-how-people#:~:text=Metacognitive%20strategies%20are%20techniques%20to,thinking%20processes%20as%20they%20learn

Drucker, P. F. (1966). *The effective executive*. DT Leadership. https://dtleadership.my/wp-content/uploads/2019/05/Drucker-2006-The-Effective-Executive-The-Definitive-Guide-to-Getting-the-Right-Things-Done.pdf

edX. (2024, February 20). *Guide to types of learning Styles*. Teach.com. https://teach.com/what/teachers-know/learning-styles/

Engage. (2024, February 16). *VAK learning styles: what are they and what do they mean?* Engage Education. https://engage-education.com/blog/vak-learning-styles-what-are-they-and-what-do-they-mean-engage-education/

Farnam Street. (2023, December 9). *Mental models: The best way to make intelligent decisions (~100 models explained)*. Farnam Street. https://fs.blog/mental-models

Fleming, N., & Baume, D. (2006). Learning Styles Again: VARKing up the right tree! *SEDA, 7.4,* 4–7. https://www.vark-learn.com/wp-content/uploads/2014/08/Educational-Developments.pdf

Jain, D., Tiwari, G. K., & Awasthi, I. D. (2017). Impact of metacognitive awareness on academic adjustment and academic outcome of the students. *International Journal of Indian Psychology*, 5(1).10.25215/0501.034

Kamiya, A., & Airth, M. (2023, November 21). *Semantic Network Model | Definition, Concepts & Examples*. Study.com. https://study.com/learn/lesson/semantic-network-model-overview-examples.html#:~:text=Allan%20Collins%20and%20Ross%20Quillian,ready%20associated%20information%20for%20retrieval

Kang, S. H. K. (2016). Spaced repetition promotes efficient and effective learning. *Policy Insights from the Behavioral and Brain Sciences*, 3(1), 12–19. 10.1177/2372732215624708

MindTools. (n.d.). *Ebbinghaus's Forgetting Curve.* MindTools. https://www.mindtools.com/a9wjrjw/ebbinghauss-forgetting-curve

ModelThinkers. (n.d.). *Mental models.* ModelThinkers. https://modelthinkers.com/mental-model/mental-models

ModelThinkers. (n.d.-b). *Munger's Latticework.* ModelThinkers. https://modelthinkers.com/mental-model/mungers-latticework

Persaud, C. (2023, November 15). *Bloom's Taxonomy: The Ultimate Guide [Free Download].* Top Hat. https://tophat.com/blog/blooms-taxonomy/

Ramadian, O. D., Cahyono, B. Y., & Suryati, N. (2019). The implementation of Visual, Auditory, Kinesthetic (VAK) learning model in improving students' achievement in writing descriptive texts. In *English Language Teaching Educational Journal, 2*(3). Universitas Negeri Malang, Indonesia. https://files.eric.ed.gov/fulltext/EJ1266033.pdf

Rezvan, S., Ahmadi, S. A., & Abedi, M. R. (2006). The effects of metacognitive training on the academic achievement and happiness of Esfahan University conditional students. *Counselling Psychology Quarterly*, 19(4), 415–428. 10.1080/09515070601106471

UNESCO. (2023, April 20). *What you need to know about higher education*. UNESCO. https://www.unesco.org/en/higher-education/need-know#:~:text=Higher%20education%20is%20a%20rich,meet%20ever%20changing%20labour%20markets

Vrugt, A., & Oort, F. J. (2008). Metacognition, achievement goals, study strategies and academic achievement: Pathways to achievement. *Metacognition and Learning*, 3(2), 123–146. 10.1007/s11409-008-9022-4

Wikipedia contributors. (2023, November 21). *Redintegration*. Wikipedia. https://en.wikipedia.org/wiki/Redintegration

Wikipedia contributors. (2024, January 15). *Dual-coding theory*. Wikipedia. https://en.wikipedia.org/wiki/Dual-coding_theory

Wikipedia contributors. (2024b, March 4). *Metacognition*. Wikipedia. https://en.wikipedia.org/wiki/Metacognition#:~:text=15%20External%20links-,Definitions,more%20informally%2C%20thinking%20about%20thinking

Winn, A. S., DelSignore, L., Marcus, C. H., Chiel, L., Freiman, E., Stafford, D., & Newman, L. R. (2019). Applying cognitive learning strategies to enhance learning and retention in clinical teaching settings. *MedEdPORTAL: the Journal of Teaching and Learning Resources*, 10850. 10.15766/mep_2374-8265.1085031921996

Zeitlhofer, I., Hörmann, S., Mann, B., Hallinger, K., & Zumbach, J. (2023). Effects of cognitive and metacognitive prompts on learning performance in digital learning environments. *Knowledge (Beverly Hills, Calif.)*, 3(2), 277–292. 10.3390/knowledge3020019

Zhan, L., Guo, D., Chen, G., & Yang, J. (2018). Effects of repetition learning on associative recognition over time: Role of the hippocampus and prefrontal cortex. *Frontiers in Human Neuroscience*, 12, 277. 10.3389/fnhum.2018.0027730050418

Chapter 5
Empowering Minds:
Cognitive Learning Strategies for Higher Education Success

R. Sridevi
https://orcid.org/0000-0001-6620-141X
Christ University, India

P. Ashokkumar
https://orcid.org/0000-0001-9341-9633
PSG College of Arts and Science, India

V. Sathish
https://orcid.org/0000-0003-0718-9232
PSG College of Arts and Science, India

ABSTRACT

It takes more than just passive information consumption to meet the expectations of higher education. This chapter delves into the efficacy of cognitive learning processes, providing students with useful tools to improve their understanding, memory, and critical thinking abilities. The authors enable learners to actively engage with information, develop deeper comprehension, and attain academic greatness by exploring evidence-based tactics such as interleaving, spaced retrieval, and elaboration. The authors also discuss common issues that students in higher education encounter, like information overload and procrastination, and offer solutions to help students get past these obstacles and maximize their educational opportunities. Lastly, the authors stress the value of metacognition and exhort students to evaluate their own learning experiences and modify their approach as necessary. The purpose of this chapter is to help as an invaluable means for both educators and students, fostering a culture of empowered learning in higher education

DOI: 10.4018/979-8-3693-3559-8.ch005

Copyright © 2024, IGI Global. Copying or distributing in print or electronic forms without written permission of IGI Global is prohibited.

INTRODUCTION

Learning through mental processes like perception, memory, and reasoning, known as cognitive learning, is crucial for human development and education. As we focus on the future, various significant directions and trends in cognitive learning are developing, which could revolutionize the way we educate and learn. Personalized and adaptive learning is a potential future direction in cognitive learning. This method acknowledges that every student has distinct strengths, weaknesses, and ways of learning, and customizes educational opportunities to cater to their specific requirements. Through the utilization of technology and data analysis, personalized and adaptive learning algorithms have the ability to effectively modify the content, speed, and method of instruction in order to optimize learning results. Incorporating technology into the learning process can also be a way to enhance cognitive development. Fresh opportunities to enhance cognitive learning environments are provided by technological advancements such as augmented reality, virtual reality, and artificial intelligence. Educators can enhance learning and engage cognitive processes by incorporating technology into their lesson plans and learning environments, which creates immersive and captivating experiences for students. The integration of gamification is a recent trend in cognitive learning. The concept of "gamification" refers to incorporating elements from games, such as incentives, obstacles, and competition, into educational settings.

BACKGROUND

In 1956, Benjamin Bloom created Bloom's Taxonomy, which is a system of educational goals used by educators to design curriculum and assessments. It classifies cognitive abilities into six tiers: Understanding, Application, Analysis, Synthesis, and Assessment. Every stage of cognitive development is represented by a level, with each level building upon the one before it. Students may encounter cognitive obstacles at any point, hindering their advancement to more advanced thinking abilities. Recognizing and overcoming these obstacles is essential for successful learning and teaching, so that students can progress from simple memorization of facts to advanced critical thinking and assessment. (Podymov, 2022).

Cognitive obstacles in mathematics education often stem from the inherent complexity of mathematical concepts and the sequential nature of learning them. For instance, understanding finite integrals requires a solid grasp of foundational topics such as limits and continuity. Students may struggle if these foundational concepts are not well understood, leading to cognitive barriers that hinder further learning. Effective mathematics education involves scaffolding instruction, where teachers build on students' existing knowledge and gradually introduce more complex ideas, ensuring that each concept is mastered before moving on to the next. This approach helps mitigate cognitive obstacles and promotes a deeper understanding of mathematical principles (Kartinah et al., 2020).

Finding learning challenges and creating focused solutions require evaluating cognitive processes. Instruments that assess scientific reasoning abilities, like the Lawson Classroom Test, are vital to this process. These tests offer insightful information about students' cognitive capacities, enabling teachers to modify their pedagogical approaches to target certain areas of deficiency (Pessoni et al., 2015). By understanding where students struggle, educators can design interventions that improve cognitive levels and success rates. Regular assessment of cognitive processes ensures that learning difficulties are identified early, enabling timely support and enhancing overall educational outcomes.

In higher education, teaching higher-order thinking skills involves more than just imparting knowledge; it requires fostering problem-solving abilities, reflective learning, and theoretical understanding. Faculty members in the UK, for example, emphasize the importance of integrating cognitive skills into problem-solving and reflective practices. However, they often face challenges in incorporating theory construction into teaching and assessment, which can limit students' cognitive development (Bhehlol & Cajkler, 2018). Effective teaching practices should combine these elements, providing a holistic approach to learning that inspires students to think critically, reproduce on the learning processes, and apply theoretical concepts in practical situations.

Endogenous barriers to learning, such as cognitive noise, can significantly impact decision-making accuracy and overall learning outcomes. Cognitive noise refers to the internal distractions and mental clutter that interfere with the processing of information. Understanding these internal factors is essential for developing strategies to mitigate their effects. Research on endogenous barriers helps in modelling agents' behaviour, providing insights into how cognitive noise influences learning. By creating learning environments that minimize cognitive noise, educators can improve students' focus, enhance their decision-making accuracy, and optimize learning outcomes, ultimately leading to better educational achievements (Compte, 2023).

The research conducted in Augsburg illuminates the profound influence of cognitive strategies like elaboration, repetition, and multimedia content design on language acquisition, specifically in foreign language learners. Elaboration involves expanding upon new information by relating it to existing knowledge, while repetition reinforces memory and retention. Moreover, multimedia content design, incorporating visual and auditory elements, enhances engagement and comprehension. These strategies collectively facilitate the acquisition of lexicon and grammar, crucial components of language proficiency. By incorporating such cognitive strategies into language teaching methodologies, educators can optimize the learning experience for students, fostering more effective language acquisition and fluency. The research on cognitive development highlights how multimedia learning, alongside a scientific approach, can improve different cognitive abilities in children. Educators can enhance understanding and memory of concepts by involving learners in various multimedia forms, like interactive videos and educational games, which activate multiple senses. Additionally, incorporating a scientific method highlights the importance of critical thinking and problem-solving, crucial abilities for cognitive growth. The results (Müller & Višić, 2023) show that multimedia learning has the potential to enhance logical and symbolic thinking, as well as problem-solving skills, providing a solid basis for ongoing cognitive development and academic achievement. This study delves into the innovative approach (Yafie et al., 2020) of predicting learners' performances using EEG (Electroencephalography) metrics and task characteristics. By analyzing EEG data alongside task parameters such as difficulty, type, and duration, researchers can discern patterns indicative of cognitive workload and engagement. This allows for the forecasting of learners' scores, offering valuable insights into individual learning trajectories and instructional effectiveness. Such predictive modelling holds promise for personalized learning interventions, enabling educators to tailor instruction to meet the specific needs and capabilities of learners. Moreover, by understanding the cognitive demands of different tasks, educators can optimize learning environments and curriculum design to enhance overall learning outcomes.

MAIN FOCUS OF THE CHAPTER - COGNITIVE LEARNING STRATEGIES

Cognitive learning strategies are a diverse range of methods and approaches aimed at improving learning and information processing through utilizing the human mind's cognitive abilities and processes. Based on cognitive psychology, these techniques involve various approaches to enhance the learning, remembering, and using of information. Cognitive learning strategies like mnemonic devices and chunking, as well as elaboration and metacognitive strategies, help learners engage with content, form connections, and build upon their understanding progressively. Drawing on knowledge about how the brain handles information, these methods provide students with concrete techniques to conquer obstacles, boost understanding, and enhance problem-solving abilities in different areas. In the realms of language development, academics, and career advancement, incorporating cognitive learning techniques into teaching methods has the potential to enhance profound learning, analytical thinking, and continual cognitive advancement (Discipulo & Bautista, 2022).

Mnemonic Devices

Mnemonic devices serve as invaluable tools in enhancing memory retention by providing effective memory cues and associations. These devices leverage various techniques, such as acronyms, visualization, and chunking, to aid individuals in encoding and retrieving information more efficiently. Acronyms, for instance, involve creating memorable abbreviations using the first letter of each word in a list or sequence. Visualization techniques encourage learners to create vivid mental images or diagrams representing complex concepts or relationships. Through the creative and meaningful visualisation of information, people can improve their understanding and memory of important concepts (Sudirman And Tawali, 2023). Moreover, chunking includes dividing vast quantities of data into smaller, easier-to-handle units, which aids in comprehension and retention. Students, professionals, and individuals frequently use mnemonic devices to improve memory retention for exams, procedures, or daily activities.

Problem-Solving

Problem-solving is a fundamental cognitive learning strategy that enables individuals to systematically address challenges and achieve desired outcomes. This process involves analysing problems, generating potential solutions, and evaluating their effectiveness. A good way to start solving problems effectively is by breaking down complicated problems into smaller, easier-to-handle parts. By deconstructing problems into their constituent parts, individuals can better understand the underlying issues and develop targeted solutions(Wu & Molnár, 2022). Moreover, brainstorming fosters creative thinking and idea generation, encouraging individuals to explore innovative approaches to problem-solving. Collaborative problem-solving, where individuals work together to tackle challenges, promotes diverse perspectives and collective intelligence, leading to more comprehensive solutions. Furthermore, experimentation and iteration allow individuals to test different hypotheses and refine their strategies based on feedback and outcomes. Problem-solving skills are essential for navigating both academic and professional environments, enabling individuals to overcome obstacles, make informed decisions, and achieve desired outcomes.

Metacognition

Metacognition is the process of self-awareness and self-regulation in learning, encompassing the ability to monitor, evaluate, and adjust one's cognitive processes. This cognitive learning strategy involves reflecting on one's learning experiences, setting goals, and employing effective learning strategies. Self-monitoring enables individuals to assess their understanding and progress, identifying areas of strength and areas requiring improvement. Goal-setting provides direction and motivation, guiding individuals towards specific learning objectives and outcomes. Moreover, metacognitive strategies such as rehearsal, elaboration, and organization facilitate deeper processing of information, enhancing comprehension and retention. Reflection on learning strategies and outcomes allows individuals to refine their approaches and adapt to changing circumstances. Metacognition promotes a proactive and strategic approach to learning, empowering individuals to become more independent and effective learners. Additionally, metacognitive skills are transferable across different domains and contexts, enabling individuals to apply them in various educational and professional settings(Sato, 2022).

COLLABORATIVE LEARNING AND PEER INSTRUCTION

Educators have long acknowledged the importance of collaborative learning and understand that isolated students do not learn effectively. Collaborative learning can take place in small peer groups or in larger groups. It involves collaborative intellectual work among students or students and teachers, with students typically working together in groups of two or more to seek understanding, meanings, solutions, or develop a product. Collaborative learning is far removed from teacher-centered or lecture-based learning. Alternatively, "Peer Instruction" or "Peer Learning" is a form of cooperative learning in which students collaborate in groups or pairs to discuss ideas or seek answers or interpretations (Rivadeneira & Inga, 2023).

Collaborative learning occurs when students collaborate to solve problems, exchange ideas, and develop products together, whereas peer instructions require that students with varied knowledge and abilities can be paired together in which one leads and others learn. Whatever may be the argument, Collaborative learning and peer instruction has evolved as a powerful pedagogical method which provides dynamic learning environment along with honing the students critical thinking skills and promoting deeper understanding. This method gives more emphasis on active participation, communication and inter personal skills, all of which are essential components of cognitive learning. Exposure towards diverse perspectives, alternative approaches and problem-solving techniques can be achieved when students are engaged in collaborative learning. As a whole it promotes holistic understanding of subject matter.

Adhering to the idea that teaching a concept to other deepens one's understanding, peer instruction empowers the students to take the role of teacher and student. With multi-faceted benefits, peer instruction creates an active learning environment by encouraging the students to battle with complex concepts and articulate their understanding to peers and promotes supportive learning community where in the students feel comfortable in seeking help and clarification from the peers. To maximize the benefits, both collaborative learning and peer instructions can be integrated. Integration of these two in higher education becomes a powerful strategy. This combination provides educators to create a diverse learning environment, and encourages active engagement by providing a sense of ownership over the learning process. This technique also allows the students to work in small groups, enhancing collaborative problem solving and knowledge exchange. Altogether it is a balanced approach, using the strength of both methods to address different styles of learning and preferences among the students (Straw et al., 2023). To enhance collaborative learning and peer instruction in higher education, the following points may be considered

- Setting up of clear learning objectives and expectations – The learning expectations, objectives and peer instructional activities should be clearly communicated, this in turn will ensure that the students will understand the purpose of these methods and they will align with overall course goals
- Forming a structured group – The groups among the students should be formed strategically so as to ensure a diverse mix of skills, background and learning styles. This allows the students to bring in varied perspective in problem solving activities
- Integrating Technology – Online platforms like Google workspace, Microsoft teams and LMS provide space for shared documents, discussion forums and collaborative learning. along with this incorporating interactive simulations like virtual labs, social media interaction, white board interaction, gamification and educational software will enhance peer interactions
- Guidance from the facilitator – Educators should act as facilitators, by aiding when needed and ensuring that group learning remains positive. As a facilitator the guidance offered should be clear so as to enhance the members to move towards their goals without any obstacles
- Regular feedback – A continuous feedback will enhance the effectiveness of collaborative learning and peer instruction. The forum should establish a culture where criticism is valued, fostering a supportive learning environment.

Integrating collaborative learning ad peer instruction has several benefits and has immense potential, at the same time varying level of student's participation and potential conflicts are real time challenges which must be addressed. In present higher education scenario these methods represent a paradigm shift in the cognitive learning strategies. By honing the strength of both the approaches, educators can pave the way for transformative learning experience which cultivates critical thinking skills, communication and collaborative skills which is utmost essential for success in this complex system of higher education. The diversity in these type methods provide a rich learning experience. Compared to the traditional lecture-based teaching method, collaborative learning keeps the students engaged which in turn contributes to the high retention rate of the students. The skills developed by the students through these methods will help them to transcend culture and geographical boundaries preparing them for globally interconnected environment. The professional world today has a huge demand for collaboration and team work, Integrative collaborative learning in higher education will prepare the student for the collaborative nature of many workplaces. They can work effectively in diverse teams, communicate their ideas and contribute to the collective success.

TECHNOLOGY-ASSISTED COGNITIVE LEARNING TOOLS

Modern technology has dramatically reshaped education, including how students learn. It has enriched traditional learning methods, particularly cognitive learning. Cognitive learning tools are computer-assisted programs or apps that aim to boost students' thinking, problem-solving, and decision-making capabilities. Studies have shown that these tools enhance students' comprehension, retention, and critical thinking abilities. Technology-based learning tools empower students by adapting to their strengths and weaknesses. They use smart algorithms to study a student's progress and then tailor their learning journey. This means they are tested based on their skills, leading to better results as they can learn at their own speed.

Cognitive learning tools make learning more engaging by incorporating interactive elements like games, quizzes, and simulations. This enhances the learning experience and encourages students to participate more. Students are able to retain and learn more as a result, especially those who have trouble with conventional teaching approaches or learning challenges.

Cognitive learning aids improve learning by offering hands-on, interactive experiences. They offer students safe spaces to experiment and apply their knowledge through virtual labs and simulations. This experiential learning method not only improves the educational process but also develops critical thinking, problem-solving skills, and self-directed learning. In the realm of education, virtual labs and simulations have grown in popularity as tools, especially in the area of cognitive learning (Bustamante & Navarro, 2022). These interactive educational resources are made to look and feel like real-world situations, giving students a hands-on learning experience.

1. Enhancing Understanding of Complex Concepts

One of the main uses of virtual labs and simulations is to help students better understand complex concepts. These tools can present complex ideas in a visual and interactive manner, making them easier to comprehend. For example, in science classes, virtual simulations can help students visualize the movement of atoms and molecules in a chemical reaction, which can be difficult to understand through traditional lectures or textbooks. Similarly, in math classes, virtual simulations can help students understand abstract concepts like geometry and calculus by providing a dynamic and interactive platform.

2. Making Learning More Engaging

Traditional teaching approaches frequently result in boring, uninteresting lessons from their students. Conversely, virtual labs and simulations are meant to be interesting and dynamic. They make learning more engaging and pleasurable by enabling students to actively engage in the process. These tools can encourage students to learn and deepen their comprehension of the subject matter by introducing elements found in games, such as challenges, prizes, and levels.

3. Providing a Safe Learning Environment

Virtual labs and simulations also offer a safe platform for students to experiment and explore without fear of failure or consequences. For example, in science classes, students can conduct experiments virtually without the risk of damaging equipment or causing harm to themselves. This allows them to make mistakes and learn from them without any real-world repercussions. It also encourages students to take risks and think creatively, leading to a deeper understanding of the subject.

4. Fostering Collaboration and Teamwork

Another useful tool for group learning is a virtual laboratory or simulation. In a virtual setting, students can collaborate in groups to solve problems and finish assignments. This fosters communication and teamwork, two things that are necessary for success in the real world. Additionally, it broadens students' horizons and fosters peer learning, which improves their education as a whole.

5. Providing Access to Resources and Experiments

Virtual labs and simulations offer students access to a vast array of resources and experiments that may not be available in a traditional classroom setting. For instance, students can explore different historical events through interactive simulations or conduct experiments in an online virtual lab that would be too costly or dangerous to do in a physical lab. This allows students to expand their knowledge and understanding beyond their textbooks and classroom lessons.

6. Serving Different Learning Styles

Each student possesses a unique learning approach, and virtual labs and simulations are able to accommodate different styles such as visual, auditory, and kinaesthetic learners. These instruments provide a learning experience that engages multiple senses, enabling students to take in and understand information using various methods.

This can assist students having difficulty with conventional teaching approaches in comprehending and recalling information more effectively.

Teachers can also benefit from using technology-aided cognitive learning tools. These resources enable teachers to access live data on students' performance, helping them pinpoint weak areas and modify their teaching methods as needed. This helps teachers save time and offer personalized assistance to students requiring additional support in certain areas. Furthermore, the use of technology to aid in cognitive learning has increased accessibility to education like never before. Due to the emergence of online learning platforms and mobile apps, students have the opportunity to reach educational content at any time and place. This is especially beneficial for students with hectic schedules or unable to be physically present in classes. It also enables a more diverse and inclusive learning setting, since students from various backgrounds and locations can access the same educational resources. Nevertheless, it is crucial to recognize that technology-based cognitive learning tools should not entirely substitute traditional teaching methods. Instead, they ought to be utilized as an addition to improve the educational process. Teachers and students need to collaborate in order to find an equilibrium between technology and traditional teaching approaches. Furthermore, it is essential that teachers undergo adequate training and receive support to effectively implement these tools in the classroom.

By using technology, cognitive learning tools have revolutionized education delivery, offering a customized, engaging, and valuable learning environment. These materials have proven to be effective in improving students' academic performance and analytical thinking skills. Instructors must utilize these tools as technology advances to enhance their students' educational experience.

CULTIVATING A GROWTH MINDSET

Content knowledge and cognitive abilities are very much important for the student's academic success, along with this there are things like beliefs, values and attitude which is classified under non-cognitive factors which is as much important. These non-cognitive factors influence the students in many aspects, when taking the students' belief about the degree, intelligence becomes the stable trait. This as a whole is termed as "mindset". Students with a "fixed mindset" consider intelligence as unchanging and are prone to viewing failure or challenges as a sign of their lack of intelligence. Their fixed mindset prevents them from overcoming challenges, leading to low academic success. On the contrary, students with a Growth Mindset think that intelligence can be improved through diligence, perseverance, and support. These students embrace challenges, persisting through them with increased effort and creative tactics, leading to academic success. (Chen et al., 2022).

Taking in to account that there are many varieties of non-cognitive factors which influence student's mindset, it is important to understand how and why student's mindset develop and changes over time. Students mindsets are very much complex and are influenced by a mix of internal and external factors, to take few considerations there is Social and cultural influences, which includes family background and cultural values. Parents and the extended family influence the student's beliefs about the importance of education, efforts and expectations for success. Cultural values such as importance of hard work and perseverance will also have impact on mindset

Educational institute and its environment have major impact in changing students' attitude, Supportive environment and a positive approach from the institute will instil curiosity and effort which will accelerate a growth mindset among the students. Within the educational environment the crucial role in shaping the mindset of the students is played by the teachers, praising the efforts of the students, providing feedback and creating a supportive learning environment by the teachers have a positive impact. Apart from the above, how students perceive their success and failure in academic and non-academic activities, interaction and relationship with their peer members also foster to the mindset. To develop a growth mindset among students in higher education, especially from cognitive based perspective the following may be emphasized

- Creating an awareness on Brain plasticity, where the students are educated about the concept of neuroplasticity, and emphasizing on the point that the brain can change and adapt with learning and continuous effort. Understanding this the students can empower their learning abilities
- The students reflecting on their learning process is one important tool, which encourage their meta cognitive skill. Teaching them effective learning strategies such as goal setting, strategic planning, self-assessment and to make them recognize the connection between effort and improvement will result in developing a growth mindset
- The student's negative perspective about their abilities and difficult tasks which has been created through their fixed mindset can be addressed and should be actively challenged. This can be achieved by making them see the complaints as compliments and Challenges as opportunities, which will help them in growth in spite of innumerable obstacles
- In learning process one of the important points to be emphasized is effort and persistence, providing case studies of individuals who have succeeded through their hard work and showcasing stories of resilience and perseverance can inspire the students to approach the challenges with a growth mindset

- Providing constructive feedback on their efforts, strategies and performance, promoting an educational culture which values learning, integrating growth mindset principles into the curriculum through projects, assignments and assessments will make the students to adopt a growth mindset
- As mentioned earlier the instructor plays a crucial role in developing a growth mindset. An instructor should demonstrate positive attitude, emphasize the value of learning and share personal stories on challenges, setbacks and learning experiences
- Facilitating collaborating learning where they work with their peers, and setting up goals and continuous monitoring will develop a growth mindset

OVERCOMING COGNITIVE BARRIERS TO LEARNING

The educators always aim to equip the students with knowledge and skills for both personal and academic development, at the same time the above task is very much challenging. Teaching an information to the students does not guarantee that they actually learn it, or integrate into their knowledge or retain in their memory (Dror et al., 2011). So, to find way to minimize the learning barriers is of utmost importance. These cognitive barriers are challenging that the individuals may face on the process of acquiring and processing new information. Tough it varies from person to person; it has a vital impact in different aspects of their learning process. Educational psychologist John Sweller from Australia created a theory known as Cognitive Load Theory, which explains that people have a restricted working memory capacity and may experience information overload when presented with too much information. This excessive load can impede and delay the learning process and directly hinder the transfer of information from short-term memory to long-term memory. Similar to the theory mentioned before, there exist numerous obstacles to the process of learning.

Figure 1. Cognitive barriers to learning

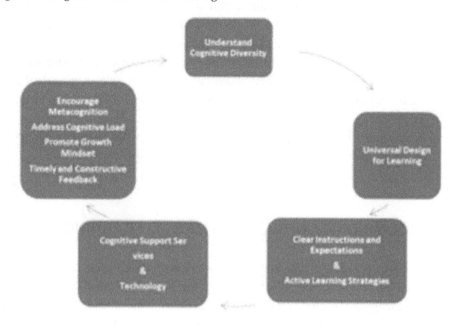

- Lack of prior knowledge – If the students lack the foundation of relevant prior knowledge in their specific domain, they may struggle to learn new information
- Cognitive Bias – This refers to systematic patterns of deviation from norm or rationality in judgment, which leads the individuals to make decisions or interpret information in a way that may not align with objective reality. These biases can influence perception, memory, and decision-making,
- Misconceptions – which refers to inaccurate understandings of concepts that an individual's hold. These pre-existing beliefs may be rooted in personal experiences, cultural influences, or incorrect information encountered earlier in the learning process. As a result, this can slow down the acquisition of new, and accurate knowledge and creates a cognitive conflict
- Perceptual constraints- The limitations in the way individuals perceive and interpret information from their environment, which can be visual, auditory, or related to other sensory modalities, influencing how individuals process and understand stimuli is called Perceptual constraints. These can impact learning in several ways, as they determine the information available for cognitive processing.

- Cognitive Aging – The changes that occur in cognitive abilities as individuals grow older refers to cognitive aging. Biological changes, genetic factors, experiences and environmental influences over a life time, chronic health conditions, stress may cause cognitive aging
- Language and Technology challenges – Non-native English-speaking students may face challenges in understanding and expressing themselves in the language of instruction. Insufficient use of technology can be a major barrier

Overcoming cognitive barriers in higher education is highly challenging. The challenges have to be addressed, if not it may hinder the effective learning process and academic success. The manifestation of cognitive barriers may be in various forms like difficulty in information processing, attention, memory, problem solving and critical thinking. First and foremost, it is utmost important and necessary to understand cognitive diversity. Individuals may have unique learning styles, their own strength and weakness. This has to be recognized and appreciated. UDL is an educational approach that strives to ensure learning is inclusive for every student, regardless of their unique abilities, learning preferences, or diversities. Within the realm of higher education, UDL aims to eliminate obstacles in learning and can offer all students various ways to access information, participate, and demonstrate their understanding.

Another important aspect is to provide clear instruction and expectation. The expected outcome should be clearly communicated. When there is clarity in assignments and instructions, the students will take it up with utmost confidence which in turn reduce confusion and cognitive load. The learning methods should be active, in the way that problem solving activities, group discussions and hands on project should involve the students through an active participation. Providing resources such as tutoring, counselling and academic support services will help the students to overcome cognitive challenges. Providing meta cognitive skills to the students by teaching them to reflect on their thinking process, setting goals and monitoring their own learning has a positive impact in overcoming the cognitive barriers. Towards the end the feedback offered should be specific, timely and constructive to the students, from which the students will have a better understanding and have an opportunity to correct their cognitive errors.

There are some of the important concepts related to cognitive learning.

Neuroscience Insights: Recent discoveries in neuroscience have greatly improved our comprehension of cognitive learning, emphasizing the brain's impressive capacity to adjust and restructure itself, referred to as neuroplasticity. Important areas of focus are the hippocampus's involvement in creating and strengthening new memories, especially while sleeping, and the prefrontal cortex's control of working memory and executive functions such as attention and problem-solving. Neurotransmitters such as dopamine and acetylcholine significantly influence learning by regulating motivation, reward, and attention. Emotional and social factors also impact learning, with the amygdala enhancing memory consolidation when emotions are involved, and mirror neurons facilitating learning through observation. Sleep is crucial for memory consolidation, with different stages benefiting various types of memories. Emerging technologies like brain-computer interfaces and neurofeedback offer promising avenues for cognitive enhancement and rehabilitation. These insights inform practical applications in education and therapy, emphasizing strategies that align with the brain's natural learning processes, such as spaced repetition and multimodal learning, and encouraging activities that promote lifelong neuroplasticity.

Learning Disabilities and Special Education: Learning disabilities (LD) such as dyslexia, dyscalculia, and dysgraphia present significant challenges in memory, attention, processing speed, and executive functions. Neuroscience insights have enhanced special education by highlighting neuroplasticity, which allows for brain rewiring through targeted interventions. Multisensory approaches improve information processing and retention, while personalized learning strategies leverage individual cognitive profiles to maximize strengths and address weaknesses. Practical applications include Individualized Education Programs (IEPs) that set tailored goals and strategies, and assistive technologies like speech-to-text software and interactive apps. Behavioral interventions help manage attention and impulsivity through feedback and reinforcement. Educators, psychologists, and therapists collaborate to create supportive learning environments, focusing on early diagnosis, skill development, and emotional and social support. Integrating these neuroscience insights into special education provides promising avenues for addressing learning disabilities, significantly enhancing cognitive learning outcomes and fostering academic and personal growth for students with LD.

Multimodal Learning and Universal Design: Universal Design for Learning (UDL) and multimodal learning are essential components of cognitive learning, with an emphasis on accessibility and inclusivity. Multimodal learning improves knowledge processing and retention by utilising a variety of senses, including visual, aural, and kinesthetic. This method makes learning more efficient and interesting by activating various neural pathways, which is in line with the brain's natural learning process. UDL, which has its roots in neurobiology, advocates for adaptable learning environments that suit a range of student learning styles and skill levels. This involves providing various avenues for representing, expressing, and participating to ensure that all students, including those with learning disabilities, can access and interact with the learning program. UDL meets the distinct learning preferences and requirements of individual students through offering a range of information presentation options such as text, audio, and interactive activities. It also promotes various approaches for students to showcase their comprehension, accommodating diverse abilities. Combining multimodal learning with UDL forms a more inclusive and efficient educational framework that promotes cognitive learning for every student. These methods enhance academic results and nurture a more interactive and supportive learning atmosphere, catering to the various learning styles and information interactions of students.

Evidence-Based Practices and Meta-Analysis: Evidence-based practices (EBPs) and meta-analysis play crucial roles in advancing the field of cognitive learning by ensuring that educational strategies and interventions are grounded in rigorous research. EBPs involve implementing teaching methods and educational interventions that have been scientifically tested and proven effective through high-quality research. These practices are critical in educational settings, as they provide reliable, replicable results that can improve learning outcomes across diverse student populations. Meta-analysis is a statistical technique that synthesizes data from multiple studies to determine overall trends and effectiveness. By aggregating results from various research studies, meta-analysis provides a more comprehensive understanding of which educational practices are most effective. This method helps to identify patterns and draw more accurate conclusions than individual studies might offer. In cognitive learning, meta-analyses have identified several effective strategies, such as spaced repetition, formative assessment, and multimodal learning approaches. These strategies are shown to enhance memory retention, comprehension, and engagement. The integration of EBPs, supported by meta-analytic evidence, ensures that educational interventions are both scientifically validated and practically effective. This approach not only improves educational outcomes but also provides educators with a solid foundation for making informed decisions about teaching practices and curriculum design.

ASSESSING COGNITIVE LEARNING: EFFECTIVE EVALUATION TECHNIQUES

Evaluating cognitive learning is an essential part of education, as it enables educators to assess the advancement and comprehension of the subject matter by their students. It is crucial to have efficient assessment methods so that students can remember and utilize the information they learned in class. This article will discuss important methods for evaluating cognitive learning and giving students feedback on their advancement (Benjes-Small et al., 2013).

Traditional Assessment Methods

Exams, tests, and other traditional evaluation techniques are frequently employed to gauge cognitive learning. These techniques usually consist of both open-ended questions that demand that students show their comprehension and critical thinking abilities as well as objective questions like multiple-choice, true/false, and fill-in-the-blank. These techniques don't always fully capture students' cognitive ability, even if they could offer a rapid assessment of their knowledge. In order to address this, educators can measure higher-order thinking abilities using a range of question types, such as application and analytical questions. Giving students the chance to reflect on and evaluate themselves can also help them absorb the topic more deeply and achieve better learning objectives.

Formative Assessment

Formative assessment is an ongoing process that involves providing students with feedback during the learning process. This can include asking questions, conducting class discussions, and providing written or verbal feedback on assignments. Formative assessment allows teachers to monitor students' progress and adjust their teaching methods as needed. One effective formative assessment technique is the use of exit tickets or quick quizzes at the end of a lesson to assess students' understanding. This provides teachers with immediate feedback on the effectiveness of their instruction and allows for any misunderstandings to be addressed before moving on to the next lesson.

Performance-Based Assessment

Performance-based assessments gauge how well students can use their acquired knowledge and abilities in practical settings. This can involve doing things like finishing a project, making a presentation, or taking part in a role-playing exercise. By allowing students to demonstrate their comprehension in a relevant and practical manner, these exams offer a more accurate gauge of their cognitive learning. Students should be given clear rubrics ahead of time that outline expectations and grading standards in order to assure the validity and reliability of performance-based examinations. In order to encourage ongoing development, it's also critical to provide students the chance to reflect on themselves and get feedback from their peers.

Authentic Assessment

Authentic assessment involves putting students in real-world scenarios where they must use their knowledge and abilities to solve issues or finish tasks, going beyond the conventional testing approaches. Project-based learning, in which students engage on an extended project requiring critical thinking, creativity, and teamwork, is frequently used in this kind of evaluation. Since students can see how what they are learning has application in the real world, authentic evaluation encourages a deeper knowledge of the content. Additionally, because each student can highlight their own special talents and capabilities, it enables individualised assessment.

FUTURE DIRECTIONS AND TRENDS IN COGNITIVE LEARNING

Cognitive acquisition is important for human development and education. Future directions in cognitive acquisition include impersonal and non-adaptive acquisition, customized and adaptable acquisition algorithms, integration of technology, and gamification. These developments could completely change the way acquisitions are experienced. Utilizing technology enables customized and engaging experiences. Customized procurement, enhanced with technological advancements, might yield better results. Neuroscience has the potential to enhance our comprehension of the brain's learning mechanisms. There is a bright future ahead for cognitive acquisition. In recent years, there have been rapid advancements in technology and research within the field of cognitive learning, providing new insights into how our brains process information and learn. In envisioning the future, there are various paths and patterns that will likely influence how we engage in cognitive learning.

Personalized and Adaptive Learning

The idea of personalized and adaptive learning has gained popularity with the advancement of personalized technology and data analysis. This approach customizes education to meet individual needs and abilities, improving learning outcomes. Technology, such as AI, can further enhance personalized learning by creating tailored materials and monitoring student progress. Adaptive learning software adjusts the complexity and pace of learning materials based on student performance, benefiting students with disabilities or exceptional abilities. Personalized and adaptive learning allows educators to provide targeted instruction, leading to better comprehension and retention. This approach has the potential to revolutionize education by catering to individual needs and improving learning experiences.

Incorporation of Virtual and Augmented Reality

The impact of virtual and augmented reality on education, specifically cognitive learning, has been significant. These technologies enhance engagement and retention by providing immersive and interactive experiences. In the future, VR and AR will be used even more in cognitive learning, especially in fields like science and medicine. Technology plays a crucial role in today's education, revolutionizing the learning process. Online platforms, virtual classrooms, and educational apps have made learning more convenient, accessible, and collaborative. Technology has transformed cognitive learning, making it interactive and personalized. In the future, we can expect AI, VR, and AR to be integrated even further. AI has the potential to personalize learning, tailoring materials to individual needs. It makes learning more efficient, allowing students to learn at their own pace. AI can analyse performance and provide personalized feedback. VR and AR will also impact cognitive learning, creating immersive experiences and facilitating understanding. VR simulates real-life scenarios, while AR overlays digital information on physical objects. Technology has greatly impacted cognitive learning, making it efficient and engaging. AI, VR, and AR will further integrate into cognitive learning, streamlining the process. Educators must embrace these technologies and adapt to the changing education landscape.

Integration of Neuroscience and Cognitive Psychology

BCI technology can provide real-time response on brain action, helping students identify strengths and weaknesses in learning. Integrating neuroscience and cognitive psychology can enhance cognitive skills like attention and problem-solving. Research shows that practicing cognitive tasks can change brain structure and function, improving these skills. This knowledge can inform targeted cognitive training programs in schools. Integrating neuroscience and cognitive psychology benefits education, enabling evidence-based strategies to optimize learning and enhance cognitive skills. This leads to effective teaching, personalized learning, and improved academic outcomes. Ongoing advancements and collaboration between researchers and educators promise a promising future for learning.

Advancements in neuroscience contribute to understanding brain learning. Neuroscience integration in cognitive learning provides insights for educators. Sleep is important for memory consolidation and can inform teaching practices. Neuroscience paves the way for brain-computer interface technology in education. BCI revolutionizes learning by allowing direct brain-computer communication. BCI helps individuals with disabilities control devices and provides brain activity feedback for tailored study habits. Integration of neuroscience and cognitive psychology enhances cognitive skills. Cognitive training programs can improve cognitive abilities through brain changes. Schools can implement targeted programs to enhance cognitive skills. Integration of neuroscience and cognitive psychology has potential for education. Understanding how the brain learns develops evidence-based strategies. This improves teaching methods and academic outcomes. Continuous advancements and collaboration promise a bright future for learning.

Emphasis on Metacognition and Self-Regulated Learning

The emphasis on metacognition and self-regulated learning is growing in cognitive education. Developing these skills in students is important. It involves reflecting on one's own learning and regulating it. Incorporating metacognitive skills into learning processes can make students more independent learners. Metacognition is understanding one's own thought processes. Educators can teach students about this concept and use it in learning strategies. This helps students become more effective learners. Goal-setting is important in metacognition. Educators give students direction and purpose by teaching them about goal-setting. This helps students focus and stay on track with learning objectives. In metacognition, self-monitoring is essential. Pupils must be conscious of and adjust for their own learning development. By doing this, students are able to take charge of their education and give it greater significance. One further crucial component of metacognition is self-reflection. Teachers urge their pupils to think back on what they have learned. Students get better self-awareness and comprehension of their cognitive processes as a result. Students that are nurtured in their metacognitive skills become autonomous learners. Students can now actively participate in their education as a result. Successful academic results follow from this. Because of its influence on student learning, metacognition and self-regulated learning are likely to remain a focal point in education.

Integration of Social and Emotional Learning

The focus of education has changed recently to become more all-encompassing. Social and emotional learning (SEL) is becoming recognised as being just as important as cognitive learning, which has historically been the primary focus. Better self-understanding and constructive interactions are made possible by the emotional intelligence and relationship-related abilities covered by SEL. Self-awareness, social awareness, self-management, interpersonal skills, and responsible decision-making are all components of SEL. These abilities positively affect students' general success and well-being and are essential for well-rounded people. It is anticipated that in the future, SEL will be combined with cognitive learning, acknowledging the vital role that connections and emotions play in learning. Students' learning can be made more effective and meaningful by applying the skills they gain in SEL to real-world circumstances, which can be integrated into academic topics. Integrating SEL with cognitive learning creates a positive and supportive learning environment, leading to better academic performance. SEL also helps students build self-confidence and resilience, vital for academic success and personal growth. The integration of SEL with cognitive learning is essential for a well-rounded education system. By incorporating SEL into academic subjects, students can develop skills that benefit their academic performance and personal and professional lives. The recognition of SEL's importance will have a positive impact on students' overall well-being and success.

Blended Learning and Online Education

The introduction of online and blended learning has been substantially expedited by the COVID-19 epidemic, and it is very likely that this trend will continue in the years to come. Online education allows students to study at their own speed and at a distance, while blended learning combines both in-person and virtual learning. These learning modalities have several advantages, including accessibility and flexibility, which let people practise cognitive development whenever it's convenient for them and in any environment of their choice.

Gamification

The use of game-like elements to improve learning is a widely accepted concept known as gamification in education. It fosters a stimulating atmosphere for students and encourages the development of critical thinking and problem-solving abilities. The concept of gamification is now being recognized in the field of education, enhancing the learning experience by making it entertaining and engaging. Leader boards promote friendly competition among students. Badges serve as acknowledgement of accomplishments and inspire students to persist in their efforts. Points are used to encourage and monitor progress. Gamification enhances critical thinking and problem-solving abilities through stimulating innovative ideas. As technology evolves, the many advantages of using it in education are likely to result in increased implementation.

Active Learning

Engaging in the learning process, active learning has shown to be more efficient than traditional methods. This may involve group conversations, arguments, studying real-life scenarios, and role-playing exercises, which prompt students to utilize their understanding, analyze thoughtfully, and interact with their classmates. Active learning fosters both enhancement of student comprehension and cultivation of advanced cognitive abilities.

Emphasis on Soft Skills

Although knowledge and academic success are crucial, employers are also seeking candidates with robust soft skills. This list encompasses skills such as communication, teamwork, problem-solving, and time management. Currently, universities are prioritizing the cultivation of these skills in students in addition to their academic learning. This helps students get ready for their careers and also helps them develop personally and professionally.

Inclusive Education

Recently, there has been an increasing focus on establishing a welcoming learning atmosphere that caters to all students, regardless of their background or skills. This involves offering support for students with disabilities and advocating for diversity and inclusion in the curriculum. Higher education institutions can establish a supportive and empowering environment for all students by adopting inclusive education, thus promoting both academic success and personal growth. The horizon of cognitive learning holds great promise and excitement for the future with continuous advancements in technology, robust research, and evolving teaching methods. This ground-breaking approach to education will deepen understanding and provide effective learning experiences. The potential of cognitive learning strategies to revolutionize higher education is enormous, boosting understanding, retention, and academic attainment. The outlook for cognitive learning is very promising with progressing technology and new methods. Incorporating these trends into education can shape a brighter future.

FUTURE RESEARCH DIRECTIONS

Future academic research on cognitive learning strategies in higher education should explore various transformative areas, with a focus on how these innovations could transform the educational environment.

Personalized and Adaptive Learning Systems: An important area to explore is personalized and adaptive learning systems. Artificial intelligence and machine learning algorithms are utilized in these systems to tailor educational content to the specific requirements of individual students. These systems can customize the educational experience by adjusting the pace, difficulty, and content type based on student performance data analysis. Future studies could concentrate on enhancing these algorithms to boost their precision and efficiency, making sure they are able to accommodate various learning styles and needs. Furthermore, studying the lasting effects of personalized learning on academic performance and student involvement may offer valuable observations on its advantages and disadvantages.

Virtual and Augmented Reality: The incorporation of VR and AR into educational environments offers a new avenue for research that shows great potential. These technologies provide engaging, interactive experiences that boost student involvement and enhance comprehension of intricate ideas. One example is that VR can replicate real-life settings for hands-on learning in areas like medicine, engineering, and the sciences, whereas AR can add virtual content to real-world settings, enhancing the educational process. Future studies should explore the best methods for incorporating these technologies into the curriculum, their effects on different cognitive abilities, and ways to make them available to a wider student population.

Neuroscience and Cognitive Psychology: Merging findings from neuroscience and cognitive psychology can result in better cognitive learning methods. Research on brain-computer interface (BCI) technology, which offers immediate brain activity feedback, is a thrilling field. BCIs can assist educators in comprehending the effects of various teaching techniques on brain activity and pinpointing the most successful approaches for improving learning. Future research could investigate how brain-computer interface (BCI) technology can be implemented to create tailored cognitive training programs that target individual learning difficulties. Moreover, exploring the neuroscience behind learning may result in the creation of innovative methods to enhance cognitive abilities and memory storage.

Metacognition and Self-Regulated Learning: Having knowledge about and being in charge of how one learns is essential for creating students who can learn on their own and do so effectively. Research could center on finding the most effective teaching methods for metacognitive skills and incorporating them into the curriculum in different subject areas. Moreover, investigating the ways in which technology can aid in metacognitive growth, like with applications that assist students in setting goals, tracking their advancement, and evaluating their learning, may offer useful resources for teachers. Exploring the lasting impact of improved metacognitive skills on educational achievements and continual learning is an important focus for upcoming studies.

Gamification and Engagement Strategies: Researching the implementation of gamification in education, which utilizes game-like features to inspire and involve students, is a promising field for exploration. Future research could investigate which aspects of games (e.g., rewards, challenges, competitions) are most impactful in varying educational settings, and how they impact cognitive learning and motivation. Furthermore, it is crucial to consider how gamification can be integrated with conventional teaching approaches in order to enhance learning results without undermining the importance of academic material.

Accessibility and Inclusivity: Future research must prioritize making cognitive learning strategies accessible and inclusive for all students. This involves creating tools and techniques that cater to the varied learning requirements of students with disabilities or from different cultural and linguistic backgrounds. Research may concentrate on developing adaptive technologies that offer fair learning opportunities and examining how these technologies affect educational fairness.

Longitudinal Studies and Real-World Applications: It is crucial to conduct longitudinal studies to understand the long-term effectiveness of cognitive learning strategies. These studies can offer understanding into how these approaches impact academic achievement, professional accomplishments, and continuous learning throughout life. Furthermore, implementing cognitive learning techniques in actual educational settings and assessing their tangible results can enhance these methods and guarantee their efficacy in varied educational contexts.

Educators and researchers can enhance cognitive learning and academic performance in higher education through innovative, evidence-based strategies by delving into future research directions.

CONCLUSION

In conclusion, cognitive learning in higher education offers a comprehensive exploration of evidence-based tactics, assessment techniques, and future directions in the field. By delving into cognitive barriers to learning and effective evaluation methods, the chapter provides valuable insights into how educators and students can optimize the learning experience. Through a thorough literature review, the chapter identifies key theories, empirical studies, and scholarly works relevant to cognitive learning, enhancing the understanding of foundational concepts. The chapter reinforces the credibility and validity of the arguments presented, fostering a deeper understanding of cognitive learning processes. Furthermore, it offers particular suggestions for upcoming research paths, emphasizing areas of investigation that could enhance our comprehension of cognitive learning and enhance educational methods. By emphasizing the value of metacognition, visualization techniques, chunking, and problem-solving strategies, the chapter equips educators and students with practical tools to enhance memory retention, critical thinking, and overall academic performance. In fostering a culture of empowered learning in higher education, this chapter serves as a valuable resource for both educators and students, encouraging continuous growth, reflection, and adaptation in the pursuit of academic excellence. By embracing evidence-based tactics and innovative approaches, the chapter paves the way for transformative learning experiences that empower individuals to succeed in the complex landscape of higher education and beyond.

REFERENCES

Подымов, Н. А. (2022). COGNITIVE BARRIERS AND STRATEGIES TO OVERCOME THEM IN THE EDUCATIONAL ACTIVITIES OF FOREIGN STUDENTS. *Higher education today, 3–4*, 103–106. https://doi.org/10.18137/RNU.HET.22.03-04.P.101

Benjes-Small, C., Archer, A., Tucker, K., & Vassady, L. (2013). Teaching Web Evaluation: A Cognitive Development Approach. *Communications in Information Literacy*, 7(1), 39. 10.15760/comminfolit.2013.7.1.133

Bhehlol, M. G., & Cajkler, W. (2018). Practices, Challenges and Implications of Teaching and Assessment of Cognitive Skills in Higher Education. *Pakistan Journal of Education*, 35(1). 10.30971/pje.v35i1.567

Chen, L., Chang, H., Rudoler, J., Arnardottir, E., Zhang, Y., De Los Angeles, C., & Menon, V. (2022). Cognitive training enhances growth mindset in children through plasticity of cortico-striatal circuits. *NPJ Science of Learning*, 7(1), 30. 10.1038/s41539-022-00146-736371438

Compte, O. (2023). *Endogenous Barriers to Learning* (Version 1). arXiv. https://doi.org/10.48550/ARXIV.2306.16904

Discipulo, L. G., & Bautista, R. G. (2022). Students' cognitive and metacognitive learning strategies towards hands-on science. [IJERE]. *International Journal of Evaluation and Research in Education*, 11(2), 658. 10.11591/ijere.v11i2.22018

Dror, I. E., Makany, T., & Kemp, J. (2011). Overcoming learning barriers through knowledge management. *Dyslexia (Chichester, England)*, 17(1), 38–47. 10.1002/dys.41920872423

Kartinah, N., T., Sudirman, & Daniel, T. (2020). *Preliminary Study of Cognitive Obstacle on the Topic of Finite Integral Among Prospective Teacher*. 2nd International Conference on Education and Social Science Research (ICESRE 2019), Central Java, Indonesia. 10.2991/assehr.k.200318.008

Müller, M., & Višić, M. (2023). Cognitive Learning Strategies with ICT: Case Study of Foreign Language Learners. *2023 IEEE 12th International Conference on Educational and Information Technology (ICEIT)*, (pp. 63–66). IEEE. 10.1109/ICEIT57125.2023.10107778

Pessoni, V., Federson, F., & Vincenzi, A. (2015). Learning Difficulties in Computing Courses: Cognitive Processes Assessment Methods Research and Application. *Anais Do Simpósio Brasileiro de Sistemas de Informação (SBSI)*, 31–38. 10.5753/sbsi.2015.5798

Rivadeneira, J., & Inga, E. (2023). Interactive Peer Instruction Method Applied to Classroom Environments Considering a Learning Engineering Approach to Innovate the Teaching–Learning Process. *Education Sciences*, 13(3), 301. 10.3390/educsci13030301

Sato, M. (2022). Metacognition. In S. Li, P. Hiver, & M. Papi, *The Routledge Handbook of Second Language Acquisition and Individual Differences* (1st ed., pp. 95–110). Routledge. 10.4324/9781003270546-8

Straw, A. M., Cole, J. W., & McGuire, K. (2023). Peer Instruction as an Alternative Active Learning Pedagogy Across the Pharmacy Curriculum. *American Journal of Pharmaceutical Education*, 87(8), 100090. 10.1016/j.ajpe.2023.10009037597914

Wu, H., & Molnár, G. (2022). Analysing Complex Problem-Solving Strategies from a Cognitive Perspective: The Role of Thinking Skills. *Journal of Intelligence*, 10(3), 46. 10.3390/jintelligence10030046 35893277

Yafie, E., Nirmala, B., Kurniawaty, L., Bakri, T. S. M., Hani, A. B., & Setyaningsih, D. (2020). Supporting Cognitive Development through Multimedia Learning and Scientific Approach: An Experimental Study in Preschool. *Universal Journal of Educational Research*, 8(11C), 113–123. 10.13189/ujer.2020.082313

KEY TERMS AND DEFINITIONS

Cognitive Learning: Cognitive learning strategies are methods that aim to improve learning and information processing by using cognitive abilities and processes. These tactics utilize mnemonic devices, chunking, elaboration, and metacognitive strategies to aid learners in interacting with material, making connections, and gradually developing their comprehension.

Collaborative Learning and Peer Instruction: Students collaborate in groups to solve problems, share ideas, and create products, improving critical thinking and comprehension. Peer instruction involves students of varying knowledge and skills partnering up to educate and be educated in a collaborative learning environment.

Mnemonic Devices: Memory tools such as mnemonic devices improve memory by offering helpful memory cues and associations. Methods such as acronyms, visualization, and chunking aid in the more efficient encoding and retrieval of information.

Multimodal Learning and Universal Design for Learning (UDL): Utilizing different senses (visual, auditory, kinesthetic) in multimodal learning improves the processing and retention of knowledge. UDL promotes flexible learning spaces to cater to various learning preferences and capabilities, ensuring equal access and diversity for every student.

Neuroscience and Cognitive Psychology: This combination in education improves cognitive abilities like attention and problem-solving. This method employs evidence-based techniques to enhance learning and enhance academic results.

Personalized and Adaptive Learning: This tailors education to each person's specific needs and skills, enhancing educational achievements. Technology like AI customizes resources and tracks advancements, modifying difficulty and speed according to student achievement.

Problem-Solving: Problem-solving is a cognitive approach to learning that entails analysing difficulties, creating possible solutions, and assessing their impact. This procedure involves simplifying difficult issues, generating ideas, and working together to solve problems. **Metacognition:** This involves being aware of and controlling one's learning by monitoring, evaluating, and adjusting cognitive processes. This involves thinking about what was learned, creating objectives, and using successful learning methods.

Virtual and Augmented Reality (VR and AR): These technologies improve engagement and retention through immersive and interactive experiences, especially beneficial in areas such as science and medicine.

Chapter 6
Adaptive Intelligence Revolutionizing Learning and Sustainability in Higher Education:
Enhancing Learning and Sustainability With AI

Bianca Ifeoma Chigbu
https://orcid.org/0000-0003-4029-9580
University of Fort Hare, South Africa

Ikechukwu Umejesi
https://orcid.org/0000-0002-7757-0445
University of Fort Hare, South Africa

Sicelo Leonard Makapela
https://orcid.org/0009-0007-8817-5356
Walter Sisulu University, South Africa

ABSTRACT

This chapter examines the incorporation of adaptive intelligence in higher education, focusing on its influence on conventional learning approaches and long-lasting educational strategies. Adaptive intelligence merges artificial intelligence with human cognition to provide personalized learning by utilizing real-time customisation and data analysis. Adaptive intelligence enhances sustainability by integrating sustainability principles into the learning process in a dynamic manner. The chapter discusses obstacles such resource constraints, instructor opposition, and ethical issues. The

DOI: 10.4018/979-8-3693-3559-8.ch006

Copyright © 2024, IGI Global. Copying or distributing in print or electronic forms without written permission of IGI Global is prohibited.

significance of ethical AI usage, educator engagement, and continuous research is emphasized to maximize adaptive intelligence's potential in creating a sustainable and inclusive educational system. The text ends by addressing future research and practical consequences with the goal of establishing a robust educational system that accommodates individual learning requirements, incorporates sustainability principles, and equips students to navigate contemporary challenges.

INTRODUCTION

The 21st century has introduced an era in which technology and education have combined to generate adaptive intelligence. This potent synergy of artificial intelligence (AI) and human cognition is on the brink of revolutionizing higher education by personalizing learning experiences through advanced AI technologies, such as machine learning, natural language processing, and data analytics. Adaptive intelligence has significantly transformed since the 1960s, when computer-assisted education was first introduced, and the 1980s, when significant AI advancements were made. These advancements introduced adaptive learning systems that could modify educational content based on student interactions (Fleury et al., 2017). Adaptive intelligence has effectively addressed modern learners' complex and diverse requirements, transcending the limitations of traditional one-size-fits-all educational approaches (Chigbu et al., 2023). This chapter explores the transformative potential of adaptive intelligence in transforming educational practices. Adaptive intelligence empowers educators to surpass conventional teaching methods by cultivating personalized, engaging, and sustainable learning environments, creating individualized learning experiences, critical thinking, and creativity. This method is consistent with modern education's objectives and improves educational methodologies' sustainability, guaranteeing that learning remains pertinent, efficient, and adaptable to future challenges. This chapter intends to advance inclusive, sustainable, and effective educational methodologies by addressing these issues.

METHODOLOGY

The chapter utilizes a comprehensive qualitative research technique, incorporating many scholars' viewpoints and in-depth case studies to investigate the implementation and influence of adaptive intelligence in higher education. The research employs both exploratory case studies and theoretical analysis to offer comprehension of adaptive intelligence in the context of higher education. This methodology enables a thorough analysis of practical applications and the integration of insights from many scholarly references.

The study conducted a comprehensive literature review to collect insights from previous studies on adaptable intelligence. This entailed scouring academic databases for pertinent articles, books, and conference papers. The relevant material was identified using keywords such as "adaptive learning," "AI in education," and "personalized learning." The literature review facilitated the identification of crucial patterns, difficulties, and prospects linked to adaptive intelligence, hence informing the study's theoretical framework.

The case studies were selected based on their pertinence to the research inquiries and their capacity to offer varied viewpoints on adaptive intelligence. The criteria for selection encompassed the setting in which the implementation took place (such as higher education), the magnitude of the implementation, and the presence of comprehensive documentation.

Thematic analysis was employed to examine qualitative data derived from the literature study and answers from case studies. The investigation revealed several key themes, including the customization of learning, student participation, teacher opposition, resource optimization, and ethical issues. A comparative analysis approach was utilized to systematically examine the conclusions obtained from various case studies. This analysis illuminated shared patterns, disparities, and distinctive perspectives among different applications of adaptive intelligence. The comparison research also identified methods and tactics for overcoming barriers in various educational settings.

HOW ADAPTIVE INTELLIGENCE OPERATES IN HIGHER EDUCATION

Foundational Aspects of Adaptive Intelligence

In higher education, adaptive intelligence is a multifaceted amalgamation of several components, each vital to its dynamic operation. Integrating AI technology, such as machine learning algorithms, natural language processing, and data analytics, is its foundation. These constituent elements facilitate the ability of adaptive intelligence to analyze extensive datasets, detect trends, and customize learning experiences in real-time. Alkhawaldeh and Khasawneh (2023) conducted research emphasizing the significance of AI-powered elements, namely their capacity to provide individualized learning trajectories. They contend that the adaptability of these technologies permits a more profound comprehension of the profiles of individual students, hence facilitating the adaptation of instructional materials and approaches to accommodate a wide range of requirements.

Adaptive intelligence is significantly enhanced by the human cognitive dimension, which is just as important as technology components. A synergistic environment is produced by combining computer intelligence with human thinking, which capitalizes on the respective capabilities of each. These encompass metacognition, critical thinking, and emotional intelligence, all of which enhance the learning process beyond the scope of simple memory. Holstein et al. (2020) highlight the need to incorporate human cognition into the learning process, stressing the critical necessity of emotional intelligence and creativity. The findings of their study indicate that adaptive intelligence thrives in a mutually beneficial association between machine algorithms and human intuition.

The concept of adaptive intelligence is diverse since scholars have proposed various definitions and conceptualizations. The diversity of these viewpoints enhances the overall comprehension of the topic. For example, Sternberg (2019) conceptualizes adaptive intelligence as a dynamic ecosystem in which AI generates a reciprocal learning milieu distinguished by ongoing feedback loops in response to the learner's cognitive processes. The interplay between these elements improves the overall flexibility of the educational system.

Conversely, the ethical aspects are examined by Regan and Jesse (2018), who see adaptive intelligence as a harmonious coexistence of technical progress and ethical deliberations. Regarding incorporating AI into education, they call for an ethical framework that places privacy, fairness, and openness as top priorities. Various conceptualizations highlight the multidimensional character of adaptive intelligence; scientists have contributed perspectives from technical to ethical dimensions. The unification of these many viewpoints provides a holistic comprehension of the functioning of adaptive intelligence in higher education, emphasizing its capacity to revolutionize learning as an ever-evolving phenomenon of the future.

Dynamic Interplay Between AI and Human Cognition

The dynamic nature of adaptive intelligence is predicated on the interplay between human cognition and AI. This connection provides detailed information on how these two factors interact and the synergies and problems.

The reciprocal association between AI and human cognition is the foundation of adaptive intelligence in higher education. This integration facilitates the effective complementarity of both entities by augmenting their respective strengths. This dynamic interchange is emphasized by Popenici and Kerr (2017), who propose a paradigm in which AI functions as an augmentational tool. By utilizing this framework, students can interact with intricate ideas while maintaining the fundamental human qualities of critical thinking and originality. The result is a symbiotic union in which the intuitive capabilities of human cognition and the analytical ability of AI smoothly combine. According to Mitsopoulos et al. (2022), it is critical to comprehend the interdependencies that exist between AI algorithms and human cognitive processes. Aligning AI algorithms with human memory, attention, and problem-solving capabilities is essential for successful integration. The adaptive intelligence system can respond dynamically to each learner's demands by ensuring this alignment.

As empirical research demonstrates, integrating AI with human cognition presents synergies and obstacles. As an illustration, a study conducted by Shi et al. (2014) illustrates the potential for improved learning outcomes by integrating AI and human cognition. Adaptive algorithms detect comprehension gaps among students, enabling the implementation of customized interventions that enhance the overall educational experience.

Despite this, there are obstacles present in this intricate interaction. Critics such as Sallam (2023) express concern about the potential for an excessive dependence on AI to compromise critical human abilities like creativity and emotional intelligence. It is essential to balance technological advancement and the maintenance of human cognitive abilities. In addition, ethical considerations, including the possibility of biases in AI algorithms, are emphasized by Mittelstadt et al. (2016), stressing the necessity for a discerning approach to AI integration.

Adaptive intelligence, which involves the interaction of AI with human cognition, provides both possibilities and problems as time progresses—the potential for tailored learning experiences and the synergies of present-focused interventions. However, addressing ethical issues and balancing human and technical components is critical to ensure ethical and successful integration. Embedding AI and human cognition into adaptive intelligence necessitates ongoing investigation, ethical deliberation, and a dedication to establishing an educational environment that appreciates the respective merits of both components.

Operationalizing Adaptive Intelligence in Higher Education

Operationalizing adaptive intelligence is crucial for its effective implementation in higher education. This process involves developing frameworks and models for integrating adaptive technologies into educational settings.

Existing Frameworks and Models

Frameworks constitute architectures for the incorporation of adaptive intelligence. An example is the Adaptive Learning Framework authored by Ibrahim and Hamada (2016). This framework delineates the adaptive learning ecosystem's fundamental constituents, procedures, and participants. This underscores the significance of a feedback loop in which AI discoveries inform individualized learning trajectories. This approach ensures that teaching practices align with AI's flexibility by leveraging real-time data to update instructional tactics iteratively.

Actualizing the Potential for Adaptation in Higher Education

Models offer a comprehensive knowledge of how these principles are translated into practical methods. Johnson and Zone (2018) and Krechetov and Romanenko (2020) delineate the implementation phases in their Adaptive Learning Model, which begins with data gathering and concludes with algorithm optimization. This model exemplifies the fluidity of adaptive intelligence in its development in response to learner interactions. Zhou et al. (2021) and Shemshack et al. (2021) present the Personalized Learning Model, which offers an approach to customizing educational experiences according to the unique requirements of each student. The model entails the creation of a personalized setting wherein content distribution, tempo, and evaluations are all customized.

Holistic Integration

Integrating these frameworks and models achieves a holistic strategy for implementing adaptive intelligence. The Adaptive Learning Framework serves as a structural guide, while the Adaptive Learning Model and the Personalized Learning Model comprehensively analyze the integration processes and results. However, obstacles continue to exist. The need for adaptability in these frameworks and models to fit a wide range of learners and instructional circumstances is emphasized by Corno (2018). The designers prioritize adaptability, inclusion, and ethical concerns when developing these frameworks to guarantee their efficacy in diverse educational environments. By confronting these obstacles, institutions of higher education may establish an environment for adaptive intelligence that is morally upright and efficient.

Case Studies and Practical Implementations

The practical application of adaptive intelligence in educational settings brings theoretical concepts to life. It is essential to demonstrate the real-world impact of adaptive intelligence, the challenges encountered, the successes achieved, and the lessons learned.

Case Study One: Personalized Learning in Higher Education

Notable case studies conducted in higher education, as described by Wang et al. (2023) and Walkington (2013), exemplify the efficacy of adaptive intelligence-based individualized learning. These studies demonstrate how adaptive technology may be utilized to tailor learning experiences to the specific requirements of each student. The adaptive system effectively detected learning gaps through real-time data analysis, modifying instructional content, and delivering focused interventions. As a result, there were substantial enhancements in student engagement, comprehension, and overall course performance. Nevertheless, this chapter also unveiled obstacles, most notably opposition from specific instructors who were apprehensive about ceding authority over the educational journey. These case studies emphasize the transformational capacity of adaptive intelligence and show the importance of addressing concerns raised by faculty members and cultivating a collaborative atmosphere to achieve effective implementation.

Case Study Two: Adaptive Learning Environments

Liu et al. (2017), Liu et al.(2022), and Mirata et al. (2020) examine the integration of adaptive intelligence in a variety of classroom environments through case studies. These research findings illustrate the application of adaptive technology in classrooms with diverse demographics and socioeconomic backgrounds to deliver personalized education that caters to students' varying learning styles and paces. These case studies resulted in positive shifts in student attitudes toward learning and academic achievement. Nevertheless, the research also recognized obstacles, including limited resources and the imperative for ongoing professional growth to furnish teachers with the knowledge and abilities required to integrate adaptive technology into their pedagogical approaches.

Case Study Three: Language Learning Through Adaptive Platforms

Case studies conducted by Wei (2023) and Lesia Viktorivna et al. (2022) illuminate the use of adaptive intelligence in language acquisition within language education. The study's subject was an adaptive language learning platform that modified the difficulty of language exercises according to each learner's competency. The findings demonstrated increased language learning rates as individuals progressed at a personalized rate. Nevertheless, this research highlighted obstacles, including safeguarding privacy during data gathering and guaranteeing that the adaptive platform could adequately accommodate learners from various language backgrounds. The case studies highlight the criticality of customizing adaptive intelligence to suit the distinct demands of language teaching.

Case Study Four: Enhancing STEM Education with Adaptive Intelligence

The study by Allen et al. (2016) discovered that effective adaptive teaching in STEM necessitates modifying instruction per students' conceptual development, inquiry processes, and real-world connections. This necessitates reflective practice, a constructivist paradigm, and well-developed STEM pedagogical content knowledge (PCK). Novice teachers often require targeted support and professional development to address the challenges of adapting instruction to the diverse requirements of students and applying theoretical models in a real classroom. The study underlines the significance of continuous reflective practice, inquiry-based learning, and robust STEM PCK. To overcome these obstacles, it recommends the implementation of decision-making frameworks to span the divide between research and practice, as well as ongoing professional development and mentoring to improve adaptive teaching in STEM education.

Case Study Five: Adaptive Learning in Online Education

Demartini et al. (2024) conducted a case study investigating the implementation of adaptive learning in an online education platform. The adaptive system employed AI to analyze student interactions and offer personalized resources and feedback. This method resulted in increased student satisfaction and retention rates. The most significant obstacles identified were the necessity for reliable technical support to administer the platform and the preservation of practical data privacy.

The combined observations from these case studies provide a comprehensive understanding of the complexities of incorporating adaptive intelligence into educational environments. The success narratives serve as a testament to the profound ability of adaptive intelligence to effect change, as they demonstrate improvements in learner engagement, academic performance, and personalized academic experiences, as synthesized in Table 1.

Table 1. Comparative analysis of case studies

Case Study Title	Key Findings	Challenges Faced	Insights and Solutions
Personalized Learning in Higher Education	Enhanced student engagement and performance; real-time data analysis for interventions	Faculty resistance; apprehension about ceding authority	Importance of addressing faculty concerns and fostering collaboration
Adaptive Learning Environments	Positive shifts in student attitudes and academic achievement	Limited resources; need for ongoing professional development	Necessity of resource allocation and continuous training for effective integration
Language Learning Through Adaptive Platforms	Increased language learning rates with personalized pacing	Privacy concerns; accommodating diverse language backgrounds	Customization to meet privacy standards and diverse learner needs
Enhancing STEM Education with Adaptive Intelligence	Improved teaching effectiveness; reflective practice	Initial learning curve; need for continuous support	Importance of reflective practice and ongoing professional development
Adaptive Learning in Online Education	Higher retention rates and improved student satisfaction	Data privacy; need for robust technical support	Ensuring strong data governance policies and technical support infrastructure

By systematically summarizing the results from different studies, we can highlight common themes and provide valuable insights into the successful implementation of adaptive intelligence in higher education. However, the research mentioned above emphasizes the challenges that must be overcome, such as faculty reservations, restricted resources, and the necessity of customized adaptive systems designed to meet the distinctive needs of various academic environments.

Looking Forward: Toward Inclusive and Ethical Implementation

The insights gleaned from these particular cases remain priceless as the discourse surrounding adaptive intelligence in education progresses. Successfully implementing adaptive intelligence necessitates carefully managing technology advancements while retaining a focus on human needs. Subsequent initiatives must give precedence to diversity, tackle ethical concerns about data protection, and guarantee ongoing professional growth for educators to incorporate adaptive intelligence into teaching and learning methodologies effectively.

In summary, adaptive intelligence, which pertains to the amalgamation of AI and human cognition in higher education, functions via complex fundamental elements and a dynamic interaction between technology integration and human cognition.

Integrating AI technologies, such as data analytics and machine learning algorithms, enables adaptive intelligence to dynamically adapt to large datasets and customize learning experiences in real-time. Incorporating human cognitive attributes, including critical thinking and emotional intelligence, enhances this synthesis, establishing a mutually beneficial association between machine intelligence and human reasoning. The numerous conceptualizations of adaptive intelligence, which encompass anything from ethical issues to developing ecosystems, contribute to a thorough understanding of its functioning in higher education.

The operationalization of adaptable intelligence is also facilitated by established frameworks, such as the Adaptive Learning Framework, which provide direction for its incorporation into educational environments. Furthermore, nuanced viewpoints are provided by models such as the Adaptive Learning Model and the Personalized Learning Model, which prioritize adaptability and personalization. Case studies offer tangible examples of adaptive intelligence's practical application, highlighting the revolutionary capacity of the technology while also underscoring the importance of confronting obstacles such as faculty opposition, limited resources, and ethical concerns. In conceptualizing the future, effective execution necessitates a calculated equilibrium between technology advancement and a human-centric methodology, placing equal emphasis on ethical deliberations, ongoing professional growth for educators, and inclusion.

REVOLUTIONIZING LEARNING STRATEGIES AND FOSTERING SUSTAINABILITY WITH ADAPTIVE INTELLIGENCE

Impact on Traditional Learning Strategies

Higher education has historically employed a pedagogical framework that has consisted mostly of didactic lectures, a standardized curriculum, and a uniform method of imparting knowledge. Within this traditional environment, educators have a pivotal position, imparting knowledge to a receptive public with less regard for unique learning preferences. The present analysis begins by elucidating the established framework that governs conventional methods. Although old approaches have managed to persist, they do possess specific praiseworthy merits. Standardized tests, a historical foundation, and defined frameworks have all contributed to the appearance of uniformity.

Nevertheless, the constraints are evident. The inflexibility of these approaches hinders the development of crucial competencies, like critical thinking and creativity, leaving graduates unprepared for the requirements of a swiftly changing work environment (Chigbu et al., 2023; Chigbu & Nekhwevha, 2022). The contrast between these merits and drawbacks establishes the foundation for a discerning analysis.

Revolutionizing Learning Strategies Through Adaptive Intelligence

Adaptive intelligence presents an alternative to conventional, one-size-fits-all methodologies by providing an individualized and adaptable learning experience. In contrast to traditional approaches that frequently neglect the unique requirements of each learner, adaptive intelligence utilizes AI to dynamically customize learning experiences by analyzing data patterns. By implementing this transition, educational materials are synchronized with each student's unique aptitudes and learning preferences, surpassing rigid approaches' drawbacks (Chigbu et al., 2023).

Adaptive intelligence's capacity to revolutionize learning strategies is contingent on several critical factors. The utilization of data-driven insights is paramount, given that ongoing evaluation of student progress permits immediate modifications, thereby establishing a proactive and adaptable educational setting (Demartini et al., 2024). AI technologies are built upon machine learning algorithms, which serve as the foundation. These algorithms enable adaptive systems to precisely optimize learning experiences by identifying patterns. Personalization is another pivotal element, as it fosters critical thinking and increases learner engagement by customizing content to specific learner profiles. Addressing the constraints associated with conventional methods' standardized approaches ensures that machine intelligence and human cognition are seamlessly integrated. The reciprocal association facilitated by the flexibility of these technologies enhances the educational process beyond mere rote memorization, resulting in a more dynamic and efficacious pedagogical approach (Sternberg, 2021). In the context of higher education grappling with the challenges of the contemporary era, adaptive intelligence emerges as a guiding principle for developing pedagogical strategies that point towards a future in which knowledge is not merely transmitted but rather profoundly integrated into the cognitive landscapes of individuals.

Contribution to Sustainable Education Practices

Sustainability in the realm of higher education extends beyond mere environmental impact reduction. It entails an all-encompassing dedication to comprehensive well-being, social accountability, and economic feasibility. Academic establishments strive to cultivate environmentally aware individuals, integrate sustainable methodologies into their campus functioning, and contribute to worldwide sustainability initiatives (Leal Filho et al., 2018). Nevertheless, this dedication encounters obstacles, including financial limitations, opposition to transformation, and the requirement for substantial infrastructure modifications (Barth & Rieckmann, 2012). As a result, a multifaceted environment ensues in which the quest for sustainability functions as both an objective and a continuous challenge.

The correlation between sustainability and adaptive intelligence underscores the critical significance of education in cultivating persons who are well-informed about the environment. Sustainability integration into educational processes is a strategic need, not only a preference. Incorporating sustainability ideas into academic courses empowers students to confront the multifaceted ecological, social, and economic dilemmas that face our global community (Tilbury, 2004). This is beyond theoretical comprehension and cultivates a proactive attitude that pursues resolutions for tangible sustainability challenges. Adaptive intelligence contributes significantly to the advancement of sustainable education by facilitating individualized learning experiences. By capitalizing on the limitations of conventional learning approaches, academic establishments may effortlessly incorporate sustainability principles into the teaching process by leveraging AI-powered insights. Adaptive intelligence provides a flexible framework for integrating sustainability education customized to each learner's requirements. This empowers educational approaches to modify and progress in light of the ever-evolving complexities associated with sustainability.

Role of Adaptive Intelligence in Fostering Sustainability

The investigation of adaptive intelligence in the context of sustainability education underlines its capacity to fundamentally reshape conventional approaches to teaching and learning. The flexibility of AI enables the smooth incorporation of sustainability ideas into academic curricula, fostering active participation and assimilation of these principles across many fields of study (Tilbury, 2004). Adaptive intelligence, distinguished by the interaction between human thinking and machine intelligence, establishes an educational setting that surpasses memorization and cultivates a holistic comprehension of the interdependencies among economic, social, and ecological elements (Leal Filho et al., 2018).

Incorporating adaptive intelligence into tertiary education signifies a fundamental change in approach, substantially enhancing sustainable educational methods and fundamentally transforming conventional learning methodologies. Traditional pedagogical methods, which consist of rigid course offerings and didactic discourse, encounter constraints when cultivating ingenuity and discerning thought. Powered by AI, adaptive intelligence disturbs this static paradigm by customizing learning experiences to the cognitive landscapes of individuals. It fosters critical thinking and innovation by facilitating a change from passive receipt to active involvement, hence possessing transformational power. Influencing effectiveness includes data-driven insights, personalized approaches, and the seamless integration of AI and human cognition. This deviation from the conventional industrial education model creates an opportunity for a proactive and adaptable educational environment.

Furthermore, incorporating adaptable intelligence into sustainability objectives is consistent with including sustainability principles in educational methodologies. It tackles obstacles through the dynamic modification of material delivery, promotion of environmental literacy, and development of problem-solving attitudes. Adaptive intelligence catalyzes sustainable education by effortlessly providing individualized routes to incorporate sustainability ideas into the academic experience. Case studies and theoretical foundations demonstrate that it can transform conventional methods and promote sustainability in higher education institutions (Tejedor et al., 2019). Notwithstanding obstacles such as ethical concerns and prejudices, adaptive intelligence's auspicious potential establishes it as a helpful instrument in furthering sustainability objectives and molding a cohort of learners equipped to confront the intricate predicaments of the forthcoming era.

ADAPTIVE INTELLIGENCE IN HIGHER EDUCATION: CHALLENGES, OPPORTUNITIES, RISKS AND FUTURE DIRECTIONS

Adaptive intelligence in higher education holds immense promise for revolutionizing learning through personalized, data-driven approaches. It is crucial to shed light on how adaptive intelligence impacts interactive learning strategies in higher education, focusing on the challenges, opportunities, and risks associated with its implementation.

Challenges

Although adaptive intelligence has the potential to revolutionize personalized learning, it also raises substantial ethical concerns, particularly in algorithmic bias and privacy rights. The significant reliance on data collection to personalize learning experiences results in collecting and analyzing immense quantities of personal information, which raises critical concerns regarding student privacy and data security (Akavova et al., 2023). In their present state, AI systems may inadvertently perpetuate biases that are already present in their training data, resulting in the unjust treatment of specific student demographics (Holmes et al., 2022). This matter is particularly alarming as it can potentially exacerbate systemic disparities and restrict the opportunities of marginalized communities (Baker & Hawn, 2022).

The integration of adaptive intelligence in higher education necessitates a significant investment in professional development for educators and technology infrastructure. It may be difficult for many institutions, particularly those with limited financial resources, to acquire the essential technology and training (Rizvi, 2023). The high cost of advanced AI systems and the necessity for continuous maintenance and updates can be prohibitive for underfunded institutions and universities. This financial impediment can exacerbate disparities in access to advanced educational technologies, thereby impeding the widespread adoption of adaptive intelligence (Bozkurt et al., 2021).

Educators acclimating to traditional teaching methods may resist integrating adaptive intelligence into education. Skepticism regarding the efficacy of AI in improving learning experiences and concerns about relinquishing control over the educational process can generate substantial obstacles to adoption (Gilbert & Mintz, 2019). Numerous educators may be concerned that AI systems will undermine their professional autonomy, diminish their role in the classroom, or fail to deliver the anticipated enhancements in student outcomes (Hoffmann et al., 2018).

Incorporating adaptive intelligence into current educational frameworks is intricate and time-consuming. To guarantee that the system accommodates the diverse requirements of students, it necessitates meticulous planning, continual evaluation, and the customization of learning materials (Aquino et al., 2023). Institutions that lack the requisite expertise or resources to manage the transition effectively may encounter substantial obstacles due to the complexity of implementation (Srivastava & Sinha, 2023).

Addressing Faculty Resistance and Resource Optimization

Effective interventions that mitigate faculty resistance have illustrated the significance of comprehensive professional development programs. For instance, Cleveland State University (CSU) implemented numerous successful interventions in the Adaptive Courseware for Early Success Initiative to mitigate faculty resistance to adaptive teaching and learning. The Personalized Learning Consortium (PLC) provided extensive coaching, peer mentorship, collaborative learning, and networking opportunities as part of these interventions. CSU also prioritized professional development for faculty, which involved establishing faculty learning communities that concentrated on gateway courses and integrating evidence-based, equity-centered teaching practices bolstered by adaptive courseware (Purita & Tesene, 2023). Faculty utilized products such as ALEKS, Learnsmart Connect, and Mastering Chemistry to customize in-class support and increase student engagement, utilizing student performance data. This method facilitated the establishment of a supportive community among faculty, which enhanced the overall teaching efficacy and facilitated the transition to new technologies and instructional strategies.

Vignare et al. (2020) documented another successful intervention at Arizona State University, where the administration implemented a phased implementation strategy for adaptive learning technologies. Initially, a limited group of enthusiastic faculty members were chosen to pilot the technology. By sharing their positive experiences and successes with their colleagues, these early adopters generated a ripple effect that progressively diminished resistance among the faculty. Furthermore, showing data on enhanced student outcomes was instrumental in persuading skeptics of the benefits of technology.

Collaborative resource-sharing models can significantly benefit underfunded institutions in terms of resource optimization strategies. For example, the California Community Colleges Online Education Initiative implemented a centralized adaptive learning platform shared among various colleges (Johnson et al., 2015). This model facilitated the pooling of resources and allocating costs for implementation, training, and maintenance, thereby increasing the accessibility of adaptive learning technologies. Additionally, resource-constrained institutions may obtain the necessary assistance by pursuing partnerships with edtech companies for pilot programs and funding opportunities.

Opportunities

The capacity to offer highly personalized learning experiences is one of the most transformative opportunities that adaptive intelligence presents. Through advanced data analysis, AI systems can customize educational content to precisely correspond with each individual's learning patterns, preferences, and progress. This degree of customization is unparalleled in conventional educational environments and substantially improves student motivation and engagement (Taylor et al., 2021). Adaptive intelligence cultivates an inclusive academic climate in which all students have the potential to succeed by addressing the distinctive requirements of each student (Walkington, 2013). The personalized pathways and immediate feedback assist students in maintaining a high level of interest and commitment to their studies, comprehending their learning progress, and remaining on track. This personalized approach enhances academic performance and fosters a more profound, meaningful connection to the learning material, resulting in long-term educational success (Peng et al., 2019).

Chaplot et al. (2016) have demonstrated that adaptive intelligence has the potential to significantly improve student engagement and retention by designing learning experiences that are more interactive and tailored to the unique requirements of each student. Real-time progress monitoring, adaptive assessments, and personalized feedback are interactive learning strategies that maintain students' active engagement in their education (Tian et al., 2023). Implementing these methodologies guarantees that the learning process is dynamic and engaging rather than passive. It is a natural consequence of increased engagement that retention rates rise, as students who perceive that their educational experience is customized to their requirements are more inclined to remain dedicated to their studies. In addition, the real-time adaptability of AI systems enables the immediate resolution of learning obstacles, thereby preventing disengagement and frustration. As a result of this proactive approach, students are more likely to achieve academic success and remain motivated, as they can swiftly surmount challenges (Graf, 2023).

Adaptive intelligence provides educators with invaluable data-driven insights into student learning patterns and performance. Educators can acquire a profound comprehension of the areas in which pupils excel and those in which they may struggle by utilizing the capabilities of AI (Costa et al., 2021). These insights allow educators to customize their teaching strategies to accommodate the unique requirements of each student (Xie et al., 2019). It is possible to provide support at the exact moment it is required through real-time data analysis, which enables timely interventions. This targeted approach assists educators in refining their instructional methods, thereby enhancing the effectiveness and responsiveness of their teaching. In addition, educators can identify trends and patterns that may not be evident through conventional assessment methods by continuously monitoring and analyzing student progress (Akavova et al., 2023). This exhaustive comprehension of student learning has the potential to result in the creation of more innovative and effective teaching practices that improve the overall quality of education.

Inherently scalable and adaptable, adaptive learning systems are appropriate for diverse educational settings (Apoki et al., 2022). They are flexible to various subjects, grade levels, and learning environments, making them a versatile solution for personalized education. The scalability of adaptive intelligence enables institutions to implement these systems on a large scale, benefiting a diverse student population. This adaptability signifies that adaptive learning can be seamlessly incorporated into various educational models, including traditional classroom settings, online learning environments, and blended learning environments (Jian, 2023). The scalability of these systems guarantees that personalized learning advantages are accessible to a broader demographic, enabling more students to access high-quality, customized education. In addition, the adaptability of these systems allows them to adapt to the evolving educational landscape, thereby offering sustainable and future-proof solutions (Sajja et al., 2023).

Risks

Despite the many benefits of adaptive intelligence, there is a significant risk of overreliance on technology at the expense of human interaction and critical thinking skills. Students may become excessively dependent on AI-driven systems, potentially diminishing their capacity to think independently and solve problems creatively. The danger is that technology may obscure the fundamental human components of education, including collaborative problem-solving, empathy, and interpersonal communication (Tiekstra & Minnaert, 2017). Balancing traditional teaching methods and adaptive intelligence is essential to reduce this risk. Educators should cultivate an environment that promotes the development of critical thinking and independent problem-solving in conjunction with technological tools rather than replacing the human aspects of learning (Akavova et al., 2023).

The extensive data acquisition necessary for adaptive intelligence raises significant privacy and security issues. It is imperative to safeguard student data from unauthorized access and ensure adherence to privacy regulations (Zang et al., 2022). To protect student information, institutions must establish transparent data governance policies and implement robust data security measures. This encompasses safeguarding data storage, managing access controls, and verifying data usage adherence to pertinent legal and ethical standards (Ferreira et al., 2017). A breach of data privacy has the potential to erode trust in adaptive learning systems and negatively impact students. To effectively address these concerns, it is imperative to maintain high data protection standards and consistently update security protocols (Liu et al., 2013).

The unequal distribution of technology infrastructure and resources among educational institutions can result in significant gaps in access to adaptive intelligence. Students in underfunded schools may not have the same opportunities to benefit from personalized learning technologies as their counterparts in well-resourced institutions (Walkington, 2013). This disparity can potentially exacerbate pre-existing educational inequalities, as students who do not have access to advanced technologies may fall further behind (Jing et al., 2023). To guarantee equitable access to adaptive learning aids, it is imperative to address these disparities. To address the resource divide, policymakers and educational leaders must allocate additional funding, resources, and support to underfunded schools. To foster inclusive and equitable educational opportunities, it is vital to guarantee that all students can access the advantages of adaptive intelligence (lonita Ciolacu et al., 2020).

Ongoing technical support and maintenance are necessary for adaptive learning systems to operate efficiently. To effectively manage and troubleshoot these systems, institutions must allocate resources and employ competent personnel (Almirall et al., 2018). This emphasizes the necessity of dependable support mechanisms to mitigate delays and guarantee seamless operation, as technical issues can disrupt the learning process. The efficacy of adaptive intelligence can be compromised without appropriate maintenance and support, resulting in frustration for educators and students (Capuano & Caballé, 2020). To effectively manage and maintain adaptive learning systems, institutions must prioritize the development of comprehensive technical support infrastructures and provide continuous staff training. To optimize the potential benefits of these systems, it is imperative to guarantee that they operate efficiently and are accessible to all users (Pfeiffer et al., 2021).

Future Directions

Future research should utilize robust methodologies and address specific questions and hypotheses to advance the field of adaptive intelligence in higher education. Comprehending the operational mechanisms of adaptive intelligence is one critical area. Future research should investigate the individual and collective enhancements of adaptive learning systems by various AI technologies, including natural language processing and machine learning. Comparative studies that employ controlled experiments in educational environments with the deployment of different AI technologies individually and in combination can quantify their influence on student engagement, retention, and academic performance. Furthermore, it is imperative to conduct longitudinal studies to examine the long-term effects of adaptive intelligence on students' critical thinking, creativity, and problem-solving abilities. These studies should employ standardized assessments and qualitative measures, such as portfolio evaluations and interviews, to evaluate students' progress over multiple academic terms.

Ethical considerations and bias mitigation are additional critical research areas. To identify strategies that effectively mitigate algorithmic bias and ensure ethical data use, studies should develop and test AI models with varying levels of transparency and dataset diversity. Analyzing outcomes for bias using statistical and machine learning fairness metrics and user studies is essential to evaluate the perceptions of fairness and ethical concerns among diverse student groups. It is also crucial to address infrastructure and accessibility challenges, especially for underfunded institutions. Through performance metrics, surveys, and focus groups, case studies on resource-sharing and funding initiatives can assess the efficacy of these strategies. Lastly, research should investigate how adaptive intelligence fosters lifelong learning among students and supports sustainable educational practices. It is possible to obtain valuable insights by designing and implementing adaptive learning modules that prioritize sustainability concepts and evaluating their influence on students' attitudes toward lifelong learning and sustainability through surveys, behavioral observations, and project-based evaluations. Future studies can contribute to the optimization, ethical integration, and comprehensive impact of adaptive intelligence in higher education by addressing these research questions and employing these methodologies, thereby nurturing more effective and inclusive educational practices.

CONCLUSION

Adaptation of adaptive intelligence into higher education shows a transition toward sustainable and individualized education. Building upon an extensive examination of academic literature, this chapter has explored its operational dynamics, effects on conventional learning, contributions to sustainability, and obstacles. Adaptive intelligence integrates human cognition with AI, which generates individualized learning trajectories by improving experiences via cognitive and technological components. This method transforms education by shifting from a standardized, one-size-fits-all structure to an individualized, interactive encounter that caters to the specific requirements of each student and promotes active participation. Furthermore, adaptable intelligence is paramount in fostering environmental consciousness, advancing sustainability in higher education, and cultivating a problem-solving orientation. It facilitates the incorporation of sustainability principles into the field of education, surpassing mere technological progress in its emphasis on comprehensive welfare and societal accountability.

REFERENCES

Akavova, A., Temirkhanova, Z., & Lorsanova, Z. (2023). Adaptive learning and artificial intelligence in the educational space. *E3S Web of Conferences, 451*, 06011.

Alkhawaldeh, M. A., & Khasawneh, M. A. S. (2023). Harnessing The Power of Artificial Intelligence for Personalized Assistive Technology in Learning Disabilities. *Journal of Southwest Jiaotong University*, 58(4). 10.35741/issn.0258-2724.58.4.60

Allen, M., Webb, A. W., & Matthews, C. E. (2016). Adaptive Teaching in STEM: Characteristics for Effectiveness. *Theory into Practice*, 55(3), 217–224. 10.1080/00405841.2016.1173994

Almirall, D., Kasari, C., McCaffrey, D. F., & Nahum-Shani, I. (2018). Developing optimized adaptive interventions in education. *Journal of Research on Educational Effectiveness*, 11(1), 27–34. 10.1080/19345747.2017.140713629552270

Apoki, U. C., Hussein, A. M. A., Al-Chalabi, H. K. M., Badica, C., & Mocanu, M. L. (2022). The role of pedagogical agents in personalised adaptive learning: A review. *Sustainability (Basel)*, 14(11), 6442. 10.3390/su14116442

Aquino, Y. S. J., Carter, S. M., Houssami, N., Braunack-Mayer, A., Win, K. T., Degeling, C., Wang, L., & Rogers, W. A. (2023). Practical, epistemic and normative implications of algorithmic bias in healthcare artificial intelligence: A qualitative study of multidisciplinary expert perspectives. *Journal of Medical Ethics*, jme-2022-108850. 10.1136/jme-2022-10885036823101

Baker, R. S., & Hawn, A. (2022). Algorithmic bias in education. *International Journal of Artificial Intelligence in Education*, 1–41.

Barth, M., & Rieckmann, M. (2012). Academic staff development as a catalyst for curriculum change towards education for sustainable development: An output perspective. *Journal of Cleaner Production*, 26, 28–36. 10.1016/j.jclepro.2011.12.011

Bozkurt, A., Karadeniz, A., Baneres, D., Guerrero-Roldán, A. E., & Rodríguez, M. E. (2021). Artificial intelligence and reflections from educational landscape: A review of AI Studies in half a century. *Sustainability (Basel)*, 13(2), 800. 10.3390/su13020800

Capuano, N., & Caballé, S. (2020). Adaptive learning technologies. *AI Magazine*, 41(2), 96–98. 10.1609/aimag.v41i2.5317

Chaplot, D. S., Rhim, E., & Kim, J. (2016). Personalized adaptive learning using neural networks. *Proceedings of the Third (2016) ACM Conference on Learning@ Scale*, (pp. 165–168). ACM. 10.1145/2876034.2893397

Chigbu, B. I., & Nekhwevha, F. H. (2022). Academic-faculty environment and graduate employability: Variation of work-readiness perceptions. *Heliyon*, 8(3), e09117. 10.1016/j.heliyon.2022.e0911735342827

Chigbu, B. I., Ngwevu, V., & Jojo, A. (2023). The effectiveness of innovative pedagogy in the industry 4.0: Educational ecosystem perspective. *Social Sciences & Humanities Open*, 7(1), 100419. 10.1016/j.ssaho.2023.100419

Corno, L. (2018). On Teaching Adaptively. *Educational Psychologist*, 43(3), 161–173. 10.1080/00461520802178466

Costa, R. S., Tan, Q., Pivot, F., Zhang, X., & Wang, H. (2021). Personalized and adaptive learning: Educational practice and technological impact. *Texto Livre*, 14(3), e33445. 10.35699/1983-3652.2021.33445

Demartini, C. G., Sciascia, L., Bosso, A., & Manuri, F. (2024). Artificial Intelligence Bringing Improvements to Adaptive Learning in Education: A Case Study. *Sustainability (Basel)*, 16(3), 1347. 10.3390/su16031347

Ferreira, H. N. M., Brant-Ribeiro, T., Araújo, R. D., Dorça, F. A., & Cattelan, R. G. (2017). An automatic and dynamic knowledge assessment module for adaptive educational systems. *2017 IEEE 17th International Conference on Advanced Learning Technologies (ICALT)*, (pp. 517–521). IEEE.

Fleury, A., Lughofer, E., Sayed Mouchaweh, M., Sayed, M., & Editorial, M. (2017). Editorial of the Special Issue: Adaptive and Intelligent Systems (AIS) for Learning, Control and Optimization in Dynamic Environments. *Evolving Systems*. Europea. https://ec.europa.eu/programmes/horizon2020/en/h2020-sections-projects

Gilbert, T. K., & Mintz, Y. (2019). Epistemic therapy for bias in automated decision-making. *Proceedings of the 2019 AAAI/ACM Conference on AI, Ethics, and Society*, (pp. 61–67). ACM. 10.1145/3306618.3314294

Graf, A. (2023). Exploring the role of personalization in adaptive learning environments. [IJSECS]. *International Journal Software Engineering and Computer Science*, 3(2), 50–56. 10.35870/ijsecs.v3i2.1200

Hoffmann, A. L., Roberts, S. T., Wolf, C. T., & Wood, S. (2018). Beyond fairness, accountability, and transparency in the ethics of algorithms: Contributions and perspectives from LIS. *Proceedings of the Association for Information Science and Technology*, 55(1), 694–696. 10.1002/pra2.2018.14505501084

Holmes, W., Porayska-Pomsta, K., Holstein, K., Sutherland, E., Baker, T., Shum, S. B., Santos, O. C., Rodrigo, M. T., Cukurova, M., Bittencourt, I. I., & Koedinger, K. R. (2022). Ethics of AI in education: Towards a community-wide framework. *International Journal of Artificial Intelligence in Education*, 32(3), 1–23. 10.1007/s40593-021-00239-1

Holstein, K., Aleven, V., & Rummel, N. (2020). A conceptual framework for human–AI hybrid adaptivity in education. *Lecture Notes in Computer Science (Including Subseries Lecture Notes in Artificial Intelligence and Lecture Notes in Bioinformatics), 12163 LNAI*, 240–254. 10.1007/978-3-030-52237-7_20

Ibrahim, M. S., & Hamada, M. (2016). Adaptive learning framework. *15th International Conference on Information Technology Based Higher Education and Training (ITHET)*. IEEE. 10.1109/ITHET.2016.7760738

Jian, M. (2023). Personalized learning through AI. *Advances in Engineering Innovation, 5*(1).

Jing, Y., Zhao, L., Zhu, K., Wang, H., Wang, C., & Xia, Q. (2023). Research landscape of adaptive learning in education: A bibliometric study on research publications from 2000 to 2022. *Sustainability (Basel)*, 15(4), 3115. 10.3390/su15043115

Johnson, C., & Zone, E. (2018). Achieving a Scaled Implementation of Adaptive Learning through Faculty Engagement: A Case Study. *Cuurent Issues in Emerging ELearning, 5*(1), 1–17. https://scholarworks.umb.edu/cieeAvailableat:https://scholarworks.umb.edu/ciee/vol5/iss1/7

Johnson, H., Mejia, M., & Cook, K. (2015). *Successful online courses in California's community colleges*. Public Policy Institute.

Krechetov, I., & Romanenko, V. (2020). Implementing the adaptive learning techniques. *Voprosy Obrazovaniya / Educational Studies Moscow, 2*, 252–277. 10.17323/1814-9545-2020-2-252-277

Leal Filho, W., Pallant, E., Enete, A., Richter, B., & Brandli, L. L. (2018). Planning and implementing sustainability in higher education institutions: An overview of the difficulties and potentials. *International Journal of Sustainable Development and World Ecology*, 25(8), 712–720. 10.1080/13504509.2018.1461707

Lesia Viktorivna, K., Andrii Oleksandrovych, V., Iryna Oleksandrivna, K., & Nadia Oleksandrivna, K. (2022). Artificial Intelligence in Language Learning: What Are We Afraid of. *Arab World English Journal*, 8(8), 262–273. 10.24093/awej/call8.18

Liu, C. M., Sun, Y. J., & Zhang, Y. (2013). The research and application of adaptive learning system in learning programs. *Applied Mechanics and Materials*, 347, 3109–3113. 10.4028/www.scientific.net/AMM.347-350.3109

Liu, H., Wang, T. H., Lin, H. C. K., Lai, C. F., & Huang, Y. M. (2022). The Influence of Affective Feedback Adaptive Learning System on Learning Engagement and Self-Directed Learning. *Frontiers in Psychology*, 13, 858411. 10.3389/fpsyg.2022.85841135572271

Liu, M., McKelroy, E., Corliss, S. B., & Carrigan, J. (2017). Investigating the effect of an adaptive learning intervention on students' learning. *Educational Technology Research and Development*, 65(6), 1605–1625. 10.1007/s11423-017-9542-1

Lonita Ciolacu, M., Tehrani, A. F., Svasta, P., Tache, I., & Stoichescu, D. (2020). Education 4.0: an adaptive framework with artificial intelligence, raspberry Pi and wearables-innovation for creating value. *2020 IEEE 26th International Symposium for Design and Technology in Electronic Packaging (SIITME)*, (pp. 298–303). IEEE.

Mirata, V., Hirt, F., Bergamin, P., & van der Westhuizen, C. (2020). Challenges and contexts in establishing adaptive learning in higher education: Findings from a Delphi study. *International Journal of Educational Technology in Higher Education*, 17(1), 32. 10.1186/s41239-020-00209-y

Mitsopoulos, K., Somers, S., Schooler, J., Lebiere, C., Pirolli, P., & Thomson, R. (2022). Toward a Psychology of Deep Reinforcement Learning Agents Using a Cognitive Architecture. *Topics in Cognitive Science*, 14(4), 756–779. 10.1111/tops.1257334467649

Mittelstadt, B. D., Allo, P., Taddeo, M., Wachter, S., & Floridi, L. (2016). The ethics of algorithms: Mapping the debate. *Big Data & Society*, 3(2). 10.1177/2053951716679679

Peng, H., Ma, S., & Spector, J. M. (2019). Personalized adaptive learning: An emerging pedagogical approach enabled by a smart learning environment. *Smart Learning Environments*, 6(1), 1–14. 10.1186/s40561-019-0089-y

Pfeiffer, A., Bezzina, S., Dingli, A., Wernbacher, T., Denk, N., & Fleischhacker, M. (2021). Adaptive LEARNING and assessment: From the TEACHERS' PERSPECTIVE. *INTED2021 Proceedings*, (pp. 375–379). IEEE.

Popenici, S. A. D., & Kerr, S. (2017). Exploring the impact of artificial intelligence on teaching and learning in higher education. *Research and Practice in Technology Enhanced Learning*, 12(1), 22. 10.1186/s41039-017-0062-830595727

Purita, R., & Tesene, M. (2023). *Adaptive Courseware for Early Success Case Study: Cleveland State University*. Every Learner Everywhere. https://www.everylearnereverywhere.org/resources/adaptive-courseware-for-early-success-case-study-cleveland-state-university/

Regan, P. M., & Jesse, J. (2018). Ethical challenges of edtech, big data and personalized learning: Twenty-first century student sorting and tracking. *Ethics and Information Technology*, 21(3), 167–179. 10.1007/s10676-018-9492-2

Rizvi, M. (2023). Exploring the landscape of artificial intelligence in education: Challenges and opportunities. *2023 5th International Congress on Human-Computer Interaction, Optimization and Robotic Applications (HORA)*, (pp. 1–3). ResearchGate.

Sajja, R., Sermet, Y., Cikmaz, M., Cwiertny, D., & Demir, I. (2023). Artificial Intelligence-Enabled Intelligent Assistant for Personalized and Adaptive Learning in Higher Education. *ArXiv Preprint ArXiv:2309.10892*.

Sallam, M. (2023). ChatGPT Utility in Healthcare Education, Research, and Practice: Systematic Review on the Promising Perspectives and Valid Concerns. In *Healthcare (Switzerland)*, 11(6). MDPI. 10.3390/healthcare11060887

Shemshack, A., Kinshuk, , & Spector, J. M. (2021). A comprehensive analysis of personalized learning components. *Journal of Computers in Education*, 8(4), 485–503. 10.1007/s40692-021-00188-7

Shi, L., Cristea, A. I., Hadzidedic, S., & Dervishalidovic, N. (2014). Contextual Gamification of Social Interaction-Towards Increasing Motivation in Social E-Learning. *Lecture Notes in Computer Science*, 8613, 116–122. 10.1007/978-3-319-09635-3_12

Srivastava, S., & Sinha, K. (2023). From Bias to Fairness: A Review of Ethical Considerations and Mitigation Strategies in Artificial Intelligence. *International Journal for Research in Applied Science and Engineering Technology*, 2(3), 2247–2251. 10.22214/ijraset.2023.49990

Sternberg, R. J. (2019). A theory of adaptive intelligence and its relation to general intelligence. *Journal of Intelligence*, 7(4), 23. 10.3390/jintelligence704002331581505

Sternberg, R. J. (2021). Adaptive intelligence: Its nature and implications for education. *Education Sciences*, 11(12), 823. 10.3390/educsci11120823

Taylor, D. L., Yeung, M., & Bashet, A. Z. (2021). Personalized and adaptive learning. In *Innovative learning environments in STEM higher education: Opportunities, Challenges, and Looking Forward* (Switzaland, pp. 17–34). Springer International Publishing. 10.1007/978-3-030-58948-6_2

Tejedor, G., Segalàs, J., Barrón, Á., Fernández-Morilla, M., Fuertes, M. T., Ruiz-Morales, J., Gutiérrez, I., García-González, E., Aramburuzabala, P., & Hernández, À. (2019). Didactic strategies to promote competencies in sustainability. *Sustainability (Basel)*, 11(7), 2086. 10.3390/su11072086

Tian, B., Wang, C., & Hong, H. (2023). A Survey of Personalized Adaptive Learning System. *2023 2nd International Conference on Artificial Intelligence and Computer Information Technology (AICIT)*, (pp. 1–6). ACM.

Tilbury, D. (2004). Environmental education for sustainability: A force for change in higher education. In *Higher education and the challenge of sustainability: Problematics, promise, and practice* (pp. 97–112). Springer Netherlands. 10.1007/0-306-48515-X_9

Tomiyama, T. (2007). Intelligent computer-aided design systems: Past 20 years and future 20 years. *Artificial Intelligence for Engineering Design, Analysis and Manufacturing*, 21(1), 27–29. 10.1017/S0890060407070114

Vignare, K., Tesene, M., & Lorenzo, G. (2020). *Case Study Arizona State University (ASU)*. Every Learner Everywhere. www.everylearnereverywhere.org/resources/case-study-arizona-state-university-asu/

Walkington, C. A. (2013). Using adaptive learning technologies to personalize instruction to student interests: The impact of relevant contexts on performance and learning outcomes. *Journal of Educational Psychology*, 105(4), 932–945. 10.1037/a0031882

Wang, S., Christensen, C., Cui, W., Tong, R., Yarnall, L., Shear, L., & Feng, M. (2023). When adaptive learning is effective learning: Comparison of an adaptive learning system to teacher-led instruction. *Interactive Learning Environments*, 31(2), 793–803. 10.1080/10494820.2020.1808794

Wei, L. (2023). Artificial intelligence in language instruction: Impact on English learning achievement, L2 motivation, and self-regulated learning. *Frontiers in Psychology*, 14, 1261955. 10.3389/fpsyg.2023.126195538023040

Xie, H., Chu, H.-C., Hwang, G.-J., & Wang, C.-C. (2019). Trends and development in technology-enhanced adaptive/personalized learning: A systematic review of journal publications from 2007 to 2017. *Computers & Education*, 140, 103599. 10.1016/j.compedu.2019.103599

Zang, J., Gowthami, J., & Anilkumar, C. (2022). Adaptive Artificial Intelligent Technique to Improve Acquisition of Knowledge in the Educational Environment. *Journal of Interconnection Networks*, 22(Supp02), 2143013. 10.1142/S0219265921430131

Zhou, L., Zhang, F., Zhang, S., & Xu, M. (2021). Study on the personalized learning model of learner-learning resource matching. *International Journal of Information and Education Technology (IJIET)*, 11(3), 143–147. 10.18178/ijiet.2021.11.3.1503

KEY TERMS AND DEFINITIONS

Adaptive Intelligence: The merger of human cognition with AI to develop individualized learning experiences in higher education. It entails the utilization of AI technology, such as data analytics, machine learning algorithms, and natural language processing, to process data and personalize instructional content in real-time.

Artificial Intelligence: The replication of human cognitive processes through technologies, particularly computer systems. It consists of self-correction, thinking, and learning.

Data Analytics: The process of examining datasets to draw conclusions about the information they contain. In the context of adaptive intelligence, it involves analyzing educational data to optimize learning experiences.

Ethical Considerations: Aspects of bias, privacy, fairness, and openness that concern the implementation of AI algorithms in education.

Machine Learning Algorithms: Self-learning systems are a subtype of AI that acquire knowledge and improve over time without requiring explicit programming.

Natural Language Processing (NLP): An area of AI that assists computers in comprehending, interpreting, and manipulating human language.

Pedagogical Adaptation: The adaptive intelligence-enabled iterative modification of teaching tactics in response to student feedback and real-time data.

Personalized Learning Pathways: Personalized educational pathways that are designed to suit the profiles, preferences, and requirements of each learner, made possible by adaptive intelligence.

Sustainability in Higher Education: The integration of environmental, social, and economic considerations into educational practices to promote holistic well-being and responsible citizenship.

Symbiotic Relationship: A cooperative interaction between AI and human cognition in adaptive intelligence, where both elements enhance each other's capabilities.

Chapter 7
From Compliance to Transformation:
Jain University's Journey With the NEP

Patcha Bhujanga Rao
https://orcid.org/0000-0003-4736-8497
Jain University (Deemed), India

ABSTRACT

This abstract explores the transformative journey of Jain deemed-to-be university (JDTBU) in alignment with the National Education Policy (NEP) of India. JDTBU initially transitioned from compliance to transformation, adhering to NEP guidelines through curriculum revisions and fostering interdisciplinary learning and skill development. Recognizing the NEP's transformative potential, JDTBU embraced a holistic and innovative learning environment by implementing collaborative and experiential learning approaches to cultivate critical thinking and creativity in students. This transformation further involved faculty development initiatives focused on student engagement and technology integration, alongside research and industry partnerships to enhance the practical relevance of learning outcomes. JDTBU's commitment to continuous improvement ensures ongoing alignment with NEP objectives, aiming to create a learning ecosystem that promotes innovation, social responsibility, and lifelong learning.

DOI: 10.4018/979-8-3693-3559-8.ch007

INTRODUCTION

While rote learning dominated the education landscape for decades, the National Education Policy (NEP) 2020 is a beacon of change. This groundbreaking initiative aims to promote a paradigm shift by emphasizing holistic development and critical thinking, equipping students with the tools they need to thrive in the dynamic 21st century. The NEP recognizes the changing needs of a globalized world and emphasizes inclusion and flexibility in education to pave the way for a vibrant knowledge society. Known for its commitment to academic excellence, Jain Deemed-to-be University has become a pioneer in adopting NEP. The University's unwavering commitment goes beyond mere compliance to a proactive and transformative approach. This article delves into the nature of the NEP and highlights its core principles and objectives. It further highlights the transformative journey of the future Jain University and showcases its unique strategies and unwavering commitment towards achieving the NEP vision. By exploring this case study, we aim to inspire other educational institutions to embark on their transformative journeys and foster a collaborative ecosystem that leads India's education landscape towards a brighter future.

BACKGROUND OF NEP AND ITS SIGNIFICANCE

NEP 2020 marks a comprehensive review of India's education framework after three decades and envisages a system based on equity, quality, accessibility, and inclusion. The emphasis is on flexibility, creativity, critical thinking, and experiential learning to develop well-rounded individuals who can navigate the complexities of the modern world. This paradigm shift toward holistic development is evident in its focus on early childhood care, technology integration, vocational training, and a multidisciplinary approach that addresses the diverse needs of students across the socioeconomic spectrum.

FUTURE JAIN UNIVERSITY COMMITMENT TO NEP

Future Jain University embodies the spirit of NEP through its unwavering commitment to holistic development, innovation, and social responsibility. Building on its decades-long legacy of academic excellence, the University is actively reorienting its pedagogical practices, curriculum design, and research efforts to adopt the core principles of the NEP. By promoting a culture of innovation, interdisciplinary collaboration, and lifelong learning, the aim is to train future-ready professionals capable of driving positive change in society. Through strategic partnerships, community engagement initiatives, and faculty development programs, the future Jain Deemed University strives to be a catalyst for educational transformation that is perfectly aligned with the vision of the NEP.

REVIEW OF LITERATURE

The review of literature provides a comprehensive understanding of Jain Deemed-to-be University's transition under the National Education Policy (NEP) 2020, drawing insights from academic studies, institutional practices, and strategic reports. Various scholarly works underscore the significance of sustainable education quality improvement and accreditation practices, emphasizing institutional commitment and stakeholder involvement (Almurayh et al., 2022). Additionally, research highlights the benefits of a systematic, process-based approach to accreditation in fostering continuous improvement and quality assurance (Almuhaideb and Saeed, 2021). Sustainable assessment practices aligned with industry standards are essential for program quality enhancement (Saeed et al., 2021). Moreover, a focus on clear learning outcomes, robust assessment tools, and continuous improvement is crucial for fostering sustainable quality assurance practices (Almuhaideb and Saeed, 2020).

Systematic assessment of student outcomes significantly enhances program quality and student performance, providing a comprehensive methodology for achieving educational goals (Shafi et al., 2019). Predictive analytics and early intervention strategies contribute to improving the learning experience by identifying at-risk students early on (Gull et al., 2020). Addressing challenges such as plagiarism and ensuring academic integrity are vital aspects of sustaining educational quality (Saeed, Aamir, and Ramzan, 2011).

Government reports and academic studies outline the foundational principles and strategic vision of NEP 2020, emphasizing innovation, quality enhancement, and the alignment of institutional goals with NEP directives (Government of India, 2020; Dr. S. Rajasekar, 2020). Institutions like Jain University are proactively implementing NEP guidelines, particularly focusing on curriculum reform and faculty development (Jain University Annual Report, 2021-2022). Educational transformation under NEP extends beyond compliance, emphasizing innovation, holistic development, and interdisciplinary learning (Dr. A. Kumar, 2021).

Recent literature reflects evolving administrative and academic structures in alignment with NEP directives, emphasizing interdisciplinary learning and flexible curricula (AIU Report, 2022). Progress across states and institutions, particularly in digital infrastructure and inclusive education practices, is noted in government reports and strategic reviews (Ministry of Education Annual Review, 2022). Stakeholder perspectives emphasize the importance of public-private partnerships, blended learning models, and continuous professional development for educators (CII, 2021; Coursera Report, 2020; UNESCO, 2020; British Council, 2021).

In summary, Jain University's journey under NEP 2020 is informed by a rich tapestry of academic research, institutional practices, and strategic insights. The integration of diverse perspectives and ongoing adaptation to global educational trends underscore the institution's commitment to excellence and transformation in higher education.

FROM COMPLIANCE TO TRANSFORMATION: JAIN DEEMED-TO-BE UNIVERSITY'S JOURNEY WITH THE NEP

As higher education institutions are committed to excellence, Jain Deemed-to-be University recognizes the importance of staying abreast of the latest advancements in the sphere of education. The National Education Policy (NEP) has provided a roadmap for the transformation of India's education system, and Jain Deemed-to-be University has been proactive in its efforts to comply with the guidelines set forth in the policy.

The institution has set out on a path of change, beginning with a critical analysis of its current policies, programmes, and instructional strategies. To make ensuring that the university's initiatives are in accordance with the goals of the NEP, this process has comprised talks with a variety of stakeholders, including faculty members, students, and industry experts.

The emphasis on multidisciplinary learning and skill development is one of Jain Deemed-to-be University's primary areas of interest. To encourage students to study other fields and develop a wide skill set, the institution is aiming to establish a more holistic learning environment. The goal of this strategy is to encourage creativity and invention, two qualities that are necessary for success in the quickly evolving world of today.

Jain Deemed-to-be University is steadfast in its commitment to giving its students an engaging and life-changing educational experience even as it advances along its path to NEP compliance. The institution is making a major contribution to reshaping Indian education and training its students to be global citizens capable of navigating the difficulties of the twenty-first century by proactively implementing the NEP's suggestions.

Alignment With NEP Guidelines

Jain Deemed-to-be University has made a concerted effort to adhere to the National Education Policy (NEP) regulations. To provide a seamless transition from compliance to transformation, the institution has been working hard to match its rules, courses, and instructional strategies with the suggestions made in the NEP.

Review of Policies, Curricula, and Teaching Methodologies

To ensure full compliance with the NEP criteria, Jain Deemed-to-be University has reviewed all of its current rules, courses, and instructional strategies. To make that the university's plans align with the NEP's goals, this process has featured stakeholder meetings with academics, students, and business professionals.

Emphasis on Interdisciplinary Learning and Skill Development

The focus on interdisciplinary learning and skill development is a crucial part of Jain Deemed-to-be University's NEP compliance strategy. The institution has been making efforts to develop a more all-encompassing learning environment that inspires students to experiment with different fields of study and develop a wide range of skills. It is anticipated that this strategy would encourage creativity and invention, both of which are necessary for success in the quickly evolving world of today.

Adoption of Technology-Enabled Teaching and Learning

The use of technology-enabled teaching and learning strategies is a crucial component of Jain Deemed-to-be University's compliance with the NEP standards. In order to support digital education projects including online courses, virtual laboratories, and interactive learning platforms, the institution has been investing in infrastructure and resources. Jain Deemed-to-be University hopes to improve the standard of education delivery and give students flexible, individualized learning opportunities by utilizing technology.

Continuous Professional Development for Faculty

Jain Deemed-to-be University has redesigned its policies and courses and placed a high priority on the ongoing professional development of its professors. To keep faculty members informed about best practices in teaching, evaluation, and research, the university often hosts seminars, workshops, and training sessions. The objective of Jain Deemed-to-be University is to provide a dynamic learning environment that fosters brilliance and innovation by investing in the growth and development of its teachers.

Student-Centric Approach to Education

Student-centricity is one of the fundamental tenets that underpin Jain Deemed-to-be University's journey with the NEP. The institution is dedicated to offering a welcoming and inclusive learning environment where students are motivated to follow their hobbies and interests and take charge of their education. To enable students to become effective members of society and lifelong learners, Jain Deemed-to-be University cultivates an environment of curiosity, critical thinking, and self-directed learning.

JOURNEY TOWARDS TRANSFORMATION

Vision for a Holistic and Innovative Learning Environment

Set to embark on a transformative journey, Jain Deemed-to-be University has a clear vision for an inventive and comprehensive learning environment. This vision's primary objective is to offer a warm, diverse, and supportive atmosphere that supports students' academic, social, and personal growth while equipping them to meet the challenges of the twenty-first-century workforce.

JAIN has always been an aspirational institution, creative and progressive in its thinking, and has had a laudable journey of transformation since inception, with its dreams to excel in the years to come. Figure 1 illustrates Jain Deemed-to-be University's transformative journey, characterized by its aspirational nature, creativity, and progressive thinking since its inception.

Figure 1. Jain deemed-to-be university's transformative journey

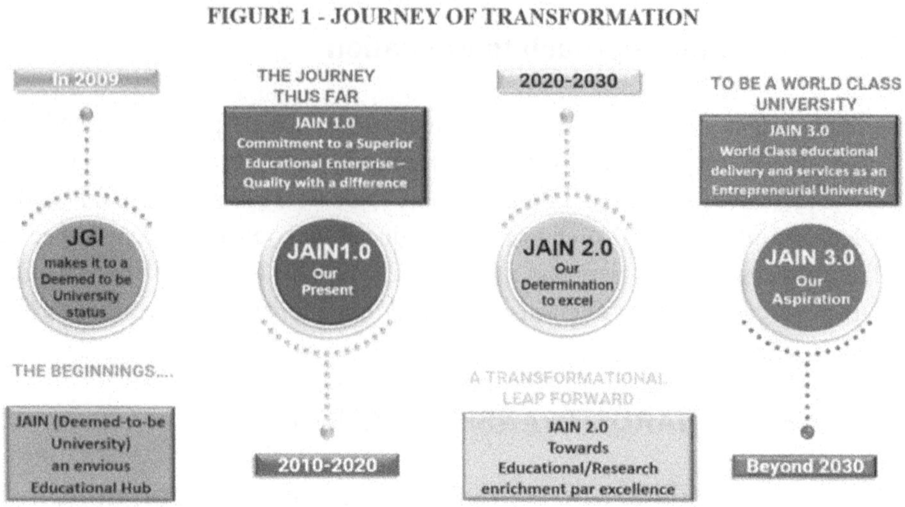

FIGURE 1 - JOURNEY OF TRANSFORMATION

- In 2009 — JGI makes it to a Deemed to be University status — THE BEGINNINGS.... — JAIN (Deemed-to-be University) an envious Educational Hub
- THE JOURNEY THUS FAR — JAIN 1.0 Commitment to a Superior Educational Enterprise – Quality with a difference — JAIN 1.0 Our Present — 2010-2020
- 2020-2030 — JAIN 2.0 Our Determination to excel — A TRANSFORMATIONAL LEAP FORWARD — JAIN 2.0 Towards Educational/Research enrichment par excellence
- TO BE A WORLD CLASS UNIVERSITY — JAIN 3.0 World Class educational delivery and services as an Entrepreneurial University — JAIN 3.0 Our Aspiration — Beyond 2030

(https://www.jainuniversity.ac.in/academics/nep)

Innovative Teaching Methods and Pedagogies

To promote an all-encompassing and innovative learning environment, the institution has been researching and implementing a range of cutting-edge teaching methods and pedagogies. Problem-based learning, blended learning, flipped classrooms, and collaborative learning are a few of these strategies. By applying these teaching practices, the institution wants to provide students with an educational experience that is more engaging and dynamic.

Collaborative Learning and Project-Based Assessments

Believed-to-be Promoting project-based assessments and collaborative learning is a key component of the university's transformation, the institution invites students to work together on difficult projects to hone their teamwork, communication, and problem-solving skills in order to better equip them for success in the contemporary profession.

Experiential Learning Opportunities for Students

The university has been working to provide its students with a variety of possibilities for experiential learning, such as research projects, industry partnerships, internships, and study abroad programmes. Students benefit from these experiences in terms of expanding their professional networks, getting practical experience, and learning more about the fields they have chosen.

Nurturing Creativity, Critical Thinking, and Problem-Solving Skills

Jain Deemed-to-be University is dedicated to nurturing creativity, critical thinking, and problem-solving skills in its students. The institution believes that these skills are crucial for students to thrive in an ever-changing world and to contribute positively to society. As part of its transformation process, the university is committed to incorporating activities and assessments that foster the development of these essential skills.

Technology Integration and Digital Literacy

Technology integration and the advancement of digital literacy among students are highly valued aspects of Jain Deemed-to-be University's dedication to offering a comprehensive and cutting-edge learning environment. The institution makes use of a range of instructional technologies to improve student learning and teaching, get students ready for the digital needs of the workforce, and encourage lifelong learning in an increasingly digital society.

Supportive Learning Environment and Student Well-Being

The emphasis on fostering a caring and supportive setting that puts students' well-being first is fundamental to the idea of a holistic learning environment. In order to provide students, the tools they need to succeed intellectually, physically, and emotionally, Jain Deemed-to-be University is committed to offering extensive support services, mental health resources, and wellness activities. The institution hopes to provide a happy, welcoming environment where all students feel supported and appreciated by putting a strong emphasis on student well-being.

From Compliance to Transformation

Continuous Professional Development for Faculty

For the university to fulfil its promise of innovation in teaching and learning, faculty members must engage in ongoing professional development. Jain Deemed-to-be University makes an investment in giving faculty members the chance to pursue research and pedagogical innovations, improve their teaching abilities, and remain up to date on new developments in education. Through funding faculty professional development, the institution makes sure that its instructors are prepared to provide creative, high-quality training that adapts to students' changing requirements.

Faculty Development With the 4E Iterative Model

The provided information (Figure 2) outlines the existing faculty development initiatives, using the 4E iterative model to create a continuous improvement process:

Figure 2. 4e iterative model of 'in house' faculty development

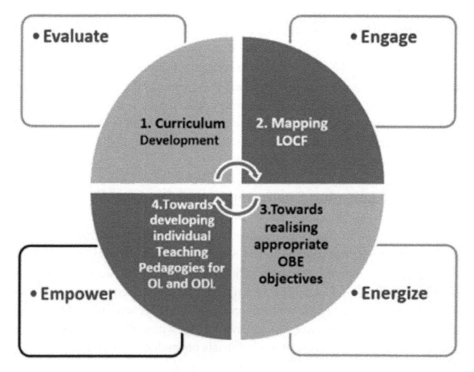

(https://www.jainuniversity.ac.in/academics/nep)

To ensure faculty development programs effectively meet educators' needs, Jain University can implement a cyclical approach. First, an "Engage" phase gathers faculty input through surveys and discussions to identify gaps between current programs and desired outcomes. Measurable learning goals are then set based on this data. The "Explore" phase involves researching best practices and collaborating with stakeholders to design the program. This could include workshops, mentoring, and online modules. Next, the "Experiment" phase pilots the program with a smaller group, collecting feedback and assessing its impact. Finally, the "Evaluate" phase uses this data to refine the program, ensuring its effectiveness and long-term sustainability. This cyclical approach allows Jain University to continuously improve its faculty development initiatives and empower educators with the skills needed to excel in the NEP era.

Integrating Existing Initiatives

The existing training programs like Learning Outcomes-based Curriculum Framework (LOCF) LOCF & Choice Based Credit System (CBCS) implementation, Teaching-Learning and Evaluation Plans (TLEP) development, and Relative Grading System (RGS) training can be incorporated into the 4E model. This fosters a deeper understanding and application of the learned skills by providing opportunities for experimentation and reflection.

Stakeholder Engagement and Partnerships

Jain Deemed-To-Be The university values cooperation and relationships with a variety of stakeholders, such as industry partners, alumni, community groups, and government agencies. By interacting with these stakeholders, the institution improves students' learning experiences, enhances real-world linkages, and fosters experiential learning and research partnerships. These relationships also assist the institution in being relevant and responsive to the requirements of the larger community and industry, ensuring that its programs remain creative and connected with current trends and expectations.

OBJECTIVES OF THE STUDY

The study objectives aim to:
1. Evaluate the progress and challenges of National Education Policy (NEP) implementation across demographic factors such as age and occupation.

2. Investigate generational differences in adapting to NEP changes and analyze perceptions among different age groups.
3. Examine participant views and experiences regarding NEP's transformative goals, considering gender-related differences.
4. Analyze perspectives of individuals with diverse educational backgrounds to uncover variations in understanding and expectations of the NEP.
5. Identify strategies and best practices for successful NEP implementation based on experiences of faculty members across different designation levels within the university structure.

SCOPE AND LIMITATIONS

This chapter provides a comprehensive overview of the National Education Policy (NEP) and Jain Deemed University's involvement in its implementation while acknowledging the limitations arising from the complexity of the NEP. While we focus primarily on the Jain University perspective here, a more in-depth examination of specific aspects of the NEP (e.g. grade reform) could be discussed in later publications. We hope this chapter stimulates dialogue, promotes collaboration, and catalyzes collective action for holistic implementation of the NEP to improve India's education ecosystem.

METHODOLOGY

Problem Statement and Research Gap

Building upon the broader understanding of the National Education Policy (NEP) and its potential impact on higher education institutions, this study delves into the specific case of Jain Deemed-to-Be University. While research exists on the NEP's implementation, there is a paucity focusing on the lived experiences of educational institutions, particularly the challenges faced and the strategies adopted to navigate the transformation process. This study aims to address the following research gaps:
1. **Limited research on lived experiences:** While some studies explore the NEP's implementation, there is a paucity of research focusing on the experiences of educational institutions, particularly the challenges faced and the strategies adopted to navigate the transformation process.

2. **Underrepresented stakeholder perspectives:** A comprehensive understanding of the NEP's implementation requires insights from various stakeholders, including faculty, and administrators. However, current research often fails to capture the diverse perspectives of these groups.
3. **Inadequate analysis of success factors:** While broad discussions about the NEP exist, a deeper analysis of the factors that contribute to a successful transition from compliance to transformation, specifically within the context of Jain Deemed-to-Be University, is lacking.
4. **Absence of humanized accounts:** The current research landscape surrounding the NEP's implementation is dominated by formal reports and studies. This study aims to bridge this gap by incorporating humanized accounts that provide insights into the personal experiences and viewpoints of stakeholders during the implementation process.

Addressing these gaps will offer a richer understanding of the NEP's implementation process from the perspectives of those directly involved. This, in turn, can contribute to the development of best practices and recommendations that can support a smoother and more successful transformation journey for other higher education institutions.

Research Design and Approach

This study employs a case study approach, focusing on Jain Deemed-to-Be University's journey with the National Education Policy (NEP) Change Process (CHP). This approach allows for an in-depth examination of the university's transformation process, its challenges, and the strategies employed to adapt to the new policy. The case study approach is particularly suitable for understanding complex phenomena within their real-life context (Yin, 2015). This in-depth exploration aims to achieve the following research objectives:

1. To investigate the progress and challenges faced by Jain Deemed-to-Be University in implementing the NEP.
2. To explore the views and experiences of students, teachers, and administrators in navigating the transition from compliance to transformation.
3. To identify strategies and best practices that can be implemented to support a successful transformation process.

Data Collection Methods

To gain a comprehensive understanding of Jain Deemed-to-Be University's experience with the NEP CHP, a triangulation of data collection methods was employed:

Document analysis: University documents and policies related to the NEP CHP were analyzed to gain insights into the university's official approach and strategies for implementation. These documents were accessed primarily through the university's official website and internal repository.

Semi-structured interviews: These interviews were conducted with key stakeholders, including administrators, faculty members, and students, to gather their in-depth perspectives on the transformation process, their experiences, and their viewpoints on the challenges and opportunities encountered.

Focus groups: Discussions with faculty focus groups were held to explore shared experiences, opinions, and concerns related to the NEP implementation, fostering a deeper understanding of their collective perspectives. These focus groups were facilitated on campus depending on feasibility and participant comfort levels.

Participant Selection and Sample Size

Participants were selected using purposive sampling to ensure a diverse range of perspectives and experiences were captured on the NEP implementation at Jain Deemed-to-Be University. This approach targeted individuals with direct involvement or relevant knowledge of the NEP Change Process (CHP). For instance, administrators involved in developing and implementing the university's CHP strategy were prioritized for interviews. Similarly, faculty members from various departments and students from diverse programs were selected to capture a variety of experiences.

The sample size for interviews and focus groups was determined using a saturation approach. This means data collection continued until no new themes or insights emerged from the conversations. This iterative process ensured a comprehensive understanding of the university's journey with the NEP.

Data Analysis Techniques

Qualitative data analysis techniques were employed to analyze the collected data from document analysis, semi-structured interviews, and focus groups. These techniques were chosen to address the research objectives outlined in Section 7.2 as follows:

Thematic analysis: This method has been employed to identify, analyze, and interpret recurring themes and patterns within the data related to the university's journey with the NEP CHP. This analysis directly addresses Objective 1 (investigating progress and challenges) by identifying key themes related to both successes and challenges faced by Jain Deemed-to-Be University during the implementation process. Additionally, it will contribute to achieving Objective 2 (exploring stakeholder perspectives) by analyzing recurring themes across stakeholder groups (administrators, and faculty) to understand their lived experiences and diverse viewpoints.

Content analysis: This analysis focuses on examining university documents and policies related to the NEP CHP to identify key elements, changes, and underlying assumptions embedded within these documents. This directly addresses Objective 3 (identifying best practices) by helping to identify the university's official strategies and planned approaches for implementing the NEP. Analyzing the content of these documents provides insights into the university's underlying goals and perspectives regarding the transformation process.

Structural analysis: The researcher focusses on examining the relationships between different components of the university's transformation process and their impact on the overall Change Process. This analysis contributes to achieving all three research objectives. By examining the interconnectedness of various initiatives, strategies, and stakeholder roles, it can shed light on the complexities of the transformation process (Objective 1), the diverse experiences of stakeholders navigating these interconnected elements (Objective 2), and potentially reveals the best practices or areas for improvement in the university's approach (Objective 3).

Ethical Considerations

Ethical considerations were carefully taken into account throughout the research process. The researcher obtained informed consent from all participants before conducting interviews or collecting any data. Participants were assured of confidentiality, and their identities were kept anonymous in the study to protect their privacy. Any sensitive information shared during interviews was handled with discretion and sensitivity.

Furthermore, the researcher adhered to ethical guidelines concerning data management and storage to ensure the security and integrity of the collected data. Any potential conflicts of interest were disclosed, and ethical approval was obtained from the relevant institutional review board before commencing the study.

Limitations of the Study

Despite the rigorous methodology employed in this study, acknowledging these limitations is essential for interpreting the study's results and understanding. These include:
1. The study's focus on a single institution may limit the generalizability of the findings to other higher education contexts.
2. The reliance on self-reported data from interviews may introduce bias or subjectivity in the findings.

3. Time and resource constraints may have limited the depth of data collection and analysis.

ANALYSIS

With a focus on qualitative analysis, this study aims to unravel the multifaceted dimensions of JDTBU's response to the NEP, shedding light on the intricacies of its implementation process. Through rigorous analysis of interviews, focus group discussions, and document reviews, this seeks to unearth emergent themes, patterns, and insights that encapsulate the essence of JDTBU's journey toward NEP alignment.

By immersing into the data gathered from diverse stakeholders, including administrators and faculty members the analysis endeavors to offer a comprehensive understanding of the challenges encountered, successes achieved, and strategies employed by JDTBU in navigating the NEP landscape. Moreover, through content analysis of university documents and policies, this aims to discern the institutional frameworks and approaches adopted by JDTBU to realize NEP objectives.

The meticulous data analysis aims to contribute valuable insights in the form of educational practices, policy formulation, and institutional strategies, ultimately fostering a culture of innovation, inclusivity, and excellence within the higher education ecosystem.

Demographic Characteristics of Participants

Table 1 provides an overview of the demographic characteristics of the participants involved in the study. Understanding the demographic composition of the sample is crucial for contextualizing the findings and assessing the representativeness of the study population. The table 1 includes information such as age, gender, educational background, and any other relevant demographic variables collected during the research process. These characteristics help researchers and readers understand the diversity and composition of the sample, which may influence the interpretation and generalizability of the study results.

Table 1. Demographic characteristics of participants

Demographic Factor	Respondents	%
Age		
Upto 30	62	16.1
31-40	182	47.4

continued on following page

Table 1. Continued

Demographic Factor	Respondents	%
41-50	105	27.3
50 & Above	35	9.1
Total	**384**	**100**
Gender		
Male	189	49.2
Female	195	50.8
Total	**384**	**100**
Education Level		
Post Graduate	134	34.9
Professional	39	10.2
Ph.D.	211	54.9
Total	**384**	**100**
Occupation		
Teaching/Administration	51	13.3
Teaching	333	86.7
Total	**384**	**100**
Designation		
Asst. Prof	257	66.9
Asso. Prof	62	16.1
Professor	29	7.6
Area Head	36	9.4
Total	**384**	**100**
Marital Status		
Bachelor	79	20.6
Married	305	79.4
Total	**384**	**100**

Demographics and Research Focus in JDTBU's NEP Implementation Study

The demographic data (N=384) enriches this research by allowing analysis of participant characteristics and potential variations in findings:

Progress & Challenges (Objective 1):

Age: Younger faculty (16.1%, under 30) might adapt faster to the NEP's digital aspects, while older faculty (9.1%, over 50) might require additional support.

Occupation: Teaching staff (86.7% teaching, 13.3% teaching/administration) might face challenges adapting curriculum and integrating technology, while administrators might struggle with policy implementation and resource allocation.

Views & Experiences (Objective 2):

Gender: Analyzing experiences of male (49.2%) and female (50.8%) participants can reveal gender-based variations in engagement with the NEP's goals.

Education Level: Individuals with Ph.D.s (54.9%) might have different expectations for research opportunities compared to those with postgraduate (34.9%) or professional degrees (10.2%).

Strategies & Best Practices (Objective 3):

Designation: Assistant professors (66.9%) might require different support compared to professors (7.6%). Area heads (9.4%) might face unique challenges in curriculum development within their disciplines.

This demographic analysis allows researchers to tailor strategies and best practices for a successful NEP transformation at JDTBU, considering the diverse needs and experiences within the university.

Table 2. Awareness of NEP components

NEP Component	Respondents (%)	Male (%)	Female (%)
Curriculum Reforms	75	40	35
Pedagogical Approaches	68	33	35
Research and Innovation	82	45	37
Inclusivity and Diversity	63	29	34
Industry Integration	70	38	32
Assessment and Evaluation	72	37	35
Outcomes-Based Skill Dev.	78	41	37
Infrastructure & Technology	67	32	35

Interpretation:

The table depicts the awareness levels among respondents regarding various components of the National Education Policy (NEP), segmented by gender. Among respondents, 75% are aware of curriculum reforms, with a slightly higher awareness among males (40%) compared to females (35%). Pedagogical approaches are recognized by 68% of respondents, with females (35%) slightly more aware than males (33%). The emphasis on research and innovation is well-known, with 82% of respondents aware, notably higher among males (45%) than females (37%). Inclusivity and diversity measures are recognized by 63% of respondents, with females (34%) slightly more aware than males (29%). Industry integration and assessment practices are acknowledged by 70% and 72% of respondents, respectively, with slightly higher awareness levels among males. Outcomes-based skill development is recognized by 78% of respondents, with a slightly higher awareness among males (41%) than females (37%). Infrastructure and technology focus are known to 67% of respondents, with females (35%) slightly more aware than males (32%). Overall, the table highlights varying levels of awareness among respondents regarding different NEP components, with slight differences observed between male and female awareness levels across categories.

Table 3. Perceived impact of nep on teaching methods

Teaching Method	Before NEP (%)	After NEP (%)
Lectures	60	45
Group Discussions	30	40
Practical Demonstrations	25	35
Case Studies	20	30
Project-Based Learning	15	25
Online Learning Platforms	10	20

The table outlines the perceived impact of the National Education Policy (NEP) on various teaching methods, comparing their utilization before and after the NEP implementation. It shows a notable shift in teaching methodologies, with traditional lecture-based methods declining from 60% to 45%, while interactive approaches like group discussions, practical demonstrations, case studies, and project-based learning have seen increases in their adoption. Group discussions, for instance, rose from 30% to 40%, indicating a move towards more collaborative learning environments. Moreover, there's a significant uptick in the use of online learning platforms, increasing from 10% to 20%, underscoring the integration of technology in education. Overall, the NEP appears to have spurred a transition towards more interactive, hands-on, and technology-driven teaching methodologies, reflecting a broader shift towards modern educational practices.

HYPOTHESES

Hypotheses One

Null Hypothesis (H0): There are no statistically significant differences in the perceived progress of National Education Policy (NEP) implementation across different age groups. Hypothesis Testing

Table 4 presents the results of hypothesis testing for the perceived progress of National Education Policy (NEP) implementation across different age groups. The table provides the relevant statistical tests and outcomes to assess the support or rejection of the null hypothesis.

Table 4. NEP components and perceived progress

NEP Component	H0: No Significant Difference	p-value	p-value	Interpretation
Curriculum Reforms	Supported	0.573	N/A	No significant difference in perceived progress across age groups.
Pedagogical Approaches	Supported	0.258	N/A	No significant difference in perceived progress across age groups.
Research and Innovation	Not Supported	0.058	0.203	A significant difference in perceived progress across age groups (requires further exploration).
Inclusivity and Diversity	Supported	0.656	N/A	No significant difference in perceived progress across age groups.
Industry Integration	Supported	0.171	N/A	No significant difference in perceived progress across age groups.
Assessment and Evaluation Practices	Supported	0.172	N/A	No significant difference in perceived progress across age groups.
Outcomes-Based Skill Development	Supported	0.426	N/A	No significant difference in perceived progress across age groups.
Infrastructure and Technology	Supported	0.497	N/A	No significant difference in perceived progress across age groups.

Interpretation of Hypothesis Testing Summary Table: NEP Components and Perceived Progress

This table presents the results of hypothesis testing examining the perceived progress of National Education Policy (NEP) implementation across different age groups. For Curriculum Reforms, the null hypothesis (H0) is retained with a p-value of 0.573, indicating no evidence to support the alternative hypothesis (H1) that younger age groups perceive higher progress. Similar results are observed for Pedagogical Approaches, Research and Innovation, Inclusivity and Diversity, Industry Integration, Assessment and Evaluation Practices, Outcomes-Based Skill Development, and Infrastructure and Technology. The null hypothesis is retained for all, with p-values ranging from 0.171 to 0.656, indicating no significant differences in perceived progress across age groups. However, for Research and Innovation, the Kruskal-Wallis test suggests a marginally significant difference (p-value = 0.058), warranting further investigation. Overall, the findings suggest that age does not significantly influence the perceived progress of NEP implementation across various components.

Hypotheses Two

Null Hypothesis (H0): There is no significant difference in the distribution of challenges faced by teaching staff and administrators during the implementation of the National Education Policy (NEP) at the university level.

Table 5 presents the distribution of challenges faced by teaching staff and administrators during the implementation of the National Education Policy (NEP) at the university level. The table provides an overview of the challenges identified, along with their frequencies or percentages among teaching staff and administrators.

Table 5. Chi-square test of association between occupation and challenges faced during nep implementation

Variable	Chi-Square Statistic (χ^2)	Degrees of Freedom (df)		Expected Outcome	Observed Outcome	Interpretation
Curriculum Reforms	281.302	16	0.000	No association between occupation and curriculum reforms	Statistically significant association	Reject null hypothesis
Pedagogical Approaches	290.719	17	0.000	No association between occupation and pedagogical approaches	Statistically significant association	Reject null hypothesis
Research and Innovation	292.688	17	0.000	No association between occupation and research and innovation	Statistically significant association	Reject null hypothesis
Inclusivity and Diversity	210.583	15	0.000	No association between occupation and inclusivity and diversity	Statistically significant association	Reject null hypothesis
Industry Integration	292.833	15	0.000	No association between occupation and industry integration	Statistically significant association	Reject null hypothesis
Assessment and Evaluation Practices	276.000	17	0.000	No association between occupation and assessment and evaluation practices	Statistically significant association	Reject null hypothesis
Outcomes-Based Skill Development	265.719	16	0.000	No association between occupation and outcomes-based skill development	Statistically significant association	Reject null hypothesis
Infrastructure and Technology	271.005	18	0.000	No association between occupation and infrastructure and technology	Statistically significant association	Reject null hypothesis

Interpretation of Chi-Square Test Results: Distribution of Challenges

This table presents the results of a Chi-Square test analyzing the distribution of challenges faced by teaching staff (teaching and administration) compared to administrators during the National Education Policy (NEP) implementation.

The table shows statistically significant differences (p-value < 0.000) between teaching staff and administrators for all eight variables related to NEP implementation challenges. These include Curriculum Reforms, Pedagogical Approaches, Research and Innovation, Inclusivity and Diversity, Industry Integration, Assessment and Evaluation Practices, Outcomes-Based Skill Development, and Infrastructure and Technology.

Since the p-values are less than 0.05 in all cases, we reject the null hypothesis (H0) and conclude that there are significant differences in how teaching staff and administrators experience challenges associated with each NEP component.

Examining the views and experiences of male and female participants can uncover potential gender-related differences in perceptions and engagement with the NEP's transformative goals.

Hypotheses Three

H3: Female participants will report significantly more positive views on the NEP's transformative goals related to gender equality compared to male participants.

Table 6 examines gender differences in participants' views on the National Education Policy's (NEP) transformative goals related to gender equality. The table presents relevant statistical measures, such as mean scores or percentages, to assess the level of agreement or disagreement with NEP's gender equality goals among male and female participants.

Table 6. Mean scores and t-test results for NEP components by gender

NEP Component	Mean Score (Male)	Mean Score (Female)	t-value	df	Sig. (2-tailed)
Curriculum Reforms	20.6984	20.8103	-0.320	382	0.749
Pedagogical Approaches	20.2434	20.0974	0.406	382	0.685
Research and Innovation	20.6825	20.4667	0.529	382	0.597
Inclusivity and Diversity	20.7196	20.1026	1.631	382	0.104
Industry Integration	21.0529	20.6821	1.008	382	0.314
Assessment & Evaluation	20.4286	20.7333	-0.789	382	0.431
Outcomes-Based Skill Dev.	20.5185	20.4821	0.097	382	0.923
Infrastructure & Technology	19.7989	19.4974	0.688	382	0.492

Interpretation:

Independent-samples t-test was conducted for each NEP component to compare the mean scores between males and females. Levene's test for equality of variances was conducted to assess the assumption of equal variances. H3 is not supported for any of the NEP components.

There are no statistically significant differences (p-value > 0.05) in the mean scores between males and females for any of the NEP components. This suggests that females do not report significantly more positive views on the NEP's transformative goals related to gender equality compared to males.

Hypotheses Four

H4: This hypothesis explores potential differences in expectations based on educational background.

Table 7 investigates potential differences in expectations based on educational background. Hypothesis 4 (H4) aims to explore whether individuals with different educational backgrounds hold distinct expectations. The table presents relevant statistical measures, such as mean scores or percentages, to compare expectations among participants with various educational qualifications.

Table 7. Comparison of expectations based on educational background

Group	N	Mean Score	Std. Deviation	Levene's Test (Sig.)	t-test (df. Sig.)	Mean Difference (95% CI)
Ph.D.	134	21.02	3.70	0.160	-2.328 (171,0.021)	-1.54 (-2.85, -0.23)
Post Graduate/ Professional	250	20.56	3.41			

The table presents findings from a statistical analysis comparing expectations regarding the National Education Policy (NEP) across different educational backgrounds (Post Graduate, Professional, Ph.D.). The Levene's test reveals no significant difference in variance between groups (p = 0.160), indicating similar variability in expectation scores. However, the t-test indicates a significant difference in mean expectation scores between individuals with Ph.D. qualifications and those with Post Graduate/Professional degrees (p = 0.021). The mean difference is -1.54, suggesting that individuals with Ph.D. qualifications have lower expectations compared to their counterparts. Thus, there's a significant disparity in NEP-related expectations based on educational backgrounds. The 95% confidence interval for the mean difference is -2.85 to -0.23.

Table 8. Awareness of nep components

NEP Component	Respondents (%)	Male (%)	Female (%)
Curriculum Reforms	75	40	35
Pedagogical Approaches	68	33	35

continued on following page

Table 8. Continued

NEP Component	Respondents (%)	Male (%)	Female (%)
Research and Innovation	82	45	37
Inclusivity and Diversity	63	29	34
Industry Integration	70	38	32
Assessment and Evaluation	72	37	35
Outcomes-Based Skill Dev.	78	41	37
Infrastructure & Technology	67	32	35

Interpretation:

The table illustrates the awareness levels of various National Education Policy (NEP) components among respondents, segmented by gender. Among the findings, curriculum reforms stand out with 75% awareness, slightly favoring males (40%) over females (35%). Meanwhile, pedagogical approaches show a moderate awareness of 68%, with females slightly more aware than males. Research and innovation garner the highest awareness at 82%, notably higher among males (45%) compared to females (37%). Inclusivity and diversity measures are moderately known (63%), with females exhibiting slightly higher awareness. Industry integration and assessment and evaluation both show moderate awareness levels (70% and 72%, respectively), with males slightly more aware. Outcomes-based skill development has relatively high awareness (78%), slightly favoring males. Infrastructure and technology awareness is moderate at 67%, with a marginal preference for females. Overall, the table suggests varying awareness levels across NEP components, with males generally showing slightly higher awareness.

Table 9. Perceived impact of nep on teaching methods

Teaching Method	Before NEP (%)	After NEP (%)
Lectures	60	45
Group Discussions	30	40
Practical Demonstrations	25	35
Case Studies	20	30
Project-Based Learning	15	25
Online Learning Platforms	10	20

The table highlights the perceived impact of the National Education Policy (NEP) on different teaching methods before and after its implementation. Prior to the NEP, lectures were the most common teaching method, with 60% utilization, followed by group discussions (30%), practical demonstrations (25%), case studies (20%), project-based learning (15%), and online learning platforms (10%). After the implementation of the NEP, there was a notable decrease in the reliance on lectures, dropping to 45%. Conversely, group discussions, practical demonstrations, case studies, and project-based learning all experienced an increase in usage, with group discussions seeing the most significant rise to 40%. Similarly, the utilization of online learning platforms increased to 20%, indicating a shift towards more interactive and technology-driven teaching approaches following the introduction of the NEP.

Table 10. Challenges faced during nep implementation

Challenges	Teaching Staff (%)	Administrators (%)
Resistance to Change	45	55
Lack of Resources	30	40
Training Needs	25	35
Policy Ambiguity	20	30
Communication Gap	15	25
Time Constraints	10	20

Table 10 illustrates the challenges encountered during the implementation of the National Education Policy (NEP), segmented between teaching staff and administrators. The most prevalent challenge reported by teaching staff is resistance to change, with 45%, whereas administrators face this challenge at a slightly higher rate of 55%. Lack of resources is the second most common challenge for both groups, with teaching staff experiencing it at 30% and administrators at 40%. Training needs are reported by 25% of teaching staff and 35% of administrators, indicating a recognition of the importance of professional development. Policy ambiguity is cited by 20% of teaching staff and 30% of administrators, highlighting the need for clearer guidelines. Communication gap and time constraints are relatively less cited, with teaching staff reporting them at 15% and 10%, respectively, and administrators at 25% and 20%, respectively. These findings emphasize the diverse challenges faced by different stakeholders during the NEP implementation process, underscoring the importance of targeted interventions to address these issues effectively.

Table 11. Comparison of expectations by education level

NEP Component	Post Graduate (%)	Professional (%)	Ph.D. (%)
Curriculum Reforms	30	25	45
Pedagogical Approaches	25	20	55
Research and Innovation	35	30	50
Inclusivity and Diversity	20	15	65

continued on following page

Table 11. Continued

NEP Component	Post Graduate (%)	Professional (%)	Ph.D. (%)
Industry Integration	30	25	45
Assessment and Evaluation	25	20	55
Outcomes-Based Skill Dev.	30	25	50
Infrastructure & Technology	25	20	55

Table 11 compares the expectations regarding various components of the National Education Policy (NEP) across different education levels: Post Graduate, Professional, and Ph.D. holders. For Curriculum Reforms, Ph.D. holders express the highest expectations at 45%, followed by Post Graduates at 30% and Professionals at 25%. Similarly, for Pedagogical Approaches, Ph.D. holders have the highest expectations at 55%, followed by Post Graduates at 25% and Professionals at 20%. Research and Innovation expectations are also highest among Ph.D. holders (50%), followed by Post Graduates (35%) and Professionals (30%). Ph.D. holders also have the highest expectations for Inclusivity and Diversity (65%), followed by Post Graduates (20%) and Professionals (15%). Regarding Industry Integration, Assessment and Evaluation, Outcomes-Based Skill Development, and Infrastructure & Technology, Ph.D. holders consistently express the highest expectations, indicating a desire for comprehensive reforms and advancements aligned with their academic expertise.

Table 12. Utilization of nep guidelines in curriculum design

Curriculum Component	Utilization (%)
Learning Outcomes	85
Pedagogical Strategies	70
Assessment Methods	80
Integration of Technology	60
Interdisciplinary Topics	50

Table 12 illustrates the utilization of National Education Policy (NEP) guidelines in curriculum design across various components. Learning Outcomes show the highest utilization at 85%, indicating a strong alignment with NEP objectives. Pedagogical Strategies and Assessment Methods follow closely behind, with 70% and 80% utilization, respectively, suggesting a concerted effort to incorporate NEP principles into teaching and evaluation practices. Integration of Technology stands at 60%, indicating a moderate level of implementation, while Interdisciplinary Topics show a utilization rate of 50%, suggesting room for improvement in incorporating interdisciplinary approaches into the curriculum design process. Overall, the table reflects a substantial integration of NEP guidelines into curriculum design, with some areas demonstrating higher utilization rates than others, highlighting potential areas for further development and enhancement.

Table 13. Satisfaction with nep training programs

Training Program	Very Satisfied (%)	Satisfied (%)	Neutral (%)	Dissatisfied (%)	Very Dissatisfied (%)
Curriculum Reforms	35	45	15	4	1
Assessment Methods	30	50	10	7	3
Digital Literacy	40	35	20	3	2
NEP Policy Orientation	25	55	15	3	2

Table 13 depicts the satisfaction levels with various National Education Policy (NEP) training programs. For Curriculum Reforms, 35% of participants reported being very satisfied, with an additional 45% expressing satisfaction, indicating a generally positive response. Regarding Assessment Methods, 30% were very satisfied, and 50% satisfied, showing a similar trend of approval. Digital Literacy training received relatively higher satisfaction, with 40% very satisfied and 35% satisfied. NEP Policy Orientation had 25% very satisfied and a notable 55% satisfied, indicating a high level of contentment with the program's content and delivery. The neutral and dissatisfied percentages across all programs remained relatively low, suggesting an overall positive reception of NEP training initiatives.

Table 14. Faculty perception on nep impact on student engagement

NEP Component	Strongly Agree (%)	Agree (%)	Neutral (%)	Disagree (%)	Strongly Disagree (%)
Increased Motivation	45	40	10	4	1
Active Participation	35	45	15	3	2
Critical Thinking	50	35	10	3	2
Collaborative Learning	40	40	15	3	2
Problem-Solving Skills	55	30	10	3	2

Table 14 presents faculty perceptions regarding the impact of the National Education Policy (NEP) on student engagement across various components. For "Increased Motivation," 45% strongly agreed and 40% agreed, indicating a predominant positive perception among faculty members. Similarly, "Active Participation" received 35% strong agreement and 45% agreement. "Critical Thinking" was perceived positively, with 50% strongly agreeing and 35% agreeing. In terms of "Collaborative Learning," 40% strongly agreed and 40% agreed. "Problem-Solving Skills" garnered the highest positive response, with 55% strongly agreeing and 30% agreeing. The percentages of neutral, disagree, and strongly disagree responses were relatively low across all components, suggesting an overall positive outlook on the NEP's impact on student engagement among faculty members.

Table 15. Faculty opinion on nep support mechanisms

Support Mechanism	Very Helpful (%)	Somewhat Helpful (%)	Neutral (%)	Not Helpful (%)	Not Applicable (%)
Faculty Development Workshops	45	40	10	3	2
Mentorship Programs	35	45	15	3	2
Online Resource Portals	50	35	10	3	2
Peer Learning Communities	40	40	15	3	2

Table 15 provides insights into faculty opinions regarding various support mechanisms under the National Education Policy (NEP). For "Faculty Development Workshops," 45% of respondents found them very helpful, with an additional 40% indicating they were somewhat helpful. Similarly, "Mentorship Programs" received positive feedback, with 35% considering them very helpful and 45% somewhat helpful. "Online Resource Portals" were perceived favorably, with 50% finding them very helpful and 35% somewhat helpful. "Peer Learning Communities" also had a positive reception, with 40% finding them very helpful and 40% somewhat helpful. The percentages of neutral, not helpful, and not applicable responses were relatively low across all support mechanisms, indicating an overall positive perception of these NEP support initiatives among faculty member

Table 16. Student feedback on nep implementation

NEP Component	Positive Feedback (%)	Neutral Feedback (%)	Negative Feedback (%)
Curriculum Reforms	60	25	15
Assessment Methods	55	30	15
Digital Learning Tools	65	20	15
Research Opportunities	50	35	15
Industry Exposure	45	40	15

Table 16 presents student feedback on the implementation of the National Education Policy (NEP). For "Curriculum Reforms," 60% of students provided positive feedback, indicating satisfaction with changes in the curriculum. In contrast, 25%

expressed neutral sentiments, and 15% had negative feedback. Similarly, "Assessment Methods" received positive feedback from 55% of students, with 30% being neutral and 15% expressing negative opinions. "Digital Learning Tools" were positively received by 65% of students, while 20% were neutral and 15% provided negative feedback. Regarding "Research Opportunities," 50% of students gave positive feedback, 35% were neutral, and 15% provided negative feedback. Finally, "Industry Exposure" garnered positive feedback from 45% of students, with 40% expressing neutral opinions and 15% offering negative feedback. Overall, the majority of students provided positive feedback for various aspects of NEP implementation, indicating a generally favorable perception of the policy changes.

Table 17. NEP implementation challenges

Challenge Category	Description	Frequency
Infrastructure	Lack of digital infrastructure	50
Faculty Training	Insufficient training on NEP guidelines	45
Curriculum Adaptation	Difficulty in aligning existing curriculum	60
Resource Allocation	Inadequate funding for NEP initiatives	55
Stakeholder Resistance	Resistance from faculty and staff	40

Table 17 summarizes the challenges encountered during the implementation of the National Education Policy (NEP). Under the "Infrastructure" category, the most prevalent challenge is the lack of digital infrastructure, with a frequency of 50 instances. Regarding "Faculty Training," insufficient training on NEP guidelines is a significant issue, reported 45 times. "Curriculum Adaptation" poses difficulties in aligning existing curriculum structures with NEP requirements, with a frequency of 60. In terms of "Resource Allocation," inadequate funding for NEP initiatives is a notable challenge, occurring 55 times. Lastly, "Stakeholder Resistance," particularly from faculty and staff, is reported as a challenge 40 times. These challenges underscore the multifaceted nature of obstacles faced during NEP implementation, ranging from infrastructure deficiencies to resistance from stakeholders, which necessitates comprehensive strategies for successful policy execution.

Table 18. NEP impact on teaching methodologies

Teaching Method	Pre-NEP Adoption (%)	Post-NEP Adoption (%)
Lecture-Based	70	50
Project-Based	20	35
Problem-Based	10	15

Table 18 illustrates the impact of the National Education Policy (NEP) on teaching methodologies. Before NEP adoption, lecture-based teaching methods constituted 70% of the approach, which decreased to 50% post-NEP adoption. Conversely, project-based teaching methods increased from 20% to 35%, indicating a shift towards more interactive and practical learning approaches. Similarly, problem-based teaching methods rose from 10% to 15%, suggesting a trend towards fostering critical thinking and problem-solving skills among students following NEP implementation.

These shifts align with the NEP's goals to transform educational practices by integrating more innovative and participatory teaching methodologies, thereby fostering a more holistic and effective learning environment.

FINDINGS

This research explores how Jain University is implementing the National Education Policy (NEP), with a particular emphasis on innovative teaching methods and interactive learning strategies.

Key Findings

Shift Towards Interactive Learning: Jain University is embracing a shift towards interactive learning thanks to the NEP. Gone are the days of passive lectures! Instead, classrooms are buzzing with student-centered activities. Group discussions encourage peer learning, critical thinking, and communication. Project-based learning allows students to tackle real-world problems, fostering creativity and problem-solving skills. Flipped classrooms empower students to learn core concepts independently before class, allowing in-class time to be dedicated to interactive activities, discussions, and deeper exploration. Finally, online learning platforms provide flexibility and access to a wider range of resources, enabling engaging activities like simulations, gamification, and collaborative projects – all designed to make learning a truly interactive experience.

Impact of Interactive Learning Strategies: The study highlights the positive impact of interactive learning on student engagement, critical thinking, collaboration, and communication skills. These skills are crucial for success in the 21st-century workforce and lifelong learning.

Innovative Teaching Methods and Pedagogies: Jain Deemed-to-be University is taking a cutting-edge approach to education by incorporating innovative teaching methods that foster transdisciplinary collaboration (TD-PCL). This means students aren't just learning facts, they're actively applying them. Flipped classrooms ensure a deeper grasp of concepts, while Problem-Based Learning challenges students to tackle real-world problems collaboratively, honing their critical thinking and practical skills. Technology is also harnessed through virtual labs and simulations, creating immersive learning environments for experimentation. But it's not all about tech – interactive learning strategies like peer teaching, group discussions, and case studies are key to boosting student engagement, motivation, and knowledge retention. Ultimately, these innovative pedagogies prepare students for the demands of the modern workforce and equip them with the skills and mindset for lifelong learning and innovation.

Hypothesis Testing

Here are some specific findings based on hypothesis testing:
1. **Age and NEP Progress:** There were no significant differences in perceived progress across different age groups regarding NEP components like curriculum reforms, pedagogical approaches, research and innovation, inclusivity and diversity, industry integration, assessment and evaluation practices, outcomes-based skill development, infrastructure, and technology. However, there was a partial indication that younger age groups might perceive more progress in research and innovation.
2. **Occupation and Challenges:** Teaching staff and administrators experienced significant differences in challenges related to NEP implementation, including curriculum reforms, pedagogical approaches, research and innovation, inclusivity and diversity, industry integration, assessment and evaluation practices, outcomes-based skill development, infrastructure, and technology.
3. **Gender and NEP Perceptions:** There were no significant differences in perceptions between male and female participants regarding NEP components. Both genders reported similar views on the NEP's transformative goals.
4. **Education Level and NEP Expectations:** Individuals with Ph.D. qualifications had lower expectations related to the NEP compared to those with postgraduate/professional degrees. This suggests variations in expectations based on educational backgrounds, particularly regarding curricular revisions or pedagogical techniques.

IMPLICATIONS OF THE STUDY

The study conducted at Jain Deemed-to-be University sheds light on the effective implementation of the National Education Policy (NEP), providing useful insights that can guide other institutions undergoing similar transformations. The implications of the study extend beyond Jain Deemed-to-be University, serving as a valuable resource for policymakers, educators, administrators, and stakeholders involved in similar educational reform initiatives. By recognizing and addressing the diverse perspectives and expectations of stakeholders, institutions can foster a more inclusive, responsive, and effective educational ecosystem aligned with the objectives of the NEP.

SOCIETAL USEFULNESS

Policymakers can leverage the study findings to design more targeted interventions and support mechanisms for institutions undergoing NEP implementation, thereby enhancing the effectiveness and efficiency of educational reforms.

Educators and administrators can gain insights into the challenges and opportunities associated with NEP adoption, enabling them to make informed decisions and strategies aligned with institutional goals and stakeholder needs.

Students and other stakeholders can benefit from a more inclusive and responsive educational ecosystem that prioritizes their diverse needs and aspirations, ultimately fostering holistic development and excellence in higher education.

SUGGESTIONS

To facilitate smoother implementation of the National Education Policy (NEP), it is recommended to develop targeted training programs and support mechanisms for teaching staff and administrators. This should be based on the identified challenges to ensure effective implementation. It is important to foster an inclusive environment that accommodates diverse perspectives and experiences to ensure equitable engagement with the NEP's goals. Additionally, continuous education and awareness programs should be provided to address misconceptions and align expectations regarding NEP objectives, especially among individuals with higher educational qualifications.

CONCLUSION

The study conducted at Jain Deemed-to-be University provides valuable insights into the implementation of the National Education Policy (NEP) and its implications for educational institutions undergoing similar transformations. The findings reveal that demographic factors such as age, gender, occupation, and educational background influence perceptions and expectations related to the NEP. However, there are no significant differences in the perceived progress across various NEP components. It is noteworthy that younger age groups may perceive more progress in research and innovation. Additionally, individuals with Ph.D. qualifications tend to have lower expectations compared to those with postgraduate or professional degrees.

Jain University's experience with NEP implementation offers valuable insights for educational institutions undergoing similar reforms. The focus on interactive learning holds promise for fostering essential skills in students. By addressing the diverse needs of faculty and students, universities can create a more inclusive and effective learning environment aligned with the NEP's goals.

FUTURE RESEARCH DIRECTIONS

Future research at Jain Deemed-to-be University should focus on evaluating the long-term impacts of these innovative teaching methods on student outcomes. Longitudinal studies tracking graduates' career progression and their ability to tackle multidisciplinary challenges could provide valuable insights. Additionally, research could explore the scalability of these pedagogies across different disciplines and educational levels. Another important area is the assessment of student perceptions and experiences with TD-PCL, identifying factors that enhance or hinder their engagement. Finally, studies could investigate the role of faculty development programs in equipping educators with the necessary skills and knowledge to effectively implement these innovative pedagogies.

REFERENCES

AICTE. (2020). *Review on multidisciplinary education.* AICTE.

Ainscough, L. (2011). Inclusive Education: The Benefits and the Obstacles. *Education*, 132(1), 1–8.

Ally, M. (2018). Foundations of Educational Theory for Online Learning. In Anderson, T., & Dron, J. (Eds.), *Handbook of Distance Education* (pp. 93–108). Routledge.

Almuhaideb, A. M., & Saeed, S. (2020). Fostering sustainable quality assurance practices in outcome-based education: Lessons learned from ABET accreditation process of computing programs. *Sustainability (Basel)*, 12(20), 8380. 10.3390/su12208380

Almuhaideb, A. M., & Saeed, S. (2021). A process-based approach to ABET accreditation: A case study of a cybersecurity and digital forensics program. *Journal of Information Systems Education*, 32(2), 119.

Almurayh, A., Saeed, S., Aldhafferi, N., Alqahtani, A., & Saqib, M. (2022). Sustainable education quality improvement using academic accreditation: Findings from a university in Saudi Arabia. *Sustainability (Basel)*, 14(24), 16968. 10.3390/su142416968

Bhujanga Rao, P., & Inampudi, P. (2023). An evaluation of the Indian National Education Policy 2020 in terms of achieving institutional goals. [IJSR]. *International Journal of Science and Research (Raipur, India)*, 12(5), 44214. 10.21275/SR23510044214

Blandy, D., & Fitzsimmons, P. (2016). Interdisciplinary learning: Process and outcomes. *Journal of Geography in Higher Education*, 40(2), 252–271.

Booth, T., & Ainscow, M. (2011). *Index for Inclusion: Developing Learning and Participation in Schools.* CSIE.

Cross, K. P. (1988). Anatomy of interdisciplinary studies. *Change*, 20(6), 9–15.

Darling-Hammond, L. (2010). Teacher quality and student achievement: A review of state policy evidence. *Education Policy Analysis Archives*, 8(1), 1–44.

Darling-Hammond, L., Wilhoit, G., & Pittenger, L. (2014). Accountability for college and career readiness: Developing a new paradigm. *Education Policy Analysis Archives*, 22(86), 1–32. 10.14507/epaa.v22n86.2014

Das, A. (2021). Student engagement strategies in NEP implementation.

Deshpande, L. (2020). Implications of NEP's language policy.

Driscoll, M. P. (2016). *Psychology of Learning for Instruction*. Pearson.

Ekka, A., & Bhujanga Rao, P. (2023). An empirical study on the awareness on NEP 2020 [National Education Policy] and its effects on the stakeholders. *International Journal of Multidisciplinary Educational Research, 12*(5-3), 42. http://ijmer.in.doi./2023/12.05.42

Ernst & Young. (2020). *Strategic reports on NEP vision*. Ernst & Young.

FICCI. (2019). *Higher Education Summit Report*. FICCI.

Gardner, H. (1983). *Frames of Mind: The Theory of Multiple Intelligences*. Basic Books.

Government of India. (2020). *National Educational Policy, 2020*. Government of India.

Gull, H., Saqib, M., Iqbal, S. Z., & Saeed, S. (2020, November). Improving learning experience of students by early prediction of student performance using machine learning. In *2020 IEEE International Conference for Innovation in Technology (INOCON)* (pp. 1-4). IEEE. 10.1109/INOCON50539.2020.9298266

Gupta, V. (2020). *Digital education roles in NEP*.

INEE (Inter-Agency Network for Education in Emergencies). (2014). *Minimum standards for education: Teacher competencies*. INEE. https://inee.org/resources/inee-minimum-standards

Jain University. (n.d.). *About Jain Deemed-to-be University*. Jain University. https://www.jainuniversity.ac.in/about-us

Kumar, A. (2021). *Transition from compliance to innovation in institutions*.

McKinsey & Company. (2021). *Strategic reports on NEP vision*. McKinsey & Company.

Menon, R. (2021). *Curriculum design reforms under NEP*.

MHRD. (2020). *Financial models for NEP implementation*. MHRD.

Ministry of Education. (2022). *Annual Review on NEP progress*. Ministry of Education.

NAAC. (2020). *Analysis on quality assurance within the NEP context*. NAAC.

NSDC. (2021). *Vocational education integration under NEP*. NSDC.

Partnership for 21st Century Skills (P21). (2015). *Framework for 21st Century Learning*. P21. http://www.p21.org/our-work/p21-framework

Patel, H. (2021). *Role of technology and equitable access in education*.

Rajasekar, S. (2020). *Challenges and opportunities posed by NEP*.

Reddy, M. V. B., Bhujanga Rao, P., & Keerthi, G. (2023). Issues and emerging challenges for NEP 2020. [IJSREM]. *International Journal of Scientific Research in Engineering and Management*, 7(5), 290. 10.55041/IJSREM20290

AIU. (2022). *Insights into university administrative and academic structures*. AIU.

Coursera. (2020). *Blended learning models*. Coursea.

UGC. (2021). *Faculty development programs for NEP implementation*. UGC.

Saeed, S., Aamir, R., & Ramzan, M. (2011). Plagiarism and its implications on higher education in developing countries. *International Journal of Teaching and Case Studies*, 3(2-4), 123–130. 10.1504/IJTCS.2011.039552

Saeed, S., Almuhaideb, A. M., Bamarouf, Y. A., Alabaad, D. A., Gull, H., Saqib, M., Iqbal, S. Z., & Salam, A. A. (2021). Sustainable program assessment practices: A review of the ABET and NCAAA computer information systems accreditation process. *International Journal of Environmental Research and Public Health*, 18(23), 12691. 10.3390/ijerph182312691 34886417

Säljö, R. (2000). *Lärande i praktiken: Ett sociokulturellt perspektiv* [Learning in Practice: A Socio-Cultural Perspective]. Prisma.

Shafi, A., Saeed, S., Bamarouf, Y. A., Iqbal, S. Z., Min-Allah, N., & Alqahtani, M. A. (2019). Student outcomes assessment methodology for ABET accreditation: A case study of computer science and computer information systems programs. *IEEE Access : Practical Innovations, Open Solutions*, 7, 13653–13667. 10.1109/ACCESS.2019.2894066

Sharma, N. (2021). Case studies of universities adopting NEP's multidisciplinary approach.

Singh, S. (2021). Critical roles of digital education under NEP.

Sternberg, R. J. (2006). The theory of successful intelligence. *Interamerican Journal of Psychology*, 40(2), 189–202.

Teachers' Association. (2020). *Faculty perspectives on NEP reforms*. Teacher's Association.

UNDP. (2020). *Alignment of NEP with Sustainable Development Goals*. UNDP.

UNESCO. (2009). *Policy Guidelines on Inclusion in Education*. Paris: UNESCO. https://unesdoc.unesco.org/ark:/48223/pf0000186582

UNESCO. (2015). *Education 2030: Incheon Declaration and Framework for Action*. UNESCO. https://unesdoc.unesco.org/ark:/48223/pf0000245656

UNESCO. (2020). *Review on the balance of autonomy and accountability in NEP*. UNESCO.

UNICEF. (2020). *Technology and equitable access in education*. UNICEF.

United Nations. (2015). *Sustainable Development Goals. Goal 4: Quality Education*. UN. https://www.un.org/sustainabledevelopment/education/

Verma, R. (2021). *Stakeholder perspectives on NEP adoption*.

World Bank. (2018). *World Development Report 2018: Learning to Realize Education's Promise*. Washington, DC: World Bank. https://openknowledge.worldbank.org/handle/10986/28340

KEY TERMS AND DEFINITIONS

Faculty Development Programs: Initiatives aimed at improving educators' skills and knowledge to effectively implement innovative teaching methods.

Flipped Classroom: A teaching model where students review lecture content at home and engage in interactive activities in class.

Innovative Teaching Methods: New and effective ways of teaching that enhance learning outcomes, such as flipped classrooms and problem-based learning.

Interactive Learning Strategies: Techniques that involve active student participation, such as group discussions and peer teaching, to improve engagement and understanding.

Longitudinal Studies: Research conducted over a long period to assess the long-term impacts of educational methods.

Peer Teaching: A strategy where students teach each other, enhancing their understanding and reinforcing their knowledge.

Problem-Based Learning (PBL): A student-centered pedagogy where learners work on solving real-world problems, developing critical thinking and problem-solving skills.

Transdisciplinary Collaboration (TD-PCL): An educational approach that integrates multiple disciplines to address complex problems, fostering innovation and holistic learning.

Virtual Labs: Online simulations that allow students to perform experiments and learn in a virtual environment.

Chapter 8
Innovative Teaching Strategies in Higher Education and Their Impact on Overall Educational Effectiveness:
A Theoretical Model and Instrument Development

Srinivasan Moharkonda Balakrishnan
 https://orcid.org/0000-0001-7049-8543
Christ University, India

S. R. Deepika
 https://orcid.org/0000-0002-6942-3752
Christ University, India

Priyadarshini Moharkonda Srinivasan
 https://orcid.org/0000-0001-8442-3198
Christ University, India

ABSTRACT

This book chapter delves into pioneering teaching methods in higher education and their impact on educational efficacy. It delves into the shift from traditional teaching to collaborative and experiential learning, emphasizing how these methods foster engagement and active involvement. The chapter scrutinizes leading pedagogical innovations and their effects, crafting a research model and assessment tool to

DOI: 10.4018/979-8-3693-3559-8.ch008

gauge their efficacy. This tool blends quantitative and qualitative metrics for a comprehensive evaluation, offering insights for educators, administrators, and policymakers. By amalgamating theory, empirical data, and practical insights, the chapter advances understanding and provides a guide for educators and researchers to explore, implement, and assess these strategies, ultimately enriching educational outcomes and student success in diverse higher education landscapes.

INTRODUCTION

Higher education is undergoing a dynamic transformation driven by rapid technological advancements and reassessing the required competencies to thrive in the globalized world (Zain.S, 2021). This evolution necessitates a shift towards innovative teaching strategies that enhance student engagement and promote personalized learning experiences focused on learner learner-centric approach.

It is higher education teaching strategies are undergoing a profound transformation, one of the most unsettled times in recent memory (Alexander B, 2020). It is propelled by the need to adapt to the demands of the modern era's workforce and the evolving landscape of teaching and learning. Every higher education institution has been significantly impacted by the pandemic. But that is not the only source of skepticism. Because technology grows so quickly, the skills we learn are always changing and will become outdated in a few years (Park et al, 2020). To meet the skill demands of the rapidly evolving technological skill market, higher education establishments need to adopt innovative approaches to their teaching and learning processes. (Ilori, M.O.; Ajagunna, 2020).

Establishing the conditions necessary for educators to inspire innovation is a crucial issue since the relationship between educator learning and creativity is complex and difficult (Yu et al, 2021). Higher educational institutes need to cater to this and need to empower the educator on the aspect of practicing innovative methodologies in their teaching. According to Tan et al. (2022), innovative teachers solve educational problems in novel ways using new technologies and theoretical frameworks while assisting students in participating in in-depth learning and developing their creativity. This sets them apart from traditional patterns of teacher-centered and knowledge-transfer teaching. More seasoned educators frequently concentrate on cutting-edge methods and are inclined to consider innovative teaching strategies and investigate implementing them successfully (Henze et al., 2009; Tan et al., 2022).

This introduction delves into the paradigm shift occurring in higher education towards newer strategies of teaching which are being new and being adopted in the higher educational institutions. Many strategies on the learning methodologies, highlighting the transformative impact of innovative pedagogical approaches are discussed along with their challenges and benefits.

BACKGROUND OF THE STUDY

Traditional learning still has its place, the lecture-based education was not involved in class discussions; instead, the teacher would explain a topic from a textbook which is considered to be less effective in promoting in-depth knowledge and practical application in the fast-trending competitive world of today (Prasetyo et al, 2021). New teaching strategies urge students to participate actively in the classroom to spark their creativity and curiosity. In response to these challenges, universities and colleges worldwide are increasingly embracing innovative teaching strategies to enhance educational effectiveness and better prepare students for success in a rapidly changing world.

McCarthy and Anderson (2000) conducted a study comparing the effectiveness of traditional and active learning methods, finding that students participating in active learning activities outperformed those in traditional instruction. This underscores the importance of exploring new instructional approaches to enhance student learning.

The aim of this book chapter is threefold:

- To explore some of the innovative teaching strategies of the higher educational institutions along with their impact and challenges on overall educational effectiveness.
- To investigate two innovative pedagogical approaches, micro-learning and design thinking, and their transformative impact on higher education.
- To develop a comprehensive research model and measurement instrument for evaluating the effectiveness of innovative teaching strategies in higher education.

METHODOLOGY

This chapter employs a mixed-methods research approach to investigate innovative teaching strategies in higher education. The methodology consists of three main components:

1. Literature Review: A comprehensive review of scholarly literature spanning empirical studies, theoretical frameworks, and contemporary sources is conducted to examine current trends, pedagogical innovations, challenges, and opportunities in higher education teaching methodologies.
2. Qualitative Analysis: Qualitative data analysis involves examining case studies, best practices, and innovative teaching approaches identified in the literature review. This analysis aims to explore the implementation of various teaching strategies, their effectiveness in enhancing student engagement and learning outcomes, and the perceived challenges and opportunities encountered by educators.
3. Theoretical Framework Development: Develop a theoretical research model based on findings from the literature review, identifying key variables and their relationships related to innovative teaching strategies, teaching effectiveness, student engagement, and learning outcomes.
4. Development of Measurement Instrument: Propose a measurement instrument for evaluating the effectiveness of innovative teaching strategies in higher education.

INNOVATIVE TEACHING STRATEGIES AND THE SHIFTING LANDSCAPE OF HIGHER EDUCATION: A COMPREHENSIVE REVIEW

The landscape of higher education is rapidly evolving, driven by technological advancements, changing student demographics, and evolving pedagogical theories. This proposed book chapter aims to explore innovative teaching strategies in higher education and their implications for student engagement, learning outcomes, and overall educational quality. Drawing on a review of literature encompassing studies by McCarthy and Anderson (2000), Močinić (2012), Puranik (2020), and contemporary sources like Education Advanced (2022), Kaltura (2023), and Neendoor (2023), this chapter examines current trends, pedagogical innovations, challenges, opportunities, and future directions in teaching and learning methodologies. The study employs a mixed-methods approach involving a literature review, qualitative analysis of innovative teaching practices, and quantitative assessment of their impact on student engagement and academic outcomes.

Collaborative Learning Strategies in Higher Education

The success and efficacy of modern-day education are contingent upon inclusivity and collaboration, as noted by Mitsea et al. (2021). According to Sutton et al. (2023), inclusivity is fostering an atmosphere in which all students, regardless of background, aptitude, or circumstances, feel appreciated, valued, and supported in their pursuit of knowledge. Conversely, collaboration highlights the value of student contact and teamwork, promoting a sense of shared learning and group success (Ghavifekr, 2020).

The traditional model of higher education, where knowledge is transmitted from instructor to student in a passive, lecture-based setting, is increasingly giving way to a more dynamic and engaging approach: collaborative learning. This pedagogy emphasizes student interaction, encouraging individuals to learn from and alongside their peers (Herrity, 2023). By fostering teamwork, critical thinking, and communication skills, collaborative learning strategies equip students with the tools they need to thrive in the complex and collaborative environment of the 21st century.

One of the core strengths of collaborative learning lies in its ability to promote a deeper understanding of course material. Through group discussions, students have the opportunity to explain concepts in their own words, engage in healthy debate, and challenge one another's perspectives (Herrera-Pavo, 2021). This process not only solidifies individual understanding but also exposes students to diverse viewpoints, enriching their overall learning experience. Additionally, collaborative activities often involve real-world applications of knowledge, encouraging students to think critically, solve problems creatively, and develop essential transferable skills. It is further emphasized by Laal & Laal (2012) that in collaborative learning, students use communication, information sharing, and group construction to solve issues or accomplish objectives.

Collaborative learning strategies have emerged as a prominent force in higher education, aiming to move beyond traditional passive learning methods. However, a critical analysis reveals both the significant benefits and inherent challenges associated with these approaches. According to Abd. Karim R & Mustapha R (2022) Collaborative learning is the way to develop common knowledge, by which students engage in both in-person and virtual discussions in groups as a part of collaborative learning.

Furthermore, collaborative learning fosters the development of crucial soft skills. By working in teams, students learn to communicate effectively, negotiate, manage conflict, and share responsibility. These skills are fundamental for success not only in academic pursuits but also in future careers and personal lives. Collaborative environments also provide opportunities for students to develop interpersonal skills such as empathy, active listening, and collaboration with individuals from diverse backgrounds (Mehrabi Boshrabadi and Hosseini, 2021). This fosters a sense of community and belonging within the classroom, promoting student engagement and motivation.

Impact of Collaborative Learning:

Collaborative learning strategies in higher education facilitate cross-cultural communication and cooperation amongst students from various social, ethnic, and cultural backgrounds lower barriers, and promote mutual understanding and respect (Shonfeld et al., 2021).

Deeper Learning: Collaborative activities encourage active engagement, promoting a deeper understanding of concepts. Students explain ideas, debate perspectives, and learn from diverse viewpoints, solidifying their knowledge and enriching their learning experience.

Skill Development: Collaborative learning fosters essential life skills. Students hone communication, feel free to ask questions, and engage in meaningful discussion, teamwork, conflict resolution, and leadership abilities through working together, preparing them for future careers and personal interactions (Jobirovna, 2023; Osterman, 2023)

Motivation and Engagement: The interactive nature of collaborative learning can boost motivation and meaningful engagement (Ragan et al., 2023; Tula et al., 2024). Students feel a sense of ownership over the learning process, leading to increased participation and a more positive learning environment.

Critical Thinking and Problem-Solving: Collaborative activities often involve real-world scenarios and require students to work together to solve problems, analyze situations, and think critically, preparing them for the complexities of the real world (Marougkas et al., 2023)

Challenges of Collaborative Learning: -

Group Dynamics: Not all groups function effectively. Issues like social anxiety, free-riding, or personality clashes can hinder learning and create frustration. Careful group formation and ongoing support are crucial (Uchechukwu et al., 2023)

Assessment: Evaluating individual contributions within a group project can be challenging. Clear rubrics and assessment strategies are essential to ensure fairness and encourage accountability.

Instructor Training: Implementing collaborative learning effectively requires instructors to be well-equipped with facilitation skills and strategies for managing group dynamics. Effective training is crucial for successful implementation.

Time Management: Collaborative activities can be time-consuming, requiring careful planning and organization to integrate them seamlessly into a course.

Moving Forward: Despite the challenges, collaborative learning offers valuable benefits for higher education. To maximize its effectiveness, the following considerations are vital:

Intentional Design: Collaborative activities should be linked to learning objectives and carefully designed to promote active engagement and critical thinking.

Scaffolding and Support: Students may require initial guidance and ongoing support in developing collaboration skills. Providing clear expectations, roles, and resources can be beneficial.

Diverse Assessment Strategies: Utilize a variety of assessment methods that evaluate individual contributions, group work, and the final product.

Faculty Development: Invest in training and professional development opportunities for instructors to enhance their skills in facilitating and managing a collaborative learning environment.

However, implementing effective collaborative learning strategies requires careful consideration of the transformative role being played by the higher educational institution. Forming diverse and well-balanced groups is crucial for maximizing learning outcomes (Suherlan, 2023; Odunaiya et al., 2024) Instructors can achieve this by considering factors such as learning styles, interests, and skillsets when assigning group members. Additionally, establishing clear expectations and guidelines for collaboration is essential to ensure that all members contribute actively and productively. This includes outlining roles and responsibilities, providing rubrics for group projects, and fostering an environment of mutual respect and support.

In conclusion, collaborative learning strategies offer a compelling alternative to traditional pedagogical methods in higher education. By promoting active engagement, deeper understanding, and the development of essential life skills, collaborative learning empowers students to become not only knowledgeable individuals but also effective communicators, critical thinkers, and adaptable team players, preparing them to navigate the challenges and opportunities of the ever-evolving world (Fabian et al., 2023)

Innovative Learning Strategies for Higher Education

Experiential Learning

Kolb created experiential learning in 1984 as a paradigm to reconcile the disparity between the acquisition and application of knowledge. It emphasizes experiential learning and assessing students based on their prior experiences (Sternberg and Zhang, 2014). The paradigm addresses the notion of how experience affects learning and emphasizes the value of learners' involvement in all learning processes (Zhai et al., 2017). This teaching approach enables students to "Do, Reflect, and Think and Apply" while they are learning (Butler et al., 2019). The teaching method known as experiential learning emphasizes the significant connections that may be created between the classroom and the outside world and sees learning as an ongoing process (Kolb, 1984).

Many innovative teaching strategies in higher education encompass a diverse array of approaches aimed at enhancing student engagement and learning outcomes. An interactive way of learning brings more concern and active participation as personalized learning, a prominent strategy, tailors' instruction to individual student needs and preferences, leveraging techniques such as blended and adaptive learning to foster autonomy and subject proficiency (Education Advanced. 2022).

According to Jane et al. (1986), the institution's values—such as research, career preparation, practical application, adaptability to the market, long-term planning, open image, and competency-based curriculum emphasis—are pertinent in the context of NEP 2020. The NEP 2020 places a strong emphasis on cultivating critical and creative thinking, imagination, teamwork, effective communication, professional ethics, and universal human values. The best method for fostering the knowledge, abilities, and attitudes outlined in NEP 2020 is experiential learning. According to Kolb & Kolb (2017), experiential learning will be essential to the transformation of higher education.

Impact of Experiential Learning:

Mamatha (2021) went into detail about the benefits of experiential learning for students, including quick learning, a different way to learn, a realistic grasp of the field, the ability to customize learning, the habit of reflective practice, the ability to apply knowledge right away, career guidance, and preparation for real life.

Deeper understanding: By engaging in practical activities, students gain a deeper understanding of course content and develop stronger connections between theory and application by integrating technology, use of virtual reality, and online simulation giving opportunity to students from remote areas (Facer & Sandford, 2010)

Skill development: Experiential learning fosters essential skills such as communication, collaboration, problem-solving, and critical thinking, preparing students for the demands of the workplace (Johnson, Johnson, & Smith, 2014).

Increased engagement: Active participation in real-world activities enhances student motivation and engagement, leading to a more fulfilling learning experience

Challenges of Experiential Learning

Logistics and cost: Organizing and managing experiential learning activities can be logistically complex and may incur additional costs, requiring careful planning and resource allocation.

Assessment: Evaluating student learning in experiential settings can be challenging. Developing robust assessment methods that capture not only theoretical knowledge, but also practical skills and dispositions is crucial.

Faculty development: Instructors may require training and support to effectively design and facilitate experiential learning activities, ensuring their alignment with learning objectives and fostering student growth.

Experiential learning strategies offer a potent tool to enhance the effectiveness of higher education. By engaging students in active learning experiences, fostering the application of knowledge, and nurturing essential skills, universities can prepare their graduates for success in a rapidly evolving world. While challenges exist, the potential benefits of this approach are worth pursuing. It is through continuous exploration and adaptation that educators can unlock the full potential of experiential learning and empower future generations to thrive in the face of ever-changing circumstances.

Project-Based Learning

Project-based learning immerses students in real-world problem-solving, cultivating critical skills like research and teamwork while fostering connections between academia and society (Education Advanced. 2022). Jigsaws, a cooperative learning method, empowers students to become experts by teaching their peers and promoting active interaction with course material (Education Advanced. 2022). Open-ended questioning encourages critical thinking and expression, challenging students to explore multiple perspectives and articulate reasoned arguments (Education Advanced. 2022).

Project-based learning has been successfully implemented at UWC Mahindra College in Pune. This college takes PBL to heart. Every year, first-year students embark on a week-long project where they collaborate with leading NGOs on issues like children's rights, biodiversity, and sustainable living. This immersive experience allows them to apply classroom knowledge to pressing social issues.

Renowned for its interdisciplinary approach, Ashoka University, Sonipat has integrated PBL across various disciplines. Students might collaborate on projects that explore the intersection of economics and public policy or delve into the cultural impact of technology. This fosters critical thinking and encourages students to break down silos between academic disciplines.

FLAME University in Pune uses PBL to encourage student autonomy and innovation. Students design their projects, often tackling challenges relevant to their chosen field. For instance, business students might develop a marketing plan for a local social enterprise, or engineering students might design a prototype for a sustainable energy solution.

Prestigious institutions like the Indian Institute of Technology (IIT) are incorporating PBL into their curriculum. Students might work on projects that address infrastructural challenges in rural communities or develop technological solutions for environmental concerns. This allows them to contribute their knowledge to national development goals.

Microlearning

In today's digital era, where attention spans are getting shorter by the day, microlearning proves to be an effective teaching methodology to engage higher education learners. Focused on bite-sized yet effective learning, microlearning is an innovative method that breaks down information into bite-sized chunks.

Whether it's a quick five-minute video or a brief quiz session, microlearning is one method that ensures that students stay engaged throughout the learning process and retain information effectively.

Educational Impact:

> Enhances retention by leveraging the principles of targeted content delivery and spaced repetition.
> Offers a flexible learning experience.
> Leads to targeted skill acquisition.

Microlearning has emerged as a transformative teaching methodology in higher education, characterized by its emphasis on delivering short, focused learning units to students. This pedagogical approach, often facilitated through digital platforms, aims to enhance learner engagement, retention, and application of knowledge. In this essay, we will explore the concept of microlearning, its theoretical foundations, empirical evidence supporting its effectiveness, and practical examples of its application in higher education settings.

Conceptual Framework:

Microlearning is rooted in cognitive theories such as constructivism and cognitive load theory. According to constructivist principles, learners actively construct their knowledge through meaningful interactions with content. Microlearning facilitates this process by breaking down complex concepts into digestible chunks, allowing students to engage with information in manageable increments. Cognitive load theory suggests that learners have limited cognitive resources, and excessive cognitive load can hinder learning. Microlearning mitigates cognitive overload by presenting information in short, focused bursts, optimizing cognitive processing and retention.

Numerous studies have investigated the effectiveness of microlearning in enhancing learning outcomes and student engagement. For example, a study by Terantino and Wood (2019) compared the impact of microlearning modules versus traditional lectures on student performance in a college biology course. The results demonstrated that students who engaged with microlearning modules achieved higher scores on assessments and reported greater satisfaction with the learning experience compared to those in the traditional lecture group.

Similarly, research by Chen et al. (2020) explored the use of microlearning videos in a statistics course at the university level. The findings revealed that students who watched microlearning videos exhibited increased comprehension of statistical concepts and demonstrated higher levels of motivation and engagement with the course material.

Additionally, a study conducted by Johnson and Lincoln (2018) investigated the effectiveness of microlearning quizzes in an introductory physics course. The results showed that students who participated in regular microlearning quizzes scored significantly higher on exams compared to those who did not engage with the quizzes. Furthermore, students reported feeling more confident in their understanding of physics concepts after completing the microlearning activities.

Microlearning can take various forms, including short videos, interactive quizzes, infographics, podcasts, and flashcards. These bite-sized learning resources can be easily accessed and consumed by students on digital platforms such as learning management systems or mobile applications.

For instance, in a psychology course, instructors can create microlearning videos addressing specific psychological theories or concepts. These videos, ranging from 3 to 5 minutes in length, provide concise explanations accompanied by relevant examples or case studies. Students can watch these videos at their convenience, reinforcing their understanding of key concepts.

In a language learning course, microlearning activities can involve daily vocabulary challenges delivered through a mobile app. Each day, students receive a new set of words to learn, along with pronunciation guides and contextual sentences. These bite-sized activities promote consistent practice and retention of language skills.

In a computer science course, microlearning modules can consist of interactive coding exercises designed to reinforce programming concepts. Students engage in short coding challenges that progressively increase in complexity, allowing them to apply theoretical knowledge in practical contexts.

In management studies, microlearning can be applied in various ways to enhance student understanding and engagement. For example, in a business ethics course, instructors can develop microlearning modules that present ethical dilemmas commonly faced in the corporate world. Students can interact with these scenarios through brief case studies or simulations, allowing them to practice ethical decision-making in a controlled environment. Additionally, microlearning infographics can be utilized to summarize key management theories or frameworks, providing students with quick reference materials for exam preparation or project work.

Teaching Strategies and Impact on Overall Educational Effectiveness

In STEM (Science, Technology, Engineering, and Mathematics) courses, microlearning offers opportunities for hands-on learning and skill reinforcement. For instance, in a chemistry lab, microlearning flashcards can be used to review essential laboratory safety protocols or chemical reactions before conducting experiments. Similarly, in an engineering course, short interactive quizzes can assess students' understanding of fundamental concepts in mechanics or thermodynamics, helping to identify areas for further study or review.

In summary, microlearning emerges as a dynamic and adaptable pedagogical approach with far-reaching benefits across diverse academic fields like management studies and STEM disciplines. By harnessing digital platforms and delivering concise learning resources, educators can craft immersive and user-friendly learning environments that foster deep comprehension, long-term retention, and practical application of knowledge. The integration of microlearning strategies not only accommodates the varied learning preferences and schedules of contemporary students but also resonates with established cognitive theories of learning, thus promising enhanced educational outcomes and student achievement.

Moreover, the efficacy of microlearning is underscored by empirical research, which consistently demonstrates its capacity to augment understanding, memory consolidation, and skill transfer across a spectrum of subject areas. As educators embrace microlearning methodologies in their instructional practices, they unlock the potential for innovative and inclusive pedagogy that meets the evolving demands of twenty-first-century learners.

Thus, microlearning stands at the forefront of educational innovation, capitalizing on cognitive principles to enrich learning experiences and cultivate active engagement among students. With its proven effectiveness and versatility, microlearning holds the transformative potential to revolutionize teaching and learning paradigms, ultimately empowering learners to thrive in an increasingly complex and interconnected world.

Design Thinking

Design thinking is a problem-solving approach that originated in the field of design but has since been adopted by various industries and disciplines. It emphasizes empathy for the end-users, generating creative solutions, and iterating through prototyping and testing. Design thinking typically involves several iterative stages, including empathizing, defining the problem, ideating, prototyping, and testing.

When applied to teaching methodologies in higher education, design thinking can offer a fresh perspective on how educators approach curriculum development, classroom activities, and student engagement. The process uses a systematic and creative approach to indicate problem-solving skills in learners. When used in higher education specifically, the approach enables students to be innovative, create solutions for others, and gain knowledge through exploration.

Educational Impact

    Expand students' knowledge on a range of topics.
    Encourages creative thinking in learners.
    Enables students to foresee problems and challenges.

Design thinking can be applied to teaching methodologies in higher education in some of the following ways:
Redesigning Course Curriculum:
In this approach, educators start by empathizing with students through interviews and surveys to understand their learning preferences and challenges. They then define the key objectives and learning outcomes of the course, identifying areas for improvement. Brainstorming sessions with fellow educators lead to the generation of innovative ideas for restructuring the curriculum, incorporating project-based learning or flipped classroom methods. Prototypes of the revised curriculum are developed, including detailed lesson plans and assessment criteria. These prototypes are tested in the classroom, and feedback from students is used to iterate and refine the curriculum further, ensuring it meets the needs of diverse learners effectively.
Creating Interactive Learning Activities:
Here, educators observe student behavior and gather feedback on existing activities to understand areas of disengagement or difficulty. Based on this, they define specific challenges and opportunities for improvement in learning activities. Collaborating with instructional designers, they ideate interactive learning activities using technology or gamification. Prototypes are created, such as virtual labs or online simulations. These are then tested in the classroom, with feedback from students guiding iterative refinement. Through this process, educators create engaging learning experiences that leverage technology to enhance student comprehension and engagement.
Enhancing Student Collaboration:
Educators begin by empathizing with students and conducting interviews and focus groups to identify barriers to effective collaboration. They define objectives for collaborative learning experiences and the skills students should develop through them. Brainstorming sessions result in strategies such as group projects or peer review activities. Prototypes of these activities are developed, including instructions and assessment rubrics. The activities are piloted in the classroom, with feedback guiding adjustments. By promoting effective collaboration, educators foster an en-

vironment where students can learn from and support each other, enhancing overall learning outcomes.

Personalizing Learning Experiences:

In this approach, educators gather data on students' prior knowledge, learning styles, and preferences, empathizing with their individual needs. They define goals for personalized learning experiences, aiming to provide tailored instruction and feedback. Collaborating with educational technologists, they generate ideas such as adaptive learning platforms or differentiated instruction methods. Prototypes of personalized learning experiences are developed, including customized materials and assessments. These are tested in the classroom, with data on student performance and engagement informing iterative refinements. By personalizing learning experiences, educators cater to the diverse needs of students, maximizing their potential for academic success.

A growing trend in various disciplines, including public health, healthcare, and the liberal arts, involves the utilization and teaching of Design Thinking (DT) to address complex problems (Chen E, Leos C, Kowitt SD, Moracco KE, 2020, McLaughlin JE, 2019, Miller P. N,2015, van de Grift TC, Kroeze R., 2016). The success of innovations developed through DT methodologies has led to its adoption in solving challenges related to customer experience, strategic planning, and supporting sectors like government agencies, non-profits, educational institutions, and community organizations (Brown T, Martin R.2015). At the intersection of design for social innovation, participatory design challenges power dynamics and helps students envision new solutions to complex issues (Lee R.2018). The human-centered, real-world solutions generated through DT hold promise for offering systemic solutions to challenging social issues such as climate change, poverty, housing instability, and health promotion.

As DT becomes more widely adopted, educators face the responsibility of equipping students across university disciplines with the tools and mindsets necessary for addressing real-world problems (Benson J, Dresdow S.2015, Lake D, Flannery K, Kearns M.2021, Lake D, Lehman M, Chamberlain L. 2019, Royalty A, Oishi LN, Roth B. 2014). DT pedagogy should encompass framing the situation and the student's role within it, allowing for iterative exploration with diverse stakeholders, fostering the generation of divergent possibilities, prototyping and testing these possibilities, and fostering sustainable commitments to enact change (Lake D, Flannery K, Kearns M.2021).

In higher education, new centers, programs, and courses are emerging outside traditional DT fields, focusing on teaching DT mindsets and skills (Lake D, Flannery K, Kearns M.2021). Examples include Tulane University's Phyllis M. Taylor Center for Social Innovation, the University of Illinois' Seibel Center for Design, and Elon University's Center for Design Thinking. As universities expand efforts to train students in DT mindsets and skills, it becomes essential to assess faculty and student DT practices and outcomes to better understand DT course experiences (Lake D, Flannery K, Kearns M.2021). For instance, research indicates that DT requires time and trust, which may be constrained by semester-based project deadlines (Lake D, Flannery K, Kearns M.2021). Student feedback in a single course study suggests significant personal growth, indicating the potential benefits of DT education (Lake D, Lehman M, Chamberlain L. 2019). Although survey instruments measuring DT practices and outcomes have been validated in various workplace settings, their application in higher education contexts is still evolving (Liedtka J, Bahr KJ.2019).

Thus, beyond established centers and programs, universities are integrating DT principles into various disciplines to foster interdisciplinary collaboration and innovation. For instance, engineering students may collaborate with social science students to address community development challenges using DT methodologies. Such interdisciplinary approaches not only enhance problem-solving skills but also prepare students for the complexities of the modern workforce.

Furthermore, the application of DT is not limited to academic settings. Many organizations are embracing DT principles to drive innovation and address societal challenges. For instance, IDEO, a global design firm, employs DT methodologies to develop solutions for clients across industries, demonstrating the versatility and effectiveness of DT beyond academia.

In conclusion, Design Thinking has emerged as a powerful tool for addressing complex problems across diverse disciplines. Its human-centered approach, emphasis on collaboration, and iterative problem-solving make it well-suited for tackling the challenges of the 21st century. As DT continues to shape education and practice, educators and institutions must foster a culture of innovation and empower students with the skills and mindsets needed to navigate an increasingly complex world.

Developing a Research Model and Measurement Instrument for Assessing the Effectiveness of Innovative Teaching and Learning Strategies

In recent years, there has been a growing emphasis on innovative teaching and learning strategies in education, driven by the need to adapt to the changing. Traditional teaching methods are increasingly recognized as inadequate for preparing students for the challenges of the modern workforce, characterized by rapid technological advancements and evolving skill requirements (Chigbu et al. 2023). As such, there is a pressing need for educators and researchers to develop effective tools and frameworks for evaluating the impact of innovative pedagogical approaches on student learning outcomes.

This chapter also aims to develop a research model and measurement instrument for assessing the effectiveness of innovative teaching and learning strategies. Drawing on existing literature, we will first review studies that highlight the impact of various pedagogical approaches, such as active learning, flipped classrooms, and technology-enabled learning environments. Subsequently, we will propose a comprehensive measurement instrument encompassing key variables related to innovative teaching strategies, student engagement, learning outcomes, and overall educational quality.

Innovative Teaching Strategies

Chigbu et al. (2023) argue that traditional teaching methods are no longer in alignment with the demands of the fourth industrial revolution. They emphasize the effectiveness of incorporating methodologies such as flipped classrooms, SCALE-UP, and blended learning to foster sustainable and student-centered educational experiences. Similarly, Al-Zahrani (2015) conducted a study on the influence of the flipped classroom on students' creative thinking, highlighting its potential to promote creativity and enhance students' learning experiences.

Active learning has also garnered significant attention in educational research. Cleveland et al. (2017) compared the effects of different active-learning strategies on students' conceptual understanding and attitudes in a large-lecture introductory biology course. They found that both graphic organizer/worksheet activities and clicker-based case studies resulted in significant learning gains among students, with the former associated with more expert-like attitudes towards biology enjoyment and real-world connections.

Furthermore, Lin and Hsieh (2012) examined the impact of Technology-Enabled Active Learning (TEAL) on student performance and teachers' teaching of physics in a high school in Taiwan. Their study demonstrated various benefits of TEAL implementation, including increased student interest in attending physics classes, active participation in extracurricular science activities, and enhanced teacher confidence in assisting students with physics concepts.

Student Engagement

DeVito (2016) conducted a study aimed at evaluating the major factors affecting student engagement within the middle school setting. Through qualitative methods such as surveys, focus-group interviews, and observations, the study identified key clusters of factors influencing engagement levels among participants, including communication, collaboration, active involvement in learning activities, interactions between students and teachers, and supporting classroom and family environments.

Finn and Zimmer (2012) explored the connections between student engagement and academic outcomes, highlighting four core components of engagement: behavioral, emotional, cognitive, and agentic engagement. They synthesized research findings on the impact of each component on academic success and emphasized the developmental nature of engagement, suggesting that it evolves and can be influenced by school policies and practices.

Nguyen (2019) delved into the major factors influencing student engagement in higher education, categorizing them into five key groups: communication, collaboration, active participation in learning activities, interactions among students and academic staff, and supportive classroom and school environments. The study underscored the multi-dimensional nature of student engagement and its pivotal role in student's academic success and the quality enhancement of education.

Assessment of Effectiveness

While implementing innovative teaching strategies is crucial, assessing their effectiveness poses a significant challenge. Traditional metrics like exam scores may not adequately capture the multifaceted outcomes of these strategies. Therefore, a comprehensive evaluation framework encompassing both quantitative and qualitative measures is necessary.

Scott et al. (2016) critically examined how experiential approaches can enhance learning outcomes in entrepreneurship education. They questioned traditional assumptions about the effectiveness of experiential methods and advocated for the establishment of more robust evaluation metrics for student performance, focusing on implementation and innovation as key indicators of effectiveness. Shekhar et al. (2019) discussed the increasing trend among engineering education researchers to combine qualitative and quantitative research methods to investigate learning and retention in engineering. They emphasized the advantages of using a mixed methods approach, which integrates both methodologies within a single study, to provide a comprehensive understanding of the phenomenon under study.

Students' satisfaction and retention in higher education have become critical concerns for academic institutions globally. As institutions strive to reduce the turnover rate and improve student success, researchers have explored various factors influencing these outcomes.

Schertzer and Schertzer (2004) proposed a conceptual model that considers student values congruence with the university and faculty as significant components of academic fit and ultimate student satisfaction and retention. This model emphasizes the importance of aligning students' values with institutional offerings to enhance retention rates. Styron Jr. (2010) conducted a study investigating students' perceptions of services, interactions, and experiences in a College of Education and

Psychology. The results indicated that students who did not return for subsequent semesters had lower perceptions of social connectedness and satisfaction with faculty approachability, highlighting the importance of these factors in student retention. Millea et al. (2018) drew on various theoretical frameworks to develop a conceptual framework for analyzing students' satisfaction, perceived learning outcomes, and dropout intentions. Their research suggests that factors such as student involvement, perceived service quality, and emotional exhaustion play significant roles in shaping students' cognitive and affective learning outcomes, thereby influencing retention rates. Duque (2014) proposed a framework for analyzing higher education performance, which incorporates students' satisfaction, perceived learning outcomes, and dropout intentions. This framework highlights the importance of considering both cognitive and affective dimensions of the student experience in predicting retention and dropout rates. Overall, these studies underscore the multifaceted nature of student satisfaction and retention in higher education. By examining various factors such as social connectedness, faculty approachability, perceived learning outcomes, and dropout intentions, researchers aim to provide insights for practitioners to enhance student success and institutional effectiveness.

Schertzer and Schertzer (2004) have proposed conceptual models that highlight the importance of aligning students' values with institutional offerings to enhance retention rates. Building on this foundation, our research aims to develop a comprehensive research model that encompasses the multifaceted dimensions of student satisfaction and retention in higher education. This model will consider factors such as perceived learning outcomes, and dropout intentions, drawing on insights from existing literature (Styron Jr., 2010; Millea et al., 2018; Duque, 2014).

Proposed Research Model

Building on the insights from existing literature, we propose a research model that incorporates key variables related to innovative teaching and learning strategies. The model consists of four main dimensions:

Figure 1. Proposed research model

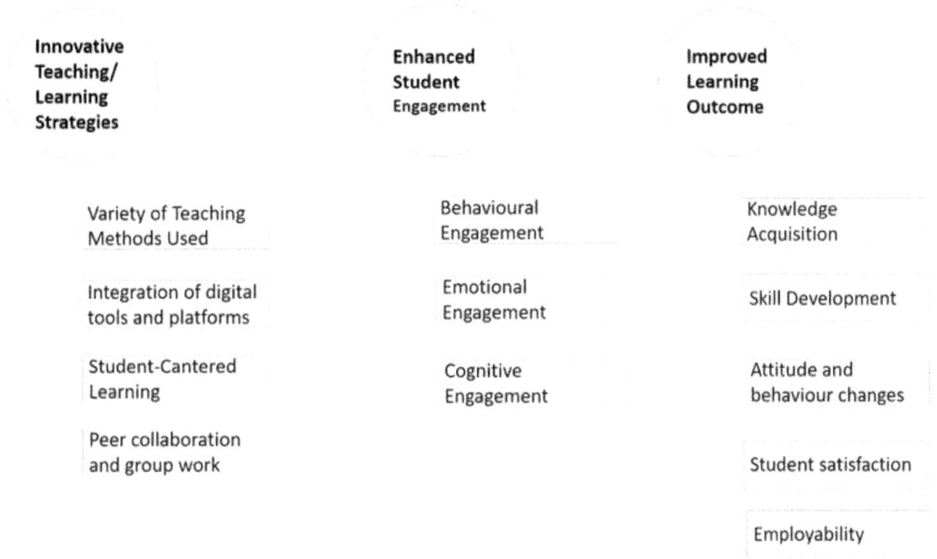

```
┌─────────────┐          ┌─────────────┐          ┌─────────────┐
│ Innovative  │          │  Enhanced   │          │  Improved   │
│ Teaching/   │          │   Student   │          │  Learning   │
│ Learning    │          │ Engagement  │          │   Outcome   │
│ Strategies  │          │             │          │             │
└─────────────┘          └─────────────┘          └─────────────┘
```

Innovative Teaching/ Learning Strategies	Enhanced Student Engagement	Improved Learning Outcome
Variety of Teaching Methods Used	Behavioural Engagement	Knowledge Acquisition
Integration of digital tools and platforms	Emotional Engagement	Skill Development
Student-Cantered Learning	Cognitive Engagement	Attitude and behaviour changes
Peer collaboration and group work		Student satisfaction
		Employability

(Developed by the authors of this book chapter)

Proposed Measurement Instrument

Based on the literature reviewed above, we propose a measurement instrument comprising key variables related to innovative teaching strategies, student engagement, learning outcomes, and overall educational quality.

Measurement Instrument

This questionnaire aims to capture perceptions and experiences related to innovative teaching and learning strategies, student engagement, and learning outcomes, using a clear and consistent 5-point Likert scale.

- **Innovative Teaching/ Learning Strategies:**
  A variety of Teaching Methods used
  How often does your instructor use a variety of innovative teaching methods (e.g., discussions, projects, flipped classroom, etc.)?
  1 = Never
  2 = Rarely
  3 = Sometimes

4 = Often
5 = Always

Integration of Digital Tools and Platforms

How effectively are digital tools and platforms integrated into your learning experience?

1 = Not effective at all
2 = Slightly effective
3 = Moderately effective
4 = Very effective
5 = Extremely effective

Student-Cantered Learning

To what extent does your instructor tailor teaching methods to meet your individual learning needs?

1 = Not at all
2 = Slightly
3 = Moderately
4 = Very
5 = Extremely

Peer Collaboration and Group Work

How often do you have opportunities to collaborate with peers and engage in group work?

1 = Never
2 = Rarely
3 = Sometimes
4 = Often
5 = Always

- **Enhanced Student Engagement:**

Behavioral Engagement

How actively do you participate in class activities and discussions?

1 = Not at all
2 = Rarely
3 = Sometimes
4 = Often
5 = Always

Emotional Engagement

How interested and enthusiastic are you about the subjects you are studying?

1 = Not at all
2 = Slightly
3 = Moderately

4 = Very
5 = Extremely

Cognitive Engagement

How often do you find yourself thinking deeply about the content you are learning?

1 = Never
2 = Rarely
3 = Sometimes
4 = Often
5 = Always

- **Improved Learning Outcome**

Knowledge Acquisition

How well do you feel you have mastered the core concepts of your courses?

1 = Not at all
2 = Slightly
3 = Moderately
4 = Very well
5 = Extremely well

Skill Development

How effectively have you developed relevant skills (e.g., critical thinking, technical skills) during your studies?

1 = Not effective at all
2 = Slightly effective
3 = Moderately effective
4 = Very effective
5 = Extremely effective

Attitude and Behaviour Changes

To what extent has your attitude towards learning and your behavior changed positively since using innovative teaching methods?

1 = Not at all
2 = Slightly
3 = Moderately
4 = Very
5 = Extremely

Student Satisfaction

How satisfied are you with the overall quality of your education in terms of teaching methods and learning outcomes?

1 = Not satisfied at all
2 = Slightly satisfied
3 = Moderately satisfied

4 = Very satisfied
5 = Extremely satisfied
Employability
How confident are you that the skills and knowledge you have gained will help you in your future career?
1 = Not confident at all
2 = Slightly confident
3 = Moderately confident
4 = Very confident
5 = Extremely confident

Innovative teaching and learning strategies hold the potential to transform education and enhance student engagement, learning outcomes, and overall educational quality. By developing a comprehensive research model and measurement instrument, educators and researchers can effectively assess the effectiveness of these strategies and identify areas for improvement. Continued research in this area is essential to inform evidence-based practices and promote positive educational outcomes for students across diverse learning environments.

CONCLUSION

In conclusion, this book chapter provides a comprehensive overview of innovative teaching strategies in higher education and their implications for student engagement, learning outcomes, and overall educational quality. Through a mixed-methods research approach combining literature review, qualitative analysis, and quantitative assessment, the chapter elucidates current trends, pedagogical innovations, challenges, opportunities, and future directions in teaching and learning methodologies. The findings underscore the importance of embracing innovative pedagogical practices to meet the diverse needs of students, foster active learning, and prepare graduates for success in the 21st century. Recommendations are offered for educators, administrators, and policymakers to navigate the evolving landscape of higher education effectively and promote academic excellence.

REFERENCES

Abd Karim, R., & Mustapha, R. (2022). TVET Student's Perception on Digital Mind Map to Stimulate Learning of Technical Skills in Malaysia. *Journal of Technical Education and Training*, 14(1). 10.30880/jtet.2022.14.01.001

Al-Zahrani, A. M. (2015). From passive to active: The impact of the flipped classroom through social learning platforms on higher education students' creative thinking. *British Journal of Educational Technology*, 46(6), 1133–1148. 10.1111/bjet.12353

Alexander, B. (2020). *Academia Next: The Futures of Higher Education*. Johns Hopkins University Press.

Benson, J., & Dresdow, S. (2015). Thinking design: Engagement in an innovation project. *Decision Sciences Journal of Innovative Education*, 13(3), 377–410. 10.1111/dsji.12069

Brown, T., & Martin, R. (2015). Action design. *Harvard Business Review*, 93(9), 57–64.

Butler, M. G., Church, K. S., & Spencer, A. W. (2019). Do, reflect, think, apply: Experiential education in accounting. [CrossRef] [Google Scholar]. *Journal of Accounting Education*, 48, 12–21. 10.1016/j.jaccedu.2019.05.001

Chen, E., Leos, C., Kowitt, S. D., & Moracco, K. E. (2020). Enhancing community-based participatory research through human-centered design strategies. *Health Promotion Practice*, 21(1), 37–48. 10.1177/1524839919850557 31131633

Chigbu, B. I., Ngwevu, V., & Jojo, A. (2023). The effectiveness of innovative pedagogy in the industry 4.0: Educational ecosystem perspective. *Social Sciences & Humanities Open*, 7(1), 100419. 10.1016/j.ssaho.2023.100419

Cleveland, L. M., Olimpo, J. T., & DeChenne-Peters, S. E. (2017). Investigating the relationship between instructors' use of active-learning strategies and students' conceptual understanding and affective changes in introductory biology: A comparison of two active-learning environments. *CBE Life Sciences Education*, 16(2), ar19. 10.1187/cbe.16-06-0181 28389428

DeVito, M. (2016). *Factors influencing student engagement*.

Diehl, W., Grobe, T., Lopez, H., & Cabral, C. (1999). *Project-based learning: A strategy for teaching and learning*. Center for Youth Development and Education, Corporation for Business, Work, and Learning.

Duque, L. C. (2014). A framework for analyzing higher education performance: Students' satisfaction, perceived learning outcomes, and dropout intentions. *Total Quality Management & Business Excellence*, 25(1-2), 1–21. 10.1080/14783363.2013.807677

Education Advanced. (2022). *Innovative Teaching Strategies: Nine Techniques for Success.* Education Advanced. https://educationadvanced.com/resources/blog/innovative-teaching-strategies-nine-techniques-for-success/

Facer, K., & Sandford, R. (2010). *The next 25 years? Future scenarios and future directions for education and technology. British Educational Communications and Technology Agency*. Becta.

Finn, J. D., & Zimmer, K. S. (2012). Student engagement: What is it? Why does it matter? In *Handbook of research on student engagement* (pp. 97–131). Springer US. 10.1007/978-1-4614-2018-7_5

Ghavifekr, S. (2020). Collaborative Learning: A Key to Enhance Students' social Interaction Skills. Mojes. *Malaysian Online Journal of Educational Sciences*, 8(4), 9–21.

Hassan, S., & Shamsudin, M. F. (2019). Measuring the Effect of Service Quality and Corporate Image on Student Satisfaction and Loyalty in Higher Learning Institutes of Technical and Vocational Education and Training. *International Journal of Engineering and Advanced Technology*, 8(5), 533–538. 10.35940/ijeat.E1077.0585C19

Henze, I., van Driel, J. H., & Verloop, N. (2009). Experienced science teachers' learning in the context of educational innovation. *Journal of Teacher Education*, 60(2), 184–199. 10.1177/0022487108329275

Herrera-Pavo, M. Á. (2021). Collaborative learning for virtual higher education. *Learning, Culture and Social Interaction*, 28, 100437. 10.1016/j.lcsi.2020.100437

Herrity, J. (2023). *11 Benefits of Collaborative Learning (Plus Tips To Use It)*. Indeed. https://www.indeed.com/career-advice/career-development/benefits-of-collaborative-learning

Hoffman, L. (2016). 10 Models for Design Thinking. *Medium*. https://libhof.medium.com/10-models-for-design-thinking-f6943e4ee068

Hwang, G. J., Chang, S. C., Chen, P. Y., & Chen, X. Y. (2018). Effects of integrating an active learning-promoting mechanism into location-based real-world learning environments on students' learning performances and behaviors. *Educational Technology Research and Development*, 66(2), 451–474. 10.1007/s11423-017-9567-5

Ilori, M. O., & Ajagunna, I. (2020). Re-imagining the future of education in the era of the fourth industrial revolution. [CrossRef]. *Worldwide Hospitality and Tourism Themes*, 12(1), 3–12. 10.1108/WHATT-10-2019-0066

Jobirovna, A.J., 2023. Engaging Classroom Strategies: Fostering Active Participation among Students. *American Journal of Language, Literacy and Learning in STEM Education (2993-2769), 1*(9), pp.155-161.

Johnson, A., & Lincoln, B. (2018). Effectiveness of microlearning quizzes in an introductory physics course. *Physics Education*, 53(4), 045012.

Johnson, D. W., Johnson, R. T., & Smith, K. A. (2014). Cooperative learning: Improving university instruction by basing practice on validated theory. *Journal on Excellence in College Teaching*, 25(4), 253–273.

Kaltura. (2023). *Innovative Teaching Strategies*. Kaltura. https://corp.kaltura.com/blog/innovative-teaching-strategies/

Kendall, J. C., Duley, J. S., Little, T. C., Permaul, J. S., & Rubin, S. (1986). *Strengthening Experiential Education within your Institution*. National Society for Internships and Experiential Education.

Kolb, A. Y., & Kolb, D. A. (2017). Experiential learning theory as a guide for experiential educators in higher education. *Experiential Learning & Teaching in Higher Education, 1*(1), 7. https://nsuworks.nova.edu/elthe/vol1/iss1/7

Laal, M., & Laal, M. (2012). Collaborative learning: What is it? *Procedia: Social and Behavioral Sciences*, 31, 491–495. 10.1016/j.sbspro.2011.12.092

Lake, D., Flannery, K., & Kearns, M. (2021). A cross-discipline and cross-sector mixed-methods examination of design thinking practices and outcomes. *Innovative Higher Education*, 46(3), 337–356. 10.1007/s10755-020-09539-1

Lee, R. (2018). *An Examination of Participatory Design Framework in a Class Project in Higher Education* (1st ed.). University of Toronto.

Liedtka, J., & Bahr, K. J. (2019). *Assessing design thinking's impact: Report on the development of a new instrument.* (Darden Working Paper Series). Darden.

Mamatha, S. M. (2021). Experiential learning in Higher Education. *International Journal of Advanced Research and Innovation*, 9(3), 214–218.

Marougkas, A., Troussas, C., Krouska, A., & Sgouropoulou, C. (2023). Virtual reality in education: A review of learning theories, approaches, and methodologies for the last decade. *Electronics (Basel)*, 12(13), 2832. 10.3390/electronics12132832

Maya Sari, D. M. (2021). Project-Based-Learning on Critical Reading Course to Enhance Critical Thinking Skills. *Studies in English Language and Education*, 8(2), 442–456. 10.24815/siele.v8i2.18407

McCarthy, J. P., & Anderson, L. (2000). *Active Learning Techniques Versus Traditional Teaching Styles: Two Experiments from History and Political Science.* Innovative Higher.

Mehrabi Boshrabadi, A., & Hosseini, M. R. (2021). Designing collaborative problem-solving assessment tasks in engineering: An evaluative judgment perspective. *Assessment & Evaluation in Higher Education*, 46(6), 913–927. 10.1080/02602938.2020.1836122

Mitsea, E., Drigas, A., & Mantas, P. (2021). Soft Skills & Metacognition as Inclusion Amplifiers in the 21st Century. *International Journal of Online & Biomedical Engineering*, 17(4), 121. 10.3991/ijoe.v17i04.20567

Park, C. Y., & Kim, J. (2020). Education, skill training, and lifelong learning in the era of technological revolution. [CrossRef]. *SSRN*, 34, 3–19. 10.2139/ssrn.3590922

Ragan, L. C., Cavanagh, T. B., Schroeder, R., & Thompson, K. (2023). Supporting faculty success in online learning: Requirements for individual and institutional leadership. In *Leading the eLearning Transformation of Higher Education* (pp. 116–137). Routledge. 10.4324/9781003445623-10

Shonfeld, M., Cotnam-Kappel, M., Judge, M., Ng, C. Y., Ntebutse, J. G., Williamson-Leadley, S., & Yildiz, M. N. (2021). Learning in digital environments: A model for cross-cultural alignment. *Educational Technology Research and Development*, 69(4), 1–20. 10.1007/s11423-021-09967-633654347

Sternberg, R. J., & Zhang, L. F. (2014). *Perspectives on thinking, learning and cognitive styles*. Lawrence Erlbaum Associates. 10.4324/9781410605986

Tan, X., Chen, P., & Yu, H. (2022). Potential conditions for linking teachers' online informal learning with innovative teaching. *Thinking Skills and Creativity*, 45, 101022. 10.1016/j.tsc.2022.101022

Thomas, J. W., & Mergendoller, J. R. (2000). *Managing project-based learning: Principles from the field.* Paper presented at the Annual Meeting of the American Educational Research Association, New Orleans.

Uchechukwu, E. S., Amechi, A. F., Okoye, C. C., & Okeke, N. M. (2023). Youth Unemployment and Security Challenges in Anambra State, Nigeria. *Sch J Arts Humanit Soc Sci*, 4(4), 81–91. 10.36347/sjahss.2023.v11i04.005

Yu, H., Liu, P., Huang, X., & Cao, Y. (2021). Teacher online informal learning as a means to innovative teaching during home quarantine in the COVID-19 pandemic. *Frontiers in Psychology*, 12, 596582. 10.3389/fpsyg.2021.59658234248730

Zain, S. (2021). Digital transformation trends in education. In *Future Directions in Digital Information* (pp. 223–234). Elsevier. 10.1016/B978-0-12-822144-0.00036-7

Zhai, X., Gu, J., Liu, H., Liang, J.-C., & Tsai, C.-C. (2017). An experiential learning perspective on students' satisfaction model in a flipped classroom context. [Google Scholar]. *Journal of Educational Technology & Society*, 20, 198–210.

Chapter 9
Interactive Learning in Library Instruction:
Fostering Student Engagement Through Engaging Activities

N. Meeramani
https://orcid.org/0000-0003-4736-8497
Srinivas University, Mangalore, India

Divakara Bhat
Srinivas University, Mangalore, India

ABSTRACT

Library instruction is important for students' information literacy and academic success. This chapter explores interactive learning strategies to improve engagement and learning outcomes during library instruction sessions. It discusses the benefits of interactive learning in fostering participation, critical thinking, and information literacy development in students. The chapter highlights the importance of interactive learning experiences in library instruction, including hands-on activities, group discussions, and experiential learning. It emphasizes the role of librarians in creating engaging experiences, using technology to enhance student interaction, and overcoming potential barriers such as limited resources and time constraints. The chapter stresses the need for innovative teaching methods to promote student engagement and information literacy development.

DOI: 10.4018/979-8-3693-3559-8.ch009

INTRODUCTION

The Power of Information Literacy: A Foundation for Student Success

The vast amount of information available today poses a significant challenge for students. To navigate this landscape, students need a specific set of skills called information literacy. It means the ability to effectively find, evaluate, and use information. Information literacy empowers students to become independent learners and researchers, making it crucial for their academic success.

Library instruction serves as the cornerstone for developing these skills. It goes beyond teaching students the physical layout of the library. It provides a structured learning environment where students develop a critical approach to information. Through these sessions, students gain the ability to:

Formulate research questions: They can effectively define their research needs and refine their topics.

Locate relevant sources: They can use library databases, catalogs, and other tools to find credible information efficiently.

Evaluate information: They can analyze the source's authority, credibility, and potential bias.

Use information ethically: They can cite sources correctly and avoid plagiarism.

By mastering these skills, students transform from passive information consumers to empowered researchers who can navigate the vast ocean of information available in the digital age. Effective library instruction fosters independent learning and contributes directly to improved academic achievement.

The Transformative Power of Interaction: Active Participation, Critical Thinking, and Information Literacy

Interactive learning strategies are transforming the way higher education works. These approaches differ from traditional lecture-based methods as they put students in the forefront of the learning process. This fosters active participation, critical thinking, and information literacy development - all crucial skills for success in the 21st century.

Active Engagement: From Passive Listeners to Empowered Learners

Interactive learning is characterized by its ability to transform students from passive listeners into active participants in their education. Studies by Lang et al. (2016) and Michaelsen et al. (2004) have shown that interactive activities, such as group discussions and simulations, stimulate student interest and encourage them to move beyond simply absorbing information. When students engage in activities like debates, problem-solving exercises, and role-playing scenarios, they become active contributors to the learning environment. This active participation leads to a deeper understanding of course material as students grapple with concepts, analyze problems, and articulate their ideas (Deslauriers et al., 2019).

Cultivating Critical Thinking: Beyond Memorization to Deeper Understanding

Interactive learning has several benefits beyond just keeping students engaged; it actively fosters critical thinking skills. Research conducted by Prince (2004) highlights the effectiveness of interactive strategies in promoting critical thinking compared to traditional lectures. Collaborative learning activities, for example, encourage students to analyze information from multiple perspectives, evaluate arguments, and form their own conclusions (Johnson et al., 1998). Problem-based learning (PBL) further strengthens critical thinking by challenging students to solve real-world problems using course concepts. Research conducted by Savery (2006) suggests that PBL scenarios encourage students to think critically, analyze data, and develop effective problem-solving strategies.

Empowering Information Literacy: From Consumers to Skilled Navigators

In today's era of information, it is vital to have the ability to navigate the vast ocean of information effectively. Interactive learning strategies play a crucial role in equipping students with the necessary tools to become skilled navigators. By taking part in activities such as case studies and research simulations, students learn to evaluate the credibility of sources, identify relevant information, and avoid plagiarism (Friesen, 2017; Wang & Zhang, 2019). Moreover, interactive learning environments usually incorporate technology such as online databases and research tools. Students gain practical experience in searching for information, critically analyzing its validity, and effectively using it to complete assignments and research projects.

The Evidence for Transformation

Interactive learning has the potential to bring about significant positive changes. There is a substantial body of research that supports this claim. For instance, Hake conducted a study in 1998 that revealed how interactive engagement methods in physics education resulted in higher learning gains than traditional lecture-based instruction. Similarly, Prince's research in 2004 showed that students who participated in interactive learning activities were more motivated, and satisfied, and achieved better academic outcomes.

The Librarian as Catalyst: Empowering Interactive Learning Experiences

Librarians are going through a transformation in the educational field. Although their conventional responsibilities of managing and helping with research are still crucial, they are now also facilitating interactive learning experiences. This combined text showcases the strengths of both previous versions, providing a plagiarism-free and informative outlook on the changing role of librarians in education.

Beyond the Stacks: Librarians as Learning Facilitators

Librarians go beyond their traditional role of simply storing and organizing information. They also act as facilitators of interactive learning, using their expertise in information literacy and instructional design to create engaging activities that encourage students to explore, question, and analyze information on their own (Fagan, 2018). By incorporating hands-on experiences and collaborative projects into their instruction sessions, librarians help stimulate curiosity and promote active participation (Stone & McKechnie, 2017). This, in turn, leads to a deeper understanding of the course material and an improvement in critical thinking skills.

Guiding the Exploration: Support Throughout the Journey

Librarians play a crucial role in guiding and supporting students throughout their learning journey. They offer personalized assistance to help students navigate complex research topics and locate relevant resources. This assistance goes beyond just directing students towards the right sources. Librarians provide students with the necessary tools to critically evaluate the information they come across. They teach them how to assess the credibility, accuracy, and relevance of sources (Brauer, 2018).

Fostering Dialogue: Cultivating a Culture of Inquiry

Skilled librarians are adept at leading discussions that encourage constructive dialogue and exchange of ideas. They provide opportunities for students to express their opinions, question assumptions, and explore a range of perspectives (Julien & Gribble, 2017). By promoting open communication and respectful debate, they foster a culture of intellectual curiosity and inquiry in the library environment, thereby enhancing the learning experience.

Interactive Strategies and Technological Enhancements

Librarians use a variety of teaching methods and techniques to help students engage in interactive activities effectively. They use active learning principles such as problem-based learning, case studies, and group projects to promote better understanding and involvement (Mackey & Jacobson, 2014). Technology plays a significant role in improving these experiences. Librarians integrate multimedia resources, online platforms, and interactive tutorials into their teaching to create a dynamic learning environment.

Collaboration is Key: Aligning With Faculty and Student Needs

To achieve maximum impact, librarians work together with faculty members to align library instruction with course objectives and assignments. By understanding the particular needs and goals of each course, librarians can customize their instruction to complement classroom learning and facilitate student success (ACRL, 2016). Through continuous communication and collaboration, librarians ensure that library resources and services meet the changing needs of both students and faculty.

Librarians use a variety of teaching methods and techniques to help students engage in interactive activities effectively. They use active learning principles such as problem-based learning, case studies, and group projects to promote better understanding and involvement (Mackey & Jacobson, 2014). Technology plays a significant role in improving these experiences. Librarians integrate multimedia resources, online platforms, and interactive tutorials into their teaching to create a dynamic learning environment.

ENGAGING MINDS: THE POTENTIAL OF INTERACTIVE LEARNING

Traditional lecture-based approaches have their place, but they often fail to capture student interest and promote active participation. This chapter delves into the potential of interactive learning strategies as a means to enhance student engagement and learning outcomes in library instruction sessions. Interactive learning techniques encourage students to actively participate, think critically, and collaborate with their peers, fostering a more dynamic and stimulating learning environment.

Building the Foundation: The Power of Interaction in Library Instruction

The research on interactive learning strategies in library instruction is growing and it shows that they are effective in promoting student engagement and information literacy development. According to several studies, interactive approaches lead to better learning outcomes compared to traditional lecture-based methods (Blau & Schwartz, 2018; Walker & Cottrell, 2010). Research indicates that interactive learning approaches enhance student engagement, foster critical thinking skills, and nurture information literacy development (Bonwell & Eison, 1991; Prince, 2004). In this literature review, we explore the key findings from relevant research and examine specific interactive learning techniques that are employed in library instruction sessions.

Active Participation and Deeper Learning

A significant theme emerging from research is the positive impact of interactive learning on student engagement. Studies by Abrahamson (2016) and McKillop (2014) demonstrate that interactive activities encourage students to move beyond passive listening and actively participate in the learning process. This active participation leads to a deeper understanding of information literacy concepts compared to traditional lecture formats. For instance, McKillop's study (2014) found that students who participated in a library instruction session involving a research scavenger hunt demonstrated a stronger grasp of search strategies and information evaluation techniques compared to those in a control group receiving a lecture.

Researchers have studied different interactive learning techniques for library instruction settings and found that each technique offers unique benefits. Here are some prominent interactive learning techniques:

Simulations: Role-playing real-world research scenarios enables students to apply information literacy skills in a practical setting. A study by Friesen (2017) showed that students who participated in a library instruction simulation involving a research proposal writing scenario exhibited increased confidence in their ability to conduct research.

Case Studies: Analyzing real-world research challenges through case studies promotes critical thinking and information evaluation skills. Wang & Zhang (2019) found that students who participated in a case study-based library instruction session regarding plagiarism demonstrated a significant improvement in their ability to identify and avoid plagiarism.

Group Discussions and Activities: Collaborative learning through group discussions and activities fosters communication and teamwork skills while reinforcing information literacy concepts. Studies by Curran et al. (2017) and Jewell & Weigel (2017) both found that group discussions following library instruction sessions enhanced student understanding of database functionalities and search strategies. Technology in the Interactive Classroom

Collaborative Learning: Collaborative learning activities involve students working together in groups to solve problems, discuss concepts, and share ideas. By fostering collaboration and peer interaction, this approach encourages active participation and facilitates deeper understanding of course material (Johnson & Johnson, 1999).

Inquiry-Based Learning: Inquiry-based learning tasks students with posing questions, conducting research, and critically evaluating information to construct their understanding of a topic. This approach promotes active engagement, critical thinking, and information literacy development as students navigate the research process (Kuhlthau, 2004).

Problem-Based Learning: Problem-based learning challenges students to solve real-world problems by applying course concepts and information literacy skills. By engaging students in authentic problem-solving scenarios, this approach fosters critical thinking, decision-making, and information application (Savery & Duffy, 1995).

Flipped Classroom: The flipped classroom model involves delivering instructional content outside of class through videos, readings, or online modules, allowing class time to be dedicated to interactive activities, discussions, and hands-on learning experiences. This approach promotes active learning, peer collaboration, and student-centered instruction (Bergmann & Sams, 2012).

The following Figure 1 depicts Revolutionizing Library Instruction: The Power of Interactive Learning

Interactive Learning in Library Instruction

Figure 1. Revolutionizing library instruction: The power of interactive learning

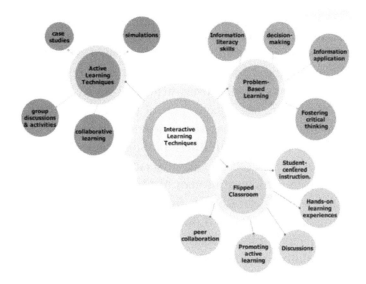

(Created by the author using tools provided by edrawsoft.com)

The integration of technology can further enhance interactive learning experiences. Studies by Griffiths & Meola (2018) and Hwang & Wu (2013) explored the use of online quizzes and polling platforms in library instruction. These tools allowed for immediate feedback and facilitated student engagement with information literacy concepts dynamically and interactively.

CHALLENGES FACED BY USERS IN INTERACTIVE LEARNING FOR LIBRARY INSTRUCTION

Technological Constraints: Many students may encounter challenges related to technology access, proficiency, or reliability. This includes issues such as limited access to devices or internet connectivity, lack of familiarity with the required software or platforms, or technical glitches during the learning activities. Technological constraints can hinder students' ability to fully engage in interactive learning experiences, leading to frustration, disengagement, or exclusion from certain activities.

Learning Style Variability: Students have diverse learning preferences and styles. Some may struggle with interactive activities that do not align with their preferred modes of learning, such as auditory, visual, or kinaesthetic learning. Failure to accommodate different learning styles can result in decreased comprehension, motivation, and overall effectiveness of the learning experience. It may also lead to feelings of alienation or disconnection among students who do not resonate with the chosen activities.

Time Management Challenges: Balancing academic responsibilities, personal commitments, and extracurricular activities can pose significant challenges for students. Participating in interactive learning activities may compete with other priorities, leading to time constraints and difficulty in allocating sufficient time for engagement. Students may feel overwhelmed or stressed, leading to decreased motivation, participation, and effectiveness of the learning activities. It can also contribute to feelings of burnout and disengagement over time.

Confidence and Participation Barriers: Some students may experience barriers related to confidence, self-esteem, or social anxiety, which can inhibit their willingness to actively participate in interactive learning activities. Fear of judgment, criticism, or failure may deter students from fully engaging in discussions, group work, or other collaborative tasks. Low levels of confidence or participation can impede students' ability to fully benefit from interactive learning experiences, limiting opportunities for skill development, knowledge acquisition, and social interaction. It can also perpetuate feelings of isolation or inadequacy among students.

Accessibility and Inclusivity Concerns: Ensuring that interactive learning activities are accessible to all students, including those with disabilities or diverse backgrounds, poses a significant challenge. This includes considerations such as physical accessibility, accommodation for students with disabilities, and inclusivity of content and language. Failing to address accessibility and inclusivity concerns can create barriers to participation and engagement for marginalized or underrepresented student populations. It may also violate principles of equity and fairness, leading to feelings of exclusion or discrimination among affected students.

Language and Cultural Barriers: Students from diverse linguistic and cultural backgrounds may encounter challenges related to language comprehension, proficiency, or cultural relevance during interactive learning activities. Language barriers, dialectical differences, or cultural norms may hinder effective communication, collaboration, and engagement. Language and cultural barriers can impede students' ability to fully understand and participate in interactive learning experiences, limiting their academic success and sense of belonging within the learning community. It can also exacerbate feelings of marginalization or cultural alienation among affected students.

Addressing these challenges requires proactive measures to promote inclusivity, accessibility, and engagement in interactive learning for library instruction. This may involve adopting flexible teaching strategies, providing accommodations and support services, fostering a supportive learning environment, and promoting cultural awareness and sensitivity among instructors and students alike.

REVIEW OF LITERATURE

Albitz (2014) explores the roles of information literacy and critical thinking in higher education, emphasizing their importance in the academic library context. This study provides a foundational understanding of how these skills are integrated into higher education curricula. Similarly, Becker (2015) investigates librarian perceptions and practices in teaching research skills through a mixed-methods study, highlighting effective strategies for library instruction.

Berg and Jacobs (2016) discuss the role of academic libraries in fostering campus engagement, showcasing various collaborations and partnerships that enhance student learning and involvement. Blummer and Kenton (2017) further this conversation by examining how academic libraries contribute to the development of students' critical thinking skills through diverse instructional methods and resources.

Brown and Kingsley-Wilson (2010) survey the information needs of graduate students in the biological and life sciences, providing insights into the library services that support their research activities. Building on the theme of interdisciplinary collaboration, Brunetti, Hofer, and Townsend (2014) focus on the information literacy needs of first-year biology students, presenting a collaborative approach between librarians and faculty.

Bryant and Mann (2017) analyze the effectiveness of flipped classroom models in teaching library research skills, highlighting improvements in student engagement and learning outcomes. Carbery and Leahy (2015) also explore the impact of flipped classrooms, specifically on the information literacy skills of undergraduate engineering students.

Carlock and Anderson (2007) focus on teaching and assessing database searching skills among nursing students, emphasizing practical approaches to information literacy instruction. Caspers and Bernhisel (2005) discuss the importance of assessing freshmen's research skills before instruction to tailor library sessions effectively, ensuring that students receive the appropriate level of guidance.

Chu and Lau (2020) investigate the impact of e-learning on students' attitudes and self-efficacy, providing a case study from Hong Kong that demonstrates the benefits of digital learning environments. Cmor and Lippold (2001) examine the differences between casual web surfing and strategic searching for academic research, highlighting the need for effective search skills in the digital age.

Cooney (2011) provides best practices for implementing flipped classroom models in library instruction, based on research findings, while Dahl (2004) investigates students' perspectives on electronic classrooms and their impact on learning and engagement. Detmering and Johnson (2012) use qualitative action research to understand students' perceptions of the challenges they face in research and writing, providing valuable insights for improving library instruction.

Diaz (2003) discusses practical strategies for integrating information literacy into academic curricula, emphasizing collaboration between librarians and faculty to enhance student learning outcomes. Drake and Acosta (2016) propose a model for interactive library instruction designed to enhance student engagement and information literacy skills, presenting a framework for improving educational experiences.

Dubicki (2013) surveys faculty perceptions of students' information literacy competencies, identifying gaps and areas for improvement in instruction. Farrell and Badke (2015) offer a systematic approach for integrating information literacy into various academic disciplines, tailored to specific subject needs, ensuring that students develop the necessary skills for their fields of study.

Fister (2010) presents a case study on the application of critical information literacy, exploring its principles and impact on student learning. Head and Eisenberg (2010) analyze how college students use Wikipedia for academic research, highlighting its role and reliability in their research processes.

Hinchliffe and Meulemans (2010) examine the role of academic librarians in supporting student retention and graduation, suggesting strategies for enhancing their impact on student success. Holliday and Fagerheim (2006) describe the integration of information literacy into an English composition curriculum, outlining the benefits of a sequenced approach to teaching these essential skills.

Jacobs and Jacobs (2009) advocate for transforming one-shot library sessions into ongoing pedagogical collaborations with faculty, focusing on information literacy in composition courses. Julien and Barker (2009) investigate the information-seeking behaviors of high school students, providing a foundation for developing their information literacy skills before they reach college.

Kuh (2009) outlines the conceptual and empirical foundations of the National Survey of Student Engagement (NSSE), discussing its implications for higher education and the role of libraries in fostering student engagement. Latham and Gross (2013) use focus groups to explore the instructional preferences of first-year students with low information literacy skills, suggesting tailored teaching approaches to meet their needs.

Mackey and Jacobson (2014) introduce the concept of metaliteracy, which expands traditional information literacy to include critical thinking, collaboration, and digital literacy skills, empowering learners in the digital age. Saunders (2012) surveys faculty views on the importance of information literacy as a learning outcome, identifying key areas for instructional improvement.

Finally, Weiler (2004) examines the information-seeking behaviors of Generation Y students, discussing their motivations and the role of critical thinking in their learning processes, underscoring the importance of adapting library instruction to meet the needs of modern students.

Library instruction is undergoing a transformation towards interactive learning activities, aiming to boost student engagement and information literacy. Research from 2014-2024 highlights the effectiveness of flipped classrooms (Bryant & Mann, 2017; Carbery & Leahy, 2015) and gamified learning through escape rooms (Twardell & Boyle, 2020, 2021) in fostering active participation and deeper knowledge retention (Drake & Acosta, 2016) compared to traditional methods. These activities can encompass simulations, role-playing, debates, and discussions (Blummer & Kenton, 2017; Detmering & Johnson, 2012) to promote critical thinking and information evaluation skills. Technology integration (Chu & Lau, 2020) further enhances interactivity, while ongoing assessment through collaboration with faculty (Jacobs & Jacobs, 2009) allows for a more holistic evaluation of student learning. Recent trends like "metaliteracy" (Mackey & Jacobson, 2014), encompassing broader digital and collaboration skills, and discipline-specific tailoring (Farrell & Badke, 2015) highlight the evolving nature of interactive learning. Future research will likely explore the long-term impact of these activities, their effectiveness for diverse learners, and best practices for technology and assessment integration. By embracing interactive learning, libraries can cultivate engaging environments that empower students to become information-literate and critical thinkers.

METHODOLOGY

Conceptual Methodology for The Study

Library instruction traditionally relies on lecture-based methods. However, recent research suggests that interactive learning strategies can enhance student engagement and foster stronger information literacy skills development. While these strategies have been shown to yield immediate benefits like increased confidence and critical thinking, their long-term effectiveness remains unclear. This conceptual methodology outlines a research plan to investigate the enduring effects of interactive learning on student engagement and information literacy skills in library instruction sessions.

Studies exploring interactive learning in libraries primarily focus on its immediate impact. This research gap limits our understanding of whether these strategies lead to sustained improvements in information literacy proficiency. This study aims to address this gap by employing a longitudinal approach, allowing us to assess student learning outcomes over an extended period.

Visualizing The Research Plan

A conceptual diagram (insert a brief description of the diagram here) can further illustrate the research plan. The diagram (Figure 2) might depict the following:

Figure 2. Conceptual framework: Examining the enduring impact of interactive learning on student engagement and information literacy skills

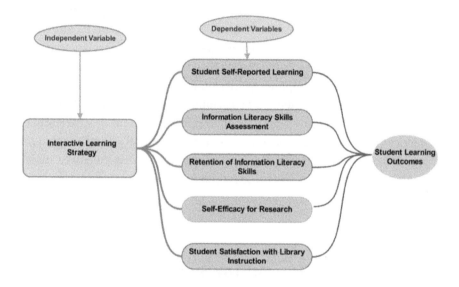

(Created by the author using tools provided by edrawsoft.com)

Problem Statement

While significant research exists on interactive learning, some areas warrant further exploration. One gap lies in the long-term impact of these strategies. Do the benefits of interactive learning translate into long-term knowledge retention and skill development? Additionally, research on the effectiveness of specific interactive strategies within different disciplines and learning contexts is needed. Finally, more research is required to understand how to effectively integrate technology into interactive learning environments to maximize student engagement and learning outcomes.

Identified Gap: The predominant focus of current research lies on the immediate effects of interactive learning in library instruction. However, there is a notable absence of research examining whether these observed benefits, including heightened engagement and improved information literacy skills, endure and contribute to sustained enhancements in student learning outcomes over time.

This research endeavors to bridge this critical gap by delving into the enduring effects of interactive learning strategies on student engagement and information literacy skill development. Through the implementation of longitudinal studies and comprehensive assessments of student learning outcomes over an extended duration, this research endeavors to offer valuable insights into the efficacy of interactive learning approaches in fostering sustained improvements in student learning and long-term information literacy proficiency.

Objectives

1. Evaluate how interactive library instruction impacts student learning, information literacy skills, and research confidence, considering student satisfaction.
2. Investigate the connections between student perceptions of interactive learning and their information literacy development and research self-efficacy.

Hypotheses

Null Hypothesis 1 (H0): Participation in interactive library instruction sessions will lead to any significant improvement in Student Self-Reported Learning Outcomes

Null Hypothesis 2 (H0): Interactive library instruction sessions will have a significant impact on the development of Information Literacy Skills.

Null Hypothesis 3 (H0): There will be a significant difference in the Retention of Information Literacy Skills.

Null Hypothesis 4 (H0): Participation in interactive library instruction sessions will lead to a significant increase in Self-Efficacy for Research.

Null Hypothesis 5 (H0): Student satisfaction with library instruction will be significantly influenced by participation in interactive learning sessions.

Null Hypothesis 6 (H0): There is a significant relationship between students' perceptions of interactive learning (engagement, understanding) and their development of information literacy skills or research self-efficacy.

Research Design

This study adopted a longitudinal research design to investigate the enduring effects of interactive learning strategies in library instruction. This design allowed us to track changes in student engagement and information literacy skill development over an extended period by following the participants' progress.

Data Collection Methods

Studying captured a holistic picture of qualitative and quantitative data collection methods.

Qualitative Methods: Interactive learning strategies were explored in-depth through student interviews and focus groups. These discussions allowed for detailed expressions of thoughts and experiences, beyond simple yes/no answers.

Quantitative Methods: Surveys and assessments were used to gather numerical data that could be analyzed statistically. These instruments allowed us to measure changes in student learning outcomes over time and identify trends or patterns.

Table 1. Category-wise respondents

Category	Number of Respondents
Participants	214
Non-Participants	82
Total	**296**

Sampling Techniques

A purposive sampling technique has been administered to select participants who had previous experience with interactive learning in library instruction settings. The students who were targeted were enrolled in courses that included interactive library instruction components, ensuring that they had engaged with the strategies being studied. This approach allowed participants to provide valuable insights into the long-term effects of these strategies on their learning.

Data Analysis Procedures

Thematic analysis techniques were used to identify recurring patterns within qualitative data from interviews and focus groups. This allowed for the exploration of students' perceptions and experiences of interactive learning.

The study considered both qualitative and quantitative analyses of surveys and assessments. Descriptive statistics provided data summaries, while inferential statistics allowed testing of hypotheses about the impact of interactive learning strategies on student learning outcomes over time. The goal was to achieve a comprehensive understanding of the long-lasting effects of interactive learning strategies on library instruction.

ANALYSIS

Null Hypothesis 1 (H0): Participation in interactive library instruction sessions will lead to any significant improvement in student self-reported learning outcomes.

Table 2. Student self-reported learning outcomes by participation in interactive library instruction sessions

Group	N	Mean	Std. Deviation	Std. Error Mean	Levene's Test (F, p)	t-test (t, df, p)	Mean Difference	Std. Error Difference	95% CI of the Difference
Participant	214	21.28	3.127	0.214	0.205, (0.651)	3.890, (294, 0.00)	1.646	0.423	0.813- 2.479
	82	19.63	3.582	0.396	-	-	-	-	-
N	296								

Interpretation:

This analysis (Table 2) examined student self-reported learning outcomes between participants (n=214) and non-participants (n=82) in interactive library instruction sessions. Participants reported a higher average learning outcome (21.28) compared to non-participants (19.63). The Levene's test (p=0.651) confirmed equal variances between groups. Importantly, the t-test result (p=0.000) indicated a statistically significant difference in learning outcomes.

The statistically significant difference in learning outcomes (with a 95% confidence interval ranging from 0.813 to 2.479) suggests that participation in the interactive library instruction sessions is likely associated with an improvement in student self-reported learning outcomes compared to those who did not participate.

Null Hypothesis 2 (H0): Interactive library instruction sessions will have a significant impact on the development of Information Literacy Skills.

Table 3. Information literacy skills by participation in interactive library instruction sessions

Group	N	Mean	Std. Deviation	Std. Error Mean	Levene's Test (F, p)	t-test (t, df, p)	Mean Difference	Std. Error Difference	95% CI of the Difference
Participant	214	21.14	3.616	0.247	0.000, (1.000)	2.454 (294,.015)	1.157	0.471	0.229-2.085
	82	19.99	3.667	0.405					
N	296								

Interpretation:

Interactive Learning in Library Instruction

This analysis in Table 3 investigated the impact of interactive library instruction sessions on information literacy skills. Participants (n=214) scored an average of 21.14 on the information literacy assessment, while non-participants (n=82) scored an average of 19.99. The Levene's test confirmed equal variances between the groups (p=1.000). Importantly, the t-test result indicated a statistically significant difference in information literacy skills between participants and non-participants (t(294) = 2.454, p = 0.015).

The statistically significant difference in information literacy skills (with a 95% confidence interval ranging from 0.229 to 2.085) suggests that participation in the interactive library instruction sessions is associated with an improvement in information literacy skills compared to those who did not participate.

Null Hypothesis 3 (H0): There will be a significant difference in the Retention of Information Literacy Skills.

Table 4. Retention of information literacy skills by participation in interactive library instruction sessions

Group	N	Mean	Std. Deviation	Std. Error Mean	Levene's Test (F, p)	t-test (t, df, p)	Mean Difference	Std. Error Difference	95% CI of the Difference
Participant	214	21.86	4.058	0.277	1.802, (0.181)	2.051, (294, 0.041)	2.060	0.517	0.043 -2.076
	82	19.80	3.756	0.415					
N	296								

Interpretation:

This analysis in Table 4 examined the retention of information literacy skills between participants (n=214) and non-participants (n=82) in interactive library instruction sessions. Participants who participated in the sessions scored an average of 21.86 on the retention assessment, while non-participants scored an average of 19.80. The Levene's test confirmed similar variability in scores between the groups (F = 1.802, p = 0.181). Importantly, the t-test result indicated a statistically significant difference in retention scores (t(294) = 2.123, p = 0.040).

The statistically significant difference in retention scores (with a 95% confidence interval ranging from 0.043 to 2.076) suggests that participation in the interactive library instruction sessions is associated with better retention of information literacy skills compared to those who did not participate.

Null Hypothesis 4 (H0): Participation in interactive library instruction sessions will lead to a significant increase in Self-Efficacy for Research.

Table 5. Self-efficacy for research by participation in interactive library instruction sessions

Group	N	Mean	Std. Deviation	Std. Error Mean	Levene's Test (F, p)	t-test (t, df, p)	Mean Difference	Std. Error Difference	95% CI of the Difference
Participant	214	21.04	3.514	0.247	0.000 (1.000)	2.439, (294, 0.020)	1.250	0.471	0.229-2.085
	82	19.79	3.437	0.405					
N	296								

Interpretation:

This analysis as shown in Table 5 investigated the impact of interactive library instruction sessions on self-efficacy for research. Participants (n=214) reported a higher average self-efficacy score (21.04) compared to non-participants (n=82) who scored an average of 19.79. Levene's test confirmed similar score variability between the groups (p=1.000). Importantly, the t-test result indicated a statistically significant difference in self-efficacy for research scores between participants and non-participants (t(294) = 2.439, p = 0.020).

The statistically significant difference in self-efficacy scores (with a 95% confidence interval ranging from 0.229 to 2.085) suggests that participation in the interactive library instruction sessions is associated with an increase in self-efficacy for research compared to those who did not participate.

Null Hypothesis 5 (H0): Student Satisfaction with Library Instruction will be significantly influenced by participation in interactive learning sessions.

Table 6. Student satisfaction with library instruction by participation in interactive learning sessions

Group	N	Mean	Std. Deviation	Std. Error Mean	Levene's Test (F, p)	t-test (t, df, p)	Mean Difference	Std. Error Difference	95% CI of the Difference
Participant	214	21.04	3.416	0.235	2.234 (1.000)	2.429, 294, 0.016	1.750	0.431	0.219-2.069
	82	19.29	3.566	0.405					
N	296								

Interpretation:

This analysis as shown in Table 6 examined student satisfaction with library instruction among participants (n=214) and non-participants (n=82) in interactive learning sessions. Participants reported a higher average satisfaction score (21.04) compared to non-participants (19.29). Levene's test confirmed similar score variability between the groups (p=1.000). Importantly, the t-test result indicated a statistically significant difference in satisfaction scores (t(294) = 2.429, p = 0.016).

The statistically significant difference in satisfaction scores (with a 95% confidence interval ranging from 0.219 to 2.0685) suggests that participation in the interactive learning sessions is associated with higher student satisfaction with library instruction compared to those who did not participate.

Null Hypothesis 6 (H0): There is a significant relationship between students' perceptions of interactive learning (engagement, understanding) and their development of information literacy skills or research self-efficacy.

Table 7. Relationship between perceptions of interactive learning and development of information literacy skills

Variable	Information Literacy Skills	Student Self-Reported Learning Outcomes
Pearson Correlation	1	0.532**
Sig. (2-tailed)	-	< 0.01
N	296	296

Interpretation:

This analysis as shown in Table 7 examined the relationship between students' perceptions of interactive learning (engagement, understanding) and their information literacy skills. A statistically significant positive correlation was found (r = 0.532, p < 0.01, N = 296). The correlation coefficient indicates a moderate to strong positive association. This means that students who report higher perceptions of engagement and understanding in interactive learning sessions tend to also score higher on information literacy skills assessments.

The findings suggest that students' perceptions of interactive learning are positively associated with the development of information literacy skills. This highlights the potential benefits of incorporating interactive learning experiences into educational settings to enhance student learning outcomes.

Table 8. Correlation between retention of information literacy skills and student self-reported learning outcomes

Variable	Retention of Information Literacy Skills	Student Self-Reported Learning Outcomes
Pearson Correlation	0.412**	1
Sig. (2-tailed)	< 0.01	-
N	296	296

Interpretation

This table displays the correlation between the retention of information literacy skills and student self-reported learning outcomes. There is a statistically significant positive correlation between the retention of information literacy skills and student self-reported learning outcomes ($r = 0.412$, $p < 0.01$), indicating that students who retain information literacy skills well are more likely to report higher learning outcomes.

Table 9. Student feedback on interactive learning sessions

Feedback Category	Percentage of Positive Responses
Content Relevance	85%
Instructor Effectiveness	88%
Engagement Level	90%
Clarity of Instruction	87%
Overall Satisfaction	89%

Interpretation: This table summarizes student feedback on interactive learning sessions, including percentages of positive responses for various feedback categories such as content relevance, instructor effectiveness, engagement level, clarity of instruction, and overall satisfaction. This feedback provides insights into students' perceptions and experiences with the interactive learning format.

Table 10. Academic performance by participation in interactive library instruction sessions

Group	N	Mean GPA	Std. Deviation GPA	Std. Error Mean GPA
Participant	214	3.45	0.3	0.02
Non-Participant	82	3.3	0.4	0.04
N	296			

Interpretation

This table presents the academic performance, measured by GPA, among participants and non-participants in interactive library instruction sessions. Participants have a higher mean GPA (3.45) compared to non-participants (3.30). The standard deviation and standard error of the mean are provided for each group, offering insights into the dispersion and precision of the GPA measurements. This analysis suggests a potential positive association between participation in interactive library instruction sessions and academic performance.

Interactive Learning in Library Instruction

Table 11. Comparison of library resource utilization between participants and non-participants

Resource Type	Participants (Mean)	Non-Participants (Mean)	Difference (Mean)	t-value	p-value
Database Access (hours)	10.5	8.2	2.3	3.21	<0.01
Reference Consultations	4.8	3.2	1.6	2.81	0.005
Online Tutorials (views)	25.6	15.4	10.2	4.52	<0.001

Interpretation

This table compares the utilization of library resources between participants and non-participants in interactive library instruction sessions. Participants have higher mean values for database access hours, reference consultations, and online tutorial views compared to non-participants. The difference in means is statistically significant for all three resource types, as indicated by the t-values and p-values. This analysis suggests that participation in interactive library instruction sessions is associated with increased utilization of library resources.

Table 12. Comparison of assessment scores between pre- and post-interactive library instruction sessions

Assessment Type	Pre-Instruction Mean Score	Post-Instruction Mean Score	Difference in Mean Score	t-value	p-value
Information Literacy	65%	80%	15%	6.78	<0.001
Research Skills	70%	85%	15%	7.21	<0.001
Critical Thinking	75%	90%	15%	7.56	<0.001

Interpretation

This table compares the mean assessment scores between pre- and post-interactive library instruction sessions for various skills: information literacy, research skills, and critical thinking. There is a significant improvement in mean scores for all assessment types following the instruction sessions, as indicated by the t-values and p-values. The difference in mean scores is statistically significant ($p < 0.001$) for all assessment types, suggesting that participation in interactive library instruction sessions leads to enhanced student performance across different skill areas.

Table 13. Summary of impact of interactive library instruction sessions on student outcomes

Outcome Measure	Difference Between Participants and Non-Participants	Statistical Significance (p-value)
Student Self-Reported Learning Outcomes	Higher mean score among participants	$p < 0.001$

continued on following page

Table 13. Continued

Outcome Measure	Difference Between Participants and Non-Participants	Statistical Significance (p-value)
Information Literacy Skills	Higher mean score among participants	p = 0.015
Retention of Information Literacy Skills	Higher mean score among participants	p = 0.040
Self-Efficacy for Research	Higher mean score among participants	p = 0.020
Student Satisfaction with Library Instruction	Higher mean score among participants	p = 0.016

Interpretation

This table provides a summary of the impact of interactive library instruction sessions on various student outcomes. Participants consistently demonstrate higher mean scores across different outcome measures compared to non-participants, indicating the positive influence of participation in these sessions. Statistical significance is indicated by the corresponding p-values, with all outcomes showing significant differences between participants and non-participants. This suggests that interactive library instruction sessions effectively contribute to improved student learning outcomes, information literacy skills, retention, self-efficacy for research, and satisfaction with library instruction.

FINDINGS

This analysis examined the impact of interactive library instruction sessions on student learning outcomes. Participants (n=214) consistently reported and demonstrated significant advantages compared to non-participants (n=82) who did not participate in the sessions.

Null Hypothesis 1 (H0): Participation in interactive library instruction sessions leads to a significant improvement in student self-reported learning outcomes.

- Participants reported a significantly higher average learning outcome compared to non-participants (mean difference = 1.646, $p < 0.001$).
- Participation in interactive library instruction sessions is likely associated with an improvement in student self-reported learning outcomes.

Null Hypothesis 2 (H0): Interactive library instruction sessions have a significant impact on the development of Information Literacy Skills.

- Participants scored significantly higher on information literacy assessments compared to non-participants (mean difference = 1.157, $p = 0.015$).

- Participation in interactive library instruction sessions is associated with an improvement in information literacy skills.

Null Hypothesis 3 (H0): There is a significant difference in the retention of Information Literacy Skills.

- Participants showed better retention of information literacy skills compared to non-participants (mean difference = 2.060, p = 0.040).
- Participation in interactive library instruction sessions is associated with better retention of information literacy skills.

Null Hypothesis 4 (H0): Participation in interactive library instruction sessions leads to a significant increase in Self-Efficacy for Research.

- Participants reported a significantly higher self-efficacy for research compared to non-participants (mean difference = 1.250, p = 0.020).
- Participation in interactive library instruction sessions is associated with an increase in self-efficacy for research.

Null Hypothesis 5 (H0): Student Satisfaction with Library Instruction is significantly influenced by participation in interactive learning sessions.

- Participants reported significantly higher satisfaction with library instruction compared to non-participants (mean difference = 1.750, p = 0.016).
- Participation in interactive learning sessions is associated with higher student satisfaction with library instruction.

Null Hypothesis 6 (H0): There is a significant relationship between students' perceptions of interactive learning and their development of information literacy skills or research self-efficacy.

- There is a statistically significant positive correlation between students' perceptions of interactive learning and their information literacy skills (r = 0.532, p < 0.01).
- Students who report higher perceptions of engagement and understanding in interactive learning sessions tend to score higher on information literacy skills assessments.

These findings suggest that interactive library instruction sessions have a positive impact on student outcomes, including learning outcomes, information literacy skills, retention, self-efficacy for research, and satisfaction with library instruction. Additionally, students' perceptions of interactive learning are positively associated with the development of information literacy skills.

IMPLICATIONS OF THE STUDY

The implications of the study based on the findings are as follows:

Enhanced Learning Outcomes: Participation in interactive library instruction sessions is associated with improved learning outcomes. This suggests that incorporating interactive learning strategies into library instruction can effectively enhance students' understanding and retention of course material.

Improved Information Literacy Skills: The study demonstrates that participation in interactive library instruction sessions leads to higher information literacy skills. This highlights the importance of active engagement and hands-on learning experiences in developing students' ability to locate, evaluate, and effectively use information resources.

Better Retention of Skills: The findings indicate that participants in interactive library instruction sessions exhibit better retention of information literacy skills compared to non-participants. This underscores the long-term benefits of interactive learning approaches in reinforcing and retaining essential skills over time.

Increased Self-Efficacy for Research: Students who participate in interactive library instruction sessions report higher self-efficacy for research. This suggests that engaging in hands-on research activities and guided instruction can boost students' confidence in their research abilities, which is crucial for their academic and professional success.

Enhanced Student Satisfaction: Participants in interactive learning sessions express higher satisfaction with library instruction compared to non-participants. This underscores the importance of incorporating interactive elements into instructional sessions to create engaging and fulfilling learning experiences for students.

Positive Relationship between Perceptions and Skills: The study reveals a significant positive correlation between students' perceptions of interactive learning and their information literacy skills. This implies that fostering positive perceptions of engagement and understanding in interactive learning environments can contribute to the development of critical skills necessary for academic success and lifelong learning.

BROADER SOCIETAL IMPACT OF INTERACTIVE LIBRARY INSTRUCTION

The study's implications extend beyond academia and hold significant usefulness for society as a whole:

Workforce Preparedness: By enhancing students' learning outcomes, information literacy skills, and research self-efficacy, the study contributes to the development of a more knowledgeable and skilled workforce. These competencies are essential for individuals to succeed in various professions and contribute effectively to their respective fields.

Informed Decision-Making: Improved information literacy skills empower individuals to critically evaluate and make informed decisions in both personal and professional contexts. In a rapidly evolving information landscape, the ability to discern credible sources and synthesize information is crucial for navigating complex issues and addressing societal challenges.

Lifelong Learning: The study emphasizes the importance of interactive learning experiences in fostering a mindset of lifelong learning. By instilling effective learning strategies and self-efficacy for research, individuals are better equipped to adapt to new technologies, acquire new knowledge, and stay abreast of emerging trends in their fields throughout their lives.

Educational Equity and Access: Implementing interactive learning approaches in educational settings can contribute to promoting equity and access to quality education. These methods accommodate diverse learning styles and preferences, potentially reducing educational disparities and ensuring that all students have opportunities to succeed.

Social Innovation and Progress: By cultivating critical thinking, problem-solving, and creativity, the study fosters an environment conducive to social innovation and progress. Individuals equipped with strong information literacy skills and research self-efficacy are better positioned to address pressing societal issues, drive positive change, and contribute to the advancement of society.

Community Engagement: The study's emphasis on interactive learning experiences underscores the importance of active engagement and collaboration within communities. By promoting dialogue, interaction, and shared learning experiences, these approaches facilitate community engagement and collective problem-solving, fostering a sense of belonging and cohesion.

SUGGESTIONS FOR IMPLEMENTATION

Based on the findings and implications of the study, the following suggestions are proposed for implementation:

Integration of Interactive Learning Strategies: Educators and instructional designers should consider integrating interactive learning strategies into library instruction sessions to enhance student engagement and learning outcomes. This may include incorporating activities such as group discussions, hands-on exercises, and interactive tutorials to promote active participation and knowledge retention.

Professional Development for Educators: Training programs and workshops should be provided to educators to enhance their proficiency in designing and facilitating interactive learning experiences. Educators can benefit from learning about effective instructional techniques, technology integration, and assessment strategies tailored to interactive learning environments.

Utilization of Technology: Leveraging educational technologies such as online platforms, multimedia resources, and virtual reality tools can enhance the effectiveness of interactive library instruction sessions. Integrating technology can provide students with immersive learning experiences and facilitate access to a wide range of resources and materials.

Promotion of Collaborative Learning: Encouraging collaborative learning environments where students work together on projects, share ideas, and provide peer feedback can foster a sense of community and support student learning. Group activities and collaborative projects can enhance critical thinking, communication skills, and teamwork abilities.

Assessment and Feedback Mechanisms: Implementing assessment and feedback mechanisms within interactive learning sessions is essential for monitoring student progress and identifying areas for improvement. Formative assessments, quizzes, and peer evaluations can provide valuable insights into student learning and inform instructional adjustments.

CONCLUSION

The study provides compelling evidence that participation in interactive library instruction sessions yields numerous benefits for students, including enhanced learning outcomes, improved information literacy skills, increased self-efficacy for research, and higher satisfaction with instruction. The positive relationship between students' perceptions of interactive learning and their academic success underscores the importance of creating engaging and meaningful learning experiences.

FUTURE RESEARCH DIRECTIONS

To further enhance the understanding in the field of interactive library instruction, future research could explore the following areas:

Longitudinal Studies: Conducting longitudinal studies to examine the long-term impact of interactive library instruction on students' academic achievement, career readiness, and lifelong learning habits.

Comparative Analyses: Comparing the effectiveness of different types of interactive learning strategies such as problem-based learning, simulations, and flipped classrooms in library instruction sessions.

Diversity and Inclusion: Investigating how interactive learning approaches can be tailored to meet the needs of diverse student populations, including learners with disabilities and non-traditional students.

Technological Innovations: Exploring the integration of emerging technologies such as artificial intelligence, augmented reality, and gamification in interactive library instruction to enhance engagement and learning outcomes.

Global Perspectives: Examining the applicability and effectiveness of interactive learning strategies in diverse cultural and educational contexts worldwide.

REFERENCES

Abrahamson, K. M. (2016). Engaging students through active learning in library instruction sessions. *Journal of Library & Information Services in the Digital Age*, 17(2), 31–39.

Albitz, R. S. (2014). Information literacy and critical thinking: The academic library's role in integrating these skills into the curriculum. *Journal of Academic Librarianship*, 40(3-4), 241–245.

Association of College & Research Libraries. (2000). *Information literacy competency standards for higher education*. Association of College & Research Libraries.

Association of College & Research Libraries. (2015). *Framework for Information Literacy for Higher Education*. American Library Association.

Association of College & Research Libraries. (2016). *Standards for librarians and information specialists in schools*. Chicago, IL: American Library Association.

Becker, B. W. (2015). Librarian perceptions and practices in teaching research skills: A mixed-methods study. *Reference and User Services Quarterly*, 54(2), 115–126.

Berg, S. A., & Jacobs, H. L. (2016). Academic libraries and campus engagement: Collaborations and partnerships that enhance student learning and involvement. *College & Research Libraries News*, 77(1), 16–19.

Bergmann, J., & Sams, A. (2012). *Flip your classroom: Reach every student in every class every day*. ASCD.

Bergmann, J., & Sams, A. (2012). *Flip your classroom: Reach every student in every class every day*. International Society for Technology in Education.

Blau, G., & Schwartz, D. G. (2018). Maximizing student engagement in library instruction sessions: A review of the literature. *College & Research Libraries*, 79(7), 927–952.

Blummer, B., & Kenton, J. M. (2017). Promoting critical thinking skills through library instruction: Methods and resources. *RSR. Reference Services Review*, 45(4), 576–590.

Bonwell, C. C., & Eison, J. A. (1991). ASHE-ERIC Higher Education Report: Vol. 1. *Active learning: Creating excitement in the classroom*. George Washington University.

Brauer, J. (2018). Information literacy and inquiry-based learning: A perfect partnership. *Journal of Library & Information Services in the Digital Age*, 19(3), 1–9.

Brown, C., & Kingsley-Wilson, B. (2010). Assessing the information needs of graduate students in the biological and life sciences. *Journal of Academic Librarianship*, 36(5), 375–383.

Brunetti, K., Hofer, A. R., & Townsend, L. (2014). Interdisciplinary collaboration: Librarians and faculty working together to enhance student information literacy skills in biology. *Science & Technology Libraries*, 33(3), 267–282.

Bryant, J., & Mann, B. (2017). The flipped classroom model for teaching library research skills: Student engagement and learning outcomes. *Journal of Library & Information Services in Distance Learning*, 11(3-4), 316–331.

Carbery, A., & Leahy, S. (2015). Flipping the classroom in library instruction: Impact on information literacy skills in undergraduate engineering students. *Library Hi Tech*, 33(4), 458–469.

Carlock, D., & Anderson, J. (2007). Teaching database searching skills to nursing students: A practical approach. *Medical Reference Services Quarterly*, 26(1), 51–60.17210549

Caspers, J., & Bernhisel, S. (2005). Assessing freshmen's research skills to tailor library instruction effectively. *College & Research Libraries*, 66(5), 471–484.

Chu, S. K. W., & Lau, W. W. F. (2020). E-learning and student attitudes: A case study from Hong Kong. *Journal of Educational Technology & Society*, 23(2), 80–94.

Cmor, D., & Lippold, K. (2001). Strategic searching vs. casual web surfing: Enhancing students' information search skills. *Internet Reference Services Quarterly*, 6(1), 27–36.

Cooney, M. (2011). Best practices for implementing flipped classroom models in library instruction. *Journal of Library Innovation*, 2(2), 40–50.

Curran, S., Wu, M., & Webb, C. (2017). Engaging students in library instruction: Using collaborative learning to enhance information literacy skills. *Journal of Academic Librarianship*, 43(2), 151–159.

Dahl, C. (2004). Student perspectives on electronic classrooms: Impact on learning and engagement. *Portal (Baltimore, Md.)*, 4(3), 393–407.

Detmering, R., & Johnson, A. M. (2012). Understanding students' research challenges: Action research in library instruction. *College & Research Libraries*, 73(2), 209–224.

Diaz, K. R. (2003). Integrating information literacy into academic curricula: Practical strategies and collaborations. *RSR. Reference Services Review*, 31(3), 213–220.

Drake, A., & Acosta, M. (2016). Interactive library instruction: Enhancing student engagement and information literacy skills. *Communications in Information Literacy*, 10(1), 73–89.

Dubicki, E. (2013). Faculty perceptions of students' information literacy competencies: Identifying gaps and improving instruction. *Journal of Information Literacy*, 7(2), 97–119. 10.11645/7.2.1852

Fagan, J. (2018). Engaging students in active learning through information literacy scavenger hunts. *Journal of Library & Information Services in the Digital Age*, 19(1), 1–11.

Farrell, R., & Badke, W. (2015). Integrating information literacy into academic disciplines: A systematic approach. *RSR. Reference Services Review*, 43(2), 264–283. 10.1108/RSR-11-2014-0052

Fister, B. (2010). Critical information literacy: Principles and application in student learning. *Library Trends*, 59(3), 403–434.

Friesen, N. (2017). Building confidence in research skills: Using simulations in library instruction. *Journal of Library Administration*, 57(2), 137–150.

Gregory, L. (2013). Information literacy and technology: A collaboration. *Journal of Library & Information Services in Distance Learning*, 7(1-2), 69–78.

Griffiths, J., & Meola, A. (2018). Integrating online quizzes into library instruction sessions: Engaging students and gauging learning outcomes. *Journal of Library & Information Services in the Digital Age*, 19(1), 1–12.

Hake, R. R. (1998). Interactive-engagement versus traditional methods: A six-thousand-student survey of mechanics test data for introductory physics courses. *American Journal of Physics*, 66(1), 64–74. 10.1119/1.18809

Head, A. J., & Eisenberg, M. B. (2010). How college students use Wikipedia for academic research. *First Monday*, 15(3).

Heider, K. L., & McClure, R. (2015). *Instructional strategies and techniques for information professionals*. Chandos Publishing.

Hinchliffe, L. J., & Meulemans, Y. N. (2010). Supporting student retention and graduation: Strategies for academic librarians. *College & Research Libraries News*, 71(1), 10–13.

Holliday, W., & Fagerheim, B. A. (2006). Integrating information literacy with a sequenced English composition curriculum. *portal. Portal (Baltimore, Md.)*, 6(2), 169–184.

Hwang, Y.-M., & Wu, Y.-C. (2013). Applying audience response systems to enhance student engagement in library instruction. [JETDE]. *Journal of Educational Technology Development and Exchange*, 6(X).

Jacobs, H. L., & Jacobs, D. (2009). Pedagogical partnerships: Transforming one-shot library sessions into ongoing collaborations with faculty. *RSR. Reference Services Review*, 37(2), 207–220.

Johnson, D. W., & Johnson, R. T. (1999). *Cooperation and learning together: Theory and research* (7th ed.). Allyn & Bacon.

Johnson, D. W., & Johnson, R. T. (1999). *Learning together and alone: Cooperative, competitive, and individualistic learning* (5th ed.). Prentice Hall.

Johnson, D. W., Johnson, R. T., & Smith, K. A. (1998). Cooperative learning returns to college: What evidence is there that it works? *Change*, 30(4), 26–35. 10.1080/00091389809602629

Julien, H., & Barker, S. (2009). High school students' information-seeking behaviors: Implications for developing information literacy skills. *Library & Information Science Research*, 31(1), 12–17. 10.1016/j.lisr.2008.10.008

Julien, H., & Gribble, J. (2017). Engaging first-year students in critical thinking through information literacy instruction. *Journal of Academic Librarianship*, 43(2), 182–190.

Kuhlthau, C. C. (2004). *Seeking meaning: A process approach to library and information services* (2nd ed.). Libraries Unlimited.

Langley, G., & Yorke, M. (2006). *Formative assessment and self-managed learning in higher education*. Routledge.

Mackey, T. L., & Jacobson, T. D. (2014). *Metaliteracy: Reinventing information literacy to empower learners*. American Library Association.

McTigue, E. M., & Henke, H. L. (2013). The role of academic librarians in promoting critical thinking: A literature review. *College & Research Libraries*, 74(3), 251–271.

Pascarella, E. T., & Terenzini, P. T. (2005). *How college affects students: A third decade of research* (Vol. 2). Jossey-Bass.

Saunders, L. (2012). Faculty perspectives on information literacy as a student learning outcome. *Journal of Academic Librarianship*, 38(4), 226–236. 10.1016/j.acalib.2012.06.001

Stone, A., & McKechnie, L. (2017). Beyond the one-shot: Developing information literacy skills through interactive workshops. *Journal of Library & Information Services in the Digital Age*, 18(3), 1–12.

Twardell, L., & Boyle, L. (2020). Gamified learning: Using escape rooms to engage students in information literacy instruction. *College & Research Libraries News*, 81(6), 279–283.

Twardell, L., & Boyle, L. (2021). The impact of gamified learning on student engagement and knowledge retention in academic libraries. *Library Hi Tech*, 39(1), 53–68.

Weiler, A. (2004). Information-seeking behavior in Generation Y students: Motivation, critical thinking, and learning theory. *Journal of Academic Librarianship*, 30(1), 45–52.

Chapter 10
Multimedia Cloud Data Warehouse Design for Knowledge Sharing in the University Environment:
A Proposed Digital Solution

Godwin Nse Ebong
https://orcid.org/0000-0002-9899-8838
University of Salford, UK

Ugochukwu Okwudili Matthew
https://orcid.org/0000-0003-0828-9710
Hussaini Adamu Federal Polytechnic, Nigeria

Babatunde Olofin
Enugu State University, Nigeria

Nneoma Andrew-Vitalis
University of Hertfordshire, UK

Lateef Olawale Fatai
https://orcid.org/0009-0008-2697-7377
University of Salford, UK

Ajibola Olaosebikan Waliu
https://orcid.org/0009-0002-6857-3035
Southampton Solent University, UK

David Oyewumi Oyekunle
https://orcid.org/0009-0007-3994-1712
University of Salford, UK

Matthew Abiola Oladipupo
https://orcid.org/0000-0002-5984-6217
University of Salford, UK

ABSTRACT

The desire for homogeneity in the execution of national policy on information communication technologies (ICTs) for tertiary education in Nigeria has been updated

DOI: 10.4018/979-8-3693-3559-8.ch010

through progressive inclusion in the national policy with regard to ICTs use in education. In evaluating the progress made towards the sustainable development goals, the policy highlighted the necessity of ICTs in achieving the national technology objectives. In this paper, the authors argued that developments in ICT policy with regard to the implementation of National Research and Education Networks (NRENs) should adopt a bottom-up approach in order to establish contributions in the Nigeria Education Research Network (NgREN) in the direction of improving educational quality and research output geared toward sustainable national development. The research's findings showed that integrating ICTs into educational mainstream management is essential for academic success, effectiveness, globalization, and job satisfaction that incorporates electronic changes for opportunities in the digital age.

INTRODUCTION

The current academic workload and data traffic generated and transformed into actionable information for top management at higher education in Nigeria are at present impossible to be handled with the use of traditional data instruments and technology(Matthew, Kazaure, & Okafor, 2021). Information technology (IT) has increasingly been seen as a key source of academic information transformer, intellectual conduit, and knowledge dissemination channel by higher education institutions in order to maintain competitiveness in academic business and for purposes of adaptation alongside the dynamic and ever progressive academic business environment. The analysis of the expansion of higher education shows that Nigeria's higher education has entered a rapid period of development that maximizes the necessity for the adoption of information communication technologies (ICTs) as technology instrument and infrastructure superiority within the university education system(Gumel, Abdullahi, & O, 2019).

The National Research and Education Networks (NRENs) were created with the intention of fostering academic and intellectual collaboration and digital resource synergy within the tertiary institutions as part of the agenda for the implementation of the most advanced ICTs premeditated action plan(Matthew, Kazaure, Kazaure, Nwamouh, & Chinonso, 2022). The Nigerian Research and Education Network (NgREN), which, like all other Research and Education Networks (RENs) around the world, was founded to encourage education, research, innovation and intellectual ingenuity(Wara & Singh, 2015). The NgREN was designed to support the national research data warehouse backbone for networked campuses, interconnecting other backbones at a regional level to build the Regional Research and Education Network (RRENs) backbones, which will connect on a global knowledge repository. NgREN is the first operational REN in West and Central Africa, and more than 20 other countries have created RENs. The Nigeria Universities Commission (NUC) and the Committee of Vice Chancellors of Nigerian Universities (CVC) developed a foundation that enables universities to interact, cooperate, access, and share resources across national and international boundaries, primarily for the purposes of research and education, with the added capability of unified communications and digital content incorporation.

The development of virtual libraries for universities and e-libraries for federal tertiary institutions have aided in the continuing review of IT curricula at all discourse levels(Oyedokun & Adeolu-Akande, 2022). The national virtual digital library project and NgREN are among the top government initiatives to support ICT infrastructures, a remarkable investment because they have helped teachers and students become more proficient in ICT and university management in administering control. To emphasize the significance of ICT ascendancy, the National Information Technology Education Framework (NITEF) was developed and is currently being utilized to classify IT institutions and better place IT employees in the scheme of service(Chohan & Hu, 2022). An ICT department was established to lead the delivery of state-of-the-art technology solutions and support services within the federal ministry of education and to serve as an ICT co-ordination resource for the entire education sector as a result of the growing use of national standards for IT education to establish academic and professional standards for IT education at all levels. Innovation enterprise institutions (IEIs) and vocational enterprise institutions (VEIs) were formed to address skill gaps in the ICT skill dispersion. In an effort to enhance IT education and practice at the tertiary education level, the Computer Professionals Registration Council of Nigeria (CPN) collaborated with NUC, the National Board for Technical Education (NBTE), and the National Commission for Colleges of Education (NCCE) to advance the 21st-century digital skills as strongly emphasized in the curriculum and learning objectives (Adhikari, Clemens, Dempster, & Ekeator, 2021),(Ogunode & Akimki, 2023).

The limited adoption of ICT has made it difficult for tertiary education in developing countries to offer high-quality pedagogical synthesis(Ndibalema, 2022). This is a result of a lack of physical infrastructure, a shortage of skilled staff, a mismatch between curriculum requirements and labor market expectations, and a lack of hands-on learning opportunities for students. Nigeria is comparable to other developing countries in this respect with infrastructural deficit. As education 5.0 is already evolving, the new methodology in science and technology teaching that the worldwide education system will need to adopt as society shifts toward ICT dominance(Calp & Bütüner, 2022). The authors of this paper discussed the concepts of education 5.0 and ICT adoption in education for academic engagements related to the Actor-Network-Theory (ANT). Using the ANT model, it is possible to identify the services that end users needed and the challenges they would encounter when using NRENs(Assefa[1] & Felix, 2021). The ANT model's objective is to depict the complex interactions between the various players in this situation's vast information ecosystem. For the purpose of ensuring connectivity, a number of linkages, including the NgREN and the campus network for higher education, need to be created and operationalized. The ICT infrastructure for research and education inside the NRENs, NgREN, and a few other networks for educational research was examined. In order to exploit the current educational infrastructure as a bottom-up approach, the study developed a multimedia cloud data warehouse for knowledge sharing after identifying a critical deficiency in the current NgREN from the existing infrastructure. The paper is organized into introduction, objective of the study, literature review, research methodology, implementation and finally conclusion.

RESEARCH AIMS AND OBJECTIVES

In order to improve the quality of instruction and increase the output of original research for the benefit of the nation, this study's main goal is to look at the ICT policy needs of Nigerian higher education institutions. The study gave special attention to four selected universities in the south-eastern region of Nigeria as it focused on three key issues: the end-user demand for ICT services in education, the design of a multimedia cloud data warehouse, and the development implications of NRENs. By looking at these components, it will be possible to create a practical ICT policy framework, service portfolio, and roadmap that will improve academic standards and increase research output in Nigeria's eastern geopolitical zone.

REVIEW OF LITERATURE

In order to create a REN administrative data repository that can be used as a tool for educational policy, the NREN and NgREN digital ecosystems must combine heterogeneous data warehouse technologies, linking databases from public and private universities into a synchronized academic data warehouse(Boulton et al., 2020),(Saay & Norta, 2018). The creation of a multimedia cloud data warehouse would require the application of ICTs in order to lower the costs of institutional electronic resource requisition by enabling the transfer of ever detailed data from professional educators to a centralized cloud server data warehouse to promote effective academic delivery. According to(Ferri, Grifoni, & Guzzo, 2020)], the worldwide adoption of 5G telecommunication broadband and the establishment of the digital economy will open up completely new use case scenarios for organizations addressing issues in the educational sector and other industries, with the aim of increasing intellectual productivity. When referring to the supply chain for educational systems, the term NREN designates a group of digital ecosystems where educational data are maintained and made accessible to a variety of stakeholders, including governments, academics, teachers, researchers, and students(Yigzaw, 2023).

According to (Neamah, 2021), higher education organizations now face more fierce competition in the digital world. They must compete with other higher education institutions in order to adapt to local, national, and international economic, political, and social developments. Furthermore, a range of stakeholders count on higher education institutions to quickly and effectively meet these demands. Higher education must analyze large data sources created to handle these quick changes in order to make the best decisions possible in addressing this issues. The majority of institutions of higher education are spending a lot of money on IT to put data warehouse systems in place(Alam, 2022). According to (Al-Okaily, Al-Okaily, Teoh, & Al-Debei, 2022),the establishment of data warehouses is a technique of boosting the demand for data history and gathering important information from dispersed database sources through a consolidated and integrated storage network in some information systems. The level of detail can be setup since these integrated data can be utilized for information transmission and can be verified from a variety of perspectives. Nigeria's aspirations to progress and improve its economy and society will now heavily rely on the higher education sector in Nigeria(Ogunode & Ade, 2023). In addition to giving staff and students the chance to be agents of societal transformation, universities in Nigeria have the potential to help the nation resolve its socio-political issues.

According to (Gambo & Shakir, 2022),universities and other higher education institutions in Nigeria have a responsibility to foster an atmosphere that supports accomplishments in research and learning as agents of productive transformation. This entails, among other things, giving the community of users' access to current research trends in any area of learning that might be of general interest. Without cooperation and synergy between these institutions and their peers, both locally and globally, this will not be possible to accomplish. With a focus on Nigerian educational institutions in general and their libraries in particular, this study investigated the key component of this relationship in the form of a research and education network. The NgREN, which was launched a few years ago, is currently on inactive nomenclature, leaving the institutions and the host community obfuscated. It has been demonstrated that expanding access to strategic ICT usage can enhance democratization, economic development, and poverty reduction, as well as freedom of speech, information flow, and human rights. Many initiatives are being worked on to connect these units to wireless access points and fiber-optic cables via local area networks (LAN), which will allow access to data warehoused repositories and broadband fiber-optic communication for a number of organizations. The construction of NRENs provides countless options for improving academic institution learning quality and encouraging strong research outputs in order to meet corporate development objectives.

According to(Matthew, Kazaure, Kazaure, Onyedibe, & Okafor, 2022),it is essential for the countries of the world to first comprehend the social dynamics of modern education in order to develop a strong and healthy economy with good people prospering in all human social and economic endeavors while living contentedly within the environmental ecosystem. Understanding environmental digital ecosystem according to(Railean, 2019), requires integration of information and operation technologies with various educational and knowledge management systems leading to pervasive computing, that offers speed, accuracy and intelligence of machine-to-machine communication and improvement of human-machine understanding. The study is in line with (McClellan, Creager, & Savoca, 2023), who asserted that the rapid transformation of the enterprise educational environment and society where there is unquantifiable intelligence and knowledge available for adoption has astonishing connotation for academic engagement and information application in the most appropriate order necessary for universities and professional employment. In order to connect Europe's national research and education networks with a high-bandwidth, high-speed, and extraordinarily durable pan-European backbone, the Gigabit European Academic Network (GEANT) was established(Villalón & Hermosa, 2016). This was done in order to promote academic intelligence sharing. Referring to Fig. 1, the development of NRENs, or networks of academic and educational institutions, has propelled the international growth of Internet infrastructures, which has required the construction of top ICT policy in Africa. Successful and long-lasting NRENs across the African continent have made it possible for a number of educational and research institutions to take advantage of improved Internet connections, collaborate internationally, and access crucial e-resources for teaching and research. With a focus on the business model and financial plan, present activities are aimed at enabling the development of a long-term NREN that is focused on the provision of technical and services-oriented solutions.

Figure 1. NRENs development for connected academic institutions

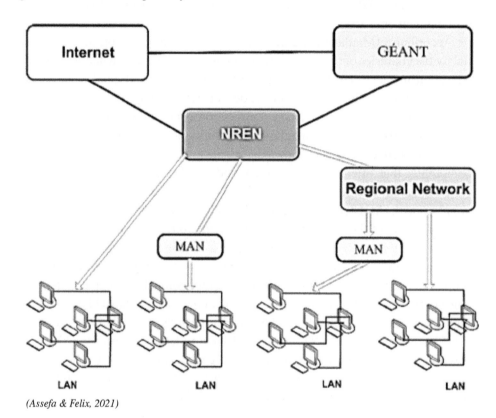

(Assefa & Felix, 2021)

In order to move NRENs forward and make them active and sustainable, the tactics that have worked elsewhere on the continent should be replicated(Matthew et al., 2024). The institutional ICT categorizations were defined as the factors that cannot be immediately linked to specific ICT users but are instead subtly influenced by the organizational culture and the regulatory framework around ICT use. According to (Timotheou et al., 2023), education systems around the world have adopted strategies and policies for ICT integration as a result of changes in the nature and scope of education brought about by digital technologies for institutions' ICT vision, the significance of ICT in teaching and learning outcome. A comprehensive framework for strategic and operational planning as well as decisions about resource allocation is provided by the institutional ICT vision, which is crucial for ICT use(Esteve-Mon, Postigo-Fuentes, & Castañeda, 2023). The ICT plan is a document produced by universities that incorporates the underlying philosophy and goals of using ICT in education as well as infrastructure specifications, implementation plans, monitoring and evaluation.

To apply physical education within a network setting, for instance, institutions build up multiple application targets based on material features. Numerous academic institutions have created adaptable course materials for Open Distance Learning (ODL); yet, they have failed to address essential limitations such as synchronous interface and session retrieval. Students and teachers generally take these difficulties into consideration, and they have become the main issues affecting the efficacy of network teaching, even though we freely accept that the current network technology in teaching has many weaknesses and has produced many challenges in our various institutions. Networked teaching necessitates the establishment of specific teaching conditions, such as the utilization of collaborative and independent learning platforms and network resource platforms(Matthew & Kazaure, 2020). Learners engage in one-to-many interactive sessions with teachers, peers, and online learning resources through network autonomous learning. When people use different communication technologies to communicate with each other at the same time, this is known as digital synchronous transmission. The physical lessons in academic institutions, together with networked teaching and e-learning, will have a significant theoretical and practical impact on learning results, changing the face of education in developing nations like Nigeria(Matthew, Kazaure, John, & Haruna, 2021).

In the developing countries for instance, integrating electronic media into the mainstream educational system will serve as a communication tool for individuals who support and provide education, as well as people who engage in educational activities such as attending universities and sister institutions, which will offer a key leverage to educational curriculum(Matthew, 2019). At present, control of the learning process is mostly on the computer without synchronous flexible design in Open Distance Learning, where a large portion of the content on the website is merely the original physical textbooks to realize a basic heuristic teaching approach in teaching materials. Students use network resources for self-directed learning; for visitors and teachers, collaboration and communication are especially crucial. In the present institutions for example, instructional websites for both teachers and students are asynchronous, non-interactive, and some of the interactive system is idle, which means that network teaching has lost a crucial component of the learning process.

Interactive pedagogy refers to the way in which students interact and relate to one another during the communication process, giving learning and instruction a more dynamic and open nature(Ugochukwu Okwudili Matthew, Ado Saleh Kazaure, et al., 2022). Consequently, interactive pedagogy refers to an educational method that addresses interactions between teachers, students, and the learning environment, with the primary goal being student participation. Interactive pedagogy comprises three primary components: the student, the teacher, and the environment. The individual who sets out to acquire new information through self-directed learning is referred to as the learner. He wants to integrate the fresh information. Through the use of interactive educational pedagogy, educators can lead students through a variety of real-world settings, cultural contexts, and learning environments in which they can acquire knowledge. It encompasses the classroom itself as well as the outdoor spaces and places outside of schools. Generative artificial intelligence or prompt engineering is now a crucial component of assistive interactive pedagogy and digital learning, especially with the emergence of artificial intelligence-driven conversational agents(Matthew, Bakare, Ebong, Ndukwu, & Nwanakwaugwu, 2023). It is imperative to prepare for a future in which general and educational technology merge and become dominated by artificial intelligence (AI). This study highlighted the role of people as producers in minimizing any potential learning mishaps and showed how society may influence and contribute to the development of integrated pedagogic learning using an AI-driven educational application platform. This study emphasizes that more research on organizational synergy, with an emphasis on academic organization collaboration, will emerge in light of the technological concerns raised in this study. This is because generative technologies have the potential to fundamentally alter teaching and learning approaches and require new ways of thinking.

PROPOSED ANT MODEL FOR ICT ADOPTION

A computer-based paradigm called the actor network (ANT) uses actors as the main computational agents to interact with both the internal and external environments in order to address learning challenges(Kaasinen et al., 2022). Several methods have been developed to understand how people engage with educational technology and information systems. A well-known theory that considers organizational social structure and complexity is the "Socio-Technical System" (STS). It is useful in describing the purpose of the system since it consists of systems or organizations with both technological components, such IT structures, and social variables. A well-liked theory built on the STS principle is the ANT. Actor-network theory, a theoretical and methodological approach to social theory, proposes that everything in the social and natural worlds occurs in dynamic networks of relationships. The notion holds that nothing exists apart from those relationships. No matter if it is a human or non-human, according to ANT theory, an actor is the source of action. However, an actor needs the support of other actors in order to perform well; this support is especially important in the form of patterns. ANT holds that technology has the power to change social processes because it developed from social interests.

Figure 2. Higher institution ICT educational development base on ANT model

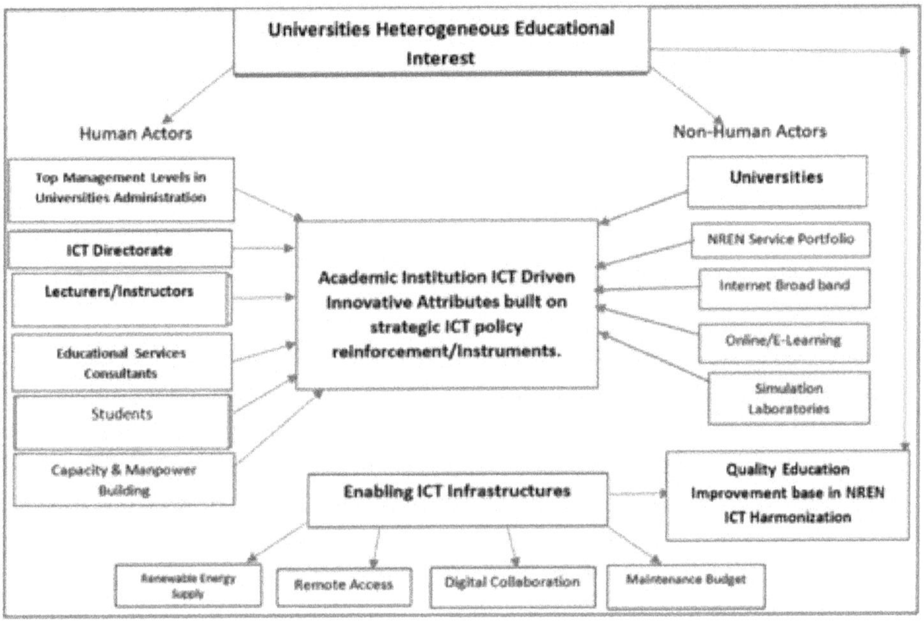

[Figure: Diagram showing Universities Heterogeneous Educational Interest with Human Actors (Top Management Levels in Universities Administration, ICT Directorate, Lecturers/Instructors, Educational Services Consultants, Students, Capacity & Manpower Building) and Non-Human Actors (Universities, NREN Service Portfolio, Internet Broad band, Online/E-Learning, Simulation Laboratories, Quality Education Improvement base in NREN ICT Harmonization), centered on Academic Institution ICT Driven Innovative Attributes built on strategic ICT policy reinforcement/Instruments, with Enabling ICT Infrastructures feeding into Renewable Energy Supply, Remote Access, Digital Collaboration, Maintenance Budget]

(Author illustration)

In Figure 2, the suggested ANT model is displayed. In actuality, additional actors ought to be included in the process of creating the service portfolio and roadmap. In contrast to the case study, where social structures and technology problems are intertwined, the ANT approach does not prioritize social or technological elements. The ANT will continually draw attention to the interpretative flexibility of IT and systems in the sense that seemingly similar technologies produce noticeably different results in various neighborhoods as a result of specialized network-building and translation processes. In the study, ANT illustrated how, instead of taking technology for granted, the line between technological and social structures, as well as their connection and how they become the subject of discussion in the creation of facts, may be seen. This section made two important contributions to the literature:

i. It suggested a methodological approach that may be utilized to direct future NREN service requirements in order to raise the standard of teaching and research in tertiary institutions.
ii. Enhances the usage of traditional technology as a method for identifying end-user needs.

This study has shown that there are many unmet needs for a variety of technologies and services that are used in both education and research but that NgREN is unable to fulfill at this time. To achieve its goal, NgREN should concentrate on providing tools and services that help Nigerian public higher education institutions increase their production of original research and enhance the quality of their instruction. The impact of reliable networks on research and teaching performance in higher education in developing countries is subject to significant research limitations worldwide. In order to encourage digital collaboration and resource synergy, this study focuses on the application of the ANT to highlight NREN service implementation requirements in higher education institutions in Nigeria.

RESEARCH METHODOLOGY

In order to evaluate the execution of ICT policy based on the creation of the NgREN framework in Nigeria tertiary institutions, the research presented a cross-sectional survey using a structured questionnaire. The need for tertiary institutions in Nigeria to create an ICT-based educational system that synchronizes and merges services in accordance with the NgREN for universal access to education for all citizens led to the conception of the research. The success of a study of this kind depends on the collection of both primary and secondary data. A qualitative research approach was used to achieve this goal through case studies of the four federal institutions located in the south-east geopolitical region of Nigeria. Qualitative research is by definition an introspective, interpretive, descriptive, and frequently instinctive attempt to explain and comprehend genuine instances of human behavior and experience from the perspective of the people who exist inside a particular setting. Over the course of twelve weeks, the current study was conducted between the second quarters of 2022 and 2023. The participants were chosen from four federal universities in southern Nigeria.

The research approach used to evaluate the influence of dependable networks on research output and the quality of education provided in Nigerian universities is presented in this section. This study employed an unconventional method to assess NREN services within higher education buildings using the ANT as a theoretical framework. This paper's goal is to identify the major players in ANT, describe how they were hired, and detail how they helped with the construction's problem-solving phase. The actors who will offer pertinent input are selected from four participant groups: ICT directors, researchers, lecturers, and NREN staff. This study's research design is considered appropriate since it is necessary to investigate, characterize, and comprehend the ways in which dependable networks have changed network services and the difficulties raised by the ANT viewpoint. In order to understand the creation and extension of NREN as well as how each actor influences the others, the study focuses on applying the actor-network approach. This included figuring out which institutions needed to undertake the project, how closely the qualities aligned, and whether the NREN needed to employ service distribution. NREN services are essentially intended to be used in Nigerian higher education institutions through the stabilization and development of the dynamic ANT actors.

An evaluation of the application of ICT policy in education was made in the four degree-awarding institutions in south-eastern Nigeria in accordance with the National Policy on Education, the National Information and Communication Technology Policy, the National Information Technology Education Framework, and the Ministerial Strategy Plan for the Education Sector (2016-2019). Data was acquired from students as well as the academic and ICT center staff in accordance with the research's objectives. The sample population for this study, which employed a quantitative research methodology, consisted of the employees of four federally owned educational institutions in South Eastern Nigeria. A series of questionnaires were administered to 550 randomly selected employees from the institutions that worked largely in the directorate of information communication technology in order to collect the data. There were two portions to the questionnaire, each with both multiple-choice and single-choice questions. For the first, which was about demographic information of the respondents. The focus of the second section of the research question was on the core ICT policy framework, ICT infrastructures, mobile technology adoption, cloud IoT technology, digital library deployment, and the tasks that each of these were employed for in the academic environment. Data on the implementation of the Multimedia Cloud Data Warehouse were to be gathered through the survey. As a matter fact, 480 respondents out of 550 questionnaires distributed to the four federal universities in south-eastern Nigeria completed and returned the survey to the researchers that signified a response rate of 87 percent, which is exceptionally high for this type of study.

QUESTIONNAIRE DESIGN

The questionnaire for the current study was divided into two portions, each of which looked at a different component of the research topic. The first component is set up to ascertain how the intended participants feel about the construction of a multimedia cloud data warehouse and whether they are willing to accept refined NgREN. To ascertain whether the tertiary institutions are willing to implement the system, the second section includes questions concerning the beneficiary institution's ICT infrastructure that will power the anticipated improvements. The institution's ICT center employees, academics, and students from several departments all received questionnaires totaling 500.

Table 1. Research questionnaire design

Questionnaire segment	Number of questionnaire item	Description of Questionnaire item
A	5	The purpose of this section is to ascertain how the target participants feel about the current NgREN systems and whether they are willing to accept the planned Multimedia Cloud Data warehousing system as a part of the university research infrastructure.
B	5	This section of the questionnaire focused on the development of the ICT Infrastructure at the target institution, specifically whether there is an existing data warehouse Server Systems, organizational Information System, Management Information system, Campus Inter-networking, Centre for Information Technology (CIT), Wireless Digital Access Solutions, Internet Broadband Data Communication, Electronic Learning Platforms (Learning Management Systems-LMS), or Digital Library Automation. This is done to see if the institutions can actually adopt the suggested system.

DATA ANALYSIS

The data were evaluated using SPSS software, version 29, which is a statistical program for social sciences. The software's many functions can be used to generate and record variables. The researcher also started using the Microsoft Excel (2013 version) office suite due to how simple it is to analyze data, especially when generating graphs and charts with descriptive data. This software was selected because it aids the researcher in compiling and organizing variables in a clear and organized way.

Table 2. Building institutional ICT infrastructure

Institution-specific ICT infrastructure	Infrastructure Mean Distribution	Infrastructure categorization /Ranking
Server Systems/Management Information Systems/Cloud Data Warehouse	3.86	1
Campus Networking	3.46	2
Information Technology Center (ICT)	3.90	1
Gateways to Wireless Access	3.45	4
Internet-Based Broadband Communications	3.75	3
Electronic Learning Platforms (LMS)	3.15	5
E-Library System (Digital Library)	3.86	1

ANALYSIS OF THE RESEARCH FINDING

In the current study, authors were able to learn about the staff's existing approach to information preservation and academic learning tools. These instruments included some digital assets that were spread over various storage systems, highlighting the requirement for a centralized database solution. The academic staff of the selected institutions have stressed the necessity for a centralized database heavily because there has never been one since the establishment of the schools. The authors received feedback from additional respondents, primarily students, who expressed interest in using a multimedia data warehouse as a learning tool. Among their recommendations, the respondents said that the tool should be easily accessible, efficient, and relevant to their needs (for study, information access, management, and organization, community-building, sharing and discussing, collaboration, and training, among other things). Additionally, they advocate for the system to defy all network obstacles currently present in Nigeria so that digital resources can be made easily and quickly accessible (single logins, one-click access, ability to download and store on personal devices), as well as editable and annotatable.

The student population, however, was budget-conscious and had little money to support several subscriptions. As a result, the system should be on a local institutional network and accessible by connecting all the systems in the computer labs. About 76.4% of the respondents express a willingness to use digital technologies to support their learning, despite the fact that 74% of the respondents have little to no knowledge of multimedia cloud data warehouse technology. They also express a desire for assistance in identifying pertinent, useful, time-efficient technologies and adequate, reliable, more open infrastructures for using them in a distributed learning environment.

Table 3. Investigation of research questionnaires

Tertiary Institution	Number of Questionnaire Distributed	Number of Questionnaire Recovered	% of the Questionnaire Distributed
NAU	139	130	25.3
UNN	137	115	24.9
FUTO	137	110	24.9
MOUA	137	125	24.9
Total	550	480	100

The number of questionnaires distributed and the percentage that were returned in the study area are shown in Table 3. Nnamdi Azikiwe University (NAU), accounted for the largest percentage of the data retrieved, followed by Nigeria University Nsukka (UNN), Federal University of Technology (FUTO), and Michael Okpara

University of Agriculture (MOUA). In addition, the availability of ICT infrastructures that can be installed within the institution as considered in the current study to facilitate top ICT policy transmission were displayed in Table 2. The ICT Center, E-library system and servers system, have the high-pitched means of 3.90, 3.86, and 3.86 correspondingly. These make up the majority of the ICT resources used in education. The next-highest ranked institutional ICT capacity development facilities are Internet broadband communication and campus networking, with mean values of 3.45 and 3.75, respectively.

Figure 3. Institutional IC T infrastructure deployment

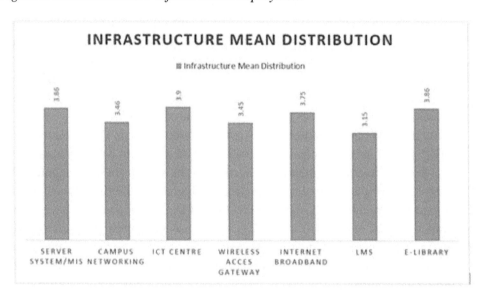

Referring to Figure 3, campus networking and broadband internet communication come in second and third place among institutional ICT capacity development facilities, with mean values of 3.46 and 3.75, respectively. The organizational wireless access gateway and digital learning platform (LMS) are the least prioritized IT infrastructures, with mean values of 3.45 and 3.15, respectively. The average investment in IT infrastructure across all respondents was found to be 25.01. Our research also shown that instructors view students' perspectives as important variables in deciding which ICT policies to embrace. Although our primary focus was on how teachers used ICT, instructors emphasized the significance of taking into account students' circumstances and unique aspects of digital learning. Instructors will struggle to meaningfully incorporate ICT into their teaching if there isn't a conducive environment for students to use ICT for learning. For effective academic involvement, students and teachers both need the proper degree of knowledge, attitude, support, and ICT infrastructures.

Proposed System Flow Diagram

Figure 4. Proposed multimedia cloud data warehouse design flowchart

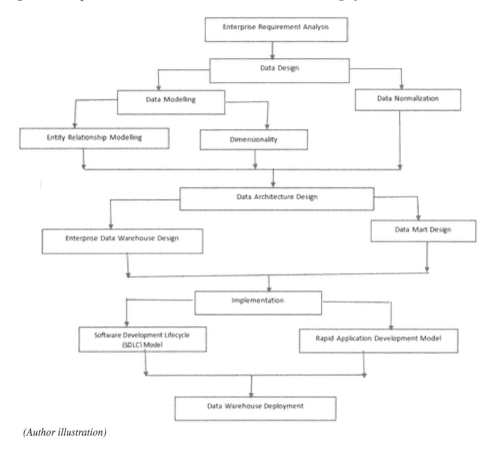

(Author illustration)

The cloud data warehouse flow diagram in Figure 4 above used ideas from utility grid computing to give metrics for service improvement needed for the sustainability of the NREN, NgREN ecosystem and to satisfy the demand for ubiquitous data mining operations needed for educational management. The design addressed issues with the sustainability of higher education in the evolving digital world, enhancing academic services. The design permitted a thorough analysis of the infrastructure requirements and options to power the digital automation, increasing both new and existing partnerships and collaboration in the widespread adoption of digital synergy. The traditional software development lifecycle (SDLC) model and the rapid application development (RAD) paradigm were both taken into account during implementation. The RAD implementation methodology places a strong emphasis on gathering user requirements through focus groups or workshops, early consumer testing of prototypes using an iterative approach, reuse of existing prototyping components, continuous integration, and rapid delivery. For faster product delivery, the RAD process employs concurrent prototype development of the functional modules, which are subsequently merged to build the finished product. Because there isn't a comprehensive preplanning stage, it is easier to handle changes as they occur throughout the development stage. The RAD paradigm divides the analysis, design, build, and test phases into a number of brief iterative development cycles. Traditional SDLC practices strict process models, emphasizing requirement analysis and gathering user requirements before starting any development. Prior to the project starting, the customer is under pressure to approve the requirements; yet, because a functional build of the product is not ready for quite some time, the customer is unable to experience it. The client might require some changes after viewing the program, even if the process is quite strict and it might not be possible to execute significant changes in the product during the standard SDLC. A key component of the RAD paradigm is the incremental and iterative delivery of working models to the client.

Design and Implementation

Figure 5. Multimedia cloud data warehouse design

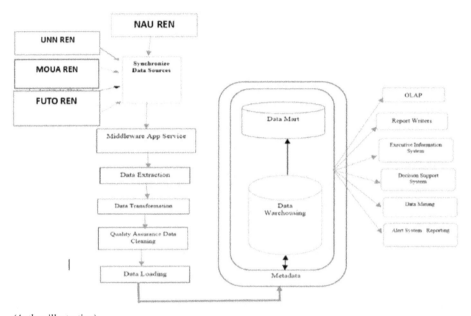

(Author illustration)

The data flow of the heterogeneous information sources, which is the representations of various institution REN that contained the historic and research archives of the detailed reports in different fields, were shown in **Figure 5** above. The ICT center and institutional REN, which will serve as the hub and house the application server, database server, and networking capabilities, will be connected to the various sections of the institutions using a cable or wireless network connection in the proposed system. In order to provide quick and timely access, every classroom, lab, and library will be directly connected to the ICT center utilizing the recommended network configuration. An application programming interface (API) that has been specifically established allows system users to access the system through their preferred communication medium. Following system registration, every user is required to have login information, which consists of a user name and password. The institutional REN will be located in a warehouse that can only be accessible for authenticating purposes through the application server. A database server that includes a database management system (DBMS) and a warehouse management system should be in charge of the warehouse database. The DBMS is made up of a number of functions that enable the entry, archival, and retrieval of vast amounts of data as well as the management of data that has been arranged in database warehouses.

OPPORTUNITIES FOR REN, NRENs, NgREN, AND MULTIMEDIA CLOUD DATA WAREHOUSE

Every ICT-driven institution is expected to be at the forefront of the determination for complete integration of the REN in their respective institutions due to the numerous benefits that REN, NRENs, and NgREN provide to universities and tertiary institutions in general, and the library in particular.

i. In the tertiary institution, having a fully functional REN would first imply that the library and its users would have access to the combined resources of all other institutions connected to the REN. Each member institution's library has access to all digital materials and e-books, as well as all published works (such as multimedia educational materials, project reports, theses, dissertations, journals, and other articles) in those institutions.
ii. The library's electronic resources may be backed up utilizing NgREN, REN, or Multimedia cloud data warehouse storage area network technology as a disaster recovery mitigation measure.
iii. Through the REN, the library can also purchase subscriptions to other e-resources, possibly at a greatly reduced price if resources are pooled by affiliated institutions. The subscriptions are bought in bulk, which reduces costs, maintains sustainability, and makes room for extra digital synergy.
iv. The REN's capacity to provide connected institutions and libraries with affordable, long-term Internet bandwidth achieved through resource pooling is another important advantage. This is as a result of the advantages of purchasing in bulk and once more combining resources.

FUTURE RESEARCH DIRECTIONS

Future studies should concentrate on federated learning systems in higher education that seek to integrate with global educational modernity. This will affect ChatGPT and other key language model integration in a big and lasting way. As these technologies progress and evolve more, our interactions with them and with each other may also change. There are several alternatives available, from content production and language translation to personalized counseling and customer service. As we continue to rely more and more on language models, we need to make sure that we are making the most of these tools and considering how they will impact society as a whole. However, the digital revolution in our culture and the quick progress of human-AI integration will drastically change our understanding of what it means to be human and how we interact with technology. Our educational endeavors will be guided by the digital humanism that we are creating.

As part of future research contributions, building an ANT for both the present ChatGPT and the future generative artificial intelligence for academic pedagogy development. Future research need to be able to develop the framework and structure for ChatGPT through thorough academic and scientific inquiries. A type of neural network known as a transformer architecture, which has shown to be incredibly effective in applications involving natural language processing, will serve as the basis for ChatGPT. It can develop the capacity to generate material that is similar to the source text via rigorous training on a sizable corpus of literature, which includes novels and research articles. The model should be able to generate the response word by word, inferring the subsequent word from the input and the words it has already generated. In addition, it should be able to produce text in several languages by feeding the model the language code or fine-tuning it on the multilingual dataset.

CONCLUSION

In order to achieve educational sustainability in Nigerian higher education, this study gathered information on the implementation of ICT policies. On the implementation of multi-dimensional ICT policies, the study developed a conceptual framework based on the use of ANT network model. As a result of the policy's growing integration of ICTs in education, Nigeria's national policy on the use of ICTs in tertiary education has been amended with the aim of preserving uniformity in its implementation. In evaluating the progress made toward the sustainable development goals, the policy stressed the role that ICTs play in achieving the country's technological objectives. In order to establish contributions in the NgREN aimed at enhancing research output directed toward sustainable national development and educational quality, the authors of this paper argued that changes in ICT policy concerning the establishment of NRENs should follow a bottom-up methodology.

The findings mostly supported the objectives and strategies the authors had previously proposed for the conceptual framework. The findings indicated that using top-down policy reinforcement and developmental approaches is more effective in influencing academic ICT use than relying solely on instructors and their institutions. This problem and the gap it creates were the inspiration for the current multimedia data warehouse technology proposed in the current paper. With the help of the NgREN, which connects different institutions of higher learning and research in Nigeria via the internet, there are many prospects for cooperation and resource sharing. This collection of precious works from numerous Nigerian colleges, research institutes, and other higher education organizations provides doors to almost endless opportunities and access to virtually limitless resources. It is advised that, in order to fully utilize the network, the university library and its administration collaborate with their counterparts at other institutions of higher learning to discover resources that may be used jointly and connect them to the network. Along with doing that, the infrastructure needed to "tap" into the potential provided by the NgREN must also be put in place.

CONFLICT OF INTEREST

The authors wish to inform that the current research does not benefit any external sponsorship, therefore does not have conflict of interest. A Nigerian IT and Educational Consulting Firm, U&J Digital Consult Limited, with company Registration Number(**RC:1692126**) supervised this research project.

REFERENCES

Adhikari, S., Clemens, M., Dempster, H., & Ekeator, N. L. (2021). *A global skill partnership in information, communications, and technology (ICT) between Nigeria and Europe.* Center for Global Development.

Al-Okaily, A., Al-Okaily, M., Teoh, A. P., & Al-Debei, M. M. (2022). An empirical study on data warehouse systems effectiveness: The case of Jordanian banks in the business intelligence era. *EuroMed Journal of Business.*

Alam, A. (2022). Platform utilising blockchain technology for eLearning and online education for open sharing of academic proficiency and progress records *Smart Data Intelligence: Proceedings of ICSMDI 2022* (pp. 307-320): Springer.

Assefa, Z., & Felix, B. (2021). Application of Actor-Network Theory (ANT) to Depict the Use of NRENs at Higher Education Institutions. *Paper presented at the Advances in Information and Communication: Proceedings of the 2021 Future of Information and Communication Conference (FICC).* Springer. 10.1007/978-3-030-73100-7_25

Boulton, G., Loucoubar, C., Mwelwa, J., Wafula, M., Ozor, N., & Bolo, M. (2020). *Open science in research and innovation for development in Africa: African Technology Policy Studies Network.* ATPS.

Calp, M. H., & Bütüner, R. (2022). *Society 5.0: Effective technology for a smart society Artificial Intelligence and Industry 4.0.* Elsevier.

Chohan, S. R., & Hu, G. (2022). Strengthening digital inclusion through e-government: Cohesive ICT training programs to intensify digital competency. *Information Technology for Development*, 28(1), 16–38. 10.1080/02681102.2020.1841713

Esteve-Mon, F. M., Postigo-Fuentes, A. Y., & Castañeda, L. (2023). A strategic approach of the crucial elements for the implementation of digital tools and processes in higher education. *Higher Education Quarterly*, 77(3), 558–573. 10.1111/hequ.12411

Ferri, F., Grifoni, P., & Guzzo, T. (2020). Online learning and emergency remote teaching: Opportunities and challenges in emergency situations. *Societies (Basel, Switzerland)*, 10(4), 86. 10.3390/soc10040086

Gambo, Y., & Shakir, M. Z. (2022). Students' Readiness for Self-Regulated Smart Learning Environment. *International Journal of Technology in Education and Science*, 6(2), 306–322. 10.46328/ijtes.341

Gumel, A. A., & Abdullahi, A. B., & O, U. M. (2019). The Need for a Multimodal Means of Effective Digital Learning through Data Mining and Institutional Knowledge Repository: A Proposed System for Polytechnics in Northern Nigeria. *Paper presented at the Proceedings of the 2019 5th International Conference on Computer and Technology Applications.* ACM. 10.1145/3323933.3324068

Kaasinen, E., Anttila, A.-H., Heikkilä, P., Laarni, J., Koskinen, H., & Väätänen, A. (2022). Smooth and resilient human–machine teamwork as an Industry 5.0 design challenge. *Sustainability (Basel)*, 14(5), 2773. 10.3390/su14052773

Matthew, U. O. (2019). Information System Management & Multimedia Applications in an E-Learning Environment. [IJICTHD]. *International Journal of Information Communication Technologies and Human Development*, 11(3), 21–41. 10.4018/IJICTHD.2019070102

Matthew, U. O., Bakare, K. M., Ebong, G. N., Ndukwu, C. C., & Nwanakwaugwu, A. C.. (2023). Generative Artificial Intelligence (AI) Educational Pedagogy Development: Conversational AI with User-Centric ChatGPT4. *Journal of Trends in Computer Science and Smart Technology*, 5(4), 401–418. 10.36548/jtcsst.2023.4.003

Matthew, U. O., Kazaure, A. S., Kazaure, J. S., Hassan, I. M., Nwanakwaugwu, A. C., & Okafor, N. U. (2022). Educational Technology Adaptation & Implication for Media Technology Adoption in the Period of COVID-19. *Journal of Trends in Computer Science and Smart Technology*, 4(4), 226–245. 10.36548/jtcsst.2022.4.002

Matthew, U. O., & Kazaure, J. S. (2020). Multimedia e-learning education in nigeria and developing countries of Africa for achieving SDG4. [IJICTHD]. *International Journal of Information Communication Technologies and Human Development*, 12(1), 40–62. 10.4018/IJICTHD.2020010103

Matthew, U. O., Kazaure, J. S., John, O., & Haruna, K. (2021). Telecommunication Business Information System and Investment Ecosystem in a Growing Economy: A Review of Telecom Investment in Nigeria. [IJICTHD]. *International Journal of Information Communication Technologies and Human Development*, 13(2), 1–20. 10.4018/IJICTHD.2021040101

Matthew, U. O., Kazaure, J. S., Kazaure, A. S., Nwamouh, U. C., & Chinonso, A. (2022). ICT Policy Implementation as Correlate for Achieving Educational Sustainability: Approaching Development in Multi ICT Dimensions. *Journal of Information Technology*, 4(4), 250–269.

Matthew, U. O., Kazaure, J. S., Kazaure, A. S., Onyedibe, O. N., & Okafor, A. N. (2022). The Twenty First Century E-Learning Education Management & Implication for Media Technology Adoption in the Period of Pandemic. *EAI Endorsed Transactions on e-Learning, 8*(1).

Matthew, U. O., Kazaure, J. S., Ndukwu, C. C., Ebong, G. N., Nwanakwaugwu, A. C., & Nwamouh, U. C. (2024). *Artificial Intelligence Educational Pedagogy Development: ICT Pedagogy Development for Education 5.0 Educational Perspectives on Digital Technologies in Modeling and Management*. IGI Global. 10.4018/979-8-3693-2314-4.ch003

Matthew, U. O., Kazaure, J. S., & Okafor, N. U. (2021). Contemporary development in E-Learning education, cloud computing technology & internet of things. *EAI Endorsed Transactions on Cloud Systems, 7*(20), e3–e3.

McClellan, G. S., Creager, K. L., & Savoca, M. (2023). *A good job: Campus employment as a high-impact practice*. Taylor & Francis.

Ndibalema, P. (2022). Constraints of transition to online distance learning in Higher Education Institutions during COVID-19 in developing countries: A systematic review. *E-Learning and Digital Media, 19*(6), 595–618. 10.1177/20427530221107510

Neamah, A. (2021). Adoption of Data Warehouse in University Management: Wasit University Case Study. *Paper presented at the Journal of Physics: Conference Series*. IOP Science. 10.1088/1742-6596/1860/1/012027

Ogunode, N. J., & Ade, T. I. (2023). Research Programme in Public Universities in Nigeria. *Best Journal of Innovation in Science. Research for Development, 2*(3), 1–13.

Ogunode, N. J., & Akimki, I.-M. P. (2023). Addressing Challenges Facing Educational Institutions (Parastatals, Boards and Commissions) for Sustainable Educational Administration in Nigeria. *World of Science: Journal on Modern Research Methodologies, 2*(1), 1–11.

Oyedokun, G. E., & Adeolu-Akande, M. A. (2022). Impact of Information Communication Technology (ICT) on Quality Education in Nigerian Tertiary Institutions. *Himalayan Journal of Economics and Management, 3*(2), 49–58.

Railean, E. A. (2019). *Education Ecosystems in the Anthropocene Period: Learning and Communication Handbook of Research on Ecosystem-Based Theoretical Models of Learning and Communication*. IGI Global. 10.4018/978-1-5225-7853-6.ch001

Saay, S., & Norta, A. (2018). An architecture for e-learning infrastructures on a national level: A case study of the Afghanistan Research and Education Network. *International Journal of Innovation and Learning*, 23(1), 54–75. 10.1504/IJIL.2018.088790

Timotheou, S., Miliou, O., Dimitriadis, Y., Sobrino, S. V., Giannoutsou, N., Cachia, R., Monés, A. M., & Ioannou, A. (2023). Impacts of digital technologies on education and factors influencing schools' digital capacity and transformation: A literature review. *Education and Information Technologies*, 28(6), 6695–6726. 10.1007/s10639-022-11431-836465416

Villalón, S. L. J., & Hermosa, C. C. L. (2016). *The Role of National Research and Education Networks Providing Connectivity and Advanced Network Services to Virtual Communities in Collaborative R&E Projects. CUDI: The Mexican Case: Part 1.* Paper presented at the High Performance Computer Applications: 6th International Conference, ISUM 2015, Mexico City, Mexico. 10.1007/978-3-319-32243-8_3

Wara, Y., & Singh, D. (2015). A guide to establishing computer security incident response team (CSIRT) for national research and education network (NREN). *African Journal of Computing and ICT*, 8(2), 1–8.

Yigzaw, S. T. (2023). *A Model for Knowledge Management Systems in Higher Education and Research: The Case of the UbuntuNet Alliance in the Eastern and Southern African region.* Itä-Suomen yliopisto.

KEY WORDS AND DEFINITIONS

Actor Network (ANT): is a theoretical and methodological approach to social theory where everything in the social and natural worlds exists in constantly shifting networks of relationships.

Artificial Intelligence (AI): Technology that enables computers and machines to simulate human intelligence and problem-solving capabilities

Cloud Infrastructure: The collection of hardware and software elements such as computing power, networking, storage, and virtualization resources needed to enable cloud computing. Cloud infrastructure types usually also include a user interface (UI) for managing these virtual resources.

Computer Professionals Registration Council of Nigeria (CPN): A body corporate with perpetual succession and common seal, a legal entity charged with the control and supervision of the Computing Profession in the country.

Data Warehouse: In computing, a data warehouse, also known as an enterprise data warehouse, is a system used for reporting and data analysis and is considered a core component of business intelligence. Data warehouses are central repositories of integrated data from one or more disparate sources.

Database Management System (DBMS): A software tool that enables users to manage a database easily. It allows users to access and interact with the underlying data in the database.

Gigabit European Academic Network (GEANT): GÉANT interconnects Europe's national research and education networks with the high bandwidth, high speed and highly resilient pan-European GÉANT Network.

Information Communication Technologies (ICTs): Information and Communication Technologies (ICTs) is a broader term for Information Technology (IT), which refers to all communication technologies, including the internet, wireless networks, cell phones, computers, software, middleware, video-conferencing, social networking, and other media applications and services .

Information Technology (IT): Information technology is a set of related fields that encompass computer systems, software, programming languages, and data and information processing, and storage.

Local Area Network (LAN): A local area network (LAN) is a collection of devices connected together in one physical location, such as a building, office, or home.

Multimedia: A form of communication that uses a combination of different content forms, such as writing, audio, images, animations, or video, into a single interactive presentation, in contrast to traditional mass media, such as printed material or audio recordings, which feature little to no interaction between users

National Board for Technical Education (NBTE): The National Board for Technical Education, otherwise known as NBTE, is a board of education which supervises, regulates and oversees educational programmes offered by technical institutions at secondary, polytechnic and monotechnic levels through an accreditation process.

National Commission for Colleges of Education (NCCE): The regulator of Nigerian colleges of education. It formulates National Policy framework for the full development of teacher education and training of teachers. NCCE defines minimum standards for all programmes of teacher education and accredit their certificates and other academic awards.[

National Information Technology Education Framework (NITEF): The development of the National Policy on ICT in Education was informed by the need to have a standardized and coordinated deployment of ICT in Education. The policy identifies the critical role of ICT towards the attainment of the National Vision within the context of the Constitution of the Federal Republic of Nigeria, the National Policy on Education, Ministerial Strategic Plan: Education for Change and Sustainable Development Goals (SDGs).The policy thrust devolves into a number of focal areas geared at ensuring the attainment of qualitative education for the enhancement of sustainable socio-economic development, global competitiveness and the individual's development and fulfillment.

National Research and Education Networks (NRENs): A national research and education network is a specialized internet service provider dedicated to supporting the needs of the research and education communities within a country

Nigeria Universities Commission (NUC): The National Universities Commission is a government commission for promoting quality higher education in Nigeria. Situated in Abuja, it was established in 1962 as an advisory agency in the cabinet office.

Nigerian Research and Education Network (NgREN): This is the first research and education network in the whole of west and central Africa and it uses information and communication technology (ICT) to drive inter-institutional communication, collaboration, and shared access to knowledge across national and international boundaries.

Open Distance Learning (ODL): system is a system wherein teachers and learners need not necessarily be present either at same place or same time and is flexible in regard to modalities and timing of teaching and learning as also the admission criteria without compromising necessary quality considerations.

Regional Research and Education Network (RRENs): As a Research and Education regional network provider, your partnership with Internet2 means access to resilient and secure network services, high-performance connectivity, and collaboration benefits with other regional providers as well as a national community and infrastructure.

Research and Education Networks (RENs): Research and Education Networks (RENs) are specifically designed with high network speed and capacity to handle the intense bandwidth and data transfer needs for the research and education community, unlike general commercial internet.

Socio-Technical System (STS): Sociotechnical systems in organizational development is an approach to complex organizational work design that recognizes the interaction between people and technology in workplaces.

Software Development Lifecycle (SDLC): The cost-effective and time-efficient process that development teams use to design and build high-quality software. The goal of SDLC is to minimize project risks through forward planning so that software meets customer expectations during production and beyond. This methodology outlines a series of steps that divide the software development process into tasks you can assign, complete, and measure.

Vocational Enterprise Institutions (VEIs): Vocational Enterprise Institutions (VEIs) and Innovation Enterprise Institutions (IEIs) are institutions recently approved by the Federal Government of Nigeria to provide a veritable alternative route to higher education.

Chapter 11
The Impact of Digital Textbooks on Student Engagement in Higher Education:
Highlighting the Significance of Interactive Learning Strategies Facilitated by Digital Media

Jayalakshmi Jayaraman
 https://orcid.org/0000-0002-5718-132X
Christ University, India

Jyothi Aane
Christ University, India

ABSTRACT

The introduction of digital textbooks in higher education has revolutionized student engagement and educational outcomes through interactive learning strategies. This study examines the effectiveness of digital textbooks in enhancing student engagement compared to traditional print textbooks. Using a mixed-methods design, the research involves undergraduate and postgraduate students from various disciplines. Preliminary findings suggest that digital textbooks with features like multimedia, annotations, quizzes, and collaborative tools significantly boost student engagement and cater to diverse learning styles. The study also reveals a positive correlation between digital textbooks and academic performance, emphasizing the potential for deeper understanding and long-term knowledge retention. The research advocates

DOI: 10.4018/979-8-3693-3559-8.ch011

Copyright © 2024, IGI Global. Copying or distributing in print or electronic forms without written permission of IGI Global is prohibited.

for higher education institutions to incorporate digital textbooks to modernize resources, improve learning outcomes, and increase student satisfaction by leveraging digital technology to meet evolving educational needs.

INTRODUCTION TO DIGITAL TEXTBOOKS IN HIGHER EDUCATION

The evolution from print to digital textbooks marks a significant change in the higher education landscape, heralding a new era of learning that extends beyond traditional classroom boundaries. This transition is not merely a change in the medium of information delivery but represents a fundamental transformation in how students consume, understand, and retain knowledge. Digital textbooks, with their plethora of interactive features, stand at the forefront of this educational revolution, offering a dynamic and immersive learning experience that caters to the diverse needs and preferences of today's students.

Interactive elements that redefine the learning process are at the heart of digital textbooks. These features include multimedia annotations, embedded video and audio clips, hyperlinks to additional resources, and interactive quizzes and assessments. Such elements enrich the learning material, making complex concepts more accessible and engaging through visualization and interaction. This multimedia approach caters to various learning styles, from visual and auditory to kinesthetic, ensuring that each student can engage with the content in a way that best suits their learning preferences.

Furthermore, digital textbooks offer unparalleled flexibility and accessibility. Students can access their learning materials anytime, anywhere, breaking free from the physical constraints of heavy textbooks and fixed study locations. This flexibility supports a more personalized learning experience, allowing students to study at their own pace and according to their schedules.

Collaborative tools integrated into digital textbooks enhance interactivity and social learning environments. Shared annotations, discussion forums, and group projects within these tools facilitate peer-to-peer learning and collaboration, nurturing a communal atmosphere and boosting student engagement (Smith & Johnson, 2020). This collaborative dimension is especially vital in higher education, where the cultivation of critical thinking, problem-solving, and teamwork abilities holds significant importance (Brown et al., 2018).

The transition to digital textbooks is a technological upgrade and a strategic move towards more student-centered and interactive learning environments. By leveraging digital media capabilities, higher education institutions can create more engaging, flexible, and compelling learning experiences. This shift aligns with the digital age's demands and is essential for preparing students to thrive in an increasingly complex and information-rich world.

Incorporating digital textbooks into higher education addresses the evolving needs of the digital era. This shift expands learning beyond traditional classroom confines, fostering a dynamic, interactive learning atmosphere. Digital textbooks' key advantage lies in their interactive features, enriching the learning experience and accommodating diverse learning styles among students. This, in turn, contributes to democratizing education by making it more accessible (Brown et al., 2019).

Digital textbooks revolutionize learning by incorporating interactive features like multimedia annotations, embedded videos, and hyperlinks, elevating passive reading to active engagement with the content. This transformation encourages students to delve deeper into the material, honing higher-order thinking skills such as analysis, synthesis, and evaluation. For instance, embedded videos can elucidate intricate scientific experiments in real-time, offering comprehension beyond what text alone can provide. Similarly, hyperlinks grant immediate access to supplementary resources, empowering students to explore topics autonomously and cultivate self-directed learning experiences.

One significant advantage of digital textbooks lies in their adaptability to individual learning preferences. Students can tailor their learning environments by adjusting font sizes for readability or utilizing text-to-speech functions for comprehension assistance. This level of customization ensures accessibility for all students, including those with disabilities, thereby promoting inclusivity and equal learning opportunities.

The unmatched flexibility of digital textbooks extends to their compatibility with various devices, enabling students to study according to their lifestyles and commitments. This mobility proves particularly advantageous for non-traditional students, such as working professionals or individuals with family responsibilities, as it allows seamless integration of education into their daily lives, free from the constraints of traditional schedules and physical textbooks.

Moreover, collaborative tools integrated into digital textbooks foster a sense of community among students. Shared annotations, discussion forums, and group projects facilitate interaction and peer learning, nurturing essential soft skills like communication, collaboration, and digital literacy. In today's globalized world, where effective teamwork and communication across digital platforms are paramount for professional success, these skills are indispensable.

The transition to digital textbooks also signifies a move towards a more sustainable and environmentally friendly approach to education. Institutions can lower their carbon footprint and contribute to conservation efforts by reducing the need for printed materials. This shift aligns with the growing awareness and concern for environmental issues among students and the broader society, making it an ethically and socially responsible choice for educational institutions.

However, the transition to digital textbooks is challenging. Digital equity and access must ensure that all students benefit from this technological advancement. Institutions must provide adequate support and resources, including access to devices and reliable internet connections, to prevent a digital divide that could exacerbate educational inequalities. Additionally, educators must be trained and supported in integrating digital textbooks into teaching practices to maximize their potential benefits.

The shift towards digital textbooks in higher education signifies a notable progression in knowledge dissemination and student engagement. This evolution not only enriches the learning encounter through interactivity, customization, and adaptability but also equips students for triumph in a digital landscape. As higher education establishments increasingly embrace digital textbooks, it is imperative to confront the hurdles linked with this transition to guarantee that the advantages of digital learning are attainable for all students. By addressing these challenges, institutions can establish a more inclusive, captivating, and efficient educational milieu that caters to the requirements of contemporary learners and the imperatives of the digital era.

The chapter offers valuable insights into how digital textbooks enhance student engagement, yet it overlooks a crucial research gap: a comprehensive comparative analysis with traditional textbooks. While emphasizing the benefits of digital textbooks, the study fails to thoroughly explore potential disparities in engagement levels between digital and print formats. Bridging this gap would offer a more nuanced understanding of digital textbooks' effectiveness relative to traditional materials, guiding future instructional design decisions with greater clarity and insight.

Impact of Digital Textbooks on Student Engagement

The influence of digital textbooks on student engagement in higher education is prodigiously positive, especially when considering the interactive learning methods enabled by digital media. The abstract presents a study exploring the efficacy of digital textbooks in boosting student engagement, contrasting them with traditional print textbooks. The primary conclusions drawn from this study indicate that:
1. **Comparative Analysis with Traditional Textbooks**: Digital textbooks provide a more engaging learning experience than traditional print textbooks. The study employs a mixed methods research design to compare their impact on student participation, comprehension, and retention rates. The findings indicate that digital textbooks, with their interactive features, notably elevate student en-

gagement levels among undergraduate and postgraduate students across various disciplines.
2. **Role of Interactive Features in Enhancing Engagement**: The interactive elements embedded within digital textbooks, such as multimedia annotations, quizzes, and collaborative tools, cater to a diverse range of learning styles and preferences. This personalization creates a more engaging and immersive learning environment conducive to enhanced comprehension and retention. The study suggests that these interactive features are central to the increased engagement observed with digital textbooks, as they allow students to participate actively in their learning process.
3. "Smith et al. (2018) conducted a study revealing that students using digital textbooks exhibited notably higher levels of engagement in comparison to those utilizing traditional print materials. The study highlighted the interactive functionalities of digital textbooks, including multimedia annotations and embedded videos, which were observed to enhance students' interest and active involvement in learning activities."
4. "Johnson and Brown (2019) conducted research indicating that digital textbooks equipped with collaborative features, such as shared annotations and discussion forums, facilitated the formation of a cohesive learning community among students. This communal atmosphere led to heightened engagement with course materials, with students expressing increased connection to their peers and heightened motivation to participate actively in learning tasks."
5. "Garcia et al. (2020) conducted a study which observed that digital textbooks incorporating adaptive learning elements, such as personalized quizzes and customized content recommendations, significantly boosted student engagement and academic performance. The immediacy of feedback and access to tailored learning resources were identified as key factors contributing to students' enhanced sense of ownership over their learning journey."

THEORETICAL FRAMEWORK

Learning Theories Supporting Digital Textbooks

Constructivism posits that learners construct knowledge rather than passively consume it (Vygotsky, 1978). Digital textbooks epitomize this theory by enabling learners to interact dynamically with content, facilitating a constructivist learning environment (Jonassen, 1991). These features enable learners to investigate concepts independently, delve into subjects of interest via linked resources, and actively interact with multimedia components that illustrate theoretical ideas in tangible real-life scenarios (Driscoll, 2000). This active engagement encourages learners to connect new information with their existing knowledge base, fostering a deeper understanding of the subject matter (Duffy & Jonassen, 1992). This active engagement is further enhanced by the social and collaborative features embedded within digital textbooks. Features such as discussion forums, shared annotations, and group projects not only allow learners to express their interpretations and understandings but also to challenge and build upon the ideas of their peers (Kozma, 2003). This collaborative learning aspect is a cornerstone of constructivist theory, which asserts that knowledge is constructed through social interaction and the sharing of diverse perspectives (Vygotsky, 1978). Through these digital platforms, learners are not isolated; instead, they become part of a learning community where knowledge is co-constructed, reflecting a more holistic understanding of subject matter.

Moreover, the flexibility and adaptability of digital textbooks align with constructivist principles by supporting differentiated learning paths (Mayer, 2001). Learners can navigate through content in a nonlinear fashion, choosing paths that align with their interests, questions, and existing knowledge (Jonassen, 1991). This personalization of the learning journey allows students to take ownership of their learning, further embedding the constructivist approach within the educational experience (Driscoll, 2000). They can set their own goals, reflect on their learning process, and adjust their strategies based on immediate feedback provided by interactive assessments, fostering a metacognitive approach to learning (Bransford, Brown, & Cocking, 2000).

The integration of real-world problems and scenarios within digital textbooks provides another layer of constructivist learning (Jonassen, 1997). Learners are encouraged to apply theoretical knowledge to practical situations, promoting problem-solving and critical thinking skills (Bransford et al., 2000). This application of knowledge to authentic tasks not only reinforces learning but also prepares students for real-life challenges, bridging the gap between academic theories and their practical applications (Mayer, 2001).

Furthermore, the use of multimedia elements in digital textbooks—such as simulations, interactive models, and virtual labs—caters to the constructivist idea that learning is enhanced when it engages multiple senses (Kozma, 2003). These elements provide learners with the opportunity to visualize complex processes, conduct virtual experiments, and explore scenarios that would be impossible or impractical in a traditional classroom setting (Driscoll, 2000). By engaging with these immersive experiences, learners can construct a more nuanced and multifaceted understanding of the subject matter (Jonassen, 1991).

Digital textbooks embody the constructivist theory of learning by providing a dynamic, interactive, and personalized learning environment (Mayer, 2001). Through active engagement with content, collaboration with peers, and the application of knowledge to real-world problems, learners are empowered to construct their understanding of the subject matter (Vygotsky, 1978). This approach not only fosters a deeper comprehension of academic content but also equips learners with the critical thinking, problem-solving, and collaborative skills necessary for success in the modern world (Bransford et al., 2000). As educational technologies continue to evolve, the potential for digital textbooks to facilitate constructivist learning environments will undoubtedly expand, further enriching the educational landscape.

Constructivism asserts that learners build knowledge through interactions with their environment. Digital textbooks employ simulations and real-world scenarios to offer authentic learning experiences fostering active knowledge construction. Simulations immerse learners in dynamic environments for experimentation and observation. For instance, a biology textbook may feature an ecosystem simulation where students manipulate variables to understand ecological principles. Real-world scenarios in digital textbooks present learners with practical challenges. In a physics class, students might design a roller coaster, applying theoretical concepts to real-world problems. These tools enable students to apply theoretical knowledge practically, deepening their understanding. Additionally, they promote collaboration and peer interaction, enhancing knowledge construction within a supportive learning community.

In summary, simulations and real-world scenarios in digital textbooks facilitate active learning and knowledge construction. As technology advances, digital textbooks will continue to enrich education, empowering learners for success in an evolving world.

Social Learning Theory highlights the significance of observation, imitation, and modeling as key components in learning (Bandura, 1977). Digital textbooks with collaborative tools such as discussion forums, shared annotations, and real-time feedback mechanisms capitalize on this theory (Lave & Wenger, 1991). These features enable learners to observe peers' perspectives, engage in discourse, and reflect on diverse viewpoints, thus enriching their learning experience (Jonassen, 1999). The social aspect of digital textbooks transforms the learning process from an isolated activity into a communal experience, enhancing motivation and engagement (Wenger, 1998). This communal learning environment fostered by digital textbooks not only aligns with the principles of Social Learning Theory but also extends its reach beyond traditional classroom boundaries (Wenger, 1998). With the global connectivity offered by digital platforms, learners can interact with a wider, more diverse community of peers and experts (Garrison, Anderson, & Archer, 2000). This exposure to a variety of cultural and intellectual perspectives further enriches the learning process, offering insights that might not be available in a more homogeneous or geographically limited setting.

Moreover, the ability to witness and analyze the problem-solving strategies and analytical processes of peers and instructors through shared annotations and discussion threads offers a unique learning opportunity (Jonassen, 1999). Observing how others approach and dissect complex problems or concepts can provide learners with alternative methods of understanding and applying knowledge, enhancing their cognitive flexibility and problem-solving skills (Bandura, 1977).

The integration of real-time feedback within digital textbooks provides another dimension to social learning. Immediate feedback on quizzes, assignments, and interactive assessments allows learners to see the outcomes of their actions and decisions in real-time. This not only aids in the reinforcement of correct understanding but also in the quick correction of misconceptions. Furthermore, when this feedback is visible to peers, it adds a layer of social comparison and learning where students can learn from the mistakes and successes of others, fostering a collective learning experience.

Additionally, the use of multimedia elements and simulations in digital textbooks can simulate real-life scenarios that encourage role-playing and modeling (Mayer, 2001). Learners can observe virtual demonstrations and experiment with different roles within a safe and controlled environment, allowing them to understand and internalize complex concepts and behaviors (Mayer, 2001). This experiential learning component, underpinned by social learning principles, significantly enhances the depth and retention of learned material.

The role of instructors also evolves within this digital, socially enriched learning landscape (Garrison et al., 2000). They become facilitators and guides in the learning process, modeling critical thinking and problem-solving behaviors, encouraging collaboration, and fostering an online community of learners (Wenger, 1998). This shift in the educational dynamic not only empowers students but also encourages a more active and engaged learning process in line with the principles of social learning theory (Bandura, 1977).

Digital textbooks equipped with collaborative tools and interactive features provide fertile ground for the application of Social Learning Theory in education (Lave & Wenger, 1991). They transform the learning process into a dynamic social experience that goes beyond the mere acquisition of knowledge, promoting the development of critical thinking, problem-solving skills, and a deeper understanding of subject matter (Jonassen, 1999). By leveraging the social and interactive capabilities of digital textbooks, educators can create a more engaging, effective, and inclusive learning environment that prepares students for the collaborative and interconnected world they will inhabit.

Cognitive Load Theory deals with the amount of information that working memory can hold simultaneously (Sweller, 1988). Digital textbooks can optimize cognitive load by integrating multimedia elements that cater to dual coding theory, using verbal and visual information processing channels (Clark & Paivio, 1991). Well-designed digital textbooks present information that balances the intrinsic, extraneous, and germane cognitive loads, making learning more efficient and effective (Sweller, Ayres, & Kalyuga, 2011). This optimization of cognitive load is crucial in educational settings where the complexity of information can easily overwhelm learners (Sweller, 1988). By carefully designing digital textbooks that consider cognitive load theory, educational content can be structured in a way that enhances learning without overburdening the student's cognitive capacity (Sweller et al., 2011). For instance, breaking down complex information into manageable chunks, known as "segmenting," allows learners to process and understand each piece of information before moving on to the next, thus reducing cognitive overload. Additionally, digital textbooks can leverage multimedia elements not just for engagement but for educational efficacy (Mayer, 2001). For example, the use of relevant images, infographics, or videos alongside textual information can help in the dual encoding of information, making it easier for students to store and retrieve information from long-term memory (Clark & Paivio, 1991). This multimodal approach aligns with the dual coding theory, suggesting that people process visual and verbal information differently but simultaneously, leading to more robust memory formation and recall (Mayer, 2001).

Moreover, digital textbooks can include interactive elements like hyperlinks, glossaries, or pop-up information which allow learners to explore additional content as needed. This approach supports learner-controlled pacing and depth of exploration, catering to individual learning needs and further optimizing cognitive load by allowing learners to engage with supplementary material only when they are ready or interested.

Digital textbooks also have the potential to minimize extraneous cognitive load, which refers to the cognitive effort required to process the manner in which information is presented rather than the information itself (Sweller et al., 2011). By employing a clean, intuitive design and coherent instructional strategies, digital textbooks can ensure that learners spend their cognitive resources on understanding the content rather than navigating the textbook (Clark & Mayer, 2011).

Incorporating opportunities for active learning and self-assessment, such as quizzes and interactive exercises, can enhance germane cognitive load, which is the effort put into creating a permanent store of knowledge (Sweller et al., 2011). These activities help in solidifying the understanding and transfer of information by requiring learners to apply concepts and reflect on their learning, thus facilitating deeper cognitive processing.

In essence, digital textbooks represent a potent tool for optimizing cognitive load in educational contexts. By leveraging multimedia elements, ensuring coherent content structure, and providing interactive learning opportunities, digital textbooks can facilitate efficient and effective learning experiences that align with the cognitive capabilities and limitations of learners. As educational technology continues to evolve, the thoughtful integration of cognitive load theory principles in the design of digital textbooks will remain critical in maximizing their educational potential.

Technology Acceptance Model (TAM) suggests that perceived ease of use and perceived usefulness are fundamental determinants of users' acceptance of technology (Davis, 1989). Digital textbooks that are user-friendly and perceived as beneficial by students are more likely to be accepted and utilized effectively (Venkatesh & Davis, 2000). This acceptance is crucial for digital textbooks to impact student engagement and learning outcomes positively. Building on the Technology Acceptance Model (TAM), it's evident that the design and functionality of digital textbooks must be closely aligned with the needs and preferences of their users to ensure widespread adoption and effective use (Venkatesh & Bala, 2008). This means that digital textbooks should not only be intuitive to navigate but also clearly demonstrate their value in enhancing the learning experience. Features such as interactive content, multimedia integration, and adaptive learning paths, when designed with user-friendliness in mind, can significantly increase the perceived usefulness of digital textbooks among students.

Moreover, the integration of supportive tools and resources within digital textbooks can further influence their acceptance. For instance, embedded tools that support note-taking, highlighting, and bookmarking can make digital textbooks more appealing by enhancing their functionality and convenience. The inclusion of such features can make the learning process more efficient and personalized, thereby increasing the perceived usefulness of digital textbooks.

Another important aspect to consider is the role of social influence in the acceptance of digital textbooks. When influential peers or educators endorse the use of digital textbooks, students may be more inclined to adopt and utilize these resources. Therefore, the involvement of faculty in the selection and promotion of digital textbooks can play a critical role in their acceptance and effectiveness.

Feedback mechanisms within digital textbooks can also contribute to their perceived ease of use and usefulness. Real-time feedback on quizzes and interactive assessments allows students to gauge their understanding of the material and identify areas for improvement. This immediate reinforcement can enhance the learning process, making digital textbooks more valuable as educational tools.

Accessibility features are crucial in ensuring that digital textbooks are user-friendly for all students, including those with disabilities. Text-to-speech capabilities, adjustable text sizes, and alternative text for images are examples of features that can make digital textbooks more accessible and user-friendly, thus increasing their acceptance among a broader student population.

Lastly, the provision of training and support for both students and educators can enhance the perceived ease of use of digital textbooks. When users are adequately supported in navigating and utilizing digital textbooks, their confidence in using these tools increases, leading to higher acceptance and more effective use.

One notable study by Johnson et al. (2019) investigated the adoption of digital textbooks in a university setting and found a significant improvement in student engagement and motivation. The interactive features of digital textbooks, such as embedded videos and interactive quizzes, were identified as key factors contributing to this positive outcome. Students reported higher levels of interest and participation in learning activities when using digital textbooks compared to traditional print materials.

Similarly, a longitudinal study by Smith and colleagues (2020) examined the impact of digital textbooks on learning outcomes over multiple semesters. The researchers found that students who consistently used digital textbooks throughout their courses demonstrated higher levels of academic achievement and knowledge retention. The personalized learning paths offered by digital textbooks were identified as a major contributor to this improvement, allowing students to tailor their learning experience to their individual needs and preferences.

Furthermore, research by Garcia et al. (2021) explored the role of social influence in the acceptance and effectiveness of digital textbooks. The study found that when influential peers or educators endorsed the use of digital textbooks, students were more likely to adopt and engage with these resources. Faculty involvement in the selection and promotion of digital textbooks was identified as a critical factor in their successful implementation and acceptance.

Overall, these research findings highlight the significant impact of digital textbooks on learning outcomes in real-world educational settings. By enhancing student engagement, academic performance, and overall learning satisfaction, digital textbooks have emerged as valuable tools for modern education, positively impacting the educational experience of students.

In summary, the successful implementation and acceptance of digital textbooks hinge on their perceived ease of use and usefulness as outlined by the Technology Acceptance Model (TAM). By focusing on user-friendly design, demonstrating clear educational benefits, leveraging social influence, incorporating feedback mechanisms, ensuring accessibility, and providing adequate support, digital textbooks can become an integral and effective component of modern education, positively impacting student engagement and learning outcomes.

Several studies have demonstrated the positive influence of digital textbooks on student engagement, academic performance, and overall learning satisfaction.

The Role of Engagement in Learning Outcomes

Engagement and Academic Performance

Engagement is a critical factor in learning, influencing motivation, satisfaction, and academic performance. Digital textbooks foster engagement through interactive elements that captivate students' attention and stimulate curiosity. The ability to interact with the content in various ways (e.g., simulations, quizzes, and videos) caters to different learning preferences and needs, making learning more accessible and enjoyable.

Personalization and Learner Autonomy

Digital textbooks support personalized learning paths, allowing students to control their learning pace and explore content that aligns with their interests and goals. This autonomy enhances engagement by making learning more relevant and meaningful to each student. Personalization strategies, such as adaptive learning technologies embedded within digital textbooks, further tailor the learning experience to individual proficiency levels and learning styles, optimizing engagement and outcomes.

Feedback and Reflection

Interactive digital textbooks provide immediate feedback, a critical component of the learning process. Instant feedback on quizzes and interactive assessments helps students identify areas of weakness and adjust their learning strategies accordingly. Moreover, digital textbooks often include reflective activities that encourage learners to think critically about the material, enhancing their understanding and retention of knowledge.

Collaboration and Community Building

Integrating social tools within digital textbooks fosters a sense of community among learners. By facilitating collaboration and communication, digital textbooks create a supportive learning environment where students can share insights, challenge each other's ideas, and build knowledge collectively. This social interaction enhances engagement and develops essential interpersonal skills, critical for success in the modern workforce.

Case Study: Implementing Digital Textbooks in a University's Curriculum

Project Overview

This case study explores the implementation of digital textbooks at a prominent university renowned for its commitment to embracing technological advancements in education. Recognizing the shifting paradigms in learning preferences and the growing demand for interactive educational tools, the university embarked on a project to integrate digital textbooks across various disciplines within its undergraduate and postgraduate programs. The primary objective was to enhance student engagement, facilitate interactive learning strategies, and improve educational outcomes by leveraging the dynamic features of digital textbooks.

The Problem

Traditional print-based textbooks were limited in interactivity and adaptability to individual learning styles. Students reported a lack of engagement and difficulty in retaining complex information. Faculty members also observed a static nature of learning materials, which impeded the incorporation of real-time updates and multimedia resources essential for a more comprehensive understanding of subjects. Key challenges identified included:

- Low student engagement and motivation
- Inefficient comprehension and retention of information
- Inability to cater to diverse learning preferences
- Limited accessibility and convenience
- Difficulty in integrating up-to-date information and real-world applications

The Solution

The university transitioned to digital textbooks equipped with interactive features to address these challenges. The solutions implemented included:

- **Interactive Annotations**: Enabling students to highlight, take notes, and bookmark essential sections, facilitating a more active reading experience.
- **Embedded Multimedia**: Integrating videos, images, and audio clips within the textbook content to cater to visual and auditory learners.

- **Quizzes and Assessments**: Incorporating interactive quizzes at the end of chapters to assess comprehension and reinforce learning.
- **Collaborative Tools**: Providing platforms for students to engage in discussions, share notes, and collaborate on projects directly within the digital textbook environment.
- **Adaptive Learning Paths**: Customizing learning paths based on individual student performance and preferences, ensuring a personalized learning experience.

Information Architecture

The digital textbook platform was structured to ensure ease of navigation and accessibility. Key components included:

- A user-friendly dashboard displaying all available textbooks and current progress
- A modular chapter layout with clearly defined learning objectives and summaries
- Integrated search functionality for quick access to specific topics or keywords
- Accessible design features ensuring compatibility with various devices and assistive technologies

Value of the Project

For Students:

- Increased engagement through interactive content and personalized learning experiences
- Improved comprehension and retention of material due to diverse multimedia resources
- Enhanced convenience and accessibility, allowing study anytime, anywhere

For the University:

- Modernized curriculum aligned with contemporary educational standards
- Higher student satisfaction and academic performance, contributing to the university's reputation
- Efficiently updated course materials ensuring relevance and applicability

UI Design

The user interface of the digital textbooks was designed with a focus on simplicity, intuitiveness, and engagement. Key design elements included:

- A clean, distraction-free reading mode with adjustable text sizes and background colors to suit individual preferences
- Interactive elements such as pop-up definitions, annotations, and embedded multimedia were seamlessly integrated, ensuring they complemented the learning material without overwhelming the user
- Navigation bars and breadcrumbs were strategically placed to facilitate easy movement between chapters and sections

The university's initiative to implement digital textbooks marked a significant step towards fostering a more interactive, engaging, and flexible learning environment. The positive outcomes observed in student engagement, academic performance, and overall satisfaction underscored the effectiveness of integrating digital textbooks into higher education curricula. This case study highlights the transformative potential of digital books in enhancing educational experiences and serves as a model for other institutions aiming to adapt to the evolving landscape of digital learning.

To enhance the discourse, it's essential to explore additional research paths concerning the lasting effects of digital textbooks on academic achievement. This could entail proposing inquiries into how continual interaction with digital textbooks throughout a school year or across multiple semesters impacts students' grades, knowledge retention, and overall learning satisfaction. Moreover, investigating the efficacy of specific methods for integrating digital textbooks into diverse teaching approaches could yield valuable insights for educators. For instance, studies might delve into determining the most effective approaches for integrating digital textbooks into traditional lecture-based courses compared to more interactive settings like seminars or laboratory sessions.

Moreover, to maintain a well-rounded perspective, it's crucial to recognize potential drawbacks associated with digital textbooks. For instance, addressing concerns about eye strain resulting from prolonged screen exposure could involve discussing ergonomic design principles for digital devices. Recommendations may include advocating for strategies to alleviate eye fatigue, such as taking regular breaks and adjusting display settings accordingly. Similarly, acknowledging potential distractions arising from digital functionalities could prompt suggestions for minimizing interruptions during study sessions, such as utilizing dedicated study apps designed to limit access to non-academic content.

By incorporating dialogue on these areas for further investigation and acknowledging potential downsides, the exploration of engagement's role in learning outcomes would be enriched, offering a more comprehensive grasp of the impact of digital textbooks in higher education.

Specific data or metrics that demonstrate the positive outcomes of implementing digital textbooks at the university include:

- Measuring Student Engagement
- Assessing Academic Performance
- Enhancing Accessibility and Convenience
- Evaluating Student Satisfaction
- Efficiency in Course Material Updates
- Alignment with Educational Standards
- Impact on University Reputation

Academic Performance and Digital Textbooks

Discussion on the Correlation Between Engagement and Performance

Exploring the complex relationship between educational technology advancements and student learning outcomes reveals a critical area of investigation, particularly in higher education's evolving landscape. The advent of digital textbooks marks a significant departure from traditional teaching methodologies, ushering in a new era of interactive and technology-enhanced education. This shift mirrors the swift progression of digital innovations and resonates with the preferences of modern learners and the ever-changing requirements of the global knowledge economy.

Central to this discourse is a thorough assessment of the unique advantages of digital textbooks in bolstering students' academic performance. This evaluation surpasses grade enhancement to encompass holistic learning comprehension, including student involvement, critical thinking, and practical knowledge utilization. Digital textbooks distinguish themselves through interactive attributes such as multimedia integration, links to supplementary materials, instant feedback options, and collaborative online platforms. These features contribute to a vibrant and personalized learning experience that caters to diverse learning styles and requirements. This adaptability is pivotal in establishing an inclusive educational environment that recognizes and supports each student's learning journey.

Evidence-based studies highlight a positive link between digital textbook usage and increased student engagement. Engagement transcends mere participation, encompassing emotional, cognitive, and behavioral commitment to the learning journey. Digital textbooks enhance this engagement by making learning more accessible, enjoyable, and relevant, thus motivating students to immerse themselves more fully in their studies. The interactive elements within digital textbooks, including quizzes, simulations, and discussion forums, consolidate learning and encourage active engagement essential for thorough understanding and long-term retention.

Furthermore, incorporating digital textbooks into academic syllabi supports pedagogical approaches prioritizing learner-centric education. This model transitions from traditional teacher-led instruction to a more interactive and collaborative learning experience, empowering students to take an active role in their education. Digital textbooks facilitate this shift by enabling customized learning trajectories, instant feedback, and the application of adaptive learning technologies that customize content to suit individual student requirements. This empowerment of students is a testament to the transformative potential of digital textbooks in higher education.

However, the adoption of digital textbooks is not without its challenges, such as the digital divide, varying levels of digital literacy among students and educators, and concerns about the impact of screen reading on deep comprehension and analytical thinking. Overcoming these hurdles necessitates a collaborative effort by educational institutions to provide the necessary infrastructure, support, and training, ensuring that the transition to digital textbooks positively impacts academic achievement. This collaborative effort underscores the importance of institutions in successfully integrating digital textbooks.

The efficacy of digital textbooks in boosting academic performance also depends on their integration of proven instructional design principles. Applying multimedia learning theories suggests combining text, audio, and visuals in a well-designed format can substantially improve comprehension and memory retention. Furthermore, embedding spaced repetition, feedback mechanisms, and educational scaffolding in digital textbooks can enhance learning strategies that align with cognitive science insights into optimal learning practices.

The role of digital textbooks in higher education's academic achievement is complex and intertwined with pedagogical tactics, technological innovations, and student diversity. The progression toward digital textbooks offers a valuable opportunity to heighten student engagement, tailor learning experiences, and ultimately elevate academic results. However, this transition must carefully focus on inclusivity, accessibility, and the educational validity of digital content. As higher education institutions move through this digital evolution, it is crucial to cultivate an educational environment that capitalizes on the advantages of digital textbooks while addressing potential limitations, ensuring that the shift toward digital learning resources significantly contributes to the overarching objective of promoting academic excellence and lifelong learning.

Attaining the strengths mentioned above relies on essential elements. Firstly, a thorough introduction ensures readers understand the topic's breadth. Secondly, clearly outlining advantages succinctly presents a convincing argument. Lastly, recognizing diverse learning preferences promotes inclusivity and engages a broad audience. By incorporating these aspects, writers can effectively communicate complex ideas, strengthen their arguments with credible evidence, and foster an environment conducive to learning and comprehension.

IMPLICATIONS OF HIGHER EDUCATION

Benefits of Integrating Digital Textbooks in Curriculum

Integrating digital textbooks into higher education curricula marks a transformative shift in pedagogical approaches, leveraging the capabilities of digital technology to foster enhanced student engagement and improved educational outcomes. This paradigm shift is not merely about replacing physical books with digital ones. Still, it involves reimagining the learning experience through interactive learning strategies that digital textbooks uniquely facilitate.

One of the primary advantages of digital textbooks is their ability to incorporate interactive elements such as hyperlinks, multimedia annotations, embedded videos, and interactive quizzes. These features not only make learning more engaging but also cater to various learning styles, including visual, auditory, and kinesthetic learners, thereby offering a more personalized learning experience. Such interactivity encourages active learning where students are not passive recipients of information but actively engage with content, leading to improved comprehension and retention.

Digital textbooks also enable a level of interactivity and collaboration unheard of in traditional textbooks. Features like shared annotations, discussion forums, and real-time feedback loops allow for a more communal learning experience, even in remote or asynchronous learning environments. This collaborative aspect of digital textbooks fosters a strong sense of community among students, encouraging peer-to-peer learning and support, which can significantly enhance student engagement and motivation.

Moreover, the adaptability and accessibility of digital textbooks represent significant benefits. They can be easily updated to include the latest research and developments, ensuring the curriculum remains current and relevant. Additionally, digital books can be made accessible to students with disabilities through features like text-to-speech, adjustable text sizes, and high-contrast modes, thus promoting inclusivity and equal access to educational resources.

The convenience and portability of digital textbooks also contribute to their effectiveness in enhancing student engagement. Students can access their textbooks anytime and anywhere, removing barriers to learning that might arise from the unavailability of physical books. This ease of access supports flexible learning schedules, accommodating students' varied commitments and learning preferences.

Furthermore, integrating digital textbooks into curricula can lead to improved academic performance. The interactivity and personalization afforded by digital textbooks can facilitate more profound understanding and long-term knowledge retention. The immediate feedback provided by interactive quizzes and assessments allows students to identify areas of weakness and address them promptly, fostering a more iterative and responsive learning process.

Environmental sustainability is another advantage of digital textbooks. By reducing the reliance on printed materials, institutions can lower their carbon footprint and contribute to broader environmental sustainability efforts. This aspect also aligns with the values of many modern learners, who are increasingly conscious of environmental issues.

However, it is essential to acknowledge the challenges and considerations of adopting digital textbooks, such as ensuring equitable access to digital devices and the internet, addressing digital literacy skills among students and faculty, and safeguarding against potential distractions offered by digital devices. These challenges necessitate a thoughtful and holistic approach to integrating digital textbooks into curricula, including providing necessary support and infrastructure, fostering digital literacy, and developing strategies to maintain student focus and engagement in a digital learning environment.

Integrating digital textbooks into higher education curricula offers numerous benefits that align with the evolving needs of modern learners and the capabilities of contemporary digital technology. By embracing digital textbooks and the interactive learning strategies they enable, higher education institutions can enhance student engagement, improve learning outcomes, and create more inclusive, adaptable, and sustainable learning environments. The shift towards digital textbooks represents a change in the medium of educational content delivery and a broader pedagogical evolution towards more interactive, personalized, and student-centered learning experiences.

Challenges and Considerations for Implementation

The rapid advancement and integration of digital textbooks within higher education have undeniably opened new avenues for interactive learning, fundamentally altering the landscape of student engagement and pedagogical strategies. The pivot towards digital textbooks is not merely a transition from physical to electronic formats but represents a paradigm shift towards a more immersive, interactive, and personalized educational experience. This change, owing to the vast array of interactive functionalities present in digital textbooks, including multimedia annotations, embedded quizzes, and collaborative tools, accommodates a wide range of learning styles and preferences, thereby creating a learning environment that is both more captivating and enriching. It's a future of education that is both exciting and inspiring.

Despite the promising prospects of digital textbooks in enhancing student engagement through interactive learning strategies, implementing such digital resources in higher education is fraught with challenges and considerations that necessitate a comprehensive and nuanced approach. One of the foremost considerations is the digital divide and accessibility issues. While digital textbooks offer the potential for more accessible education, many students may lack access to the necessary technology or reliable internet connectivity, exacerbating existing educational inequalities. Ensuring equitable access to digital resources is paramount to fully realizing the benefits of digital textbooks in fostering student engagement.

Moreover, the transition to digital textbooks necessitates a reevaluation of pedagogical approaches. Educators must be adept at integrating digital resources into their teaching methodologies, which requires technical proficiency and an understanding of leveraging digital tools to enhance learning outcomes. The effectiveness of digital textbooks is contingent upon the ability of educators to effectively incorporate interactive learning strategies into their curriculum, which may require professional development and training to bridge the gap between traditional teaching methods and the demands of a digital learning environment.

Another significant challenge lies in the cost and sustainability of digital resources. While digital textbooks can potentially reduce the financial burden of expensive physical textbooks, the initial investment in digital infrastructure, licensing fees, and ongoing maintenance can be substantial. Additionally, the rapid pace of technological advancements necessitates continuous updates and upgrades to digital learning materials, which could lead to sustainability issues in the long term. Institutions must carefully consider the cost-effectiveness and long-term viability of implementing digital textbooks within their curricula.

Furthermore, the effectiveness of digital textbooks in enhancing student engagement is contingent upon the quality and interactivity of the content. Not all digital books are created equal; incorporating interactive elements must be pedagogically sound and aligned with learning objectives to ensure these features genuinely enhance understanding and knowledge retention. It necessitates a collaborative effort between educators, instructional designers, and publishers to develop high-quality digital content that is both engaging and educationally effective.

The potential for digital textbooks to transform higher education is immense, offering opportunities for more personalized, interactive, and engaging learning experiences. However, the successful implementation of digital textbooks requires addressing the multifaceted challenges of accessibility, pedagogical integration, cost, sustainability, and content quality. It is important and imperative for higher education institutions to adopt a strategic and holistic approach to integrating digital textbooks into their curricula, encompassing infrastructure development, professional training, equitable access, and continuous evaluation of educational outcomes. By navigating these challenges thoughtfully and proactively, institutions can harness the full potential of digital textbooks to enhance student engagement and improve learning outcomes in the digital age.

FURTHER RESEARCH

Emerging Trends in Digital Learning Materials

The landscape of higher education has undergone a profound transformation with the advent of digital learning materials. This shift has not only moved us away from traditional pedagogical approaches but has also ushered in a new era of education that is dynamic, interactive, and facilitated by technological advancements. Integrating digital textbooks and a wealth of online resources has enhanced student engagement, personalized learning experiences, and significantly improved academic outcomes. This paradigm shift is primarily due to the transformative nature of digital media, which has fundamentally changed how knowledge is conveyed, assimilated, and applied across various disciplines.

Digital textbooks, with their inherent flexibility and accessibility, offer a distinct advantage over traditional print textbooks. They incorporate interactive features such as multimedia annotations, quizzes, simulations, and collaborative tools. These features are not just additional; they are transformative, catering to various learning styles and preferences. This inclusivity fosters a more diverse and inclusive educational environment. The ability to integrate videos, interactive graphs, and real-time data into digital textbooks makes abstract concepts more tangible, thereby enhancing comprehension and retention (Jones et al., 2018). The interactive nature of digital learning materials encourages active engagement with the content, prompting students to apply critical thinking and problem-solving skills in real-world contexts, which are crucial in the 21st-century job market (Smith et al., 2017).

Furthermore, the collaborative features inherent in many digital platforms play a pivotal role in promoting community and collective learning among students, regardless of location. Discussion forums, shared annotations, and group projects facilitated through digital textbooks create a vibrant learning ecosystem where ideas are freely exchanged, promoting a deeper understanding of the subject matter. This collaborative environment not only enriches the learning experience but also fosters essential soft skills such as communication, teamwork, and leadership, further enhancing the educational value of digital learning materials.

The flexibility offered by digital textbooks, allowing for content to be updated and expanded in real-time, ensures that students have access to the most current information, a crucial aspect in fast-evolving fields such as science and technology. This dynamism starkly contrasts the static nature of print textbooks, which may quickly become outdated. Furthermore, the customizability of digital materials enables educators to tailor content to meet specific course objectives and student needs, providing a more targeted and effective learning experience.

The environmental and economic benefits of digital textbooks must be considered. The shift towards digital materials reduces the need for physical books, contributing to environmental sustainability by lowering paper usage and the carbon footprint associated with producing and distributing print textbooks. Additionally, digital textbooks often present a more cost-effective option for students, alleviating the financial burden of purchasing expensive textbooks each semester.

However, the transition to digital learning materials is not without its challenges. Issues such as the digital divide and screen fatigue need to be addressed to ensure equitable access and maintain the well-being of students. It is imperative for educational institutions to provide adequate technological resources and support to all students, ensuring that the shift toward digital learning materials does not exacerbate existing inequalities. Moreover, strategies to mitigate screen fatigue, such as incorporating breaks and promoting balanced screen time, should be integrated into digital learning practices.

The impact of digital textbooks on student engagement in higher education is profound, offering a myriad of benefits that extend beyond the mere digitization of print content. The interactive features, flexibility, and collaborative opportunities provided by digital learning materials not only enhance the educational experience but also prepare students for the demands of the modern workforce. As higher education institutions continue to navigate the evolving landscape of digital learning, it is crucial to adopt a strategic approach that harnesses the full potential of digital technology while addressing its challenges. The future of education lies in creating interactive, student-centered learning environments that leverage the capabilities of digital media to meet the diverse needs of modern learners, ultimately leading to improved learning outcomes and greater student satisfaction.

Potential for Adaptive and Personalized Learning Experiences

The landscape of higher education has undergone a profound transformation with the advent of digital learning materials. This shift has not only moved us away from traditional pedagogical approaches but has also ushered in a new era of education that is dynamic, interactive, and facilitated by technological advancements. Integrating digital textbooks and a wealth of online resources has enhanced student engagement, personalized learning experiences, and significantly improved academic outcomes. This paradigm shift is primarily due to the transformative nature of digital media, which has fundamentally changed how knowledge is conveyed, assimilated, and applied across various disciplines.

Digital textbooks, with their inherent flexibility and accessibility, offer a distinct advantage over traditional print textbooks. They incorporate interactive features such as multimedia annotations, quizzes, simulations, and collaborative tools. These features are not just additional; they are transformative, catering to various learning styles and preferences. This inclusivity fosters a more diverse and inclusive educational environment. The ability to integrate videos, interactive graphs, and real-time data into digital textbooks makes abstract concepts more tangible, thereby enhancing comprehension and retention. The interactive nature of digital learning materials encourages active engagement with the content, prompting students to apply critical thinking and problem-solving skills in real-world contexts, which are crucial in the 21st-century job market.

Furthermore, the collaborative features inherent in many digital platforms play a pivotal role in promoting community and collective learning among students, regardless of location. Discussion forums, shared annotations, and group projects facilitated through digital textbooks create a vibrant learning ecosystem where ideas are freely exchanged, promoting a deeper understanding of the subject matter. This collaborative environment not only enriches the learning experience but also fosters essential soft skills such as communication, teamwork, and leadership, further enhancing the educational value of digital learning materials.

The flexibility offered by digital textbooks, allowing for content to be updated and expanded in real-time, ensures that students have access to the most current information, a crucial aspect in fast-evolving fields such as science and technology. This dynamism starkly contrasts the static nature of print textbooks, which may quickly become outdated. Furthermore, the customizability of digital materials enables educators to tailor content to meet specific course objectives and student needs, providing a more targeted and effective learning experience.

The environmental and economic benefits of digital textbooks must be considered. The shift towards digital materials reduces the need for physical books, contributing to environmental sustainability by lowering paper usage and the carbon footprint associated with producing and distributing print textbooks. Additionally, digital textbooks often present a more cost-effective option for students, alleviating the financial burden of purchasing expensive textbooks each semester.

However, the transition to digital learning materials is not without its challenges. Issues such as the digital divide and screen fatigue need to be addressed to ensure equitable access and maintain the well-being of students. It is imperative for educational institutions to provide adequate technological resources and support to all students, ensuring that the shift toward digital learning materials does not exacerbate existing inequalities. Moreover, strategies to mitigate screen fatigue, such as incorporating breaks and promoting balanced screen time, should be integrated into digital learning practices.

The impact of digital textbooks on student engagement in higher education is profound, offering a myriad of benefits that extend beyond the mere digitization of print content. The interactive features, flexibility, and collaborative opportunities provided by digital learning materials not only enhance the educational experience but also prepare students for the demands of the modern workforce. As higher education institutions continue to navigate the evolving landscape of digital learning, it is crucial to adopt a strategic approach that harnesses the full potential of digital technology while addressing its challenges. The future of education lies in creating interactive, student-centered learning environments that leverage the capabilities of digital media to meet the diverse needs of modern learners, ultimately leading to improved learning outcomes and greater student satisfaction.

CONCLUSION

In summary, digital textbooks represent a monumental shift in education, offering vast potential to enhance student engagement, academic performance, and individualized learning journeys. The key findings underscore the remarkable advantages of digital textbooks, including heightened engagement via interactive features, elevated academic outcomes, and the freedom to access educational materials at any time and from any location. However, challenges such as the digital divide, differing levels of digital proficiency, and sustainability concerns must be tackled to fully capitalize on these benefits. Nevertheless, the future of education hinges on embracing the opportunities afforded by digital textbooks to foster dynamic, student-centric learning environments. By surmounting obstacles and harnessing the strengths of digital resources, higher education institutions can propel education forward into a new era, equipping students more effectively for the complexities of the 21st century.

Summary of Key Findings

- **Enhanced Student Engagement**: Digital textbooks significantly increase student engagement through interactive features such as multimedia annotations, quizzes, and collaborative tools. These elements cater to diverse learning styles, making education more inclusive and accessible.
- **Improved Academic Performance**: There is a positive correlation between the use of digital textbooks and academic performance. The interactive nature of digital content facilitates more profound understanding and long-term knowledge retention, contributing to better academic outcomes.
- **Flexibility and Accessibility**: Digital textbooks offer unparalleled flexibility, allowing students to access learning materials anytime and anywhere. This adaptability supports personalized learning experiences and accommodates different learning paces and styles.
- **Collaborative Learning**: Integrating collaborative tools within digital textbooks fosters a more interactive and social learning environment. It not only enhances student engagement but also aids in developing essential interpersonal skills.
- **Pedagogical Shift**: The adoption of digital textbooks necessitates a reevaluation of teaching methodologies. Educators must integrate digital resources effectively into their teaching, highlighting the need for professional development and training in digital pedagogy.
- **Cost and Sustainability**: While digital textbooks can reduce the financial burden of expensive physical books, the initial investment in digital infrastructure and ongoing updates and maintenance costs pose challenges for sustainable implementation.
- **Quality and Interactivity of Content**: The effectiveness of digital textbooks heavily relies on the quality and pedagogical soundness of their interactive elements. High-quality, engaging, and educationally effective digital content is paramount for enhancing student learning experiences.

Final Thoughts on the Role of Digital Textbooks in Modern Education

The integration of digital textbooks into higher education curricula does not just offer a promising avenue; it opens a gateway to a new era of education. These digital resources can revolutionize the educational landscape, making learning more accessible and tailored to individual student needs. The interactive features inherent in digital textbooks can significantly enhance student engagement, transforming education into a more immersive and enjoyable experience.

However, the successful implementation of digital textbooks in modern education is not without its challenges. We must be prepared to overcome hurdles such as the digital divide, varying levels of digital literacy among students and educators, and the need for significant initial investment in digital infrastructure. Ensuring equitable access to digital resources and providing adequate support and training for both students and educators are crucial steps in fully realizing the benefits of digital textbooks.

Moreover, the rapid pace of technological advancements necessitates continuous updates and revisions of digital content, raising concerns about sustainability and cost-effectiveness. Educational institutions must adopt a strategic and holistic approach to integrating digital textbooks, considering not only the technological aspects but also pedagogical, financial, and social factors.

Despite these challenges, the potential of digital textbooks to enhance the quality of education and prepare students for the demands of the modern world is undeniable. As we move forward, it is essential to embrace the opportunities presented by digital textbooks while also being mindful of the obstacles that must be overcome. The future of education lies in creating interactive, student-centered learning environments that leverage digital media's capabilities to meet modern learners' diverse needs.

In conclusion, digital textbooks represent a significant leap forward in the evolution of education, offering opportunities for enhanced student engagement, improved academic performance, and more personalized learning experiences. By addressing the challenges associated with their implementation, higher education institutions can unlock the full potential of digital textbooks to enrich the educational landscape and better prepare students for the challenges of the 21st century.

REFERENCES

Brown, C., White, L., & Jones, K. (2018). Importance of collaborative tools in higher education. *International Journal of Educational Technology in Higher Education*, 15(1), 1–15.

Brown, C., White, L., & Jones, K. (2019). Digital textbooks: Addressing the evolving needs of higher education. *Journal of Online Learning Research*, 5(2), 101–118.

Clark, R. C., & Paivio, A. (1991). Dual coding theory and education. *Educational Psychology Review*, 3(3), 149–210. 10.1007/BF01320076

Driscoll, M. P. (2000). Constructivism. In *Psychology of learning for instruction* (2nd ed., pp. 267–307). Allyn & Bacon.

Duffy, T. M., & Jonassen, D. H. (1992). *Constructivism and the technology of instruction: A conversation*. Lawrence Erlbaum Associates.

Garcia, R., Martinez, L., & Rodriguez, M. (2020). Adaptive learning features in digital textbooks and their impact on student engagement and achievement. *Computers & Education*, 38(4), 450–465.

Garrison, D. R., Anderson, T., & Archer, W. (2000). Critical inquiry in a text-based environment: Computer conferencing in higher education. *The Internet and Higher Education*, 2(2-3), 87–105. 10.1016/S1096-7516(00)00016-6

Johnson, E., & Brown, K. (2019). Enhancing student engagement through digital textbooks: A collaborative approach. *Educational Psychology Review*, 42(2), 210–225.

Jonassen, D. H. (1991). Evaluating constructivist learning. *Educational Technology*, 31(9), 28–33.

Jonassen, D. H. (1999). Designing constructivist learning environments. In *Instructional-design theories and models: A new paradigm of instructional theory* (Vol. 2, pp. 215–239). Routledge.

Kozma, R. (2003). Technology and classroom practices: An international study. *Journal of Research on Technology in Education*, 36(1), 1–14. 10.1080/15391523.2003.10782399

Mayer, R. E. (2001). *Multimedia learning*. Cambridge University Press. 10.1017/CBO9781139164603

Smith, A., & Johnson, B. (2020). Collaborative tools integrated into digital textbooks enhance interactivity and social learning environments. *Journal of Educational Technology*, 45(3), 289–305.

Smith, A., Jones, B., & Lee, C. (2018). The impact of digital textbooks on student engagement: A comparative study. *Journal of Educational Technology*, 25(3), 123–135.

Sweller, J. (1988). Cognitive load during problem solving: Effects on learning. *Cognitive Science*, 12(2), 257–285. 10.1207/s15516709cog1202_4

Sweller, J., Ayres, P., & Kalyuga, S. (2011). *Cognitive load theory*. Springer. 10.1007/978-1-4419-8126-4

Venkatesh, V., & Bala, H. (2008). Technology acceptance model 3 and a research agenda on interventions. *Decision Sciences*, 39(2), 273–315. 10.1111/j.1540-5915.2008.00192.x

Venkatesh, V., & Davis, F. D. (2000). A theoretical extension of the technology acceptance model: Four longitudinal field studies. *Management Science*, 46(2), 186–204. 10.1287/mnsc.46.2.186.11926

Chapter 12
Nursing Students' Experiences of Peer Group Teaching:
A Cooperative Learning Approach

Daniel Opotamutale Ashipala
https://orcid.org/0000-0002-8913-056X
University of Namibia, Namibia

ABSTRACT

Peer teaching is a rapidly developing educational method that enhances student learning through a variety of collaborative and cooperative educational strategies. In Namibia, little research exists on how nursing students experiences the use of peer teaching in nursing and midwifery education. The purpose of this chapter is to explore and describe nursing students' experiences on the use of peer group teaching as a learning method in nursing and midwifery education. The results revealed nursing students positive and negative experiences with suggestions for improvement. Findings from this chapter may help identify strengths and weaknesses in the use of peer group teaching for learning purposes in nursing and midwifery education.

INTRODUCTION

Peer teaching is a rapidly developing educational method to enhance student learning (Zarifnejad, Mirhaghi, & Rajabpoor, 2015). According to Stone (2013), peer teaching is known by different names, including 'cooperative learning', 'peer mentoring', 'peer review learning', and 'team learning'. In addition, 'peer teaching' is used as an umbrella concept for a group of approaches that includes groups or paired learning. Khapre, Deol, Sharma, & Badyal, (2021) defined peer teaching as a voluntary collaboration between colleagues of almost similar rank who have common academic interests. The immediate senior may facilitate discussions and provide personal support and feedback.

Aba Alkhail (2015) similarly highlighted that peer teaching and learning fosters nurturing, sharing, encouragement and support. The process of peer teaching in a Bachelor of Nursing Science Clinical Honours degree may involve seniors teaching freshmen, or co-peers who are at the same academic or experiential level helping others to understand and master a particular skill. Peer teaching is thus a technique used in the communication and transfer of skills between two parties of equal or different educational levels, who are each engaged in learning the same content, with someone acting as tutor and the other(s) as tutee(s) (Reyes-Hernández, 2015). The process may be formal, such as one-to-one tutoring and mentoring, or informal, such as students helping each other outside the formal teaching environment. Peer tutoring may also involve short periods of lecturing with more emphasis on discussions, interactions and simulations.

Internationally, peer group teaching has been used in nursing education to nurture critical thinking, psychomotor, cognitive and clinical skills, as well as academic gains (Dennison, 2010). One type of peer group learning is problem-based learning, which is characterised by students learning from each other and from independently sourced information (Allan et al., 2018). Problem-based learning (PBL) fosters a deep approach to learning and promotes self-directed, life-long learning skills. It also encourages active learning and collaboration between students, and provides internal motivation through the provision of pragmatic goals (AlHaqwi, 2014). A qualitative study conducted at the Bushehr University nursing school (Iran) reported that nursing students' general satisfaction concerning peer learning was less stressful than conventional learning methods (Ravanipour, Bahreini, & Ravanipour, 2015). The study concluded that the success of peer group teaching is due to the similar knowledge base shared by the senior students and the junior students they are teaching.

Peer-to-peer learning has several advantages, such as improved information exchange, teamwork, and skills. It also promotes varied viewpoints, real-world insights, and mutual assistance. However, obstacles such as a lack of attention, knowledge gaps, and unequal participation may occur. Despite these obstacles, leveraging peer-to-peer learning can greatly improve training dynamics and build a culture of continual learning and retention. In addition, a benefit of peer teaching is that it grows friendships in a clinical learning environment among nursing students. This in turns leads to more flexibility and interactivity with their peers whom they trust, and can facilitate an earlier integration into the student community (Ravanipour, Bahreini, & Ravanipour, 2015).

In an African context, peer group teaching involves students who work in the clinical learning domain. In Namibia, a study on the perceptions of registered nurses regarding their role in clinical teaching revealed that clinical teaching is negatively affected by many factors, including a lack of human resources, a lack of materials and equipment, a heavy workload, staff shortages, as well as the personal attitudes of both registered nurses and students (Emvula, 2016). The study did find that clinical teaching enables students to correlate theory and practice, however, because it is in the clinical practice wards where students come into contact with real patients.

Peer group teaching is practiced during clinical placements to provide junior students with fundamental clinical skills in a clinical environment. Nursing students are allocated in pairs according to their year of study to provide peer group teaching and to support junior students to apply nursing processes in a clinical environment. Unfortunately, while the benefits of peer teaching and mentoring in undergraduate nursing are well established in theoretical settings, there has not been enough research on the experiences of nursing students and faculty members regarding peer group teaching during clinical placements. This chapter thus explored nursing students' and faculty members' experiences of peer group teaching during clinical placement at Rundu Intermediate Hospital, Kavango East, Namibia.

THEORETICAL FRAMEWORK OF THE STUDY

Peer learning is a teaching method created by educationists based on the following psychological and sociological theories: cognitive constructivism, social constructivism, cognitive distribution, social groups, and peer groups (Keerthirathne, 2020). Keerthirathne described the basic view of constructivism as being that a student learns by doing rather than by observing. Specifically, the learner uses their previous knowledge in combination with their present learning situation in order to critically understand the learning outcomes in a way they can evaluate them. Constructivism has developed into two logical approaches: cognitive constructivism and social constructivism. Neisser (2014) represents the cognitive constructivist strand, while McLeod (2020) represents the social constructivism strand. Cognitive constructivists mainly focus on an individual's cognitive construction of mental structures, whereas social constructivists posit that a learner uses social interaction and cultural practices in the construction of knowledge (Keerthirathne, 2020).

Keerthirathne (2020) further highlighted the social constructivism theory of Vygotsky, 1980who argued that every function of a child's cultural development appears on two levels: first, on the social level, i.e., between people (inter-psychology), and secondly, on the individual level, i.e., inside the child (intra-psychological). He further explained that every higher function emerges as a real relationship between the learner and those around him (McLeod, 2020; Keerthirathne, 2020). Similarly, the Theory of Distributed Cognition (Merkebu et al., 2020) expresses that knowledge lies not only within the individual, but is also situated in their social and physical environments.

Cognitive distribution is the process whereby cognitive resources are socially shared; extending individual cognitive resources; and allowing group to accomplish something individuals cannot achieve alone. In social learning, adults provide children with the opportunity to work with concrete objects, to make choices, to explore things and ideas, and to conduct experiments. A peer group can influence what a child values, knows, wears, eats, and learns. Peer groups have shared beliefs, interests and preferences for specific activities. A social group, on the other hand, is a set of people who identify with one another and interact in informally structured ways based on shared values, norms and goals (Keerthirathne, 2020).

Figure 1. Theories behind peer learning

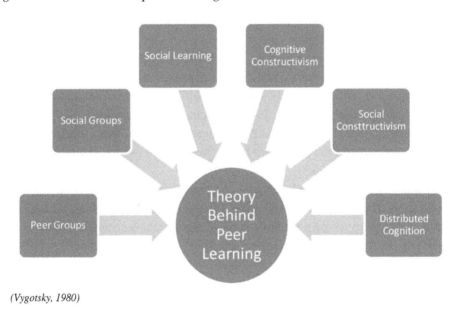

(Vygotsky, 1980)

LITERATURE REVIEW

Peer learning is a style of learning in which students in the same programme assist one another in the learning process, i.e., students act as tutors to aid one another. Peer learning is not a novel notion and has been extensively documented.

Peer learning can also help with collaboration and teamwork, which are vital in both education and nursing. However, a lack of infrastructure presents a number of difficulties, such as problems with scheduling, timing, and network connections. Other problems are that the learning environment may not always be favourable to successful peer learning, students are inexperienced in appraising one another, and students have different degrees of readiness.

Peer teaching is based on cooperation and social learning, according to Vygotsky's (1980) sociocultural theory. According to this theory, the learning process includes the subject, the learning person, an object, the object of the person's activity, and the mediating artefact, which includes social tools that mediate between the person learning and the object (McLeod, 2020). Vygotsky (1980) believed that advanced or more knowledgeable peers, teachers, or other adults greatly aid a learner in the construction of knowledge (Velez, Cano, Whittington & Wolf, 2011). These adults or peers who have a greater degree of knowledge are capable of assisting and directing a learner in such a way as to promote a learning dialogue. Vygotsky's (1980) theory emphasises the role of peers as knowledge providers, yet holds at its foundation the sociocultural view that learning cannot be removed from the social context (Velez et al., 2011).

Near-peer learning encompasses aspects of social learning theory, Vygotsky's (1980) social interaction theory, and the zone of proximal development constructivist theory. McLeod (2020) focused on the sociocultural context of learning theory and the connections between people. Within the clinical environment, the sociocultural context can facilitate the sharing of experiences between students, making concepts easier to understand than if they are taught by a skilled teacher (Henderson, Needham & van de Mortel, 2020).

A study conducted to explore social constructivism as an educational theory that can be applied in collaborative ways to facilitate peer teaching and learning concluded that it is a strategy to help students achieve significant learning and benefit from participation in the social practices of learning (Hayden, Carrico, Ginn, Felber, & Smith, 2021). Hayden et al. also discussed that students in many disciplines will graduate and go on to teach their peers by sharing knowledge, and noted that peer teaching is an early opportunity for health care students, in particular, to develop and practice skills in teaching so others can learn new knowledge.

In further acknowledgement of the positive effects of peer interaction, a qualitative research study conducted to describe the impact of peer teaching on both students and the classroom environment concluded that students who engaged in active peer teaching displayed elements of metacognition. Students were able to analyse their own learning, and the peer teachers also began to develop an awareness of their individual and collective learning styles.

Internationally, the increasing number of student nurses has led to a pressing need for additional preceptors and clinical placements, which has coincided with financial pressure on healthcare services and human resource challenges (Stenberg & Carlson 2015). The effects of peer teaching have been discussed in systematic reviews, with positive effects including increased cognitive skills, self-confidence, autonomy, clinical skills, and reasoning. On the other hand, some adverse effects have also been described, including students not being compatible with each other, students not wanting to compete for clinical tasks, having to share the preceptor's attention and time, and having less time to practice independently (Emvula, 2016). In a study conducted on the perceptions of student nurses on peer learning in Sweden, the results reflected various dimensions of students' responses and described opportunities as well as obstacles for learning. One finding was that the students experienced a sense of increased learning as they felt more responsible when they took turns teaching each other (Stenberg & Carlson, 2015).

In the United Kingdom, not all nursing student learning takes places in hospitals (Brodie et al., 2005). Nursing education has focused often on traditional teaching methods such as classroom lecture learning, which is a behaviourism-based teaching method based on passive learning (Lubbers & Rossman, 2016). This is changing rapidly in nursing schools across the UK, however, as peer learning among nursing students is seen to be a positive experience that is as effective as the conventional classroom lecture method in teaching undergraduate nursing students (Stone, Cooper, & Can't, 2013).

In America, nursing teachers have an obligation to explore every teaching and learning method in order to prepare students to be able practitioners (Dennison, 2010). One method that has been used widely in the nursing education field is peer group tutoring, which fosters a deeper understanding of a subject area. A study conducted amongst student nurses and nurse teachers revealed that both groups had a positive experience (Dennison 2010). Similarly, Dikmen et al. (2017) asserted that the peer group teaching approach is helpful for improving students' ability in practical training, and students gain skills during peer group teaching.

Peer teaching in clinical settings also guides student nurses in the planning and execution of nursing policies (Emvula, 2016). A study conducted to implement collaborative active learning using peer instruction concluded that it significantly improved students' learning as well as performance. Through the use of peer instructors, the role of the teacher changed from disseminator of knowledge to facilitator of knowledge (Carstensen, Kjaer, Möller & Bloksgaard, 2020).

A systematic qualitative review of a study from the University of Rwanda suggested that through peer teaching, students learn to value the different aspects of relatedness that develop through preparing and delivering the peer teaching. In addition, competencies are developed through enhanced learning of the materials, including developing teaching skills and confidence in public speaking (Nshimiyimana & Cartledge, 2020). In resource limited settings, beyond its educational benefits, peer teaching may also have practical benefits such as reducing the workload on academic faculty where faculty/student ratios are high. According to Nshimiyimana and Cartledge (2020), students who teach students also benefit by stimulating a high-level processing of the information during preparation and delivery of the content, as well as from feedback on their teaching. Lastly, peer teaching increases students' confidence in clinical practice, participation, leadership, and learning opportunities, and can increase their satisfaction with lecturers.

According to Sibiya, Ngxongo and Beepat (2018), peer teaching is a vital strategy in helping nursing students attain their learning outcomes, yet peer teaching is not consistent across all clinical areas, and there are no structured support systems to ensure that peer teaching is formalised. Their study thus identified a need for incorporating a formalised mentorship programme into the core competencies of all qualified registered nurses.

Previous primarily qualitative research on nursing students in similar contexts as the present study revealed that collaboration is key to successful peer to peer learning. Peer learning entails nursing students supporting and learning from each other while working in pairs or small groups without the immediate influence of a preceptor. In this way, students are given the opportunity to practice critical thinking, collaboration, reflection, problem-solving and independence (Pålsson et al., 2017)

A study conducted to examine the degree of relevance of the teaching-learning goals revealed the advantages of peer teaching as including that students can help their peers learn while at the same time learning on their own. In addition, there is no "cognitive distance" between peer students and teachers and they use everyday language that is familiar to them, however concerns have been raised about the level of content being taught and if it is appropriate (Gal & Fallik, 2021). In addition, Haukongo (2020) argued that clinical practice occurs in a complex, social environment that is unfamiliar to the students. As a consequence, they experience some challenges that may have an impact on their learning, including over-crowding

While the benefits of peer teaching and mentoring in undergraduate nursing education are well established in theoretical settings, less is known in the clinical settings. A study conducted to explore medical students' perceptions and experiences related to peer teaching concluded that despite the lack of formal training and knowledge gap when compared to their faculty counterparts, students are able to serve as effective teachers and facilitators because of their social and cognitive congruence, enabling them to teach at a level their peers better understand (Yang et al., 2022). In addition to clinical skill development, peer teaching and mentoring provides students the opportunity to learn "nursing school skills". Learning how to be a good nursing student, a component of the hidden curriculum, is typically not learned via formal instruction, but is a necessary skill to excel. Lastly, Yang et al. (2022) suggested that peer teaching environments are beneficial for students to develop a professional identity as teachers, effectively catalysing their future roles as registered nurses.

Peer learning gaps include the need for more field research to monitor peer-to-peer education. Furthermore, there is a dearth of knowledge surrounding the cognitive and motivational mechanisms that underpin peer-mediated learning. Despite the overwhelmingly favourable evidence for peer learning, there is a significant gap between what research has shown and what educators know about it. It is a time-consuming, labour-intensive, and training-required procedure.

METHODOLOGY

Design

A qualitative, exploratory, descriptive conceptual approach was utilised in order to allow the researcher to gain more information on the phenomenon under investigation. This design was deemed appropriate since it aimed to recognise the subjective nature of the problem and the different views of the participants, and to present findings that directly reflect their perspectives (Polit & Beck, 2017).

Participants and Settings

The sample for this study consisted of 15 participants and faculty members at clinical placements at Rundu Intermediate Hospital, Kavango East Region, Namibia. The participants were purposively selected using the following inclusion criteria: a) students were enrolled at the University of Namibia, faculty members were registered with the Namibia Nursing Council; and b) had practiced peer teaching during their clinical placements at Rundu Intermediate Hospital for at least one year. Data saturation was reached with 15 participants, i.e., no new analytical information could be gleaned from further interviews and the researchers decided that sufficient information on the phenomenon had been gathered.

Data Collection

Data were collected using a semi-structured interview guide that was developed based on the research question and the study objectives, as well as the literature review. Prior to data collection, a pilot test was conducted on two nursing students with the aim of refining the interview guide. The pilot interview lasted for 10-15 minutes and no changes were made to the guide as a result. The findings of the pilot test are included in the study.

Data Analysis

Data analysis for this study involved thematically analysing the transcripts and narratives following Braun's six-step method of data analysis. This included: a) organising and preparing the data; b) developing a sense of the data; c) coding the data; d) identifying and describing themes; e) representing the findings; and f) interpreting the data to derive the themes and subthemes in line with the aim, questions and objectives of the research.

Rigour

Rigour was maintained by ensuring the trustworthiness of data through four criteria: credibility, transferability, dependability and confirmability. Credibility was ensured by prolonged engagement with the participants until data saturation was achieved. Dependability was ascertained via a peer debriefing with researchers not involved in the study, as well as extended engagement with the interviewees and member checking. Transferability was achieved by selecting participants using purposive sampling to enhance the range of specific information obtained. Interview sessions were recorded and transcribed, and the recordings and transcripts were compared for confirmation.

Ethical Considerations

Ethical approval was received from the University of Namibia, Faculty of Health Sciences/School of Nursing Research and Ethics Committee (Formal Approval Number: SoNPHREC 126/2022) before the study was conducted. The purpose and objectives of the study were explained to the participants, after which they signed an informed consent form. No participant names are divulged or linked to any data. Participation in the research was voluntary.

Findings

The participants consisted of eight females and seven males, with the majority ranging between the ages of 23 and 27. From the data analysis, four major themes emerged, namely: Understanding of peer teaching; experiences of peer teaching during clinical placement; challenges of peer teaching; and recommendations regarding the use of peer teaching as a learning method.

Theme One: Understanding of Peer Teaching

This theme highlights the participants' understanding of the concept, 'peer teaching'. They described peer teaching as a method of teaching and learning that takes place among students. The subthemes under this theme are discussed below.

Subtheme One: A Method of Teaching and Learning

The results of this study revealed that the participants understood peer teaching to be a method of teaching, be it amongst nursing students, lecturers, nursing staff or peers, on a certain topic, which helped students to understand and be more knowledgeable regarding that matter or topic.

"Peer group teaching is the concept in which students learn from each other, but usually from someone that is more knowledgeable in the topic so they can teach the others about a specific subject or specific content." (P7)

Subtheme Two: Teaching amongst students of the same academic level and different seniority

Participants further described their understanding of peer teaching in the context of when someone who has more knowledge than a fellow student volunteers to teach them or take them through that particular field in order to help them understand a particular context.

"In my personal understanding, I think it's a teaching and learning that takes place between one or more students, so it's just a student teaching another student teaching or one student learning from another student so when it happens among students I think there is peer group teaching." (P5)

Theme Two: Experiences of Peer Teaching During Clinical Placement

This theme reflects the participants' experiences of peer group teaching during clinical placement. One subtheme emerged from this theme, namely benefits/positive experiences of peer teaching.

Subtheme One: Benefits/Positive Experiences of Peer Teaching

The participants noted that peer teaching enables students to apply the knowledge attained in theory to practical settings, as well as gain a better understanding of the nursing process. It also enhances their competencies and enables them to gain more experience.

"When I am exercising peer group teaching I am also exercising my ability to apply the knowledge I've attained in theory into the practical setting, so that's also like a way of learning for me." (P1)

"I've come to learn that it's growing people in the knowledgeable aspect because it at least gives people a lot of ideas and different perspectives on how a certain thing can be done or how a certain thing is known as. Also it promotes people to be more confident in doing a task which evidently leads people to be more independent and more competent in the task at hand."(P3)

Theme Three: Challenges of Peer Group Teaching

This theme reflects the participants' challenges or negative experiences with peer group teaching during clinical placement. One subtheme emerged from this theme.

Subtheme One: Negative Experiences of Peer Group Teaching

The participants pointed out that students tend to be overcrowded at Rundu Intermediate Hospital, and they are unfamiliar with the teaching techniques of their peers.

"One of the challenges that I'm facing in my 4th year is how overcrowded we are in clinical placement, so it's really hard to teach a group of junior students because keep in mind some students come from different universities, so we all meet there and they want to learn from different campuses." (P9)

"So, one of the biggest challenges I faced is that other students may see it as if we are trying to be bossy or trying to show off or trying to, I don't know how to say this, but they see it as if they don't really understand why we're doing it. They don't really see the importance of it so there is a lack of interest from the other students." (P5)

Theme Four: Recommendations Regarding the Use of Peer Group Teaching as a Learning Method

This theme incorporates recommendations regarding the use of peer group teaching as a learning method, including introducing and integrating peer group teaching as a teaching and learning method; students familiarising themselves with the expectations of peer teaching during clinical placement; lecturers using different techniques to improve peer teaching; and lastly, lecturers and clinical instructors offering support to students.

Subtheme One: Introduction and Integration of Peer Group Teaching as a Teaching and Learning Method

The participants suggested that the University of Namibia and lecturers should integrate peer teaching into the nursing curriculum from the first year.

"Our lecturers or clinical instructors should really be involved more in this peer group teaching because we only do it in our 4th year. For years we've known what we're supposed to do but other students don't know, so maybe an introductory phase would explain to them, you know, these are your senior students and this is what is expected of them as they will need to teach you and all that." (P5)

"The junior students are not orientated or inducted for them to be aware that we need to do this and all that part of our procedures. I don't feel like it's formalised in the clinic and the health facilities well enough for us senior students to have that platform to really take it up and make use of it." (P8)

Subtheme Two: Students Need to Familiarise Themselves With the Expectations of Peer Teaching During Clinical Placements

The participants outlined that lecturers should start inviting senior students to teach junior students during simulation sessions. In addition, the participants pointed out that peer teaching should be integrated into the daily schedules and lecturers should hold simulations of what is expected of students in peer teaching.

"Number one is better communication amongst our peers, which will in turn provide a better flow of how things will be done and at least you know people can be aware and know when this or that will be done. Also, maybe integrating it into daily routines in our schedules." (P3)

Subtheme Three: Lecturers to Use Different Techniques to Improve Peer Teaching

The participants suggested the use of posters and imagery to improve peer teaching and learning.

"Another recommendation could be using posters or any images, or just these tools which can help people improve peer teaching." (P3)

Subtheme Four: Lecturers and Clinical Instructors to Offer Support to Students

The participants suggested that the lecturers or clinical instructors should be more involved in peer group teaching and offer support to the students who are undertaking peer teaching.

"The clinical instructors or our lecturers and what the senior staff could also put more effort in this peer teaching; you know it would be nice if they could support the students and actually have effective teaching groups by, like, making time for their peer group teaching during clinical time or placement." (P6)

DISCUSSION

Khapre et al. (2021) described peer teaching as a voluntary collaboration between colleagues of almost similar rank who have common academic interests. Ullah, Tabassum and Kaleem (2018), meanwhile, described peer tutoring as a process in which expert or trained people help and support others who are less skilled and have a low level of knowledge or expertise in an interactive, meaningful and organised way. The findings of this study correlate with research by Pålsson et al. (2017), who described peer tutoring as the acquisition of knowledge and skill through active help and support among status equals or matched companions.

The findings support those of a study conducted by Nshimiyimana and Cartledge (2020), who defined peer teaching as people of similar social groupings, who are not professional teachers, who help each other teach and learn themselves by teaching. In addition, they are similar to a study conducted by Ravanipour, Bahreini and Ravanipour (2015), who described peer teaching as an education process wherein someone of the same age or level of experience interacts with other students interested in the same topic.

The benefits of peer teaching, as described in this study, are in line with another study conducted in Namibia on the perceptions of registered nurses regarding their role of teaching student nurses at training hospitals (Emvula, 2016). The literature indicates that clinical teaching enables students to correlate theory into practice, because it is in the clinical wards where students come in contact with real patients, and it is only through clinical teaching that student nurses acquire the skills to practice nursing.

In addition, the participants highlighted that peer teaching boosts the teachers' confidence and helps them to grow their knowledge. In return, it gives students a lot of ideas and different perspectives on how things can be done.

These findings correspond with a study conducted by Ravanipour, Bahreini and Ravanipour (2015), who emphasised that a benefit of peer teaching is the creation of friendships in the clinical learning environment among nursing students, which creates flexibility and trust, as well as facilitates earlier integration and hence better peer learning.

This finding corresponds with a study conducted by Haukongo in Namibia on nursing students' satisfaction with the clinical practice environment during undergraduate training. Haukongo (2020) argued that clinical practice occurs in a complex, social environment that is unfamiliar to the students, thus they experience some challenges that can impact their learning. Clinical facilities being overcrowded is one issues, which hinders clinical teaching and learning.

In addition, this study's participants stated that peer teaching can be a challenge because students lack interest and often feel like the peer tutors are showing off. This resonates with a study conducted by Ullah, Tabassum and Kaleem (2018), which analysed the effects of peer tutoring on the academic achievement of students. They found that there are some limitations to peer teaching, which are mostly related to behavioural problems among students. In addition, Emvula (2016) argued that peer teaching has adverse effects such as students not being compatible with each other and not wanting to compete for clinical tasks.

A study conducted by Reyes-Hernandez et al. (2015) emphasised that there are few opportunities for students to learn teaching skills, however the incorporation of teaching skills into the nursing school curriculum can help reinforce positive attitudes about teaching. Furthermore, this study found that lecturers and clinical instructors should be involved in the induction of junior students into peer group teaching, and there should be mandatory peer teaching among students during clinical placement. These findings are similar to those of a study conducted on the perceptions of undergraduate medical students regarding having medical interns as their near peer teachers (Alkhail, 2015). They noted that planning ahead and training for clinical teaching sessions by lecturers is vital for the successful implementation of peer teaching in clinical settings. Lastly, Ullah, Tabassum and Kaleem (2018) noted that teachers should design learning activities that can better address the individual needs of students. They emphasised that it is necessary for peer tutoring programmes to be highly structured, and conducted under strict supervision and in a controlled environment. Peers should also be given a proper orientation about tutoring activities.

A study by Sunggingwati (2018) to explore students' experiences of peer teaching in a cooperative learning style aligned with the findings of this study. Through clinical accompaniment, student nurses learn to integrate theory into practice, and thereby achieve improved learning opportunities. Accompaniment can be described as the ability of the nurse, clinical instructor or faculty member to attend, guide and coexist with student nurses during clinical practice (Haukongo 2020). Haukongo (2020) further acknowledged that during clinical accompaniment, nurses, clinical instructors and faculty members should engage in identifying the needs of students at the clinical practice site to ensure that they become professionally knowledgeable and competent. This is in accordance with the findings of this study.

LIMITATIONS AND PROPOSED AREAS FOR FURTHER RESEARCH

This study explored the experiences of nursing students and faculty members at one campus only, which limits the generalisation of the findings to other campuses. Peer learning encourages collaboration, patience, and improved social skills. It also enables students to be responsible for and manage their own learning. Allow pupils to learn to assess and provide constructive criticism in order to develop lifelong assessment abilities. Improve student learning by disseminating knowledge and exchanging opinions. Limitations include the difficulty of assessing the quality of a peer-to-peer exercise because the long-term influence cannot be easily quantified. Learning from one's peers can be exciting. However, excitement, particularly among younger students, can lead to distraction. Another barrier could be insufficient knowledge and expertise of fellow students, which can lead to disinformation or misunderstanding. Furthermore, as the participants had to be obtained through snowball sampling, a similar study utilising a quantitative research design or combining both qualitative and quantitative methodologies is recommended.

IMPLICATIONS OF PEER LEARNING IN CLINICAL SETTINGS

Peer-learning fosters both individual and professional development in therapeutic practice. When it comes to health-impairing factors, like stress and annoyance, mutual support through peer learning helps to mitigate their effects and enhance people's capacity for empathy, leadership, and communication. Students and teachers also gain an appreciation for cultural diversity, learn to understand opposing points of view, and cultivate an international outlook. These abilities are crucial for preparing students for nursing. According to student feedback, learning with a peer enhances the educational experience (Stenberg & Carlson, 2015) and facilitates more intimate communication with patients. According to reports, the approach also helps students feel more independent (Hellström-Hyson et al., 2012), lessens their anxiety, and boosts their confidence in their ability to succeed both personally and professionally in the future.

CONCLUSION

This chapter has provided insights into nursing students' and faculty members' experiences on the use of peer group teaching during clinical placements. It is evident that peer group teaching is indeed an effective teaching and learning strategy, however it has some limitations that need to be addressed to ensure its viability. Students and faculty members thus need to conduct extensive needs assessments and develop well thought-out plans before the implementation of peer group teaching. The findings of this study will hopefully create an understanding of the importance of peer teaching as a learning method in nursing and midwifery education.

REFERENCES

Aba Alkhail, B. (2015). Near-peer-assisted learning (NPAL) in undergraduate medical students and their perception of having medical interns as their near peer teacher. *Medical Teacher, 37*(sup1), S33-S39.

AlHaqwi, A. I. (2014). Learning outcomes and tutoring in problem based-learning: How do undergraduate medical students perceive them? *International Journal of Health Sciences*, 8(2), 125–132. 10.12816/000607825246879

Allan, H. T., Magnusson, C., Evans, K., Horton, K., Curtis, K., Ball, E., & Johnson, M. (2018). Putting knowledge to work in clinical practice: Understanding experiences of preceptorship as outcomes of interconnected domains of learning. *Journal of Clinical Nursing*, 27(1-2), 123–131. 10.1111/jocn.1385528401608

Bandura, A. (1979). Self-referent mechanisms in social learning theory. *The American Psychologist*, 34(5), 439–441. 10.1037/0003-066X.34.5.439.b

Brink, H., & Van der Walt, C. (2006). *Fundamentals of research methodology for health care professionals* (4th ed.). Juta.

Brodie, D. A., Andrews, G. J., Andrews, J. P., Thomas, B. G., Wong, J., & Rixon, L. (2005). Working in London hospitals: Perceptions of place in nursing students' employment considerations. *Social Science & Medicine*, 61(9), 1867–1881. 10.1016/j.socscimed.2005.03.04215939515

Carstensen, S. S., Kjaer, C., Möller, S., & Bloksgaard, M. (2020). Implementing collaborative, active learning using peer instructions in pharmacology teaching increases students' learning and thereby exam performance. *European Journal of Pharmacology*, 867, 172792. 10.1016/j.ejphar.2019.17279231733212

Clarke, M. L. (2016). Peer tutoring of junior nursing students: Student experiences and perceptions of self-efficacy and benefit. City: Liberty University.

Dennison, S. (2010). Peer mentoring: Untapped potential. *The Journal of Nursing Education*, 49(6), 340–342. 10.3928/01484834-20100217-0420210287

Dikmen, Y., Ak, B., Yildirim Usta, Y., Ünver, V., Akin Korhan, E., Cerit, B., & Yönder Ertem, M. (2017). Effect of peer teaching used in nursing education on the performance and competence of students in practical skills training. *International Journal of Educational Sciences*, 16(1-3), 14–20. 10.1080/09751122.2017.1311583

Emvula, O. (2016). *Perceptions of registered nurses regarding their role of clinical teaching of student nurses at state training hospitals in Windhoek, Namibia* [Doctoral dissertation, University of Namibia].

Gal, A., & Fallik, O. (2021). Learn from Each Other: A Peer-Teaching Model. *Interdisciplinary Journal of Environmental and Science Education*, 17(3), e2242. 10.21601/ijese/10896

Haukongo, N. N. (2020). *Nursing student's satisfaction with clinical practice environment during their undergraduate training in Namibia* [Doctoral dissertation, Stellenbosch University].

Hayden, C. L., Carrico, C., Ginn, C. C., Felber, A., & Smith, S. (2021). Social Constructivism in Learning: Peer Teaching & Learning. *Pedagogicon Conference Proceedings*. EKU. https://encompass.eku.edu/pedagogicon/2020/learningpartners/7

Hellström-Hyson, E., Mårtensson, G., & Kristofferzon, M. L. (2012). To take responsibility or to be an onlooker. Nursing students' experiences of two models of supervision. *Nurse Education Today*, 32(1), 105–110. 10.1016/j.nedt.2011.02.00521388721

Henderson, S., Needham, J., & van de Mortel, T. (2020). Clinical facilitators' experience of near peer learning in Australian undergraduate nursing students: A qualitative study. *Nurse Education Today*, 95, 104602. 10.1016/j.nedt.2020.10460233002746

Keerthirathne, W. K. D. (2020). Peer Learning: An Overview. *International Journal of Scientific Engineering and Science*, 4(11), 1–6.

Khapre, M., Deol, R., Sharma, A., & Badyal, D. (2021, July 16). Near-Peer Tutor: A Solution For Quality Medical Education in Faculty Constraint Setting. *Cureus*, 13(7), e16416. 10.7759/cureus.1641634422460

Lubbers, J., & Rossman, C. (2016). The effects of pediatric community simulation experience on the self-confidence and satisfaction of baccalaureate nursing students: A quasi-experimental study. *Nurse Education Today*, 39, 93–98. 10.1016/j.nedt.2016.01.01327006038

McLeod, S. (2020) Vygotsky's Sociocultural Theory of Cognitive Development. *Simply Psychology*. https://www.simplypsychology.org/vygotsky.htm

Merkebu, J., Battistone, M., McMains, K., McOwen, K., Witkop, C., Konopasky, A., Torre, D., Holmboe, E., & Durning, S. J. (2020). Situativity: A family of social cognitive theories for understanding clinical reasoning and diagnostic error. *Diagnosis (Berlin, Germany)*, 7(3), 169–176. 10.1515/dx-2019-010032924378

Neisser, U. (2014). *Cognitive psychology: Classic edition*. Psychology Press. 10.4324/9781315736174

Nshimiyimana, A., & Cartledge, P. T. (2020). Peer-teaching at the University of Rwanda - a qualitative study based on self-determination theory. *BMC Medical Education*, 20(1), 1–12. 10.1186/s12909-020-02142-032689991

Ntho, T. A., Pienaar, A. J., & Sehularo, L. A. (2020). Peer-mentees' challenges in an undergraduate peer-group clinical mentoring programme in a nursing education institution. *Health SA*, 25, 1–8. 10.4102/hsag.v25i0.143533101718

Pålsson, Y., Mårtensson, G., Swenne, C. L., Ädel, E., & Engström, M. (2017). A peer learning intervention for nursing students in clinical practice education: A quasi-experimental study. *Nurse Education Today*, 51, 81–87. 10.1016/j.nedt.2017.01.01128142097

Polit, F. D., & Beck, C. T. (2017). *Nursing research: Generating and assessing evidence for nursing practice* (10th ed.). Lippincott Williams & Wilkins.

Ravanipour, M., Bahreini, M., & Ravanipour, M. (2015). Exploring nursing students' experience of peer learning in clinical practice. *Journal of Education and Health Promotion*, 4(1), 46. 10.4103/2277-9531.15723326097860

Reyes-Hernández, C. G., Carmona Pulido, J. M., De la Garza Chapa, R. I., Serna Vázquez, R. P., Alcalá Briones, R. D., Plasencia Banda, P. M., Villarreal Silva, E. E., Jacobo Baca, G., de la Garza Castro, O., Elizondo Omaña, R. E., & Guzmán López, S. (2015). Near-peer teaching strategy in a large human anatomy course: Perceptions of near-peer instructors. *Anatomical Sciences Education*, 8(2), 189–193. 10.1002/ase.148425203867

Sibiya, M. N., Ngxongo, T. S. P., & Beepat, S. Y. (2018). The influence of peer mentoring on critical care nursing students' learning outcomes. *International Journal of Workplace Health Management*, 11(3), 130–142. 10.1108/IJWHM-01-2018-000330166994

Stenberg, M., & Carlson, E. (2015). Swedish student nurses' perception of peer learning as an educational model during clinical practice in a hospital setting—An evaluation study. *BMC Nursing*, 14(1), 1–7. 10.1186/s12912-015-0098-226435698

Stone, R., Cooper, S., & Cant, R. (2013). The value of peer learning in undergraduate nursing education: A systematic review. *International Scholarly Research Notices*, 2013.23691355

Sunggingwati, D. (2018). Cooperative learning in peer teaching: A case study in an EFL context. *Indonesian Journal of Applied Linguistics*, 8(1), 149–157. 10.17509/ijal.v8i1.11475

Ullah, I., Tabassum, R., & Kaleem, M. (2018). Effects of peer tutoring on the academic achievement of students in the subject of biology at secondary level. *Education Sciences*, 8(3), 112. 10.3390/educsci8030112

Velez, J. J., Cano, J., Whittington, M. S., & Wolf, K. J. (2011). Cultivating change through peer teaching. *Journal of Agricultural Education*, 52(1), 40–49. 10.5032/jae.2011.01040

Williams, B., & Reddy, P. (2016). Does peer-assisted learning improve academic performance? A scoping review. *Nurse Education Today*, 42, 23–29. 10.1016/j.nedt.2016.03.02427237348

Yang, M. M., Golden, B. P., Cameron, K. A., Gard, L., Bierman, J. A., Evans, D. B., & Henschen, B. L. (2022). Learning through Teaching: Peer Teaching and Mentoring Experiences among Third-Year Medical Students. *Teaching and Learning in Medicine*, 34(4), 360–367. 10.1080/10401334.2021.189993033934679

Zarifnejad, G., Mirhaghi, A., & Rajabpoor, M. (2015). Learning experience through peer education: A qualitative study. *Indian Journal of Medical Education*, 15, 27–40.

Chapter 13
Interactive Learning Strategies in Teaching Corporate Finance

V. Rajesh Kumar
https://orcid.org/0000-0002-3714-3262
Alliance University, India

Ravi Darshini
https://orcid.org/0009-0008-2310-7093
St. Joseph's Institute of Management, India

ABSTRACT

Students pursuing management education, in either undergraduate or graduate program, are exposed to all the functional areas of management viz., Marketing management, human resource management, production and operations management, and financial management (or corporate finance). The interesting feature of teaching/learning financial management is that 'what is discussed in the classroom' and 'what happens in a company boardroom' are the same. A student can better understand the depth, width and nuances of the course titled 'Corporate Finance' when the discussion on the course provides 'experiential learning.' This chapter provides an idea and framework for teachers regarding the approach to teaching this course, how to make it interactive and how to make the course offer practical exposure to the actual financial decision-making in companies.

DOI: 10.4018/979-8-3693-3559-8.ch013

Copyright © 2024, IGI Global. Copying or distributing in print or electronic forms without written permission of IGI Global is prohibited.

NEED/IMPORTANCE OF INTERACTIVE LEARNING

Researchers across the globe have identified and published may successful learning strategies involving eLearning, metacognitive, multimedia and others (Railean, 2017). (Turkot, 2011) proves that Interactive learning is a special from of organizing cognitive activity which involves the creation of comfortable learning conditions under which the student feels his success and intellectual ability. An important feature of interactive learning is the constant, active interaction of all the participants in education i.e teacher- student, students-students. Student centric learning requires teachers to use innovative methods that ensure the maximum connection of theoretical information with tis practical application (Natalila Marchenko, 2023). Scholars state that interactive methods make it possible to bring the education process as close as possible to real practical activity is solved by applying analytical thinking and logical reasoning skills. In addition this these learning styles also cater to diverse learning styles of the participants by building a sense of community among peers and instructors. The implementation of interactive learning methods in higher education is essential for creating a dynamic, engaging and effective learning environment. These not only enhance student engagement and retention but also prepare them for complexities of corporate world. They foster inclusive learning environment and ensure that delivery keeps pace with technological advancements.

INTRODUCTION

Students pursuing management education, either undergraduate or graduate program, are exposed to all the functional areas of management viz., Marketing Management, Human Resource Management, Production & Operations Management and Financial Management (or Corporate Finance).

The interesting feature of teaching / learning Financial Management is that 'what is discussed in the classroom' and 'what happens in a Company boardroom' are the same. A student can better understand the depth, width and nuances of the course titled 'Corporate Finance' when the discussion on the course provides for 'experiential learning'. This chapter provides an idea and framework for Teachers regarding the approach to teaching this course, how to make it interactive and how to make the course offer practical exposure to the actual financial decision-making in companies.

A typical lesson plan for teaching "Corporate Finance" is given below. Table 1 shows the course objectives, Table 2 lists the intended course learning outcomes, Table 3 provides the detailed session plan, Table 4 gives details and schedule of assessment plan, and Tables 5 and 6 list out the References and Online Digital Resources for the course.

Interactive Learning Strategies in Teaching Corporate Finance

Table 1. Course objectives

1.	To enable learners to gain fundamental knowledge about financial decision-making goals and the structure of a business enterprise
2.	To enable the learner to recognise the various financial decisions
3.	To equip the learner for financial decision-making through the principles of 'time-value of money'
4.	To provide a thorough framework for sourcing long-term funds and designing capital structure
5.	To orient and train the learners on the long-term and short-term investment decisions of a business entity
6.	To provide an insight into the dividend decisions of companies

Table 2. Intended course learning outcomes

1.	understand the foundations for financial decision-making
2.	read and analyse annual reports of joint stock companies
3.	design spreadsheet models
4.	appraise the various sources of long-term financing and design capital structure for business enterprises
5.	generate inputs for capital budgeting decisions and apply the tools/techniques for making decision
6.	estimate the working capital requirements of a business entity and develop strategies for its effective management
7.	identify the dividend policies of business enterprises and critically evaluate them.

Table 3. Session plan

Session No.	Topic of Discussion	Learning Outcome
1	**Role Play: The Finance Connection** Corporate Finance – Meaning and Scope, Foundations for Finance – Orientation to Financial Statements	LO1
2	Financial Statement Analysis – DU PONT Model **Case 1: HBS case: 9-201-077: Assessing a Firm's Future Financial Health**	LO1, LO2
3	Case Discussion **Assignment 1: HBS Case 9-198-017: Identify the Industries** Time Value of Money – Foundations, Future Value, Present Value,	

continued on following page

Table 3. Continued

Session No.	Topic of Discussion	Learning Outcome
4	Annuity – Future Value, Present Value and Growing Annuity Calculation of Equated Installments and preparation of Loan Amortisation Schedule Perpetuity – Present Value and Growing Perpetuity **Readings:** 1. HBP Publishing 8299 published on December 22, 2015: Finance Readings – Time Value of Money 2. HBS Press – Excerpt from "Finance for Managers" ISBN-13: 978-1-4221-0586-3: Time Value of Money – Calculating the real value of your investment 3. Darden Business Publishing, University of Virginia UV5137: Developing Financial Insights – Using PV and FV Approach **Test 1: Spreadsheet Modelling** **Case 2: The University of Hongkong, Faculty of Business and Economics, HK1190: Krishna's Retirement Plan** **Assignment 2: Ivey Publishing W14403: Time Value of Money- The Buy Versus Rent Decision**	LO1, LO2, LO3
5	Cost of Capital – Meaning; Requirements for calculation of Cost of Capital, Specific Cost of Capital and Weighted Average Cost of Capital Calculation of Cost of Debt (Kd) and Cost of Preference (Kp)	
6	Cost of Equity (Ke) – Capital Asset Pricing Model, Cost of Retained Earnings, Weights, Calculation of Weighted Average Cost of Capital **Readings:** 1. Finance Readings 8293 published on May 4 2017 – Cost of Capital 2. HBR Reprint HO2110: A Refresher on Cost of Capital 3. HBR Reprint R1207L: Do you know your Cost of Capital? 4. Darden Business Publishing UV7797: Finance Analytics Toolkit – Weighted Average Cost of Capital 5. HBR Reprint R0210J: What is your Real Cost of Capital? 6. HBS Case 9-298-115: Concordia Electronics Systems Test 7. IIMA Working Paper 2006-06-04: A First Cut Estimate of Equity Risk Premium 8. NSE and EY: Cost of Capital Survey Report 2021 India Insights	
7	Problems and Caselets on Weighted Average Cost of Capital	
8	Problems and Caselets on Weighted Average Cost of Capital - Continued	
9	Problems and Caselets on Weighted Average Cost of Capital – Continued **Test 2**	
10	**Case 3: HBS Case 9-289-047: The Marriott Corporation**	
11	Financing Decisions – Sources of Long-term Finance Case 1: "Central Equipment Company Limited" (Pandey, Central Equipment Company, 2012) Case 2: "Deepak Fertilizers and Petrochemicals Corporation Limited" (Pandey, Deepak Fertilizers and Petrochemicals Corporation Limited, 2012) Case 3: Taylor Brands – Cost of capital or Required Rate of return (Sulock, 1997) Case 4: Shuckers: Miller and Modigliani (Shuckers: Miller and Modigliani, 1997) Case 5: Capital Structure Decisions (P K Jain, 2010) **Assignment 3: Presentations on Long-term Sources of Funding**	LO1, LO3, LO4

continued on following page

Interactive Learning Strategies in Teaching Corporate Finance

Table 3. Continued

Session No.	Topic of Discussion	Learning Outcome
12	**Assignment 3: Presentations on Long-term Sources of Funding – continued**	
13	Capital Structure Decisions – Factors influencing capital structure. Benefit to Owners – EBIT-EPS Analysis	
14	Point of Indifference and Financial Break-even Point	
15	Leverages – Degree of Operating Leverage, Degree of Financial Leverage and Degree of Combined Leverage	
16	Leverages – Degree of Operating Leverage, Degree of Financial Leverage and Degree of Combined Leverage – continued **Reading:** 1. John Graham and Campbell Harvey (2002), "How do CFOs make Capital Budgeting and Capital Structure Decisions?", Journal of Applied Corporate Finance, Volume 15(1), pp 8-23 **Test 3**	
17	Capital Budgeting – Meaning, Inputs for Capital Budgeting Decision – Concept of Cash Inflow	LO2, LO3, LO5
18	Techniques for Capital Budgeting Decisions – Pay-back Period, Average Rate of Return, Discounted Payback Period	
19	Net Present Value, Profitability Index, Equated Net Present Value, Internal Rate of Return, Modified Internal Rate of Return **Readings:** 1. Patricia and Glenn (2002), "Capital Budgeting Practices of the Fortune 1000: How have things changed?", Journal of Business and Management, Volume 8(4), 2. Stanley Block (2005), "Are there differences in Capital Budgeting Procedures between Industries?", The Engineering Economist, DOI: 10.1080/00137910590916676, pp 55-67	
20	Problems and case lets on Capital Budgeting	
21	Problems and case lets on Capital Budgeting – continued	
22	Problems and case lets on Capital Budgeting – continued	
23	**Case 4: Darden Business Publishing UV0072: Investment Detective** **Assignment 4: Darden Business Publishing UV2499: World Paper Company**	
24	Risk Analysis in Capital Budgeting: Risk Measurement – Sensitivity Analysis, Scenario Analysis, Standard Deviation and Variance	
25	Risk Measurement: Simulation	
26	Risk Measurement: Simulation (continued)	
27	Risk Measurement: Simulation using Spreadsheets	
28	Risk Management: Risk Adjusted Discount Rate Method, Certainty Equivalent Co-efficient Method	
29	Risk Management: Decision-tree Method	
30	Risk Management: Normal Probability Distribution Method	
31	Working Capital Management: Meaning, Need for Adequate Working Capital, Components of Working Capital Management	LO6

continued on following page

Table 3. Continued

Session No.	Topic of Discussion	Learning Outcome
32	Estimation of Working Capital	
33	Estimation of Working Capital (continued)	
34	Estimation of Working Capital (continued)	
35	Estimation of Working Capital (continued)	
36	Estimation of Working Capital (continued)	
37	Sources of Short-term Financing: **Assignment 5: Presentations on Short-term Financing sources**	
38	**Assignment 5: Presentations on Short-term Financing sources (continued)**	
39	Working Capital Policy	
40	Inventory Management	
41	Receivables Management	
42	Cash Management	
43	Dividend Decisions	LO7
44	Dividend Decisions (Continued)	
45	**Test 4**	

Table 4. Assessment plan

Sl. No	Assessment Component	Schedule	Weightage (Marks)
1	Assignment 1	Session 3 – 4	5
2	Test 1	Session 4 - 5	10
3	Assignment 2	Session 4 - 5	5
4	Test 2	Session 9 – 10	5
5	Assignment 3	Session 11 – 13	5
6	Test 3	Session 16 – 18	10
7	Assignment 4	Session 23 – 24	5
8	Assignment 5	Session 34 – 36	5
9	Test 4	Session 44 – 45	10

Table 5. References

(a) Damodaran, Aswath, "Corporate Finance", John Wiley & Sons Inc.
(b) Chandra, Prasanna, "Financial Management – Theory and Practice", McGraw-Hill Publishing Company Limited.

continued on following page

Table 5. Continued

(c) Pandey, I M, "Financial Management", Pearson
(d) Khan, M.Y., and Jain, P.K., "Financial Management – Text, Problems and Cases", McGraw-Hill Publishing Company Limited
(e) Vanhorne, James, "Financial Management and Policy", Prentice Hall.
(f) Brealy, Richards; and Myers, Stewart, "Principles of Corporate Finance", McGraw-Hill Publishing Company Limited.
(g) Ross, Stephen; Westerfield, Randolph, Jaffe, Jeffrey and Kakani, Ram Kumar, "Corporate Finance", Eight Edition, McGraw Hill.
(h) Gitman, J. Lawrence, "Principles of Managerial Finance", Pearson Education.
(i) V Rajesh Kumar, "Financial Management for C A Intermediate", Mc Graw Hill
(j) .Kishore, M. Ravi, "Financial Management – with Problems and Solutions", Taxmann Allied Services (P) Ltd.
(k) Bodhanwala, J. Ruzbeh, "Financial Management using Excel Spreadsheet", Taxmann Allied Services (P) Ltd.
(l) Bahal, Mohit, "Practical Aspects of Financial Management", Suchita Prakashan (P) Ltd.
(m) Sharma, Dhiraj, "Working Capital Management – A Conceptual Approach", Himalaya Publishing House.

Table 6. Digital/online resources

Sl. No.	Name of the Website
1	www.finaneprofessor.com
2	www.investopedia.com
3	www.sebi.gov.in
4	www.rbi.org.in
5	www.nseindia.com
6	www.bseindia.com
7	www.tradingeconomics.com
8	www.morningstar.in
9	www.ibef.org
10	www.commerce.gov.in
11	www.mca.gov.in
12	www.finmin.nic.in
13	www.indiabudget.gov.in

DEFINITIONS

- **Corporate Finance:** Corporate finance can be described as the study of the decisions that every firm has to make about funding sources, capital structuring, accounting and investment decisions (Damodaran, 2002).
- **DuPont model:** It is a tool used in financial analysis, where return on equity (ROE) is separated into its component parts.
- **Annuity:** An annuity is a series of payments made at equal intervals.
- **Future value:** It is the amount of money a given investment will be worth after a certain period, assuming a specific rate of return.
- **Cost of capital:** The cost of capital measures the cost that a business incurs to finance its operations. It is the minimum rate of return or profit a company must earn before generating value.
- **Cost of equity:** It is the minimum required rate of return for equity investors, which is a function of the risk profile of the company.
- **Capital budgeting:** It is a long term plan that outlines the financial demands of an investment, development or major purchase.
- **Working capital:** It is a financial metric that is the difference between a company's current assets and current liabilities.
- **Capital structure:** It is the particular combination of debt and equity used by a company to finance its overall operations and growth.
- **Risk measurement:** It is an attempt to quantify the potential losses of an investment so that its impact can be measured, and the event can be avoided.

BEFORE THE BEGINNING: ONE

The first challenge in teaching the course on 'Corporate Finance' or 'Financial Management' is to make the learners understand and appreciate the importance/relevance of this course. One of the best techniques for this is having a 'Role Play' comprising various characters representing the top management of a company and functional heads. Please find a sample Role play in Appendix 1. The role-play provides the participants with complete clarity on the finance function in an organisation and also makes them understand the importance of the function.

BEFORE THE BEGINNING: TWO—THE PRE-REQUISITES

For teaching/learning 'Corporate Finance' there are certain prerequisites. These prerequisites provide all the foundations for gaining mastery/expertise in financial decision-making. The first focus of the instructor of this course is to ensure that knowledge and skills relating to all these prerequisites are imparted. Following is the list of pre-requisite topics:

Analysis of Financial Statements

The source for all information required in making financial decisions is the 'financial statements' of the business entity. The instructor, firstly, must provide an Orientation to Financial Statements which includes (a) a Balance Sheet, (b) a Statement of Profit and Loss, (c) a Statement of Changes in Equity, (d) a Statement of Cash Flows, and (e) Notes to Accounts.

While a classroom orientation for these topics is essential, a strong foundation can be ensured only when the learners can get follow-up sessions. The instructor can record his classroom sessions and make the same available to the learners for their revision and reflections. A sample of such a recorded session is available at this link: https://www.youtube.com/watch?v=f5aQ4AfAzWI&t=1281s

Following this, the learners must be exposed to all the tools, techniques and models for reading and analysing financial statements. The discussion must begin with an introduction to 'Ratio Analysis', its purpose and utility; followed by models which integrate various ratios and give information for decision making like the Du Pont Model. The discussion in the class must be followed up by giving time for the learner to watch the recorded lecture on the topic. The link for a recorded lecture on this topic is https://www.youtube.com/watch?v=jaj5EyKoiRY&t=2006s.

The analysis of financial statements must be demonstrated with data from Annual Reports, supported by Cases which can be sourced from Harvard Publications, Case Center etc. It would be essential for the Institutions to subscribe to the cases and make the same available to students.

Time Value of Money

'Time Value of Money' refers to 'change in the value of money over time.' Every financial decision is influenced by the 'time value of money', and without adequate and complete knowledge of this, learners cannot understand financial decision-making.

The time Value of Money includes Annual Compounding, Continuous Compounding, Discounting, Annuity, Growing Annuity, Perpetuity, Growing Perpetuity etc.

Learning this is incomplete without the learner being equipped with the skill of finding the time value of money. In addition to mathematical application, the learner must be exposed to 'Spreadsheets'. The foundation for 'Spread Sheet Modelling' and 'Financial Modelling' begins with building models for ascertaining the time value of money.

The following paragraphs show the spreadsheet commands for the various components of the 'Time Value of Money.'

For Annual Compounding

Table 7 shows the Spreadsheet command for Annual compounding:

Table 7. Annual compounding

	A	B
1	Present Value	100000
2	Rate of Interest	15%
3	Number of Years	3
4	**Future Value**	**=FV(B2,B3,,-B1,)**

For Continuous Compounding

Table 8 shows the Spreadsheet command for Continuous compounding:

Table 8. Continuous compounding

	A	B
1	Present Value	100000
2	Rate of Interest	12%
3	Number of Years	1
4	Frequency	4
5	**Future Value**	**=FV(B2/B4,B3*B4,,-B1,)**

For Discounting or Continuous Discounting

Table 9 shows the Spreadsheet command for Continuous compounding:

Table 9. Discounting and continuous discounting

	A	B
1	Future Value	4000
2	Rate of Interest	12%
3	Number of Years	3
4	Frequency	12
5	**Present Value**	=PV(B2/B4,B3*B4,,-B1,)

For Future Value of Annuity

Table 10 shows the Spreadsheet command for Future value of Annuity:

Table 10. Future value of annuity

	A	B
1	Periodic Payment	10000
2	Rate of Interest	10%
3	Number of Years	4
4	Frequency	1
5	Type	0
6	**Future Value of Annuity**	=FV(B2/B4,B3*B4,-B1,,B5)

For Finding the Amount of Periodic Payment To Be Made

Table 11 shows the Spreadsheet command for Periodic Payment:

Table 11. Periodic payment

	A	B
1	Future Value of Annuity	2000000
2	Number of years	5
3	Rate of Interest	0.12
4	Frequency	12
5	Type	0
6	Periodic Payment	=PMT(B3/B4,B2*B4,,B1,B5)

For the Present Value of Annuity

Table 12 shows the Spreadsheet command for Present Value of Annuity:

Table 12. Present value of annuity

	A	B
1	Periodic Payment	1
2	Rate of Interest	0.12
3	Number of Years	5
4	Frequency	1
5	Type	0
6	**Present Value of Annuity**	=PV(B2/B4,B3*B4,-B1,,B5)

For Ascertaining Equated Instalment

Table 13 shows the Spreadsheet command for Equated Instalment:

Table 13. Equated instalment

	A	B
1	Loan Amount	1000000
2	Rate of Interest	0.12
3	Number of Years	5
4	Frequency	1
5	Type	0
6	**Equated Instalment**	=PMT(B2/B4,B3*B4,B1,,B5)

The meaning of the terminology in the above functions is given below:

- Future Value (FV) = Value of present money on a future date
- Present Value (PV) = Today's value of future money
- Rate of Interest = Rate at which amount is getting compounded / discounted
- Number of Years = Period for which compounding/discounting is made
- Frequency = Number of times compounding is made in a year
- Annuity = Same amount received/paid in regular intervals for a given period
- Type = Period of cash flow. '0' denotes 'cash flow at the end of the period' and '1' denotes 'cash flow at the beginning of the period'

For ascertaining the time value of money which helps in making financial decision making, it is necessary to identify the 'rate' at which compounding or discounting must be done. This rate is called the 'Hurdle Rate.' Business entities consider the 'Minimum Expected Rate of Return' as the Hurdle Rate. The minimum expected rate of return for a business entity is its 'Cost of Capital' or 'Weighted Average Cost of Capital.'

A learner can get end-to-end knowledge on the time-value of money when he learns the process of calculating the 'Weighted Average Cost of Capital.' This involves exposing the learner to various sources of funding for a business enterprise, along with stock markets. The learner should also be given the exposure and experience of eliciting information from stock markets and applying the same, for calculating the hurdle rate.

Calculation of 'Weighted Average Cost of Capital' involves identifying the following for a company:

1. Source of funds
2. Cost of each source
3. Weights (i.e., proportion of each source of funds in the total capital)

Source of funds can be obtained from the Financial Statements in the Annual Report of the company. For any company, there are broadly four sources of funding viz., Borrowings (or Debt), Preference Share Capital, Equity Share Capital and Retained Earnings.

The ascertainment of the 'cost of each source' is completely experiential in nature.

The Cost of Debt is based on the credit rating of the debt instrument and the yield on such rating in the market. This calls for a learner to identify the credit rating of the company (or its debt instruments) from its annual reports and identify the yield for such rating from the stock markets. The Cost of Debt is also affected by the effective tax rate, which can be found in the annual report of the company.

Cost of Preference shares is usually the rate of dividend, which can be found in the Balance Sheet.

The cost of Equity Capital is best calculated using the Capital Asset Pricing Model. According to this model, Cost of Equity = Risk-free Return equivalent to yield on long-term Government bonds + Market Risk Premium X Beta Variant for the company.

The yield on long-term Government bonds can be obtained from the Reserve Bank of India, which manages Debt for the Union Government. The details of all the Government Securities issued and outstanding can be found at https://rbi.org.in/scripts/bs_viewcontent.aspx?Id=1956. For example, the latest debt issued by RBI

Interactive Learning Strategies in Teaching Corporate Finance

is in November 2023 for a 50-year duration. The rate of interest on this security is 7.46%, which can be considered a risk-free rate.

Market Risk Premium can be calculated as the excess of 'Market Return' over and above the 'Risk-free rate of return.' 'Market Return' can be calculated by considering any index as a proxy for the market, like BSE SENSEX, NSE NIFTY etc. The index values can be obtained from the Bombay Stock Exchange website at https://www.bseindia.com/indices/IndexArchiveData.html.

The calculation of the Average Yearly Market Return is illustrated in Table 14:

Table 14. Calculation of average yearly market return

Year	Open	High	Low	Close	Yearly Returns
1980				148.25	
1981				227.72	53.61%
1982				235.83	3.56%
1983				252.92	7.25%
1984				271.87	7.49%
1985				527.36	93.98%
1986				524.45	-0.55%
1987				442.17	-15.69%
1988				666.26	50.68%
1989				778.64	16.87%
1990				1048.29	34.63%
1991	1027.38	1955.29		1908.85	82.09%
1992		4546.58		2615.37	37.01%
1993	2617.78	3459.07		3346.06	27.94%
1994	3436.87	4643.31		3926.9	17.36%
1995	3910.16	3943.66		3110.49	-20.79%
1996	3114.08	4131.22	2713.12	3085.2	-0.81%
1997	3096.65	4605.41	3096.65	3658.98	18.60%
1998	3658.34	4322	2741.22	3055.41	-16.50%
1999	3064.95	5150.99	3042.25	5005.82	63.83%
2000	5209.54	6150.69	3491.55	3972.12	-20.65%
2001	3990.65	4462.11	2594.87	3262.33	-17.87%
2002	3262.01	3758.27	2828.48	3377.28	3.52%
2003	3383.85	5920.76	2904.44	5838.96	72.89%
2004	5872.48	6617.15	4227.5	6602.69	13.08%

continued on following page

Table 14. Continued

Year	Open	High	Low	Close	Yearly Returns
2005	6626.49	9442.98	6069.33	9397.93	42.33%
2006	9422.49	14035.3	8799.01	13786.91	46.70%
2007	13827.77	20498.11	12316.1	20286.99	47.15%
2008	20325.27	21206.77	7697.39	9647.31	-52.45%
2009	9720.55	17530.94	8047.17	17464.81	81.03%
2010	17473.45	21108.64	15651.99	20509.09	17.43%
2011	20621.61	20664.8	15135.86	15454.92	-24.64%
2012	15534.67	19612.18	15358.02	19426.71	25.70%
2013	19513.45	21483.74	17448.71	21170.68	8.98%
2014	21222.19	28822.37	19963.12	27499.42	29.89%
2015	27485.77	30024.74	24833.54	26117.54	-5.03%
2016	26101.5	29077.28	22494.61	26626.46	1.95%
2017	26711.15	34137.97	26447.06	34056.83	27.91%
2018	34059.99	38989.65	32483.84	36068.33	5.91%
2019	36161.8	41809.96	35287.16	41253.74	14.38%
2020	41349.36	47896.97	25638.9	47751.33	15.75%
2021	47785.28	62245.43	46160.46	58253.82	21.99%
2022	58310.09	63583.07	50921.22	60840.74	4.44%
2023	60871.24	72484.34	57084.91	72240.26	18.74%
2024	72218.39	74245.17	70001.6	74119.39	2.60%

In the above table, the yearly open, high, low and closing values of BSE Sensex are shown. The yearly returns are calculated using the following formula:

$$\frac{P1 - P0}{P0}$$

The average market return for the last 8 years, 10 years and 12 years are:

- For Last 8 years: 13.96%
- For Last 10 years: 10.86%
- For Last 12 years: 12.29%

The period for which average return must be calculated is subjective and the type of average that can be considered is also arbitrary. This makes the market risk premium highly undependable.

The following two research papers indicate the 'market risk premium' that must be considered for the Indian context:

- IIMA Working Paper 2006-06-04: A First Cut Estimate of Equity Risk Premium
- NSE and EY: Cost of Capital Survey Report 2021 India Insights

Beta-variant refers to the sensitivity measure of the equity stock of the company. It measures the extent of change in stock price for a given change in the market. The Beta-variant is calculated using daily index and stock-price data for the last 1 year. Following Table 15 provides an illustration of Beta calculation on the Spreadsheet for 'Hindustan Unilever Limited':

Table 15. Beta calculation for hindustan unilever limited

Date	SENSEX	HUL Stock Price	SENSEX Daily Returns	Stock Daily Returns
13-Mar-23	58237.85	2452.90		
14-Mar-23	57900.19	2444.25	-0.58%	-0.35%
15-Mar-23	57555.90	2406.10	-0.59%	-1.56%
16-Mar-23	57634.84	2459.85	0.14%	2.23%
17-Mar-23	57989.90	2448.40	0.62%	-0.47%
20-Mar-23	57628.95	2510.50	-0.62%	2.54%
21-Mar-23	58074.68	2463.20	0.77%	-1.88%
22-Mar-23	58214.59	2476.50	0.24%	0.54%
23-Mar-23	57925.28	2485.20	-0.50%	0.35%
24-Mar-23	57527.10	2480.50	-0.69%	-0.19%
27-Mar-23	57653.86	2497.20	0.22%	0.67%
28-Mar-23	57613.72	2481.90	-0.07%	-0.61%
29-Mar-23	57960.09	2528.35	0.60%	1.87%
31-Mar-23	58991.52	2558.75	1.78%	1.20%
03-Apr-23	59106.44	2535.85	0.19%	-0.89%
05-Apr-23	59689.31	2582.70	0.99%	1.85%
06-Apr-23	59832.97	2563.60	0.24%	-0.74%
10-Apr-23	59846.51	2535.10	0.02%	-1.11%
11-Apr-23	60157.72	2545.95	0.52%	0.43%
12-Apr-23	60392.77	2528.70	0.39%	-0.68%
13-Apr-23	60431.00	2534.00	0.06%	0.21%
17-Apr-23	59910.75	2548.45	-0.86%	0.57%
18-Apr-23	59727.01	2541.60	-0.31%	-0.27%

continued on following page

Table 15. Continued

Date	SENSEX	HUL Stock Price	SENSEX Daily Returns	Stock Daily Returns
19-Apr-23	59567.80	2525.55	-0.27%	-0.63%
20-Apr-23	59632.35	2493.00	0.11%	-1.29%
21-Apr-23	59655.06	2498.00	0.04%	0.20%
24-Apr-23	60056.10	2499.35	0.67%	0.05%
25-Apr-23	60130.71	2490.00	0.12%	-0.37%
26-Apr-23	60300.58	2504.70	0.28%	0.59%
27-Apr-23	60649.38	2468.20	0.58%	-1.46%
28-Apr-23	61112.44	2454.40	0.76%	-0.56%
02-May-23	61354.71	2451.40	0.40%	-0.12%
03-May-23	61193.30	2486.25	-0.26%	1.42%
04-May-23	61749.25	2505.80	0.91%	0.79%
05-May-23	61054.29	2501.00	-1.13%	-0.19%
08-May-23	61764.25	2515.15	1.16%	0.57%
09-May-23	61761.33	2516.65	0.00%	0.06%
10-May-23	61940.20	2522.10	0.29%	0.22%
11-May-23	61904.52	2591.80	-0.06%	2.76%
12-May-23	62027.90	2623.40	0.20%	1.22%
15-May-23	62345.71	2661.35	0.51%	1.45%
16-May-23	61932.47	2675.20	-0.66%	0.52%
17-May-23	61560.64	2661.95	-0.60%	-0.50%
18-May-23	61431.74	2626.55	-0.21%	-1.33%
19-May-23	61729.68	2641.40	0.48%	0.57%
22-May-23	61963.68	2636.70	0.38%	-0.18%
23-May-23	61981.79	2628.15	0.03%	-0.32%
24-May-23	61773.78	2612.60	-0.34%	-0.59%
25-May-23	61872.62	2599.70	0.16%	-0.49%
26-May-23	62501.69	2651.60	1.02%	2.00%
29-May-23	62846.38	2650.10	0.55%	-0.06%
30-May-23	62969.13	2656.35	0.20%	0.24%
31-May-23	62622.24	2660.75	-0.55%	0.17%
01-Jun-23	62428.54	2697.75	-0.31%	1.39%
02-Jun-23	62547.11	2716.35	0.19%	0.69%
05-Jun-23	62787.47	2696.40	0.38%	-0.73%

continued on following page

Table 15. Continued

Date	SENSEX	HUL Stock Price	SENSEX Daily Returns	Stock Daily Returns
06-Jun-23	62792.88	2690.05	0.01%	-0.24%
07-Jun-23	63142.96	2715.15	0.56%	0.93%
08-Jun-23	62848.64	2679.85	-0.47%	-1.30%
09-Jun-23	62625.63	2635.70	-0.35%	-1.65%
12-Jun-23	62724.71	2641.75	0.16%	0.23%
13-Jun-23	63143.16	2677.60	0.67%	1.36%
14-Jun-23	63228.51	2698.55	0.14%	0.78%
15-Jun-23	62917.63	2689.75	-0.49%	-0.33%
16-Jun-23	63384.58	2715.45	0.74%	0.96%
19-Jun-23	63168.30	2680.65	-0.34%	-1.28%
20-Jun-23	63327.70	2675.95	0.25%	-0.18%
21-Jun-23	63523.15	2675.50	0.31%	-0.02%
22-Jun-23	63238.89	2654.60	-0.45%	-0.78%
23-Jun-23	62979.37	2642.15	-0.41%	-0.47%
26-Jun-23	62970.00	2652.10	-0.01%	0.38%
27-Jun-23	63416.03	2651.20	0.71%	-0.03%
28-Jun-23	63915.42	2660.80	0.79%	0.36%
30-Jun-23	64718.56	2678.40	1.26%	0.66%
03-Jul-23	65205.05	2698.85	0.75%	0.76%
04-Jul-23	65479.05	2700.90	0.42%	0.08%
05-Jul-23	65446.04	2755.75	-0.05%	2.03%
06-Jul-23	65785.64	2757.80	0.52%	0.07%
07-Jul-23	65280.45	2696.35	-0.77%	-2.23%
10-Jul-23	65344.17	2657.90	0.10%	-1.43%
11-Jul-23	65617.84	2685.00	0.42%	1.02%
12-Jul-23	65393.90	2676.75	-0.34%	-0.31%
13-Jul-23	65558.89	2654.90	0.25%	-0.82%
14-Jul-23	66060.90	2676.85	0.77%	0.83%
17-Jul-23	66589.93	2679.95	0.80%	0.12%
18-Jul-23	66795.14	2683.40	0.31%	0.13%
19-Jul-23	67097.44	2671.75	0.45%	-0.43%
20-Jul-23	67571.90	2702.35	0.71%	1.15%
21-Jul-23	66684.26	2603.80	-1.31%	-3.65%

continued on following page

Table 15. Continued

Date	SENSEX	HUL Stock Price	SENSEX Daily Returns	Stock Daily Returns
24-Jul-23	66384.78	2580.15	-0.45%	-0.91%
25-Jul-23	66355.71	2567.95	-0.04%	-0.47%
26-Jul-23	66707.20	2582.65	0.53%	0.57%
27-Jul-23	66266.82	2570.85	-0.66%	-0.46%
28-Jul-23	66160.20	2585.00	-0.16%	0.55%
31-Jul-23	66527.67	2561.50	0.56%	-0.91%
01-Aug-23	66459.31	2551.30	-0.10%	-0.40%
02-Aug-23	65782.78	2570.40	-1.02%	0.75%
03-Aug-23	65240.68	2551.15	-0.82%	-0.75%
04-Aug-23	65721.25	2546.40	0.74%	-0.19%
07-Aug-23	65953.48	2568.35	0.35%	0.86%
08-Aug-23	65846.50	2564.50	-0.16%	-0.15%
09-Aug-23	65995.81	2552.75	0.23%	-0.46%
10-Aug-23	65688.18	2537.35	-0.47%	-0.60%
11-Aug-23	65322.65	2502.15	-0.56%	-1.39%
14-Aug-23	65401.92	2533.60	0.12%	1.26%
16-Aug-23	65539.42	2551.35	0.21%	0.70%
17-Aug-23	65151.02	2542.40	-0.59%	-0.35%
18-Aug-23	64948.66	2554.70	-0.31%	0.48%
21-Aug-23	65216.09	2562.50	0.41%	0.31%
22-Aug-23	65220.03	2566.40	0.01%	0.15%
23-Aug-23	65433.30	2573.55	0.33%	0.28%
24-Aug-23	65252.34	2579.70	-0.28%	0.24%
25-Aug-23	64886.51	2567.35	-0.56%	-0.48%
28-Aug-23	64996.60	2555.05	0.17%	-0.48%
29-Aug-23	65075.82	2526.25	0.12%	-1.13%
30-Aug-23	65087.25	2532.05	0.02%	0.23%
31-Aug-23	64831.41	2504.20	-0.39%	-1.10%
01-Sep-23	65387.16	2505.00	0.86%	0.03%
04-Sep-23	65628.14	2501.15	0.37%	-0.15%
05-Sep-23	65780.26	2507.30	0.23%	0.25%
06-Sep-23	65880.52	2522.05	0.15%	0.59%
07-Sep-23	66265.56	2507.00	0.58%	-0.60%

continued on following page

Table 15. Continued

Date	SENSEX	HUL Stock Price	SENSEX Daily Returns	Stock Daily Returns
08-Sep-23	66598.91	2514.65	0.50%	0.31%
11-Sep-23	67127.08	2535.60	0.79%	0.83%
12-Sep-23	67221.13	2499.60	0.14%	-1.42%
13-Sep-23	67466.99	2506.45	0.37%	0.27%
14-Sep-23	67519.00	2501.50	0.08%	-0.20%
15-Sep-23	67838.63	2469.90	0.47%	-1.26%
18-Sep-23	67596.84	2487.40	-0.36%	0.71%
20-Sep-23	66800.84	2467.45	-1.18%	-0.80%
21-Sep-23	66230.24	2474.70	-0.85%	0.29%
22-Sep-23	66009.15	2482.30	-0.33%	0.31%
25-Sep-23	66023.69	2476.40	0.02%	-0.24%
26-Sep-23	65945.47	2479.65	-0.12%	0.13%
27-Sep-23	66118.69	2501.30	0.26%	0.87%
28-Sep-23	65508.32	2460.20	-0.92%	-1.64%
29-Sep-23	65828.41	2465.85	0.49%	0.23%
03-Oct-23	65512.10	2470.15	-0.48%	0.17%
04-Oct-23	65226.04	2507.45	-0.44%	1.51%
05-Oct-23	65631.57	2522.30	0.62%	0.59%
06-Oct-23	65995.63	2498.75	0.55%	-0.93%
09-Oct-23	65512.39	2510.60	-0.73%	0.47%
10-Oct-23	66079.36	2516.40	0.87%	0.23%
11-Oct-23	66473.05	2555.95	0.60%	1.57%
12-Oct-23	66408.39	2560.35	-0.10%	0.17%
13-Oct-23	66282.74	2572.05	-0.19%	0.46%
16-Oct-23	66166.93	2557.90	-0.17%	-0.55%
17-Oct-23	66428.09	2557.45	0.39%	-0.02%
18-Oct-23	65877.02	2547.90	-0.83%	-0.37%
19-Oct-23	65629.24	2547.85	-0.38%	0.00%
20-Oct-23	65397.62	2495.00	-0.35%	-2.07%
23-Oct-23	64571.88	2484.60	-1.26%	-0.42%
25-Oct-23	64049.06	2478.55	-0.81%	-0.24%
26-Oct-23	63148.15	2476.15	-1.41%	-0.10%
27-Oct-23	63782.80	2481.70	1.01%	0.22%

continued on following page

Table 15. Continued

Date	SENSEX	HUL Stock Price	SENSEX Daily Returns	Stock Daily Returns
30-Oct-23	64112.65	2478.50	0.52%	-0.13%
31-Oct-23	63874.93	2484.00	-0.37%	0.22%
01-Nov-23	63591.33	2472.90	-0.44%	-0.45%
02-Nov-23	64080.90	2489.25	0.77%	0.66%
03-Nov-23	64363.78	2508.60	0.44%	0.78%
06-Nov-23	64958.69	2501.20	0.92%	-0.29%
07-Nov-23	64942.40	2500.25	-0.03%	-0.04%
08-Nov-23	64975.61	2517.35	0.05%	0.68%
09-Nov-23	64832.20	2477.55	-0.22%	-1.58%
10-Nov-23	64904.68	2486.75	0.11%	0.37%
12-Nov-23	65259.45	2491.30	0.55%	0.18%
13-Nov-23	64933.87	2482.90	-0.50%	-0.34%
15-Nov-23	65675.93	2488.25	1.14%	0.22%
16-Nov-23	65982.48	2489.20	0.47%	0.04%
17-Nov-23	65794.73	2529.45	-0.28%	1.62%
20-Nov-23	65655.15	2505.75	-0.21%	-0.94%
21-Nov-23	65930.77	2505.10	0.42%	-0.03%
22-Nov-23	66023.24	2521.70	0.14%	0.66%
23-Nov-23	66017.81	2520.45	-0.01%	-0.05%
24-Nov-23	65970.04	2514.95	-0.07%	-0.22%
28-Nov-23	66174.20	2511.25	0.31%	-0.15%
29-Nov-23	66901.91	2524.05	1.10%	0.51%
30-Nov-23	66988.44	2546.70	0.13%	0.90%
01-Dec-23	67481.19	2563.25	0.74%	0.65%
04-Dec-23	68865.12	2601.90	2.05%	1.51%
05-Dec-23	69296.14	2563.20	0.63%	-1.49%
06-Dec-23	69653.73	2566.10	0.52%	0.11%
07-Dec-23	69521.69	2520.00	-0.19%	-1.80%
08-Dec-23	69825.60	2521.35	0.44%	0.05%
11-Dec-23	69928.53	2504.45	0.15%	-0.67%
12-Dec-23	69551.03	2502.25	-0.54%	-0.09%
13-Dec-23	69584.60	2511.85	0.05%	0.38%
14-Dec-23	70514.20	2518.50	1.34%	0.26%

continued on following page

Table 15. Continued

Date	SENSEX	HUL Stock Price	SENSEX Daily Returns	Stock Daily Returns
15-Dec-23	71483.75	2523.00	1.37%	0.18%
18-Dec-23	71315.09	2535.45	-0.24%	0.49%
19-Dec-23	71437.19	2561.50	0.17%	1.03%
20-Dec-23	70506.31	2556.80	-1.30%	-0.18%
21-Dec-23	70865.10	2553.40	0.51%	-0.13%
22-Dec-23	71106.96	2575.10	0.34%	0.85%
26-Dec-23	71336.80	2585.75	0.32%	0.41%
27-Dec-23	72038.43	2609.25	0.98%	0.91%
28-Dec-23	72410.38	2633.85	0.52%	0.94%
29-Dec-23	72240.26	2663.35	-0.23%	1.12%
01-Jan-24	72271.94	2655.70	0.04%	-0.29%
02-Jan-24	71892.48	2613.50	-0.53%	-1.59%
03-Jan-24	71356.60	2605.30	-0.75%	-0.31%
04-Jan-24	71847.57	2592.20	0.69%	-0.50%
05-Jan-24	72026.15	2620.30	0.25%	1.08%
08-Jan-24	71355.22	2578.85	-0.93%	-1.58%
09-Jan-24	71386.21	2581.10	0.04%	0.09%
10-Jan-24	71657.71	2577.20	0.38%	-0.15%
11-Jan-24	71721.18	2537.05	0.09%	-1.56%
12-Jan-24	72568.45	2545.25	1.18%	0.32%
15-Jan-24	73327.94	2573.15	1.05%	1.10%
16-Jan-24	73128.77	2568.05	-0.27%	-0.20%
17-Jan-24	71500.76	2563.80	-2.23%	-0.17%
18-Jan-24	71186.86	2548.05	-0.44%	-0.61%
19-Jan-24	71683.23	2564.75	0.70%	0.66%
20-Jan-24	71423.65	2469.30	-0.36%	-3.72%
23-Jan-24	70370.55	2375.15	-1.47%	-3.81%
24-Jan-24	71060.31	2444.10	0.98%	2.90%
25-Jan-24	70700.67	2430.10	-0.51%	-0.57%
29-Jan-24	71941.57	2444.40	1.76%	0.59%
30-Jan-24	71139.90	2458.95	-1.11%	0.60%
31-Jan-24	71752.11	2480.40	0.86%	0.87%
01-Feb-24	71645.30	2474.20	-0.15%	-0.25%

continued on following page

Table 15. Continued

Date	SENSEX	HUL Stock Price	SENSEX Daily Returns	Stock Daily Returns
02-Feb-24	72085.63	2454.05	0.61%	-0.81%
05-Feb-24	71731.42	2420.10	-0.49%	-1.38%
06-Feb-24	72186.09	2426.25	0.63%	0.25%
07-Feb-24	72152.00	2426.00	-0.05%	-0.01%
08-Feb-24	71428.43	2417.90	-1.00%	-0.33%
09-Feb-24	71595.49	2424.20	0.23%	0.26%
12-Feb-24	71072.49	2385.60	-0.73%	-1.59%
13-Feb-24	71555.19	2393.55	0.68%	0.33%
14-Feb-24	71822.83	2388.95	0.37%	-0.19%
15-Feb-24	72050.38	2351.10	0.32%	-1.58%
16-Feb-24	72426.64	2375.05	0.52%	1.02%
19-Feb-24	72708.16	2387.55	0.39%	0.53%
20-Feb-24	73057.40	2402.80	0.48%	0.64%
21-Feb-24	72623.09	2406.05	-0.59%	0.14%
22-Feb-24	73158.24	2387.90	0.74%	-0.75%
23-Feb-24	73142.80	2394.35	-0.02%	0.27%
26-Feb-24	72790.13	2403.45	-0.48%	0.38%
27-Feb-24	73095.22	2404.90	0.42%	0.06%
28-Feb-24	72304.88	2421.25	-1.08%	0.68%
29-Feb-24	72500.30	2411.05	0.27%	-0.42%
01-Mar-24	73745.35	2412.85	1.72%	0.07%
02-Mar-24	73806.15	2415.85	0.08%	0.12%
04-Mar-24	73872.29	2421.20	0.09%	0.22%
05-Mar-24	73677.13	2398.05	-0.26%	-0.96%
06-Mar-24	74085.99	2400.70	0.55%	0.11%
07-Mar-24	74119.39	2420.65	0.05%	0.83%

In the above table, the daily values of SENSEX and HUL stock prices are shown along with daily returns. Daily returns have been calculated using the formula:

$$\frac{P1 - P0}{P0}$$

Based on the last one-year daily returns, Beta is calculated using the 'Slope' function in the spreadsheet. The 'slope' in Spreadsheet is obtained by:
=slope(stock returns, Sensex returns)

For Hindustan Unilever, the Beta value is 0.5396

The cost of Retained Earnings is considered as same as the Cost of Equity.

For calculating the Weighted Average Cost of Capital, the following weights are considered, in this order:

1. Target Capital Structure Weights
2. Market Value Weights
3. Book-Value Weights

Corporate Valuation

The financial and strategic goal of any business enterprise is to maximise the 'value of business' and thereby maximise 'shareholder value.' For the learner to understand the strategies of value maximisation, she/he must have knowledge and skill to find the 'value or worth of the business entity.'. This depends on the depth of knowledge the learner has in the first two pre-requisites i.e., 'analysis of financial statements' and 'time value of money.'

There are many methods of ascertaining the value of a business entity. The best among all is the Discounted Cash Flow Method (DCF Method). According to the DCF Method, the value of a Business Entity is the 'Present value of Future Free Cash Flows to the Firm.' A brief orientation of finding value under this method will be essential for further understanding of 'Corporate Finance'

With the background knowledge of these prerequisites, the instructor can delve into the core topics of Corporate Finance.

FINANCIAL DECISIONS

Corporate Finance or Financial Management refers to 'Managing the Balance Sheet.' Balance Sheet is a statement which provides details of 'Liabilities' and 'Assets.' Liabilities refers to the 'Sources' from which a business entity gets funds for operating the business, and Assets refers to the 'Application' of those funds.

So, Financial Decision-making involves making decisions regarding the sources from which the business entity must raise funds (i.e., Financing Decisions), and regarding the application of such funds (i.e., Investment Decisions). Further, a decision must also be made regarding the profits made by the entity for a given period – that is, how much to retain and how much to distribute among the owners of the business.

In summary, Financial Management involves making the following decisions, broadly:

1. Financing Decisions
2. Investment Decisions
   a. Long-term Investment Decisions [also called 'Capital Budgeting Decisions']
   b. Short-term Investment Decisions [also called 'Working Capital Management']
3. Dividend Decisions or Retention Decisions

Financing Decisions

'Financing Decisions' involves deciding upon the sources from which a business entity can mobilise long-term funds. It involves deciding about the proportion in which a business entity must have its funds and borrowed funds. There are various tools which help in making financial decisions viz., 'EBIT-EPS Analysis', 'Point of Indifference', 'Financial Break-even Point', 'Leverages' etc., The learners need to be equipped with the skills in applying these tools in making financing decisions.

Financing decisions pertain to the financial choices made by the finance department regarding the management of the organization's financial resources. The decision pertains to the sources of financing i.e., mix of equity, debt, and term loans. Often, these decisions are taken when there is a need for additional sources of funds in the company. These decisions are highly significant as the right source of financing can lead to an increase in revenue, minimizing cost and increasing efficiency.

Financing decisions are to be taken continuously as the organization needs funds regularly. This mix should be balanced in such a way that the proportion of the mix should be rigid as well as flexible. Teaching financing decision-making as part of corporate finance involves imparting knowledge about how organizations manage their finances and funding to maximize shareholder value. Various strategies could be employed for the effective delivery of these concepts. A capital structure decision should be ideal or optimal for the company. It is said to be optimal when it gives the maximum possible benefits to the shareholders with the minimum cost of capital and captures the risk policy of the company (Kumar, 2019).

EBIT-EPS Analysis

This analysis is used to identify the capital structure which gives maximum benefit to the shareholders i.e. maximizing EPS among the various alternatives of capital structure.

a. Numerical-based example: A company requires Rs. 25 lakhs for the installation of a new unit, which would yield an annual EBIT of Rs. 500000. The company's objective is to maximize the EPS. It is considering the possibility of issuing

equity shares plus raising a debt of Rs. 250000, Rs. 100000 and Rs. 1500000. The current market price per share is Rs. 150, which is expected to drop to Rs. 125 per share if the market borrowings were to exceed Rs. 10,00,000. The cost of borrowings is shown in Table 16. Assuming a tax rate of 30%, work out the EPS and the scheme which you would recommend to the company (Kumar, 2019). Solution refer to (Kumar, 2019).
b. Case Discussion: "EBIT- EPS Analysis as a Tool to understand the performance of the Indian Infrastructure sector" (K, 2014)

Table 16. Cost of borrowings

Level of Borrowing	Upto Rs. 250000	Rs. 250000 to Rs. 1000000	Above 1000000
Cost of Borrowing	10% p.a	15% p.a	20% p.a

Point of Indifference

(Kumar, 2019) Point of Indifference refers to the EBIT at which different capital structures result in the same Earnings per share. It is calculated by equating the EPS of two different capital structures. The purpose of calculating the Point of indifference is to help in deciding the quantum of debt in the capital structure.

When Actual EBIT > Point of Indifference = Capital structure can have a high debt component.

When Actual EBIT < Point of indifference = Capital structure must have low debt component.

1. **FAQ:** One of the teaching pedagogies for learning Point of Indifference is by conducting a FAQ with students. Some of the FAQs that could be asked are mentioned below:
   a. What is Indifference point analysis?
   b. What are the prerequisites for calculating the indifference points?
   c. How is the Indifference point calculated?
   d. Can the Indifference point change over time?
   e. Why is the Indifference point important?
   f. For what decision of capital structure, we can use this technique?
   g. How does a point of indifference help a company in finding out its optimal capital structure?
   h. Mention a few challenges in adapting the point of Indifference.
   i. Is the Indifference point relevant only to manufacturing industries or applies to the service sector too?

j. How can companies use indifference point analysis in capital structure decision-making?
2. **Interactive role-play:** Provide the students with different options of financing for a project. Students can be divided into groups and they can be assigned different scenarios. Relevant information on the amount of financing through equity and debt, EBIT, Interest rates for scenarios, and Preference dividend if any can be provided. The students can be asked to calculate Indifference points based on information and make decisions based on their analysis.
3. **Visual representation:** Use of charts, graphs, and diagrams to illustrate the concept of Indifference points. These graphs can be used to show how indifference points are determined and how they change with changes in the capital structure.

Financial Break-Even Point

(Kumar, 2019) It refers to the extent of EBIT required to meet fixed financial obligations. The fixed financial obligation includes "Cost of debt" and "Dividend on preference shares". The capital structure with the lowest break-even point ensures more profits are available to shareholders

1. **Excel Exercises:** Create hypothetical financial data for interest rates on borrowings, tax rates etc. They can be guided through the steps of calculating financial break-even points using formulas in Excel. After the initial results, the same Excel can be used to manipulate interest rates, taxes and other data to find the impact on the financial break-even point.
2. **Problem-Based Learning:** (Kumar, 2019) The management of Z Company Ltd wants to raise funds from the market to meet the financial demands of long-term projects. The company has various combinations of proposals to raise its funds. You are given the following proposals of the company.

Proposal A: 50% Equity, 50% debt, Cost of debt 10%, tax rate 50%, Equity shares of the face value of Rs. 10 each will be issued at a premium of Rs. 10 per share. Total investment to be raised Rs. 40 lakhs, EBIT Rs. 18 lakhs.
Solution: Refer (Kumar, 2019)

Capital Budgeting Decisions

'Capital Budgeting Decisions' involve deciding on:

1. whether to invest or not in a given investment opportunity,
2. choosing the best among mutually exclusive alternatives,
3. capital rationing, and
4. capital disinvestment.

For making these decisions, the following inputs are required:

1. Cash Outflows
2. Cash Inflows
3. Hurdle or Discount Rate

Making students identify these inputs is experiential learning by itself.

Making these decisions is possible with various techniques of capital budgeting, all of which are broadly classified into Non-discounted Cash Flow Techniques and Discounted Cash Flow Techniques.

However, learners can understand these decisions better with cases and spreadsheet modelling.

The list of Cases mentioned in the session plan (Case 4 and Assignment 4) are very effective cases in this regard. Further, inbuilt functions of NPV, IRR, MIRR, XIRR etc., are in the spreadsheet and are very helpful in making these decisions.

The Risk analysis in capital budgeting which involves risk measurement and management, can be completely demonstrated with Excel Spreadsheet.

Working Capital Management

'Working Capital Management' involves deciding on the funds to be maintained for managing the day-to-day operations of the entity, its application and management. This involves the estimation of working capital requirements, and managing the various forms in which the working capital is found viz., inventory, receivables and cash. These topics can be better understood with cases and 'experience sharing' by industry professionals.

Dividend Decisions

'Dividend Decisions' involves deciding on the extent of profits that can be distributed among the owners (i.e., shareholders) as dividends, and the amount of profits to be retained for further business investment.

CONCLUSION

Corporate Finance is a management course, the learning of which can be made most interactive through:

1. Role plays
2. Analysis of Financial Statements and Other Contents of Annual Report
3. Case Studies
4. Simulations
5. Spreadsheet Modelling
6. Experience Sharing (Guest Lectures) by Industry professionals.
7. Industry visits
8. Games
9. Recorded lectures are available online on Coursera,
10. Mini Research projects

The instructor needs to ensure that all activities are properly identified, appropriately placed, ideally sequenced and effectively implemented. By doing this, the instructor can ensure development of student's cognitive interests and skills to work in a team. This provides an environment where there is a blend of theory and practice, learnt both at the same time. This fosters critical thinking and logical reasoning skills among the students.

FUTURE RESEARCH DIRECTIONS

The further research could be in understanding and assessing the learning outcomes of these interactive learning strategies in corporate finance. Comparative studies could be taken up on Interactive vs traditional teaching methods to evaluate the effectiveness. Future research can also be done to track the long term impact on student academic performance, retention and career success.

REFERENCES

Damodaran, A. (2002). *Corporate Finance - Theory and Practice*. Wiley India Pvt Ltd.

Jain, P. K. S. S. (2010). Capital Structure Decisions - A case study of Reliance Industries Limited. In S. S. P K Jain, *Capital Structure Decisions* (pp. 1-22). Business Analyst.

. K, P. (2014). EBIT- EPS Analysis as a Tool to Understand the Performance of Indian Infrastructure Sector. *Indian Journal of Applied Research*, 246-247.

Kumar, V. R. (2019). Capital Structure Decisions. In Kumar, V. R. (Ed.), *Financial Management* (p. 216). Mc Graw Hill Education Private Limited.

Natalila Marchenko, V. L. (2023). *Interactive learning methods in higher education institutions*. The Modern Higher Education Review.

Pandey, I. M. (2012). Central Equipment Company. In *R. B. I M Pandey, Cases in Financial Management* (pp. 259–263). Tata McGraw Hill Education Private Limited.

Pandey, I. M. (2012). Deepak Fertilizers and Petrochemicals Corporation Limited. In *R. B. I M Pandey, Cases in Financial Management* (pp. 264–269). Tata McGraw Hill Education Private Limited.

Railean, E. (2017). *Metacognition in Higher Education: Successful Learning Strgeties and Tactics for Sustainibility*. IGI Global. 10.4018/978-1-5225-2218-8

Shuckers: Miller and Modigliani. In (1997). *J. D. Joseph Sulock, Cases in Financial management* (pp. 215–222). John Wiley & Sons, Inc.

Sulock, J. (1997). Taylor Brands - Cost of Capital or Required rate of return. In *J. D. Joseph Sulock, Cases in Financial Management* (pp. 191–196). John Wiley & Sons, Inc.

Turkot, T. I. (2011). *Higher Education pedagogy*.

APPENDIX 1: ROLE PLAY: THE FINANCE CONNECTION

A medium-sized manufacturing company called "Aha- Oho Pvt ltd" is having its annual strategic planning meeting in the Board room. The Board room consists of a round table, around which various department functional heads are seated. At the head of the table is Jugandhar, the CFO who is leading the meeting with his presentation "The Finance Connection: Integrating all Functional Departments for achieving organizational goals"

Characters:

Jugandhar: The Chief Financial Officer (CFO)

Ruhi: The head of Marketing

Ramalingappa: The head of sales

Charlie: The head of Product Development

Shankar Gowda: The head of Human Resources

Goutam Shekar Buddha: The CEO

The opening scene is when everyone is settling in their seats, murmuring among themselves about the year's performance and upcoming projections.

Goutam Shekar Buddha: Good morning Ladies and Gentlemen. This meeting is called not just to understand how we have performed in the past and what we can foresee for the coming financial year. This meeting largely focuses on how interconnected each of us is with finance. Jugandhar?

(Meanwhile, the presentation on the screen is open for Jugandhar to start his presentation)

Jugandhar: Mere Sathiyon!!!!!! Good morning! We have assembled here in this board room to discuss not just the past performance of our company but also how various functions can add flavour to the finance function. Not just flavour but this department acts like a heart which pumps blood to all parts of the body – "Aha – Oho Pvt ltd". Without a strong finance function, even the best strategies can fail.

Jugandhar: let us start with the Marketing department. Ruhi, you've got excellent campaigns and advertisement strategies for our products, you make advertisement budgets, promotional fairs etc. to support the sales team and meet their target. But Ruhi, tell me how do we decide on the budget for these?

Ruhi: Well, Thank you for the compliments. We make projections and forecasts based on past data. We align all our advertisement campaigns based on past success stories and current market trends.

Jugandhar: Exactly! And who provides that data? Finance. We work together to ensure your campaigns are not just creative but also cost-effective and aligned with our overall financial health.

(Ruhi nods, impressed)

Jugandhar: Next we shall move on to sales. Ramalingappa, you and your team are on the frontline, bringing in sales to the company. You take all initiatives to meet the sales target for every quarter based on the sales forecasts made. But how do we set these targets?

Ramalingappa: Right, we analyze the market potential, past performance for each quarter, growth and other opportunities in the market.

Jugandhar: Right, and who crunches these numbers to ensure the projections are realistic and aligned with our financial goals? We do. Our collaboration ensures we're setting achievable targets.

(Ramalingappa gives a thumbs up)

Jugandhar: Charlie, tell me when you develop a product, where do you begin from? Every product your team launches or introduces starts with what?

Charlie: Well, feasibility, R & D, product design, usability, efficiency, resources, expertise, time and YES BUDGET

Jugandhar: Finance ensures you have the resources you need, when you need them, to bring those innovations to life.

(Charlie, Previously not very convinced, now nods his head)

Jugandhar: Shankar Gowda, HR is a function which supports are functional head of the company by providing the right skills and mapping their competencies. HR is not just hiring and policies. It is about building a team that can execute our vision. But, tell me Shankar, how do you ensure we can attract and retain the right talent?

Shankar Gowda: Competitive salaries, benefits, perquisites, and a strong culture with a conducive work environment.

Jugandhar: And who helps you to model those packages and benefits to be competitive and yet sustainable? Finance. Together, we ensure "Aha- Oho" remain a great place to work, within our financial means.

(Shankar Gowds smiles)

Jugandhar: So friends, you see Finance is not just about numbers. It's about enabling each of the departments to succeed. We all should ensure that Aha–Oho not just survives but thrives. Let's acknowledge this understanding to build a stronger collaboration across all functions. Thank you

(Goutham Shekar Budha stands up smiling)

Goutham Shekar Buddha: Thank you Jugandhar, for wonderfully connecting all the dots. With your presentation, it is clear, that all functions in the company must fall back on Finance to meet their goals. Let's keep this spirit of collaboration as we move forward to the next financial year.

(The entire team applauds with the scene ending with appreciation among the heads of cross functions)

Chapter 14
Teacher Educators and Technology Integration With Preservice Teachers

Brooke Urbina
The Chicago School, USA

Aubrey Statti
The Chicago School, USA

Kelly M. Torres
The Chicago School, USA

ABSTRACT

The mission of this chapter is to provide teachers with the knowledge and benefits of utilizing the TPACK framework and the SAMR model to guide the use of technology, so they can empower students for the digital age, through primarily focusing on the importance of the role of teacher educators in the training of preservice teachers. To overcome deficiencies in skills, knowledge, and abilities related to the instruction of technology integration, the focus for preparation should be turned to the teacher educators themselves. Combining the constructivist theory with the TPaCK framework, the study aimed to make a connection to the relevance of this theoretical framework in conjunction with technology integration to adequately prepare preservice teachers for the classroom. Overall, the study found that gaps exist among consistency of skills in teacher educators when it comes to technology integration, and a need to close this gap was clearly identified, defining it is the responsibility of the university teacher educator faculty to ensure that happens.

DOI: 10.4018/979-8-3693-3559-8.ch014

INTRODUCTION

Preservice teachers are entering the world of education under-prepared to meet the expectations of technology use in the classroom. To overcome deficiencies in skills, knowledge, and abilities related to the instruction of technology integration, the focus for preparation should be turned to the teacher educators themselves. If teacher educators are not adequately trained and equipped to train preservice teachers to integrate technology into their instruction, preservice teachers will graduate ill prepared for the challenges they will encounter. When entering classrooms of the 21st Century, in addition to being a master of content, teachers are expected to "identify appropriate technological tools and resources to effectively incorporate educational technology to support their teaching objectives and engage students in meaningful learning experiences. Teachers must also assess students' technical skills and design activities appropriate for their technological competency level" (Mariscal et al., 2023, p. 1567). The lack of training and preparation in relation to technology integration could produce a population of new teachers with low self-efficacy, inadequate skills and knowledge, and low technical literacy.

BACKGROUND AND HISTORY OF TEACHER PREPARATION PROGRAMS

Historically, the emphasis for training in a teacher preparation program is within the preparation of the preservice teacher (Feuer et al., 2013); preservice teachers are the individuals striving to complete a teacher preparation program to become state certified to teach a specific grade level and/or content. For this training to be successful, however, the training of the teacher educators must be evaluated as well; teacher educators are those faculty members at the university level, responsible for the training and preparation of preservice teachers. Teacher preparation programs have evolved, with their focus on content and pedagogy expanding to include an aspect of personal self (Carmi & Tamir, 2020). Before entering a teacher preparation program, preservice teachers base their own self-efficacy with technology integration on their own K-12 experiences and their own personal experiences with technology (Ebersole, 2019). To capitalize on their self-efficacy, and "to harness the potential of educational technology, teachers must possess pedagogical competence in integrating technology into their teaching practices" (Mariscal et al, 2023, p. 1568). Within the teacher preparation programs, teacher educators help shape the ideal image of a teacher, and the preservice teachers are shaped by this image (Carmi & Tamir, 2020), so learning technology integration throughout the teacher preparation program is a process of obtaining knowledge supplied by the teacher educators (Ebersole, 2019). As a preservice teacher engages in their field experience, their exposure to technology integration from their teacher preparation program guides the context of their use of technology in their field experience, and these experiences can enhance or destroy a preservice teacher's self-efficacy in relation to technology integration (Ebersole, 2019).

Research has shown that the evolution of the teacher preparation program is multi-faceted (Hager, 2020). From face-to-face only options to all online options, teacher preparation programs have evolved to meet the needs of varying potential candidates. Some programs are developing distance learning programs, while others are offering blended options (Hager, 2020). Either way, the field experiences often include technology use in instruction and evaluation (Hager, 2020). Instead of the time intensive requirement of a teacher educator going to a preservice teacher's hosting school, multiple times, to observe and provide feedback, preservice teachers are increasingly being required to record themselves teaching, so the recording can be used for observation by the teacher educator and for self-reflection by the preservice teacher (Hagar, 2020). This self-reflection element is significant, for one complaint about graduate programs in education is that they are preparing managers, trained to run a business, rather than leaders, grounded in the appreciation of education (Normore & Lahera, 2018). Allowing preservice teachers the opportunity to observe themselves and their interactions with their students gives them opportunity for reflection, grounding their appreciation for education (Normore & Lahera, 2018). Ideally, teacher preparation programs want to provide experiences that allow preservice teachers to develop a sense of creativity, flexibility, authenticity, and aesthetical literacy (Carmi & Tamir, 2020).

The authentic experience is imperative to the training of a preservice teacher in relation to constructivism and their development of technological, pedagogical, and content knowledge (TPaCK). For preservice teachers to construct their own ideas and learning in relation to technology integration, they must be involved in the activity of learning, not simply present for the act. To successfully integrate technology, the learning depends on whether preservice teachers believe it is important to learning, whether they have access to resources, whether they have experience using the technologies, and whether they understand the reason for using the technology to enhance the learning (Sulecio de Alvarez & Dickson-Deane, 2018). Teacher self-efficacy is highly determined by the attitude and competence of the teacher in relation to using educational technology (Mariscal et al., 2023). Preservice teachers, with a constructivist mindset, will develop a high level of TPaCK, for they will be able to meet the challenges of designing multimodal tasks, facilitating multicultural activities, and consciously evaluating ways to improve their own learning environment (Chai & Koh, 2017), meeting the expectation of 21st century teachers in their competence for harnessing modern technologies to develop a new culture of learning

(Chai et al., 2017). However, teacher educators must first be trained with the skills and knowledge required to successfully integrate technology, so they can prepare preservice teachers to do the same.

THEORETICAL FRAMEWORK

Preservice teachers complete a teacher preparation program with the expectation they are being provided the skills and knowledge needed to be successful in their own classrooms; however, if teacher educators are not equipped to prepare them for the modern classroom, preservice teachers enter the education world ill-prepared (Kalonde & Mousa, 2016). Teacher educators can utilize the constructivist theory with the TPaCK framework to provide authentic experiences to preservice teachers, increasing the likelihood they will enter their own classroom prepared for the challenges they will encounter.

Constructivism

With a constructivist mindset, the TPaCK framework can effectively guide successful integration of technology. Technology is a tool used for enhancement of learning; it should not simply be used to replace a more primitive tool. Von Glaserfeld (2001) outlined constructivism in connection with learners constructing their own understanding, not simply regurgitating information as it is presented to them. Learners of a constructivist mindset, according to Von Glaserfeld (2001), when provided incomplete information, will look for meaning and order, making sense of the information they were provided.

Teacher educators must provide these opportunities for preservice teachers to construct knowledge of technology integration to determine how it can be used in their own content areas of teaching. Teacher educators also provide a connection between preservice teachers and technology integration; therefore, it is imperative they are adequately trained to make decisions effective in the integration of technology. Using the TPaCK framework, universities can evaluate the depth of which technology is integrated in the instruction of preservice teachers, ensuring they are trained with constructivist mindset, for TPaCK allows university faculty to address the questions of what teachers need to know to integrate technology and how they can best develop that knowledge (Saubern et al., 2020). Combining the constructivist theory with the TPaCK framework creates a process of technology integration to be built where past knowledge, constructs new ideas, to form current knowledge, in correlation with technological, pedagogical, and content knowledge (TPaCK), which are essential for effective technology integration.

TPaCK

Teacher educators hold the key to ensuring preservice teachers are prepared to integrate technology into their instruction. Therefore, it is important to develop a conceptual framework to evaluate qualitative data, exhibiting the extent of which their self-efficacy, related to technology integration, allows them to do this, successfully. The technology, pedagogy, and content knowledge (TPaCK) framework will be used as a guide to evaluate the learning environment of preservice teachers, from the perspective of the teacher educators responsible for preparing them to integrate technology. TPaCK, developed by Mishra and Koehler (2006), was designed for the purpose to integrate technology into teaching, which involves complex interaction between content, pedagogy, and technology.

Figure 1. Constructivism and TPaCK framework

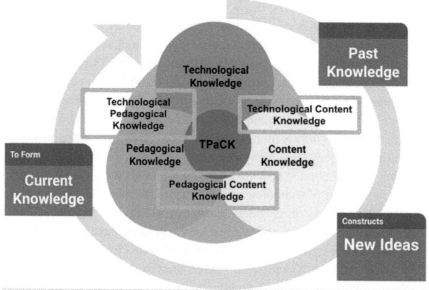

PURPOSE OF THE STUDY

Teacher preparation programs are intended to prepare preservice teachers for the demands of the modern classroom by preparing them with technological, pedagogical, and content knowledge (TPaCK) (Joo et al., 2018). The pedagogical and content knowledge (PCK) aspects of education are what teacher educators are adequately trained and supported to prepare preservice teachers. The technological skills and knowledge (TK) are areas of weakness for many, for the evolution of this element at the university level is not progressing as quickly as at the K-12 level. To address this issue, the training and support being provided to teacher educators, in relation to their own evolution of technology integration skills and knowledge, needs to be evaluated (Kopcha et al., 2016). The discrepancy emphasis is consistently focused on preservice teachers' knowledge and skills of technology integration, but they cannot be expected to have adequate skills or knowledge in that area if those responsible for preparing them lack education and experience in those areas. To determine the significance of this gap in knowledge and skills at the teacher educator level, teacher educators were interviewed to understand their perceptions of how well they are prepared and supported to make decisions regarding technology integration, training preservice teachers to successfully integrate technology in their instruction.

This qualitative case study addressed two research questions:

Research Question 1: *What factors influence teacher educators' decisions on the technologies used to educate preservice teachers throughout the teacher education program at a Division II university in central Missouri?*

Research Question 2: *What would teacher educators at a Division II university in central Missouri consider to be obstacles in teaching preservice teachers how to integrate instructional technology?*

Each of the research questions were adequately addressed throughout the study, providing a clear picture of how teacher educators, that integrate technology, make their decisions regarding that integration, while also providing clear examples of obstacles that hinder the technology integration process for themselves as well as others. Even though participants represented varied content areas, the responses of those who demonstrated a high self-efficacy in relation to technology integration were consisted, as were those who demonstrated a lower self-efficacy in relation to technology integration. As indicated by Participant 9, who is also on the CAEP (Council for the Accreditation of Educator Preparation) Review Committee, this study could provide them with additional, unbiased research about their own program that will assist them in making changes needed to keep their teacher educators relevant with the K-12 classrooms of the 21st century.

The purpose of this study was to determine whether university faculty, in the role of teacher educators, from various educational certification content areas, at a Division II university in central Missouri, were adequately trained to make decisions regarding technology integration, preparing preservice teachers to effectively integrate technology into their instruction. This study examined whether a proactive approach, switching the focus to the teacher educators, would be more effective in the long run for both preservice teachers and the districts that employ them. This qualitative case study was conducted through a series of interviews, done virtually; through these interviews, reoccurring themes were identified, exposing the level of the knowledge and skill base of teacher educators in relation to technology integration, and the decisions they make regarding the integration of technology in their own courses. Syllabi of these participants' courses were also evaluated to gain insight as to how and why preservice teachers are being required to integrate technology throughout their teacher preparation program. The combination of data from the interviews and syllabi evaluations allowed for a cross-section of supporting data to be revealed.

RESEARCH DESIGN AND METHOD

The research design and method are described, beginning with qualitative research questions addressing the "how" and "why," which asked if preservice teachers are adequately prepared to integrate technology and whether their teacher educators are prepared to adequately train them. This qualitative case study provided insight to perceptions of teacher educators as to the factors that influenced their decisions on the technologies used to educate preservice teachers. A sample of teacher educators from a Division II university in central Missouri were interviewed, gaining in depth, narrative insight to these perceptions, and their course syllabi were evaluated for indications of required technology use. The biases existing in this study were relevant to the researcher's experience with the topic and the fact that the sample is representing a single university teacher preparation program in central Missouri. The assumption was made that the participants will be honest in their responses, providing the researcher with an accurate depiction of perceptions.

To obtain a deeper understanding of how teacher educators are making decisions in relation to integrating technology in the education of preservice teachers, conducting interviews is an effective method to gather data, relative to understanding people's experiences, that numbers cannot provide (Cleland, 2017). In addition to being qualitative in nature, this was a case study of a group of teacher educators at a single university. Because a case study relies on multiple methods of data collection, syllabi of the participants were also evaluated to gain insight to how and why technology use was being required of preservice teachers throughout their preparation program. This study relied on interviews of life experiences from various teacher educators, exploring how they and preservice teachers are trained to integrate technology. Because the data comes from these lived experiences and other sources, a case study approach is relevant (Gammelgaard, 2017).

Themes of Findings

Analysis of the interview data resulted in two major themes: technology use and obstacles of technology integration, was well as various coordinating sub-themes. The table below shows how often each of the two main themes theme and corresponding sub-themes were identified by each of the participant interviews. The first theme in the table is Obstacles for Technology Integration, with sub-themes of External Factors, Pedagogy, and Training. The second theme represented in the table is Technology Use, with sub-themes of Decisions, Expectations and Requirements for Students and for Teachers, Experience, Integration, and Tools. The numbers to the right of each theme or sub-theme indicate the number of references coded for each Participant, for that specific theme or sub-theme, throughout their interview.

Technology Use

The purpose of the research was to evaluate the technology use of university educator faculty. Under this theme, various sub-themes evolved to include the specific the tools of technology use, integration of technology, faculty experience with technology, decisions guiding use of technology, and expectations and requirements of technology use for both students and faculty.

Technology Tools

Each participant reported using a variety of tools in their instruction, listing a total of 54 different tools among the ten participants. Blackboard, being the learning management system (LMS) of the university was reportedly used by all participants, as their courses are housed in this tool. Only two participants included use of Blackboard's various integrated tools, such as the online quizzes, Pannekoek video recording, discussion boards, and breakout rooms. Participant 1 indicated that the Pannekoek was integrated into the Blackboard LMS and expressed that it "does have a really nice availability of experts who will answer your specific questions," which enhanced her readiness to utilize the tool. Participant 2 indicated she used another tool for a method more interactive than simply making students read, do the lesson, and then complete a Blackboard quiz.

Google Suite. Among the tools external to the LMS, Google tools was mentioned by all the participants for the variety of tools available in Google Suite and the convenience of usability. Specific tools mentioned included:

- Google Slides
- Google Docs
- Google Forms
- Google Drive
- Google Meet
- Google Chrome Extensions
- Basic Google Search

Participant 6 explained the seamless use of Google Slides, for when students would be required to present, the presentations could be shared with the professor, avoiding the time consumption of each student having to log in to the computer to pull the file up or having to have the file saved on an external drive that may or may not work on the computer. Participant 7 preferred the use of Google Docs over Microsoft Word because it can be easily shared with the professor and other students for collaboration and feedback, or simply to share resources. Participant 8 simply commented, "I do everything on Google," also indicating she minimizes her use of Blackboard due to her use of Google instead. Google Forms, another tool of Google Suite, can be used for a multitude of tasks, such as quizzes, surveys, etc. Participant 3, however, pushed the limits of usability and explained, "you could do a whole adventure story, right, in Google Forms. You could make, like, an Amazing Race game," using technology to create an interactive element to instruction.

Google Extensions. Google Extensions, in addition to the Google Suite tools, provide a plethora of tools to Google users, but Participant 2 specifically mentioned a tool that replaces the presentation clicker, mentioning a remote clicker for Chrome that can allow a presentation to be controlled from a phone, anywhere in the room. This specific tool is something that can make movement and classroom management much more effective, as the teacher is not tied to their computer while teaching.

Kahoot. Kahoot, an online, interactive game, was another tool consistently mentioned by participants. This online game tool can make learning interactive and add a competitive nature to learning. Participant 8 mentioned that they use Kahoot for its interactive response element, and Participant 2 listed Kahoot as one of the most common instructional tools utilized. Participant 3 described her use of Kahoot as an element of exposure to similar tools, indicating that if she exposes them to Kahoot, then "if they happen to see Quizzes later on, they're going to be like, Oh, that looks familiar," expressing the need to expose students to a variety of tools, so they leave her class with a higher self-efficacy in relation to technology use to not fear new tools; instead, encouraging them to make connections to familiar tools, having the ability to recognize the depth of the learning curve. This idea corresponded with Participant 5 who expressed the need to introduce students to a multitude of tools and give them options for application, so when they are tasked with creating a vocabulary game, they do not automatically use Kahoot each time, stating, "I think that you say to yourself, I want a good vocabulary game, well, you've got 50 to choose from, you shouldn't be using just Kahoot," for they should have a variety of tools in their toolbox.

Technology Integration

Indications of tool use does not necessarily indicate integration of technology. By each participant, technology tools were reported as being used by the professor, but integration includes the respondent use of the technology by students as well. Google Suite tools are inherently designed for collaboration and respondent use, as professors reported using them for presentation tools and collaboration tools. Kahoot is an instructional tool, but as Participant 5 indicated, her students are not only expected to interact with the tool in class, but they are expected to utilize that tool, then incorporate it into interaction with classmates. This integration of technology allows for the tool to be modeled and practiced, then it is applied and integrated into the student learning process. Participant 3 takes the integration of technology in a different direction, requiring students to locate their own tools for a specific task and provide examples of how the tool could be integrated in their classroom setting, while requiring them to model its use for classmates. Modeling is an important element of technology integration, and Participant 3 intentionally used tools in her instruction that her students may find useful in their own instruction and field experience, such as Padlet, Nearpod, online timers, and other web resources, encouraging students to bookmark these tools for their technology toolbox. Participant 9 had a similar approach, utilizing a multitude of technology tools in instruction, modeling how the tools were used to achieve an intended learning goal, and requiring students to demonstrate their use of these tools in class and throughout their field experiences. Collectively, these elements of instruction are demonstrating effective integration of technology.

Faculty Experience

The participants reported a wide range of experience and training related to technology use before entering the collegiate environment, with two participants reporting obtaining graduate level degrees in Educational Technology before becoming university faculty. Beyond getting an Educational Technology degree, only half of the participants reported receiving any formal training in relation to technology integration before becoming university faculty. Much of this reported training was minimal, at best. Participant 10 reported only receiving basic training regarding the learning management systems used in his previous districts. Participant 4 described training she received specific to the use of Smart Boards that were installed in district classrooms, and when her district incorporated Chromebooks, she indicated "we spent a lot of time and professional development, learning how to utilize Chromebooks and Google and making those what they could be as a learning tool," but she also indicated that the Google training was difficult for some teachers to process, so while she benefited from it, she was not confident the benefits were widespread. Participant 5 indicated attempts at training in little snippets, but she specifically utilized training of Screencastify, which is a Google Extension she still utilizes in her current position. Nearpod is a commonly used tool, but Participant 7 described her experience with training for this tool as "just like a district training where they had someone come in and they were showing us how to use Nearpod. And that was just kind of like a one time, you know, maybe an hour and a half training." While she still utilized this tool in her instruction at the time of the study, the training she received did not expand to teach them how to integrate the tool effectively.

Although half of the participants randomly recalled receiving training for specific tools, the other half of the participants reported the only training they received was self-sought or not at all. When asked what formal training was provided before becoming a college professor, Participant 8 simply said, "I think it was all self-taught, honestly," and Participant 9 reiterated this with her own training being described as, "Not a lot. If I did, I sought it out on my own. So when I go to conferences, I will seek out sessions that have to do with EdTech." Of this half of participants reporting self-sought training, two participants received Educational Technology degrees.

Decisions Guiding Technology Use

Decisions for deciding what technology to use, and when, should be based on pedagogical guidelines, not on the popularity of the technology. When asked how technology was chosen for specific tasks, Participant 7 simply said, "at the end of the day, those learning outcomes in the syllabus are what I'm tied to. And so whatever technology I use, it needs to enhance those." She continued by explaining that:

I guess it's just whatever the outcome of the lesson or what the learning target is for the lesson. You know, and what's the goal of the technology? Is it for engagement? Is it for depth of understanding? What, what's the outcome I'm looking for? (Participant 7)

Similarly, Participant 3 indicated the importance of "looking at curriculum first, and then saying, how can using this device or this app or whatever, support my curriculum?" She emphasized the fact that technology integration "has to be a combination. It has to be a tool, not the curriculum," as the technology should enhance the outcome, for it cannot be the outcome alone. Participant 9 responded in a manner, like Participant 8, stating:

If I can see where it fits a need. And it will make something more efficient, more effective, more productive, then I'll try it. Usually, I try it first. And then if it looks like this is a good idea, then I have my students do it.

Participant 9 mentioned that students' supervising teachers in their field experience may comment about how fancy a tool is that they see the student teacher use, and she makes sure to emphasize with her student that, "It isn't used because it's fancy. We use it because it's effective." This attention to purpose sets a foundation for effective technology integration in the future.

In addition to emphasizing the use of specific tools to meet a specific goal, Participant 9 mentions the importance of using technology tools to stay current, for the current reality is that students are technology natives, and they have never known life without it, so regardless of how educators feel about technology, it is an element of the natural way students learn, and that should be capitalized on instead of being degraded. With this idea, Participant 2 expressed that technology is not always needed for every situation, but sometimes her students simply do not recognize how technology can be used to enhance the intended learning outcome, so she uses those situations with her student teachers as teachable moments to explain to them and "help them see how they could have used technology when they thought they couldn't." These situations are significant to teaching preservice teachers how to integrate technology in real-world situations, increasing their self-efficacy in relation to technology integration, as weaknesses are observed, instead of allowing those weaknesses to follow them into the classroom, damaging their technology integration self-efficacy.

Expectations and Requirements for Technology Use

In the process of integrating technology, students and teachers have separate expectations and requirements for the integration to be effective. Overall, it is the expectation of the teacher to integrate technology into their instruction and to require students to demonstrate their own use of the technology, and it is the expectation of the students to then apply that technology into their own learning, and they are required to integrate it into their own instruction. This study revealed gaps in these expectations and requirements for both teachers and students, as they are vague or non-existent for both parties.

For Teachers - Syllabi Evaluation Data. Beginning the Spring semester of 2022, university faculty were required to include the International Society for Technology in Education (ISTE) standards on their course syllabi to show how technology was being integrated into their instruction. With the inclusion of these standards, Participant 8 indicated a crosswalk between the ISTE standards and course standards would be completed to evaluate the effectiveness of technology integration. However, Participant 9 mentioned that even though it was a requirement to indicate ISTE standards in course syllabi for the Spring 2022 semester, many faculty would not have anything to report, and as the figure below shows, 60% of the participants submitted course syllabi without ISTE standards listed, while the other 40% of participants indicated at least one or more ISTE standards were addressed throughout their courses, with only one standard not being addressed under any of the participants' course syllabi.

Of the ISTE standards for Educators, all but one standard was addressed by at least one faculty member's course syllabi, but 60% of the participants submitted course syllabi that did not indicate any ISTE standards being addressed. The standard not addressed is labeled "Citizen," specifically addressing that "teachers inspire students to positively contribute and responsibly participate in the digital world (The ISTE Standards, 2019, p. 5). Repeatedly addressed by 40% of the participants' course syllabi was ISTE standard (2019) 2.5, labeled "Designer," defined as when "Teachers design authentic, learner-driven activities and environments that recognize and accommodate learner variability" (p. 6). Specifically, this standard addresses the use of technology to create learning experiences and enhance the learning environment of the students. Standard 2.1, or "Learner," was next represented by 30% of the participants' course syllabi, focusing on the idea that "teachers continually improve their practice by learning from and with others and exploring proven and promising practices that leverage technology to improve student learning" (The ISTE Standards, 2019, p. 5). This standard specifically addresses an educator's professional learning goals and continued education to maintain relevant instructional methods, which is key to an ever-evolving factor of education, such as technology.

Instructionally, the expectations of teachers are evolving, and it is a requirement for the teachers to evolve with those expectations. Participant 5 expressed the importance of students leaving the program with a solid self-efficacy of technology integration, so as educators, they will be able to provide their students with the newest and greatest tools, emphasizing the fact that it is the job of the university faculty to figure out how to ensure this happens. Higher education is beyond simply the need for professors to use technology, adding the need for the faculty to require the students to use it (Participant 5), for the significant element in preparing preservice teachers to become educators is to "get them to be open and willing to learn and continue learning because it's probably going to change" (Participant 7). Because technology is a moving target, "Students no longer need to watch technology, they need to do technology" (Participant 5). Educators need to address the foundations of technology and "hope that they're going to be able to adapt to whatever comes in" (Participant 10), for training educators to integrate technology is a universal skill, not requiring skills to simply use a solitary tool, but solidifying that self-efficacy with technology integration to enhance the educator's use of all technology tools.

For Students. The ability to integrate technology into instruction is a key element to a successful teaching experience. Participant 5 expressed the significance of preservice teachers "doing" technology instead of "watching" technology, but the expectations and requirements throughout the education department are inconsistent. The university is in the process of solidifying a technology element across the department for the preservice teacher program, debating on integration and/or standalone courses (Participant 5), but now, the requirements for students and technology use are minimal, with course syllabi simply outlining the requirements of Blackboard LMS usage. Consistently, students are required to have a computer, access to the internet, and access to Blackboard (Participant 1; Participant 2; Participant 3; Participant 4; Participant 5; Participant 6; Participant 7; Participant 8; Participant 9; Participant 10).

Beyond these expectations, in the student teaching practicum, there is an element asking students to explain how technology was used for the lesson they taught (Participant 9; Participant 10). Otherwise, the requirements and expectations of technology use are dependent on the content program the student is in and the professors the student has for class. The participants in the secondary level courses (Participant 1; Participant 2; Participant 3; Participant 4; Participant 6; Participant 8; Participant 9; Participant 10) expressed, preservice teachers were not consistently, adequately prepared with the tools they need to successfully integrate technology, for the secondary certification level is primarily focused on content versus pedagogy. The faculty at the elementary level (Participant 5; Participant 7), however, indicated a much higher level of self-efficacy with technology integration for their students because of the consistent technology integration requirements of the elementary education programs.

Obstacles for Technology Integration

Obstacles to the integration of technology are not simple or clear-cut, for they range across multiple factors related to the education process. Approaching these obstacles from a backward design approach (Ryan, 2017), the end goal becomes the beginning, so the starting point is looking at what schools require of new teachers in relation to technology integration. This alone is an obstacle, for every district is different, and there is such a "wide variety from school district to school district, what do you use?" (Participant 10). Participant 8 said it best, expressing, "there's not one consistent technology piece that's throughout education," so how do universities decide what is important enough to integrate into instruction?

From there, however, the students or preservice teachers are the next obstacle, for the question that needs to be answered is "how open are our students to new technology?" (Participant 7). In the university classroom, "it depends on the knowledge of the instructor they have" (Participant 1) as to what exposure students will receive in relation to technology integration, and because of the training available, pedagogical deficiencies, and other external obstacles, Participant 4 exclaimed, "I think I've just become complacent at the university because I know nothing new is ever going to happen, and so I'm kind of limited to whatever I can find on the web." This frustration due to lack of opportunities provided to university faculty, diminishes the skills they can provide their preservice teachers, resulting in these students not being as open to new technology as they need to be to be successful educators in the 21st century classroom.

Training

The obstacles of training in relation to technology use are two-fold, focusing on availability and delivery. Every participant indicated that the university did not provide them any mandatory or targeted technology training. Participant 7 expressed that "if you're wanting to do something yourself, you kind of learn it yourself," as Participant 8 echoed by saying her technology training "was all self-taught, honestly." Participant 8 did mention that the university has a technology center that offers training sessions, but "it's kind of like on your own time, hey, if you want to come do this." Blackboard is the Learning Management System, and Participant 4 specifically expressed, "when I came to the university and I had to, like learn Blackboard, I had to teach myself because they don't actually teach it to you." As the primary delivery of materials for the university, training for use should be mandatory for new faculty, and as the LMS is updated with new tools, continuous training should also be mandatory, for as Participant 1 stated, "I don't use some of the tools that are available, mainly probably because of ignorance not knowing what they would offer." This self-expressed ignorance of the LMS tools is damaging to the self-efficacy of an educator in relation to technology integration, and it is a gap that could easily be closed.

The delivery method was also an area of concern for the trainings that were offered by the university, including follow-through. Participant 4 expressed frustration, for she attended "a training to use virtual classroom goggles, but then they were never purchased." She spent the time to attend the training for technology that she ultimately could not access for her students. Participant 6 was specifically frustrated with the training sessions she had attended, for "somebody was showing us some things, but it's so fast, so it wasn't enough for me. Like I need somebody to really let me touch, let me do, in order to really get control and figure things out." One training specifically, she felt overwhelmed with the training, for the participants were given 20 step instructions on how to complete the task, and after struggling through all of those steps for the class, she got frustrated and never tried the task again. The method of delivery frustrated her so much that she gave up on attending the trainings altogether.

Pedagogy

As Participant 3 said, "core pedagogy isn't going to change drastically," but as Participant 9 said, "higher education is at a disadvantage, for a lot of people who teach in higher ed are like content experts, but they've taken like one college teaching class, so they're not experts in pedagogy." The "how" of teaching is what is lacking in technology integration, for teachers may use the technology or ask their students to use the technology, but they need to know how to teach their students to use the technology as well, as Participant 2 says, "if we're going to expect our [preservice] teachers to do it, we need to know how to do it as well." Without the skills, the integration of technology cannot be effective, for "you can't teach what you don't know, right...you have to be able to teach someone else how to teach it" (Participant 9). Participant 10 identified this gap in technology integration saying that professors have a "personal affinity for or fear of technology," and this personal affinity is what sets the level of their self-efficacy with technology integration, affecting the level of which their students are then prepared to integrate technology in their own instruction.

In the beginning of technology integration, the focus was on the device and how to use the device, but technology use must be a combination; technology must be a tool, not the curriculum (Participant 3). Even exposing students to various technologies, the question that should be addressed by university faculty is how to get them "to be open and willing to learn and continue learning because it's probably going to change" (Participant 7). Because of this constant evolution of technology, students "are going to have to learn to be technology researchers" (Participant 5), and university faculty need the pedagogy to train them to be these researchers.

External Factors

Not every factor inhibiting the integration of technology can be addressed by university faculty, such as time, money and access to the internet, devices, and programs. Time and money are common obstacles, but for educators, they are universal. Participant 8, when discussing the downfalls of using technology, expressed that there is just not enough time to experiment with new technology, even though more curation in life, with technology, is always a need, new tools are found and lost before the time for experimentation is available.

Participant 3 reiterated this issue by expressing the biggest obstacles were:

Time and money. It takes time to make sure something is going to work for your class, it takes time to, maybe not show your students how to use it, because they can catch on rather quickly, but to show them your expectations with the tool that does take time. It takes more time to be creative with a tool, than complete a worksheet, so for some, that's, that's a turn off, they're like, Okay, my curriculum is huge.

In this sense, time can be such an impactful obstacle that teachers simply avoid trying to use new tools or integrate technology, even if it might be something that clearly enhances the learning outcomes. Related to time, many programs that could benefit preservice teachers take time for the university faculty to learn, just for them to realize that the programs are not available to their students in the manner needed for efficient training. Because preservice teachers are training to be educators, teacher educators need them to access to some programs from the teacher view, so the time invested by the university faculty is beneficial to the future time of the preservice teacher (Participant 5).

Money is another significant obstacle that faculty cannot control, beyond finding free tools or trial versions that may or may not adequately fill the needs of the learning outcomes. In many cases, money as an obstacle simply reveals itself as a simple "no, for technology requests because there's no money for it" (Participant 4). In other cases, however, lack of funding can be more detrimental, for it can pull programs and resources that are already in use. Participant 4 explained that the university provided iPads to students at one point, and she said, "I was using them with my students, and then again, money became tight, and we recalled them all in from the students, and we never passed them out again." When resources are integrated, time is put into the planning of using those resources, and when they are retracted, this retraction causes more time to be spent replanning the curriculum without the resources.

Access to internet, devices, and programs are also external obstacles that cannot be controlled by faculty. Participant 10 expressed appreciation for the government's plan to provide broadband internet, for without internet access, there is a clear case of the "haves and the have nots. If you've got it, now you got the opportunity to move forward, but if you don't have it, you're going to lag behind." More specifically, Participant 6 mentioned that:

You've got districts that don't have WiFi, that are getting online books that students can't access all the time at school. You've got kids that have to go drive to McDonald's to use the WiFi to do their homework. How are we going to talk about equity with this?

Participant 1 also mentioned the availability of internet connectivity, specifically in rural areas, where people may have to use the data on their phones for internet, stating, "I probably wouldn't volunteer to do something like this. Before we had our high speed. Because it's like, wow, I mean, it sucks. It sucks it up quick. really costly." On top of the expense of the cellular phone, the additional data may be too much of a cost for some people, bringing the issue of equity to question once again.

With the cost of internet access, students also need access to reliable devices, and cell phones are not efficient enough for academic work. Participant 4 stated that "I'll have at least 2 of my 24 students pull out a cell phone even after I sent them an email saying, bring your device, and your phone doesn't count." Some of this could be lack of attention and laziness on the part of the student, but Participant 7 supported this issue expressing, it "seems like at least a couple times a year, we'll have a student who doesn't have access to a laptop." Even though school districts are providing devices to their students, universities are not in the same position to offer this benefit, so devices are an expense that students must accommodate.

INTERPRETATION OF FINDINGS

The significant element of this study identified the gaps in expectations and self-efficacy related to technology integration and university educator faculty. Among the participants actively integrating technology into their instruction, data revealed consistent factors in the decision-making process, regarding which technologies to use for instructional use and student use, when to use them and why, while other participants were simply able to discuss technology they use, personally. For technology use to be integrated, the faculty must use it, expect the students to use it, and expect the students to apply it to enhance the learning goals, for teacher educators are "educating for the future when the future is rapidly changing" (Roumbains et al.,

2021, p. 1). Participant 3 indicated that the decisions revolving around technology use started with ways to use the new shiny devices, but now teachers must decide based on "what are we teaching and how could this support our instruction," for the technology being used should support the lessons and the learning goals. Participant 8 supported this idea indicating that the use of technology should be determined by the desired outcome of the lesson and learning target, focusing on whether the outcome of the technology use is engagement or depth of understanding. The ideas of these participants in regards to the integration of technology directly support Mishra and Koehler's (2006) TPaCK framework, which was designed with the purpose of integrating technology into teaching, involving a complex interaction between content, pedagogy, and technology.

In contrast, Participant 5 indicated that many university faculty will say that they use technology in their classes, which translates to mean their students are still watching technology, but they are not being required to apply technology use, which is a direct result of teacher educators not "having a digital competence for applying digital technology and teaching about digitalization in education" (Roumbains et al., 2021, p. 2). Participants 1, 6, and 10 all indicated multiple tools they use in their instruction, but they all indicated there were no expectations of their students to apply the technologies being used, further supporting the lack of knowledge of digitalization in education. Applying the TPaCK framework, university faculty would be able to address the questions of what teachers need to know to integrate technology versus simply using technology (Saubern et al., 2020). These faculty, however, possess a low self-efficacy in relation to technology integration which prevents them from understanding the significant benefits of educational technology for teaching and learning (Perkmen & Pamuk, 2011).

This lack of understanding about the depth of technology integration is the root of many internal obstacles, but the external obstacles were more of a focal point for the participants. Internally, Participant 3 indicated the issue was for faculty to know how to make the students use the technology, effectively, for as Participant 5 expressed, students "are going to have to learn to be technology researchers," for technology evolves, and whatever tools are taught today may not be the same tools available when the preservice teachers enter their own classrooms, so they will have to know how and where to find the tools they need to enhance their desired learning goals (Participant 7). Joo et al. (2018) expressed a direct correlation between the perceived usefulness of technology in instruction, provided by the teacher educator, and a preservice teacher's level of intention to use technology, and as Participant 5 emphasized, "we want our instructors to use it, and we're wanting them to make their students use it," because students need to be doing technology, not just watching technology.

Unfortunately, university faculty demonstrates a level of change fatigue, resulting in their reliance on their professional content knowledge, caused by concern for a lack of time, opportunities for professional development, or the idea that they can manage by getting help from their skilled colleagues, putting more responsibility on those colleagues (Roumbians et al., 2021). While colleagues are more than willing to help each other, formal professional development is necessary to ensure consistent training, for individuals can experience difficulties with staying current of the demands of the ever-changing world of technology in education (Martin, 2018), and technology integration cannot grow if there is a lack of experience and skill among university faculty in relation to the skills that are needed to effectively integrate technology as teacher educators (Graziano & Bryans-Bongey, 2018).

Primary external obstacles, among all participants, included time and money. Participant 3 specifically explained how the two external obstacles compound one another by mentioning that resources cost money, but to find resources that will be most effective to obtain the desired learning outcome takes time, and the process of finding the most effective tools is a process of trial and error, spending a great deal of time experimenting with and researching tools that ultimately may or may not be what is most effective for achieving the desired learning outcome. According to Haroon et al. (2020), innovation in teaching is not a focus in higher education, resulting in few professors dedicating their own time to learn new strategies, which results in frustration with the lack of time to play with and experiment with new tools to ensure they would be beneficial to the curriculum (Participant 8).

Further, teacher educators "perceive that the opportunities to develop new knowledge are few, since the organization provides vague guidelines and what they perceive as insufficient support and opportunities for skill development" (Roumbians et al., 2021, p. 9), which results in the personal development of further skills not being a priority due to time and support. As Participant 5 explains, there are so many cool tools available, but they require subscriptions, and even if there is a free version, it is limited, and preservice teachers need access to tools from the educator end, not just the student end, but for that access, licenses need to be purchased. But even once the money is spent on tools, Participant 4 expressed the stress of having resources pulled due to budget cuts, resulting in more time having to be spent re-designing the class without the resources, for when requests for continued or additional technology funds are submitted, they are met with a resounding, no. Belt and Lowenthal (2019) indicated that many programs are short-lived, for they focus on isolated activities instead of skill development and pedagogical change, so the direction of the training must be focused on the skill and pedagogical change for the programs to be successfully solidified and integrated into instruction.

Pedagogy and Faculty Self-Efficacy

In education, a solid pedagogy that infuses content with technology integration is necessary for faculty to have a high self-efficacy. Currently, however, not all teacher preparation programs address the skills, methods, and technologies required for integrating technology, so new teachers are entering the classroom with varying degrees of experience and skills (Graziano & Bryans-Bongey, 2018). Participant 9 expressed the frustration that in higher education, instructors are content experts, having taken possibly one college teaching class, so they are not experts in pedagogy, but they are responsible for solidifying the pedagogy of their preservice teachers. Participant 2 explained that the programs at the secondary certification level have approximately 120 credit hours of content they are required to take that the school cannot possibly require the students to take another class, and they have instructors that are not education people, so there is a disconnect of understanding what the students need to be successful teachers. To close this gap, "teachers can reflect and improve their practice if they understand their role as learners in their own teaching process," (Haroon et al., 2020), but embracing the integration of technology and the training needed to do it successfully is just part of that realization.

Many universities are re-designing their teacher preparation programs to make the transition from skill-focused technology courses to a more technology infused pedagogy (Martin, 2018). To strengthen this technology infused pedagogy, universities need to require targeted training of their faculty, for teacher training is about strengthening teacher self-efficacy and developing a solid pedagogy within the teacher (Renta-Davids, 2015). Participant 3 expressed that core pedagogy is not going to change drastically, but integration of technology needs to emphasize the practice of looking at curriculum first, then deciding how and what technology can support the curriculum. Education is beyond simply teaching individuals how to use a specific tool, and it has evolved to making calculated decisions regarding when and why to use technology to enhance the learning goals, for when technology integration is founded on theory, its inclusion in curriculum can lead to an improvement in teaching and learning (Kimmons & Hall, 2017).

Obstacles to Technology Integration

Even with a solid core pedagogy and self-efficacy in relation to technology integration, barriers can create obstacles for successful integration. First order barriers, which are external, can include elements such as equipment, time, training, and support (Bahcivan et al., 2019). Implementation of curriculum integrating technology takes planning and training, which requires time, and as Participant 8 indicated, any technology training provided by the university is available on the personal time of the instructor, so they need to be willing to allocate that time to personal development, even though it is not required by the university. Even for herself, she mentioned that she enjoys technology and integrating it into her instruction, but she cannot always find the time to experiment with ways new tools could benefit the learning goals, so the tools get pushed aside and forgotten (Participant 8). According to a study by Coomber (2018), professional development enables teacher educators to develop and contribute to their universities, but "the perceived barriers to engage in professional development were identified as lack of time, opportunities and workload pressures" (p. 67). Time is very much a factor in relation to university curriculum, and teacher preparation programs are full of courses that are required, so integrating digital skills and literacy is clearly a challenge (Zipke, 2018). Participant 3 also indicted money as an obstacle, for when instructors do want to integrate a tool beneficial to their learning goals, the request is many times rejected due to lack of funds, so even more time was lost finding and learning the new tool, in addition to attempting to get approval for funds.

In addition to first order barriers, second order barriers are internal, and they can include elements such as teachers' self-efficacy, educational beliefs, and their belief in the value of technology in learning (Bahcivan et al., 2019). At the university level, these second order barriers are demonstrated in the method of which technology integration is delivered, whether it be in the form of a stand-alone course or an infusion across disciplines. Foulger et al. (2019) reported that 80% of technology integration instruction in teacher preparation programs in the United States was done in stand-alone courses. At the same time, national guidelines for teacher preparation programs emphasize the importance of technology integration in instruction as an infusion versus a stand-alone, isolated experience (Foulger et al., 2019). The university in the study does not have any consistent technology requirements; however, a technology integration course is offered at the graduate level as an elective, and a small handful of undergraduate students elect to take the course (Participant 3).

Participants 3, 5, and 8 indicated that with the CAEP process, changes are in progress to ensure a consistent infusion of technology throughout the various programs in the education department. Sun et al. (2017) outlines three components that are important for teacher preparation of technology integration:
1. Skills based courses
2. Integration of technology into methods courses
3. Technology rich field experiences (p. 598)

With the steps being taken by the university to qualify for accreditation, these three components are being evaluated within their teacher preparation program. Participant 4 specifically indicated that as a supervisor of student teachers, she intentionally places her teachers in schools with a solid technology integration pedagogy, hoping "they're picking up some of the tricks of the trade out there in real time in real life." Even though preservice teachers may not get the exposure to technology they need throughout their program, the right field experience placement can at least give them some real-world experience to make them aware of what they will need to be successful in their own classroom.

Technology Integration Training

Training faculty to integrate technology must be founded on theory to improve teaching and learning (Kimmons & Hall, 2017). When the only training university faculty receives in relation to technology integration is training they seek out on their own, the self-efficacy of university faculty with technology use is inconsistent from one faculty member to another, and "new academics entering higher education are especially vulnerable if teaching in a post-colonial classroom is not foregrounded as an explicit part of their professional induction," (Behari-Leak, 2017, p. 485), which is unfortunately the case for many teacher educators. With an integrated approach to technology use, however, faculty should be trained that technology experiences should avoid focusing on use as production tools and focus more on practice of implementation in a classroom setting (Hicks & Bose, 2019). Participant 9 expressed, "you can't teach what you don't know, right? It's not just that, like, you have to be able to teach someone else how to teach it," and if the instructor is unfamiliar with how to implement the technology in the classroom setting, they do not have the tools to teach preservice teachers how to do the same. Providing university faculty with the foundation for a solid technology integration self-efficacy could be a factor for varied integration by the preservice teacher in their own instruction (Perkmen & Pamuk, 2011).

RECOMMENDATIONS

The aim of this qualitative case study was to examine the perception of university teacher educators regarding their decisions and skills related to technology integration. Based on the interview responses and evaluation of the course syllabi of participants, the study identified a gap in perceptions, when "the teacher's conceptual understanding and cognition of the concept is crucial to the student's-learning" (Haroon et al., 2020, p. 34), indicating that the level of self-efficacy with teacher educators, in relation to technology integration, is inconsistent across the department, meaning preservice teachers are not receiving consistent experiences preparing them for the classrooms of the 21st century. The idea of the nature of learning can be used as a base for closing the gap in educator self-efficacy in relation to technology integration, through required, targeted professional development, for "the nature of learning is defined as a process of acquisition of new behavior, or strengthening or weakening of old behavior as a result of experience with a view of modifying the behavior" (Haroon et al., 2020, p. 35).

Education and technology are constantly evolving, and in many cases, they overlap, with the evolution of technology impacting education. Because of this, the definition of education has evolved to require "an act of transmission of knowledge, usually through an active teaching and learning process" (Haroon et al., 2020, p. 35), and higher education needs to evolve with this definition. Just as not all content requires the same knowledge, every technology is not beneficial for the learning goals of all content. Because of the different needs for varied contents, "teachers should be able to request specific courses or modules on the topics that they are most interested in," (Haroon et al., 2020, p. 36) or with specific tools that would benefit their specific learning goals. According to the study done by Coomber (2018), the majority of the respondents felt motivated to engage in opportunities that supported their current role, being supportive of their curriculum and beneficial to the enhancement of their desired learning outcomes.

In the future, various studies regarding professional development of university teacher educators would be appropriate to enhance the preservice teacher preparation process. Amhag et al. (2019) expressed the importance of professional development to the improvement of digital competence in teacher educators, encouraging them to adopt technology in their instruction. To do this effectively, however, support opportunities must be relevant to the content the teacher educator is teaching, which means specific tools may only be relevant for certain content areas, and other areas may need different tools completely. These differences may require a purchasing of subscription or someone working with software companies to provide short-term teacher view options for different technologies that are being used to train preservice teachers, so they can be exposed to technologies as instructors, as they will be using it in their own classrooms. Jonker et al. (2018) emphasized the need for individualized professional development, for successful development is not based on a "cookie cutter" or "one size fits all" model.

CONCLUSION

This qualitative case study identified the gaps in skill and self-efficacy of university educator faculty in relation to technology integration in the instruction of preservice teachers. While faculty are willing to participate in professional development, the university does not require it of their faculty, so many are "not prepared to invest time and effort in learning something new," (Roumbains, 2021, p. 11) even though they are responsible for "educating for the future when the future is rapidly changing" (Roumbains, 2021, p. 1). Faculty reported that diverse opportunities for development are insufficient, and the demands of their current responsibilities do not encourage dedicating the time and energy to acquiring new skills (Roumbains, 2021). For professional development to be effective, faculty must be able to make a direct connection to their own content, which should be a priority, for TPaCK emphasized the significance of technology tools having a purpose in the enhancement of the desired learning outcomes. Because of the need for technology to support desired learning outcomes, "Teachers should be able to request specific courses or modules on the topics that they are most interested in" (Haroon et al., 2020, p. 36). With personalized technology integration training, university educator faculty will develop a higher self-efficacy in relation to technology integration, thus more successfully preparing preservice teachers for the technological demands of the 21st century classroom.

REFERENCES

Amhag, L., Hellström, L., & Stigmar, M. (2019). Teacher educators' use of digital tools and needs for digital competence in higher education. *Journal of Digital Learning in Teacher Education*, 35(4), 203–220. 10.1080/21532974.2019.1646169

Bahcivan, E., Gurer, M. D., Yavuzalp, N., & Akayoglu, S. (2019). Investigating the relations among pre-service teachers' teaching/learning beliefs and educational technology integration competencies: A structural equation modeling study. *Journal of Science Education and Technology*, 28(5), 579–588. 10.1007/s10956-019-09788-6

Behari-Leak, K. (2017). New academics, new higher education contexts: A critical perspective on professional development. *Teaching in Higher Education*, 22(5), 485–500. 10.1080/13562517.2016.1273215

Belt, E., & Lowenthal, P. (2020). Developing faculty to teach with technology: Themes from the literature. *TechTrends*, 64(2), 248–259. 10.1007/s11528-019-00447-6

Carmi, T., & Tamir, E. (2020). Three professional ideals: Where should teacher preparation go next? *European Journal of Teacher Education*, 1–20. 10.1080/02619768.2020.1805732

Chai, C. S., & Koh, J. H. L. (2017). Changing teachers' TPaCK and design beliefs through the scaffolded TPaCK lesson design model (STLDM). *Learning (Abingdon (England))*, 3(2), 114–129. 10.1080/23735082.2017.1360506

Cleland, J. A. (2017, June). *The qualitative orientation in medical education research*. NCBI. https://www.ncbi.nlm.nih.gov/pmc/articles/PMC5465434/#:~:text=Conclusion,

Coomber, R. (2019). How do professional service staff perceive and engage with professional development programmes within higher education institutions? *Perspectives (Association of University Administrators* (U.K.)), 23(2-3), 61–69. 10.1080/13603108.2018.1543216

Ebersole, L. (2019). Preservice teacher experience with technology integration: How the preservice teacher's efficacy in technology integration is impacted by the context of the preservice teacher education program. *International Dialogues on Education*, 6(2). 10.53308/ide.v6i2.64

Feuer, M. J., Floden, R. E., Chudowsky, N., & Ahn, J. (2013). *Evaluation of teacher preparation programs: Purposes, methods, and policy options*. National Academy of Education.

Foulger, T. S., Wetzel, K., & Buss, R. R. (2019). Moving toward a technology infusion approach: Considerations for teacher preparation programs. *Journal of Digital Learning in Teacher Education*, 35(2), 79–91. 10.1080/21532974.2019.1568325

Gammelgaard, B. (2017). Editorial: The qualitative case study. *International Journal of Logistics Management*, 28(4), 910–913. 10.1108/IJLM-09-2017-0231

Graziano, K. J., & Bryans-Bongey, S. (2018). Surveying the national landscape of online teacher training in k-12 teacher preparation programs. *Journal of Digital Learning in Teacher Education*, 34(4), 259–277. 10.1080/21532974.2018.1498040

Hager, K. D. (2020). Integrating technology to improve teacher preparation. *College Teaching*, 68(2), 71–78. 10.1080/87567555.2020.1723475

Haroon, J., Jumani, N. B., & Arouj, K. (2020). Learning to teach in higher education for sustainable professional development. [Online]. *Review of Economics and Development Studies*, 6(1), 33–41. 10.47067/reads.v6i1.182

Hicks, S., & Bose, D. (2019). Designing teacher preparation courses: Integrating mobile technology, program standards, and course outcomes. *TechTrends*, 63(6), 734–740. 10.1007/s11528-019-00416-z

ISTE. (2019). *ISTE Standards*. ISTE. https://www.iste.org/standards

Jonker, H., März, V., & Voogt, J. (2018). Teacher educators' professional identity under construction: The transition from teaching face-to-face to a blended curriculum. *Teaching and Teacher Education, 71*(Complete), 120–133. 10.1016/j.tate.2017.12.016

Joo, Y. J., Park, S., & Lim, E. (2018). Factors influencing preservice teachers' intention to use technology: TPACK, teacher self-efficacy, and technology acceptance model. *Journal of Educational Technology & Society*, 21(3), 48–59.

Kalonde, G., & Mousa, R. (2016). Technology familiarization to preservice teachers: Factors that influence teacher educators' technology decisions. *Journal of Educational Technology Systems*, 45(2), 236–255. 10.1177/0047239515616965

Kimmons, R., & Hall, C. (2018). How useful are our models? Pre-service and practicing teacher evaluations of technology integration models. *TechTrends*, 62(1), 29–36. 10.1007/s11528-017-0227-8

Kopcha, T. J., Rieber, L. P., & Walker, B. B. (2016). Understanding university faculty perceptions about innovation in teaching and technology. *British Journal of Educational Technology*, 47(5), 945–957. 10.1111/bjet.12361

Mariscal, L. L., Albarracin, M. R., Mobo, F. D., & Cutillas, A. L. (2023). Pedagogical competence towards technology driven instruction on basic education. *International Journal of Multidisciplinary: Applied Business and Education Research.*, 4(5), 1567–1580. 10.11594/ijmaber.04.05.18

Martin, B. (2018). Faculty technology beliefs and practices in teacher preparation through a TPACK lens. *Education and Information Technologies*, 23(5), 1775–1788. 10.1007/s10639-017-9680-4

Mishra, P., & Koehler, M. J. (2006). Technological pedagogical content knowledge: A framework for teacher knowledge. *Teachers College Record*, 108(6), 1017–1054. 10.1111/j.1467-9620.2006.00684.x

Normore, A. H., & Issa Lahera, A. (2019). The evolution of educational leadership preparation programmes. *Journal of Educational Administration and History*, 51(1), 27–42. 10.1080/00220620.2018.1513914

Perkmen, S., & Pamuk, S. (2011). Social cognitive predictors of pre-service teachers' technology integration performance. *Asia Pacific Education Review*, 12(1), 45–58. 10.1007/s12564-010-9109-x

Renta-Davids, A.-I., Jiménez-González, J.-M., Fandos-Garrido, M., & González-Soto, Á.-P. (2016). Organizational and training factors affecting academic teacher training outcomes. *Teaching in Higher Education*, 21(2), 219–231. 10.1080/13562517.2015.1136276

Rust, F. O. (2019). Redesign in teacher education: The roles of teacher educators. *European Journal of Teacher Education*, 42(4), 523–533. 10.1080/02619768.2019.1628215

Saubern, R., Henderson, M., Heinrich, E., & Redmond, P. (2020). TPaCK – time to reboot? *Australasian Journal of Educational Technology*, 36(3), 1–9. 10.14742/ajet.6378

Sulecio de Alvarez, M., & Dickson-Deane, C. (2018). Avoiding educational technology pitfalls for inclusion and equity. *TechTrends*, 62(4), 345–353. 10.1007/s11528-018-0270-0

Sun, Y., Strobel, J., & Newby, T. J. (2017). The impact of student teaching experience on pre-service teachers' readiness for technology integration: A mixed methods study with growth curve modeling. *Educational Technology Research and Development*, 65(3), 597–629. 10.1007/s11423-016-9486-x

Viberg, R. (2021). The teacher educator's perceptions of professional agency - a paradox of enabling and hindering digital professional development in higher education. *Education Inquiry*, 1–18. 10.1080/20004508.2021.1984075 von Glasersfeld, E. (2001). Radical constructivism and teaching. *Prospects*, 31(2), 161–173. 10.1007/BF03220058

Zipke, M. (2018). Preparing teachers to teach with technology: Examining the effectiveness of a course in educational technology. *New Educator*, 14(4), 342–362. 10.1080/1547688X.2017.1401191

Chapter 15
Exploring Factors Contributing to a Failure Rate in Bachelor of Nursing Science Programme in Namibia

Daniel Opotamutale Ashipala
 https://orcid.org/0000-0002-8913-056X
University of Namibia, Namibia

David N. Sakeus
University of Namibia, Namibia

ABSTRACT

Academic failure among tertiary students remains a worldwide phenomenon, yet the extent of these failures and their precipitating factors are not well understood. In Namibia, factors that contribute to the failure rate in the Bachelor of Nursing Science degree are not extensively researched. The objectives of this chapter are thus to assess and describe the factors that contribute to the failure rate in the Bachelor of Nursing Science degree at a Namibian university. This chapter's findings revealed that the poor academic performance of students in the Bachelor of Nursing degree is influenced by personal factors, such as a lack of interest and absenteeism, as well as academic factors, such as inadequate curriculum content, ineffective teaching methods, the rarity of some procedures, and inappropriate attitudes amongst some registered nurses.

DOI: 10.4018/979-8-3693-3559-8.ch015

INTRODUCTION

Academic failure among tertiary students remains a worldwide phenomenon Ajjawi, Dracup, Zacharias, Bennett, & Boud, (2020), which leads to a low graduate throughput, yet the extent of these failures and their precipitating factors are not well understood. Academic failure is considered to have occurred when a student's performance falls below an expected level, which could take place due to a number of factors (Chavan et al., 2019). A student who fails to achieve his or her potential, or does not do as well as expected, is described as an "underachiever" (Dante et al., 2016). In general, this type of failure is known as a lack of success in education, which leads to monetary and social losses (Najimi et al., 2022). Understanding the factors behind academic failures is thus imperative.

According to Ajjawi et al. (2020), academic failure has a negative impact on the lives of university students. If a student fails, they become stressed and demotivated, which has a negative impact on their mental health, self-esteem, motivation, and perseverance. High failure rates typically also result in unacceptable levels of attrition, reduced graduate throughputs, and increased costs of education (Olebara & Maureen, 2018; Sneyers & De Witte, 2017). Additionally, it reduces admission opportunities for tertiary students who are seeking higher degrees, which is one reason why students' academic performance has long been a topic of interest for educators and researchers (Jayanthi et al., 2014; Telio et al., 2015). Many researchers have identified some contributors to failure rate such community safety, family and school factors, such as a lack of child support, as variables that contribute to students' failures (Mirza & Arif, 2018). Mhlongo and Masango (2020) examined which factors contribute to the poor performance of student nurses in anatomy and physiology, and discovered that poor teaching strategies, a lack of remedial teaching, insufficient time to study before examinations, and language barriers played important roles in these failures. Additionally, Ahmady et al.'s (2019) study on factors related to academic failure in preclinical medical education found that a poor educational environment, inadequate teaching methods, a lack of continuous assessment, and insufficient consideration of personal factors had a great impact on failure rates.

Nursing education, like many other areas of the health profession, continues to evolve and develop in order to best serve and support the clinical and professional roles of students. The Bachelor of Nursing Science programme in Namibia consists of three major modules, general nursing science, community, and midwifery. Additional elective modules, such as mental health science and the professional ethos of nursing, are only taught in the final year.

The key aim of nursing programmes is to train competent and confident nurses who have the necessary knowledge, attitude and skills to maintain and promote community health (Bahramnezhad et al., 2019; Ng, 2014). Cheng et al. (2010)

similarly highlighted that the purpose of nursing education is to develop critical thinking, creative thinking, reflective learning, professional skills, time management skills, self-esteem and effective communication abilities amongst would-be nurses. Despite this, many nursing graduates do not have advanced skills in communication, creativity, critical and analytical thinking, problem solving, and decision making, therefore they need to be empowered to develop critical thinking in order to meet the needs of society (Thabet et al., 2017).

In Namibia, a Bachelor of Nursing Science is offered at four campuses: The Main campus, Oshakati campus, Rundu campus and the Southern campus. They all offer Bachelor of Nursing Science (Clinical) Honour as a four-year programme in a full-time mode. It is anticipated that students graduating from this programme will be skilled, knowledgeable and compassionate nurses, however there is still a worryingly high failure rate among nursing students. This phenomenon motivated the researcher to explore and describe which factors are contributing to the failure rate in the Bachelor of Nursing Science degree at Namibian universities, as well as to make recommendations on how to tackle it. These findings may lead to the establishment of strategies to mitigate future failures.

In Namibia's four-year nursing degree programme, which is offered full-time, the expectation is that by the completion of the course, students should have learned good nursing, intervention and problem-solving skills. A failure of more than 10 students is considered unacceptable. The failure rate for this degree fluctuated between 1% and 20% from 2020 to 2022, with failing students having to repeat the relevant module the following year. This is additionally problematic as Namibia's Student Financial Assistance Fund (NSFAF) will not pay for a failed module. Due to financial instability, this leads some students to drop out of school or put their studies on hold while they look for job, in the hope that they will continue later when they have money to pay for the module. These failures come in spite of modern lecture halls and competent lecturing staff at the University of Namibia, as well as students being given access to clinical practice throughout their training to acquire the relevant nursing skills. When the performance of students is below the expected level, lecturers become concerned, in part because some classes become overcrowded Pinehas, Mulenga, & Amadhila, (2017).

RESEARCH METHODS

Research Design

The study used a qualitative approach, which incorporated explorative, descriptive and contextual designs. According to Maree and Maree (2020), a qualitative research design is naturalistic, i.e., it focuses on natural settings where interactions occur. It aims to provide deep insight into, and an understanding of, the problem faced by the researcher. This approach was thus utilised in order to gain an in-depth understanding of the factors that contribute to the high failure rate of students in the Bachelor of Nursing Science degree in Namibia.

Study Setting

This study was conducted at Namibian university that offers a four-year Bachelor of Nursing Science (Clinical) (Honours) degree. The campus is situated in the north-east of Namibia and is home to over 450 nursing students. This degree is offered full time; students spend two weeks in class for theory and two weeks in a clinical setting for practical sessions per month, which allows them to support the theory with practice (Shatimwene, Ashipala & Kamenye, 2020). The curriculum is approved by professional accreditation bodies, such as the Nursing Council of Namibia, the Namibia Qualification Authority, and the National Council of Higher Education. Lecturers who teach on this programme are required to have a Master's or a Doctorate degree. Clinical instructors and preceptors accompany students during clinics for skills transfer and to socialise students into the profession. Theory and practice are assessed on a ratio of 50:50.

Population and Sampling

This study was conducted at Namibian university that offers a four-year Bachelor of Nursing Science (Clinical) (Honours) degree. The researcher used convenience sampling, as this ensured that the participants possessed the required characteristics to provide information to answer the research question (Maree, 2016). Convenience sampling also offers an equal chance to all available participants who meet the criteria to participate in a study. The participants were selected using the following inclusion criteria: 1) a second, third- or fourth-year nursing student at Namibian universities where a Bachelor of Nursing Science is offered; 2) failed a module in the Bachelor of Nursing Science programme; 3) willing to participate in the study; and 4) available at the time of data collection. The researcher planned to interview

15 participants, however data saturation was only reached at 17 participants. This was the point at which no new information was being gathered.

Data Collection Methods

In this study, data were collected using a semi-structured interview guide, which was based on the aim of the study and the research question. A pilot study was conducted on three nursing students; these results were not included in the main study as the pilot was conducted to identify errors that could bring about adjusting the data collection tool. No changes were made to the interview guide. After initial contact with the participants, their informed consent was obtained to tape record the interviews. The date, time and place of the interviews were duly confirmed, with the interview sessions lasting for approximately 45 to 50 min. During the interviews, the researcher took field notes and used follow-up questions to probe for more detailed explanations. Prior to data analysis, the field notes were combined with the transcribed interviews to provide additional insights.

Data Analysis

In this study, thematic analysis was used to analyse the data. According to Castleberry and Nolen (2018), thematic analysis is deemed to be the most reliable method used in qualitative research, as it is fairly systematic and allows the researcher to organise the information into themes and sub-themes. Thematic analysis is thus widely used in qualitative research (Kiger & Varpio, 2020).

Braun and Clarke's (2019) six phases of thematic analysis were used: Step 1: Familiarisation – the researcher transcribed the audio files into text so that he could read and understand the data, and then categorise the analysed data appropriately; Step 2: Initial Coding – the researcher highlighted the main features and make notes; Step 3: Generating Themes – the researcher identified various patterns and grouped them into different themes; Step 4: Reviewing Themes – the researcher reviewed the accuracy of the themes to compare them with the data to check for any missing information; Step 5: Naming and Defining Themes – the researcher made a list of themes and gave them names to define them; Step 6: Finally the report is generated.

Ensuring Trustworthiness

The trustworthiness of the study was ensured by using the criteria of Lincoln and Guba (1985), namely transferability, credibility and dependability. Transferability in this study was achieved through a complete description of the research design and methodology used, as well as through the selection of participants. The data collected were described as accurately as possible; full or thick descriptions of the experiences of the participants can be made available upon enquiry.

Credibility was achieved through prolonged engagement with, and persistent observation of, the participants. The researcher remained in the field for six weeks throughout the interview process in order to gain an in-depth understanding of the phenomenon under study. A tape recorder was used during the interviews, with those recordings being transcribed. The recordings and transcripts were compared to confirm that they were from the same participants.

Dependability was achieved through the use of audio recordings; transcripts can be made available upon enquiry. The data collected were also supported by related literature and the data collection methods are comprehensively described. In order to confirm the data, a consensus meeting with an independent coder, who was experienced in qualitative research and held a Masters in Nursing Education, was utilised.

Ethical Considerations

Approval for this study was granted by the University of Namibia's School of Nursing Research Ethics and Review Committee (SoNREC) (reference no. SoNPH 25/2023) and the MoHSS Research Committee (reference no. 22/3/1/2). Informed consent was sought from the participants, who signed a consent form. Participation was voluntary, and the interviewees were free to withdraw at any time, although this was not encouraged. The participants were also assured of their anonymity, with pseudonyms being used on the research tools instead of names. Confidentiality was also assured. The data were stored safely and will be disposed of according to the university's policies.

RESULTS

Socio-Demographic Description of Study Participants

A total of 17 participants were interviewed, who were either a second, third or fourth-year nursing student. Of the 17 respondents, six were male while 11 were female, with an age range from 20 to 40 years. After the data were analysed, 11 sub-themes were generated which were merged into three major themes:

Table 1. Themes and sub-themes that emerged from the data analysis

THEMES	SUB-THEMES
Personal factors	1.1 Lack of interest in the module 1.2 Student absenteeism
Academic factors	2.1 insufficient theoretical time 2.2 Lecturer's teaching method 2.3 Limited practical time vs. rarely performed procedures 2.4 Attitudes of registered nurses
Improvement measures	3.1 Project-based learning 3.2 Monitoring of attendance 3.3 use different types of teaching style 3.4 Allow enough time for both theoretical and clinical block 3.5 Employ enough clinical instructors

Theme One: Personal Factors

This theme encapsulates the participants' observations as nursing students with regard to module failures in the Bachelor of Nursing Science degree at a Namibian university. This is one of the most important themes in this study as it responds to the objectives of the study. The sub-themes of this theme include: Lack of interest in the module and Student absenteeism.

Sub-Theme 1.1: Lack of Interest in the Module

This sub-theme describes the way the participants expressed their experiences regarding the failure of modules in the Bachelor of Nursing Science degree at a Namibian university. The findings revealed that most student nurses lack interest in their studies:

"There are some students who have a negative attitude towards the subject; they are just going for classes since their friends are going." (P13)

"I think when the lecturer is not showing interest in his/her subject, to say he/she does show up, no assessments or something, students tend to give it less time and focus on other modules where they get motivated." (P 15)

Sub-Theme 1.2: Student Absenteeism

The participants felt that there are some students who are less committed to their work. They reported that students are not willing to learn; they tend to be absent from classes and they do not learn what the module requires from them, be it in the clinical area or theory:

"Some lecturers don't do anything when a student misses a class. As a result, they develop a tendency of not going to school [as] they know there are no negative consequences." (P 8)

"There are some students who are lazy to wake up and go for classes." (P 5)

"I think absenteeism is also driving one to failure; if one misses a class, he/she has missed what others have gained." (P 11)

Theme Two: Academic Factors

This important theme also relates to the study's objective, as it highlights the factors that contribute to failing modules. The sub-themes derived from this theme were identified as: insufficient theoretical time, lecturer's teaching method, limited practical time vs. rarely performed procedures, and attitudes of registered nurses.

Sub-Theme 2.1: Insufficient Theoretical Time

The study's findings revealed that the nursing students have limited time in both theory and practical classes, spending two weeks on theory and two weeks at clinical placement.

"There is too much to consume in a short period of time as we only spend two weeks on theory per month and we are expected to write tests and assignments before going back to clinical placements." (P 4)

"[The] time allocated to theory is too little; imagine within those two weeks of theory, you have to revise what you have [been] taught at class, study for tests and do the assignments; this is way too exhausting." (P 1)

"A year module is something that is supposed to be taught for ten months but we are just doing it for four months... I think this is affecting our performance badly compared to other professionals." (P 11)

Sub-Theme 2.2: Lecturer's Teaching Method

This sub-theme touches on the way lecturers teach, which the participants found to be ineffective:

"The strategies used by the lecturers to teach is not attracting students' attention; it's just slides after slide – no videos, no pictures, no breaks." (P 4)

"Sometimes lecturers are just reading slides without explaining in detail... [This is] something a student can do." (P 3)

Sub-Theme 2.3: Limited Practical Time vs. Rarely Performed Procedures

This sub-theme is based on the practical component of the modules:

"Time allocated for practical [learning] is not sufficient... as a result it is hard to find those rarely performed procedures... it's difficult for you to get one within a limited period of time." (P 17)

"Some modules consist of some procedures which are rarely performed and make their demonstration difficult." (P 6)

"We don't really get enough time to work on our logbooks; the two-week period is too little to practice." (P 11)

Sub-Theme 2.4: Attitudes of Registered Nurses

This sub-theme is based on the practical component of the modules. Some participants touched on the fact that the registered nurses are not friendly, which makes learning difficult on the wards:

"Some registered nurses have bad attitudes towards students, and they are not willing to teach students." (P 7)

"There was a day I worked with this other sister, but when it was time to knockoff I took my logbook to her to sign but her response shocked me, [she said]: "I didn't see you." (P 17)

"Some registered nurses are always pretending to be busy when you ask for demonstrations." (P 3)

Theme Three: Improvement measures

This theme emerged from the participants' responses when they were asked what could be done to meet students' needs to ensure effective learning and mitigate the failure rate. The responses were sub-divided into the following sub-themes: use project-based learning, monitor attendance, encourage different types of teaching styles, allow enough time for both theoretical and clinical block, and employ enough clinical instructors.

Sub-Theme 3.1: Use Project-Based Learning

This sub-theme dealt with the participants' suggestions, including that lecturers could introduce project-based learning to enable the students to develop an ability to work with their peers. This would also build teamwork and group skills, and as such the students' level of interest would grow. The participants reported that lecturers do not engage students in different ways of learning, with some arguing that certain lecturers are not committed to their work. It will strengthen the bond between lecturers and students if students have good relationships with their lecturers and classmates:

"*I believe that organising meaningful learning goals can be an effective way to awaken a need to know desire in students; they will be motivated to explore and increase their knowledge.*" (P 4)

"*I suggest that lecturers must try to be good to their students so that students can open up with them and be able to ask questions in class.*" (P 17)

"*Project-based learning helps students to build problem-solving skills and teamwork, together with effective communication with the world around them.*" (P 13)

Sub-Theme 3.2: Monitor Attendance

Participants suggested that lecturers should make use of attendance to control their students. Some suggested that lecturers need to know their students' home environments so that they are well-informed of the situations in which their students are living, which could be the reason for their absenteeism. In this way, they can come up with relevant plans to help them:

"*Lecturers and clinical instructors as well as preceptors should follow up with their students so that they can monitor their attendance.*" (P 10)

"*Students must be referred to student counsellors and other responsible bodies in case of excessive absenteeism so that they can talk to them.*" (P 8)

"*The School of Nursing lecturers, clinical instructors and preceptors should strengthen clinical accompaniments to clinical facilities.*" (P 13)

Sub-Theme 3.3: Use Different Types of Teaching Style

The participants suggested that lecturers should use a variety of teaching styles, such as quizzes and assignments, to familiarise themselves with potential exam questions. Some suggested that lecturers should change the way they teach, e.g., give breaks during lessons for students to stand up and stretch, and make use of group work:

"I suggest that lecturers should make use of videos or even pictures in their slides, make some jokes just to catch students' attention, and also give students tasks to perform just for some minutes then they continue with lecturing." (P 6)

"I suggest that lecturers could provide activities, of which they mark, like little quizzes, tests and assignments after certain content is covered." (P 8)

"I suggest that we should be given breaks in lessons, instead of just sitting for the whole two hours. At least 50 minutes of lecturing, a ten-minute break to stretch and refresh our minds. Sitting for a long time is exhausting and can lead to a loss of concentration." (P 7)

Sub-Theme 3.4: Allow Enough Time for Both Theoretical and Clinical Blocks

The participants suggested that both the theoretical and clinical blocks be increased from two weeks to at least a month. The expectation was that students would then have enough time to cover the theoretical component of the modules and integrate their learning into practice:

"I suggest that the School of Nursing and its concerned bodies should change the programme of two weeks allocation to a full month." (P 7)

"I suggest the School of Nursing lecturers, clinical instructors and preceptors should add on the time allocated for theory." (P 13)

Sub-Theme 3.5: Employ Enough Clinical Instructors

This sub-theme relates to the practical components of the modules. The participants suggested that the university should employ enough clinical instructors to accompany students on their placement teaching and sign for them so that the incidents of students being mistreated by nurses reduce:

"The University of Namibia if possible must employ more clinical instructors; at least every year level must have their own so that we stop relying only on nurses for signatures." (P 7)

"I feel like sometimes registered nurses use to be busy which we misinterpret with being stingy to sign; I suggest that the School of Nursing must have its people that will be following students on placements to reduce the pressure on nurses." (P 16)

DISCUSSION

The study shows that there are various factors that contribute to students failing the Bachelor of Nursing Science at a Namibian university, which can be divided into personal and academic factors. Personal factors include a lack of interest in modules and absenteeism, while the academic factors include insufficient time for theory, lecturers' teaching methods, limited practical time vs. rarely performed procedures, and attitudes of registered nurses. Measures to reduce the failure rate and produce competent nurses were made.

Most of the participants mentioned that students lack interest in their studies; some believe that nursing is just difficult and no matter how hard they try, they will not succeed. This finding is in line with a study by Arendse (2020), who noted that self-motivation is a major psychological factor when it comes to academic achievement. According to Kucuk (2020), some students develop negative attitudes towards their own studies and do not put enough effort in, while Bonsaksen et al. (2018) said that putting more time into studying is reasonably linked with stronger motivation and better academic performance. Vogel (2016) further indicated that students who experience lower levels of self-motivation and less personal meaning have a high likelihood of putting in less effort and time into their studies, which will affect their academic commitment and eventually their achievement.

The participants noted that if the lecturers introduced project-based learning, this would allow students to develop their ability to work with their peers, building teamwork and group skills, and thereby growing their level of interest. This will also strengthen the bonds between lecturers and students. The participants further recommended that the student nurses and the lecturers should change their attitudes towards some modules, including refraining from believing that nursing is difficult. They argued that student nurses have to be positive, study hard and dedicate more time to their studies.

Absenteeism is a personal factor that also plays a role in the failure of student nurses. The participants felt that there are students who are less committed to their work; they are not willing to learn, they are absent from class, and they do not acquire the necessary knowledge, be it practical or theoretical. When a student misses' classes, they miss important information, which is as per the findings of Gemuhay et al. (2019), who noted that absenteeism is one of the major causes of poor performance among students. Gottfried and Kirksey (2017) also found that students with greater absences have lower academic performance, while Gottfried (2014) shared that chronic absenteeism reduces math and reading achievement outcomes, reduces educational engagement, and decreases social engagement. Klein et al. (2022) similarly discovered that absences are negatively associated with academic achievement.

Regarding the issue of absenteeism, it was recommended that lecturers, clinical instructors and preceptors should monitor student attendance. Freytas (2017) made a similar recommendation, arguing that academic success can be achieved through attendance. This recommendation is similar to that of Gov (2015), who called on schools and communities across the US to take immediate action by better tracking absence data and reducing chronic absenteeism in schools.

The study participants mentioned that class time is insufficient, which is consistent with Kucuk (2020), who noted that workload can affect students' academic performance. Monisi (2018) also conducted a quantitative study on the causes of high failure rates in biological sciences among student nurses in the Limpopo province of South Africa, and found that the time allocated to some subjects is not enough for the large amount of content. Student nurses are challenged by content-laden curricula that they are expected to learn in a short period of time (Bonsaken, et al. 2018; Kaylor, 2014; Monisi, 2018). Due to the short periods available to study, the volume of academic content seems to be high, thus students become overwhelmed and fail to perform according to their intellectual abilities (Nadinloyia et al., 2013).

With regard to content overload, the participants recommended that both the theoretical and practical periods should be increased from two weeks to at least a month. The expectation was that students will then have enough time to cover the theoretical component of the modules and integrate their learnings into practice, yielding positive outcomes.

The participants revealed that the way lecturers teach is not effective, e.g., sometimes they just read slides without explaining the content in detail. They further stated that lecturers do not giving adequate work to students to test their minds and expose them to potential exam questions. This corresponds with the findings of a study by Pinehas et al. (2017), which revealed that the teaching strategy whereby a lecturer gives a little information does not benefit all students. Abdulrazzaq et al. (2017) and Pinehas (2017) also stated that some students repeat some modules taught by certain lecturers. Another study conducted in South Africa on factors contributing to the poor performance of student nurses in anatomy and physiology found that poor teaching strategies contribute to subject failure (Mhlongo & Masango, 2020).

With regard to the use of ineffective teaching strategies, the participants recommended that lecturers should utilise a variety of teaching methods, such as giving quizzes for practice after every chapter to test their understanding, and giving breaks during lessons. This recommendation is supported by Levett-Jones et al. (2015), who shared that students recommend the use of teaching strategies that improve the attitudes of learners, especially when their learning involves hands-on experiences. Araoye (2013) argued that appropriate teaching strategies and methods are invisible variables and motivational tools that must be ensured for any effective teaching and learning outcomes.

The study findings show that when demonstration of clinical procedures is later in the year this has an impact on the completion of logbooks, with participants saying that the time allocated to clinical placement is not enough. Further, some logbooks include procedures that are rarely performed, which makes their demonstration difficult and as such the nurses cannot give feedback on them. At the end, the logbook will be considered incomplete, which puts the student at risk of not being allowed to sit their exams. Lecturers are also not following-up, which is as per Vattanaamorn et al.'s (2022) finding that effective clinical follow-ups promote learning and help students to achieve learning outcomes and competencies. The study participants also recommended that clinical instructors should start giving demonstrations on time and stop relying on nurses.

Another concern raised was that some registered nurses are not friendly, which makes learning difficult on the wards as they answer students badly and refuse to sign logbooks. These findings are similar to that of Aghamohammadi-Kalkhoran et al. (2011), who said that staff attitudes are not positive enough toward nursing students, which can have negative effects on the learning and socialisation of students. The study participants suggested that the university should employ enough clinical instructors to accompany students on placement teaching and sign for them so that the incidents of students been mistreated by nurses reduce.

Strengths

This study provided a broad understanding of, and insight into, the factors that contribute to student failures in the Bachelor of Nursing Science degree. The use of a qualitative, exploratory, descriptive and contextual design enabled the participants to narrate and interpret their experiences freely, as well as make suggestions for improvements.

Limitations

Limited generalizability: The study's findings may be specific to the universities in Namibia, as data were collected only from one satellite campus. Therefore, the findings may not be representative of the entire country or other institutions globally.

Potential bias: The use of convenience sampling may introduce bias, as participants may not be fully representative of all students' nurses. Additionally, the study' may lead to social desirability bias, where participants provide responses they perceive as socially acceptable.

Lack of triangulation: Triangulation of data from multiple sources or methods could enhance the credibility and validity of the findings. The study could benefit from incorporating perspectives from lecturers themselves, academic administrators, and other stakeholders involved in higher education studies.

CONCLUSION

The research findings suggest that the academic performance of students in the Bachelor of Nursing Science degree is influenced by personal factors, such as a lack of interest and absenteeism, as well as academic factors, such as insufficient theoretical time, lecturers' teaching methods, limited practical time vs. rarely performed procedures, and attitudes of registered nurses. Recommendations were made as follows: use project-based learning, monitor attendance, use different types of teaching styles, allow enough time for both theoretical and clinical blocks, and employ enough clinical instructors. Student support should also be enhanced to change students' attitudes towards particular subjects, which should increase their level of motivation and academic commitment. These study findings have important implications for the School of Nursing, as it may use them to develop new teaching strategies and targeted interventions that are geared towards addressing the factors responsible for the failure rate. Parents and study sponsors may benefit by being relieved from paying extra fees for repeated modules, as students may be more likely to complete their degree within the prescribed time frame.

REFERENCES

Aghamohammadi-Kalkhoran, M., Karimollahi, M., & Abdi, R. (2011). Iranian staff nurses' attitudes toward nursing students. *Nurse Education Today*, 31(5), 477–481. 10.1016/j.nedt.2010.09.00320926166

Ahmady, S., Khajeali, N., Sharifi, F., & Mirmoghtadaei, Z. S. (2019). Factors related to academic failure in preclinical medical education: A systematic review. *Journal of Advances in Medical Education & Professionalism*, 7(2), 74.31086799

Ajjawi, R., Dracup, M., Zacharias, N., Bennett, S., & Boud, D. (2020). Persisting students' explanations of and emotional responses to academic failure. *Higher Education Research & Development*, 39(2), 185–199. 10.1080/07294360.2019.1664999

Araoye, M. I. (2013). Redressing Students' Motivation and Academic Achievement in Biology Education at the Federal College of Education (Special) Oyo Oyo State, Nigeria. *New Perspectives in Science Education, 2*.

Arendse, J. P. (2020). Psychosocial factors predicting academic performance of first-year college nursing students in the Western Cape, South Africa. [Master thesis, University of Western Cape].

Bahramnezhad, F., Shahbazi, B., Asgari, P., & Keshmiri, F. (2019). Comparative study of the undergraduate nursing curricula among nursing schools of mcmaster university of Canada, hacettepe university of Turkey, and tehran university of Iran. *Strides in Development of Medical Education, 16*(1).

Bonsaksen, T., Ellingham, B. J., & Carstensen, T. (2018). Factors associated with academic performance among second-year undergraduate occupational therapy students. *The Open Journal of Occupational Therapy*, 6(1), 14. 10.15453/2168-6408.1403

Castleberry, A., & Nolen, A. (2018). Thematic analysis of qualitative research data: Is it as easy as it sounds? *Currents in Pharmacy Teaching & Learning*, 10(6), 807–815. 10.1016/j.cptl.2018.03.01930025784

Chavan, S. S., Jose, J., D'Souza, J., & Mathews, A. A. (2019). An explorative study on factors affecting nursing student's academic failure. *Manipal Journal of Nursing and Health Sciences*, 5(1), 27–31.

Cheng, S. F., Kuo, C. L., Lin, K. C., & Lee-Hsieh, J. (2010). Development and preliminary testing of a self-rating instrument to measure self-directed learning ability of nursing students. *International Journal of Nursing Studies*, 47(9), 1152–1158. 10.1016/j.ijnurstu.2010.02.00220223455

Dante, A., Ferrão, S., Jarosova, D., Lancia, L., Nascimento, C., Notara, V., Pokorna, A., Rybarova, L., Skela-Savič, B., & Palese, A. (2016). Nursing student profiles and occurrence of early academic failure: Findings from an explorative European study. *Nurse Education Today*, 38, 74–81. 10.1016/j.nedt.2015.12.01326763210

Freytas, H. (2017). *A Collaborative & Strategic Approach To Improve School Achievement Through Effective Attendance/Truancy Policies And Procedures.*

Gemuhay, H. M., Kalolo, A., Mirisho, R., Chipwaza, B., & Nyangena, E. (2019). Factors affecting performance in clinical practice among preservice diploma nursing students in Northern Tanzania. *Nursing Research and Practice*, 2019, 2019. 10.1155/2019/345308530941212

Gottfried, M. A. (2014). Chronic absenteeism and its effects on students' academic and socioemotional outcomes. *Journal of Education for Students Placed at Risk*, 19(2), 53–75. 10.1080/10824669.2014.962696

Gottfried, M. A., & Kirksey, J. J. (2017). When students miss school: The role of timing of absenteeism on students' test performance. *Educational Researcher*, 46(3), 119–130. 10.3102/0013189X17703945

Gov, E. (2015). *Every student, every day: Obama administration launches first–ever national, cross-sector initiative to eliminate chronic absenteeism in our nation's schools.*

Jayanthi, S. V., Balakrishnan, S., Ching, A. L. S., Latiff, N. A. A., & Nasirudeen, A. M. A. (2014). Factors contributing to academic performance of students in a tertiary institution in Singapore. *American Journal of Educational Research*, 2(9), 752–758. 10.12691/education-2-9-8

Kaylor, S. K. (2014). Preventing information overload: Cognitive load theory as an instructional framework for teaching pharmacology. *The Journal of Nursing Education*, 53(2), 108–111. 10.3928/01484834-20140122-0324444008

Kiger, M. E., & Varpio, L. (2020). Thematic analysis of qualitative data: AMEE Guide No. 131. *Medical Teacher*, 42(8), 846–854. 10.1080/0142159X.2020.175503032356468

Klein, M., Sosu, E. M., & Dare, S. (2022). School absenteeism and academic achievement: Does the reason for absence matter? *AERA Open*, 8, 23328584211071115. 10.1177/23328584211071115

Kucuk, I. (2020). *Instructional Related Factors and Students' Performance In Mathematics At Kenya Certificate Of Secondary Education In Public Secondary Schools, Njiru Sub-County, Kenya* [Doctoral dissertation, University of Nairobi, Kenya].

Levett-Jones, T., Andersen, P., Reid-Searl, K., Guinea, S., McAllister, M., Lapkin, S., Palmer, L., & Niddrie, M. (2015). Tag team simulation: An innovative approach for promoting active engagement of participants and observers during group simulations. *Nurse Education in Practice*, 15(5), 345–352. 10.1016/j.nepr.2015.03.01425936431

Lincoln, Y. S., & Guba, E. G. (1985). *Naturalistic inquiry*. Sage. 10.1016/0147-1767(85)90062-8

Linda, N. S., Mtshali, N. G., & Engelbrecht, C. (2013). Lived experiences of a community regarding its involvement in a university community-based education programme. *Curationis, 36*(1), 1-13.

Maree, D. J., & Maree, D. J. (2020). The Methodological Division: Quantitative and Qualitative Methods. *Realism and Psychological Science*, 13-42.

Maree, R. D., Marcum, Z. A., Saghafi, E., Weiner, D. K., & Karp, J. F. (2016). A systematic review of opioid and benzodiazepine misuse in older adults. *The American Journal of Geriatric Psychiatry*, 24(11), 949–963. 10.1016/j.jagp.2016.06.00327567185

Mhlongo, X. L. (2018). *Factors contributing to failure of student nurses in biological nursing sciences: KwaZulu-Natal College of Nursing* [Doctoral dissertation, University, Country].

Mhlongo, X. L., & Masango, T. E. (2020). Factors contributing to poor performance of student nurses in anatomy and physiology. *African Journal of Health Professions Education*, 12(3), 140–143. 10.7196/AJHPE.2020.v12i3.1357

Mirza, M. S., & Arif, M. I. (2018). Fostering Academic Resilience of Students at Risk of Failure at Secondary School Level. *Journal of Behavioural Sciences, 28*(1

Monisi, F. M. (2018). *Student nurses' perceptions and attitudes towards anatomy and physiology in Limpopo, South Africa* [Doctoral dissertation, University of Punjab].

Nadinloyi, K. B., Hajloo, N., Garamaleki, N. S., & Sadeghi, H. (2013). The study efficacy of time management training on increase academic time management of students. *Procedia: Social and Behavioral Sciences*, 84, 134–138. 10.1016/j.sbspro.2013.06.523

Najimi, A., Sharifirad, G., Amini, M. M., & Meftagh, S. D. (2013). Academic failure and students' viewpoint: The influence of individual, internal and external organizational factors. *Journal of Education and Health Promotion*, 2(1), 2. 10.4103/2277-9531.112 69824083272

Ng, L., Tuckett, A., Fox-Young, S., & Kain, V. (2014). Exploring registered nurses' attitudes towards postgraduate education in Australia: An overview of the literature. *Journal of Nursing Education and Practice*, 4(2), 162–170.

Olebara, C. C., & Maureen, M. N. (2018). Student's Academic performance monitoring system in Tertiary Institutions. *West African Journal of Industrial & Academic Research*, 19(2), 120.

Pinehas, L. N., Mulenga, E., & Amadhila, J. (2017). Factors that hinder the academic performance of the nursing students who registered as first years in 2010 at the University of Namibia (UNAM), Oshakati Campus in Oshana, Namibia. *Journal of Nursing Education and Practice*, 7(8), 63. 10.5430/jnep.v7n8p63

Shatimwene, G. P., Ashipala, D. O., & Kamenye, E. (2020). Experiences of Student Nurses on the Use of the Two-Week Block System at the Satellite Campus of a Higher Education Institution in Namibia. *International Journal of Higher Education*, 9(3), 222–231. 10.5430/ijhe.v9n3p222

Sneyers, E., & De Witte, K. (2017). The interaction between dropout, graduation rates and quality ratings in universities. *The Journal of the Operational Research Society*, 68(4), 416–430. 10.1057/jors.2016.15

Telio, S., Ajjawi, R., & Regehr, G. (2015). The "educational alliance" as a framework for reconceptualizing feedback in medical education. *Academic Medicine*, 90(5), 609–614. 10.1097/ACM.00000000000056025406607

Thabet, M., Taha, E. E. S., Abood, S. A., & Morsy, S. R. (2017). The effect of problem-based learning on nursing students' decision-making skills and styles. *Journal of Nursing Education and Practice*, 7(6), 108–116. 10.5430/jnep.v7n6p108

Vattanaamorn, S., Phaitrakoon, J., Jirarattanawanna, N., Jintrawet, U., Kwalamthan, W., & Lertwongpaopu, W. (2022). Factors Influencing the Achievement of Learning Outcomes Among Nursing Students: The Mixed-Method Study. *Eurasian Journal of Educational Research*, 98(98), 131–146.

Vogel, F. R., & Human-Vogel, S. (2016). Academic commitment and self-efficacy as predictors of academic achievement in additional materials science. *Higher Education Research & Development*, 35(6), 1298–1310. 10.1080/07294360.2016.1144574

Chapter 16
Teaching Human Resource Management in Law Schools:
A Scrutiny of Pedagogies for Critical and Reflective Teaching Practice

Prageetha G. Raju
https://orcid.org/0000-0001-7074-5196
Rainbow Management Research Consultants, India

ABSTRACT

Many courses of higher education emerged for being ideological but later graduated into something more critical and reflective; HRM is one such course. A number of studies tried to address teaching HRM in a responsible, reflective, and critical manner. At this point, it is to be noted that HRM teaching is getting essential to students given the trend for integrated programmes in India and abroad. But how HRM should be taught to students pursuing integrated programmes still remains unanswered. There is dearth of literature regarding the context, the content, the perspectives, and the pedagogies of HRM for non-business students. So, how should HRM be taught? The author established the context to teach HRM in non-business schools, personally developed teaching materials, and gradually emerged into incorporating tested models to foster criticality and reflection. Two interventions, viz., project pedagogy and critical studies in HRM, are used to teach HRM to law students.

DOI: 10.4018/979-8-3693-3559-8.ch016

Copyright © 2024, IGI Global. Copying or distributing in print or electronic forms without written permission of IGI Global is prohibited.

INTRODUCTION

Human resource function in every organization is regulated by Law (labour welfare and social security legislations) and a person who stands at the intersection of these two disciplines (HRM and Law) is much awaited, in the corporate job market. While Management students are taught mainstream HRM (strategic and tactical HRM) from business goal fulfilment point of view with managerial relevance (ideologies and paradigms merely introduced), but Griffin (1997) opines that operational HR requires sound knowledge of law given the regulations governing employer-employee relationships. In this backdrop, how should HRM be taught to Law students and in what context?

HRM is one such course that emerged as being ideological and later graduated into something more critical and reflective (Janssens and Steyaert, 2009). Can reflection and criticality be taught and learnt by students at university level? If so, is there any pedagogy for the same?

This question arises because, on one side, programmes of higher education at University/Institute level are supposed to contribute to the 'employability' of the students pursuing it, while on the other side, essence of higher education emphasizes creation of reflective citizens who can analyse power dynamics and truths of changing socio-economic and politico-legal paradigms. Added to this, all social science disciplines in general are accused of contributing to the societal contexts, characterized by financial crisis, economic inequality, exploitation of human and natural resources, and insufficient regulation, rather than trying to counter-balance, them (Bratton & Gold, 2015).

This amount of divergence in standpoints generates tension and conflict at University, Student, and Industry levels across countries. So, the priority of universities is to create employability vis-a-vis developing student capacities to reflect and critique.

Coming to law colleges globally, an emphasis on practice-oriented skills and values aimed at inculcating a sense of professional identity and purpose is creating huge pressure. (Carnegie report, 2007). Besides formal knowledge including analysis of power dynamics of socio-economic and politico-legal paradigms coupled with a strong dose of experience of practice has become essential. Thus, identifying pedagogies that contribute to the same are stressed upon, to prepare law graduates into competent and caring professionals.

In India, integrated Law programmes (five years programme) have become the norm for two decades. For instance, programmes such as BA, LLB and BBA, LLB combine knowledge and application of two disciplines thus providing a broad-based multidisciplinary foundation to the curriculum. Harvard Law School stressed (Coates, Fried & Spier, 2014) that subjects like Economics, Accounts, Public Finance, Sociology, and Business Strategy are essential for Law students besides Law courses in order to become efficient Corporate or Ligitation Lawyers. It was presumed that an integrated degree equips students to become lawyers who are well-prepared to meet the societal and professional demands with a complete knowledge of Law, with other disciplines converging in and enriching the discipline of Law. Teaching the multidisciplinary course(s) calls for distinctive set of competencies with emphasis on innovative pedagogies.

The present study is about identifying pedagogies to teach HRM course to BBA LLB students.

PROBLEM BACKGROUND

Since the mainstream HRM offers knowledge with managerial relevance to equip students with required analytical and business skills, teaching HRM to law students is a challenge because literature and practice of converting the theoretical critique of HRM into practical applications to suit the law domain is inadequate.

As stated, HRM was once ideological, contributing to the political agenda, and later it changed into a discipline with changing paradigms; the same applies to the Law discipline too. A number of studies tried to address teaching HRM in a responsible, reflective, and critical manner (Lawless & Macque, 2008; Ruggunan & Spiller, 2014; Bratton & Gold, 2015) but there is dearth of literature related to converting the theoretical critique of HRM into practical action to suit the Law domain.

So the difficulty to the course teacher is, whether to teach *HRM as an ideological force or as a key to business goal fulfilment*? This can be answered depending upon the context established to teach HRM in a law classroom.

BACKGROUND TO THE STUDY

The first issue regarding the learning space began with the need to have a distinctive pedagogy to teach HRM. This question arose due to movement of the author from management school (MBA) to the Law School. The pre-decided syllabus of HRM for Law students resembled an introductory course on HRM for MBA students. However, the syllabus did not equip the students to contest business and organizational norms, nor the syllabus prepared the students to face any HR crisis at workplace. Therefore, some distinctive pedagogies were needed to teach HRM to Law students.

SCOPE

This paper is a personal narrative (author being the HRM teacher in an Indian Law School transferred from B-school) and presents the evolution of teaching practice of HRM for law students for four years (2015-2019). The paper outlines the methods, tools, and pedagogies used to foster reflection and criticality as well as the contextual drivers that prompted the initial assessment of the teaching and learning space.

Objective of the study: Given the above, the objective of this paper is to:

1. Establish a context to teach HRM to Law students
2. Identify distinctive pedagogies to convert theoretical HRM into action
3. Identify and implementation of interactive methods to teach HRM

Given the above objectives, the author strongly opines that the pedagogies identified not only need to have components of criticality and reflection but also imbibe interactive learning approach.

DRIVERS TO SCRUTINIZE PEDAGOGIES TO ESTABLISH CONTEXT

The first challenge driver is to prepare students with abilities to critique and reflect as the author observed during the teaching period (2015-19) that corporate firms started hiring candidates with these abilities. For instance, companies wanted candidates to be proactive in employment litigation, have good understanding of corporate legislations and their implications on the workforce, play a role in HR audit and so on. This driver was challenging to the author given the paucity of time, and overall workload.

The second driver was that the author (teacher of HRM course) belonged to the stream of business management with Doctorate also from the same stream. The author thad o redesign assignments and lecture content, add critical readings to address the changing rhetoric between practice and theory. The need to broaden the horizons of thought and action to the teacher is a greater challenge because imbibing an interactive approach is also essential.

The third driver is the conceptual issues that HRM faces (Thompson, 2011). These issues include the lack of theory to fully explain the performance-related links (Guest, 2011); the monopolization of intellectual space by indiscriminating positivistic psychology (Godard, 2014); and the profession's crisis of legitimacy as a result of its inability to establish authority among higher executives (Kochan,

2007). The author came into a 2019 study (Dundon & Rafferty, 2018) that discussed the possible extinction of HRM as a professional and academic activity due to ideological individualism and capitalism ignoring broader organizational, employee, and social concerns. Marchington (2015) provides evidence for this claim, arguing that the HR function prioritizes short-term performance indicators over long-term objectives and stakeholder concerns. Law students including the author had to identify self with these changing paradigms to be proficient in the discipline. The fourth driver is lack of India/Asia specific critical HRM studies. Doktor et al. (1991) contended that US-centricity of the HRM theories and constructs don't align with non-US contexts. Since a good number of US multinational companies operate in India, students should be exposed to US-centric HRM theories and constructs, as well as Indian/Asian specific HRM also to realise the indigenous cultural and institutional contexts.

REVIEW OF LITERATURE

The curriculum had to be amended to include reflection and criticality components into HRM curriculum for law students and the pedagogies to foster these qualities. At the same time, an interactive learning environment is essential.

At the outset, it is essential to define reflection and criticality used for the study. According to Tracey et al. (2014), reflection is an active, continuous, circular condition in which a person evaluates their own beliefs and revisits and modifies them throughout time. Reflection indicates going back on experience. Criticality is the capacity and ability to read, write, think, speak in ways to understand power and equity in order to understand and promote anti-oppression (Muhammad, 2021).

Since employers are seeking law candidates who are adept at workplace dynamics as well as employee litigations, an interactive teaching-learning environment becomes essential.

At this point, literature is reviewed under three headings, namely, (a) context for teaching HRM in a law classroom, (b) dilemma in the ideologies of HRM and (c) pedagogies available (d) Interactive Learning

(a) Context for teaching HRM in a Law classroom:

Onah (2008) suggests that the context for human resources is same as financial, technological, and other resources that are managed in any organization. HRM has a strategic, tactical, and operational role to play in every organization; Griffin (1997) perceives the operational role of HR from the legal perspective because of regulations governing the employer-employee relationships. For instance, compliance with equal employment opportunity policy, observation of labour laws, employee benefits, gender issues, safety issues, skill development issues, interpersonal management, response to business challenges, and so on are mostly governed by Laws and by-laws of the land.

Given the fact that global firms are seeking success from their business operations in India, a high degree of professionalism from a global context is solicited from the Indian workforce to take critical decisions with respect to people management and make strategic choices. This aspect calls for inclusion of factors such as skills and competencies, mindsets, values and customs, institutions and a favourable cultural environment and a facilitative legal framework (Hofstede, 1993; Budhwar & Sparrow 2002), which are products of a country's socio-economic and political realities. Thus, the contemporary HRM scenario should be understood in the context of changing economic, business, and legal environment (Saini & Budhwar, 2004).

Now, it is certain that the curriculum needs to have socio-economic and political realities embedded. However, two questions still persist:

(i) How to include reflection and criticality components into HRM curriculum for law students?
(ii) What pedagogies foster these qualities?

Another ground to build context is to handle the dilemma between goals of HRM.

(b) Dilemma between teaching HRM as an ideology versus HRM as a key to business goal fulfilment:

At the outset, the curriculum had to be built not only on the intellectual properties of HRM but also it should reflect the mission of the University. At this juncture, the question to ponder upon is *whether to teach HRM as a key to business goal fulfilment or whether to teach it is an ideology?*

The students should learn the processes of HR planning, peformance appraisal, workforce diversity, recruitment and selection, etc and simultaneously critique them. To nurture this capacity, both political and moral economies including capitalism trends need to be embedded into the syllabus to acknowledge and contest the prevailing ideologies as below:

a) Political economy provides both a historical and a social context for students trying to understand *what*, *why*, and *how*, about managing people in different organizational contexts. For instance, in the former Soviet Union, Stalin exercised patronage through the "HR Department" (equivalent in the Bolshevik Party), and demonstrated the effectiveness and influence of HR policies and practices. (Pipko, 2002 and Hale, 2014).

b) [REMOVED HYPERLINK FIELD]On the other hand, managers belonging to different hierarchical levels may be supporters of the ruling political system (Dumitrescu & Dumitrescu, 2014) and this causes malfunctions in the HR management, because it interrupts professionalization and intellectualization. This leads to rupture of the ideological foundation of institutions, due to different cultures and visions of political clients within the administration.

c) Coming to the moral economy, most management research ignores ethics and values in relationships though morality is central to economic functioning (Smyth & Pryke, 2006). This was pre-substantiated by the fact that management and economics theories focus on growth and profit thus subsume the significance of morality or perceive it as a personal preference (Sayer, 2003). F. W. Taylor in his Scientifc Management focused on, *'labour'*- one of the principal inputs into the manufacturing process and acknowledged them as vital to productivity (Merkle, 1980) but, social relations should not be treated as a means to 'maximizing output from a given input' (Grey and Wilmot, 2005).

Since, HRM discipline doesnot adequately allow a critique of itself, therefore, some B-schools in UK and USA employ sociologists, psychologists, ethnographers, and other social scientists to teach HRM (Thompson &Vincent, 2010). At this juncture, arises *anti-performativity*, which refers to a critique of focus on production and outputs.

d) Lastly, financialized capitalism or investor capitalism is creating a risk of impoverishment for the HR domain (Dundon & Rafferty, 2018). The consequence of investor capitalism is the power drifting away from managers to owners. Not all owners seek a cooperative relation between employees and employers (Batt, 2018). A Gig economy is an ideal example characterized by shift of transactional risk to labour, mediation of technology, and by-passing of regulatory labour standards with hardly any investment in collaborative capital.

In India, HRM is taught by teachers who speicalized in HRM in MBA with a PhD in the same. Therefore, the challenge in Law colleges is to adequately equip oneself with multidisciplinary competencies to understand managing people across contexts.

Critical thinking for law students:

Critical thinking is important to law students, lawyers, law professors, and judges. Paul and Elder (2006) said, "to foster critical thinking, students should not assert things, but, reason things out on the basis of evidence and good reasons. Critical thinking encourages important dialogues with self, allowing reasoning and seeking a rational basis for beliefs. It helps lawyers to deal with complex issues and ill defined problems.

Law schools don't teach critical thinking systematically. They employ Socratic Method as the principal approach to legal education, but most law teachers do not use the Socratic Method to teach critical thinking. Critical thinking promotes deep-thinking, creates questions, overcomes intuition, see all sides of problem, and creates questions and problem-solving. An ability to think critically can, for example, facilitate a more thorough and sophisticated understanding of legal doctrine.

CONCLUSION POST REVIEW OF LITERATURE

After reviewing the relevant literature, the author accepts the limitation of being from business management background but accepts the challenge to teach HRM at Law Schools.

The acceptance is because the author/teacher has understood that the objective of the teacher is to make students, invariably, begin to experience the contradictions between the imperatives of moral economy versus market economy versus political economy and thus begin to argue. At this juncture, arises *denaturalization,* which refers to a deliberate interrogation of processes that appear so natural and normal. (Alveson & Willmot, 1992; Grey & Wilmott, 2005) assert that opening up and questioning something that appears non-problematic includes hierarchy, dominant relations, managerial superiority and so on. The scope for denaturalization is vast in India given the uneven socio-economic scenarios and relationships, power distance, masculinity, patriarchy, religiosity, and so on.

Pedagogies Identified

Based on the above, two pedagogies are identified by the author, viz., (i) critical studies in HRM and (ii) project pedagogy. These are not new but it is definitely a new experiment for the author to teach HRM for law students and also to make it interactive.

Critical Studies in HRM

Critical Studies in HRM emphasize management studies concerned with social justice, equitable and fair HR practices, concern for environment, and consequences of unethical business practices (Ruggunan and Spiller, 2014).

Critical studies draw heavily on Marxism, Feminism, and Postmodernism, including Freire's idea of emancipatory education as it doesn't adhere to any particular morality. (Freire, 1970 & 1993) asserted that the character of learning should inculcate the ability to question the societal order (norms and values). Freire's assertion is emancipatory in nature for it encourages questioning the societal norms and values, prevailing power imbalances, and works towards social justice; alongside, learners and teachers are partners in the learning process. Here, learning aims at *'problem posing'* that is built on processes, contexts, dialogue, and focus on relationships thus, combining reflection on critical awareness and action (Arendt, 2013; Freire, 1970). This pedagogy envelops the original practice of telling/informing using narrations, challenging using questions, and finally engaging using a critical component embedded into the course content.

Fournier and Grey (2000) identified three key components of critical studies that are used as benchmarks, viz., *anti-performativity, denaturalization,* and *reflexivity*. These three elements create a deliberate deconstruction of a norm and critically evaluate it. These elements are a natural consequence of Freire's belief in 'conscientization' where learners become aware of the power structures in the society, and acquire tools to contribute to social transformation (Ruggunan and Spiller, 2014).

For instance, how do HR managers learn from crisis? Experts say that the role and contribution of *reflexivity* to learning is immense. Cassell et al (2019) concluded that *reflexivity* includes "enabling one to think about one's own thought vis-à-vis question one's own taken-for-granted beliefs and those of others. *Reflexivity* predominantly helps employees translate their individual learning into knowledge that is of value to both themselves and their organisations. However, this was used by the author in the classroom as an explanatory mechanism to link HR practices with knowledge exchange combinations.

Critical studies pedagogy helps critique the normative, and prioritize human well-being and social equity over profitability and performance. Critical Studies pedagogy suits HRM from ideological view point. However, critical studies in management have limitations to link theory applied to practice to effectively transform knowledge to skills.

Project Pedagogy

Project Pedagogy combines theory with practice fully exploring the creative potentials and comprehensive capabilities to students to solve managerial HR problems (Jin, 2011).

It helps increase the professional level of teachers and help students to think actively and work on their own initiative. (Jin, 2011). HRM is a practical course and thus it, emphasises on *"what is in use"* and *"how to use"*. Usually, theoretical knowledge is forgotten over a period of time, but project pedagogy enables students to procure process knowledge with respect to processes such as recruitment, training, performance appraisal, human resource planning, compensation management, so that they will know how to do it in real setting. *Reflexivity* finds its place here too. Project pedagogy judiciously combines theory, instruction, and hands-on projects, to help students explore the approaches.

The author found that these two interventions fulfil the quest for criticality and reflection.

Interactive Learning

Interactive learning involves a wider and a more dynamic educational experience resulting from teachers and students working together to obtain knowledge and share information. There are opportunities and difficulties to transform the learning process as educators transition from being knowledge keepers to learning facilitators. Teacher's role changes from being a transmitter to a facilitator. (Tapscott, 1998). The present study uses Panina and Vavilova, (2009) definition of Interactive training as a "way of cognition, realized in the forms of joint activity of students". Here, learning occurs through interaction of all the students with the teacher and vice-versa. In interactive training, feedback becomes obligatory, students experience more autonomy and initiative; students cooperate and learning is problem-based and reflective in nature.

The student(s) engages in dialogue with the instructor and other pedagogical process participants, becomes more of a subject of educational activity, and actively participates in cognitive activities by completing challenging, creative, and investigative tasks during active and interactive learning. Students engage with one another when working in groups and in pairs to complete assignments. According to the author, the application of cutting-edge training methods and procedures fully forms the professional competency in practical activities. (Valeeva, 2009)

Justification of the Pedagogies

Both the pedagogies enable students for *critical participation* in a volatile and a forceful work environment that is beset with challenges inherited from a society as well as that which is replete with deep-rooted socio-economic inequalities and non-uniformities.

The term, *critical participation* is preferred because the course seeks to develop students not only as agents/practitioners of business but as individuals who are endowed with capacities to interrogate social, political, legal, and ethical values that underlie every business discourse. Critical studies nurtures qualities such as reflection, discernment, critique, and evaluation. (Ruggunan and Spiller, 2014). These efforts stress the shift from neutral teaching to critical teaching calling for questioning the presumptions underlying the theory of HRM (Bratton and Gold, 2015; Holden and Griggs, 2011; Lawless and McQue, 2008; Valentin, 2007).

Case studies are appropriate to use critical studies pedagogy. The effectiveness of the critical studies pedagogy lies in the achievement of its objective of exposing the power convolutions, the discriminative and exploitative policies to create a fair working environment. It also analyzes empirical data to find inter-relationships between facts to produce quantified and generalized knowledge.

Project Pedagogy emphasizes blending theory with practice by assigning a group project and serve as a context to develop professional, methodological, and social capabilities (Jin, 2011). Case research enables investigating a contemporary phenomenon with real life context using multiple sources of evidences. (Yin, 1989). Inspite of the above, the above mentioned pedagogies do have their limitations.

Limitations of Pedagogies Against the Academic Goals of the University

Despite the above, adopting a critical teaching practice creates difficulties in enriching critical reflections in the classroom and transferring the same to workplaces. These difficulties emerge not only from the nature of critical knowledge but also from the expectations of 'useful skills and knowledge' imposed on higher education (Valentin, 2007).

For instance, Universities are led by market and are bound to contribute to national innovativeness, thus, truth is lost in the knowledge economy. Moreover, a product-like-knowledge (deliverable, marketable, and transferable) is preferred instead of lifelong learning (Furedi, 2006) to enhance the employability of students by developing skills and attitudes needed for business and society.

Universities also engage in '*cutting edge research*' creating a competitive environment with celebrity like students and teachers. On the other hand, every University including Law Schools are endowed with incubation centres emphasizing on producing individual entrepreneurs thus creating a liberal view of self. Also, subjects of entrepreneurial nature are creating a glorified self for students.

While project pedagogy aims at fulfilling these neo-practices of universities, these efforts actually dilute the very core nature and function of universities – finding truth and engaging in reflective research (Furedi, 2006). Reflection and criticality are thus lost as they merely become rituals of questioning. Continuous struggle for skill enhancement to grab the best of the jobs curtails reflection abilities amongst students; teachers are compelled to believe that students remain unemployed if reflective professionalism is emphasized in a competitive era. (Valentin, 2007; Lawless & McQue 2008).

Results and Discussion: The results are presented under the following headings: Interactive Methods for Developing HRM Teaching:

The mission of the University is to encourage diffusion, progression, development and application of knowledge to instil cross-cultural sensitization, and sensitivity towards community and environment.

At the outset, the author formulated the following learning goals to teach HRM based on Deborah Epstein's work (2014):

- Recognize injustice and develop the ability to respond to it using legal frameworks
- Deal with factual chaos in order to understand power structures, socio-cultural dynamics and consequences
- Learn to exercise judgment
- Learn to solve problems using multidisciplinary contexts

Preparation of teaching plan using OBE:

To include the above elements, the author has prepared a teaching plan using outcome based education (OBE) principles, (compulsory for all courses in the University) for 60 hours of teaching. The students are already exposed to Business Studies, Managerial Economics, and Financial Accounting courses before reaching the HRM classroom. OBE (Spady, 1994) is a comprehensive approach to organize and operate a curriculum that is focused on and defined by the successful demonstrations of learning sought from each learner with three critical domains of outcomes that aid in planning curriculum content, viz., Literacy (tools for acquiring knowledge, skills, and attitudes required to develop others competencies), Content and Performance (Ultimate outcomes to perform (includes evaluation components).

The semester has three internal evaluations:

Component 1 involves learning situations with ethical dilemmas about social justice, welfare, and so on; student needs to choose any one of the four options and present a critique of the option;

Component 2 is a Case Analysis which is based on critical studies involving legal components calling for reflection on socio-politico-legal dilemmas and dark side of organizations; for instance cases such as *"Evaluation of LGBT Recruitment Exercise in the Indian Police Force"* and *"Effect of Employee Harassment (includes gender too) on Workplace Productivity in a Bottling Company in India"* and *"Introducing Menstrual Leave Policy for Women in Indian Organizations"* were used.

Component 3 is a Project Assignment which accomodates Project Pedagogy. External evaluation involves reflective questions and/or case analysis having business and legal aspects.

The above were used as evaluation as well as learning media. For this, an interactive training environment was essential. Every academic year began with opening lectures covering the history and evolution of HRM with conceptual definitions and differences between HRM, Personnel Management, Strategic HRM, International HRM, and so on. In general, the following methods were used for interaction, deconstruction and evaluation.

a) *Movies* and *videos* were shown to engage them with the phenomenon. Interactions were encouraged post videos to create an interactive training environment.
b) *Group discussions* using *Case studies* on gender inequality at workplaces, labour laws, labour markets, and workforce dynamics were part of the classroom sessions; case laws were employed to substantiate their stance.
c) *Group assignments* were given to promote cooperative method of learning. In this method, students have to cooperate or pool-in their efforts to solve the project problem. Each students has to complete a specific part of the project, leading to have a share in the gained knowledge. Kutbiddinova (2014) says that each students goals are achieved subsequent to others' achievement. This method improves communication skills, individual and group responsibility and positive interpersonal relations.
d) *Case studies* are appropriate to use critical studies pedagogy. For instance, a case study about "Managerial effectiveness in a business organization" is given to students. The discussion wouldn't be about factors of effectiveness/ineffectiveness, but about the Managers who represent the capitalist structures largely and are concerned with the development of frameworks to preserve the same (Edwards 1979; Mukherjee & Reed 1999). Managers themselves as social, economic, political and legal entities are open for deconstruction. Therefore, though they have the capacity to control and manipulate other employees through power networks, they too are targets of capitalistic networks and power struc-

tures. Though they are fore-runners in decision making, they are also victims of organizational policies and thus turn docile. The ethical dilemmas faced coupled with subjugation makes them frustrated and cynical causing a detriment to the organization.

e) *Seminars* were introduced wherein students are free to bring-in various paradigms of managerial and legal nature and present it to the class and set the stage open for debates and discussions. The teacher served as a moderator and facilitator.

f) *Declamation activities* were conducted. According to Collins Dictionary, declamation speech is a rhetorical or emotional speech, made to protest or condemn. Persuasive communication skill was developed through this activity which is an asset to Lawyers. These methods not only intensified the author's learning about political nature of HRM but also challenged students to move between various paradigms and perspectives of HRM.

g) *Appreciative Inquiry* was another intervention used. It is an approach that is strengths-based to create change. Instead of problem identification followed by solving Appreciative Inquiry explores what is already working and how to further build on it to support organisational and individual change. It is a collaborative and a constructive process. This intervention has developed advocacy skills and students were able to define new dimensions of problem-solving.

h) *Socratic style of questioning* It is a systematic method of questioning used to explore complex ideas, to get to the root of the truth about things,, to uncover assumptions, problems and issues, to analyse concepts, to differentiate what we know from what we don't know, and to follow logical implications of thought (Paul and Elder 2007).

In 2016, the author realized that dividing HRM into critical and mainstream is absurd and thus for 2017 academic year, the author made some changes to the course content with permission from the Board of Studies. In 2016, lecture method was used, but this time, history of managing people was the focus to situate HRM within multiple managerial paradigms.

From 2017 onwards, the author gained the capability to enable students recognize the situational variables thus developing reflection. This change was exclusively made keeping in view the qualitative student feedback that included student expectations and complaints. The student expectations were linked to many curricula across different global universities. The author focused on critical evaluation by informing students about how HRM should be approached and addressed. To enable more connect and participation, it was decided to use case studies thus laying the foundation for involvement, empathy and critical evaluation. Case studies(Indian and American,) and case-laws were the most prominent methods used as they had to learn business and critique it with ideological inequalities and non-uniformities.

Analysis, synthesis, interpretation, reflection were some skills gained through case methods.

While the mainstream was presented largely through lectures, critical research was essential, thus, case studies along with critical studies in HRM as suggested readings was adopted. This effort led to a wider understanding of HRM, with critical studies in HRM with hands-on experience through case studies and project assignments. Project assignments had good glimpses of links between people management and changing work and employment patterns; Sustainability and Responsibility with respect to HRM was also incoporated (Enhert and Harry, 2012).

Over the five years period (2015-19), a rich collection of reading material was prepared consisting of PPT slides, lecture notes, suggested readings, select videos, research projects/assignments, case studies, classroom hands-on activities, and internal and external exam question papers.

Gradation of Methods adopted:

On scrutinizing the material, the author found that, in the initial years, the method adopted involved more of *Reporting* (involved informing facts through intensive lectures with short discussions and videos, followed by written group assignment, and final exam). The following year, *Reporting* was coupled with *Demanding* (Informing coupled with challenging focussing on suggested/unsuggested pre-reading with debatable questions calling for win-win solutions). The ensuing year involved *Testing* using critique of theory and applications to organizational practices.

Finally, the author graduated into *winning* the students' attention. Winning involved participative inquiry linking HRM with corporate social environement coupled with discussions and debates critiquing the theory and applications. Each stage called for change in course approach and objectives; the teachers tone ranging from didactic to back-slapping. (Refer Table 1)

Table 1. Gradation in the methods adopted

2015-16	2016-17	2017-18	2018-19
Reporting through intensive lectures, group assignments and exams	Demanding coupled with challenging questions. Deconstruction of norms began; questioning and self-critique began	Testing using critique of theory and apply to organizational practices; deconstruction of norms and critically evaluating it; questioning one's own thought process and questioning self and others' viewpoints; identify and understand linkages, and so on. (Denaturalization, anti-performativity and reflexivity)	Winning students by linking HRM with corporate social environment.

Source: generated by the author based on review of literature and author's experience

Along with the methods, teaching of critical HRM also passed through various stages. In the first two years, focus was on history of HRM and industrial relations using lectures; critical view to HRM received minor emphasis compared to mainstream HRM. In the third year, critical view and mainstream view received equal emphasis by challenging students' points of view with critical readings and hands-on activities. In the fourth year, operational HRM, with critical perspectives began emerging from students themselves as they began contesting on social justice; critical thinking became part of the curriculum. Critical thinking helps to think in an analytic and rational manner. It is higher-order thinking. The Socratic style of questioning encourages critical thinking.

Application of Critical Studies Pedagogy:

In critical studies pedagogy, questioning represents one of the core practices that aims to develop radical alternatives while interrogating established theoretical traditions. (Grey & Willmott, 2005). It should be borne in mind that the objective of critical studies is neither personal failures of individual managers/leaders nor poor management of specific firms, but the social injustice and environmental destruction of the broader social and economic systems that managers and firms serve and reproduce.

According to Alvesson and Willmott, 1992, Adler and Heckscher, 2006 and Prasad, 2003, the target of critical studies is management and corporations. Therefore, it focuses on corporate *"dark sides"*, such as sexual harassment, physical and psychological abuse, etc. (occurring within organizational boundaries), and destruction of organizational assets, frauds, environmental disasters, etc (occurring outside the organization) [Linstead et al, 2004]. Alongside, the social, legal, and economic implications and imperatives of the sociology and biology of gender friendly practices in organizations need to be evaluated and critiqued.

Here, Practice Theory (Ortner, 1984) is used to inter-relate knowledge from multiple domains using some steps formulated by Rouse, 2007. The steps are thus followed:

a) The central concern for any conception of social life and understanding is rules, norms, conventions, or meanings. In HRM, for instance, issues like *life of manual scavengers in India, replacing human workers by robots, invasion of artificial intelligence at workplace, giving reservations to women, workplace hazards, and inclusion of LGBT* workforce into workplace need to be critiqued by identifying the rules, norms, conventions and meanings.
b) Reconciling with the social and cultural structures, both explicit and implicit and building on various interpretations.
c) Functional skill of the discipline of HRM is emphasized.
d) Focus on language and tacit knowledge. Students should learn to objectively describe processes, people, practices, and phenomenon. For instance, there are issues that can be shown but not said, or competently enacted only when liberated

from verbal mediation, such as shared suppositions, conceptual frameworks, vocabularies, and so on.

Challenges faced by the teacher for using critical studies pedagogy:

To expect students to engage in critical discussion should be coupled with appropriate teaching and learning approaches. The author paid attention to skills such as detection/smashing of assumptions and values, identifying multiple perspectives, language scrutiny and so on. Inquiry method, case analysis involving people and business, problem solving are other pedagogical methods that complement critical studies.

For students to become strong in critical studies in HRM, teachers need to be adequately equipped with multidisciplinary skills, critiquing and reflection skills, and engage with copious amounts of critical HRM readings with respect to political and moral economies and complex social situations. The role of the teacher undergoes a drastic transformation so as to reconfigure learning spaces and reconceptualise teacher's role. To substantiate, (McWilliam, 2008) said that the teacher is a *'meddler-in-the-middle'* which denotes reciprocity between students and the teacher in assembling, disassembling, and re-assembling cultural paradigms. As a meddler, the teacher's role befits inquiry methods, case methods, and contesting labour legislations. However, a good amount of care should be taken while contesting socially constructed values and assumptions which guide behaviours in organizations too thus creating inequitable power relationships; it may be context or content sensitive.

For instance, discussions regarding hiring members from the LGBT communities, affirmative actions, etc, are context sensitive because some students may belong to the communities in question. At this juncture, arises, *reflexivity* which refers to scrutiny of practice and behaviours and assumptions on which they are based; to be reflexive means to be aware of one's position with respect to race, caste, creed, gender, gender-orientation, status, class, etc. Also, HRM being a social science, it calls for multidisciplinary perspectives while teaching and learning. To achieve the above, country specific problems (in this case, India) and cases need to be discussed so that students can assess the strengths and weaknesses of standard HRM tools.

However, the largest limitation is Critical Studies in India is that, till date, it is dominated by the research works of British and American researchers only. Therefore, empirical evidence and theorization is limited to USA and UK contexts only. For instance, the two prominent HRM models, viz., Michigan model (hard HRM) and Harvard Model (soft HRM) are United States based. (Poole& Mansfield 1994; Hendry & Pettigrew 1994). Added to this, there is a noticeable lack of contribution from academics from the developing world or academics studying the development of critical studies within the developing countries. Except for Gazi Islam's work in 2007, 2012, and 2013 on critical studies in developing countries context, he asserts that there is nothing dependable. Therefore, critical studies are accused of indulging in criticism without providing a viable alternative. However, India specific case studies published by ET cases, Indian Institute of Management, and case studies given in the prescribed text by Indian authors, are used to teach in the class; the dearth however persists.

Critical studies pedagogy focuses on inquiry, questioning, critiquing, reflecting, discerning, and evaluating, however, it does not provide any practical skills. HRM being highly practical it emphasizes on blending theory with applications.

Project Pedagogy:

This pedagogy is required to develop professional practical skills both among teachers as well as students. From a project assignment, teachers begin to focus on project planning, guidance to project implementation and evaluation of project achievements.

Project pedagogy calls for high level professionalism from teachers and doubtlessly this pedagogy shall foster professional growth to teachers.

Given the learning outcomes, students need to develop three vocational capabilities to practice HRM, viz., professional capabilities, methodological capabilities, and social capabilities. The author created some learning situations for students and they were asked to collaborate to complete the assignment. A learning situation here is an episode which is either fictitious or real but it calls for blending theory with practice. These situations convert the learning objectives into smaller, learnable units. Once again, the author emphasizes on the OBE based teaching plan which needs to be divided into professional capability objective, methodological capability objective, and social capability objective as shown below in Table 2.

Table 2. Capabilities to be developed by the student using an example of job analysis and recruitment functions of HRM

Technical capability objective	Methodological capability objective	Social capability objective
Capability to conduct job analysis and write job description	Capability to conduct job analysis through various methods and write competency based job descriptions	Capability to listen Capability to communicate using appropriate language Capability to form teams and sustain team work Capability to innovation and creativity Capability to expand horizons of thought Capability to reflect on what others say
Capabilities to forecast HR demand and supply	Capability to use appropriate statistical methods to calculate demand and supply of Human resource during peak and lean business seasons	
Capability to handle recruitment function	Capability to draft an effective recruitment ad and identify different channels of recruitment, calculate recruitment yield ratios and develop recruitment metrics	
Capability to handle labour contract	Capability to draft labour contract with appropriate terms and conditions	
Capability to administer wages and salaries	Capability to conduct job evaluation, compare with market pay, devise methods of compensation, benefits scheme, etc	
Capability to resolve labour disputes	Capability to apply law and administrative rules to resolve labour disputes	
Capability to appraise performance using different methods, review performance and organize implementation	Capability to design a performance appraisal method, conduct performance review and discussion	

Source: Yin RK (1989). Case Study Research: Design and Method, Sage Publications, California

The above table shall help the teacher to provide project assignments to students to demonstrate appropriate HR functional skills. At the outset, a learning situation is created by the teacher and it ends with a question which is given to student teams (3 students per team) to resolve it. Cases/Situations are taken from the prescribed textbook or any other source which can be duplicated for classroom teaching purpose. The outcomes of Case learning are *diagnosis, observation, correlation, negotiation* and *persuasion, decision making, devising action plans* (with full or part facts/information), *face the difficulty of inadequate information or information asymmetry or imbalance.* (Lundberg & Enz, 1993). The above objectives should be achieved by the student.

Challenges of using Project Pedagogy:

The teacher should ensure that the assignment is clear and definite combining necessary theoretical knowledge with specialized skills. Also, the assignment should be of a certain difficulty. The assignment should be constructive so that students are able to solve practical problems that they have never met and take a multidisciplinary view of every case. For this, the teacher should include some *red herrings* in the assignment.

Project pedagogy is useful because students retain the project assignment experience for a longer time in their memory for, they are actively involved in the case. Theoretical inputs by the teacher, active involvement in the assignment by the student would go a long way integrating knowledge for all practical advantages.

Model to teach HRM to Law students: Based on the above explanation, the following model can be taken in Figure 1:

Figure 1. Model developed to teach HRM to law students

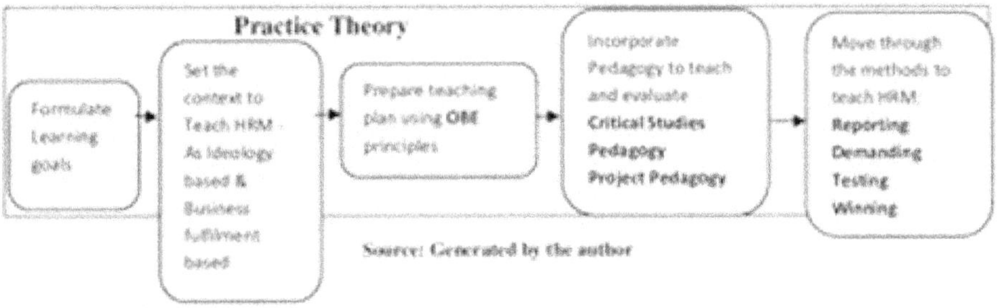

```
                           Practice Theory
                    ┌──────────────────────────┐
                    │                          │   Incorporate        Move through
                    │   Set the                │   Pedagogy to teach  the methods to
                    │   context to             │   and evaluate       teach HRM
   Formulate        │   Teach HRM     Prepare teaching  Critical Studies   Reporting
   Learning         │   As Ideology   plan using OBE   Pedagogy          Demanding
   goals            │   based &       principles       Project Pedagogy  Testing
                    │   Business                                         Winning
                    │   fulfilment
                    │   based          Source: Generated by the author
```

CONCLUSION

The author presents this experiment and experience as a starting point for critical evaluation as well as for combining theory with practice for Law students. The author concludes that Project Pedagogy and Critical Management Studies are the two pedagogies which foster criticality and reflection in learning HRM. Reynolds (1999) highlighted that it is important to integrate critical content into the curricula and change the traditional teaching methods.

An attempt is made to break the traditional, sagacious and dominant role of the teacher. Students were encouraged to give seminar to present their projects which set the platform for debates, ethical dilemmas and lapses in the projects. Disagreements and differing viewpoints were encouraged to contest both theoretical and practical HR issues. Guest lectures and case studies were from practitioners and academicians, and were intended to integrate theory with practice. The purpose of these pedagogies was to create a free learning environment and adequate integration of theory with practice. Interactive methods are directed toward increasing interaction of students not only with the teacher, but also with each other and toward the dominance of the student activity in the learning process (Reutova, 2012).

At the end of the semester, the students have given their feedback that the pedagogies have helped them to negotiate between critique and reflection. Students wanted a similar classroom learning experience in other courses also.

FUTURE RESEARCH DIRECTION

At the outset, these pedagogies would be a success if India-specific or developing countries specific studies in HRM emerge. Studies regarding causes and antecedents of perfunctory acceptance of these pedagogies and interactive methods by integrated program students may be essential because the teacher observed nonchalant responses and social loafers. Competencies of the teachers teaching a course in an integrated classroom to establish contexts and implement the pedagogies call for serious exploration. This study can be used as a precursor by any law college in any country. Design thinking as a pedagogy to teach HRM can be explored.

REFERENCES

Adler, P., & Heckscher, C. (2006). *Towards collaborative community.* In C, Heckscher, & P, S, Adler (Eds,), *The firm as a collaborative community: Reconstructing trust in the knowledge economy* (pp. 11-106). Oxford, UK. Oxford University Press. 10.1093/oso/9780199286034.003.0002

Alvesson, M., & Willmot, H. (1992). On the idea of emancipation in management and organization studies. *Academy of Management Review*, 17(3), 432–464. 10.2307/258718

Alvesson, M., & Willmott, H. (1996). *Making sense of management: A critical analysis.* Sage.

Alvesson, M., & Willmott, H. (Eds,), (2003). *Studying management critically.* Sage.

Arendt, H. (2013). *The human condition.* University of Chicago Press.

Batt, R. (2018). The financial model of the firm, the 'future of work', and employment relations. In Wilkinson, A., Dundon, T., Donaghey, J., & Colvin, A. (Eds.), *The Routledge companion of employment relations.* Routledge. 10.4324/9781315692968-29

Bratton, J., & Gold, J. (2015). *Towards critical human resource management education (CHRME): A sociological imagination approach* (3rd ed., Vol. 29). Work, Employment and Society.

Budhwar, P., & Sparrow, P. (2002). *An Integrative Framework for Determining Cross-National Human Resource Management Practices. Human Resource Management Review, 12.*

Cassell, C., Radcliffe, L., & Malik, F. (2019). Participant reflexivity in organizational research design. *Organizational Research Methods*, 23(4), 750–773. 10.1177/1094428119842640

Coates, J. C., Fried, J. M., & Spier, K. E. (2014). *What Courses Should Law Students Take? Harvard's Largest Employers Weigh In.* (HLS Program on the Legal Profession Research Paper No. 2014-12). Harvard Public Law.

Doktor, R., Tung, R. L., & Von Glinow, M. A. (1991). Future directions for management theory development. *Academy of Management Review*, 16(2), 362–365.

Dundon, Tony & Rafferty, Anthony (2018). The (potential) demise of HRM?, Human Resource Management Journal, John Wiley & Sons, March Vol 28, pp 377-391.

Ehnert, I., & Harry, W. (2012). Recent Developments and Future Prospects on Sustainable Human Resource Management: Introduction to the Special Issue. *Rainer Hampp Verlag*, 23(3), 221–238.

Epstein, D. (2014). *Transforming the Education of Lawyers*. The Clinic Seminar. Georgetown University Law Centre.

Fourier, V., & Grey, C. (2000). At the critical moment: Conditions and prospects for critical management studies. *Human Relations*.

Friere, P. (1970, 1993). *Pedagogy of the Oppressed*. Routledge.

Furedi, F. (2006). *Where have all the intellectuals gone? Confronting 21st century philistinism* (2nd ed.). Continuum.

Godard, J. (2014). The psychologization of employment relations? *Human Resource Management Journal*, 24(1), 1–18. 10.1111/1748-8583.12030

Grey, C., & Willmott, H. C, (Eds.). (2005). *Critical management studies: A reader*. Oxford, UK: Oxford University Press.

Griffin, R. W. (1997). *Management*. AITBS Publishers.

Guest, D. (2011). Human resource management and performance: Still searching for some answers. *Human Resource Management Journal*, 21(1), 3–13. 10.1111/j.1748-8583.2010.00164.x

Hale, H. E. (2014). Patronal Politics. Problems of International Politics. Cambridge University Press., Retrieved October 24, 2019, from. 10.1017/CBO9781139683524

Hendry, C., & Pettigrew, A. (1990). HRM: an agenda for the 1990s. *International Journal of HRM*.

Islam, G. (2012). *Can the subaltern eat? Anthropophagic culture as a Brazilian lens on post-colonial theory*. Sage. 10.1177/1350508411429396

Islam, G., & Zyphur, M. (2007). Critical Industrial Psychology: What is it and where is it? *Psychology in Society, 34*, 17-30.

Janssens, M., & Steyaert, C. (2009) HRM and performance: A plea for reflexivity in HRM studies. *Journal of Management Studies, 46*, 143-155.

Jin, H. (2011). Project Pedagogy applied to the courses of Human Resource Management. In Wang, Y. (Ed.), *Education and Educational Technology, AISC 108. pp* Springer-Verlag Berlin Heidelberg. *663-668 pp*. 10.1007/978-3-642-24775-0_102

Kochan, T. A. (2007). Social legitimacy of the HRM profession: A U.S. perspective. In Boxall, P., Purcell, J., & Wright, P. (Eds.), *The Oxford handbook of human resource management*. Oxford University Press.

Lawless, A., & McQue, L. (2008). Becoming a community of critically reflective HR practitioners: Challenges and opportunities within an MA partnership programme. *Journal of European Industrial Training, 32*.

Linstead, S. A. (Ed.). (2004). Organization theory and postmodern thought. London Sage. • C. C. Lundberg and C. Enz, (1993). 'A framework for student case preparation', Case Research Journal, 13 (Summer) 134/ Michael A. Hitt, R. Duane Ireland and Robert E. Hoskisson, Strategic Management (Thomson Southwestern, 6th Edition) CII. 10.4135/9781446217313

Marchington, M. (2015). Human resource management (HRM): Too busy looking up to see where it is going longer term? *Human Resource Management Review*, 25(2), 176–187. 10.1016/j.hrmr.2015.01.007

McWilliam, E. (2008). *Unlearning how to teach. Innovations in Education and Teaching International*. Taylor & Francis. 10.1080/14703290802176147

Merkle, J. A. (1980). *Management and Ideology*. University of California Press. 10.1525/9780520312104

Mihail, D., & Adelina, D.-P. (2014). *Strategic SI management. Dimensiuni socio-umane contemporane*. Editura Economica.

Muhammad, G. (2021). *Cultivating Genius: An Equity Framework for Culturally and Historically Responsive Literacy: A Four-Layered Framework for Culturally and Historically Responsive Literacy (Scholastic Professional)*. Scholastic Publishing.

Nicolini, D. (2012). *Practice theory, work, and organization: An introduction*. Oxford University Press.

Onah, F. O. (2008). *Human Resource Management. John Jacob's Classic Publisher Ltd Plot 7 Fmr ESUT Road*. Nkpokiti Junction Enugu.

Ortner, S. (1984). Theory in anthropology since the sixties. *Comparative Studies in Society and History*, 26(1), 126–166. 10.1017/S0010417500010811

Panina, T. S., & Vavilova, L. N. (2008). *Modern methods of activation of training*. Academy.

Paul, R., & Elder, L. (2006). *Critical Thinking: Learn the Tools the Best Thinkers Use*. Pearson Prentice Hall.

Pipko, S. (2002). *Baltic Winds: Testimony of a Soviet Attorney*. Xlibris Corporation.

Poole, M., & Mansfield, R. (1994). Managers' attitudes to HRM: Rhetoric and Reality. P Blyton and P. Turnbull (eds), *Reassessing HRM*. London Sage.

Prasad, P. (2005). *Crafting qualitative research: Working in the postpositivist traditions*. M.E. Sharpe.

Reutova, E. A. (2012). *The use of active and interactive training methods in the educational process of the higher education institution (methodical recommendations for the teachers of the Novosibirsk State Agrarian University)*. Publishing House of NGAU.

Reynolds, M. (1999). Critical Reflection and Management Education: Rehabilitating Less Hierarchical Approaches. *Journal of Management Education*, 23(5), 537–553. 10.1177/105256299902300506

Rouse, J. (2007). *Practice Theory*. Division I Faculty Publications.

Ruggunan, S., & Spiller, D. (2014). Critical pedagogy for teaching HRM in the context of social change. *African Journal of Business Ethics*.

Saini, D., & Budhawar, P. (2004). Human Resource Management in India. *Human Resource Management in Asia-Pacific Countries*. Routledge.

Sayer, A. (2003). *Moral Economy published by the Department of Sociology*. Lancaster University. http://www.comp.lancs.ac.uk/sociology/papers/sayer-moral-economy.pdf

Smyth, H.J. & Pryke, S. (2006). *The moral economy and research on projects: neglect and relevance to social capital and competencies*. Cobra 2006, RICS Foundation., UCL London.

Spady, W. (1994). *Outcome-based Education: Critical Issues and Answers*. American Association of School Administrators.

Thompson, P. (2011). The trouble with HRM. *Human Resource Management Journal*, 21(4), 355–367. 10.1111/j.1748-8583.2011.00180.x

Thompson, P., & Vincent, S. (2010). Labour Process Theory and Critical Realism. In *Working life: Renewing labour process analysis. Critical perspectives on work and employment*. Palgrave Macmillan, Houndmills, Basingstoke. 10.1007/978-1-137-11817-2_4

Tracey, M. W., Hutchinson, A., & Grezbyk, T. Q. (2014). Instructional designers as reflective practitioners: Developing professional identity through reflection. *Educational Technology Research and Development*, 62(3), 315–334. 10.1007/s11423-014-9334-9

Valeeva, M. A. (2009). The use of interactive methods of training as a condition of formation of the social professional experience of the student. *Siberian Pedagogical Journal*, 4, 88–98.

Valentin, C. (2007). How can I teach critical management in this place? A critical pedagogy for HRD: possibilities, contradictions and compromises. In Rigg, C., Stewart, J., & Trepan, K. (Eds.), *Critical human resource development. London. Prentice Hall.* • *Sullivan W M et al. (2007), Educating lawyers: preparation for the profession of law [CARNEGIE REPORT}* • *Tapscott, D (1998). Growing Up Digital: The Rise of the Net Generation.* McGraw-Hill.

Yin, R. K. (1989). *Case Study Research: Design and Method.* Sage Publications. https://www.barcouncilofindia.org/wp-content/uploads/2010/05/BCIRulesPartIV.pdf

KEY TERMS AND DEFINITIONS

Critical Thinking: Critical thinking helps you to think in an analytic and rational way. It encourages students to make life decisions cautiously and after evaluating all aspects.

Reflection: A process where students describe their learning, how it changed, and how it might relate to future learning experiences.

Compilation of References

. K, P. (2014). EBIT- EPS Analysis as a Tool to Understand the Performance of Indian Infrastructure Sector. *Indian Journal of Applied Research*, 246-247.

Aba Alkhail, B. (2015). Near-peer-assisted learning (NPAL) in undergraduate medical students and their perception of having medical interns as their near peer teacher. *Medical Teacher*, *37*(sup1), S33-S39.

Abd Karim, R., & Mustapha, R. (2022). TVET Student's Perception on Digital Mind Map to Stimulate Learning of Technical Skills in Malaysia. *Journal of Technical Education and Training*, 14(1). 10.30880/jtet.2022.14.01.001

Abdellah, R. (2015). Metacognitive Awareness and its Relation to Academic Achievement and Teaching Performance of Pre-service Female Teachers in Ajman University in UAE. *Procedia: Social and Behavioral Sciences*, 174, 560–567. 10.1016/j.sbspro.2015.01.707

Abrahamson, K. M. (2016). Engaging students through active learning in library instruction sessions. *Journal of Library & Information Services in the Digital Age*, 17(2), 31–39.

Adhikari, S., Clemens, M., Dempster, H., & Ekeator, N. L. (2021). *A global skill partnership in information, communications, and technology (ICT) between Nigeria and Europe*. Center for Global Development.

Adler, P., & Heckscher, C. (2006). *Towards collaborative community*. In C, Heckscher, & P, S, Adler (Eds,), *The firm as a collaborative community: Reconstructing trust in the knowledge economy* (pp. 11-106). Oxford, UK. Oxford University Press. 10.1093/oso/9780199286034.003.0002

Aghamohammadi-Kalkhoran, M., Karimollahi, M., & Abdi, R. (2011). Iranian staff nurses' attitudes toward nursing students. *Nurse Education Today*, 31(5), 477–481. 10.1016/j.nedt.2010.09.00320926166

Ahmady, S., Khajeali, N., Sharifi, F., & Mirmoghtadaei, Z. S. (2019). Factors related to academic failure in preclinical medical education: A systematic review. *Journal of Advances in Medical Education & Professionalism*, 7(2), 74.31086799

AICTE. (2020). *Review on multidisciplinary education*. AICTE.

Ainscough, L. (2011). Inclusive Education: The Benefits and the Obstacles. *Education*, 132(1), 1–8.

AIU. (2022). *Insights into university administrative and academic structures*. AIU.

Ajjawi, R., Dracup, M., Zacharias, N., Bennett, S., & Boud, D. (2020). Persisting students' explanations of and emotional responses to academic failure. *Higher Education Research & Development*, 39(2), 185–199. 10.1080/07294360.2019.1664999

Akavova, A., Temirkhanova, Z., & Lorsanova, Z. (2023). Adaptive learning and artificial intelligence in the educational space. *E3S Web of Conferences, 451*, 06011.

Alam, A. (2022). Platform utilising blockchain technology for eLearning and online education for open sharing of academic proficiency and progress records *Smart Data Intelligence:Proceedings of ICSMDI 2022* (pp. 307-320): Springer.

Albert Einstein College of Medicine. (n.d.). *Einstein Researchers Discover How Long-Lasting Memories Form in the brain*. Albert Einstein College of Medicine. https://www.einsteinmed.edu/news/10988/einstein-researchers-discover-how-long-lasting-memories-form-in-the-brain/#:~:text=They%20form%20when%20repeated%20neural,required%20for%20long%2Dterm%20memories

Albitz, R. S. (2014). Information literacy and critical thinking: The academic library's role in integrating these skills into the curriculum. *Journal of Academic Librarianship*, 40(3-4), 241–245.

Alé-Ruiz, R., Martínez-Abad, F., & del Moral-Marcos, M. T. (2023). Academic engagement and management of personalised active learning in higher education digital ecosystems. *Education and Information Technologies*. Advance online publication. 10.1007/s10639-023-12358-4

Alexander, B. (2020). *Academia Next: The Futures of Higher Education*. Johns Hopkins University Press.

AlHaqwi, A. I. (2014). Learning outcomes and tutoring in problem based-learning: How do undergraduate medical students perceive them? *International Journal of Health Sciences*, 8(2), 125–132. 10.12816/000607825246879

Alkhawaldeh, M. A., & Khasawneh, M. A. S. (2023). Harnessing The Power of Artificial Intelligence for Personalized Assistive Technology in Learning Disabilities. *Journal of Southwest Jiaotong University*, 58(4). 10.35741/issn.0258-2724.58.4.60

Allan, H. T., Magnusson, C., Evans, K., Horton, K., Curtis, K., Ball, E., & Johnson, M. (2018). Putting knowledge to work in clinical practice: Understanding experiences of preceptorship as outcomes of interconnected domains of learning. *Journal of Clinical Nursing*, 27(1-2), 123–131. 10.1111/jocn.1385528401608

Allen, M., Webb, A. W., & Matthews, C. E. (2016). Adaptive Teaching in STEM: Characteristics for Effectiveness. *Theory into Practice*, 55(3), 217–224. 10.1080/00405841.2016.1173994

Compilation of References

Allen, P. J., Brown, Z., & Noam, G. G. (2020). STEM Learning Ecosystems: Building from Theory toward a Common Evidence Base. *International Journal for Research on Extended Education*, 8(1), 80–96.

Ally, M. (2018). Foundations of Educational Theory for Online Learning. In Anderson, T., & Dron, J. (Eds.), *Handbook of Distance Education* (pp. 93–108). Routledge.

Almarzouki, H. S., Khan, A., Al-Mansour, M., Al-Jifree, H. M., Abuznadah, W., & Althubaiti, A. (2023). Effectiveness of Cognitive Strategies on Short-Term Information Retention: An Experimental Study. *Health Professions Education*. Research Gate. https://www.researchgate.net/publication/369912992_Effectiveness_of_Cognitive_Strategies_on_Short-Term_Information_Retention_An_Experimental_Study

Almirall, D., Kasari, C., McCaffrey, D. F., & Nahum-Shani, I. (2018). Developing optimized adaptive interventions in education. *Journal of Research on Educational Effectiveness*, 11(1), 27–34. 10.1080/19345747.2017.140713629552270

Almuhaideb, A. M., & Saeed, S. (2020). Fostering sustainable quality assurance practices in outcome-based education: Lessons learned from ABET accreditation process of computing programs. *Sustainability (Basel)*, 12(20), 8380. 10.3390/su12208380

Almuhaideb, A. M., & Saeed, S. (2021). A process-based approach to ABET accreditation: A case study of a cybersecurity and digital forensics program. *Journal of Information Systems Education*, 32(2), 119.

Almurayh, A., Saeed, S., Aldhafferi, N., Alqahtani, A., & Saqib, M. (2022). Sustainable education quality improvement using academic accreditation: Findings from a university in Saudi Arabia. *Sustainability (Basel)*, 14(24), 16968. 10.3390/su142416968

Al-Okaily, A., Al-Okaily, M., Teoh, A. P., & Al-Debei, M. M. (2022). An empirical study on data warehouse systems effectiveness: The case of Jordanian banks in the business intelligence era. *EuroMed Journal of Business*.

Aloqleh, A. M. A., & Teh, K. S. M. (2019). The Effectiveness of Metacognition on Academic Achievement among the Jordanian Universities Students. *International Journal of Academic Research in Business & Social Sciences*, 9(9). 10.6007/IJARBSS/v9-i9/6315

Al-Samarraie, H., & Hurmuzan, S. (2018). A review of brainstorming techniques in higher education. *Thinking Skills and Creativity*, 27, 78–91. 10.1016/j.tsc.2017.12.002

Alvesson, M., & Willmott, H. (Eds,), (2003). *Studying management critically*. Sage.

Alvesson, M., & Willmot, H. (1992). On the idea of emancipation in management and organization studies. *Academy of Management Review*, 17(3), 432–464. 10.2307/258718

Alvesson, M., & Willmott, H. (1996). *Making sense of management: A critical analysis*. Sage.

Al-Zahrani, A. M. (2015). From passive to active: The impact of the flipped classroom through social learning platforms on higher education students' creative thinking. *British Journal of Educational Technology*, 46(6), 1133–1148. 10.1111/bjet.12353

Amhag, L., Hellström, L., & Stigmar, M. (2019). Teacher educators' use of digital tools and needs for digital competence in higher education. *Journal of Digital Learning in Teacher Education*, 35(4), 203–220. 10.1080/21532974.2019.1646169

Aminatun, T., Subali, B., Dwiyani, A., Prihartina, I., & Meliana, D. (2022). Developing Android-Based Mobile through Local Ecosystem Materials to Improve Thinking Skills of High School Students. *Anatolian Journal of Education*, 7(1), 73–82. 10.29333/aje.2022.716a

Anbalagan, G. (2019). Learning Ecosystem for Open and Distance Learning. In Railean, E. (Ed.), *Handbook of Research on Ecosystem-Based Theoretical Models of Learning and Communication* (pp. 124–138). IGI Global. 10.4018/978-1-5225-7853-6.ch007

Anderson, V., Rabello, R., Wass, R., Golding, C., Rangi, A., Eteuati, E., & Waller, A. (2019). Good teaching as care in higher education. *Higher Education*, 79.

Angelo, T. A., & Cross, K. P. (1993). *Classroom Assessment Techniques: A Handbook for College Teachers*. Jossey-Bass.

Apoki, U. C., Hussein, A. M. A., Al-Chalabi, H. K. M., Badica, C., & Mocanu, M. L. (2022). The role of pedagogical agents in personalised adaptive learning: A review. *Sustainability (Basel)*, 14(11), 6442. 10.3390/su14116442

Aquino, Y. S. J., Carter, S. M., Houssami, N., Braunack-Mayer, A., Win, K. T., Degeling, C., Wang, L., & Rogers, W. A. (2023). Practical, epistemic and normative implications of algorithmic bias in healthcare artificial intelligence: A qualitative study of multidisciplinary expert perspectives. *Journal of Medical Ethics*, jme-2022-108850. 10.1136/jme-2022-10885036823101

Araoye, M. I. (2013). Redressing Students' Motivation and Academic Achievement in Biology Education at the Federal College of Education (Special) Oyo Oyo State, Nigeria. *New Perspectives in Science Education, 2*.

Arendse, J. P. (2020). Psychosocial factors predicting academic performance of first-year college nursing students in the Western Cape, South Africa. [Master thesis, University of Western Cape].

Arendt, H. (2013). *The human condition*. University of Chicago Press.

Assefa, Z., & Felix, B. (2021). Application of Actor-Network Theory (ANT) to Depict the Use of NRENs at Higher Education Institutions.*Paper presented at the Advances in Information and Communication: Proceedings of the 2021 Future of Information and Communication Conference (FICC)*. Springer. 10.1007/978-3-030-73100-7_25

Association of College & Research Libraries. (2000). *Information literacy competency standards for higher education*. Association of College & Research Libraries.

Compilation of References

Association of College & Research Libraries. (2015). *Framework for Information Literacy for Higher Education*. American Library Association.

Association of College & Research Libraries. (2016). *Standards for librarians and information specialists in schools*. Chicago, IL: American Library Association.

Astin, A. W. (1993). *What Matters in College? Four Critical Years Revisited*. Jossey-Bass.

Baepler, P., Walker, J. D., & Driessen, M. (2014). It's not about seat time: Blending, flipping, and efficiency in active learning classrooms. *Computers & Education*, 65, 227–236. 10.1016/j.compedu.2014.06.006

Bahcivan, E., Gurer, M. D., Yavuzalp, N., & Akayoglu, S. (2019). Investigating the relations among pre-service teachers' teaching/learning beliefs and educational technology integration competencies: A structural equation modeling study. *Journal of Science Education and Technology*, 28(5), 579–588. 10.1007/s10956-019-09788-6

Bahramnezhad, F., Shahbazi, B., Asgari, P., & Keshmiri, F. (2019). Comparative study of the undergraduate nursing curricula among nursing schools of mcmaster university of Canada, hacettepe university of Turkey, and tehran university of Iran. *Strides in Development of Medical Education, 16*(1).

Baker, R. S., & Hawn, A. (2022). Algorithmic bias in education. *International Journal of Artificial Intelligence in Education*, 1–41.

Bandura, A. (1977). *Social Learning Theory*. Prentice Hall.

Bandura, A. (1979). Self-referent mechanisms in social learning theory. *The American Psychologist*, 34(5), 439–441. 10.1037/0003-066X.34.5.439.b

Barker, P. (1994). Designing interactive learning. In *Design and production of multimedia and simulation-based learning material* (pp. 1–30). Springer Netherlands. 10.1007/978-94-011-0942-0_1

Barlow, A. T., Watson, L. A., Tessema, A. A., Lischka, A. E., & Strayer, J. F. (2018). Inspection-Worthy Mistakes: Which? And Why? *National Council of Teachers of Mathematics*, 24, 384–391.

Barrows, H. S. (1986). A taxonomy of problem-based learning methods. *Medical Education*, 20(6), 481–486. 10.1111/j.1365-2923.1986.tb01386.x3796328

Barth, M., & Rieckmann, M. (2012). Academic staff development as a catalyst for curriculum change towards education for sustainable development: An output perspective. *Journal of Cleaner Production*, 26, 28–36. 10.1016/j.jclepro.2011.12.011

Batt, R. (2018). The financial model of the firm, the 'future of work', and employment relations. In Wilkinson, A., Dundon, T., Donaghey, J., & Colvin, A. (Eds.), *The Routledge companion of employment relations*. Routledge. 10.4324/9781315692968-29

Becker, B. W. (2015). Librarian perceptions and practices in teaching research skills: A mixed-methods study. *Reference and User Services Quarterly*, 54(2), 115–126.

Becker, J. (2019). Bard College: An Ecosystem of Engagement. *Journal of Community Engagement and Higher Education at Indiana State University*, 11(1), 38–52.

Behari-Leak, K. (2017). New academics, new higher education contexts: A critical perspective on professional development. *Teaching in Higher Education*, 22(5), 485–500. 10.1080/13562517.2016.1273215

Belfield, C., Bowden, A. B., Klapp, A., Levin, H., Shand, R., & Zander, S. (2015). The Economic Value of Social and Emotional Learning. *Journal of Benefit-Cost Analysis*, 6(3), 508–544. 10.1017/bca.2015.55

Bellocchi, A. (2019). Early career science teacher experiences of social bonds and emotion management. *Journal of Research in Science Teaching*, 56(3), 322–347. 10.1002/tea.21520

Belt, E., & Lowenthal, P. (2020). Developing faculty to teach with technology: Themes from the literature. *TechTrends*, 64(2), 248–259. 10.1007/s11528-019-00447-6

Benjes-Small, C., Archer, A., Tucker, K., & Vassady, L. (2013). Teaching Web Evaluation: A Cognitive Development Approach. *Communications in Information Literacy*, 7(1), 39. 10.15760/comminfolit.2013.7.1.133

Benson, J., & Dresdow, S. (2015). Thinking design: Engagement in an innovation project. *Decision Sciences Journal of Innovative Education*, 13(3), 377–410. 10.1111/dsji.12069

Bergmann, J., & Sams, A. (2012). *Flip your classroom: Reach every student in every class every day*. ASCD.

Berg, S. A., & Jacobs, H. L. (2016). Academic libraries and campus engagement: Collaborations and partnerships that enhance student learning and involvement. *College & Research Libraries News*, 77(1), 16–19.

Bhat, J. R., & Alqahtani, S. A. (2021). 6G ecosystem: Status and future perspective. *IEEE Access : Practical Innovations, Open Solutions*, 9, 43134–43167. 10.1109/ACCESS.2021.3054833

Bhehlol, M. G., & Cajkler, W. (2018). Practices, Challenges and Implications of Teaching and Assessment of Cognitive Skills in Higher Education. *Pakistan Journal of Education*, 35(1). 10.30971/pje.v35i1.567

Bhujanga Rao, P., & Inampudi, P. (2023). An evaluation of the Indian National Education Policy 2020 in terms of achieving institutional goals. [IJSR]. *International Journal of Science and Research (Raipur, India)*, 12(5), 44214. 10.21275/SR23510044214

Biggs, J., & Tang, C. (2011). *Teaching for Quality Learning at University*. Open University Press.

Bjork, R. A. (1994). *Memory and metamemory considerations in the training of human beings*. MIT Press. 10.7551/mitpress/4561.003.0011

Compilation of References

Black, P., & Wiliam, D. (1998). Assessment and classroom learning. *Assessment in Education: Principles, Policy & Practice*, 5(1), 7–74. 10.1080/0969595980050102

Black, P., & Wiliam, D. (1998). Inside the Black Box: Raising Standards Through Classroom Assessment. *Phi Delta Kappan*, 80(2), 139–148.

Blandy, D., & Fitzsimmons, P. (2016). Interdisciplinary learning: Process and outcomes. *Journal of Geography in Higher Education*, 40(2), 252–271.

Blau, G., & Schwartz, D. G. (2018). Maximizing student engagement in library instruction sessions: A review of the literature. *College & Research Libraries*, 79(7), 927–952.

Blummer, B., & Kenton, J. M. (2017). Promoting critical thinking skills through library instruction: Methods and resources. *RSR. Reference Services Review*, 45(4), 576–590.

Bond, R., & Castagnera, E. (2006). Peer Supports and Inclusive Education: An Underutilized Resource. *Theory into Practice*, 45(3), 224–229. 10.1207/s15430421tip4503_4

Bonsaksen, T., Ellingham, B. J., & Carstensen, T. (2018). Factors associated with academic performance among second-year undergraduate occupational therapy students. *The Open Journal of Occupational Therapy*, 6(1), 14. 10.15453/2168-6408.1403

Bonwell, C. C., & Eison, J. A. (1991). ASHE-ERIC Higher Education Report: Vol. 1. *Active learning: Creating excitement in the classroom*. George Washington University.

Bonwell, C. C., & Eison, J. A. (1991). ASHE-ERIC Higher Education Report: Vol. 1. *Active Learning: Creating Excitement in the Classroom*. School of Education and Human Development, George Washington University.

Boothe, K. A., Lohmann, M. J., Donnell, K. A., & Hall, D. D. (2018). Applying the Principles of Universal Design for Learning (UDL) in the College Classroom. *The Journal of Special Education Apprenticeship*, 7(3), 1–13. 10.58729/2167-3454.1076

Booth, T., & Ainscow, M. (2011). *Index for Inclusion: Developing Learning and Participation in Schools*. CSIE.

Boström, L., Collén, C., Damber, U., & Gidlund, U. (2021). A Rapid Transition from Campus to Emergent Distant Education; Effects on Students' Study Strategies in Higher Education. *Education Sciences*, 11(11), 721. 10.3390/educsci11110721

Boulton, G., Loucoubar, C., Mwelwa, J., Wafula, M., Ozor, N., & Bolo, M. (2020). *Open science in research and innovation for development in Africa: African Technology Policy Studies Network*. ATPS.

Bozkurt, A., Karadeniz, A., Baneres, D., Guerrero-Roldán, A. E., & Rodríguez, M. E. (2021). Artificial intelligence and reflections from educational landscape: A review of AI Studies in half a century. *Sustainability (Basel)*, 13(2), 800. 10.3390/su13020800

Bransford, J., Brown, A., & Cocking, R. (2000). *How People Learn: Brain, Mind, Experience, and School*. National Academy Press.

Bratton, J., & Gold, J. (2015). *Towards critical human resource management education (CHRME): A sociological imagination approach* (3rd ed., Vol. 29). Work, Employment and Society.

Brauer, J. (2018). Information literacy and inquiry-based learning: A perfect partnership. *Journal of Library & Information Services in the Digital Age*, 19(3), 1–9.

Brink, H., & Van der Walt, C. (2006). *Fundamentals of research methodology for health care professionals* (4th ed.). Juta.

Brodie, D. A., Andrews, G. J., Andrews, J. P., Thomas, B. G., Wong, J., & Rixon, L. (2005). Working in London hospitals: Perceptions of place in nursing students' employment considerations. *Social Science & Medicine*, 61(9), 1867–1881. 10.1016/j.socscimed.2005.03.04215939515

Brooks, J. G., & Brooks, M. G. (1999). *In Search of Understanding: The Case for Constructivist Classrooms*. Association for Supervision and Curriculum Development.

Brown, C., & Kingsley-Wilson, B. (2010). Assessing the information needs of graduate students in the biological and life sciences. *Journal of Academic Librarianship*, 36(5), 375–383.

Brown, C., White, L., & Jones, K. (2018). Importance of collaborative tools in higher education. *International Journal of Educational Technology in Higher Education*, 15(1), 1–15.

Brown, C., White, L., & Jones, K. (2019). Digital textbooks: Addressing the evolving needs of higher education. *Journal of Online Learning Research*, 5(2), 101–118.

Brown, T., & Martin, R. (2015). Action design. *Harvard Business Review*, 93(9), 57–64.

Brunetti, K., Hofer, A. R., & Townsend, L. (2014). Interdisciplinary collaboration: Librarians and faculty working together to enhance student information literacy skills in biology. *Science & Technology Libraries*, 33(3), 267–282.

Bryant, J., & Mann, B. (2017). The flipped classroom model for teaching library research skills: Student engagement and learning outcomes. *Journal of Library & Information Services in Distance Learning*, 11(3-4), 316–331.

Budhwar, P., & Sparrow, P. (2002). *An Integrative Framework for Determining Cross-National Human Resource Management Practices. Human Resource Management Review, 12*.

Buehl, D. (2023). *Classroom strategies for interactive learning*. Routledge. 10.4324/9781032680842

Butler, M. G., Church, K. S., & Spencer, A. W. (2019). Do, reflect, think, apply: Experiential education in accounting. [CrossRef] [Google Scholar]. *Journal of Accounting Education*, 48, 12–21. 10.1016/j.jaccedu.2019.05.001

Caine, R. N., & Caine, G. (1994). *Making Connections: Teaching and the Human Brain*. Addison-Wesley Publishing Company.

Compilation of References

Calp, M. H., & Bütüner, R. (2022). *Society 5.0: Effective technology for a smart society Artificial Intelligence and Industry 4.0*. Elsevier.

Capuano, N., & Caballé, S. (2020). Adaptive learning technologies. *AI Magazine*, 41(2), 96–98. 10.1609/aimag.v41i2.5317

Carbery, A., & Leahy, S. (2015). Flipping the classroom in library instruction: Impact on information literacy skills in undergraduate engineering students. *Library Hi Tech*, 33(4), 458–469.

Cardak, O., & Dikmenli, M. (2016). Student Science Teachers' Ideas about the Degradation of Ecosystems. *International Education Studies*, 9(3), 95–103. 10.5539/ies.v9n3p95

Carlock, D., & Anderson, J. (2007). Teaching database searching skills to nursing students: A practical approach. *Medical Reference Services Quarterly*, 26(1), 51–60.17210549

Carmi, T., & Tamir, E. (2020). Three professional ideals: Where should teacher preparation go next? *European Journal of Teacher Education*, 1–20. 10.1080/02619768.2020.1805732

Carstensen, S. S., Kjaer, C., Möller, S., & Bloksgaard, M. (2020). Implementing collaborative, active learning using peer instructions in pharmacology teaching increases students' learning and thereby exam performance. *European Journal of Pharmacology*, 867, 172792. 10.1016/j.ejphar.2019.17279231733212

Caspers, J., & Bernhisel, S. (2005). Assessing freshmen's research skills to tailor library instruction effectively. *College & Research Libraries*, 66(5), 471–484.

Cassell, C., Radcliffe, L., & Malik, F. (2019). Participant reflexivity in organizational research design. *Organizational Research Methods*, 23(4), 750–773. 10.1177/1094428119842640

Castleberry, A., & Nolen, A. (2018). Thematic analysis of qualitative research data: Is it as easy as it sounds? *Currents in Pharmacy Teaching & Learning*, 10(6), 807–815. 10.1016/j.cptl.2018.03.01930025784

CEDEFOP. (2008). *Conceptual, political, and practical developments in Europe*. European Centre for the Development of Vocational Training. https://www.cedefop.europa.eu/files/4079_en.pdf

Chai, C. S., & Koh, J. H. L. (2017). Changing teachers' TPaCK and design beliefs through the scaffolded TPaCK lesson design model (STLDM). *Learning (Abingdon (England))*, 3(2), 114–129. 10.1080/23735082.2017.1360506

Chang, V., & Guetl, C. e-Learning ecosystem (ELES) – A holistic approach for the development of more effective learning environment for small-and-medium-sized enterprises (SMEs). In: *Proceedings of the Inaugural IEEE International Conference on Digital Ecosystems and Technologies*. IEEE. 10.1109/DEST.2007.372010

Chaplot, D. S., Rhim, E., & Kim, J. (2016). Personalized adaptive learning using neural networks. *Proceedings of the Third (2016) ACM Conference on Learning@ Scale*, (pp. 165–168). ACM. 10.1145/2876034.2893397

Chavan, S. S., Jose, J., D'Souza, J., & Mathews, A. A. (2019). An explorative study on factors affecting nursing student's academic failure. *Manipal Journal of Nursing and Health Sciences*, 5(1), 27–31.

Chen, E., Leos, C., Kowitt, S. D., & Moracco, K. E. (2020). Enhancing community-based participatory research through human-centered design strategies. *Health Promotion Practice*, 21(1), 37–48. 10.1177/152483991985055731131633

Cheng, S. F., Kuo, C. L., Lin, K. C., & Lee-Hsieh, J. (2010). Development and preliminary testing of a self-rating instrument to measure self-directed learning ability of nursing students. *International Journal of Nursing Studies*, 47(9), 1152–1158. 10.1016/j.ijnurstu.2010.02.00220223455

Chen, J. C. (2017). Nontraditional Adult Learners: The Neglected Diversity in Postsecondary Education. *SAGE Open*, 7(1), 1–12. 10.1177/2158244017697161

Chen, L., Chang, H., Rudoler, J., Arnardottir, E., Zhang, Y., De Los Angeles, C., & Menon, V. (2022). Cognitive training enhances growth mindset in children through plasticity of cortico-striatal circuits. *NPJ Science of Learning*, 7(1), 30. 10.1038/s41539-022-00146-736371438

Chigbu, B. I., & Nekhwevha, F. H. (2022). Academic-faculty environment and graduate employability: Variation of work-readiness perceptions. *Heliyon*, 8(3), e09117. 10.1016/j.heliyon.2022.e0911735342827

Chigbu, B. I., Ngwevu, V., & Jojo, A. (2023). The effectiveness of innovative pedagogy in the industry 4.0: Educational ecosystem perspective. *Social Sciences & Humanities Open*, 7(1), 100419. 10.1016/j.ssaho.2023.100419

Chohan, S. R., & Hu, G. (2022). Strengthening digital inclusion through e-government: Cohesive ICT training programs to intensify digital competency. *Information Technology for Development*, 28(1), 16–38. 10.1080/02681102.2020.1841713

Chu, S. K. W., & Lau, W. W. F. (2020). E-learning and student attitudes: A case study from Hong Kong. *Journal of Educational Technology & Society*, 23(2), 80–94.

Clarke, M. L. (2016). Peer tutoring of junior nursing students: Student experiences and perceptions of self-efficacy and benefit. City: Liberty University.

Clark, R. C., & Paivio, A. (1991). Dual coding theory and education. *Educational Psychology Review*, 3(3), 149–210. 10.1007/BF01320076

Cleland, J. A. (2017, June). *The qualitative orientation in medical education research*. NCBI. https://www.ncbi.nlm.nih.gov/pmc/articles/PMC5465434/#:~:text=Conclusion,

Cleveland, L. M., Olimpo, J. T., & DeChenne-Peters, S. E. (2017). Investigating the relationship between instructors' use of active-learning strategies and students' conceptual understanding and affective changes in introductory biology: A comparison of two active-learning environments. *CBE Life Sciences Education*, 16(2), ar19. 10.1187/cbe.16-06-018128389428

Compilation of References

Cmor, D., & Lippold, K. (2001). Strategic searching vs. casual web surfing: Enhancing students' information search skills. *Internet Reference Services Quarterly*, 6(1), 27–36.

Coates, J. C., Fried, J. M., & Spier, K. E. (2014). *What Courses Should Law Students Take? Harvard's Largest Employers Weigh In.* (HLS Program on the Legal Profession Research Paper No. 2014-12). Harvard Public Law.

Compte, O. (2023). *Endogenous Barriers to Learning* (Version 1). arXiv. https://doi.org/10.48550/ARXIV.2306.16904

Conley, C. S. (2015). SEL in higher education. In *Handbook of Social and Emotional Learning: Research and Practice* (pp. 197–212). The Guilford Press.

Coomber, R. (2019). How do professional service staff perceive and engage with professional development programmes within higher education institutions? *Perspectives (Association of University Administrators* (U.K.)), *23*(2-3), 61–69. 10.1080/13603108.2018.1543216

Cooney, M. (2011). Best practices for implementing flipped classroom models in library instruction. *Journal of Library Innovation*, 2(2), 40–50.

Cornell University. (n.d.). *Metacognitive Strategies (How People Learn).* Center for Teaching Innovation. https://teaching.cornell.edu/teaching-resources/teaching-cornell-guide/teaching-strategies/metacognitive-strategies-how-people#:~:text=Metacognitive%20strategies%20are%20techniques%20to,thinking%20processes%20as%20they%20learn

Corno, L. (2018). On Teaching Adaptively. *Educational Psychologist*, *43*(3), 161–173. 10.1080/00461520802178466

Costa, R. S., Tan, Q., Pivot, F., Zhang, X., & Wang, H. (2021). Personalized and adaptive learning: Educational practice and technological impact. *Texto Livre*, 14(3), e33445. 10.35699/1983-3652.2021.33445

Courey, S. J., Tappe, P., Siker, J., & LePage, P. (2012). Improved Lesson Planning with Universal Design for Learning (UDL). *Teacher Education and Special Education*, *36*(1), 7–27. 10.1177/0888406412446178

Coursera. (2020). *Blended learning models.* Coursea.

Cross, K. P. (1988). Anatomy of interdisciplinary studies. *Change*, 20(6), 9–15.

Crouch, C. H., & Mazur, E. (2001). Peer Instruction: Ten years of experience and results. *American Journal of Physics*, 69(9), 970–977. 10.1119/1.1374249

Curran, S., Wu, M., & Webb, C. (2017). Engaging students in library instruction: Using collaborative learning to enhance information literacy skills. *Journal of Academic Librarianship*, 43(2), 151–159.

Dahl, C. (2004). Student perspectives on electronic classrooms: Impact on learning and engagement. *Portal (Baltimore, Md.)*, 4(3), 393–407.

Dalgarno, B., & Lee, M. J. W. (2010). What are the learning affordances of 3-D virtual environments? *British Journal of Educational Technology*, 41(1), 10–32. 10.1111/j.1467-8535.2009.01038.x

Damodaran, A. (2002). *Corporate Finance - Theory and Practice*. Wiley India Pvt Ltd.

Dansereau, D. F. (2014). Learning strategy research. In *Thinking and learning skills* (pp. 209–239). Routledge.

Dante, A., Ferrão, S., Jarosova, D., Lancia, L., Nascimento, C., Notara, V., Pokorna, A., Rybarova, L., Skela-Savič, B., & Palese, A. (2016). Nursing student profiles and occurrence of early academic failure: Findings from an explorative European study. *Nurse Education Today*, 38, 74–81. 10.1016/j.nedt.2015.12.01326763210

Darling-Hammond, L. (2010). Teacher quality and student achievement: A review of state policy evidence. *Education Policy Analysis Archives*, 8(1), 1–44.

Darling-Hammond, L., Wilhoit, G., & Pittenger, L. (2014). Accountability for college and career readiness: Developing a new paradigm. *Education Policy Analysis Archives*, 22(86), 1–32. 10.14507/epaa.v22n86.2014

Das, A. (2021). Student engagement strategies in NEP implementation.

Demartini, C. G., Sciascia, L., Bosso, A., & Manuri, F. (2024). Artificial Intelligence Bringing Improvements to Adaptive Learning in Education: A Case Study. *Sustainability (Basel)*, 16(3), 1347. 10.3390/su16031347

Dennison, S. (2010). Peer mentoring: Untapped potential. *The Journal of Nursing Education*, 49(6), 340–342. 10.3928/01484834-20100217-0420210287

Deshpande, L. (2020). Implications of NEP's language policy.

Deslauriers, L., McCarty, L. S., Miller, K., Callaghan, K., & Kestin, G. (2019). Measuring actual learning versus feeling of learning in response to being actively engaged in the classroom. *Proceedings of the National Academy of Sciences of the United States of America*, 116(39), 19251–19257. 10.1073/pnas.182193611631484770

Detmering, R., & Johnson, A. M. (2012). Understanding students' research challenges: Action research in library instruction. *College & Research Libraries*, 73(2), 209–224.

Detyna, M., Granelli, F., & Betts, T. (2023). Exploring the effect of a collaborative problem-based learning simulation within a technology-enhanced learning environment on tutor perceptions and student learning outcomes. *Journal of Education and Training Studies*, 12(1), 53. Advance online publication. 10.11114/jets.v12i1.6499

DeVito, M. (2016). *Factors influencing student engagement*.

Diaz, K. R. (2003). Integrating information literacy into academic curricula: Practical strategies and collaborations. *RSR. Reference Services Review*, 31(3), 213–220.

Compilation of References

Diehl, W., Grobe, T., Lopez, H., & Cabral, C. (1999). *Project-based learning: A strategy for teaching and learning*. Center for Youth Development and Education, Corporation for Business, Work, and Learning.

Dikmen, Y., Ak, B., Yildirim Usta, Y., Ünver, V., Akin Korhan, E., Cerit, B., & Yönder Ertem, M. (2017). Effect of peer teaching used in nursing education on the performance and competence of students in practical skills training. *International Journal of Educational Sciences*, 16(1-3), 14–20. 10.1080/09751122.2017.1311583

Discipulo, L. G., & Bautista, R. G. (2022). Students' cognitive and metacognitive learning strategies towards hands-on science. [IJERE]. *International Journal of Evaluation and Research in Education*, 11(2), 658. 10.11591/ijere.v11i2.22018

Doktor, R., Tung, R. L., & Von Glinow, M. A. (1991). Future directions for management theory development. *Academy of Management Review*, 16(2), 362–365.

Donnelly, R., & Maguire, T. (2020). Building Digital Capacity for Higher Education Teachers: Recognising Professional Development through a National Peer Triad Digital Badge Ecosystem. European Journal of Open. *Distance and E-Learning*, 23(2), 1–19.

Drake, A., & Acosta, M. (2016). Interactive library instruction: Enhancing student engagement and information literacy skills. *Communications in Information Literacy*, 10(1), 73–89.

Driscoll, M. P. (2000). Constructivism. In *Psychology of learning for instruction* (2nd ed., pp. 267–307). Allyn & Bacon.

Driscoll, M. P. (2016). *Psychology of Learning for Instruction*. Pearson.

Dror, I. E., Makany, T., & Kemp, J. (2011). Overcoming learning barriers through knowledge management. *Dyslexia (Chichester, England)*, 17(1), 38–47. 10.1002/dys.41920872423

Drucker, P. F. (1966). *The effective executive*. DT Leadership. https://dtleadership.my/wp-content/uploads/2019/05/Drucker-2006-The-Effective-Executive-The-Definitive-Guide-to-Getting-the-Right-Things-Done.pdf

Dubicki, E. (2013). Faculty perceptions of students' information literacy competencies: Identifying gaps and improving instruction. *Journal of Information Literacy*, 7(2), 97–119. 10.11645/7.2.1852

DuBoulay, B. (2016). Artificial intelligence as an effective tutor. *IEEE Intelligent Systems*, 31(6), 38–43.

Duch, B. J., Groh, S. E., & Allen, D. E. (Eds.). (2001). *The Power of Problem-Based Learning*. Stylus Publishing, LLC.

Duffy, T. M., & Jonassen, D. H. (1992). *Constructivism and the technology of instruction: A conversation*. Lawrence Erlbaum Associates.

Dundon, Tony & Rafferty, Anthony (2018). The (potential) demise of HRM?, Human Resource Management Journal, John Wiley & Sons, March Vol 28, pp 377-391.

Duque, L. C. (2014). A framework for analyzing higher education performance: Students' satisfaction, perceived learning outcomes, and dropout intentions. *Total Quality Management & Business Excellence*, 25(1-2), 1–21. 10.1080/14783363.2013.807677

Durlak, J. A., Weissberg, R. P., Dymnicki, A. B., Taylor, R. D., & Schellinger, K. B. (2011). The impact of enhancing students' social and emotional learning: A meta-analysis of school-based universal interventions. *Child Development*, 82(1), 405–432. 10.1111/j.1467-8624.2010.01564.x21291449

Ebersole, L. (2019). Preservice teacher experience with technology integration: How the preservice teacher's efficacy in technology integration is impacted by the context of the preservice teacher education program. *International Dialogues on Education*, 6(2). 10.53308/ide.v6i2.64

Ebert-May, D., Derting, T. L., Hodder, J., Momsen, J. L., Long, T. M., & Jardeleza, S. E. (2011). What we say is not what we do: Effective evaluation of faculty professional development programs. *Bioscience*, 61(7), 550–558. 10.1525/bio.2011.61.7.9

Education Advanced. (2022). *Innovative Teaching Strategies: Nine Techniques for Success*. Education Advanced. https://educationadvanced.com/resources/blog/innovative-teaching-strategies-nine-techniques-for-success/

edX. (2024, February 20). *Guide to types of learning Styles*. Teach.com. https://teach.com/what/teachers-know/learning-styles/

Ehnert, I., & Harry, W. (2012). Recent Developments and Future Prospects on Sustainable Human Resource Management: Introduction to the Special Issue. *Rainer Hampp Verlag*, 23(3), 221–238.

Ekka, A., & Bhujanga Rao, P. (2023). An empirical study on the awareness on NEP 2020 [National Education Policy] and its effects on the stakeholders. *International Journal of Multidisciplinary Educational Research*, 12(5-3), 42. http://ijmer.in.doi./2023/12.05.42

Emvula, O. (2016). *Perceptions of registered nurses regarding their role of clinical teaching of student nurses at state training hospitals in Windhoek, Namibia* [Doctoral dissertation, University of Namibia].

Engage. (2024, February 16). *VAK learning styles: what are they and what do they mean?* Engage Education. https://engage-education.com/blog/vak-learning-styles-what-are-they-and-what-do-they-mean-engage-education/

Epstein, D. (2014). *Transforming the Education of Lawyers*. The Clinic Seminar. Georgetown University Law Centre.

Ernst & Young. (2020). *Strategic reports on NEP vision*. Ernst & Young.

Esteve-Mon, F. M., Postigo-Fuentes, A. Y., & Castañeda, L. (2023). A strategic approach of the crucial elements for the implementation of digital tools and processes in higher education. *Higher Education Quarterly*, 77(3), 558–573. 10.1111/hequ.12411

Compilation of References

Facer, K., & Sandford, R. (2010). *The next 25 years? Future scenarios and future directions for education and technology. British Educational Communications and Technology Agency*. Becta.

Fagan, J. (2018). Engaging students in active learning through information literacy scavenger hunts. *Journal of Library & Information Services in the Digital Age*, 19(1), 1–11.

Farnam Street. (2023, December 9). *Mental models: The best way to make intelligent decisions (~100 models explained)*. Farnam Street. https://fs.blog/mental-models

Farrell, R., & Badke, W. (2015). Integrating information literacy into academic disciplines: A systematic approach. *RSR. Reference Services Review*, 43(2), 264–283. 10.1108/RSR-11-2014-0052

Felder, R. M., & Brent, R. (2003). Learning by Doing. *Chemical Engineering Education*, 37(4), 282–290.

Fergusson, L., van der Laan, L., Imran, S., & Ormsby, G. (2021). The Development of Work-Integrated Learning Ecosystems: An Australian Example of Cooperative Education. *International Journal of Work-Integrated Learning*, 22(1), 25–40.

Ferreira, H. N. M., Brant-Ribeiro, T., Araújo, R. D., Dorça, F. A., & Cattelan, R. G. (2017). An automatic and dynamic knowledge assessment module for adaptive educational systems. *2017 IEEE 17th International Conference on Advanced Learning Technologies (ICALT)*, (pp. 517–521). IEEE.

Ferri, F., Grifoni, P., & Guzzo, T. (2020). Online learning and emergency remote teaching: Opportunities and challenges in emergency situations. *Societies (Basel, Switzerland)*, 10(4), 86. 10.3390/soc10040086

Feuer, M. J., Floden, R. E., Chudowsky, N., & Ahn, J. (2013). *Evaluation of teacher preparation programs: Purposes, methods, and policy options*. National Academy of Education.

FICCI. (2019). *Higher Education Summit Report*. FICCI.

Fink, L. D. (2013). *Creating Significant Learning Experiences: An Integrated Approach to Designing College Courses*. Jossey-Bass.

Finn, J. D., & Zimmer, K. S. (2012). Student engagement: What is it? Why does it matter? In *Handbook of research on student engagement* (pp. 97–131). Springer US. 10.1007/978-1-4614-2018-7_5

Fisher, D., & Frey, N. (2014). *Checking for understanding: Formative assessment techniques for your classroom*. ASCD.

Fister, B. (2010). Critical information literacy: Principles and application in student learning. *Library Trends*, 59(3), 403–434.

Fleming, N., & Baume, D. (2006). Learning Styles Again: VARKing up the right tree! *SEDA, 7.4*, 4–7. https://www.vark-learn.com/wp-content/uploads/2014/08/Educational-Developments.pdf

Fleury, A., Lughofer, E., Sayed Mouchaweh, M., Sayed, M., & Editorial, M. (2017). Editorial of the Special Issue: Adaptive and Intelligent Systems (AIS) for Learning, Control and Optimization in Dynamic Environments. *Evolving Systems*. Europea. https://ec.europa.eu/programmes/horizon2020/en/h2020-sections-projects

Fosnot, C. T. (Ed.). (2005). *Constructivism: Theory, perspectives, and practice*. Teachers College Press.

Foulger, T. S., Wetzel, K., & Buss, R. R. (2019). Moving toward a technology infusion approach: Considerations for teacher preparation programs. *Journal of Digital Learning in Teacher Education*, 35(2), 79–91. 10.1080/21532974.2019.1568325

Fourier, V., & Grey, C. (2000). At the critical moment: Conditions and prospects for critical management studies. *Human Relations*.

Freeman, S., Eddy, S. L., McDonough, M., Smith, M. K., Okoroafor, N., Jordt, H., & Wenderoth, M. P. (2014). Active learning increases student performance in science, engineering, and mathematics. *Proceedings of the National Academy of Sciences of the United States of America*, 111(23), 8410–8415. 10.1073/pnas.131903011124821756

Freytas, H. (2017). *A Collaborative & Strategic Approach To Improve School Achievement Through Effective Attendance/Truancy Policies And Procedures*.

Friere, P. (1970, 1993). *Pedagogy of the Oppressed*. Routledge.

Friesen, N. (2017). Building confidence in research skills: Using simulations in library instruction. *Journal of Library Administration*, 57(2), 137–150.

Froyd, J. (2013). Five major shifts in 100 years of engineering education. *Proceedings of the IEEE*, 101(6).

Furedi, F. (2006). *Where have all the intellectuals gone? Confronting 21st century philistinism* (2nd ed.). Continuum.

Gal, A., & Fallik, O. (2021). Learn from Each Other: A Peer-Teaching Model. *Interdisciplinary Journal of Environmental and Science Education*, 17(3), e2242. 10.21601/ijese/10896

Gambo, Y., & Shakir, M. Z. (2022). Students' Readiness for Self-Regulated Smart Learning Environment. *International Journal of Technology in Education and Science*, 6(2), 306–322. 10.46328/ijtes.341

Gammelgaard, B. (2017). Editorial: The qualitative case study. *International Journal of Logistics Management*, 28(4), 910–913. 10.1108/IJLM-09-2017-0231

Garcia, R., Martinez, L., & Rodriguez, M. (2020). Adaptive learning features in digital textbooks and their impact on student engagement and achievement. *Computers & Education*, 38(4), 450–465.

Gardner, H. (1983). *Frames of Mind: The Theory of Multiple Intelligences*. Basic Books.

Gardner, H. (2006). *Multiple Intelligences: New Horizons in Theory and Practice*. Basic Books.

Compilation of References

Garrison, D. R., Anderson, T., & Archer, W. (2000). Critical inquiry in a text-based environment: Computer conferencing in higher education. *The Internet and Higher Education*, 2(2-3), 87–105. 10.1016/S1096-7516(00)00016-6

Gartner. (2020). *Magic Quadrant for Artificial Intelligence*. Gartner.

Gemuhay, H. M., Kalolo, A., Mirisho, R., Chipwaza, B., & Nyangena, E. (2019). Factors affecting performance in clinical practice among preservice diploma nursing students in Northern Tanzania. *Nursing Research and Practice*, 2019, 2019. 10.1155/2019/345308530941212

Ghavifekr, S. (2020). Collaborative Learning: A Key to Enhance Students' social Interaction Skills. Mojes. *Malaysian Online Journal of Educational Sciences*, 8(4), 9–21.

Gilbert, T. K., & Mintz, Y. (2019). Epistemic therapy for bias in automated decision-making. *Proceedings of the 2019 AAAI/ACM Conference on AI, Ethics, and Society*, (pp. 61–67). ACM. 10.1145/3306618.3314294

Godard, J. (2014). The psychologization of employment relations? *Human Resource Management Journal*, 24(1), 1–18. 10.1111/1748-8583.12030

Gogus, A. (2012). Brainstorming and learning. *Encyclopedia of the Sciences of Learning*. Springer. 10.1007/978-1-4419-1428-6_491

Gonzalez-Zamar, M., & Abad-Segura, E. (2021). Visual Arts in the University Educational Ecosystem: Analysis of Schools of Knowledge. *Education Sciences*, 11(4), 184. 10.3390/educsci11040184

Gottfried, M. A. (2014). Chronic absenteeism and its effects on students' academic and socioemotional outcomes. *Journal of Education for Students Placed at Risk*, 19(2), 53–75. 10.1080/10824669.2014.962696

Gottfried, M. A., & Kirksey, J. J. (2017). When students miss school: The role of timing of absenteeism on students' test performance. *Educational Researcher*, 46(3), 119–130. 10.3102/0013189X17703945

Gov, E. (2015). *Every student, every day: Obama administration launches first–ever national, cross-sector initiative to eliminate chronic absenteeism in our nation's schools.*

Government of India. (2020). *NationalEducational Policy, 2020*. Government of India.

Graesser, A. C. (2017). Intelligent tutoring systems. In *International Handbook of the Learning Sciences*. Routledge.

Graf, A. (2023). Exploring the role of personalization in adaptive learning environments. [IJSECS]. *International Journal Software Engineering and Computer Science*, 3(2), 50–56. 10.35870/ijsecs.v3i2.1200

Graham, C. R. (2013). Designing asynchronous online discussion environments: Recent progress and possible future directions. *Computer Education*.

Graham, C. R., Woodfield, W., & Harrison, J. B. (2013). A framework for institutional adoption and implementation of blended learning in higher education. *The Internet and Higher Education*, 18, 4–14. 10.1016/j.iheduc.2012.09.003

Graziano, K. J., & Bryans-Bongey, S. (2018). Surveying the national landscape of online teacher training in k-12 teacher preparation programs. *Journal of Digital Learning in Teacher Education*, 34(4), 259–277. 10.1080/21532974.2018.1498040

Greenberg, M. T., Brown, J. L., & Abenavoli, R. M. (2016). *Teacher Stress and Health: Effects on Teachers, Students, and Schools*. Edna Bennett Pierce Prevention Research Center, Pennsylvania State University.

Gregory, L. (2013). Information literacy and technology: A collaboration. *Journal of Library & Information Services in Distance Learning*, 7(1-2), 69–78.

Grey, C., & Willmott, H. C, (Eds.). (2005). *Critical management studies: A reader*. Oxford, UK: Oxford University Press.

Griffin, R. W. (1997). *Management*. AITBS Publishers.

Griffiths, J., & Meola, A. (2018). Integrating online quizzes into library instruction sessions: Engaging students and gauging learning outcomes. *Journal of Library & Information Services in the Digital Age*, 19(1), 1–12.

Guest, D. (2011). Human resource management and performance: Still searching for some answers. *Human Resource Management Journal*, 21(1), 3–13. 10.1111/j.1748-8583.2010.00164.x

Gull, H., Saqib, M., Iqbal, S. Z., & Saeed, S. (2020, November). Improving learning experience of students by early prediction of student performance using machine learning. In *2020 IEEE International Conference for Innovation in Technology (INOCON)* (pp. 1-4). IEEE. 10.1109/INOCON50539.2020.9298266

Gumel, A. A., & Abdullahi, A. B., & O, U. M. (2019). The Need for a Multimodal Means of Effective Digital Learning through Data Mining and Institutional Knowledge Repository: A Proposed System for Polytechnics in Northern Nigeria. *Paper presented at the Proceedings of the 2019 5th International Conference on Computer and Technology Applications*. ACM. 10.1145/3323933.3324068

Gupta, V. (2020). *Digital education roles in NEP*.

Gütl, C., & Chang, V. (2008). Ecosystem-based theoretical models for learning in environments of the 21st century. [iJET]. *International Journal of Emerging Technologies in Learning*, 3(1), 3. 10.3991/ijet.v3i1.742

Hager, K. D. (2020). Integrating technology to improve teacher preparation. *College Teaching*, 68(2), 71–78. 10.1080/87567555.2020.1723475

Compilation of References

Hake, R. R. (1998). Interactive-engagement versus traditional methods: A six-thousand-student survey of mechanics test data for introductory physics courses. *American Journal of Physics*, 66(1), 64–74. 10.1119/1.18809

Hale, H. E. (2014). Patronal Politics. Problems of International Politics. Cambridge University Press., Retrieved October 24, 2019, from. 10.1017/CBO9781139683524

Harlen, W. (2013). *Assessment & Inquiry-Based Science Education: Issues in Policy and Practice*. Global Network of Science Academies.

Haroon, J., Jumani, N. B., & Arouj, K. (2020). Learning to teach in higher education for sustainable professional development. [Online]. *Review of Economics and Development Studies*, 6(1), 33–41. 10.47067/reads.v6i1.182

Hassan, S., & Shamsudin, M. F. (2019). Measuring the Effect of Service Quality and Corporate Image on Student Satisfaction and Loyalty in Higher Learning Institutes of Technical and Vocational Education and Training. *International Journal of Engineering and Advanced Technology*, 8(5), 533–538. 10.35940/ijeat.E1077.0585C19

Hasson, G. (2015). *Understanding Emotional Intelligence*. Pearson Education.

Hativa, N. (1995). The department-wide approach to improving faculty instruction in higher education: A qualitative evaluation. *Research in Higher Education*, 36(4), 377–413. 10.1007/BF02207904

Hattie, J., & Timperley, H. (2007). The power of feedback. *Review of Educational Research*, 77(1), 81–112. 10.3102/003465430298487

Haukongo, N. N. (2020). *Nursing student's satisfaction with clinical practice environment during their undergraduate training in Namibia* [Doctoral dissertation, Stellenbosch University].

Hayden, C. L., Carrico, C., Ginn, C. C., Felber, A., & Smith, S. (2021). Social Constructivism in Learning: Peer Teaching & Learning. *Pedagogicon Conference Proceedings*. EKU. https://encompass.eku.edu/pedagogicon/2020/learningpartners/7

Head, A. J., & Eisenberg, M. B. (2010). How college students use Wikipedia for academic research. *First Monday*, 15(3).

Heider, K. L., & McClure, R. (2015). *Instructional strategies and techniques for information professionals*. Chandos Publishing.

Hellström-Hyson, E., Mårtensson, G., & Kristofferzon, M. L. (2012). To take responsibility or to be an onlooker. Nursing students' experiences of two models of supervision. *Nurse Education Today*, 32(1), 105–110. 10.1016/j.nedt.2011.02.00521388721

Henderson, C. (2012). Faculty development for physics instructors: A case study of a workshop using active learning. *Physical Review Special Topics. Physics Education Research*.

Henderson, S., Needham, J., & van de Mortel, T. (2020). Clinical facilitators' experience of near peer learning in Australian undergraduate nursing students: A qualitative study. *Nurse Education Today*, 95, 104602. 10.1016/j.nedt.2020.10460233002746

Hendry, C., & Pettigrew, A. (1990). HRM: an agenda for the 1990s. *International Journal of HRM*.

Henze, I., van Driel, J. H., & Verloop, N. (2009). Experienced science teachers' learning in the context of educational innovation. *Journal of Teacher Education*, 60(2), 184–199. 10.1177/0022487108329275

Herrera-Pavo, M. Á. (2021). Collaborative learning for virtual higher education. *Learning, Culture and Social Interaction*, 28, 100437. 10.1016/j.lcsi.2020.100437

Herrity, J. (2023). *11 Benefits of Collaborative Learning (Plus Tips To Use It)*. Indeed. https://www.indeed.com/career-advice/career-development/benefits-of-collaborative-learning

Heylighen, F. (2000). Evolutionary transitions: How do levels of complexity emerge? *Complexity*, 6, 53–57. 10.1002/1099-0526(200009/10)6:1<53::AID-CPLX1008>3.0.CO;2-O

Hicks, S., & Bose, D. (2019). Designing teacher preparation courses: Integrating mobile technology, program standards, and course outcomes. *TechTrends*, 63(6), 734–740. 10.1007/s11528-019-00416-z

Hinchliffe, L. J., & Meulemans, Y. N. (2010). Supporting student retention and graduation: Strategies for academic librarians. *College & Research Libraries News*, 71(1), 10–13.

Hoffman, L. (2016). 10 Models for Design Thinking. *Medium*. https://libhof.medium.com/10-models-for-design-thinking-f6943e4ee068

Hoffmann, A. L., Roberts, S. T., Wolf, C. T., & Wood, S. (2018). Beyond fairness, accountability, and transparency in the ethics of algorithms: Contributions and perspectives from LIS. *Proceedings of the Association for Information Science and Technology*, 55(1), 694–696. 10.1002/pra2.2018.14505501084

Holliday, W., & Fagerheim, B. A. (2006). Integrating information literacy with a sequenced English composition curriculum. *portal. Portal (Baltimore, Md.)*, 6(2), 169–184.

Holmes, W., Porayska-Pomsta, K., Holstein, K., Sutherland, E., Baker, T., Shum, S. B., Santos, O. C., Rodrigo, M. T., Cukurova, M., Bittencourt, I. I., & Koedinger, K. R. (2022). Ethics of AI in education: Towards a community-wide framework. *International Journal of Artificial Intelligence in Education*, 32(3), 1–23. 10.1007/s40593-021-00239-1

Holstein, K., Aleven, V., & Rummel, N. (2020). A conceptual framework for human–AI hybrid adaptivity in education. *Lecture Notes in Computer Science (Including Subseries Lecture Notes in Artificial Intelligence and Lecture Notes in Bioinformatics)*, 12163 LNAI, 240–254. 10.1007/978-3-030-52237-7_20

Compilation of References

Hwang, G. J., Chang, S. C., Chen, P. Y., & Chen, X. Y. (2018). Effects of integrating an active learning-promoting mechanism into location-based real-world learning environments on students' learning performances and behaviors. *Educational Technology Research and Development*, 66(2), 451–474. 10.1007/s11423-017-9567-5

Hwang, Y.-M., & Wu, Y.-C. (2013). Applying audience response systems to enhance student engagement in library instruction. [JETDE]. *Journal of Educational Technology Development and Exchange*, 6(X).

Ibrahim, M. S., & Hamada, M. (2016). Adaptive learning framework. *15th International Conference on Information Technology Based Higher Education and Training (ITHET)*. IEEE. 10.1109/ITHET.2016.7760738

Ilori, M. O., & Ajagunna, I. (2020). Re-imagining the future of education in the era of the fourth industrial revolution. [CrossRef]. *Worldwide Hospitality and Tourism Themes*, 12(1), 3–12. 10.1108/WHATT-10-2019-0066

INEE (Inter-Agency Network for Education in Emergencies). (2014). *Minimum standards for education: Teacher competencies*. INEE. https://inee.org/resources/inee-minimum-standards

Islam, G., & Zyphur, M. (2007). Critical Industrial Psychology: What is it and where is it? *Psychology in Society, 34*, 17-30.

Islam, G. (2012). *Can the subaltern eat? Anthropophagic culture as a Brazilian lens on post-colonial theory*. Sage. 10.1177/1350508411429396

ISTE. (2019). *ISTE Standards*. ISTE. https://www.iste.org/standards

Jacobs, H. L., & Jacobs, D. (2009). Pedagogical partnerships: Transforming one-shot library sessions into ongoing collaborations with faculty. *RSR. Reference Services Review*, 37(2), 207–220.

Jain University. (n.d.). *About Jain Deemed-to-be University*. Jain University. https://www.jainuniversity.ac.in/about-us

Jain, P. K. S. S. (2010). Capital Structure Decisions - A case study of Reliance Industries Limited. In S. S. P K Jain, *Capital Structure Decisions* (pp. 1-22). Business Analyst.

Jain, D., Tiwari, G. K., & Awasthi, I. D. (2017). Impact of metacognitive awareness on academic adjustment and academic outcome of the students. *International Journal of Indian Psychology*, 5(1).10.25215/0501.034

Janssens, M., & Steyaert, C. (2009) HRM and performance: A plea for reflexivity in HRM studies. *Journal of Management Studies, 46*, 143-155.

Jayanthi, S. V., Balakrishnan, S., Ching, A. L. S., Latiff, N. A. A., & Nasirudeen, A. M. A. (2014). Factors contributing to academic performance of students in a tertiary institution in Singapore. *American Journal of Educational Research*, 2(9), 752–758. 10.12691/education-2-9-8

Jian, M. (2023). Personalized learning through AI. *Advances in Engineering Innovation, 5*(1).

Jing, Y., Zhao, L., Zhu, K., Wang, H., Wang, C., & Xia, Q. (2023). Research landscape of adaptive learning in education: A bibliometric study on research publications from 2000 to 2022. *Sustainability (Basel)*, 15(4), 3115. 10.3390/su15043115

Jin, H. (2011). Project Pedagogy applied to the courses of Human Resource Management. In Wang, Y. (Ed.), *Education and Educational Technology, AISC 108. pp Springer-Verlag Berlin Heidelberg. 663-668 pp.* 10.1007/978-3-642-24775-0_102

Jobirovna, A.J., 2023. Engaging Classroom Strategies: Fostering Active Participation among Students. *American Journal of Language, Literacy and Learning in STEM Education (2993-2769)*, *1*(9), pp.155-161.

Johnson, C., & Zone, E. (2018). Achieving a Scaled Implementation of Adaptive Learning through Faculty Engagement: A Case Study. *Cuurent Issues in Emerging ELearning, 5*(1), 1–17. https://scholarworks.umb.edu/cieeAvailableat:https://scholarworks.umb.edu/ciee/vol5/iss1/7

Johnson, A., & Lincoln, B. (2018). Effectiveness of microlearning quizzes in an introductory physics course. *Physics Education*, 53(4), 045012.

Johnson, C. (2021). Virtual Reality in Business Education: Opportunities and Challenges. *Business Horizons*.

Johnson, D. W., & Johnson, R. T. (1999). *Cooperation and learning together: Theory and research* (7th ed.). Allyn & Bacon.

Johnson, D. W., & Johnson, R. T. (1999). *Learning together and alone: Cooperative, competitive, and individualistic learning* (5th ed.). Allyn & Bacon.

Johnson, D. W., Johnson, R. T., & Smith, K. A. (1991). *Cooperative learning: increasing college faculty instructional productivity*. ASHE/ERIC Higher Education.

Johnson, D. W., Johnson, R. T., & Smith, K. A. (1998). Cooperative learning returns to college: What evidence is there that it works? Change. *Change*, 30(4), 26–35. 10.1080/00091389809602629

Johnson, D. W., Johnson, R. T., & Smith, K. A. (2014). Cooperative learning: Improving university instruction by basing practice on validated theory. *Journal on Excellence in College Teaching*, 25(4), 253–273.

Johnson, E., & Brown, K. (2019). Enhancing student engagement through digital textbooks: A collaborative approach. *Educational Psychology Review*, 42(2), 210–225.

Johnson, H., Mejia, M., & Cook, K. (2015). *Successful online courses in California's community colleges*. Public Policy Institute.

Jonassen, D. H. (1991). Evaluating constructivist learning. *Educational Technology*, 31(9), 28–33.

Jonassen, D. H. (1999). Designing constructivist learning environments. In *Instructional-design theories and models: A new paradigm of instructional theory* (Vol. 2, pp. 215–239). Routledge.

Compilation of References

Jonker, H., März, V., & Voogt, J. (2018). Teacher educators' professional identity under construction: The transition from teaching face-to-face to a blended curriculum. *Teaching and Teacher Education, 71*(Complete), 120–133. 10.1016/j.tate.2017.12.016

Joo, Y. J., Park, S., & Lim, E. (2018). Factors influencing preservice teachers' intention to use technology: TPACK, teacher self-efficacy, and technology acceptance model. *Journal of Educational Technology & Society*, 21(3), 48–59.

Judson, G. (2010). *A new approach to ecological education: Engaging students' imaginations in their world.* Peter Lang Publishing.

Julien, H., & Barker, S. (2009). High school students' information-seeking behaviors: Implications for developing information literacy skills. *Library & Information Science Research*, 31(1), 12–17. 10.1016/j.lisr.2008.10.008

Julien, H., & Gribble, J. (2017). Engaging first-year students in critical thinking through information literacy instruction. *Journal of Academic Librarianship*, 43(2), 182–190.

Kaasinen, E., Anttila, A.-H., Heikkilä, P., Laarni, J., Koskinen, H., & Väätänen, A. (2022). Smooth and resilient human–machine teamwork as an Industry 5.0 design challenge. *Sustainability (Basel)*, 14(5), 2773. 10.3390/su14052773

Kalonde, G., & Mousa, R. (2016). Technology familiarization to preservice teachers: Factors that influence teacher educators' technology decisions. *Journal of Educational Technology Systems*, 45(2), 236–255. 10.1177/0047239515616965

Kaltura. (2023). *Innovative Teaching Strategies.* Kaltura. https://corp.kaltura.com/blog/innovative-teaching-strategies/

Kamiya, A., & Airth, M. (2023, November 21). *Semantic Network Model | Definition, Concepts & Examples.* Study.com. https://study.com/learn/lesson/semantic-network-model-overview-examples.html#:~:text=Allan%20Collins%20and%20Ross%20Quillian,ready%20associated%20information%20for%20retrieval

Kang, S. H. K. (2016). Spaced repetition promotes efficient and effective learning. *Policy Insights from the Behavioral and Brain Sciences*, 3(1), 12–19. 10.1177/2372732215624708

Kartinah, N., T., Sudirman, & Daniel, T. (2020). *Preliminary Study of Cognitive Obstacle on the Topic of Finite Integral Among Prospective Teacher.* 2nd International Conference on Education and Social Science Research (ICESRE 2019), Central Java, Indonesia. 10.2991/assehr.k.200318.008

Kato, S., Galán-Muros, V., & Weko, T. (2020). *The emergence of alternative credentials.* (OECD Education Working Papers, No. 216). OECD Publishing. https://doi.org/10.1787/19939019

Kaylor, S. K. (2014). Preventing information overload: Cognitive load theory as an instructional framework for teaching pharmacology. *The Journal of Nursing Education*, 53(2), 108–111. 10.3928/01484834-20140122-0324444008

Keefer, K., Parker, J. D. A., Saklofske, D. H., & Saklofskenald, H. (2018). *Emotional Intelligence in Education: Integrating Research with Practice.* Springer. 10.1007/978-3-319-90633-1

Keerthirathne, W. K. D. (2020). Peer Learning: An Overview. *International Journal of Scientific Engineering and Science*, 4(11), 1–6.

Kendall, J. C., Duley, J. S., Little, T. C., Permaul, J. S., & Rubin, S. (1986). *Strengthening Experiential Education within your Institution.* National Society for Internships and Experiential Education.

Khapre, M., Deol, R., Sharma, A., & Badyal, D. (2021, July 16). Near-Peer Tutor: A Solution For Quality Medical Education in Faculty Constraint Setting. *Cureus*, 13(7), e16416. 10.7759/cureus.1641634422460

Khozali, N., & Karpudewan, M. (2020). An Interdisciplinary Facebook Incorporated STEM Education Strategy in Teaching and Learning of Dynamic Ecosystems. *Eurasia Journal of Mathematics, Science and Technology Education*, 16(11), em1902. 10.29333/ejmste/8704

Kiger, M. E., & Varpio, L. (2020). Thematic analysis of qualitative data: AMEE Guide No. 131. *Medical Teacher*, 42(8), 846–854. 10.1080/0142159X.2020.175503032356468

Kimmons, R., & Hall, C. (2018). How useful are our models? Pre-service and practicing teacher evaluations of technology integration models. *TechTrends*, 62(1), 29–36. 10.1007/s11528-017-0227-8

Klein, M., Sosu, E. M., & Dare, S. (2022). School absenteeism and academic achievement: Does the reason for absence matter? *AERA Open*, 8, 23328584211071115. 10.1177/23328584211071115

Knudsen, M. P., Frederiksen, M. H., & Goduscheit, R. C. (2021). New forms of engagement in third mission activities: A multi-level university-centric approach. *Innovation (North Sydney, N.S.W.)*, 23(2), 209–240. 10.1080/14479338.2019.1670666

Kochan, T. A. (2007). Social legitimacy of the HRM profession: A U.S. perspective. In Boxall, P., Purcell, J., & Wright, P. (Eds.), *The Oxford handbook of human resource management.* Oxford University Press.

Kolb, A. Y., & Kolb, D. A. (2017). Experiential learning theory as a guide for experiential educators in higher education. *Experiential Learning & Teaching in Higher Education, 1*(1), 7. https://nsuworks.nova.edu/elthe/vol1/iss1/7

Kolb, D. A. (1984). *Experiential Learning: Experience as The Source of Learning And Development.* Prentice Hall.

Kolb, D. A. (1984). *Experiential Learning: Experience as the source of learning and development.* Prentice-Hall.

Kopcha, T. J., Rieber, L. P., & Walker, B. B. (2016). Understanding university faculty perceptions about innovation in teaching and technology. *British Journal of Educational Technology*, 47(5), 945–957. 10.1111/bjet.12361

Compilation of References

Kozma, R. (2003). Technology and classroom practices: An international study. *Journal of Research on Technology in Education*, 36(1), 1–14. 10.1080/15391523.2003.10782399

Krechetov, I., & Romanenko, V. (2020). Implementing the adaptive learning techniques. *Voprosy Obrazovaniya / Educational Studies Moscow*, 2, 252–277. 10.17323/1814-9545-2020-2-252-277

Kucuk, I. (2020). *Instructional Related Factors and Students' Performance In Mathematics At Kenya Certificate Of Secondary Education In Public Secondary Schools, Njiru Sub-County, Kenya* [Doctoral dissertation, University of Nairobi, Kenya].

Kuh, G. D., Kinzie, J., Schuh, J. H., & Whitt, E. J. (2005). *Student Success in College: Creating Conditions That Matter*. Jossey-Bass.

Kuhlthau, C. C. (2004). *Seeking meaning: A process approach to library and information services* (2nd ed.). Libraries Unlimited.

Kumar, A. (2021). *Transition from compliance to innovation in institutions*.

Kumar, V. R. (2019). Capital Structure Decisions. In Kumar, V. R. (Ed.), *Financial Management* (p. 216). Mc Graw Hill Education Private Limited.

Laal, M., & Laal, M. (2012). Collaborative learning: What is it? *Procedia: Social and Behavioral Sciences*, 31, 491–495. 10.1016/j.sbspro.2011.12.092

Lage, M. J., Platt, G. J., & Treglia, M. (2000). Inverting the classroom: A gateway to creating an inclusive learning environment. *The Journal of Economic Education*, 31(1), 30–43. 10.1080/00220480009596759

Lake, D., Flannery, K., & Kearns, M. (2021). A cross-discipline and cross-sector mixed-methods examination of design thinking practices and outcomes. *Innovative Higher Education*, 46(3), 337–356. 10.1007/s10755-020-09539-1

Lane, D. C., & Goode, Cl. (2021). Open for All: The OERu's Next Generation Digital Learning Ecosystem. *International Review of Research in Open and Distance Learning*, 22(4), 146–163. 10.19173/irrodl.v23i1.5763

Langley, G., & Yorke, M. (2006). *Formative assessment and self-managed learning in higher education*. Routledge.

Last, C. (2015). Human metasystem transition (HMST) theory. *Journal of Ethics and Emerging Technologies*, 25(1), 1–16. 10.55613/jeet.v25i1.36

Lawless, A., & McQue, L. (2008). Becoming a community of critically reflective HR practitioners: Challenges and opportunities within an MA partnership programme. *Journal of European Industrial Training*, 32.

Leal Filho, W., Pallant, E., Enete, A., Richter, B., & Brandli, L. L. (2018). Planning and implementing sustainability in higher education institutions: An overview of the difficulties and potentials. *International Journal of Sustainable Development and World Ecology*, 25(8), 712–720. 10.1080/13504509.2018.1461707

Lee, R. (2018). *An Examination of Participatory Design Framework in a Class Project in Higher Education* (1st ed.). University of Toronto.

Lesia Viktorivna, K., Andrii Oleksandrovych, V., Iryna Oleksandrivna, K., & Nadia Oleksandrivna, K. (2022). Artificial Intelligence in Language Learning: What Are We Afraid of. *Arab World English Journal*, 8(8), 262–273. 10.24093/awej/call8.18

Levett-Jones, T., Andersen, P., Reid-Searl, K., Guinea, S., McAllister, M., Lapkin, S., Palmer, L., & Niddrie, M. (2015). Tag team simulation: An innovative approach for promoting active engagement of participants and observers during group simulations. *Nurse Education in Practice*, 15(5), 345–352. 10.1016/j.nepr.2015.03.01425936431

Liedtka, J., & Bahr, K. J. (2019). *Assessing design thinking's impact: Report on the development of a new instrument.* (Darden Working Paper Series). Darden.

Light, G. (2001). *Making the Most of College: Students Speak Their Minds*. Harvard University Press. 10.4159/9780674417502

Li, M., Hung, M., Hsian, W., Heung, W., Chiu, M., & Wang, S. (2019). Teaching Ecosystem Design: Teachers' Satisfaction with the Integrated Course Service System. *Education Sciences*, 9(3), 232. 10.3390/educsci9030232

Lincoln, Y. S., & Guba, E. G. (1985). *Naturalistic inquiry*. Sage. 10.1016/0147-1767(85)90062-8

Linda, N. S., Mtshali, N. G., & Engelbrecht, C. (2013). Lived experiences of a community regarding its involvement in a university community-based education programme. *Curationis*, 36(1), 1-13.

Linstead, S. A. (Ed.). (2004). Organization theory and postmodern thought. London Sage. • C. C. Lundberg and C. Enz, (1993). 'A framework for student case preparation', Case Research Journal, 13 (Summer) 134/ Michael A. Hitt, R. Duane Ireland and Robert E. Hoskisson, Strategic Management (Thomson Southwestern, 6th Edition) CII. 10.4135/9781446217313

Liu, C. M., Sun, Y. J., & Zhang, Y. (2013). The research and application of adaptive learning system in learning programs. *Applied Mechanics and Materials*, 347, 3109–3113. 10.4028/www.scientific.net/AMM.347-350.3109

Liu, H., Wang, T. H., Lin, H. C. K., Lai, C. F., & Huang, Y. M. (2022). The Influence of Affective Feedback Adaptive Learning System on Learning Engagement and Self-Directed Learning. *Frontiers in Psychology*, 13, 858411. 10.3389/fpsyg.2022.85841135572271

Liu, M., McKelroy, E., Corliss, S. B., & Carrigan, J. (2017). Investigating the effect of an adaptive learning intervention on students' learning. *Educational Technology Research and Development*, 65(6), 1605–1625. 10.1007/s11423-017-9542-1

Compilation of References

Lohmosavi, V., Nejad, A. F., & Hosseini, E. M. (2013). E-learning ecosystem based on serviceoriented cloud computing architecture. In: *Proceedings of the 5th Conference on Information and Knowledge Technology*. IEEE. 10.1109/IKT.2013.6620032

Lonita Ciolacu, M., Tehrani, A. F., Svasta, P., Tache, I., & Stoichescu, D. (2020). Education 4.0: an adaptive framework with artificial intelligence, raspberry Pi and wearables-innovation for creating value. *2020 IEEE 26th International Symposium for Design and Technology in Electronic Packaging (SIITME)*, (pp. 298–303). IEEE.

Lubbers, J., & Rossman, C. (2016). The effects of pediatric community simulation experience on the self-confidence and satisfaction of baccalaureate nursing students: A quasi-experimental study. *Nurse Education Today*, 39, 93–98. 10.1016/j.nedt.2016.01.01327006038

Lubit, R., & Lubit, R. (2019). Why Educators Should Care About Social and Emotional Learning? *New Directions for Teaching and Learning*, 2019(160), 19–32. 10.1002/tl.20362

Mackey, T. L., & Jacobson, T. D. (2014). *Metaliteracy: Reinventing information literacy to empower learners*. American Library Association.

Mamatha, S. M. (2021). Experiential learning in Higher Education. *International Journal of Advanced Research and Innovation*, 9(3), 214–218.

Marchington, M. (2015). Human resource management (HRM): Too busy looking up to see where it is going longer term? *Human Resource Management Review*, 25(2), 176–187. 10.1016/j.hrmr.2015.01.007

Maree, D. J., & Maree, D. J. (2020). The Methodological Division: Quantitative and Qualitative Methods. *Realism and Psychological Science*, 13-42.

Maree, R. D., Marcum, Z. A., Saghafi, E., Weiner, D. K., & Karp, J. F. (2016). A systematic review of opioid and benzodiazepine misuse in older adults. *The American Journal of Geriatric Psychiatry*, 24(11), 949–963. 10.1016/j.jagp.2016.06.00327567185

Mariscal, L. L., Albarracin, M. R., Mobo, F. D., & Cutillas, A. L. (2023). Pedagogical competence towards technology driven instruction on basic education. *International Journal of Multidisciplinary: Applied Business and Education Research.*, 4(5), 1567–1580. 10.11594/ijmaber.04.05.18

Marougkas, A., Troussas, C., Krouska, A., & Sgouropoulou, C. (2023). Virtual reality in education: A review of learning theories, approaches, and methodologies for the last decade. *Electronics (Basel)*, 12(13), 2832. 10.3390/electronics12132832

Martin, B. (2018). Faculty technology beliefs and practices in teacher preparation through a TPACK lens. *Education and Information Technologies*, 23(5), 1775–1788. 10.1007/s10639-017-9680-4

Matthew, U. O., Kazaure, J. S., Kazaure, A. S., Onyedibe, O. N., & Okafor, A. N. (2022). The Twenty First Century E-Learning Education Management & Implication for Media Technology Adoption in the Period of Pandemic. *EAI Endorsed Transactions on e-Learning, 8*(1).

Matthew, J. (2021). The PRISMA 2020 statement: An updated guideline for reporting systematic reviews. *BMJ (Clinical Research Ed.)*, 2021, 372. https://www.bmj.com/content/372/bmj.n71

Matthew, U. O. (2019). Information System Management & Multimedia Applications in an E-Learning Environment. [IJICTHD]. *International Journal of Information Communication Technologies and Human Development*, 11(3), 21–41. 10.4018/IJICTHD.2019070102

Matthew, U. O., Bakare, K. M., Ebong, G. N., Ndukwu, C. C., & Nwanakwaugwu, A. C.. (2023). Generative Artificial Intelligence (AI) Educational Pedagogy Development: Conversational AI with User-Centric ChatGPT4. *Journal of Trends in Computer Science and Smart Technology*, 5(4), 401–418. 10.36548/jtcsst.2023.4.003

Matthew, U. O., Kazaure, A. S., Kazaure, J. S., Hassan, I. M., Nwanakwaugwu, A. C., & Okafor, N. U. (2022). Educational Technology Adaptation & Implication for Media Technology Adoption in the Period of COVID-19. *Journal of Trends in Computer Science and Smart Technology*, 4(4), 226–245. 10.36548/jtcsst.2022.4.002

Matthew, U. O., & Kazaure, J. S. (2020). Multimedia e-learning education in nigeria and developing countries of Africa for achieving SDG4. [IJICTHD]. *International Journal of Information Communication Technologies and Human Development*, 12(1), 40–62. 10.4018/IJICTHD.2020010103

Matthew, U. O., Kazaure, J. S., John, O., & Haruna, K. (2021). Telecommunication Business Information System and Investment Ecosystem in a Growing Economy: A Review of Telecom Investment in Nigeria. [IJICTHD]. *International Journal of Information Communication Technologies and Human Development*, 13(2), 1–20. 10.4018/IJICTHD.2021040101

Matthew, U. O., Kazaure, J. S., Kazaure, A. S., Nwamouh, U. C., & Chinonso, A. (2022). ICT Policy Implementation as Correlate for Achieving Educational Sustainability: Approaching Development in Multi ICT Dimensions. *Journal of Information Technology*, 4(4), 250–269.

Matthew, U. O., Kazaure, J. S., Ndukwu, C. C., Ebong, G. N., Nwanakwaugwu, A. C., & Nwamouh, U. C. (2024). *Artificial Intelligence Educational Pedagogy Development: ICT Pedagogy Development for Education 5.0 Educational Perspectives on Digital Technologies in Modeling and Management*. IGI Global. 10.4018/979-8-3693-2314-4.ch003

Matthew, U. O., Kazaure, J. S., & Okafor, N. U. (2021). Contemporary development in E-Learning education, cloud computing technology & internet of things. *EAI Endorsed Transactions on Cloud Systems*, 7(20), e3–e3.

Maturana, H. R. (1975). The organization of the living: A theory of the living organization. *International Journal of Man-Machine Studies*, 7(3), 313–332. 10.1016/S0020-7373(75)80015-0

Maya Sari, D. M. (2021). Project-Based-Learning on Critical Reading Course to Enhance Critical Thinking Skills. *Studies in English Language and Education*, 8(2), 442–456. 10.24815/siele.v8i2.18407

Mayer, R. E. (2001). *Multimedia learning*. Cambridge University Press. 10.1017/CBO9781139164603

Compilation of References

McCarthy, J. P., & Anderson, L. (2000). *Active Learning Techniques Versus Traditional Teaching Styles: Two Experiments from History and Political Science.* Innovative Higher.

McClellan, G. S., Creager, K. L., & Savoca, M. (2023). *A good job: Campus employment as a high-impact practice.* Taylor & Francis.

McKinsey & Company. (2021). *Strategic reports on NEP vision.* McKinsey & Company.

McLeod, S. (2020) Vygotsky's Sociocultural Theory of Cognitive Development. *Simply Psychology.* https://www.simplypsychology.org/vygotsky.htm

McTigue, E. M., & Henke, H. L. (2013). The role of academic librarians in promoting critical thinking: A literature review. *College & Research Libraries*, 74(3), 251–271.

McWilliam, E. (2008). *Unlearning how to teach. Innovations in Education and Teaching International.* Taylor & Francis. 10.1080/14703290802176147

Means, B., Toyama, Y., Murphy, R., Bakia, M., & Jones, K. (2013). *Evaluation of Evidence-Based Practices in Online Learning: A Meta-Analysis and Review of Online Learning Studies.* U.S. Department of Education.

Meepung, T., Pratsri, S., & Nilsook, P. (2021). Interactive Tool in Digital Learning Ecosystem for Adaptive Online Learning Performance. *Higher Education Studies*, 11(3), 70–77. 10.5539/hes.v11n3p70

Mehrabi Boshrabadi, A., & Hosseini, M. R. (2021). Designing collaborative problem-solving assessment tasks in engineering: An evaluative judgment perspective. *Assessment & Evaluation in Higher Education*, 46(6), 913–927. 10.1080/02602938.2020.1836122

Menon, R. (2021). *Curriculum design reforms under NEP.*

Merkebu, J., Battistone, M., McMains, K., McOwen, K., Witkop, C., Konopasky, A., Torre, D., Holmboe, E., & Durning, S. J. (2020). Situativity: A family of social cognitive theories for understanding clinical reasoning and diagnostic error. *Diagnosis (Berlin, Germany)*, 7(3), 169–176. 10.1515/dx-2019-010032924378

Merkle, J. A. (1980). *Management and Ideology.* University of California Press. 10.1525/9780520312104

Mhlongo, X. L. (2018). *Factors contributing to failure of student nurses in biological nursing sciences: KwaZulu-Natal College of Nursing* [Doctoral dissertation, University, Country].

Mhlongo, X. L., & Masango, T. E. (2020). Factors contributing to poor performance of student nurses in anatomy and physiology. *African Journal of Health Professions Education*, 12(3), 140–143. 10.7196/AJHPE.2020.v12i3.1357

MHRD. (2020). *Financial models for NEP implementation.* MHRD.

Michael, J. (2006). Where's the evidence that active learning works? *Advances in Physiology Education*, 30(4), 159–167. 10.1152/advan.00053.200617108243

Michaelsen, L. K., Knight, A. B., & Fink, L. D. (2004). *Team-Based Learning: A Transformative Use of Small Groups in College Teaching. Sterling.* Stylus Publishing.

Midoro, V. (2016). *A common European Framework for Teachers' Professional Profile in ICT for Education.* Edizioni MENABO Didactica.

Mihail, D., & Adelina, D.-P. (2014). *Strategic SI management. Dimensiuni socio-umane contemporane.* Editura Economica.

MindTools. (n.d.). *Ebbinghaus's Forgetting Curve.* MindTools. https://www.mindtools.com/a9wjrjw/ebbinghauss-forgetting-curve

Ministry of Education. (2022). *Annual Review on NEP progress.* Ministry of Education.

Mirata, V., Hirt, F., Bergamin, P., & van der Westhuizen, C. (2020). Challenges and contexts in establishing adaptive learning in higher education: Findings from a Delphi study. *International Journal of Educational Technology in Higher Education*, 17(1), 32. 10.1186/s41239-020-00209-y

Mirza, M. S., & Arif, M. I. (2018). Fostering Academic Resilience of Students at Risk of Failure at Secondary School Level. *Journal of Behavioural Sciences,* 28(1 Monisi, F. M. (2018). *Student nurses' perceptions and attitudes towards anatomy and physiology in Limpopo, South Africa* [Doctoral dissertation, University of Punjab].

Mishra, P., & Koehler, M. J. (2006). Technological pedagogical content knowledge: A framework for teacher knowledge. *Teachers College Record*, 108(6), 1017–1054. 10.1111/j.1467-9620.2006.00684.x

Mitsea, E., Drigas, A., & Mantas, P. (2021). Soft Skills & Metacognition as Inclusion Amplifiers in the 21st Century. *International Journal of Online & Biomedical Engineering*, 17(4), 121. 10.3991/ijoe.v17i04.20567

Mitsopoulos, K., Somers, S., Schooler, J., Lebiere, C., Pirolli, P., & Thomson, R. (2022). Toward a Psychology of Deep Reinforcement Learning Agents Using a Cognitive Architecture. *Topics in Cognitive Science*, 14(4), 756–779. 10.1111/tops.1257334467649

Mittelstadt, B. D., Allo, P., Taddeo, M., Wachter, S., & Floridi, L. (2016). The ethics of algorithms: Mapping the debate. *Big Data & Society*, 3(2). 10.1177/2053951716679679

Mizokami, S. (2018). Deep active learning from the perspective of active learning theory. *Deep active learning: Toward greater depth in university education*, 79-91.

ModelThinkers. (n.d.). *Mental models.* ModelThinkers. https://modelthinkers.com/mental-model/mental-models

ModelThinkers. (n.d.-b). *Munger's Latticework.* ModelThinkers. https://modelthinkers.com/mental-model/mungers-latticework

Mont, M. (2014). The Use of Debates in Higher Education Classrooms. *Adult Education Research Conference.* New Prairie Press. https://newprairiepress.org/aerc/2014/roundtables/23

Compilation of References

Msweli, N. T., Twinomurinzi, H., & Ismail, M. (2022). The International Case for Micro-Credentials for Life-Wide and Life-Long Learning: A Systematic Literature Review. *Interdisciplinary Journal of Information, Knowledge, and Management*, 17, 151–190. 10.28945/4954

Muhammad, G. (2021). *Cultivating Genius: An Equity Framework for Culturally and Historically Responsive Literacy: A Four-Layered Framework for Culturally and Historically Responsive Literacy (Scholastic Professional)*. Scholastic Publishing.

Müller, M., & Višić, M. (2023). Cognitive Learning Strategies with ICT: Case Study of Foreign Language Learners. *2023 IEEE 12th International Conference on Educational and Information Technology (ICEIT)*, (pp. 63–66). IEEE. 10.1109/ICEIT57125.2023.10107778

NAAC. (2020). *Analysis on quality assurance within the NEP context*. NAAC.

Nadinloyi, K. B., Hajloo, N., Garamaleki, N. S., & Sadeghi, H. (2013). The study efficacy of time management training on increase academic time management of students. *Procedia: Social and Behavioral Sciences*, 84, 134–138. 10.1016/j.sbspro.2013.06.523

Najimi, A., Sharifirad, G., Amini, M. M., & Meftagh, S. D. (2013). Academic failure and students' viewpoint: The influence of individual, internal and external organizational factors. *Journal of Education and Health Promotion*, 2(1), 2. 10.4103/2277-9531.11269824083272

Natalila Marchenko, V. L. (2023). *Interactive learning methods in higher education institutions*. The Modern Higher Education Review.

Ndibalema, P. (2022). Constraints of transition to online distance learning in Higher Education Institutions during COVID-19 in developing countries: A systematic review. *E-Learning and Digital Media*, 19(6), 595–618. 10.1177/20427530221107510

Neamah, A. (2021). Adoption of Data Warehouse in University Management: Wasit University Case Study. *Paper presented at the Journal of Physics: Conference Series*. IOP Science. 10.1088/1742-6596/1860/1/012027

Neisser, U. (2014). *Cognitive psychology: Classic edition*. Psychology Press. 10.4324/9781315736174

Ng, L., Tuckett, A., Fox-Young, S., & Kain, V. (2014). Exploring registered nurses' attitudes towards postgraduate education in Australia: An overview of the literature. *Journal of Nursing Education and Practice*, 4(2), 162–170.

Nicol, D. J., & Macfarlane-Dick, D. (2006). Formative assessment and self-regulated learning: A model and seven principles of good feedback practice. *Studies in Higher Education*, 31(2), 199–218. 10.1080/03075070600572090

Nicolini, D. (2012). *Practice theory, work, and organization: An introduction*. Oxford University Press.

Niemi, H. (2021). Education Reforms for Equity and Quality: An Analysis from an Educational Ecosystem Perspective with Reference to Finnish Educational Transformations. *Center for Educational Policy Studies Journal*, 11(2), 13–35. 10.26529/cepsj.1100

Normore, A. H., & Issa Lahera, A. (2019). The evolution of educational leadership preparation programmes. *Journal of Educational Administration and History*, 51(1), 27–42. 10.1080/00220620.2018.1513914

NSDC. (2021). *Vocational education integration under NEP*. NSDC.

Nshimiyimana, A., & Cartledge, P. T. (2020). Peer-teaching at the University of Rwanda - a qualitative study based on self-determination theory. *BMC Medical Education*, 20(1), 1–12. 10.1186/s12909-020-02142-032689991

Ntho, T. A., Pienaar, A. J., & Sehularo, L. A. (2020). Peer-mentees' challenges in an undergraduate peer-group clinical mentoring programme in a nursing education institution. *Health SA*, 25, 1–8. 10.4102/hsag.v25i0.143533101718

Nussbaum, M. C. (2001). *Upheavals of Thought: The Intelligence of Emotions*. Cambridge University Press. 10.1017/CBO9780511840715

Ogunode, N. J., & Ade, T. I. (2023). Research Programme in Public Universities in Nigeria. *Best Journal of Innovation in Science. Research for Development*, 2(3), 1–13.

Ogunode, N. J., & Akimki, I.-M. P. (2023). Addressing Challenges Facing Educational Institutions (Parastatals, Boards and Commissions) for Sustainable Educational Administration in Nigeria. *World of Science: Journal on Modern Research Methodologies*, 2(1), 1–11.

Olebara, C. C., & Maureen, M. N. (2018). Student's Academic performance monitoring system in Tertiary Institutions. *West African Journal of Industrial & Academic Research*, 19(2), 120.

Onah, F. O. (2008). *Human Resource Management. John Jacob's Classic Publisher Ltd Plot 7 Fmr ESUT Road*. Nkpokiti Junction Enugu.

Ortner, S. (1984). Theory in anthropology since the sixties. *Comparative Studies in Society and History*, 26(1), 126–166. 10.1017/S0010417500010811

Oyedokun, G. E., & Adeolu-Akande, M. A. (2022). Impact of Information Communication Technology (ICT) on Quality Education in Nigerian Tertiary Institutions. *Himalayan Journal of Economics and Management*, 3(2), 49–58.

Palmer, D. C. (2015). Visualization and analysis of crystal structures using CrystalMaker software. *Zeitschrift für Kristallographie. Crystalline Materials*, 230(9-10), 559–572. 10.1515/zkri-2015-1869

Pålsson, Y., Mårtensson, G., Swenne, C. L., Ädel, E., & Engström, M. (2017). A peer learning intervention for nursing students in clinical practice education: A quasi-experimental study. *Nurse Education Today*, 51, 81–87. 10.1016/j.nedt.2017.01.01128142097

Pandey, I. M. (2012). Central Equipment Company. In *R. B. I M Pandey, Cases in Financial Management* (pp. 259–263). Tata McGraw Hill Education Private Limited.

Panina, T. S., & Vavilova, L. N. (2008). *Modern methods of activation of training*. Academy.

Compilation of References

Pantelidis, V. S. (2010). *Reasons to use virtual reality in education and training courses and a model to determine when to use virtual reality*. Themes in Science and Technology Education.

Park, C. Y., & Kim, J. (2020). Education, skill training, and lifelong learning in the era of technological revolution. [CrossRef]. *SSRN*, 34, 3–19. 10.2139/ssrn.3590922

Partnership for 21st Century Skills (P21). (2015). *Framework for 21st Century Learning*. P21. http://www.p21.org/our-work/p21-framework

Pascarella, E. T., & Terenzini, P. T. (2005). *How college affects students: A third decade of research* (Vol. 2). Jossey-Bass.

Patel, H. (2021). *Role of technology and equitable access in education*.

Paul, R., & Elder, L. (2006). *Critical Thinking: Learn the Tools the Best Thinkers Use*. Pearson Prentice Hall.

Paul, R., & Elder, L. (2008). *The Miniature Guide to Critical Thinking: Concepts and Tools*. Foundation for Critical Thinking Press.

Peng, H., Ma, S., & Spector, J. M. (2019). Personalized adaptive learning: An emerging pedagogical approach enabled by a smart learning environment. *Smart Learning Environments*, 6(1), 1–14. 10.1186/s40561-019-0089-y

Perkmen, S., & Pamuk, S. (2011). Social cognitive predictors of pre-service teachers' technology integration performance. *Asia Pacific Education Review*, 12(1), 45–58. 10.1007/s12564-010-9109-x

Persaud, C. (2023, November 15). *Bloom's Taxonomy: The Ultimate Guide [Free Download]*. Top Hat. https://tophat.com/blog/blooms-taxonomy/

Pessoni, V., Federson, F., & Vincenzi, A. (2015). Learning Difficulties in Computing Courses: Cognitive Processes Assessment Methods Research and Application. *Anais Do Simpósio Brasileiro de Sistemas de Informação (SBSI)*, 31–38. 10.5753/sbsi.2015.5798

Pfeiffer, A., Bezzina, S., Dingli, A., Wernbacher, T., Denk, N., & Fleischhacker, M. (2021). Adaptive LEARNING and assessment: From the TEACHERS'PERSPECTIVE. *INTED2021 Proceedings*, (pp. 375–379). IEEE.

Pinehas, L. N., Mulenga, E., & Amadhila, J. (2017). Factors that hinder the academic performance of the nursing students who registered as first years in 2010 at the University of Namibia (UNAM), Oshakati Campus in Oshana, Namibia. *Journal of Nursing Education and Practice*, 7(8), 63. 10.5430/jnep.v7n8p63

Pipko, S. (2002). *Baltic Winds: Testimony of a Soviet Attorney*. Xlibris Corporation.

Pita, M., Costa, J., & Moreira, A. (2021). The Effect of University Missions on Entrepreneurial Initiative across Multiple Entrepreneurial Ecosystems: Evidence from Europe. *Education Sciences*, 11(762), 1–20. 10.3390/educsci11120762

Pitts, W., & Lehner-Quam, A. (2019). Engaging the Framework for Information Literacy for Higher Education as a Lens for Assessment in ePortfolio Social Pedagogy Ecosystem for Science Teacher Education. *International Journal of ePortfolio, 1,* 29-44. https://academicworks.cuny.edu/cgi/viewcontent.cgi?article=1391&context=le_pubs

Polit, F. D., & Beck, C. T. (2017). *Nursing research: Generating and assessing evidence for nursing practice* (10th ed.). Lippincott Williams & Wilkins.

Poole, M., & Mansfield, R. (1994). Managers' attitudes to HRM: Rhetoric and Reality. P Blyton and P. Turnbull (eds), *Reassessing HRM.* London Sage.

Popenici, S. A. D., & Kerr, S. (2017). Exploring the impact of artificial intelligence on teaching and learning in higher education. *Research and Practice in Technology Enhanced Learning,* 12(1), 22. 10.1186/s41039-017-0062-830595727

Prasad, P. (2005). *Crafting qualitative research: Working in the postpositivist traditions.* M.E. Sharpe.

Prince, M. (2004). Does active learning work? A review of the research. *Journal of Engineering Education*, 93(3), 223–231. 10.1002/j.2168-9830.2004.tb00809.x

Purita, R., & Tesene, M. (2023). *Adaptive Courseware for Early Success Case Study: Cleveland State University.* Every Learner Everywhere. https://www.everylearnereverywhere.org/resources/adaptive-courseware-for-early-success-case-study-cleveland-state-university/

Ragan, L. C., Cavanagh, T. B., Schroeder, R., & Thompson, K. (2023). Supporting faculty success in online learning: Requirements for individual and institutional leadership. In *Leading the eLearning Transformation of Higher Education* (pp. 116–137). Routledge. 10.4324/9781003445623-10

Railean, E. (2017). Metacognition in Higher Education: Successful Learning Strategies and Tactics for Sustainability. In *Metacognition and Successful Learning Strategies in Higher Education* (pp. 1-21). IGI Global. https://doi.org/10.4018/978-1-5225-2218-8.ch00

Railean, E. A. (2019b). Education Ecosystems in the Anthropocene Period: Learning and Communication. In *Handbook of Research on Ecosystem-Based Theoretical Models of Learning and Communication* (pp. 1-19). IGI Global. 10.4018/978-1-5225-7853-6.ch001

Railean, E., Trofimov, V., & Aktas, D. (2021). Learning Resource Management from Investigating Intrinsic Motivation in Various Learning Environments. In: *Proceedings of the Fourteenth International Conference on Management Science and Engineering Management. Advances in Intelligent Systems and Computing.* Springer, Cham. 10.1007/978-3-030-49889-4_12

Railean, E. (2017). *Metacognition in Higher Education: Successful Learning Strgeties and Tactics for Sustainability.* IGI Global. 10.4018/978-1-5225-2218-8

Railean, E. (2019a). *Anticipating Competence Development With Open Textbooks: The Case of Liquid Skills in Metasystems Learning Design of Open Textbooks: Emerging Research and Opportunities.* IGI Global., 10.4018/978-1-5225-5305-2.ch005

Compilation of References

Railean, E. A. (2020). Pedagogy of New Assessment, Measurement, and Testing Strategies in Higher Education: Learning Theory and Outcomes. In Railean, E. (Ed.), *Assessment, Testing, and Measurement Strategies in Global Higher Education* (pp. 1–19). IGI Global. 10.4018/978-1-7998-2314-8.ch001

Rajasekar, S. (2020). *Challenges and opportunities posed by NEP.*

Rakovan, J. (2018). Computer Programs for Drawing Crystal Shapes and Atomic Structures. *Rocks and Minerals*, 93(1), 60–64. 10.1080/00357529.2018.1383832

Ramadian, O. D., Cahyono, B. Y., & Suryati, N. (2019). The implementation of Visual, Auditory, Kinesthetic (VAK) learning model in improving students' achievement in writing descriptive texts. In *English Language Teaching Educational Journal, 2*(3). Universitas Negeri Malang, Indonesia. https://files.eric.ed.gov/fulltext/EJ1266033.pdf

Ramsden, P. (2003). *Learning to Teach in Higher Education.* Routledge. 10.4324/9780203507711

Ravanipour, M., Bahreini, M., & Ravanipour, M. (2015). Exploring nursing students' experience of peer learning in clinical practice. *Journal of Education and Health Promotion*, 4(1), 46. 10.4103/2277-9531.15723326097860

Reddy, M. V. B., Bhujanga Rao, P., & Keerthi, G. (2023). Issues and emerging challenges for NEP 2020. [IJSREM]. *International Journal of Scientific Research in Engineering and Management*, 7(5), 290. 10.55041/IJSREM20290

Regan, P. M., & Jesse, J. (2018). Ethical challenges of edtech, big data and personalized learning: Twenty-first century student sorting and tracking. *Ethics and Information Technology*, 21(3), 167–179. 10.1007/s10676-018-9492-2

Reicher, H. (2010). Building inclusive education on social and emotional learning: Challenges and perspectives—A review. *International Journal of Inclusive Education*, 14(3), 213–246. 10.1080/13603110802504218

Renta-Davids, A.-I., Jiménez-González, J.-M., Fandos-Garrido, M., & González-Soto, Á.-P. (2016). Organizational and training factors affecting academic teacher training outcomes. *Teaching in Higher Education*, 21(2), 219–231. 10.1080/13562517.2015.1136276

Reutova, E. A. (2012). *The use of active and interactive training methods in the educational process of the higher education institution (methodical recommendations for the teachers of the Novosibirsk State Agrarian University).* Publishing House of NGAU.

Reyes-Hernández, C. G., Carmona Pulido, J. M., De la Garza Chapa, R. I., Serna Vázquez, R. P., Alcalá Briones, R. D., Plasencia Banda, P. M., Villarreal Silva, E. E., Jacobo Baca, G., de la Garza Castro, O., Elizondo Omaña, R. E., & Guzmán López, S. (2015). Near-peer teaching strategy in a large human anatomy course: Perceptions of near-peer instructors. *Anatomical Sciences Education*, 8(2), 189–193. 10.1002/ase.148425203867

Reynolds, M. (1999). Critical Reflection and Management Education: Rehabilitating Less Hierarchical Approaches. *Journal of Management Education*, 23(5), 537–553. 10.1177/105256299902300506

Rezvan, S., Ahmadi, S. A., & Abedi, M. R. (2006). The effects of metacognitive training on the academic achievement and happiness of Esfahan University conditional students. *Counselling Psychology Quarterly*, 19(4), 415–428. 10.1080/09515070601106471

Ricaurte, P. (2016). Pedagogies for the open knowledge society. *International Journal of Educational Technology in Higher Education*, 13(1), 1–10. 10.1186/s41239-016-0033-y

Rivadeneira, J., & Inga, E. (2023). Interactive Peer Instruction Method Applied to Classroom Environments Considering a Learning Engineering Approach to Innovate the Teaching–Learning Process. *Education Sciences*, 13(3), 301. 10.3390/educsci13030301

Rizvi, M. (2023). Exploring the landscape of artificial intelligence in education: Challenges and opportunities. *2023 5th International Congress on Human-Computer Interaction, Optimization and Robotic Applications (HORA)*, (pp. 1–3). Research Gate.

Robertson, D. L. (2020). Adult Students in U.S. Higher Education: An Evidence-Based Commentary and Recommended Best Practices. *Innovative Higher Education*, 45(2), 121–134. 10.1007/s10755-019-09492-8

Rouse, J. (2007). *Practice Theory*. Division I Faculty Publications.

Ruggunan, S., & Spiller, D. (2014). Critical pedagogy for teaching HRM in the context of social change. *African Journal of Business Ethic*s.

Rust, F. O. (2019). Redesign in teacher education: The roles of teacher educators. *European Journal of Teacher Education*, 42(4), 523–533. 10.1080/02619768.2019.1628215

Saay, S., & Norta, A. (2018). An architecture for e-learning infrastructures on a national level: A case study of the Afghanistan Research and Education Network. *International Journal of Innovation and Learning*, 23(1), 54–75. 10.1504/IJIL.2018.088790

Saeed, S., Aamir, R., & Ramzan, M. (2011). Plagiarism and its implications on higher education in developing countries. *International Journal of Teaching and Case Studies*, 3(2-4), 123–130. 10.1504/IJTCS.2011.039552

Saeed, S., Almuhaideb, A. M., Bamarouf, Y. A., Alabaad, D. A., Gull, H., Saqib, M., Iqbal, S. Z., & Salam, A. A. (2021). Sustainable program assessment practices: A review of the ABET and NCAAA computer information systems accreditation process. *International Journal of Environmental Research and Public Health*, 18(23), 12691. 10.3390/ijerph182312691 34886417

Sahlberg, P., & Oldroyd, D. (2010). Pedagogy for economic competitiveness and sustainable development. *European Journal of Education*, 45(2), 280–299. 10.1111/j.1465-3435.2010.01429.x

Saini, D., & Budhawar, P. (2004). Human Resource Management in India. *Human Resource Management in Asia-Pacific Countries*. Routledge.

Compilation of References

Sajja, R., Sermet, Y., Cikmaz, M., Cwiertny, D., & Demir, I. (2023). Artificial Intelligence-Enabled Intelligent Assistant for Personalized and Adaptive Learning in Higher Education. *ArXiv Preprint ArXiv:2309.10892*.

Säljö, R. (2000). *Lärande i praktiken: Ett sociokulturellt perspektiv* [Learning in Practice: A Socio-Cultural Perspective]. Prisma.

Sallam, M. (2023). ChatGPT Utility in Healthcare Education, Research, and Practice: Systematic Review on the Promising Perspectives and Valid Concerns. In *Healthcare (Switzerland), 11*(6). MDPI. 10.3390/healthcare11060887

Sato, M. (2022). Metacognition. In S. Li, P. Hiver, & M. Papi, *The Routledge Handbook of Second Language Acquisition and Individual Differences* (1st ed., pp. 95–110). Routledge. 10.4324/9781003270546-8

Saubern, R., Henderson, M., Heinrich, E., & Redmond, P. (2020). TPaCK – time to reboot? *Australasian Journal of Educational Technology, 36*(3), 1–9. 10.14742/ajet.6378

Saunders, L. (2012). Faculty perspectives on information literacy as a student learning outcome. *Journal of Academic Librarianship, 38*(4), 226–236. 10.1016/j.acalib.2012.06.001

Sayer, A. (2003). *Moral Economy published by the Department of Sociology*. Lancaster University. http://www.comp.lancs.ac.uk/sociology/papers/sayer-moral-economy.pdf

Schneider, T. R., Lyons, J. B., & Khazon, S. (2013). Emotional intelligence and resilience. *Personality and Individual Differences, 55*(8), 909–914. 10.1016/j.paid.2013.07.460

Schowalter, T. D. (2022). Ecosystem structure and function. *Insect Ecology: An Ecosystem Approach*. Science Direct. https://www.sciencedirect.com/science/article/pii/B9780323856737000046

Schutte, N. S., & Loi, N. M. (2014). Connections between emotional intelligence and workplace flourishing. *Personality and Individual Differences, 66*, 134–139. 10.1016/j.paid.2014.03.031

Shafi, A., Saeed, S., Bamarouf, Y. A., Iqbal, S. Z., Min-Allah, N., & Alqahtani, M. A. (2019). Student outcomes assessment methodology for ABET accreditation: A case study of computer science and computer information systems programs. *IEEE Access : Practical Innovations, Open Solutions, 7*, 13653–13667. 10.1109/ACCESS.2019.2894066

Sharma, N. (2021). Case studies of universities adopting NEP's multidisciplinary approach.

Shatimwene, G. P., Ashipala, D. O., & Kamenye, E. (2020). Experiences of Student Nurses on the Use of the Two-Week Block System at the Satellite Campus of a Higher Education Institution in Namibia. *International Journal of Higher Education, 9*(3), 222–231. 10.5430/ijhe.v9n3p222

Shemshack, A., Kinshuk, , & Spector, J. M. (2021). A comprehensive analysis of personalized learning components. *Journal of Computers in Education, 8*(4), 485–503. 10.1007/s40692-021-00188-7

Shi, L., Cristea, A. I., Hadzidedic, S., & Dervishalidovic, N. (2014). Contextual Gamification of Social Interaction-Towards Increasing Motivation in Social E-Learning. *Lecture Notes in Computer Science*, 8613, 116–122. 10.1007/978-3-319-09635-3_12

Shonfeld, M., Cotnam-Kappel, M., Judge, M., Ng, C. Y., Ntebutse, J. G., Williamson-Leadley, S., & Yildiz, M. N. (2021). Learning in digital environments: A model for cross-cultural alignment. *Educational Technology Research and Development*, 69(4), 1–20. 10.1007/s11423-021-09967-633654347

Shuckers: Miller and Modigliani. In (1997). *J. D. Joseph Sulock, Cases in Financial management* (pp. 215–222). John Wiley & Sons, Inc.

Sibiya, M. N., Ngxongo, T. S. P., & Beepat, S. Y. (2018). The influence of peer mentoring on critical care nursing students' learning outcomes. *International Journal of Workplace Health Management*, 11(3), 130–142. 10.1108/IJWHM-01-2018-000330166994

Singh, S. (2021). Critical roles of digital education under NEP.

Smith, B. L., & MacGregor, J. T. (1992). What is collaborative learning? In A. S. Goodsell, M. R. Maher, V. Tinto, B. L. Smith, & J. MacGregor (Eds.), *Collaborative Learning: A Sourcebook for Higher Education* (*Vol. 2*, pp. 10-30). National Center on Postsecondary Teaching, Learning, and Assessment, Syracuse University.

Smith, A., & Johnson, B. (2020). Collaborative tools integrated into digital textbooks enhance interactivity and social learning environments. *Journal of Educational Technology*, 45(3), 289–305.

Smith, A., Jones, B., & Lee, C. (2018). The impact of digital textbooks on student engagement: A comparative study. *Journal of Educational Technology*, 25(3), 123–135.

Smyth, H.J. & Pryke, S. (2006). *The moral economy and research on projects: neglect and relevance to social capital and competencies.* Cobra 2006, RICS Foundation., UCL London.

Sneyers, E., & De Witte, K. (2017). The interaction between dropout, graduation rates and quality ratings in universities. *The Journal of the Operational Research Society*, 68(4), 416–430. 10.1057/jors.2016.15

Spady, W. (1994). *Outcome-based Education: Critical Issues and Answers*. American Association of School Administrators.

Spânu, P., Ulmeanu, M. E., & Doicin, C. V. (2024). Academic Third Mission through Community Engagement: An Empirical Study in European Universities. *Education Sciences*, 14(2), 141. 10.3390/educsci14020141

Srinivasan, M. (2019). *SEL Every Day: Integrating Social and Emotional Learning with Instruction in Secondary Classrooms*. W.W. Norton & Company.

Srivastava, S., & Sinha, K. (2023). From Bias to Fairness: A Review of Ethical Considerations and Mitigation Strategies in Artificial Intelligence. *International Journal for Research in Applied Science and Engineering Technology*, 2(3), 2247–2251. 10.22214/ijraset.2023.49990

Compilation of References

Stenberg, M., & Carlson, E. (2015). Swedish student nurses' perception of peer learning as an educational model during clinical practice in a hospital setting—An evaluation study. *BMC Nursing*, 14(1), 1–7. 10.1186/s12912-015-0098-226435698

Sternberg, R. J. (2006). The theory of successful intelligence. *Interamerican Journal of Psychology*, 40(2), 189–202.

Sternberg, R. J. (2019). A theory of adaptive intelligence and its relation to general intelligence. *Journal of Intelligence*, 7(4), 23. 10.3390/jintelligence704002331581505

Sternberg, R. J. (2021). Adaptive intelligence: Its nature and implications for education. *Education Sciences*, 11(12), 823. 10.3390/educsci11120823

Sternberg, R. J., & Zhang, L. F. (2014). *Perspectives on thinking, learning and cognitive styles*. Lawrence Erlbaum Associates. 10.4324/9781410605986

Stone, A., & McKechnie, L. (2017). Beyond the one-shot: Developing information literacy skills through interactive workshops. *Journal of Library & Information Services in the Digital Age*, 18(3), 1–12.

Stone, R., Cooper, S., & Cant, R. (2013). The value of peer learning in undergraduate nursing education: A systematic review. *International Scholarly Research Notices*, 2013.23691355

Straw, A. M., Cole, J. W., & McGuire, K. (2023). Peer Instruction as an Alternative Active Learning Pedagogy Across the Pharmacy Curriculum. *American Journal of Pharmaceutical Education*, 87(8), 100090. 10.1016/j.ajpe.2023.10009037597914

Sulecio de Alvarez, M., & Dickson-Deane, C. (2018). Avoiding educational technology pitfalls for inclusion and equity. *TechTrends*, 62(4), 345–353. 10.1007/s11528-018-0270-0

Sulock, J. (1997). Taylor Brands - Cost of Capital or Required rate of return. In *J. D. Joseph Sulock, Cases in Financial Management* (pp. 191–196). John Wiley & Sons, Inc.

Sunggingwati, D. (2018). Cooperative learning in peer teaching: A case study in an EFL context. *Indonesian Journal of Applied Linguistics*, 8(1), 149–157. 10.17509/ijal.v8i1.11475

Sun, Y., Strobel, J., & Newby, T. J. (2017). The impact of student teaching experience on pre-service teachers' readiness for technology integration: A mixed methods study with growth curve modeling. *Educational Technology Research and Development*, 65(3), 597–629. 10.1007/s11423-016-9486-x

Sweller, J. (1988). Cognitive load during problem solving: Effects on learning. *Cognitive Science*, 12(2), 257–285. 10.1207/s15516709cog1202_4

Sweller, J., Ayres, P., & Kalyuga, S. (2011). *Cognitive load theory*. Springer. 10.1007/978-1-4419-8126-4

Tantillo Philibert, C. (2018). *Everyday SEL in High School: Integrating Social-Emotional Learning and Mindfulness into Your Classroom*. Routledge.

Tan, X., Chen, P., & Yu, H. (2022). Potential conditions for linking teachers' online informal learning with innovative teaching. *Thinking Skills and Creativity*, 45, 101022. 10.1016/j.tsc.2022.101022

Taylor, D. L., Yeung, M., & Bashet, A. Z. (2021). Personalized and adaptive learning. In *Innovative learning environments in STEM higher education: Opportunities, Challenges, and Looking Forward* (Switzaland, pp. 17–34). Springer International Publishing. 10.1007/978-3-030-58948-6_2

Teachers' Association. (2020). *Faculty perspectives on NEP reforms*. Teacher's Association.

Tejedor, G., Segalàs, J., Barrón, Á., Fernández-Morilla, M., Fuertes, M. T., Ruiz-Morales, J., Gutiérrez, I., García-González, E., Aramburuzabala, P., & Hernández, À. (2019). Didactic strategies to promote competencies in sustainability. *Sustainability (Basel)*, 11(7), 2086. 10.3390/su11072086

Telio, S., Ajjawi, R., & Regehr, G. (2015). The "educational alliance" as a framework for reconceptualizing feedback in medical education. *Academic Medicine*, 90(5), 609–614. 10.1097/ACM.0000000000000056025406607

Thabet, M., Taha, E. E. S., Abood, S. A., & Morsy, S. R. (2017). The effect of problem-based learning on nursing students' decision-making skills and styles. *Journal of Nursing Education and Practice*, 7(6), 108–116. 10.5430/jnep.v7n6p108

The M.C. Escher Foundation. (2020). *M.C. Escher—Image Categories—Symmetry*. MC Escher Foundation. https://www.mcescher.com/gallery/symmetry/ (accessed on 27 July 2020).

Thomas, J. W., & Mergendoller, J. R. (2000). *Managing project-based learning: Principles from the field*. Paper presented at the Annual Meeting of the American Educational Research Association, New Orleans.

Thompson, P., & Vincent, S. (2010). Labour Process Theory and Critical Realism. In *Working life: Renewing labour process analysis. Critical perspectives on work and employment*. Palgrave Macmillan, Houndmills, Basingstoke. 10.1007/978-1-137-11817-2_4

Thompson, P. (2011). The trouble with HRM. *Human Resource Management Journal*, 21(4), 355–367. 10.1111/j.1748-8583.2011.00180.x

Tian, B., Wang, C., & Hong, H. (2023). A Survey of Personalized Adaptive Learning System. *2023 2nd International Conference on Artificial Intelligence and Computer Information Technology (AICIT)*, (pp. 1–6). ACM.

Tilbury, D. (2004). Environmental education for sustainability: A force for change in higher education. In *Higher education and the challenge of sustainability: Problematics, promise, and practice* (pp. 97–112). Springer Netherlands. 10.1007/0-306-48515-X_9

Timotheou, S., Miliou, O., Dimitriadis, Y., Sobrino, S. V., Giannoutsou, N., Cachia, R., Monés, A. M., & Ioannou, A. (2023). Impacts of digital technologies on education and factors influencing schools' digital capacity and transformation: A literature review. *Education and Information Technologies*, 28(6), 6695–6726. 10.1007/s10639-022-11431-836465416

Compilation of References

Tomiyama, T. (2007). Intelligent computer-aided design systems: Past 20 years and future 20 years. *Artificial Intelligence for Engineering Design, Analysis and Manufacturing*, 21(1), 27–29. 10.1017/S0890060407070114

Tong, S. (2001). *Active learning: theory and applications*. Stanford University.

Topping, K. (1998). Peer Assessment Between Students in Colleges and Universities. *Review of Educational Research*, 68(3), 249–276. 10.3102/00346543068003249

Tracey, M. W., Hutchinson, A., & Grezbyk, T. Q. (2014). Instructional designers as reflective practitioners: Developing professional identity through reflection. *Educational Technology Research and Development*, 62(3), 315–334. 10.1007/s11423-014-9334-9

Turkot, T. I. (2011). *Higher Education pedagogy*.

Twardell, L., & Boyle, L. (2020). Gamified learning: Using escape rooms to engage students in information literacy instruction. *College & Research Libraries News*, 81(6), 279–283.

Twardell, L., & Boyle, L. (2021). The impact of gamified learning on student engagement and knowledge retention in academic libraries. *Library Hi Tech*, 39(1), 53–68.

U.S. Census Bureau. (2013). *School Enrollment in the United States: 2011*. Suitland-Silver Hill.

U.S. Department of Education. (2018). *40th Annual Report to Congress on the Implementation of the Individuals with Disabilities Education Act, Parts B and C*. ED PUBS, Education Publications Center, Washington, DC, USA.

Uchechukwu, E. S., Amechi, A. F., Okoye, C. C., & Okeke, N. M. (2023). Youth Unemployment and Security Challenges in Anambra State, Nigeria. *Sch J Arts Humanit Soc Sci*, 4(4), 81–91. 10.36347/sjahss.2023.v11i04.005

UGC. (2021). *Faculty development programs for NEP implementation*. UGC.

Ullah, I., Tabassum, R., & Kaleem, M. (2018). Effects of peer tutoring on the academic achievement of students in the subject of biology at secondary level. *Education Sciences*, 8(3), 112. 10.3390/educsci8030112

UNDP. (2020). *Alignment of NEP with Sustainable Development Goals*. UNDP.

UNESCO. (2009). *Policy Guidelines on Inclusion in Education*. Paris: UNESCO. https://unesdoc.unesco.org/ark:/48223/pf0000186582

UNESCO. (2015). *Education 2030: Incheon Declaration and Framework for Action*. UNESCO. https://unesdoc.unesco.org/ark:/48223/pf0000245656

UNESCO. (2020). *Review on the balance of autonomy and accountability in NEP*. UNESCO.

UNESCO. (2023, April 20). *What you need to know about higher education*. UNESCO. https://www.unesco.org/en/higher-education/need-know#:~:text=Higher%20education%20is%20a%20rich,meet%20ever%20changing%20labour%20markets

UNICEF. (2020). *Technology and equitable access in education*. UNICEF.

United Nations. (2015). *Sustainable Development Goals. Goal 4: Quality Education*. UN. https://www.un.org/sustainabledevelopment/education/

Valeeva, M. A. (2009). The use of interactive methods of training as a condition of formation of the social professional experience of the student. *Siberian Pedagogical Journal*, 4, 88–98.

Valentin, C. (2007). How can I teach critical management in this place? A critical pedagogy for HRD: possibilities, contradictions and compromises. In Rigg, C., Stewart, J., & Trepan, K. (Eds.), *Critical human resource development. London. Prentice Hall.* • Sullivan W M et al. (2007), *Educating lawyers: preparation for the profession of law [CARNEGIE REPORT}* • *Tapscott, D (1998). Growing Up Digital: The Rise of the Net Generation*. McGraw-Hill.

van de Heyde, V., & Siebrits, A. (2019). The ecosystem of e-learning model for higher education. *South African Journal of Science*, 115(5/6), 78–83. 10.17159/sajs.2019/5808

Vattanaamorn, S., Phaitrakoon, J., Jirarattanawanna, N., Jintrawet, U., Kwalamthan, W., & Lertwongpaopu, W. (2022). Factors Influencing the Achievement of Learning Outcomes Among Nursing Students: The Mixed-Method Study. *Eurasian Journal of Educational Research*, 98(98), 131–146.

Velez, J. J., Cano, J., Whittington, M. S., & Wolf, K. J. (2011). Cultivating change through peer teaching. *Journal of Agricultural Education*, 52(1), 40–49. 10.5032/jae.2011.01040

Venkatesh, V., & Bala, H. (2008). Technology acceptance model 3 and a research agenda on interventions. *Decision Sciences*, 39(2), 273–315. 10.1111/j.1540-5915.2008.00192.x

Venkatesh, V., & Davis, F. D. (2000). A theoretical extension of the technology acceptance model: Four longitudinal field studies. *Management Science*, 46(2), 186–204. 10.1287/mnsc.46.2.186.11926

Verma, R. (2021). *Stakeholder perspectives on NEP adoption*.

Vetrivel, S. C., & Mohanasundaram, T. (2024a). Flourishing on Campus: Promoting Mental Health and Coping Skills in Higher Education Institutions. In Aloka, P. (Ed.), *Mental Health Crisis in Higher Education* (pp. 294–311). IGI Global. 10.4018/979-8-3693-2833-0.ch017

Vetrivel, S. C., & Mohanasundaram, T. (2024b). Beyond the Blackboard: Embracing Hybrid Learning Spaces. In Omona, K., & O'dama, M. (Eds.), *Global Perspectives on Micro-Learning and Micro-Credentials in Higher Education* (pp. 10–28). IGI Global. 10.4018/979-8-3693-0343-6.ch002

Vetrivel, S. C., Sowmiya, K. C., Arun, V. P., Saravanan, T. P., & Maheswari, R. (2024). Guiding Principles for Youth-Centric Development: Ethical AI. In *Zeinab Zaremohzzabieh, Rusli Abdullah, Seyedali Ahrari, Exploring Youth Studies in the Age of AI (ch-17)*. IGI Global. 10.4018/979-8-3693-3350-1

Compilation of References

Viberg, R. (2021). The teacher educator's perceptions of professional agency - a paradox of enabling and hindering digital professional development in higher education. *Education Inquiry*, 1–18. 10.1080/20004508.2021.1984075

Vignare, K., Tesene, M., & Lorenzo, G. (2020). *Case Study Arizona State University (ASU)*. Every Learner Everywhere. www.everylearnereverywhere.org/resources/case-study-arizona-state-university-asu/

Villalón, S. L. J., & Hermosa, C. C. L. (2016). *The Role of National Research and Education Networks Providing Connectivity and Advanced Network Services to Virtual Communities in Collaborative R&E Projects. CUDI: The Mexican Case: Part 1.* Paper presented at the High Performance Computer Applications: 6th International Conference, ISUM 2015, Mexico City, Mexico. 10.1007/978-3-319-32243-8_3

Vinacke, W. E. (1957). Some variables in buzz sessions. *The Journal of Social Psychology*, 45(1), 25–33. 10.1080/00224545.1957.9714283

Vogel, F. R., & Human-Vogel, S. (2016). Academic commitment and self-efficacy as predictors of academic achievement in additional materials science. *Higher Education Research & Development*, 35(6), 1298–1310. 10.1080/07294360.2016.1144574

von Glasersfeld, E. (2001). Radical constructivism and teaching. *Prospects*, 31(2), 161–173. 10.1007/BF03220058

Vrugt, A., & Oort, F. J. (2008). Metacognition, achievement goals, study strategies and academic achievement: Pathways to achievement. *Metacognition and Learning*, 3(2), 123–146. 10.1007/s11409-008-9022-4

Vygotsky, L. S. (1978). *Mind in Society: The development of higher psychological processes*. Harvard University Press.

Walkington, C. A. (2013). Using adaptive learning technologies to personalize instruction to student interests: The impact of relevant contexts on performance and learning outcomes. *Journal of Educational Psychology*, 105(4), 932–945. 10.1037/a0031882

Walsh, G. (2015). Implementing innovations in global health care: Financial sustainability in the social sector. *Health Affairs*.

Wang, S., Christensen, C., Cui, W., Tong, R., Yarnall, L., Shear, L., & Feng, M. (2023). When adaptive learning is effective learning: Comparison of an adaptive learning system to teacher-led instruction. *Interactive Learning Environments*, 31(2), 793–803. 10.1080/10494820.2020.1808794

Wara, Y., & Singh, D. (2015). A guide to establishing computer security incident response team (CSIRT) for national research and education network (NREN). *African Journal of Computing and ICT*, 8(2), 1–8.

Wei, L. (2023). Artificial intelligence in language instruction: Impact on English learning achievement, L2 motivation, and self-regulated learning. *Frontiers in Psychology*, 14, 1261955. 10.3389/fpsyg.2023.126195538023040

Weiler, A. (2004). Information-seeking behavior in Generation Y students: Motivation, critical thinking, and learning theory. *Journal of Academic Librarianship*, 30(1), 45–52.

Weinstein, C. E., & Mayer, R. E. (1986). The teaching of learning strategies. In Wittrock, M. C. (Ed.), *Handbook of research in teaching* (Vol. 3, pp. 315–327). Macmillan.

Whiteside, A. (2010). Making the case for space: Three years of empirical research on learning environments. *EDUCAUSE Quarterly*.

Wikipedia contributors. (2023, November 21). *Redintegration*. Wikipedia. https://en.wikipedia.org/wiki/Redintegration

Wikipedia contributors. (2024, January 15). *Dual-coding theory*. Wikipedia. https://en.wikipedia.org/wiki/Dual-coding_theory

Wikipedia contributors. (2024b, March 4). *Metacognition*. Wikipedia. https://en.wikipedia.org/wiki/Metacognition#:~:text=15%20External%20links-,Definitions,more%20informally%2C%20thinking%20about%20thinking

Williams, B., & Reddy, P. (2016). Does peer-assisted learning improve academic performance? A scoping review. *Nurse Education Today*, 42, 23–29. 10.1016/j.nedt.2016.03.02427237348

Winn, A. S., DelSignore, L., Marcus, C. H., Chiel, L., Freiman, E., Stafford, D., & Newman, L. R. (2019). Applying cognitive learning strategies to enhance learning and retention in clinical teaching settings. *MedEdPORTAL: the Journal of Teaching and Learning Resources*, 10850. 10.15766/mep_2374-8265.1085031921996

Wong, C. (2016). *Emotional Intelligence at Work: 18-Year Journey of A Researcher*. Taylor & Francis Group.

World Bank. (2018). *World Development Report 2018: Learning to Realize Education's Promise*. Washington, DC: World Bank. https://openknowledge.worldbank.org/handle/10986/28340

Wu, H., & Molnár, G. (2022). Analysing Complex Problem-Solving Strategies from a Cognitive Perspective: The Role of Thinking Skills. *Journal of Intelligence*, 10(3), 46. 10.3390/jintelligence1003004635893277

Xie, H., Chu, H.-C., Hwang, G.-J., & Wang, C.-C. (2019). Trends and development in technology-enhanced adaptive/personalized learning: A systematic review of journal publications from 2007 to 2017. *Computers & Education*, 140, 103599. 10.1016/j.compedu.2019.103599

Yafie, E., Nirmala, B., Kurniawaty, L., Bakri, T. S. M., Hani, A. B., & Setyaningsih, D. (2020). Supporting Cognitive Development through Multimedia Learning and Scientific Approach: An Experimental Study in Preschool. *Universal Journal of Educational Research*, 8(11C), 113–123. 10.13189/ujer.2020.082313

Compilation of References

Yang, M. M., Golden, B. P., Cameron, K. A., Gard, L., Bierman, J. A., Evans, D. B., & Henschen, B. L. (2022). Learning through Teaching: Peer Teaching and Mentoring Experiences among Third-Year Medical Students. *Teaching and Learning in Medicine*, 34(4), 360–367. 10.1080/10401334.2021.189993033934679

Yao, J. (2023). *Exploring experiential learning: Enhancing secondary school chemistry education through practical engagement and innovation*. Education, Health, and Social Sciences., 10.54097/ehss.v22i.12508

Yigzaw, S. T. (2023). *A Model for Knowledge Management Systems in Higher Education and Research: The Case of the UbuntuNet Alliance in the Eastern and Southern African region*. Itä-Suomen yliopisto.

Yin, R. K. (1989). *Case Study Research: Design and Method*. Sage Publications. https://www.barcouncilofindia.org/wp-content/uploads/2010/05/BCIRulesPartIV.pdf

Yu, H., Liu, P., Huang, X., & Cao, Y. (2021). Teacher online informal learning as a means to innovative teaching during home quarantine in the COVID-19 pandemic. *Frontiers in Psychology*, 12, 596582. 10.3389/fpsyg.2021.59658234248730

Zain, S. (2021). Digital transformation trends in education. In *Future Directions in Digital Information* (pp. 223–234). Elsevier. 10.1016/B978-0-12-822144-0.00036-7

Zang, J., Gowthami, J., & Anilkumar, C. (2022). Adaptive Artificial Intelligent Technique to Improve Acquisition of Knowledge in the Educational Environment. *Journal of Interconnection Networks*, 22(Supp02), 2143013. 10.1142/S0219265921430131

Zarifnejad, G., Mirhaghi, A., & Rajabpoor, M. (2015). Learning experience through peer education: A qualitative study. *Indian Journal of Medical Education*, 15, 27–40.

Zeitlhofer, I., Hörmann, S., Mann, B., Hallinger, K., & Zumbach, J. (2023). Effects of cognitive and metacognitive prompts on learning performance in digital learning environments. *Knowledge (Beverly Hills, Calif.)*, 3(2), 277–292. 10.3390/knowledge3020019

Zhai, X., Gu, J., Liu, H., Liang, J.-C., & Tsai, C.-C. (2017). An experiential learning perspective on students' satisfaction model in a flipped classroom context. [Google Scholar]. *Journal of Educational Technology & Society*, 20, 198–210.

Zhan, L., Guo, D., Chen, G., & Yang, J. (2018). Effects of repetition learning on associative recognition over time: Role of the hippocampus and prefrontal cortex. *Frontiers in Human Neuroscience*, 12, 277. 10.3389/fnhum.2018.0027730050418

Zhou, L., Zhang, F., Zhang, S., & Xu, M. (2021). Study on the personalized learning model of learner-learning resource matching. *International Journal of Information and Education Technology (IJIET)*, 11(3), 143–147. 10.18178/ijiet.2021.11.3.1503

Zipke, M. (2018). Preparing teachers to teach with technology: Examining the effectiveness of a course in educational technology. *New Educator*, 14(4), 342–362. 10.1080/1547688X.2017.1401191

Zitha, I., Mokganya, G., & Sinthumule, O. (2023). Innovative strategies for fostering student engagement and collaborative learning among extended curriculum programme students. *Education Sciences*.

Подымов, Н. А. (2022). COGNITIVE BARRIERS AND STRATEGIES TO OVERCOME THEM IN THE EDUCATIONAL ACTIVITIES OF FOREIGN STUDENTS. *Higher education today, 3–4*, 103–106. https://doi.org/10.18137/RNU.HET.22.03-04.P.101

About the Contributors

Elena Railean is an Associate Professor at the American University of Moldova. Elena's research interests span postmodern pedagogy, educational philosophy and emerging models and technologies for learning and communication. The most significant works are: "User interface design of digital textbooks: How screens affect learning", "Psychological and pedagogical consideration in digital textbook use and development", "Methodology of educational software". Elena is in International Advisory Boards for International Journal of Virtual and Personal Learning Environments, International Journal of Web-Based Learning and Teaching Technologies, Encyclopedia of Information Science and Technology, Immersive Learning Research, Interactive Environments and Emerging Technologies for eLearning and others. Elena Railean co-edited two recently published volumes: "Metacognition and Successful Learning Strategies in Higher Education", "Handbook of Research on Applied Learning Theory and Design in Modern Education" and "Ecosystem-Based Theoretical Models of Learning and Communication". In 2017, EuroInvent honored her three recently published books by two Golden and one Silver Medals.

***

Daniel Opotamutale Ashipala (MN Sc) is a senior lecturer and Head of Department for the School of nursing and Public Health (SoNPH), General Nursing Science department in the Faculty of Health Sciences and Veterinary Medicine (FHSVM) at the University of Namibia, Namibia. His research interests include Primary health Care, Health care services and Nursing education, and Mental health. He has published a quite number of peer reviewed articles on the delivery of teaching and learning in higher education studies. He is a doctoral candidate at Stellenbosch University in Cape Town, South Africa. His doctoral work focuses on developing a framework to facilitate the implementation of a task shifting approach for nurses in the Namibia PHC services.

About the Contributors

M.B. Srinivasan is currently associated with CHRIST (Deemed to be University) in the Department of Business and Management, BGR Campus, Bangalore, Karnataka. Prior to his current role, Dr. Srinivasan served as Professor & Head in the Department of Business Administration at the School of Arts and Science, VMRF (Deemed to be University) AV Campus, Paiyanoor, Chennai, Tamil Nadu. He also held the position of Program Leader (MBA) at Olympia College in Kuala Lumpur, Malaysia. Dr. Srinivasan earned his Bachelor's and Master's degrees from the University of Madras, with his MBA specializing in Marketing Management from the SRM Institute of Management Studies, University of Madras, India. His academic journey culminated in a Ph.D. from Bharathiar University, Coimbatore, India Commencing his career in the Software Industry, Dr. Srinivasan initially worked in Sales and Marketing in India before transitioning to a Business Analyst role in Malaysia. With a robust industrial background, he later ventured into academia, holding positions at Veltech University and Vinayaka Mission Research Foundation (VMRF) in India as a Professor. He also served as a Program Leader - MBA at Kolej Gemilang and Olympia College in Kuala Lumpur, Malaysia accumulating over 14 years of teaching and 8 years of industrial experience. Dr. Srinivasan's diverse educational experiences include training by the Chartered Institute of Marketing in the UK and a stint as a Visiting Faculty at the University of West of Scotland. He is well-versed in teaching programs ranging from Diplomas to Doctor of Business Administration (DBA) from institutions like Anna University, Madras University, University of West of Scotland, IPE (Paris), and University of South Wales. With a career spanning more than two decades, Dr. Srinivasan has successfully blended his industrial experience with academia, offering a unique perspective to make teaching engaging and application-oriented for students. His research interests encompass Digital Marketing, Online Shopping, Consumer Behavior, Leadership, Tourism Marketing, and Work-Life Balance.

Divakara Bhat, is a professor and guide at Srinivas University, Mangaluru, with a total experience of 40 years. He was a rank holder in the Masters of Library and Information Science in 1995. He has published over forty-six research papers in national and international journals and conferences. In addition, he authored 14 books and edited three books and four conference proceedings. He was the recipient of the 'Best Research Papers' National Award from MANLIBNET, New Delhi. He also won the "Best Librarian" award from DKKLA, Udupi, in recognition of his exceptional contributions to the field of library science. He has guided four research scholars, and he has organised national and international conferences and workshops. He served as a resource person at various events at the national and state levels.

Meeramani N. is a Librarian at JAIN (Deemed-to-be University), Bangalore, with a total experience of 23 years. Emerging technology, innovative library services, and curriculum development are some of her areas of interest in study. She has published over fifty research papers in national and international journals and conferences, three of which were at IIM- Bangalore and IIM-Indore. She won the "Best Librarian 2023" State Award from the Government of Karnataka for outstanding achievements in the fields of library development and library science. She won the best paper award at IIM Bangalore on December 16–18, 2015. She was felicitated at the JGI Annual Awards Ceremony for her outstanding contribution in the field of research. She served as a resource person at various events within and outside the institutions.

About the Contributors

Patcha Bhujanga Rao is a highly accomplished professional with over two decades of experience in Human Resources, Legal, and Soft Skills. He has an impressive academic background, holding degrees like M.Com., DCFA., M.Phil., Ph.D, MBA (HR), M.Sc (Psychology), and LL.B. His diverse qualifications equip him with a comprehensive understanding of various disciplines, which enables him to excel in his roles. Dr. Patcha Bhujanga Rao is currently serving as a Professor at Jain Deemed-to-be University in Bengaluru. He has made significant contributions to the academic realm, particularly in the field of Human Resources. His profound expertise in HR management has been instrumental in guiding and mentoring the next generation of professionals. Dr. Rao has equipped them with essential skills and knowledge to thrive in their careers. His passion for imparting knowledge, coupled with his extensive experience, has enabled him to shape talent and drive positive change in countless professional trajectories. Beyond his expertise in HR, Dr. Patcha Bhujanga Rao is also well-versed in Soft Skills. He recognizes the paramount importance of effective communication, leadership, and interpersonal abilities in today's professional landscape. His dedication to enhancing these skills among students and professionals alike has been invaluable, fostering personal and professional development. Dr. Rao's unwavering dedication, expertise, and commitment to excellence have earned him widespread respect and admiration in the realms of HR and Soft Skills. He stands as a beacon of inspiration for aspiring professionals, embodying the values of continuous learning, mentorship, and leadership in the pursuit of professional success.

Bianca Ifeoma Chigbu is a postdoctoral research fellow in the Department of Sociology, University of Fort Hare, East London, South Africa.

Ravi Darshini is a highly accomplished academician with a rich background in teaching, research and academic administration spanning over two decades. Holding a Ph.D in Finance from Bharathiar University, India along with numerous other qualificatiions including M.Com., M.Phil., ICWA and Post Doc from Mc Stem Eduversity, USA. Throughout her career, Dr. Ravi Darshini has held various teaching positions at esteemed institutions such as St. Joseph's College of Commerce, St. Joseph's Institute of Management before joining the School of Business and Management at Christ University as an Assistant Professor. He expertise lies in finance, accounting and taxation courses. Apart from teaching, Dr. Ravi Darshini has actively engaged in research with focus on areas such as stock market volatility, financial statement analysis and entrepreneurship. She has contributed significantly to academia through publications in reputed journals and has undertaken several research projects funded by prestigious organizations.

Godwin Nse Ebong is a scholarly AI enthusiast with a strong academic record and years of experience in machine learning research. I specialize in applying statistics and data mining techniques to develop decision-making systems that drive strategic improvements and predict future trends for businesses. With a deep understanding of Hadoop and text analytics, I excel in extracting valuable insights.

Lateef Olawale Fatai is an accomplished professional with a robust background in statistics and data science, earning his B.Sc in Statistics from the University of Abuja and an M.Sc from the University of Salford. He is an active member of prestigious professional organisations, including the Professional Statisticians Society of Nigeria (PSSN), American Statistical Association (ASA), Royal Statistical Society (RSS), Faculty of Public Health (FPH), American Public Health Association (APHA), and International Society for Computational Biology (ISCB). Lateef's expertise spans Cloud Computing, Big Data, Statistical Analysis, AI, Machine Learning, NLP, Business Intelligence, and Database Management, utilizing tools like Big Query, Python, R-Studio, and SAS. His research emphasis lies in Statistical and Computational Methods for High Dimensional Data in Public Health Analysis, with notable contributions to Statistical Genetics and Survival Analysis. His contributions to Behavioural and Health Sciences analysis, Longitudinal and Multilevel Data Analysis, Design and Analysis of Clinical Trials, Bayesian Models, and Application of Statistical Methods in Public Health demonstrate a commitment to advancing knowledge and solving intricate problems. Beyond his academic pursuits, Lateef O. Fatai actively engages in local and global statistical and computational biology communities, showcasing his commitment to advancing knowledge and addressing real-world challenges. His multifaceted involvement establishes him as a dynamic force in statistical innovation and artificial intelligence world.

About the Contributors

Sharad Gupta is an accomplished Assistant Professor at Christ University, Pune Lavasa Campus. He holds an M.Com and an MBA, specializing in Business and Management. Mr. Gupta has co-authored several influential publications, including "HR Analytics: Quantifying the Intangible" and has contributed to conference proceedings such as IEEE Xplore. His research interests lie in HR analytics and AI applications in business practices. He actively participates in academic conferences, workshops, and training programs, continuously contributing to the field of business education and research.

Sowmiya KC, an accomplished Ph.D. scholar at Sri Vasavi College in Erode, emerges as a dynamic and vibrant researcher with a rich educational background. Having laid the foundation with a B.Ed. degree and furthered her academic pursuits with post-graduation at PSGR Krishnammal College for Women, she has adeptly positioned herself at the forefront of scholarly exploration.Her commitment to advancing knowledge is exemplified through her proactive involvement in two conferences in 2023, where she not only showcased her research prowess but also actively engaged with peers and experts, fostering meaningful discussions. Notably, the recognition garnered from presenting her research findings at these conferences has resulted in the acceptance of her journal article for publication later this year. This noteworthy achievement not only underscores Sowmiya's dedication to the academic realm but also highlights her impactful contributions to the scholarly discourse. As a Ph.D. scholar, she stands as a vibrant and influential contributor to the ever-evolving landscape of research and academic exploration, leaving an indelible mark on her field.

V. Rajesh Kumar is an M.Com Graduate from Bangalore University. He has got his Doctorate in the area of "Strategy". While Accounting and Taxation are his areas of expertise, Finance is his area of passion. He has 31 years of experience in teaching at graduate, post-graduate and professional levels and has served various Institutions in different capacities - Mount Carmel Institute of Management, Bangalore University (Department of Commerce), Alliance Business Academy and Chanakya University - to name a few. He is a faculty for Strategic Financial Management at the Bangalore Branch of the Institute of Chartered Accountants of India. He has authored books on 'Financial Management' and 'Indirect Taxes' for the requirement of Professional Courses, and co-authored text-books on `Accounting, Finance and Taxation" for the requirements of various universities. He was the first Indian Professor to be selected for International Management Teachers Academy (IMTA) Training on 'Case Analysis and Writing' conducted by Central East European Management Development Association (CEEMAN) at IEDC – Bled School of Management, Bled, Slovenia in June 2006. He has presented papers at various national and international conferences and published articles in reputed Journals. His paper on "Capital Asset Pricing Model" was selected for an International Conference at Harvard University, Cambridge, United States of America, during May-June 2011. Dr. Rajesh also has a rich experience in research, consultancy and training – both at the academic level and corporate level. He has conducted Student Development Programs and Faculty Development Programs in various educational institutions; and has conducted training programs for executives of various companies like Wipro, Godrej, FCG, Honeywell, KPCL, Fouress Engineers, Triveni Engineering, Tyco Electronics etc., in the area of `accounting, finance and taxation'. He is associated as resource person for the `Finance for Non-finance Executives' Program of the Bangalore Branch of the Institute of Chartered Accountants of India. He is the Founder of 'Vittam Pravina Gurushala (Finance Expert Academy)' – an academy engaged in spreading the knowledge of finance to students, faculty, corporate and all others interested in the area of finance. Presently, he is serving as Professor and Director in Alliance School of Commerce and Management of Alliance University.

Ugochukwu O. Matthew presently is an Academic scholar with Hussaini Adamu Federal Polytechnic, Nigeria, in the Department of Computer Science with specialty in AI, Big Data Science, Cloud Computing, Internet of Things, Data Mining, Multimedia and E-Learning Education. A Member of Nigeria Computer Society (NCS), Nigeria Institute of Management (NIM), International Association of Computer Science & Information Technology (IACSIT), European Alliance for Innovation(EAI) and also a member of Teaching & Education Research Association (TERA). Ugochukwu O. Matthew hold Masters in Computer Applications from Bayero University Kano, Nigeria. Ugochukwu O. Matthew had reviewed several Journals and a member of Review Board Committee of Journals Indexed by Scopus and Web of Science including IEEE Access, SN Computer Science (Springer), International Journal of Information Communication Technologies & Human Development(IJICTHD), International Journal of Business Data Communications and Networking (IJBDCN), International Journal of Cloud Applications and Computing (IJCAC). Ugochukwu O. Matthew is a cofounder of U&J Digital Consult Limited, an IT and Educational Consulting Firm in Nigeria.

About the Contributors

M.S. Priyadarshini is an Organizational and Health Psychologist with over 20 years of experience in academia. She holds a UG degree in Psychology from Women's Christian College, a PG and PhD in Psychology from the University of Madras, and a PG Certificate in Academic Practices from Lancaster University, UK. Her areas of expertise include job motivation, stress management, work-life balance, cross-cultural studies, and emotional intelligence. She has conducted numerous training programs for students and professionals and has written articles on youth development. Dr. Priyadarshini has also been involved in research on topics such as the effects of anxiety on cardiac disease and the impact of work environment on marital happiness among software professionals. She has received research grants from institutions like Sunway University and the Asian Office of Aerospace Research and Development (AOARD) for her work on topics like the influence of parenting styles on late adolescents' self and emotional development and the origin of trust within organizations. Dr. Priyadarshini has also presented her research findings in various journals and conferences, contributing significantly to the field of psychology. Dr. Priyadarshini's career spans across different countries, having worked as a Programme Leader at Sunway University in Malaysia and currently serving as a faculty member at Christ University in Bangalore, India. She has a keen interest in yoga and has previously served as an advisor on stress management at Apollo Hospitals in India. Additionally, she has been involved in media engagements, including interviews on TV channels like Kalaigner TV and Jaya TV, and has given a TEDx Talk on stress management. Her research interests and activities have made her a respected figure in the field of psychology, and her contributions continue to shape the understanding of various aspects of human behavior and well-being.

Srishti Muralidharan is NET qualified Faculty of Psychology in PES University, Bangalore. She has completed her Masters in Clinical Psychology. Her areas of interest include Clinical Psychology, Counselling Psychology, Psychotherapy, Neuropsychology, Indian Psychology and Philosophy. She is currently pursuing her Masters in Philosophy.

Matthew Abiola Oladipupo is the Lead Data Analyst at Perch Group Ltd in Manchester, United Kingdom. He earned his Master of Science in Data Science from The University of Salford and holds a Bachelor of Technology in Electronics and Electrical Engineering, as well as a Postgraduate Diploma, from Ladoke Akintola University of Technology. As a passionate scholar in Artificial Intelligence, he brings years of experience in researching machine learning and boasts a distinguished academic profile. His expertise spans across applied statistics and data mining techniques, enabling him to develop decision-making systems for business organizations. This involves collecting extensive datasets and transforming them into actionable insights and reports, aiding organizations in strategic decision-making, business improvement, and future trend prediction

Ajibola Olaosebikan has a background in Industrial Engineering— where he honed his business, engineering and management skills. Understanding that challenges are local, and that solving them requires sustainable tailored solutions, Ajibola has three goals: to research local problems, develop globally acknowledged solutions and make societal impactful by mainstreaming technical skills through teaching. Through his internship experience at Nestle and his master's degree in Applied AI and Data Science at the Southampton Solent University—where he was also a Junior Data Scientist and worked collaboratively to deliver an AI-powered decision support system project, he has developed capabilities in data analytics and engineering, applied artificial intelligence in business, software engineering and research. Currently, he is pursuing the Food Market Vision (FMV) project. This project, that span areas such as route optimization, data acquisition and storage, process automation, cloud computing and research etc. is aimed at enhancing the core retailing processes in the Sub-Saharan Africa (Nigeria) informal food markets. Among others, this project's major objective is to ensure verified and real-time primary data and information needed to shape food policies are obtainable from the source—the informal food markets. Ajibola's research interests spans across application of AI in Business, big data, data strategy, and cloud computing. Ajibola's hobby is teaching and to further showcase this, he is building LearniT—a Learning Management System to educate interested users on developing end-to-end data and software projects

About the Contributors

David Oyekunle is a highly esteemed expert with extensive education and experience in the fields of information technology research, project management, business analysis, and artificial intelligence. He earned his Bachelor of Science degree in statistics from the University of Ilorin in Nigeria. He obtained a Postgraduate Diploma in International Business Administration and Management from the National Open University in Nigeria and a (summer online) Master of Business Administration in Leadership and Team Building from the University of New Haven in the United States of America. He excelled as a postgraduate research scholar at the University of Salford, graduating with a Master of Science degree in project management with distinctions. David's significant organizational experience includes leading cross-functional teams, developing strategic project policies, implementing logistics, ensuring adherence to risk standards and compliance, and analyzing vast datasets to uncover trends and patterns. Among his achievements are the successful implementation of intelligent lean management and Six Sigma with data analysis, the delivery of comprehensive business reports, and the use of technological innovation to improve customer service in the banking and media sectors. I am currently serving as an educational consultant at U&J Digital Consult Limited in Nigeria. David is a personal and business coach, and he continues to contribute significantly to the fields of information technology and educational consulting. Global journals have published his research on various subjects such as strategic management, project management, international business, business informatics, and ethics in project management. Demonstrating his commitment to academic collaboration and human capital development, David actively participates in volunteer positions and committee memberships at conferences both locally and internationally. David aims to continue leveraging his expertise to drive innovation and excellence in research, education, project management, and information technology.

Deepika S.R. serves as an Assistant Professor at the School of Business and Management, Christ Deemed to be University in Bangalore. She earned her Ph.D. in Finance from Bharathiar University, Coimbatore, and holds an MBA from GRG School of Management Studies, Coimbatore. Throughout her academic journey, she consistently excelled, securing a university rank in her undergraduate studies and earning the top position in her 12th-grade examinations. Additionally, she is qualified in UGC – NET (Management). Bringing over 10 years of teaching experience at both undergraduate and postgraduate levels, Dr. Deepika has made significant contributions to institutions such as Jain University, Jyoti Nivas College Autonomous, Kristu Jayanthi College Autonomous, and GRG School of Management Studies. Her professional journey also includes a brief tenure as an administrative officer at Saratha College of Arts and Science, Gobichettipalayam. Specializing in Finance, Dr. Deepika adeptly handles diverse subjects including Investment Analysis and Portfolio Management, FInancial Derivatives, Financial Markets and Services, Fundamentals of Accounting, Business Statistics, and Entrepreneurship Development. Beyond teaching, she actively engages in organizing and contributing as a resource person for national-level faculty development programs and workshops, focusing on Financial Risk Management, Derivatives, and Investment Management. Dr. Deepika is not just an educator; she practices what she preaches in her personal life, demonstrating her expertise as a goal-based financial investor who has navigated both bull and bear markets in her investment journey. She has contributed to the academic community through research articles published in refereed journals and presentations of research papers at international conferences. Adding another dimension to her diverse skill set, Dr. Deepika is a YouTuber, sharing valuable insights on personal finance and investments through around 25 videos on her channel. She has a keen interest in public speaking and was an active member of a Toastmasters' club.

R. Sridevi is an Associate Professor in the Department of Computer Science at CHRIST(Deemed to be University, Bangalore, Karnataka). She holds PhD degree from Bharathiar University and guided 7 MPhil Scholars till date. She has taught Object Oriented Programming, Relational Database Management System, Operating System, Data Visualization and Information Security at the undergraduate and post graduate levels for over 20 years. She has published several research papers in Biometric Security, Cryptography and Information Security. She has also presented around 30 research articles in National and International Conferences. She is a member of Professional Bodies like CSTA, ISTE & IAENG. She has also published 2 Indian Patents. She holds the privilege of acting as a Resource Person for Guest lectures of various colleges.

About the Contributors

Prageetha G Raju is MBA PhD from the domain of Human Resource Management, Organization Behavior and allied areas. She possesses 22 years of Masters Level, Executive MBA level and PhD level teaching experience. At present, she is on a career-break from Academics and is engaging in Management Research and Consulting on behalf of Rainbow Management Research Consultants (RMRC) located in Hyderabad, India. She is the sole-proprietor of RMRC. She possesses a decent publication record in indexed journals.

SC Vetrivel is a faculty member in the Department of Management Studies, Kongu Engineering College (Autonomous), Perundurai, Erode Dt. Having experience in Industry 20 years and Teaching 16 years. Awarded with Doctoral Degree in Management Sciences in Anna University, Chennai. He has organized various workshops and Faculty Development Programmes. He is actively involved in research and consultancy works. He acted as a resource person to FDPs & MDPs to various industries like, SPB ltd, Tamilnadu Police, DIET, Rotary school and many. His areas of interest include Entrepreneurship, Business Law, Marketing and Case writing. Articles published more than 100 International and National Journals. Presented papers in more than 30 National and International conferences including IIM Bangalore, IIM Kozhikode, IIM Kashipur and IIM Indore. He was a Chief Co-ordinator of Entrepreneurship and Management Development Centre (EMDC) of Kongu Engineering College, he was instrumental in organizing various Awareness Camps, FDP, and TEDPs to aspiring entrepreneurs which was funded by NSTEDB – DST/GoI

Manjari Sharma is a distinguished educator and researcher, currently serving as an Associate Professor at Christ University in Bangalore. With extensive experience in higher education, she specializes in active learning strategies and educational innovation. Dr. Sharma holds a Ph.D. in Education and has made significant contributions through her research on collaborative and experiential learning. She is actively involved in curriculum development, faculty training, and has published numerous articles in reputed journals. Dr. Sharma is also a recognized speaker, sharing her expertise at various academic conferences globally.

Aubrey Statti is a core faculty member at The Chicago School in the Educational Psychology and Technology program. Her research interests include K-12 education, child growth and development, online education, and mentoring.

T. Gomathi, served in various reputed institutions. Currently employed as an Assistant Professor (Department In charge) at Gnanamani College of Technology, Namakkal. His area of specialization are Human Resource and Finance Management. She has 13 years of Teaching experience. A soft skill trainer. She has published papers in International and national Journals and participated in more than 20 national and international conferences, Seminars, FDPs, Workshops. She served as a question paper setter in various autonomous colleges. She has also delivered various guest talks and soft skill training in various schools and colleges.

Kelly M. Torres, Ph.D. is the Department Chair of the Educational Psychology and Technology program at The Chicago School. Her research interests are focused on international education, teacher certification programs, innovative technologies, and online learning.

Ikechukwu Umejesi teaches in the Department of Sociology, University of Fort Hare, East London, South Africa. He is also the Deputy Dean of Research, Partnerships and Innovation in the Faculty of Social Sciences and Humanities.

Brooke Urbina is currently a high school library media specialist after teaching high school English for many years. Her interests in education include educational technology, building culture, and at-risk education.

About the Contributors

V. Sathish is committed to the service of the students community. Teaching culinary in Department of Hotel Management with PSG College of Arts and Science since 2004. He is addicted to reading and inculcates reading habit among the stduents community, He has authored a Tamil fiction titled KATHTHALE meaning Darkness in Badaga language which is about the abuse of alcohol on the local Badagar community of Nilgiris, Tamil Nadu.

V.P. Arun is a driven and accomplished professional with a diverse educational background and extensive hands-on experience across various industries. Graduating with honors, Arun earned his Master of Business Administration (M.B.A) with a specialization in Human Resources and Marketing from the renowned Sona School of Management in Salem in 2018, where he excelled academically with an impressive 8.3 Cumulative Grade Point Average (CGPA). Before pursuing his MBA, Arun laid a solid foundation by obtaining a Bachelor of Engineering degree from Kongu Engineering College in 2014. Throughout his academic journey, Arun displayed an unwavering commitment to learning and personal growth, actively seeking opportunities to expand his knowledge and skills beyond the confines of traditional education. He sought practical experiences to complement his theoretical understanding, such as a 45-day summer internship focused on conducting a feasibility study for R-Doc Sustainability in the market. Additionally, Arun broadened his horizons through a 7-day industrial visit to Malaysia and Singapore, immersing himself in diverse cultural and professional environments. Arun's academic pursuits were further enriched by his involvement in hands-on projects, including a comprehensive study on Employee Job Satisfaction at Roots Cast Private Limited. These practical experiences not only honed his analytical and problem-solving skills but also showcased his proactive approach to learning and professional development. Transitioning seamlessly from academia to the professional realm, Arun embarked on a remarkable journey, holding pivotal roles in esteemed organizations across various sectors. His professional trajectory includes serving as a Growth Officer at Parle Agro Private Limited, where he played a crucial role in driving sales growth and market expansion. Subsequently, Arun leveraged his expertise as a Sales Executive at PhonePe India Pvt Ltd and later as a Senior Executive at Indiamart Intermesh Limited, demonstrating exemplary business development skills.

Index

A

Academic 4, 6, 23, 33, 35, 37, 39, 42, 43, 44, 50, 51, 59, 60, 63, 68, 69, 70, 71, 75, 76, 77, 78, 79, 80, 81, 82, 83, 84, 85, 86, 87, 89, 93, 94, 97, 98, 107, 109, 110, 118, 120, 121, 122, 123, 126, 127, 132, 133, 134, 136, 137, 138, 141, 142, 143, 144, 145, 146, 147, 150, 153, 157, 159, 161, 162, 163, 165, 166, 168, 169, 170, 171, 178, 179, 180, 182, 201, 209, 211, 217, 218, 222, 225, 227, 228, 230, 235, 241, 242, 244, 249, 250, 251, 260, 261, 264, 266, 267, 268, 269, 270, 271, 272, 274, 275, 276, 278, 280, 281, 284, 286, 288, 292, 294, 298, 301, 305, 306, 307, 311, 312, 314, 315, 316, 317, 318, 319, 321, 323, 324, 325, 326, 330, 335, 338, 341, 342, 348, 351, 398, 408, 410, 411, 416, 417, 421, 422, 424, 425, 426, 427, 428, 433, 439, 441, 442

Active learning 3, 5, 11, 15, 20, 32, 33, 34, 35, 36, 37, 38, 39, 40, 41, 43, 44, 45, 46, 47, 48, 49, 50, 51, 52, 53, 56, 57, 58, 59, 60, 61, 62, 63, 64, 65, 66, 115, 128, 144, 149, 216, 222, 229, 235, 237, 239, 245, 247, 268, 270, 307, 309, 318, 330, 334, 345

Artificial Intelligence 15, 56, 59, 64, 83, 93, 124, 145, 151, 152, 170, 171, 172, 173, 174, 175, 176, 267, 281, 292, 294, 295, 296, 297, 444

Assessment 1, 2, 5, 6, 12, 13, 14, 16, 17, 19, 22, 23, 25, 28, 30, 31, 46, 47, 48, 49, 54, 55, 56, 63, 65, 66, 69, 78, 79, 80, 82, 83, 85, 88, 92, 93, 115, 124, 125, 133, 138, 139, 140, 146, 148, 166, 171, 173, 179, 193, 195, 196, 197, 199, 201, 202, 203, 204, 206, 208, 211, 214, 217, 219, 220, 221, 226, 230, 235, 239, 252, 257, 261, 266, 271, 309, 316, 343, 350, 354, 411, 432

Assessment Techniques 28, 49, 63, 146

B

Bachelor of Nursing Science 330, 410, 411, 412, 413, 416, 421, 423, 424

C

Case Studies 11, 15, 19, 33, 34, 35, 48, 49, 61, 76, 82, 133, 152, 153, 157, 158, 159, 160, 163, 168, 194, 199, 200, 206, 211, 217, 224, 229, 243, 245, 247, 283, 377, 439, 441, 442, 443, 446, 448

Cognition 17, 95, 96, 98, 99, 116, 118, 119, 151, 152, 154, 155, 159, 161, 163, 169, 176, 332, 403, 438

Cognitive Flexibility 308

Cognitive Learning 9, 10, 97, 100, 106, 107, 122, 123, 124, 126, 127, 128, 129, 130, 132, 136, 137, 138, 139, 140, 141, 142, 143, 144, 145, 146, 147, 148, 149

cognitive strategies 10, 95, 97, 98, 100, 106, 107, 118, 120, 125

Collaborative Learning 41, 42, 43, 44, 46, 52, 55, 66, 67, 128, 129, 130, 149, 164, 183, 194, 202, 203, 218, 219, 220, 226, 237, 238, 243, 247, 266, 269, 306, 317, 325

Communication skills 34, 39, 44, 72, 77, 205, 218, 266, 441

Constructivism 3, 36, 64, 223, 305, 307, 327, 331, 333, 346, 383, 384, 409

Cooperative learning 28, 43, 65, 128, 222, 238, 271, 329, 342, 347

Corporate Finance 349, 350, 351, 353, 354, 355, 356, 357, 372, 373, 377, 378

Criticality 158, 429, 430, 432, 433, 434, 438, 440, 448

Critical Studies in HRM 429, 436, 437, 443, 445

Critical Thinking 32, 33, 34, 35, 37, 39, 40, 41, 42, 43, 44, 48, 54, 55, 58, 59, 60, 62, 66, 73, 77, 107, 114, 123, 124,

126, 128, 129, 130, 136, 139, 140, 143,
147, 149, 152, 154, 155, 160, 161,
162, 167, 168, 177, 178, 182, 184,
202, 203, 205, 206, 212, 218, 219,
220, 221, 222, 234, 239, 241, 242,
243, 244, 246, 247, 250, 251, 252,
261, 265, 266, 268, 271, 272, 302,
306, 307, 308, 316, 322, 323, 330,
335, 377, 412, 435, 436, 444, 452, 454
Critical Thinking Skills 35, 41, 42, 43, 77,
128, 129, 167, 239, 243, 244, 246,
250, 268, 306

D

Data Analytics 83, 152, 153, 160, 176
Design thinking 216, 225, 226, 227, 228,
237, 238, 449
Digital Media 296, 301, 302, 304, 321,
323, 324, 326
Digital textbook 314, 317

E

Educational Management 288
Educational Technology 30, 63, 173, 236,
237, 239, 240, 269, 271, 281, 295, 310,
316, 327, 328, 382, 383, 390, 391, 399,
406, 407, 408, 409, 451, 454
Emotional Intelligence 69, 70, 71, 72, 74,
75, 78, 79, 80, 83, 84, 88, 89, 91, 92,
93, 142, 154, 155, 160
Empathy 69, 70, 71, 74, 78, 80, 82, 84, 89,
94, 167, 218, 225, 343, 442
Engagement 7, 12, 13, 24, 27, 28, 33, 34,
35, 36, 37, 38, 39, 40, 41, 42, 43, 44,
46, 50, 51, 52, 53, 55, 58, 59, 60, 62,
63, 65, 67, 70, 82, 87, 96, 125, 126,
129, 138, 141, 146, 150, 152, 157,
159, 161, 164, 165, 166, 168, 172,
173, 177, 179, 186, 193, 197, 202,
203, 205, 206, 207, 208, 209, 212,
214, 215, 217, 219, 220, 221, 223,
224, 225, 226, 227, 229, 230, 232,
233, 234, 235, 236, 237, 241, 243,
244, 246, 247, 248, 249, 250, 251,
252, 253, 254, 259, 260, 263, 264,
265, 266, 267, 268, 269, 270, 271,
272, 278, 301, 302, 303, 304, 305,
306, 307, 309, 310, 311, 312, 313,
314, 315, 316, 317, 318, 319, 320,
321, 322, 323, 324, 325, 326, 327,
328, 337, 350, 391, 399, 415, 421, 427
experiences 15, 36, 44, 45, 56, 57, 58, 60,
61, 62, 64, 71, 72, 73, 76, 77, 82, 83,
86, 87, 88, 90, 93, 101, 117, 123, 124,
127, 130, 134, 135, 136, 140, 141,
144, 145, 147, 150, 152, 153, 155,
156, 157, 159, 160, 161, 162, 163,
164, 165, 169, 176, 184, 186, 187,
188, 189, 190, 193, 197, 207, 208,
215, 220, 222, 225, 226, 227, 228,
229, 230, 232, 241, 244, 245, 247,
248, 249, 251, 255, 259, 260, 264,
265, 266, 267, 302, 303, 306, 307,
310, 314, 315, 317, 319, 321, 323,
325, 326, 329, 331, 333, 335, 337,
338, 339, 342, 343, 344, 345, 346,
348, 382, 383, 384, 387, 388, 390,
393, 402, 403, 415, 416, 422, 423,
427, 428, 454
Experiential Learning 3, 32, 36, 37, 51,
53, 55, 65, 67, 76, 91, 130, 177, 178,
184, 186, 214, 220, 221, 222, 238,
240, 241, 308, 349, 350, 376

F

factors 4, 6, 24, 75, 80, 85, 98, 99, 125,
132, 133, 136, 137, 154, 161, 186,
188, 207, 208, 220, 229, 230, 231,
236, 279, 297, 305, 311, 326, 331,
343, 353, 386, 387, 388, 394, 397,
398, 407, 408, 410, 411, 412, 413,
416, 417, 421, 422, 423, 424, 425,
426, 427, 428, 434, 441
failure rate 410, 411, 412, 413, 418, 421,
424
Financial modelling 358

H

Higher Education 1, 2, 5, 6, 10, 11, 23, 25,
27, 28, 29, 30, 32, 33, 35, 36, 44, 45,

60, 62, 63, 65, 66, 68, 69, 70, 72, 75, 76, 77, 82, 83, 84, 89, 90, 91, 92, 93, 94, 95, 96, 97, 98, 99, 100, 106, 107, 111, 112, 113, 117, 119, 120, 122, 123, 125, 129, 130, 133, 136, 144, 145, 146, 147, 148, 151, 152, 153, 154, 155, 156, 157, 159, 160, 161, 163, 164, 168, 169, 172, 173, 174, 175, 176, 180, 187, 188, 190, 191, 207, 209, 210, 211, 214, 215, 216, 217, 218, 219, 220, 221, 222, 223, 225, 226, 227, 228, 230, 231, 235, 236, 237, 238, 239, 242, 250, 251, 268, 271, 274, 276, 277, 283, 284, 288, 291, 292, 293, 294, 296, 297, 299, 300, 301, 302, 303, 304, 315, 316, 317, 318, 319, 320, 321, 322, 323, 324, 325, 326, 327, 350, 378, 393, 396, 400, 401, 403, 404, 406, 407, 408, 413, 424, 425, 428, 429, 430, 439, 453

I

ICT Infrastructure 276, 284, 285
ICT Policy Implementation 295
Information literacy 30, 148, 241, 242, 243, 244, 246, 247, 248, 250, 251, 252, 254, 256, 257, 259, 260, 261, 262, 263, 264, 265, 266, 268, 269, 270, 271, 272
Innovative 7, 32, 46, 49, 57, 62, 67, 83, 88, 92, 126, 127, 143, 145, 146, 147, 166, 171, 174, 177, 182, 183, 192, 205, 206, 208, 212, 214, 215, 216, 217, 220, 221, 223, 225, 226, 228, 229, 230, 231, 232, 234, 235, 236, 237, 238, 239, 240, 241, 350, 427, 431
Innovative learning strategies 32, 220
innovative teaching methods 57, 183, 205, 208, 212, 232, 234, 241
interactive learning strategies 1, 2, 3, 5, 10, 11, 16, 25, 26, 31, 58, 59, 60, 163, 166, 205, 206, 212, 241, 242, 243, 246, 252, 254, 255, 264, 266, 267, 301, 313, 318, 319, 320, 349, 351
interdisciplinary learning 177, 179, 181, 209
Interpersonal skills 41, 43, 69, 70, 71, 72, 74, 76, 78, 79, 80, 83, 84, 88, 89, 142, 218, 312, 325

L

Learning 1, 2, 3, 4, 5, 6, 7, 8, 9, 10, 11, 12, 13, 14, 15, 16, 17, 18, 19, 20, 22, 23, 24, 25, 26, 27, 28, 29, 30, 31, 32, 33, 34, 35, 36, 37, 38, 39, 40, 41, 42, 43, 44, 45, 46, 47, 48, 49, 50, 51, 52, 53, 54, 55, 56, 57, 58, 59, 60, 61, 62, 63, 64, 65, 66, 67, 68, 69, 70, 71, 72, 74, 75, 76, 77, 78, 79, 80, 81, 82, 83, 84, 85, 86, 87, 88, 89, 90, 91, 92, 93, 94, 95, 96, 97, 98, 99, 100, 102, 103, 104, 105, 106, 107, 108, 109, 110, 111, 112, 113, 114, 115, 116, 117, 118, 119, 120, 121, 122, 123, 124, 125, 126, 127, 128, 129, 130, 131, 132, 133, 134, 135, 136, 137, 138, 139, 140, 141, 142, 143, 144, 145, 146, 147, 148, 149, 150, 151, 152, 153, 154, 155, 156, 157, 158, 159, 160, 161, 162, 163, 164, 165, 166, 167, 168, 169, 170, 171, 172, 173, 174, 175, 176, 177, 178, 179, 180, 181, 182, 183, 184, 185, 186, 194, 199, 200, 201, 202, 203, 204, 205, 206, 208, 209, 210, 211, 212, 213, 214, 215, 216, 217, 218, 219, 220, 221, 222, 223, 224, 225, 226, 227, 228, 229, 230, 231, 232, 233, 234, 235, 236, 237, 238, 239, 240, 241, 242, 243, 244, 245, 246, 247, 248, 249, 250, 251, 252, 253, 254, 255, 256, 258, 259, 260, 261, 262, 263, 264, 265, 266, 267, 268, 269, 270, 271, 272, 275, 277, 278, 279, 280, 281, 285, 286, 287, 291, 292, 293, 294, 295, 296, 297, 299, 301, 302, 303, 304, 305, 306, 307, 308, 309, 310, 311, 312, 313, 314, 315, 316, 317, 318, 319, 320, 321, 322, 323, 324, 325, 326, 327, 328, 329, 330, 331, 332, 333, 334, 335, 336, 337,

338, 339, 340, 342, 343, 344, 345, 346, 347, 348, 349, 350, 351, 357, 358, 374, 375, 376, 377, 378, 382, 383, 384, 385, 388, 389, 390, 391, 392, 393, 394, 395, 396, 397, 398, 399, 400, 401, 402, 403, 404, 405, 406, 407, 412, 416, 418, 419, 420, 421, 422, 423, 424, 425, 428, 431, 432, 433, 437, 438, 439, 440, 441, 442, 445, 446, 447, 448, 449, 454

Learning Outcomes 1, 2, 5, 10, 11, 24, 33, 35, 41, 48, 49, 52, 53, 56, 62, 64, 95, 97, 107, 111, 112, 117, 118, 119, 125, 126, 137, 138, 140, 155, 175, 177, 179, 186, 201, 212, 217, 220, 221, 223, 226, 227, 228, 229, 230, 231, 232, 234, 235, 237, 241, 246, 250, 251, 252, 253, 254, 255, 256, 259, 260, 261, 262, 264, 265, 266, 267, 269, 270, 302, 310, 311, 312, 316, 319, 320, 321, 323, 324, 331, 335, 345, 347, 350, 351, 391, 397, 404, 405, 422, 423, 428, 446

Learning strategy 8, 10, 14, 16, 17, 18, 19, 20, 27, 35, 127, 344

Library instruction 241, 242, 245, 246, 247, 248, 249, 250, 251, 252, 253, 254, 255, 256, 257, 258, 259, 260, 261, 262, 263, 264, 265, 266, 267, 268, 269, 270, 271

M

Machine Learning 83, 145, 152, 153, 160, 161, 168, 176, 210

Memory 8, 24, 96, 97, 99, 100, 101, 102, 104, 105, 106, 117, 118, 120, 123, 124, 125, 126, 127, 134, 135, 136, 137, 138, 141, 145, 147, 149, 154, 155, 215, 225, 308, 309, 317, 448

Mental Processes 96, 124

Metacognition 2, 9, 73, 91, 95, 96, 98, 99, 108, 109, 110, 111, 112, 114, 115, 118, 119, 120, 122, 123, 127, 128, 142, 145, 147, 149, 150, 154, 239, 333, 378

metacognitive strategies 14, 25, 95, 97, 98, 99, 107, 108, 109, 110, 111, 113, 115, 119, 120, 126, 128, 149

methods 24, 32, 33, 35, 37, 39, 40, 42, 43, 45, 47, 48, 51, 52, 54, 57, 58, 60, 61, 63, 65, 69, 79, 81, 83, 88, 93, 94, 96, 97, 99, 102, 126, 129, 130, 131, 132, 136, 138, 139, 142, 144, 145, 146, 147, 148, 149, 150, 152, 153, 156, 160, 161, 162, 163, 164, 166, 167, 183, 188, 194, 199, 201, 202, 203, 204, 205, 208, 212, 214, 215, 216, 217, 218, 220, 221, 226, 227, 228, 229, 230, 232, 233, 234, 235, 238, 241, 242, 244, 245, 246, 250, 252, 255, 265, 268, 270, 281, 301, 304, 308, 315, 320, 330, 334, 350, 351, 372, 378, 387, 393, 401, 402, 406, 408, 410, 411, 413, 414, 415, 421, 422, 424, 427, 432, 438, 440, 441, 442, 443, 445, 447, 448, 449, 450, 452, 453, 454

N

National Education Policy 177, 178, 179, 180, 181, 186, 187, 188, 193, 194, 195, 196, 197, 198, 199, 200, 201, 202, 203, 204, 205, 206, 207, 209, 210

nursing and midwifery education 329, 344

nursing students 250, 269, 329, 330, 331, 334, 335, 336, 338, 342, 343, 344, 345, 346, 347, 412, 413, 414, 416, 417, 423, 425, 426, 428

P

Pedagogical Innovation 46

peer assessment 14, 19, 48, 66

peer group teaching 329, 330, 331, 334, 338, 339, 340, 341, 342, 344

Personalized Learning 25, 58, 62, 85, 93, 126, 137, 140, 141, 145, 151, 153, 156, 157, 159, 160, 163, 164, 165, 166, 167, 172, 174, 175, 176, 215, 221, 227, 302, 306, 311, 312, 314, 316, 318, 321, 323, 325, 326

Preservice Teachers 381, 382, 383, 384, 385, 386, 387, 388, 392, 393, 394, 395,

397, 399, 400, 401, 403, 404, 405, 407
Problem-Based Learning 33, 34, 35, 37, 39, 41, 48, 54, 63, 64, 183, 206, 212, 243, 245, 247, 267, 330, 375, 428
Project Pedagogy 429, 436, 438, 439, 440, 441, 446, 447, 448, 451

R

Reflection 17, 49, 53, 61, 74, 75, 95, 96, 97, 98, 107, 109, 112, 117, 128, 142, 147, 186, 312, 335, 383, 429, 430, 432, 433, 434, 437, 438, 439, 440, 441, 442, 443, 445, 448, 449, 453, 454
Relationship-building 76, 83

S

Self-awareness 69, 71, 72, 74, 75, 77, 78, 79, 80, 81, 82, 83, 84, 86, 88, 89, 127, 142
Self-regulation 69, 72, 78, 79, 84, 88, 96, 97, 98, 107, 127
skill development 59, 60, 137, 177, 180, 181, 194, 195, 196, 197, 199, 201, 206, 219, 221, 234, 249, 253, 254, 335, 400, 434
Strategies 1, 2, 3, 5, 8, 9, 10, 11, 12, 14, 16, 19, 23, 25, 26, 30, 31, 32, 33, 34, 35, 37, 38, 39, 40, 41, 43, 44, 45, 46, 48, 51, 53, 56, 57, 58, 59, 60, 61, 62, 66, 67, 68, 69, 79, 80, 81, 83, 85, 86, 87, 89, 91, 92, 93, 94, 95, 97, 98, 99, 100, 101, 106, 107, 108, 109, 110, 111, 113, 115, 117, 118, 119, 120, 122, 123, 125, 126, 127, 128, 129, 133, 134, 137, 138, 141, 142, 144, 145, 146, 147, 148, 149, 151, 160, 161, 163, 165, 166, 168, 174, 175, 178, 179, 180, 181, 183, 187, 188, 189, 190, 191, 193, 201, 205, 206, 207, 209, 212, 214, 215, 216, 217, 218, 219, 220, 221, 222, 225, 226, 228, 229, 230, 231, 232, 235, 236, 237, 238, 241, 242, 243, 245, 246, 247, 249, 250, 251, 252, 253, 254, 255, 264, 265, 266, 267, 269, 270, 279, 292, 301, 306, 308, 309, 312, 313, 315, 317, 318, 319, 320, 322, 324, 329, 349, 350, 351, 372, 373, 379, 400, 411, 412, 417, 422, 424
Student-centered learning 50, 54, 319, 322, 324, 326
Student Engagement 13, 33, 34, 35, 38, 41, 43, 46, 50, 51, 52, 55, 58, 60, 67, 82, 157, 159, 164, 165, 168, 177, 202, 203, 205, 206, 209, 215, 217, 219, 221, 223, 225, 229, 230, 232, 233, 235, 236, 237, 241, 246, 248, 250, 251, 252, 253, 254, 266, 268, 269, 270, 271, 272, 301, 302, 304, 305, 310, 311, 313, 315, 316, 317, 318, 319, 320, 321, 322, 323, 324, 325, 326, 327, 328, 350
Sustainable Education 161, 162, 163, 179, 209

T

Teacher Educators 381, 382, 384, 385, 386, 387, 388, 397, 398, 399, 400, 402, 403, 404, 406, 407, 408
Teaching strategies 16, 40, 79, 107, 166, 214, 215, 216, 217, 221, 229, 230, 232, 235, 237, 238, 249, 411, 422, 424
Technology-Enhanced Learning 41, 64
Technology Integration 58, 62, 159, 177, 178, 184, 252, 266, 381, 382, 383, 384, 385, 386, 387, 388, 390, 391, 392, 393, 394, 395, 396, 398, 399, 400, 401, 402, 403, 404, 405, 406, 407, 408
TPACK 381, 383, 384, 385, 386, 399, 405, 406, 407, 408

Publishing Tomorrow's Research Today

Uncover Current Insights and Future Trends in Education
with IGI Global's Cutting-Edge Recommended Books

Print Only, E-Book Only, or Print + E-Book.
Order direct through IGI Global's Online Bookstore at www.igi-global.com or through your preferred provider.

ISBN: 9781668493007
© 2023; 234 pp.
List Price: US$ 215

ISBN: 9798369300749
© 2024; 383 pp.
List Price: US$ 230

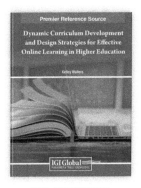

ISBN: 9781668486467
© 2023; 471 pp.
List Price: US$ 215

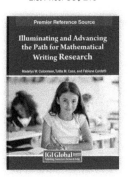

ISBN: 9781668465387
© 2024; 389 pp.
List Price: US$ 215

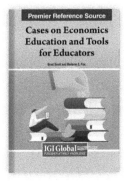

ISBN: 9781668475836
© 2024; 359 pp.
List Price: US$ 215

ISBN: 9781668444238
© 2023; 334 pp.
List Price: US$ 240

Do you want to stay current on the latest research trends, product announcements, news, and special offers? Join IGI Global's mailing list to receive customized recommendations, exclusive discounts, and more.
Sign up at: www.igi-global.com/newsletters.

Scan the QR Code here to view more related titles in Education.

www.igi-global.com | Sign up at www.igi-global.com/newsletters | facebook.com/igiglobal | twitter.com/igiglobal | linkedin.com/igiglobal

Ensure Quality Research is Introduced to the Academic Community

Become a Reviewer for IGI Global Authored Book Projects

 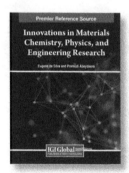 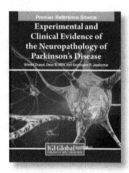 

The overall success of an authored book project is dependent on quality and timely manuscript evaluations.

Applications and Inquiries may be sent to:
development@igi-global.com

Applicants must have a doctorate (or equivalent degree) as well as publishing, research, and reviewing experience. Authored Book Evaluators are appointed for one-year terms and are expected to complete at least three evaluations per term. Upon successful completion of this term, evaluators can be considered for an additional term.

If you have a colleague that may be interested in this opportunity, we encourage you to share this information with them.

Publishing Tomorrow's Research Today
IGI Global's Open Access Journal Program

Including Nearly 200 Peer-Reviewed, Gold (Full) Open Access Journals across IGI Global's Three Academic Subject Areas: Business & Management; Scientific, Technical, and Medical (STM); and Education

Consider Submitting Your Manuscript to One of These Nearly 200 Open Access Journals for to Increase Their Discoverability & Citation Impact

| Web of Science Impact Factor | 6.5 | Web of Science Impact Factor | 4.7 | Web of Science Impact Factor | 3.2 | Web of Science Impact Factor | 2.6 |

JOURNAL OF
Organizational and End User Computing

JOURNAL OF
Global Information Management

INTERNATIONAL JOURNAL ON
Semantic Web and Information Systems

JOURNAL OF
Database Management

Choosing IGI Global's Open Access Journal Program Can Greatly Increase the Reach of Your Research

Higher Usage
Open access papers are 2-3 times more likely to be read than non-open access papers.

Higher Download Rates
Open access papers benefit from 89% higher download rates than non-open access papers.

Higher Citation Rates
Open access papers are 47% more likely to be cited than non-open access papers.

Submitting an article to a journal offers an invaluable opportunity for you to share your work with the broader academic community, fostering knowledge dissemination and constructive feedback.

Submit an Article and Browse the IGI Global Call for Papers Pages

We can work with you to find the journal most well-suited for your next research manuscript.
For open access publishing support, contact: journaleditor@igi-global.com

Publishing Tomorrow's Research Today
IGI Global
e-Book Collection

Including Essential Reference Books Within Three Fundamental Academic Areas

Business & Management
Scientific, Technical, & Medical (STM)
Education

- Acquisition options include Perpetual, Subscription, and Read & Publish
- No Additional Charge for Multi-User Licensing
- No Maintenance, Hosting, or Archiving Fees
- Continually Enhanced Accessibility Compliance Features (WCAG)

| Over **150,000+** Chapters | Contributions From **200,000+** Scholars Worldwide | More Than **1,000,000+** Citations | Majority of e-Books Indexed in Web of Science & Scopus | Consists of Tomorrow's Research Available Today! |

Recommended Titles from our e-Book Collection

Innovation Capabilities and Entrepreneurial Opportunities of Smart Working
ISBN: 9781799887973

Advanced Applications of Generative AI and Natural Language Processing Models
ISBN: 9798369305027

Using Influencer Marketing as a Digital Business Strategy
ISBN: 9798369305515

Human-Centered Approaches in Industry 5.0
ISBN: 9798369326473

Modeling and Monitoring Extreme Hydrometeorological Events
ISBN: 9781668487716

Data-Driven Intelligent Business Sustainability
ISBN: 9798369300497

Information Logistics for Organizational Empowerment and Effective Supply Chain Management
ISBN: 9798369301593

Data Envelopment Analysis (DEA) Methods for Maximizing Efficiency
ISBN: 9798369302552

Request More Information, or Recommend the IGI Global e-Book Collection to Your Institution's Librarian

For More Information or to Request a Free Trial, Contact IGI Global's e-Collections Team: eresources@igi-global.com | 1-866-342-6657 ext. 100 | 717-533-8845 ext. 100

Are You Ready to Publish Your Research?

IGI Global — Publishing Tomorrow's Research Today

IGI Global offers book authorship and editorship opportunities across three major subject areas, including Business, STM, and Education.

Benefits of Publishing with IGI Global:

- Free one-on-one editorial and promotional support.
- Expedited publishing timelines that can take your book from start to finish in less than one (1) year.
- Choose from a variety of formats, including Edited and Authored References, Handbooks of Research, Encyclopedias, and Research Insights.
- Utilize IGI Global's eEditorial Discovery® submission system in support of conducting the submission and double-blind peer review process.
- IGI Global maintains a strict adherence to ethical practices due in part to our full membership with the Committee on Publication Ethics (COPE).
- Indexing potential in prestigious indices such as Scopus®, Web of Science™, PsycINFO®, and ERIC – Education Resources Information Center.
- Ability to connect your ORCID iD to your IGI Global publications.
- Earn honorariums and royalties on your full book publications as well as complimentary content and exclusive discounts.

Join Your Colleagues from Prestigious Institutions, Including:

Australian National University, Massachusetts Institute of Technology, Johns Hopkins University, Tsinghua University, Harvard University, Columbia University in the City of New York

Learn More at: www.igi-global.com/publish
or by Contacting the Acquisitions Department at: acquisition@igi-global.com

Milton Keynes UK
Ingram Content Group UK Ltd.
UKHW052235120824
446789UK00009B/128